Reference in Discourse

OXFORD STUDIES IN TYPOLOGY AND LINGUISTIC THEORY

GENERAL EDITORS: Ronnie Cann, *University of Edinburgh*; William Croft, *University of New Mexico*; Martin Haspelmath, *Max Planck Institute for Evolutionary Anthropology*; Nicholas Evans, *University of Melbourne*; Anna Siewierska, *University of Lancaster*

PUBLISHED

Classifiers: A Typology of Noun Categorization Devices
Alexandra Y. Aikhenvald

Imperatives and Commands
Alexandra Y. Aikhenvald

Auxiliary Verb Constructions
Gregory D.S. Anderson

Pronouns
D. N. S. Bhat

Subordination
Sonia Cristofaro

The Paradigmatic Structure of Person Marking
Michael Cysouw

Adpositions: Function Marking in Languages
Claude Hagège

Indefinite Pronouns
Martin Haspelmath

Anaphora
Yan Huang

Reference in Discourse
Andrej A. Kibrik

The Emergence of Distinctive Features
Jeff Mielke

Applicative Constructions
David A. Peterson

Copulas
Regina Pustet

The Noun Phrase
Jan Rijkhoff

Intransitive Predication
Leon Stassen

Predicative Possession
Leon Stassen

Co-Compounds and Natural Coordination
Bernhard Wälchli

PUBLISHED IN ASSOCIATION WITH THE SERIES

The World Atlas of Language Structures
edited by Martin Haspelmath, Matthew Dryer, Bernard Comrie, and David Gil

IN PREPARATION

Reciprocals
Nicholas Evans

Reference in Discourse

ANDREJ A. KIBRIK

(Institute of Linguistics of the Russian Academy of Sciences and Moscow State University)

OXFORD
UNIVERSITY PRESS

OXFORD
UNIVERSITY PRESS

Great Clarendon Street, Oxford OX2 6DP

Oxford University Press is a department of the University of Oxford.
It furthers the University's objective of excellence in research, scholarship,
and education by publishing worldwide in

Oxford New York

Auckland Cape Town Dar es Salaam Hong Kong Karachi
Kuala Lumpur Madrid Melbourne Mexico City Nairobi
New Delhi Shanghai Taipei Toronto

With offices in

Argentina Austria Brazil Chile Czech Republic France Greece
Guatemala Hungary Italy Japan Poland Portugal Singapore
South Korea Switzerland Thailand Turkey Ukraine Vietnam

Oxford is a registered trade mark of Oxford University Press
in the UK and in certain other countries

Published in the United States
by Oxford University Press Inc., New York

© Andrej A. Kibrik 2011

The moral rights of the author have been asserted
Database right Oxford University Press (maker)

First published 2011

All rights reserved. No part of this publication may be reproduced,
stored in a retrieval system, or transmitted, in any form or by any means,
without the prior permission in writing of Oxford University Press,
or as expressly permitted by law, or under terms agreed with the appropriate
reprographics rights organization. Enquiries concerning reproduction
outside the scope of the above should be sent to the Rights Department,
Oxford University Press, at the address above

You must not circulate this book in any other binding or cover
and you must impose the same condition on any acquirer

British Library Cataloguing in Publication Data
Data available

Library of Congress Cataloging in Publication Data
Library of Congress Control Number: 2011929256

Typeset by SPI Publisher Services, Pondicherry, India
Printed in Great Britain
on acid-free paper by
MPG Books Group, Bodmin and King's Lynn

ISBN 978–0–19–921580–5

1 3 5 7 9 10 8 6 4 2

For Aleksandr Kibrik,
who originally proposed this research topic to me
and who has done so much for linguists and linguistics

Concise contents

Detailed contents	ix
List of figures	xviii
Abbreviations in text	xx
Abbreviations in glosses	xxi
Preface	xxvi
Acknowledgements	xxix

Part I. Preliminaries   1

1 Introduction	3
2 Basics of reference in discourse	30

Part II. Typology of Reduced Referential Devices   71

3 Major types of reduced referential devices	73
4 Pronouns and related devices	120
5 Sensitivities of reduced referential devices	159
6 Challenges of bound pronouns	185
7 The rise and fall of bound tenacious pronouns	238
Concluding remarks to Part II	284

Part III. Typology of Referential Aids   287

8 Referential aids	289
9 How functional are referential aids?	334
Concluding remarks to Part III	361

Part IV. The Cognitive Multi-Factorial Approach to Referential Choice   363

10 The cognitive multi-factorial approach	365
11 Referential choice in Russian narrative prose	396
12 Referential choice in English narrative prose	428
13 Cognitive inferences from the linguistic study of reference in discourse	445
14 Further studies based on the cognitive multi-factorial approach	459
Concluding remarks to Part IV	497

Part V. Broadening the Perspective ... 499

15 Reference and visual aspects of discourse ... 501
   Concluding remarks to Part V ... 549

16 Conclusion ... 550

Appendix 1: Questionnaire on referential systems for descriptive grammars ... 564
Appendix 2: Map of languages mentioned in the book ... 567
References ... 570
Index of languages ... 635
Index of terms ... 640

Detailed contents

List of figures	xviii
Abbreviations in text	xx
Abbreviations in glosses	xxi
Preface	xxvi
Acknowledgements	xxix

Part I. Preliminaries — 1

1 Introduction — 3

- Overview — 3
- 1.1. The nature of reference — 3
- 1.2. The importance of reference — 8
- 1.3. Reference as a discourse phenomenon — 9
- 1.4. Linguistic discourse analysis — 11
  - 1.4.1. Taxonomy of discourses — 11
  - 1.4.2. Discourse structure — 13
  - 1.4.3. Influence of discourse factors upon smaller linguistic constituents — 14
- 1.5. The cognitive approach in discourse analysis — 15
- 1.6. Discourse analysis and linguistic typology — 19
- 1.7. Typological and cognitive perspectives — 21
- 1.8. Methodology — 23
- 1.9. Terminology — 26
- Summary — 28

2 Basics of reference in discourse — 30

- Overview — 30
- 2.1. Limits and kinds of reference — 30
  - 2.1.1. Referents among the types of concepts — 31
  - 2.1.2. Specific definite and other referential statuses — 31
- 2.2. Types of specific definite reference — 34
- 2.3. Types of referential devices — 37
  - 2.3.1. Full vs. reduced referential devices — 38
  - 2.3.2. Locutors vs. non-locutors — 42
  - 2.3.3. Overt vs. zero reduced referential devices — 43

2.3.4. Position of referential devices: clause participant vs. other	44
2.3.5. Reference, prosody, and gesture	46
2.4. Referential choice and alternative notions	48
2.5. The cognitive approach to referential choice: activation in working memory	52
2.6. The speaker's and the addressee's minds: referential strategies	56
2.7. Multi-factorial approach	60
2.8. Referential conflict and referential aids	62
2.9. The structure of the subsequent parts of the book	67
Summary	69

Part II. Typology of Reduced Referential Devices 71

3 Major types of reduced referential devices	73
Overview	73
3.1. Three major types of reduced referential devices	73
3.2. Free pronouns	78
3.2.1. Free pronouns can be tenacious	80
3.2.2. Free pronouns and pronominal clitics are one category	81
3.2.3. How to distinguish free pronouns from bound pronouns?	86
3.2.4. Genealogical and geographical distribution	89
3.2.5. Free pronouns and related typological features	90
3.3. Bound (affixal) pronouns	92
3.3.1. Pronominal arguments	94
3.3.2. Tenacity	95
3.3.3. Status of noun phrases	97
3.3.4. Genealogical and geographical distribution	101
3.3.5. Bound pronouns and related typological features	102
3.4. Zero reference	104
3.4.1. Zeroes can take various positions in a clause	108
3.4.2. Role markers associated with zeroes	111
3.4.3. Genealogical and geographical distribution	112
3.4.4. Zero reference and related typological features	113
3.5. Frequencies of pure language types among the languages of the world	115
3.6. Type of dominant referential device and morphological complexity	117
Summary	118

4 Pronouns and related devices	120
Overview	120
4.1. Pronouns and pronominal categories	120
4.2. Functional analogues of personal pronouns	123
4.2.1. Demonstratives	124
4.2.2. Classifiers	127
4.2.3. Social status nouns	133
4.2.4. Pronouns vs. their functional analogues	135
4.3. Double reference pronouns	136
4.4. Pronouns marked for clausal categories	140
4.5. Strong pronouns	147
4.5.1. Free pronoun languages without morphologically specialized strong pronouns	149
4.5.2. Strong pronouns in bound pronoun languages	151
4.5.3. Strong pronouns in zero reference languages?	153
4.5.4. Functions of strong pronouns	153
4.5.5. Frequency of strong pronouns	155
Summary	157
5 Sensitivities of reduced referential devices	159
Overview	159
5.1. Inconsistency and sensitivity in referential choice	159
5.2. Different levels of activation	161
5.3. Different clause participant positions	168
5.3.1. Principal vs. Patientive as the optimal pair of contrastive clause participant positions	168
5.3.2. An alternative suggestion: Agentive vs. Absolutive	171
5.3.3. A typology of sensitivities based on clause participant position	172
5.4. Various specific contexts	176
Summary	183
6 Challenges of bound pronouns	185
Overview	185
6.1. Boundness does not equal tenacity	186
6.1.1. The case of Spanish	187
6.1.2. Boundness vs. tenacity	190
6.2. Free tenacious pronouns	191
6.2.1. Principal	191
6.2.2. Patientive	193
6.2.3. Both Principal and Patientive	195

	6.3. Bound alternating pronouns	197
	6.3.1. Patientive	198
	6.3.2. Both Principal and Patientive	199
	6.4. Free tenacious and bound alternating pronouns	200
	6.5. Boundness and tenacity	201
	6.6. Bound pronouns are not agreement markers	204
	6.6.1. What is agreement?	207
	6.6.2. Languages with polypersonal verbs	208
	6.6.3. Languages with monopersonal verbs	210
	6.6.4. Languages with bipersonal verbs	213
	6.7. Verbal person agreement	214
	6.7.1. How common is the Germanic pattern?	216
	6.7.2. Germanic person markers can occasionally be referential	221
	6.7.3. Germanic agreement participates in reference as an ancillary	225
	6.7.4. Is agreement functional?	228
	6.8. Bound zeroes	231
	Summary	236
7	The rise and fall of bound tenacious pronouns	238
	Overview	238
	7.1. The diachrony of referential systems	238
	7.2. Athabaskan, with focus on Navajo	239
	7.2.1. Northern Athabaskan	240
	7.2.2. Navajo	243
	7.2.3. The rise of the Navajo pattern	246
	7.3. Romance, with focus on French	248
	7.3.1. Spanish and general Romance	248
	7.3.2. French: from medieval to modern standard	249
	7.3.3. Colloquial French	253
	7.3.4. The French story	259
	7.4. Slavic, with focus on Russian	260
	7.4.1. Old Slavic	260
	7.4.2. South Slavic	261
	7.4.3. Russian	264
	7.4.4. The rise of the Russian pattern	267
	7.4.5. Slavic and Germanic	274
	7.5. Evolutionary paths of gaining and losing bound tenacious pronouns	275

7.5.1. Major types of reduced referential devices	276
7.5.2. Increase in boundness and tenacity (rightward evolution)	279
7.5.3. Decrease in boundness and tenacity (leftward evolution)	280
7.5.4. Do bound pronouns give way to zero reference?	281
Summary	282
Concluding remarks to Part II	284

Part III. Typology of Referential Aids — 287

8 Referential aids — 289

Overview	289
8.1. Referential aids as deconflicters	290
8.2. Ad hoc vs. conventional referential aids	291
8.3. Absolute stable sortings	295
8.3.1. Marking on free pronouns	296
8.3.2. Marking on bound pronouns	298
8.3.3. Number and person as absolute stable sortings?	299
8.3.4. Verbal marking	300
8.4. Relative stable sortings	304
8.4.1. The animacy hierarchy	304
8.4.2. The honorific hierarchy	306
8.5. Current sortings: broad domain	308
8.6. Current sortings: narrow domain	314
8.6.1. Logophoricity, or perspective taking	315
8.6.2. Topicality and subjecthood	320
8.6.3. Degree of activation	327
Summary	332

9 How functional are referential aids? — 334

Overview	334
9.1. How many referent sortings in one language?	335
9.2. Site of expression and the functioning of referential aids	337
9.3. Functions of referent sortings	338
9.3.1. Switch-reference	339
9.3.2. The current sorting based on the degree of activation	342
9.3.3. Noun classes	345
9.4. Noun class and reference in Pulaar	347
9.4.1. Strength of noun classes as a referential aid	348
9.4.2. Weakness of noun classes as a referential aid	350
9.4.3. Other conventional referential aids in Pulaar	353

9.5.	Noun class and reference in Sereer	355
	Summary	359
Concluding remarks to Part III		361

Part IV. The Cognitive Multi-Factorial Approach to Referential Choice   363

10	The cognitive multi-factorial approach	365
	Overview	365
10.1.	Cognitive analyses of reference: achievements and stumbling blocks	366
10.2.	Attention and working memory in cognitive psychology and cognitive neuroscience	367
	10.2.1. Attention	368
	10.2.2. Working memory	369
	10.2.3. Attention and working memory	372
	10.2.4. The neural grounds of attention and working memory	374
10.3.	Attention and working memory as the basis for reference in discourse	375
	10.3.1. Attention determines mention	376
	10.3.2. Activation in working memory determines referential choice	377
	10.3.3. Interaction of attention and WM activation	381
	10.3.4. Alternative hypotheses on the cognitive basis of referential choice	384
10.4.	The problem of circularity	389
10.5.	Multiplicity of factors and their interaction	390
10.6.	Properties of the cognitive multi-factorial approach to referential choice	393
	Summary	394
11	Referential choice in Russian narrative prose	396
	Overview	396
11.1.	The discourse sample	397
11.2.	Referential devices in Russian	398
11.3.	Distribution of referential devices in the sample discourse	400
11.4.	Activation factors	402
	11.4.1. The diversity of activation factors	402
	11.4.2. Correlations between candidate activation factors and referential options	406
	11.4.3. Structure of individual activation factors	407

11.5.	Referential mapping. Calculations of activation scores	416
11.6.	Minor referential devices	420
	11.6.1. *Tot* pronouns	420
	11.6.2. Zeroes	422
11.7.	World boundary filter	423
11.8.	Referential conflict filter	424
	Summary	425

12 Referential choice in English narrative prose — 428

	Overview	428
12.1.	The discourse sample. Distribution of referential devices	429
12.2.	Categorical vs. alterable referential devices	431
12.3.	Judgements on referential alternatives	432
12.4.	Referential mapping	434
12.5.	Activation factors	435
12.6.	Examples of activation score calculations	441
12.7.	Constructing a cognitive multi-factorial model	441
	Summary	444

13 Cognitive inferences from the linguistic study of reference in discourse — 445

	Overview	445
13.1.	Three classic puzzles of working memory	445
13.2.	Working memory capacity	446
	13.2.1. Working memory for specific referents	446
	13.2.2. The content of working memory: items or standard units?	447
	13.2.3. Grand activation	448
13.3.	Control of working memory	451
13.4.	Forgetting from working memory	454
13.5.	Linguistics and cognitive science	457
	Summary	458

14 Further studies based on the cognitive multi-factorial approach — 459

	Overview	459
14.1.	The neural network study	460
	14.1.1. Shortcomings of the calculative method	460
	14.1.2. Proposed solution: a neural network method	461
	14.1.3. Simulation 1: full data set	464
	14.1.4. Simulation 2: pruning	464

14.1.5. Simulation 3: reduced data set	466
14.1.6. Simulation 4: cheap data set	466
14.1.7. Comparison with the calculative approach	468
14.1.8. Comparison with Strube and Wolters (2000)	469
14.1.9. Prospects for further neural network research on referential choice	469
14.2. A corpus-based study of referential choice	470
14.2.1. The RefRhet corpus	471
14.2.2. Measuring rhetorical distance	474
14.2.3. First results from the new corpus	479
14.2.4. Preliminary results of a statistical machine learning study	483
14.2.5. Additional candidate activation factors	485
14.3. Another language: Japanese	490
14.4. Activation score, working memory capacity, and reference understanding: psycholinguistic experimental studies	493
Summary	495
Concluding remarks to Part IV	497

Part V. Broadening the Perspective 499

15 Reference and visual aspects of discourse	501
Overview	501
15.1. Deixis, exophora, and pointing	501
15.1.1. Deixis	502
15.1.2. Pointing	506
15.1.3. Exophora	510
15.1.4. Relations between deixis, exophora, and anaphora	513
15.1.5. Pointing in deixis and exophora	516
15.1.6. Recapitulation	521
15.2. Reference in a sign language	521
15.2.1. Pointing signs in Russian Sign Language	523
15.2.2. The constructed space and virtual pointing	526
15.2.3. Referential choice in Russian Sign Language	531
15.2.4. Recapitulation	536
15.3. Virtual pointing in speaking	537
15.3.1. Virtual pointing and activation	537
15.3.2. Organization of space in virtual pointing	540
15.3.3. Perspective taking	544

	15.3.4. How informative is virtual pointing?	545
	15.3.5. Recapitulation	546
	Summary	547
Concluding remarks to Part V		549
16 Conclusion		550
	16.1. What has been achieved	550
	16.2. What was disregarded	553
	16.2.1. Types of reference	553
	16.2.2. Domains of reference	556
	16.2.3. Approaches	557
	16.3. What is particularly fascinating in future research	560

Appendix 1. Questionnaire on referential systems for descriptive grammars	564
Appendix 2. Map of languages mentioned in the book	567
References	570
Index of languages	635
Index of terms	640

List of figures

1.1.	The out-of-the-window scene in Leipzig, at different times	4
1.2.	Linking of referents and referential devices	5
1.3.	Schematic representation of linking	6
2.1.	The timing of activation cost with relation to speaker and listener	57
2.2.	The cognitive multi-factorial model of referential choice (the first pass)	61
2.3.	The cognitive multi-factorial model of referential choice (the second pass)	64
3.1.	Linking of free pronouns, such as English *he* in (3.3b)	75
3.2.	Linking of bound pronouns, such as Navajo *dz-* in (3.2b)	76
3.3.	Linking of referential zeroes, such as Japanese Ø in (3.4b)	76
3.4.	Linking of the coreferential full NP and bound pronoun, both referring to 'the sons', in Abkhaz, example (3.14c)	97
3.5.	A comparison of global distribution of three typological features: predisposition to bound pronouns, head-marking, and polysynthesis	104
3.6.	A disallowed use of the zero convention	105
3.7.	Frequency of the three types of dominant reduced referential devices plotted against the degree of verb inflectional synthesis	117
4.1.	Double linking of the portmanteau Dan-Gwèètaa pronoun, referring to both 'Jean' and 'the bread', examples (4.12c, d)	137
6.1.	Linking of Principal referential devices in Lyélé (example 3.5i), German (6.32i), and Latin (6.29ii): referent non-activated	226
6.2.	Linking of Principal referential devices in Lyélé (example 3.5i), German (6.32ii), and Latin (6.29i): referent activated	226
7.1.	Routes of historical development of reduced referential devices, attested in Athabaskan, Germanic, Romance, and Slavic	281
8.1.	Ranges of activation appropriate for the Russian third person pronoun *on* and the lesser activation demonstrative *tot*	331
8.2.	A classification of referential aids	332
10.1.	Dependency of the probability of a reduced referential form upon the degree of referent's activation in WM: four thresholds	380
10.2.	The cognitive multi-factorial model of referential choice (the third pass)	394
11.1.	Examples of rhetorical tree fragments	404
11.2.	Examples of rhetorical tree fragments	404

12.1.	Averaged judgements on referential alternatives	434
12.2.	Rhetorical graph representing excerpt (12.7)	437
13.1.	The dynamics of two protagonist referents' activation and of grand activation in an excerpt from the English story (lines 1401 to 2104)	450
13.2.	The dynamics of two protagonist referents' activation and of grand activation in an excerpt from the English story (lines 201 to 903)	450
13.3.	The quartet of cognitive and linguistic phenomena	452
13.4.	The interplay of focal attention and high activation in cognition and in discourse	454
14.1.	Net from Simulation 3	467
14.2.	Windows of the MMAX2 program	473
14.3.	A fragment of a rhetorical graph from the RST Discourse Treebank	475
14.4.	Mononuclear vs. multinuclear structures	475
14.5.	A reinterpretation of discourse units, connected to multinuclear groups	476
14.6.	A multilayer multinuclear structure	477
14.7.	An example of a rhetorical graph from the RST Discourse Treebank	478
15.1.	Elements of a canonical pointing act	507
15.2.	The situation in which (15.13) can be uttered	524
15.3.	Spaces employed in referential choice in RSL	527
15.4.	An episode from the Pear Film	528
15.5.	A screenshot for the pointing gesture in (15.20b)	538
15.6.	Screenshots for the pointing gestures in (15.21b, c)	539
15.7.	A moment from the Pear Film retold in (15.21)	540
15.8.	Screenshots for the illustrative gesture in (15.22b)	541
15.9.	Screenshots for the illustrative gesture in (15.22c)	542
15.10.	Screenshots for the two pointing gestures in (15.22d)	542
16.1.	Dynamics of a single referent's activation	560

Abbreviations in text

AS	activation score
CMF	cognitive multi-factorial
DS	different-subject
EDU	elementary discourse unit
LinD	linear distance
NP	noun phrase
ParaD	paragraph distance
RhD	rhetorical distance
RSL	Russian Sign Language
RST	Rhetorical Structure Theory
SS	same-subject
WM	working memory

Abbreviations in glosses[1]

1	first person
2	second person
3	third person
4	fourth person
A	Agentive
ABL	ablative
ABS	absolutive
ACC	accusative
ACT	Actor
ADDR	addressive
ADV	adverb
AG	agentive (case)
ALL	allative
AN	animate
ANAPH	anaphoric
ANT	anterior
AOR	aorist
ART	article
ASSERT	assertion
ASSOC	associative
AUX	auxiliary
CAUS	causative
CJT	conjoint
CL	classifier, noun class
COMIT	comitative
COMPL	completive
COND	conditional
CONJ	conjunctive

[1] As is now conventional in typological work, I generally follow the Leipzig glossing rules when providing morpheme-by-morpheme glosses in examples (see http://www.eva.mpg.de/lingua/resources/glossing-rules.php). Additional conventions, such as the use of colon and underscore, are explained in footnotes on first appearance.

CONN	connective
CONR	connector
CONS	consecutive
CONT	continuity
CONTIN	continuous
CONV	converb
COP	copula
DAT	dative
DECL	declarative
DEF	definite
DEM	demonstrative
DEP	dependent
DET	determiner
DIM	diminutive
DIST	distal
DISTR	distributive
DM	discourse marker
DS	different-subject
DU	dual
DYN	dynamic
EMPH	emphatic
EPENTH	epenthetic
ERG	ergative
EVID	evidential
EX	exclamative
EXCL	exclusive
EXDEM	extended demonstrative
EXIST	existential
EYEWPRES	eyewitness present
F	feminine
FACT	factative (tense)
FOC	focus
FRUST	frustrative
FS	false start
FUT	future
GEN	genitive
GENER	generic

GER	gerund(ive)
H	human
HES	hesitation
HIST	historical (tense)
HORT	hortative
IDPH	ideophone
ILL	illative
IMP	impersonal
IMPER	imperative
IMPF	imperfect
IMPFV	imperfective
INAL	inalienable possession
INAN	inanimate
INC	inceptive
INCL	inclusive
INCOMPL	incompletive
INDEF	indefinite
INF	infinitive
INFR	inferred
INSTR	instrumental
INTRANS	intransitive
INV	inverse
INVIS	invisible
IRREAL	irrealis
ITER	iterative
KIN	kinship term
LIG	ligature
LOC	locative
LOCAL	local referential device
LOG	logophoric (pronoun)
LOGHR	hearer-oriented logophoric (pronoun)
M	masculine
N	neuter
NARR	narrative (case)
NEG	negation, negative
NEUT	neutral (aspect)
NF	non-feminine

NH	non-human
NMZR	nominalizer
NOM	nominative
NPAST	non-past
NPOSS	non-possessed
NPRES	non-present
NSG	non-singular
NSUBJ	non-subject
NVIS	non-visual
OBJ	object
OBL	oblique
OBV	obviative
OPT	optative
P	Patientive
PARTIC	participle
PASS	passive
PAT	patientive (case)
PAUS	pausal
PEG	pegative (case)
PF	perfect
PFV	perfective
PL	plural
PLPF	pluperfect
POSS	possessive
POSTCL	postpositive noun class marker
POT	potential
PRECL	prepositive noun class marker
PREF	prefix (not specified)
PRES	present
PRO	pronoun
PROG	progressive
PROL	prolative
PROTAG	discourse protagonist
PROX	proximate
PTCL	particle (not specified)
PURP	purposive
PV	preverb

QU	question marker
QUOT	quotative
REAL	realis
RECPAST	recent past
REDUP	reduplication
REFDIR	referential directive
REFL	reflexive
REFPART	referential partitive
REL	relative, relativizer
REMPAST	remote past
SBJV	subjunctive
SBRD	subordinate
SG	singular
SS	same-subject
SUBJ	subject
SUFF	suffix (not specified)
SUP	supine
TERM	terminal
TOP	topic
TOPADV	topic advancing (voice)
TOPP	topical Patientive
TRANS	transitive
TRANSF	transformative
TRI	trial
TRPOSS	transfer of possession
UND	Undergoer
VALINCR	valency increase
VERBZR	verbalizer
VERT	vertical
VIS	visible
VN	verbal noun

Preface

As people talk, they constantly refer, that is, they mention persons or objects. The process of reference is among the most central and ubiquitous phenomena in the functioning of natural languages. When a speaker has made the decision to mention a certain referent, the question of referential choice arises: what linguistic form to employ for referring to the given referent – for example, a full noun phrase, such as *my neighbour from downstairs*, or a reduced device, such as the pronoun *he*. Reference and referential choice are what this book attempts to describe and explain.

Reference and referential choice are inherently discourse-oriented linguistic processes. That is, they are part of normal discourse production and comprehension as performed by language users in everyday communication, and can be properly understood only as such. Treating reference as an essentially syntactic or logical phenomenon may be an amusing intellectual exercise but it has little in common with how actual speakers and listeners make use of referential expressions.

Two main issues are discussed in this book. The first one is **linguistic diversity** found in the realm of reference in discourse, that is, what linguistic resources are employed in the typologically diverse languages of the world for reference and referential choice. The second issue is the **cognitive foundations** of reference in discourse: how the speaker's mind operates as he or she refers and performs referential choice. These two issues constitute traditionally separate but factually interrelated facets of reference. Considering them in conjunction paves the path for a comprehensive account of reference in discourse. The cognitive approach tells us what basic and presumably universal processes underlie a single act of reference in an individual speaker, while the typological view provides the range and limits of diversity in how human languages handle the omnipresent referential function. In fact, I believe that any theoretical issue in linguistics is better explored through the combination of cognitive and cross-linguistic analysis. This provides both small-scale and grand-scale perspectives, which in conjunction give a truer picture. This particularly applies to discourse-oriented phenomena, related to online language use.

This book summarizes my studies of reference in discourse over the years from the early 1980s to the present. It is actually embarrassing that the preparation of this monograph has taken so long, even though the time was shared with other projects. But better late than never. Of course, the ideas expounded here differ substantially (and, hopefully, positively) from what was proposed a quarter of a century ago in my early Russian-language studies such as Kibrik (1983, 1987a, or 1988). However, I must say that the most important tenets, including the discourse nature of reference and the combination of cognitive and typological perspectives have remained the same.

My research in discourse reference was influenced from the very beginning by such studies as Chafe (1976), Hirst (1981), and Lyons (1975), and a bit later Givón (1983a), Tomlin (1987), and Fox (1987a). Later on, my work continued in parallel with that of these and other authors. This book is more problem-oriented than approach-oriented, so for the most part I am expounding my own current ideas. Where appropriate, however, I compare my approach with those of other authors.

This book consists of five parts. The introductory Part I includes two chapters. Chapter 1 provides a general characterization of reference in discourse, as well as the basics of the cognitive approach in discourse analysis and a relation between discourse studies and linguistic typology. Chapter 2 introduces the main premises of my approach to referential phenomena, including the difference between reference as such and referential choice, as well as the underlying cognitive processes of attention and activation in working memory. I draw a distinction between two kinds of linguistic resources involved in reference, namely referential devices and referential aids. Referential devices perform reference per se; particularly important for this book are reduced referential devices, such as pronouns. Referential aids are linguistic devices that do not refer themselves but help the referential process by discriminating between two or more concurrently activated referents.

Parts II and III are devoted to cross-linguistic aspects of reference. Part II (Chapters 3 to 7) focuses on the typology of reduced referential devices, that is, the elements that perform the referential function. Part III (Chapters 8 and 9) treats referential aids which are, essentially, various kinds of referent sortings. Generally, Parts II and III discuss **what** referential resources are found in human languages.

In contrast, Part IV (Chapters 10 to 14) looks at referential phenomena from a more dynamic perspective: **how** reference is performed in discourse. In this part an explicitly cognitive approach is taken, and an attempt is made to use positive knowledge from related sciences about the cognitive processes immediately related to reference in discourse.

Part V, consisting of Chapter 15, offers a more encompassing picture of referential phenomena, involving the visual aspects of discourse. A more detailed preview of Parts II–V appears at the end of Chapter 2. The concluding Chapter 16 summarizes the main findings and outlines possible avenues of further research.

Acknowledgements

During my years of study of reference in discourse, and the preparation of this book in particular, I had a chance to benefit from the help of numerous colleagues and friends. It is difficult to mention each of them here, but I would like to note at least the most important and the most recent aides who helped this book to become better, or to come into being at all. Of course, all of the individuals mentioned below are absolved of any responsibility for any flaws or errors found in this book.

In the first place, I would like to thank three colleagues of mine whose help over the years has been extremely important for my work, including that on reference in discourse, namely Bernard Comrie, Tom Givón, and Martin Haspelmath. In particular, Bernard Comrie supported a number of projects of mine that made the completion of this book possible.

Anna Siewierska originally proposed that I submit a monograph on reference to the series Oxford Studies in Typology and Linguistic Theory. It took a long time before it became a reality, but I am very grateful to Anna for that initiative.

Among the colleagues who read the pre-final version of this book I would like to single out two: Martin Haspelmath and Olga Fedorova. Martin took on the immense labour of reading through the manuscript with careful attention and came up with hundreds of valuable and ingenious comments. Olga read the whole manuscript, many parts of it twice or more, and gave me tremendous help at various stages of my work, including insightful comments on many chapters and sections, suggestions about relevant literature as well as editing. I am infinitely grateful to both Martin and Olga for their contributions.

The following people have read all of the manuscript or some chapters or sections and provided numerous and valued comments: Anna Siewierska, Maria Falikman, Tore Nesset, Søren Wichmann, Mira Bergelson, Ekaterina Delikishkina, Antonina Koval, Marianne Mithun, Andriy Myachykov, Julija Nikolaeva, and Elena Shamaro. Olga Fedorova, Elena Shamaro, Yuri Koryakov, Ekaterina Delikishkina, and Anna Jurčenko helped to compile the indexes for this book, Yuri Koryakov created the map that appears as Appendix 2. Olga Fedorova, Marina Raskladkina, Evgenija Prozorova, Julija Nikolaeva, and Marija Melitickaja provided indispensable assistance with certain editorial issues. I would like to express my sincere gratitude to all of them.

Over the years, I had multiple conversations and extensive correspondence with colleagues who helped to clarify certain issues discussed in this book. It is impossible to list here all who contributed in this or that way, but I vividly remember useful discussions with Wally Chafe, Matthew Dryer, Barbara Fox, André Grüning, Aleksandr Kibrik, Johanna Nichols, Ekaterina Pechenkova, Ted Sanders, James Sawusch, Irina Sekerina, Mike Tomasello, Russ Tomlin, Robert Van Valin, Boris Velichkovsky, Valentin Vydrine, as well as with many of the colleagues already mentioned above. Of course, I am very thankful to all of them for their help. Many specific acknowledgements related to local points are provided in footnotes to the chapters below.

It was a great pleasure to communicate with the Oxford University Press people throughout the preparation of this project. I would especially like to thank John Davey, Julia Steer, Elmandi du Toit, Jenny Lunsford, and Brendan Mac Evilly for their kindness, patience, and professionalism. Enormous support was provided at the proofs stage by Andrew Woodard, an extremely interested and competent reader of this work.

I also thank all colleagues from the institutions where I work or where I visited, including the Institute of Linguistics of the Russian Academy of Sciences, Moscow State University, the University of California at Santa Barbara, the University of Oregon, the University of Alaska Fairbanks, and the Max Planck Institute for Evolutionary Anthropology in Leipzig. My interaction with them was highly beneficial and enriching, including discussions of my talks related to the topics of this book. Other talks and presentations at conferences and seminars, too numerous to be listed here, also helped to improve some of the ideas proposed below.

Of course, this project could never have been completed without the help and support of my family, both nuclear and extended. Thank you all very much for assistance and encouragement. Enormous support was provided at the proofs stage by Andrew Woodard, an extremely interested and competent reader of this work.

Research projects underlying various parts of this book were supported by a number of grants, including a grant from the Wenner-Gren Foundation for Anthropological Research (1993), grant ZZ 5000/324 from the International Science Foundation (1994), grants 98-06-80442, 03-06-80241, and 09-06-00390 from the Russian Foundation for Basic Research, the OIFN RAN project 'Discourse structure, grammar, and their interaction: typological aspects', and the Russian Foundation for the Humanities grant 11–04–00153. Decisive for launching the write-up stage was my stay in Germany in 2006–07, financially supported by the Alexander von Humboldt Foundation and by the Department of Linguistics of the Max Planck Institute for Evolutionary Anthropology, Leipzig. I cordially thank all of the above-mentioned institutions for their support.

Part I
Preliminaries

1

Introduction

Overview

Reference is among the central and omnipresent phenomena in language and in language use. In this chapter I present the most preliminary account of the nature of referents and reference (section 1.1) and demonstrate their importance (section 1.2). Reference is, first and foremost, a discourse phenomenon (section 1.3) and can properly be understood only as a part of a larger enterprise – the linguistic discipline known as discourse analysis (section 1.4). The approach to reference adopted in this book is cognitive in nature – that is, overt linguistic phenomena are explained in terms of underlying cognitive processes (section 1.5). But this book is also typological, that is, interested in linguistic diversity (section 1.6). The combination of the discourse perspective with cognitive interpretation and with the panoramic typological picture, outlined in section 1.7, constitutes the spirit of this book. Sections 1.8 and 1.9 address methodological and terminological issues, respectively.

1.1 The nature of reference

Human cognition represents a large part of our experience in terms of entities, or referents. As I am writing these words, sitting at my desk in Leipzig, Germany, I can look out of my window and observe a number of referents, as well as events and states they participate in. Across the street, there is a building of the Institute for animal breeding and reproduction. This building is a large, complex entity. Some of its parts can also be perceived as referents – in particular, its magnificent red tile roof. This roof attracts my visual attention every time I look out of the window. But now the most prominent figure in the scene is a man who is working on this very steep roof, a safety rope on his waist. Despite the man being very tiny compared to the whole scene, and the roof in particular, the fact that he is moving and my knowing that he is animate attract my attention to him very strongly. The man is fixing tiles, sometimes relocating his ladder along the edge of the roof with movements that look quite

4   I. Preliminaries

FIGURE 1.1. The out-of-the-window scene in Leipzig, at different times

dangerous to me. Apart from the tiler, the picture is quite static. Occasionally a car, a tram, or a cyclist rush by, and rain clouds are moving through the sky. But the man is the obvious protagonist of this scene. Now I observe that he has disappeared from the roof through a dormer window. But his ladder is still there, so probably he is going to come back. He comes back the next morning, now working on the ridge of the roof. Another change from yesterday is that the weather is sunny, and I can occasionally see other kinds of moving objects – aircraft in the sky leaving a trail behind them. A couple of pictures illustrating the scene in question are shown in Figure 1.1.

A number of **referents** have been mentioned in the above description of the out-of-the-window scene: the building, its roof, vehicles, clouds, the man, his ladder, aircraft and their trails. The anthropocentric human cognition treats some of these referents – in particular, the man – as more prototypical than the rest of them. There are other ways in which referents can be less than fully prototypical. For example, the roof may be viewed as a location rather than a referent or object (see below). Clouds and aircraft trails are very transient compared to prototypical referents that are relatively stable across time. People also have the ability to treat as referents those concepts that are actually not referents at all – for example, the weather is a state of the environment rather than a referent.

So the boundaries of the category 'referent' are not clear-cut, but most often we know when we encounter a referent. This knowledge is partly gained through language: in language use, people mention referents by nominal expressions, such as nouns and pronouns. Referents do not have to be perceived entities of the external world; they can be brought to mind not only from perception but also from long-term memory or imagination. Throughout this book I understand 'referent' to be an image in a person's mind, and it will not be relevant whether a referent has an independent physical existence.

This book is about referents and especially about their use in speech or writing. The process of mentioning referents came to be called **reference** or **referring**. Linguistic elements that perform a mention of a referent are called **referential/referring expressions** or **referential devices**. Thus the speaker, when performing an act of reference, links a referential expression to a referent. In order to illustrate this kind of linking, Figure 1.2 repeats an element of the above description once again, and couples it with a picture containing several referents.

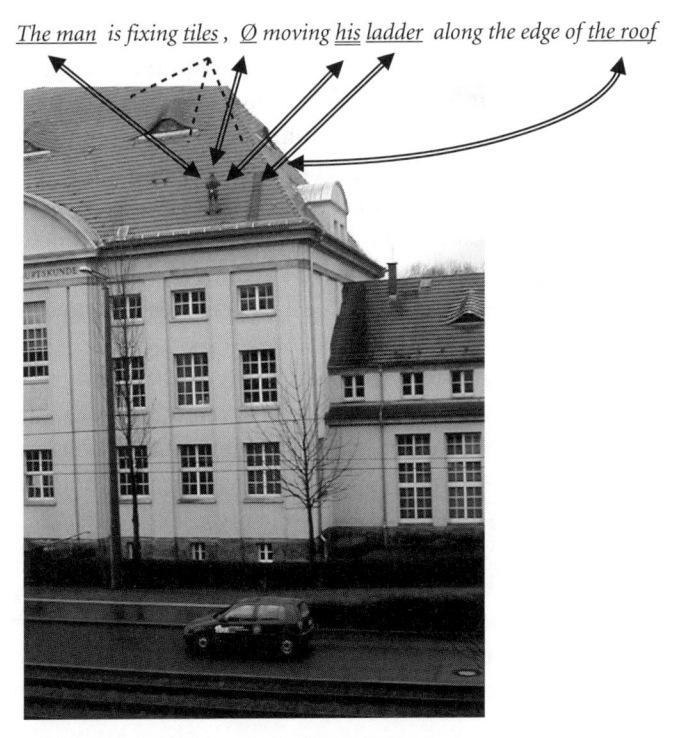

FIGURE 1.2. Linking of referents and referential devices

In Figure 1.2, the photograph of the scene stands for a mental representation that I have while writing or editing or rereading my description of the scene I saw out of the window. So I use this picture as a substitute for imagery that I have in my mind when I think about certain referents.

In various chapters of this book, I will be using schemes depicting linking between referential expressions and referents. (This kind of linking is termed 'referral' by Schiffrin 2006: 18.) As the scheme in Figure 1.3 illustrates, there can be multiple mentions of a single referent in discourse. The brace line, connecting three referential expressions (*the man*, the zero mention accompanying the gerund, and *his*), indicates that all of these expressions link to the same referent.

All three mentions of the referent 'the man', represented in Figure 1.3, are instances of specific definite reference, when a clearly delineated individual is meant. An example of a less prototypical kind of reference can be seen in Figure 1.2 – this is the nominal *tiles*, linking to a rather fuzzy subset of roof elements; this kind of less than clear-cut linking is indicated by dotted lines in Figure 1.2. In this book, I will be mostly interested in specific definite reference; the issue is further elaborated in Chapter 2.

Besides referents, there are other kinds of concepts evoked when I think or talk, especially events and states. A number of these were mentioned in the above description – for example, the event of the man disappearing was mentioned, and the state of the man looking tiny. Events and states are more complex concepts than referents in the sense that referents participate in events and states – for example, the referent 'the man' is the central participant of both the disappearance event and the looking tiny state. In the linguistic structure, type events/states are represented by predicates, in particular verbs, and token events/states by clauses. Referents that are event/state participants are represented by referring expressions that are clause participants themselves.

Events/states are usually thought of as being more central in linguistic structure compared to referents. They are conveyed by predicates that are heads of clauses. On the other hand, referents are simpler and more

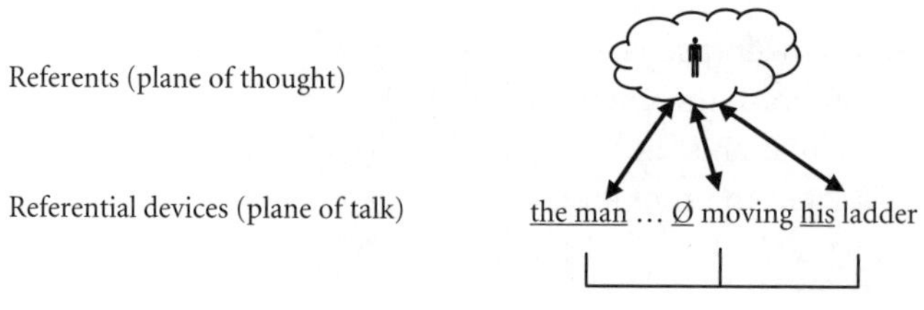

Referents (plane of thought)

Referential devices (plane of talk)   the man ... Ø moving his ladder

FIGURE 1.3. Schematic representation of linking

elementary concepts compared to events/states. They have more of an independent existence. We can think of a referent, such as 'my car' or 'the ladder' irrespective of any event/state it would participate in. But it is difficult to think of a disappearance event, or of a state of being tiny, in general, that is, without any, at least vague, idea of a participating referent. So understanding reference and referents, which this book attempts to contribute to, is a necessary prerequisite for understanding language.

This book is based on the assumption that the distinction between referents and events/states is very fundamental. It is reflected in the distinction between nominal and verbal expressions. The universality of this distinction is sometimes questioned, but in most languages and in most instances differentiating between referents and events/states is relatively unproblematic, so even if this assumption is too strong as a universal I will still accept it here.

As has already been pointed out above, speakers occasionally represent states and events as referents. For example, the expression *the weather*, even though being a nominal, hardly evokes a genuine referent; rather it is a state. Also consider the expression *movements* in the above description of the scene. The man's movements are not an entity, they are a series of events, but they are conventionally and conveniently represented as if they were entitites. What we observe in such instances is a manifestation of a conceptual metaphor in the sense of Lakoff and Johnson (1980): the metaphor EVENT/STATE IS AN ENTITY. Such metaphorical usages should not prevent us from understanding the basic difference between referents, states, and events.

Apart from referents, events, and states, other fundamental kinds of concepts are times and locations. People (and human languages) often conceptualize times and locations as referents – this is a lot more common than conceptualizing events/states as referents. In the scene description above there were multiple mentions of times (*morning, yesterday*) and locations (*the edge, the sky*) that are treated by the language as if they were referents.

Thus all kinds of concepts are closely interwoven and interact with each other. Reference is not an autonomous module of language as referents, first, may border on other kinds of concepts and, second, participate in events/states. Therefore, discussing referents to the exclusion of other types of concepts is an inevitably simplified approach. However, as a common Russian saying goes, 'One cannot embrace the unembraceable'.[1] So the discussion in this book will be focused on referents and reference, although occasionally we will touch upon issues related to other kinds of concepts, for example times and events.

---

[1] This aphorism belongs to Kozma Prutkov, a fictional author invented in mid-19th century by Aleksey Tolstoy and the Zhemchuzhnikov brothers.

1.2 The importance of reference

Reference is a ubiquitous phenomenon in language use (cf. Schiffrin 2006: 33). This is true in terms of both the informational load carried by referential expressions and their frequency. As for the former, Biber et al. (1999: 230–232) have proposed a simple but telling manipulation of a text: removing all nominal elements (roughly equivalent to referential expressions) and seeing what remains of the overall meaning of this text. (1.1) is an extract from a conversation between two persons.

(1.1)   A: Well I thought you were going to talk to me about Christmas presents.
        B: I have spoken to you about Christmas presents. I've told you about all I can tell you. Why don't you, why don't you sit down and tell me what you want for Christmas. I mean that would be useful.

Now, (1.2) is a transformed version of the same extract where only nominal elements have been retained (including those of a hierarchically complex internal structure), while in (1.3), on the other hand, all such nominal elements have been removed but all other linguistic elements preserved:

(1.2)   A: I   you   me   Christmas presents.
        B: I   you   Christmas presents. I   you   all I can tell you.   you   you   me what you want for Christmas. I   that.

(1.3)   A: Well   thought   were going to talk to   about   .
        B: have spoken to   about   .   've told   about. Why don't   , why don't   sit down and tell   .   mean   would be useful.

Comparing these two manipulated sequences with the original in (1.1) makes it quite obvious that a huge amount of information contained in the sample of language use is implemented in referential expressions. As Biber et al. (1999: 232) put it, 'the versions with only nominal elements ... are far more informative because of the *referential specification* [original emphasis – A.K.] given by the nominal elements. That is, the nominals, which normally play key roles as clause elements ... specify who and what the text is about.'

As concerns the frequency of referential expressions in language use, it is also overwhelming. According to Biber et al. (1999: 235), nouns and pronouns in four registers of English discourse (conversation, fiction, news, and academic prose) constitute between 30% and 40% of the words in their corpora. (Figures are not provided, these are my assessment of the diagram in this source.) That is, about every third word in natural discourse is a referential expression. In fact, the figures must be even higher, given that some very frequent words (such as articles and prepositions) are also a part of referential expressions. In extract (1.1) cited above, 26 graphic words out of 53, that is almost 50%, belong to nominal expressions. It is easy to find even more extreme examples. Consider a quite different kind of language use, the following limerick (Edward Lear. *Complete nonsense.* Wordsworth editions, 1994.):

(1.4) There was a <u>Young Lady of Bute</u>,
      <u>Who</u> played on <u>a silver-gilt fute;</u>
        <u>She</u> played <u>several jigs</u>
        To <u>*her* uncle's white pigs</u>,
    <u>That amusing Young Lady of Bute</u>

In this limerick there are eleven referent mentions per 28 words. (Of course, there are much fewer different referents.) In the example, each referent mention is indicated by a separate emphasis. The eleven referent mentions account for 22 words, while only six words do not participate in any referential expression.

Clearly, referring is among the most fundamental skills of language users, and linguistic communication would never be possible without this skill.

1.3 Reference as a discourse phenomenon

As we have seen in Figures 1.2 and 1.3 above, there can be multiple referential expressions linking to one and the same referent. Obviously, this situation is extremely frequent. After a referent is introduced, speakers often mention it and mention it again over and over. There is a long tradition in linguistics and other language disciplines (philosophy, psychology, artificial intelligence) to think of this kind of repeated reference as a very local phenomenon. To use the already familiar example,

(1.5) The man is fixing tiles, Ø moving his ladder along the edge of the roof.

the first mention of the referent (*the man*) can be thought of as being referentially independent, while the subsequent mentions (Ø, *his*) as being dependent on the first one. According to this approach, a dependent referential expression does not link to the referent directly but rather picks up its reference from an independent expression. This is because the first mention is the subject of the clause, that is, a position superordinate to the ones in which Ø and *his* occur. In other words, the dependent and the independent expressions are within a single syntactic domain, and the use of the dependent expressions can be possibly explained by certain syntactic rules. This approach may be defendable in this particular instance, but it cannot be generalized to most other instances of repeated mention. Consider another extract from my scene description above:

(1.6) But <u>the man</u> is the obvious protagonist of this scene. Now I observe that <u>he</u> has disappeared from the roof through a dormer window. But <u>his</u> ladder is still there, so probably <u>he</u> is going to come back. <u>He</u> comes back the next morning, now working on the ridge of the roof.

In this case, there is a supposedly independent mention *the man* at the beginning of this extract, and four subsequent mentions by means of third person pronouns (as well as some additional zero mentions). Note that one of them (*his* in *his ladder*) is very similar to the one we just discussed as possibly a syntactically-based use. None of these four third person pronouns can be explained with the help of syntactic rules, for the simple reason that they appear in different sentences and are thus beyond the reach of syntactic rules. The usage of referential expressions such as those in (1.6) is guided by discourse-based, rather than syntactic, rules.

Reference is a fundamentally discourse-oriented phenomenon, and there are generally no strict rules regarding the distance or structural relationships between subsequent pronominal mentions of the same referent. As will be discussed at several points in this book, subsequent mentions appearing within one and the same syntactic domain, as in (1.5), do occur, and in such instances one can in principle get along with syntactic rules alone. But it must be understood very clearly that this is nothing but a special case of a more general discourse phenomenon.

Examples (1.5) and (1.6), taken in conjunction, give an approximate idea of the relative frequencies of clearly discourse-based and potentially syntactic occurrences of referential expressions. Even when two mentions occur in one and the same sentence, as in the third sentence of (1.6), both can still be unequivocally discourse-based, as it is hard to think of a syntactic rule explaining one of these mentions through the other one. (The relationship between purely discourse-based and partly syntactic uses of referential devices is further discussed in section 2.2.)

Throughout this book, reference will be viewed as a discourse-based phenomenon. The principles underlying the use of referential expressions will to a great extent build upon the structure of discourse and other discourse-oriented factors. The relationship between discourse and reference is strong in the other direction as well: reference constitutes one of the most salient and persistent discourse phenomena.

At this point I leave the focused discussion of reference for a while and will return to it, in a more detailed way, in Chapter 2. The remainder of this chapter is devoted to the general framework of this study, beginning with discourse analysis in section 1.4.

1.4 Linguistic discourse analysis

Since reference is a discourse phenomenon, this book is an exercise in discourse analysis. Reviewing discourse analysis as a discipline is beyond my goal here, but some foundational studies that have laid the groundwork for its modern state include Propp (1928), Mathesius (1939), Figurovskij (1948). Harris (1952), Hartmann (1964), van Dijk (1972), Sacks (1974), Grimes (1975), Chafe (1976), Givón (ed.) (1979), Nikolaeva (1978), Galperin (1981), Longacre (1983a), and Brown and Yule (1983). Discourse analysis is a huge, rapidly expanding, interdisciplinary field (see e.g. van Dijk (ed.) 1985, Mann and Thompson (eds.) 1992, Chafe 1994, van Dijk 1997, Schiffrin et al. (eds.) 2001, Dooley and Levinsohn 2001, Makarov 2003, Johnstone 2002, Graesser et al. (ed.) 2003, Renkema 2004, Paltridge 2006, Biber et al. 2007, Renkema (ed.) 2009). A variety of disciplines, including linguistics, psychology, sociology, anthropology, and many others, contribute to discourse analysis. Here we are interested in **linguistic discourse analysis** – a part of linguistics belonging to the paradigm of constituent-oriented fields, such as phonetics/phonology, morphology, and syntax. Linguistic discourse analysis deals with linguistic constituents of the maximal, unlimited size, that is whole discourses.

Linguistic discourse analysis has three main issues of concern (Kibrik 2003, 2011). The first question, common in the study of any natural phenomenon, is the question of classification, or taxonomy: what kinds of this phenomenon are found? The second question concerns the internal organization of a phenomenon: what is its structure? The third question is: how can the given phenomenon be characterized with respect to other related phenomena? It is useful to briefly overview these three parts of linguistic discourse analysis.

1.4.1 *Taxonomy of discourses*

There are several ways in which particular discourses can differ from each other. The first major taxonomy is based on the **mode** of discourse, that is, the opposition between spoken and written discourse. A systematic comparison of spoken and written discourse began only in the last several decades; see Zemskaja et al. (1981), Chafe (1982), Miller and Weinart (1998). Written discourse is secondary to the oral use of language in all respects, and thus must be viewed as an adaptation of the basic features of language to the graphic/visual mode of presentation. Sometimes one also speaks about the internal mode of discourse (Vygotsky 1934/1994) and about the electronic mode (Herring (ed.) 1996, Baron 2000), although the latter is actually a submode within the written mode. In discourse studies it is useful to always control for whether data comes from spoken or written language use, as discourse processes, including reference, may be sensitive to mode. Part IV of this book deals with written discourse, and some studies reported in Part V with spoken discourse. In the typological Parts II and III I try to distinguish between spoken and written evidence, but that is not always possible, as descriptive studies of various languages are frequently indeterminate on the spoken/written status of cited data. Finally, it should be noted that, besides spoken languages, there exist signed languages. One study reported in Part V addresses data of a signed language.

The second central taxonomy of discourse is a classification into **genres** (Bakhtin 1953/1986, Swales 1990, Martin and Rose 2008). Discourse genres are classes of discourses that correspond to certain standard communicative goals, typical of particular discourse communities. As has been pointed out by Bakhtin, knowledge of genres is as important for using a language as knowing its grammar. 'If speech genres did not exist ... linguistic communication would be almost impossible' (Bakhtin 1953/1986: 449). Discourse genres crosscut the modes: for example, the genre of a story can appear in the spoken mode and in the written mode, still being the same genre. Genres can be defined in terms of underlying genre schemata – templates that generalize the order of meaningful components, or 'moves', in a token of the given genre. For example, according to Chafe (1994: 128), stories told by interlocutors follow the following schema: (a) orientation; (b) complication; (c) climax; (d) denouement; (e) coda. For another discussion of a genre schema, see Kong (1998) on the slight variation in schemata for business letters. It has been suggested sometimes that genres can be identified on the basis of their lexico-grammatical peculiarities. As the study by Biber (1989) has revealed, this is not viable: from the point of view of lexico-grammatical characteristics, the discourse of one genre can be very heterogeneous.

This latter observation brings us to the next taxonomy of discourse, this time concerning not whole discourses but their parts or **passages.** The following types of passages have been identified by Longacre (1983a): narrative, descriptive, expository, argumentative, and instructive. See also Graesser and Goodman (1985); for a more recent discussion and a somewhat different repertoire of passages, see Smith (2003). Passages are much more homogeneous than genres in terms of their lexico-grammatical characteristics. For example, narrative passages largely consist of clauses whose verbal predicates are past tense and perfective. Genres are not monotonous in terms of types of passages they consist of. For example, moves (b) through (d) of the story schema cited above are typically narrative, while move (a) is typically descriptive, that is, consists of descriptions of states rather than of temporally sequenced events. It is, therefore, not surprising that genres are heterogeneous from a lexico-grammatical point of view: a combination of various passages within a discourse of a given genre gives rise to a mixture of lexico-grammatical patterns. The data used in this book largely consist of stories and, most of the time, the narrative type of passages. In this sense the findings of this book may be somewhat limited, but it should be emphasized that narrative is among the most fundamental and universal types of discourse, stemming from the distinctly human ability to recollect experiences; see Prince (1982), Longacre (1983a), Bamberg (1987), Bergelson (2007), Tomasello (2008: Ch. 6). Also note that narratives are convenient for referential studies because referents typically recur in narratives more consistently than in many other discourse types.

Other differences between kinds of discourse, crosscutting the ones just discussed, relate to the so-called **functional style** and **degree of formality**. The notion of functional style, developed in Russian linguistics (see e.g. Solganik 2003, Dolinin 2004; cf. also Ädel and Reppen (eds.) 2008) correspond to typical social domains, such as lay, official, commercial, political, learned, etc. Degree of formality depends on the kind of social relationship between discourse participants, including their relative status, gender, age, etc., and is closely related to the phenomena often subsumed under the notion of politeness (Brown and Levinson 1987, Scollon and Scollon 2001, Bergelson 2007). Both functional styles and formality are reflected in many lexical, grammatical, and phonetic choices made by the speaker, and the chance is high that they can affect referential processes as well.

The diversity of discourse types is not exhausted by the distinctive features briefly discussed above. The variation of discourse is vast, and its further discussion is far beyond the goals of this book (cf. Kibrik 2009a). An overarching term sometimes used to capture all possible discourse types (identified on the basis of any or all of the distinctive features) is **register**; see e.g. Biber (2006).

1.4.2 *Discourse structure*

The second major issue in linguistic discourse analysis is discourse structure. It is useful to distinguish between the global and the local structure of discourse (van Dijk and Kintsch 1983). Global discourse structure is the segmentation of discourse into its immediate constituents or large chunks, such as paragraphs in an article (see e.g. Brown and Yule 1983) or groups of adjacent and interrelated turns in a conversation (Schegloff 1973, Baranov and Krejdlin 1992). Local discourse structure is the structure consisting of minimal units that belong to the level of discourse. In spoken discourse, such units are what is variously called syntagms (Shcherba 1955), intonation groups (Cruttenden 1986), intonation units (Chafe 1994), or prosodic phrases/units (Chafe 2001); they are usually identified through a cluster of prosodic properties, including single intonation contour, single accent centre, tempo and loudness patterns, and pausing. I prefer the term **elementary discourse units** (EDUs) (Kibrik 2001b, Kibrik and Podlesskaya (eds.) 2009; see also Carlson et al. 2003 on EDUs in written discourse), because it emphasizes the functional nature of these units and allows for a unified approach to spoken and written discourse. EDUs are minimal steps in which discourse progresses ahead. They prototypically coincide with clauses (Chafe 1994, Thompson and Couper-Kuhlen 2005, Kibrik and Podlesskaya 2006, Wouk 2008). In this respect discourse can properly be understood as a network of clauses. This is true of both spoken and written discourse.

There is of course no firm boundary between global and local discourse structures; these are simply two poles in a continuum. Thinking top-down, global discourse structure is gradually broken into smaller and smaller units that eventually lead to the local structure. There are some frameworks that provide a unified account for discourse structure, without making a strong distinction between global and local structure. One remarkable framework of this kind is Rhetorical Structure Theory developed by Mann and Thompson (1988; see also Taboada and Mann 2006), that represents discourse as a hierarchical network of nodes ranging from one clause to a large discourse chunk; nodes are connected by one and the same kind of discourse-semantic ('rhetorical') relations, irrespective of the size of the node. In this book, I rely to a great extent on the idea that discourse is a hierarchically organized network of clauses. Rhetorical Structure Theory is used as a descriptive tool in certain parts of the book.

1.4.3 *Influence of discourse factors upon smaller linguistic constituents*

Finally, the third central issue in discourse analysis is the influence of discourse factors upon more local, small-scale linguistic constituents: grammatical, lexical, and phonetic. There is a great variety of such discourse-driven, relatively local phenomena, including word order, choice between finite and non-finite verb forms, use of articles, use of connectors and other cohesion devices, discourse markers, location of pitch accents, location and length of pauses, etc. In addition, there are also non-vocal linguistic devices, in particularly illustrative gestures, that are also largely motivated by discourse context (McNeill 1992).

Influence of discourse factors upon small-scale linguistic phenomena can be described with the help of the theoretical notion of **choice** (Kibrik 2006, in press b). When a speaker is using language, grammar cues him/her to particular choices: which word order to use, where to place a discourse marker and which one, etc. Thus grammar is actually a system that guides a speaker's choices. Some choices are relatively rule-based, whereas other choices are rather probabilistic. Discourse-related choices mostly belong to the latter kind: a certain option is not strictly required or strictly ruled out, and more than one option is to a certain extent permissible.

This book is devoted to one lexico-grammatical phenomenon that is basically discourse-driven, namely the choice of referential expression for a referent in question. **Referential choice** is made by the speaker on the basis of a variety of factors, including discourse factors. What kinds of factors are these?

First and foremost, these are factors related to discourse structure. As will be seen particularly in Part IV, hierarchical and linear discourse structure has a critical impact upon referential choice. As for the influence of discourse type, it is also relevant; a number of authors have pointed out that referential processes are not neutral to discourse types. Fox (1987a) proposed different sets of principles underlying reference in spoken and written English. Toole (1996) is an unusual study looking specifically into referential differences between genres; see also Ariel (2006). In this book, possible effects of discourse type upon reference will be kept in mind. However, I will assume that, for a given language, the core patterns of the referential system are fundamentally the same in all kinds of language use, whereas discourse type may somewhat modify these basic patterns.

Referential choice is one of the most prominent phenomena explored in discourse analysis. It specifically pertains to the third area of discourse analysis – influence of discourse factors upon lexico-grammatical choices. But it also relates to the other two subfields of discourse analysis, as both discourse structure and discourse type affect this choice.

1.5 The cognitive approach in discourse analysis

Cognitive linguistics is the study of how language relates to the human mind. Definitional for this line of research is the so-called cognitive commitment, formulated by Lakoff (1990: 40). This is the commitment to coordinate linguistic research with what is known about the mind and brain from the neighbouring sciences also exploring cognition, in particular psychology and neuroscience.[2] Other important (and early) formulations of similar ideas in modern linguistics belong, inter alia, to Chafe (1974), Kacnel'son (1972), Zvegincev (1996) (written in the 1970s), A. E. Kibrik (1983), van Dijk and Kintsch (1983). Actual work done under the official heading of cognitive linguistics does not always live up to the standards of the cognitive commitment, but it seems that having this criterion in mind is extremely important. After all, boundaries between sciences are often accidental, arbitrary, of a historical nature, while the object of study – the mind – is one and undivided.

Language has two major functions and two corresponding modes of existence that can be called, using the computer metaphor, online and offline. The online mode of language is communicative transfer of various kinds of information between individuals. The central phenomenon belonging to this mode is natural discourse as it unfolds dynamically in real time. The offline mode of language is information storage. One of the central phenomena characteristic of this mode is the relatively stable system of lexical semantics. Grammar is also often viewed in an offline way, as a system of mappings between forms and functions.

Cognitive linguistics, as an established trend of thought in modern science, has mostly addressed offline phenomena. This is true of the well-known work of Lakoff (1987) and Langacker (1987/1991) that is considered foundational for cognitive linguistics. Most of the time, the practice of cognitive linguistics has ignored natural discourse data, and not been interested in discourse phenomena. Two recent introductions to cognitive linguistics (Croft and Cruse 2004, Evans and Green 2006), 355 and 830 pages long respectively, do not mention 'discourse' in their subject indexes. The same applies to another introduction, Geeraerts (ed.) (2006). Some exceptions to this tendency have been collected in Goldberg (ed.) 1996, van Hoek et al. (eds.) 1999, Németh (ed.) 2001. See also the important article Langacker 2001 and the analysis of reference within the framework of Langacker's Cognitive Grammar proposed by van Hoek 1997. Geeraerts and Cuyckens (eds.) (2007) seems to be the first handbook of cognitive linguistics paying attention to the analysis of discourse.

---

[2] This commitment is actually definitional for singling out cognitive linguistics among other kinds of linguistic thought. In particular, generative linguists also claim to be doing cognitive science, but as they believe that language is separate from other cognitive domains their actual agenda is not so much affected by what is known in other disciplines exploring mind and brain.

In turn, those practising discourse studies quite rarely use explicit cognitive explanations of observed phenomena. For example, in the 851-page-long handbook Schiffrin et al. (eds.) (2001), terms containing the epithet 'cognitive' appear on 13 pages only (according to the handbook's index, see p. 820); among these, cognitive linguistics and cognitive psychology are mentioned once each.

This mutual neglect of cognitive linguists and discourse analysts may suggest that the communicative online use of language somehow is 'less cognitive' than information storage and conceptualization. But this is obviously false. Discourse is produced in and by a speaker's cognitive system, and a prerequisite for producing it is the speaker's assumption that the addressee will properly process it in his/her cognitive system. Online linguistic phenomena are as cognitive as are offline phenomena. Excluding discourse processes from the agenda of cognitive linguistics is not justified at all. The adherence of mainstream cognitive linguistics, as we know it, to offline phenomena is a mere historical accident, due to the genetic connection of its founders to generative linguistics. Despite such limitation in scope, the crucial role of cognitive linguistics has been calling attention to cognitive explanation of linguistic phenomena as the central type of explanation.

In fact, the only way to adequately understand discourse processes is through understanding the underlying elements of the cognitive system, such as memory, attention, consciousness, knowledge representation, or categorization. Some remarkable examples of cognitively oriented explorations of discourse are provided by multiple studies by Wallace Chafe and Russell Tomlin. In particular, Chafe (1994) is a consistent account of discourse structure and a number of lexico-grammatical and prosodic phenomena as a reflection of information flow in the speaker's consciousness or working memory. Tomlin (1995) is an experimental study building an important connection between the choice of grammatical subject and the cognitive process of attention-focusing. The cognitive pespective is also characteristic of the work by Teun van Dijk, one of those responsible for the formation of discourse analysis as a discipline (see e.g. van Dijk and Kintsch 1983).

The cognitive approach in linguistics belongs to a broader class of approaches that are called functional(ist) (see Nichols 1984, Van Valin 1990, Newmeyer 1991, Givón 1995, Kibrik and Plungian 1997, Nuyts 2007). The common idea of functionalist approaches is that language is to be understood as a system adjusted for communication and information processing rather than as a collection of arbitrary symbolic units. Structural properties of language are derivative from its function, like the anatomy of an organism is adjusted, through physiology, to an ecological context in which this organism operates. Unlike cognitive linguistics in the narrow sense, functionalists have given much attention to the online side of language, that is, discourse processes. (See Nuyts 2007 for a thorough analysis of commonalities and differences of the cognitive linguistics and functionalist agendas.) The analyses proposed in this book are based to a large extent on functionalist work.

Besides cognitive linguistics, another research tradition that is interested in cognition of language is psycholinguistics. This is a primarily experimental discipline testing linguistic hypotheses with more or less numerous experiment participants. Among the innumerable textbooks and introductions, see Cutler (ed.) (2005) for a recent multi-dimensional account of the most topical issues in modern psycholinguistics. Methodologically, psycholinguistics is a branch of psychology or, perhaps, an even broader discipline inquiring into human physiology and behaviour. Psycholinguists, due to their affiliation with psychology, are sometimes more informed about general cognitive issues than cognitive linguists. However, not all of the psycholinguists are specifically associated with the label 'cognitive'. To mention some of the explicitly cognitively-oriented psycholinguistic work, consider such studies as Bates and MacWhinney (eds.) (1989), Slobin (2003), Tomasello (2008), Pickering and Garrod (2004), inter alia. Particularly interesting in this connection is the study by Sanders and Spooren (2007), authors with a psycholinguistic background, who provided a detailed discussion of the relationships between discourse studies and cognitive linguistics. They conclude with suggestions that are very much in line with my approach: 'We consider the level of discourse a "new frontier" for Cognitive Linguistics' (p. 935). There is also a nascent line of neuroimaging research in discourse; see van Berkum (in press).

Generally this book is an exercise in the discipline that might be called **cognitive discourse analysis** (outlined in Kibrik 2001b, Kibrik 2003). The approaches used in different parts of this book will be explicitly cognitive to various extents, but I generally aim to demonstrate that cognitive discourse analysis is:

- as legitimate as the cognitive approach in semantics
- useful for both the cognitive linguistic agenda and the theory of discourse
- building new links with related disciplines, including cognitive psychology and cognitive neuroscience
- shedding light on fundamental cognitive phenomena such as memory, attention, knowledge representation, etc.

The specifics of my cognitive approach to referential processes will be provided in Chapters 2 and 10.

1.6 Discourse analysis and linguistic typology

In this book I intend to crossbreed discourse analysis not only with the cognitive approach but also with another dimension of linguistic research: linguistic grammatical typology. Typology is a systematic study of linguistic diversity, as well as of the limits of such diversity. During the last thirty years or so linguistic typology has witnessed remarkable progress. A number of studies have appeared that rest on worldwide cross-linguistic databases that make knowledge of what is general and what is unique about human languages much more robust than before (see e.g. Tomlin 1986, Dryer 1992b, Nichols 1992, Bybee et al. 1994). An especially spectacular achievement of modern large-scale typology is the World Atlas of Language Structures (Haspelmath et al. (eds.) 2005, Haspelmath et al. (eds.) 2008), various parts of which are cited in this book on many occasions. See also the project 'Jazyki mira' [Languages of the World] of the Institute of Linguistics, Russian Academy of Sciences, aiming at describing as many languages as possible in accordance with a unified typologically-oriented template; 16 volumes have been published by now within the framework of this project on various languages of Eurasia, for example Moldovan et al. (eds.) (2005), and a database for quantitative studies has been created (Polyakov and Solovyev 2006).

Beside large-scale typology, building upon samples of hundreds of languages, there is also small-scale linguistic typology. Its main tenet is looking at specific phenomena in specific languages (or small groups of languages) from a typological point of view, that is, as realizations of particular cross-linguistic options.[3] An advantage of this kind of typological approach is the combination of an in-depth expert analysis of specific language phenomena with a broad, encompassing view. Progress in this kind of typology is manifested by the appearance of language grammars that are typologically minded, that is, present the data of an individual language as instantiations of typological options (see e.g. A. E. Kibrik and Testelets (eds.) 1999) – in contrast to more traditional descriptive grammars, whose authors' horizons were often limited to the studies of the given language or of the language family at best.

---

[3] In my understanding, typology, including small-scale typology, is more than simply a cross-linguistic comparison. The typological approach presumes putting the features of a given language or languages into a deductively or inductively constructed space of options. That is, unlike the more general cross-linguistic approach – collecting observations on a number of languages – the typological approach requires positing a calculus, however tentative, of possible options. If this principle is implemented, even analysing one individual language may be typologically minded.

From my perspective, focused small-scale typological work is no less important than more superficial large-scale studies. The former is responsible for the qualitative progress in linguistics, and the latter mostly for the quantitative coverage. Both are crucial for an adequate understanding of linguistic diversity and its limits. Typological thinking certainly enriches any kind of linguistic work, from purely theoretical to purely descriptive.

Many results of contemporary typology are summarized in the handbook Haspelmath et al. (eds.) (2001). Typological approaches to language and languages are closely interwoven with the functionalist research agenda mentioned in the previous section; the state of the art functional-typological view of language is presented in Shopen (ed.) (2007).

Most of linguistic typology is focused on grammatical properties of languages. Naturally, the more sizeable and complex a phenomenon, the less amenable it is to typologization. There is much typological knowledge about word-internal phenomena, such as specific inflectional categories, quite a lot about clause-wide phenomena, and less about extra-clausal phenomena, such as complex constructions. Typological studies of discourse-related phenomena are in their incipient stage. As was aptly pointed out by Myhill and Hibiya (2001), scientific programmes of discourse analysis and typology are ideologically compatible, as both fields are empirically oriented. But the problem is that few languages have been accounted for in detail as far as discourse phenomena are concerned. So there is simply little factual basis for typological discourse analysis. The existing discourse typological studies are usually cross-linguistic comparisons of discourse strategies in two or several languages, such as the comparative analysis of repairs in English and Japanese in Fox et al. (1996), or a study of placeholders by Podlesskaya (2010). As for research in reference, notable typologically oriented studies include Clancy (1980) and especially the paradigm of quantititave exploration of discourse phenomena initiated in Givón (ed.) (1983) and further developed in dozens of studies. Some other typologically minded studies of reference will be discussed in the appropriate places in Parts II and III of this book. Very close to the concerns of this book are typological studies Siewierska (2004), Helmbrecht (2004), Dryer (2005a), and Corbett (2006).

The typological purport of this book is variable across its different parts. As was explained in section 1.4, referential devices are ambivalent. On the one hand, they are very local, related to a particular lexical (or grammatical) choice at a given point. On the other hand, they can be understood only on the basis of a rather wide discourse context, not limited to constituents such as clause or sentence. In accordance with such ambivalence, various aspects of referential phenomena are readily prone to typologization to a variable extent. Typological Parts II and III mostly deal with local properties of referential devices, such as morphological status, clause argument position, number of referent representation in a clause, etc. (In this sense, the existing knowledge about grammatical typology is often relevant to the topic of this book.) In Part IV of the book, a detailed discourse analysis of referential devices and involved factors will be provided, but only with respect to two languages. Hopefully, such analysis will pave the way for a further fully-fledged typology of reference, including the whole array of discourse factors.

In the typological Parts II and III I rely, in the first place, on in-depth analyses of a number of languages I am familiar with, particularly through my own fieldwork. In addition to that, I have used the data of about two hundred other languages, relying on descriptions by other authors. Using these additional languages was possible to the extent that relevant, sufficient and clear information on referential phenomena was available in language descriptions, which was certainly not always the case.

I feel that the typological genre of this study lies somewhere between large-scale and small-scale typology. I have tried to include as many language areas as possible and provide comments on genealogical and geographical spread of the phenomena and the patterns discussed. Even though no formal language sampling procedure is used in this study, I feel that the approach taken – given the scarcity of readily available information in language descriptions – is generally faithful to the following recommendations about the sampling principles: 'Achieve a reasonable practical compromise between depth and breadth of coverage' (Comrie 1989a: 11); 'The choice of the best SIZE of the sample is easiest: one simply has to select the relation between breadth and depth... that best suits one's goals.... The deeper the questions are, the fewer languages can be handled' (Haspelmath 1997: 15).

In Appendix 1 I make suggestions on what aspects of referential systems should be covered in descriptive studies of particular languages, and what could be a format for such coverage in language descriptions. When, or if, such data is available for a substantial number of languages, a more comprehensive typology of referential phenomena may become possible.

1.7 Typological and cognitive perspectives

This book attempts to combine cognitive and typological aspects of referential processes. This is in a stark contrast to the situation in modern linguistics, where the cognitively and the typologically oriented studies are two entirely independent enterprises. The focus of cognitive approaches, including studies in discourse phenomena, is to understand how language is processed or represented in the human mind. This orientation usually – and naturally – leads to a certain degree of universalism, that is, the assumption that differences between languages are negligible when we are tackling the general properties of the cognition of Homo sapiens. (There are some exceptions, of course. Some leading figures in cognitive linguistics include a substantial cross-linguistic or typological component in their work; see Talmy 2003, Croft 2001.) The same applies to the work of psycholinguists – being interested in linguistic cognition, it is quite rare that they address linguistic diversity. (But cf. cross-language psycholinguistic research reported in Bates et al. 2001, Slobin 2003, Boroditsky 2003, von Stutterheim and Nüse 2003.)

In contrast, the central concern of typology is often descriptive rather than explanatory. Typologists generally aim at looking at as many languages as possible, and tacitly presume that some commonsense understanding of how language relates to mind is sufficient for doing informed linguistics of this kind. There are some exceptions here as well. In particular, A. E. Kibrik (1998, 2003) explicitly called for the creation of 'cognitively oriented typology'. Similar suggestions for closer links between cognitive linguistics and typology are put forward by van der Auwera and Nuyts (2007), who said that cognitive linguists and typologists, although having compatible research agendas, 'remain separated strands on the linguistic scene' (p. 1086). These authors also analyse the historical and psychological reasons for the typologists' 'cognitive modesty' (p. 1082).

In this book, I am attempting to bring together the strong sides of both perspectives on language: the cognitive and the typological ones. This idea was already present in my dissertation Kibrik 1988. The cognitive and the typological perspectives are complementary rather than separate. If one strives for a realistic and comprehensive theory of human language, one needs to both accept the cognitive commitment (see section 1.5) and be positively aware of linguistic diversity. The universal cognitive organization of Homo sapiens and the extent to which linguistic reifications of thought can vary constitute the two constraining and defining parameters that must underlie any integral linguistic model. The psychological groundedness of the cognitive approach and the cross-linguistically informed character of the typological approach complement each other and give rise to a complete picture.

In this sense coupling cognitive and typological aspects is not just one of a number of possible theoretical twists but rather a sheer necessity. Linguistics simply must bring together the knowledge of language diversity and the knowledge of elementary cognitive processes underlying language use by an individual speaker. To draw an analogy with a more developed empirical science, linguistics avoiding such a combination is similar to a biology that refuses to acknowledge both the classification of species and the basic chemical processes in an individual organism.

Even though combining the typological and the cognitive perspectives is extremely rare in empirical linguistic studies, there are some important precedents that I would like to mention. The monograph Tomlin (1986), devoted to the typology of word order, put forward a set of explanatory functional principles underlying the observed regularities. This early typological study demonstrated an unusual degree of informedness about the cognitive system and its components, and some of the proposed functional principles were cognitive in nature. The same applies, to an even greater extent, to a number of Tomlin's later studies (see list of references) devoted to cross-linguistic variation. Another monumental study, Chafe (1994), in fact provides a cognitive theory of discourse production. This study, though not being typological per se, certainly stems from Chafe's extensive and prolonged work with multiple and diverse languages, often quite 'exotic'. The convincing power of this work owes a lot to this tacit typological awareness.

In the domain of referential processes, these two authors have also contributed a lot to the formulation of the cognitive-typological approach; see Chafe (1976, 1994: Ch. 6), Tomlin and Pu (1991). A number of other important studies of reference, also including a cognitive theme and emphasizing cross-linguistic analysis include Clancy (1980), Givón (1983a, 1993), Ariel (1988), Gundel et al. (1993). However, few of these studies have been cognitive in the technical sense of the word, and none has been literally typological.

Thus the main intent of this book is to bring together cognitive and typological aspects of reference in discourse. This is important for a general understanding of how discourse reference works, but also for the adequate analysis of individual facts. In order to come up with a proper account of referential device R in language L one needs to keep in mind:

- how referential devices operate across languages in general
- how cognition operates.

All in all, looking at linguistic diversity and its limits (=typology) and looking at the cognitive bases of language are parts of one and the same enterprise. In this book this combined perspective is applied to a specific subject matter, that is, reference in discourse.

1.8 Methodology

The two major methodologies employed in empirical sciences are observation and experimentation. In **observation**, one watches natural phenomena and analyses genuine data in a natural environment. In linguistics, observational data primarily consist of natural discourse, as discourse is the ecologically normal form of language's existence. The modern corpus methods are an extension of the observational ideology. A problem with observation is that it is often hard to get necessary data – instead one often gets lots of data that are irrelevant to one's research goal; in this sense, this can be a costly methodology. Another problem is that instead of clear analytic categories one often encounters non-prototypical realizations and intermediate instances. A third problem is that causal relationships between events are not obvious and not immediately verifiable.

Experimentation allows one to properly control data and potentially relevant conditions, as well as test cause–effect relationships. 'The essence of experimentation consists simply of the recognition that our ordinary observations of the world may often be misleading and our beliefs about if faulty' (Derwing 1994). There exist a wide variety of ways to construct data in experiments; see e.g. Schütze (2006). A typical – even though not always recognized as such – instance of experimentation is elicitation of constructed examples from language speakers. The downside of experimentation is that there is always a risk of distorting natural processes, losing touch with reality and studying faked, artificial data. In the context of modern linguistics in which very powerful traditions are based exclusively on artificially constructed data, some linguists have emphasized the priority of natural data; see e.g. Heath (1984), Chafe (1994, 2008). The central role of natural data is particularly clear in the domain of discourse phenomena, including reference. For this kind of phenomena, the experimental approach is frequently misleading because it is very difficult to artificially construct a situation of online language use that would simulate a real and natural situation.

In brief, the opposition between observation and experimentation amounts to the opposition of messy reality, with all its highs and lows, on the one hand, and clean but somewhat fictitious constructed data, on the other. My position regarding this dilemma consists of two points. First, observation is the more basic, more fundamental methodology. Observation is the source of explanatory hypotheses. One should always keep in mind that what one wants to describe and explain is the given natural phenomenon and not a lab situation.

Second, experimentation can be a very useful complement to observation. If the experimenter is commited to as natural and easy-to-process experimental designs as possible, then the controlled character of the data and the conditions affecting it may specify and verify observational results. A comprehensive understanding of linguistic phenomena is attainable if a combination of both methodologies and both of the kinds of data is implemented. The two approaches complement each other rather than contradict each other. A combination of natural and experimental data is a universal recipe, allowing one to go between the Scylla of messy reality and the Charybdis of experimental artefacts.

That said, I must confess that this book is methodologically less consistent than I might want it to be. Generally, I follow the two principles just outlined. Most of the time, preference is given to natural discourse data. Sometimes constructed examples are used, however, thus requesting the reader to conjecture the relevant discourse context. Besides the substantial reasons mentioned above, an additional reason for that is that natural discourse examples are so long, that an unlimited use of them would render this book far too heavy. So I sometimes opt for simpler and shorter constructed examples at the cost of losing some naturalness. Even where such examples are used, I still believe that a real discourse situation is approximated, so the discourse-oriented approach remains in place. The final point to make here is that in the typological Parts II and III of this book I inevitably had to often rely on data whose status in terms of naturalness/artificialness was not clear enough.

Part IV of the book actually employs a method, additional to the two discussed so far. This is the method of **modelling**, that is, creating a simulation of the actual online process of discourse production. What is modelled is the choice of an appropriate referential expression for a given referent. Factors putatively affecting the actual choice in a real speaker are enumerated and quantitatively weighted, and a reconstruction of their interaction, leading to the ultimate output, is proposed.

A final comment is due about the quantitative analyses of the observational and experimental data, discussed in various parts of this book. In many empirical sciences, use of statistics is a must, if one wants to objectively assess a given regularity as being significant or not. This is probably a positive tenet, but the case is that linguistics has no established tradition of applying specific statistical tests. Without such a tradition, using a certain test to demonstrate significance of a hypothesis or a correlation has little persuasive power. As is well known, even in the disciplines with an extensive statistical background, selection of an appropriate test for a given task is, to a great extent, a kind of social contract or a widely held belief rather than an objective truth. A perfunctory transfer of this practice into linguistics can possibly produce an impression but can hardly substantially raise research standards. Developing linguistically meaningful statistics is an important goal, but it cannot be attained in this book. Instead, I generally use the following, rather generous, assessment of quantitative significance: if two numerical values, such as frequencies of discourse uses, differ by approximately one order of magnitude, this is taken as a clear indication that the difference is significant. If the difference is less than that, definitive conclusions about significance are taken to be tentative.

1.9 Terminology

Terminology is important. In fact, it is our window upon real phenomena, and our view of the phenomena will be clear to the degree our window is clean and transparent (as opposed to blurry and distorted). As is well known (Lakoff and Johnson 1980, Lakoff and Núñez 2000), it is nearly impossible to think about abstract matters without employing certain metaphors. It is not neutral to our understanding of nature what kind of metaphors we use: some metaphors are more adequate and beneficial than others. In particular, I will be arguing at certain places in this book that the transformational metaphor, instantiated in terms such as 'pronoun', is cognitively misleading, and the metaphor of choosing an appropriate referential device is much more illuminating. However, using an optimal metaphor or conceptual framework is not the only concern; there are other concerns, such as simplicity and tradition.

In this book I try to keep terminology as simple and straightforward as possible. Preference is given to generally adopted terms, with the exception of those instances where I believe that traditional terms significantly distort the reality. Some new terms are proposed, particularly for those notions that do not have traditional labels. Such novel terms are introduced in the course of the book where appropriate.

There is one conceptual domain, however, that needs to be addressed straight away. This is the notoriously complex and convoluted domain of clause participant terminology. It includes terms such as argument, actant, oblique, adjunct, agent, subject, A, P (or O), S, accusative, ergative, etc. The use of terms in this domain (or domains) varies so strongly and unpredictably across various strands of linguistics that I find it important to explicitly outline here the conceptual system I follow in the book.

Addressing this domain is important because referents do not just occur in discourse but typically occur as clause participants. Clause participant status may be important for referential processes in a number of ways. For example, as discussed in Chapter 5, referential choice may depend on clause participant position of the referent. For another example, as discussed in Part IV, clause participant status of a previous mention of the referent may affect referential choice at the current point in discourse. In order to introduce clause participant terminology, let us use an exemplary English clause (1.7):

(1.7)   John sold the book to Mary in the market place.

A typical **participants** the clause contains the predicate and one or more *participants*; the clause in (1.7) is headed by the predicate *sold* and has four participants. Clause participants fall into **arguments** [=actants, complements] (*John, Mary, the book*) and **non-arguments** [=adjuncts, circumstants, circumstantials] (*in the marketplace*). (Note that drawing a dividing line between arguments and adjuncts may be difficult; cf. the case of comitative, see Arkhipov 2009.)

In certain languages arguments may be divided into **core** and **non-core** arguments. Core arguments are those that are morphosyntactically privileged compared to other (non-core) arguments – for example, the core arguments *John* and *the book* do not require prepositional markers, while the non-core argument *to Mary* does. Sometimes I use the term **obliques**, if I need to group adjuncts and non-core arguments together.

All clause participants bear certain **semantic roles**, such as agent (*John*), patient (*the book*), recipient (*Mary*), location (*in the marketplace*). Semantic roles are understood in this book quite broadly: in order to not overcomplicate things, I do not differentiate, for example, between agent and effector or patient and theme (see Van Valin 1993: 41, inter alia). I also occasionally use terms such as 'agent-like' or 'patient-like' participant, referring to clause participants that are the closest analogues of agent or patient in the given clause. For example, in the clause *Mary sees John* the participant *Mary*, even though it is an experiencer in terms of a thorough semantic analysis, counts as an agent-like participant as the given clause contains no participant resembling agent more than *Mary*.

Core arguments may be morphosyntactically clustered in accordance with various **alignments**. In the accusative alignment, agent-like arguments cluster together, in terms of their morphosyntactic encoding, with core arguments of intransitive clauses, and are contrasted to patient-like arguments of transitive clauses. Alignment may be marked not only by inflectional cases on nouns or noun phrases but also by other means, including verbal affixes (see Chapter 3, subsection 3.3.1) and constituent order. The latter applies to English: agents – both transitive, as in (1.7), and intransitive (as in *John plays*) – and intransitive patients (as in *The book fell*) all are coded by preverbal noun phrases, while transitive patients (such as *the book* in (1.7)) by postverbal noun phrases.

Clusters of roles, after A. E. Kibrik (1997), are termed **hyperroles**. The terms for specific hyperroles, also borrowed from the same article, are as follows: for the accusative alignment – Principal and Patientive; for the ergative alignment – Agentive and Absolutive; for the 'active' alignment – Actor and Undergoer. Sometimes the hyperrole Sole is also necessary – it includes any core argument of an intransitive clause. In terms of the Comrie's well-known

(1989a: 105) terminology, Agentive equals A, Patientive equals P, Sole equals S, Principal equals A+S, and Absolutive equals P+S.

Languages differ in which hyperroles they highlight. In English, with its accusative alignment, almost always the only relevant hyperroles are Principal and Patientive. In some languages different sets of hyperroles are relevant in different constructions. Hyperroles are taken to be inferrable from morphosyntactic coding, such as inflectional cases or constituent order. Following A. E. Kibrik (1997), I assume that syntactic roles, such as subject and direct object, are not universal. Relevance of syntactic roles can only be based on an in-depth exploration of NPs' syntactic behaviour (for example, in passive constructions or in relative clause constructions). When such information for language L is not readily available, I only talk about it in terms of hyperroles. That is, knowing that language L displays the accusative alignment is not sufficient for assuming it has the subject and the direct object syntactic relations, but is sufficient for talking about Principal and Patientive.

Hyperroles are different not only from syntactic relations but also from morphosyntactic marking as such. For example, in an accusative language with inflectional case, such as Russian, Principal is likely to be encoded by the nominative, but this is not a one-to-one correspondence. On the one hand, some Principals that are experiencers may be coded by the dative case (as in *Ivanu xolodno* Ivan-DAT cold 'Ivan is cold'). On the other hand, the nominative case may be used in forms of address that are not clausal at all.

Summary

The notion of reference, as many other linguistic notions, is highly ambiguous, and various writers understand it differently and emphasize its different aspects. In this chapter I have sketched my understanding of referents and reference as they will figure in the rest of the book. Referents are among the most basic concepts represented in language and in cognition. Reference is overwhelming in natural language use – both quantitatively and qualitatively. It is among the central skills of language users. Reference makes sense only in natural discourse and can only be understood in a discourse context. So the linguistic discipline discourse analysis is the inclusive enterprise and framework for explaining reference. In this book, the discourse perspective is combined with two other theoretical components. One of them that can be called microscopic is the cognitive approach allowing us to connect individual occurrences of discourse reference with underlying cognitive processes. The other component, rather of a panoramic nature, is the typological approach addressing cross-linguistic diversity of referential forms. In my view, this combination is a necessary prerequisite for a comprehensive account of reference, as well as other linguistic phenomena, and this is the constitutive feature of the book. Methodologically, the book is also organized in an amalgamated way, as several major scientific methods are employed in different parts. The greatest emphasis is placed on the observational methodology, but experimentation and modelling are used in certain places as well. The chapter concluded with several notes on terminology. In the following chapter I proceed with a more focused discussion of reference in discourse.

2

Basics of reference in discourse

Overview

This chapter presents the basics of reference in discourse and introduces the reader to my understanding of reference. The phenomenon of reference is highly multifaceted and is understood very differently in different traditions, so it is necessary to delimit the understanding that is pursued in this book (section 2.1). There is also a great variety of linguistic expressions used as referential devices, and these are reviewed in sections 2.2 and 2.3. The chief aspect to which this book is devoted is referential choice between the available referential options (section 2.4). I approach this choice from the speaker's perspective, and referential choice is guided by referents' activation in the speaker's working memory (section 2.5). In section 2.6 I discuss the extent to which an addressee's cognitive system is important for understanding referential choice. While activation in working memory is the immediate predictor of referential choice, many discourse factors have been claimed to affect this choice; the multiplicity of factors and their integration are addressed in section 2.7. Sometimes referents that are sufficiently activated still cannot be mentioned by reduced referential devices because of the threat of a referential conflict, or ambiguity. However, a potential referential conflict is often precluded by one of the referential aids – linguistic devices helping to tell referents apart (section 2.8). Section 2.9 explains the logic of the subsequent parts of this book.

2.1 Limits and kinds of reference

The term 'reference' has a long tradition in philosophy, logic, linguistics, and other disciplines dealing with human language. So it is useful to delineate how the term is understood in the book and to delimit the intended understanding of 'reference' from other possible understandings. It is equally important to discuss which types of reference are particularly central to the concerns of the book.

2.1.1 Referents among the types of concepts

As has been pointed out in Chapter 1, several of the most basic ontological kinds of concepts typical of the human mind and language (and probably reflecting objective reality in some way) include:

- entities, or referents
- locations
- times
- states
- events.

This classification is not a rigid taxonomy but more like a cline – from most stable, most entity-like concepts, such as 'my sister' or 'this apple', to the most transient, most event-like concepts such as 'jumped' or 'is washing'. The term 'reference', in some of its uses, describes relationships between linguistic expressions and any of these kinds of concepts that can be present in humans' minds (as reflecting or not reflecting objective external reality). However, in present-day linguistics it became customary to reserve the term 'reference' as applied to entities, or referents, in the first instance. I adhere to this kind of usage in the book (but see subsection 16.2.1 in the concluding chapter). I mostly focus on entities (referents), but locations and times may also enter the scene occasionally. It should be noted, however, that events and states conceptualized as entities in language (such as *The Great French Revolution* or *my salary*) will also be included in the domain of reference.

In my approach, referents are concepts in the speakers' and addressees' minds. In the traditions of logic and philosophy of language, referents are often said to be entities in the external world. Logicians and logic-minded linguists, at least since Russell (1905), have spent much effort trying to see if language treats a real being, such as a rhinoceros, differently from imaginary beings, such as a unicorn. In fact, language is totally indifferent to this distinction. There is no evidence that Tolstoy in 'War and Peace' uses different referential strategies for Napoleon, who was an actual historical character, and Pierre Bezukhov who was created by the writer's imagination. It is more reasonable to view reference as a relation of words to things in the mind rather than to things in the external world (cf. Givón 2001: Vol. I, 438–439).

2.1.2 Specific definite and other referential statuses

Of course, there is a prototypical correlation between the ontological types of concepts and elements of linguistic structure. Referents are typically conveyed by nominal elements (such as nouns with or without modifiers, pronouns, or pronominal morphemes; see section 2.3). However, nominal elements may be used in various ways. The most prototypical use is specific definite reference. This is how both the initial noun phrase and the personal pronoun are used in this constructed example:

(2.1) <u>My neighbour from downstairs</u> was an alcoholic. <u>He</u> used to start rows in the yard.

Specific reference means that a noun phrase connects to the concept of an individuated, specific person in the speaker's mind and evokes a ditto concept in an addressee's mind.

A comprehensive classification of types of reference, or referential statuses of noun phrases, was proposed by Paducheva (1985: Ch. IV). Omitting some secondary details, her classification looks as follows.

(2.2) (1) Specific
   a. Definite (*I, the book, this red book, my book, the book you gave me, Socrates*)
   b. Indefinite (*someone, a foreigner*)
(2) Non-specific
   a. Existential (<u>*Some people*</u> *are afraid of mice*)
   b. Universal (<u>*All children*</u> *love ice cream*)
   c. Attributive (*Even* <u>*the strongest person in the world*</u> *cannot lift over 200 kilograms*)
   d. Generic (*He prefers* <u>*train*</u> *as the means of transportation;* <u>*Lions*</u> *live in Africa*)
(3) Predicative (*My mother is* <u>*a doctor*</u>)
(4) Autonymous (*Her sister was named* <u>*Tatiana*</u>)

It is no chance that the specific referential statuses (specific definite and specific indefinite) took just single noun phrases to provide an illustration while further statuses required the context of at least a clause. Specific referents are the most frequent and prototypical ones, and there are conventionalized ways to convey them in English, as well as in other languages. Although no referential statuses are excluded from consideration outright, I will mostly discuss class 1a of the above classification, namely specific definite referents and their mentions. Note that the epithet 'definite' here includes personal pronouns, NPs with possessive pronouns, and proper names – all of these types of NPs, while being semantically definite (identifiable, in terms of Chafe 1994: Ch. 8), lack a definite article in English and are sometimes excluded from definite NPs in Anglocentric terminology.

The latter approach is untenable for the simple reason that not all languages have anything like definite articles.

After Quine (1953), in some terminological systems (including Paducheva's original Russian-language terminology) the specific use of an NP is called 'referential' or 'referring', thus rendering all other statuses in (2.2) non-referential. This probably suggests that the corresponding NPs do not refer, or do not have referents. I rather suggest that they do refer and do have referents, but those referents are not specific. Consider the oft-cited example of Donnellan (1966) *The murderer of Smith is insane*. The difference between the 'attributive' understanding of the NP in this sentence (relevant in the situation when someone has obviously murdered Smith, but the identity of this person is totally unknown) and its 'referential' understanding is usually taken to be absolute in logic; several books were devoted to this distinction; see e.g. Ishikawa (1998) and the bibliographical list occupying nearly one third of page 11.

From my perspective, this distinction is a matter of degree: degree of how much is known about that person. Under the attributive usage knowledge about the person is minimal (the fact that the person murdered Smith) while under the specific definite usage it is much greater, but it is never complete. What would suffice for an NP such as *the murderer of Smith* to be 'referential' in Donnellan's terms? Knowing the person by face? Knowing his/her name? A whole detective novel can be built around a gradual accretion of knowledge about a murderer. One's knowledge of any referent, even of oneself, is partial. Identities change over time. So thinking of the 'attributive vs. referential' difference as absolute is an illusion. This distinction is not binary but simply pinpoints two ends of a huge continuous scale – minimal knowledge and supposedly complete knowledge.

Likewise other statuses, such as indefinite specific or generic, can be demonstrated to be referential in a way. For example, generic NPs can corefer and, therefore, refer; cf. *Lions are predators. They live in Africa.* So I may occasionally talk about reference of nominal expressions other than specific definite ones. Notoriously complicated are the issues of reference in indefinite pronouns (Seliverstova 1988, Haspelmath 1997), negative pronouns (Miestamo 2005), quantified noun phrases (Gil 1993, Tatevosov 2002, Abbott 2010: Ch. 4). Of course, truly non-referring nominal expressions do occur – these are, for example, dummy elements, such as *it* in English *It is raining*.

Note that correspondences between referential statuses and types of referring expressions are far from trivial. We have just considered several examples of noun phrases, based on common nouns or 'descriptions', that belong to different statuses. Personal pronouns, often assumed to be fundamentally specific, can be used in a non-specific way. This is quite obvious regarding *you, they,* and *it*. But much more exotic occurrences take place. Mühlhäusler et al. (1990: 168) quote the following passage by Margaret Thatcher: 'When I got there (Oxford) I think the first thing I learned was that for the first time in my life you were totally divorced from your background. You go there as an individual. So what did we learn?' (interview of 29 March 1983). At first sight, it seems that *I* and *my* are used in the normal, specific way. But this is much less obvious with respect to subsequent *you* and *we*. At the same time, all of these pronouns evoke one and the same referent (or referents). How are we to unequivocally establish its referential status? Such peripheral effects are mostly beyond my focus of interest in this book.

There are good reasons for concentrating on specific definite reference in the first place. This kind of reference is the most frequent one in discourse, and, accordingly, the most central in the linguistic system. Consider the following counts from the large corpus-based study Biber et al. (1999). In English, the proportion of full NPs with the definite article to those with the indefinite article varies approximately from 3:2 to 3:1 (interpretation of data in Biber et al. 1999: 267), depending on discourse register. The proportion of specific definite NPs to generic NPs (with a definite article) varies from 36:1 to 17:1 (Biber et al. 1999: 266). Note that these counts were obtained for NPs headed by common nouns alone; if other kinds of definite NPs (such as pronouns and proper names) were included in the comparison, the contrasts would become much sharper. I believe that an understanding of peripheral and exotic types of reference should be based on a prior understanding of the most canonical type. Throughout this book, 'reference' without further subcategorization should be taken to mean 'specific definite reference'.

2.2 Types of specific definite reference

A fundamental and universal property of human discourse is that one and the same referent recurs as discourse unfolds. For example, if we have a tale about Hansel and Gretel, there will be multiple mentions of these referents in the tale. Dozens of other referents will be mentioned more than once too. There are also some referents that do not recur.

Prior discourse mention is an important source of what is known as givenness (see e.g. Chafe 1976, 1994). Referents that have already been on the interlocutors' minds at the time of mention are usually termed given, and those that have not are termed new. To see a simple example, consider a randomly chosen piece of natural discourse – an excerpt from the second paragraph of Fareed Zakaria's article 'What the world really wants' (Newsweek, 29 May 2006, http://www.fareedzakaria.com/ARTICLES/newsweek/052906.html):

(2.3) Well, consider <u>Vice President Cheney</u>'s speech on May 4 in Lithuania, in which <u>he</u> accused Russia of backpedaling on democracy. <u>Cheney</u> was correct in <u>his</u> specific criticisms. If anything, <u>he</u> was coming a little late to this party. Senators like John McCain and Joe Lieberman have been making this case for more than a year.

The referential device *Vice President Cheney* at the beginning of this excerpt conveys new information, for the simple reason that it is the first mention of this referent in this particular discourse. In contrast, the four subsequent mentions of the same referent represent given information. Let us take the last of these four mentions – *he* in the third sentence of the excerpt. Evidently, when the writer mentions the referent 'Cheney' at this point in discourse, he should be able to let the addressee know that the referent is identical to the one that is already given to the addressee due to prior discourse. How does the writer ensure that the pronoun *he* is understood as referring to the referent 'Cheney'? However straightforward this process may seem at first blush, it is in fact far from trivial and involves many complex aspects. One of the main goals of this book is to offer an answer to this question.

All of the underlined mentions are said to be **coreferential** to each other; sometimes one talks about coindexation. The phenomenon of repeated mention of a referent in discourse is known as **anaphora** (see some comments about this term in section 2.4). Anaphora fundamentally depends on the activation of the referent derived from prior mentions. (The notion of activation will be elaborated below in section 2.5.) Each of the four anaphoric mentions in (2.3) is in some way dependent on the fact that there were prior mentions of the same referent. Anaphoric mentions are conventionally called **anaphors**.[1] An anaphor typically has one or more **antecedents**; for example, the pronoun *he* in the sentence *If anything, he was coming …* has several antecedents, and the pronoun *his* in the previous sentence is the immediate antecedent. Anaphors do not have to be pronouns. The proper name *Cheney* in the second sentence is also anaphoric as it relies on the existence of prior mentions of the referent (see section 2.4).

---

[1] I mean here the traditional understanding of the terms 'anaphora', 'anaphor', not the generativist usage that has completely mutilated the original meaning of these terms. In generative literature it is often claimed or presumed (see e.g. Barss (ed.) 2003: ix) that no tradition of the study of anaphora existed before generative grammarians took note of them.

As was argued in Chapter 1 (section 1.3), reference is a discourse phenomenon. Understanding instances of anaphoric reference such as in (2.3) is not possible unless we understand the organization of discourse, for example, the distance to the antecedent along the discourse structure. This claim is at odds with the tradition in linguistics that views anaphora as a syntactic phenomenon. By definition of syntax, a syntactically governed phenomenon must be fully located within the borders of a sentence. Obviously, some of the anaphors in (2.3), such as the already discussed *he* in the third sentence, are separated from their antecedents by a sentence boundary and cannot possibly be explained by syntactic rules. So the discourse nature of reference is indisputable.

However, as has again been pointed out in section 1.3, there are some instances of anaphora that are somehow more syntactic than others. In (2.3), this concerns, for example, the pronoun *he* in the first sentence. Such uses can possibly be explained by means of syntactic rules that formulate structural relations between the position of the antecedent and the anaphor; in this example it may matter that the antecedent is the possessor of the predicate noun *speech* (on some interpretations, a deep subject), while the anaphor is contained in a relative clause modifying that noun.

One possible solution to this apparent difference between the two kinds of anaphors is to offer separate, independent accounts for them: discourse-based in one case and syntactic in the other. My position, however, is that syntax, specifically inter-clausal syntax, is a subcase of discourse. Syntactic patterns are largely grammaticalizations of discourse patterns. So, as the general solution I will assume that one should seek general discourse rules and understand syntactic patterns as instantiations of these general rules. Even where a syntactic rule may account for an anaphoric phenomenon within the bounds of a sentence, most of the time more encompassing discourse-oriented principles exist that allow us to treat such an instance as a special case of a more general phenomenon.

In the book I focus on discourse anaphora and those instances of syntactic anaphora that are derivative with respect to discourse anaphora. There exist certain referential phenomena that are intrinsically syntactic, for example for the reason that they are limited to the scope of a single clause, such as usual reflexivization. One expects to find such instances in the domain of intra-clausal syntax, and less so in inter-clausal syntax. Purely syntactic patterns will remain outside of the scope of this book. But when no conclusive evidence on such purely syntactic status is available, by default all instances of anaphora are treated as discourse-based.

In (2.3), recurring reference to 'Cheney' is possible due to prior mentions of the same referent in discourse. However, there are kinds of reference that formally resemble anaphora but do not depend on prior mentions. They are possible due to the perceptual availability of the referent in the environment. Imagine the situation when a police officer tells his subordinate about a suspect, standing in front of their eyes:

(2.4)   Get him!

If the officer draws his addressee's attention to the referent in question, for example by pointing at him concurrently with this utterance, this type of reference is usually called deixis. If both of the interlocutors have attended to the person before the utterance in (2.4), this is an instance of exophora. Empirical study of deixis and exophora can only be based on corpora of videomaterials. Although this book is generally devoted to reference based on prior discourse mentions, I will return to deixis and exophora in Chapter 15.

Deixis and exophora are, in a way, simpler referential processes than anaphora because they rely on perceptually given referents, equally available to the speaker and the addressee. In contrast, anaphora presupposes thinking about referents that are recalled or imagined. This ability to reflect on entities and events that are not present here and now was once called displacement by Hockett (1958: 354–355) (see also Chafe 1994, Levinson 2004) and is presumably exclusively human and not shared by other animals. So, when studying reference in discourse one inquires into foundational properties of human cognition.

2.3 Types of referential devices

Referents are conveyed in linguistic structure by means of various kinds of referring/referential expressions, or referential devices. Grammatically, referential devices are nominal elements – most typically, noun phrases (NPs). Nominal referential expessions fall into two basic types with further subdivisions:

(2.5)   (1) Full referential devices
            a. proper names
            b. common nouns (with or without modifiers), or descriptions
        (2) Reduced referential devices
            a. pronouns
            b. zero forms.

2.3.1 Full vs. reduced referential devices

Full referential devices thus split into two major subclasses, proper names and common nouns (with or without modifiers). The term 'full' implies that characterization of the referent provided by an NP of this kind is relatively informative, that the referent is lexico-semantically specified and categorized. There is a great variety of further subdivisions in full NPs, especially within type 1b. In particular, a common noun can appear bare (or with an article in a language such as English), with a demonstrative (*this apple*), with a short modifier (*the red apple, the two men*), with a long modifier such as a relative clause (*the apple I ate this morning*), etc. These complications of NP structure are independent of each other, so they can stack up, and in addition each of them can redouble. Furthermore, a mixture of a common and a proper noun in one full NP is possible; for example, the first mention of the referent 'Cheney' in the Newsweek story cited in example (2.3) above is *Vice President Cheney*. The class of full NPs is thus extremely heterogeneous.

Theoretically a full NP can amplify to infinity, but in fact complex NPs are very rare in discourse. For example, in the corpus of spoken Russian 'Night Dream Stories' (Kibrik and Podlesskaya (eds.) 2009) only 2% of all NPs are longer than three words. Despite the great, almost unlimited variety of different full NPs applicable to one and the same referent, in a given discourse the ways that the referent is mentioned is subject to severe restrictions. Consider an example, consisting of the third paragraph of the same Newsweek story as example (2.3) above (Newsweek, 29 May 2006; http://www.fareedzakaria.com/ARTICLES/newsweek/052906.html):

(2.6) In Cheney's narrative, Russia was a blooming democracy during the 1990s, but in recent years it has turned into a sinister dictatorship where people live in fear. In castigating Vladimir Putin, Cheney believes that he is speaking for the Russian masses. He fancies himself as Reagan at the Berlin wall. Except he isn't. Had Cheney done his homework and Ø consulted a few opinion polls, which are extensive and reliable in Russia, he would have discovered that Putin has a 75 percent approval rating, about twice that of President Bush.

In this excerpt, whenever a full NP reference to 'Cheney' occurs, it consists of the last name alone. In the whole article only three variants of a full NP mention of the referent occur: *Cheney* (six times), *Vice President Cheney* (once, introductory), and *Dick Cheney* (once). Evidently, in this particular discourse this particular referent can be assigned what Boguslavskaya and Muravyeva (1987: 88–89) termed 'model form of mention' (Russian *ètalonnaja nominacija*), and it has the form *Cheney*. According to the results of Vieira and Poesio (1999), in a corpus of written English discourse nearly every full NP with a definite article that is expected to have an antecedent has one with the same head noun. So it appears that each referent has a very limited number of potential full NP mentions in the given discourse. Most of the time, choosing a full NP mention for a referent is equivalent to using the model form, fixed for the given referent in this discourse. For this reason one can justifiably view full NPs as one lump category. As a first approximation, differences between various full NPs can be disregarded, and a full NP in general can be viewed as one of the two main options in **basic referential choice**. In this book I will be primarily interested in this basic referential choice, and only occasionally internal differences between full NPs will come up in the discussion.

The opposite of full NPs are **reduced** referential devices (class 2 in (2.5)). The term 'reduced' suggests that these referential expressions are semantically leaner and can be attributed to an individual referent only in a very specific communicative context. While there is a relatively obvious class of referents that can all be named *the apple* (or likewise *the person* or even *the object*), it would be odd to talk about the class of referents that are all instances of *I* or *it*. (For substantiation of the notion of linguistic reduction see Bergelson and A. E. Kibrik 1981.) A variety of alternative terms have been used instead of 'reduced'. In particular, Chafe (1994: 75) employed the term 'attenuated', and Payne (1993) wrote about weak (as opposed to strong, that is full) referential expressions. Here is yet another alternative formulation: 'If you intend coreference, you should make the referring expression short or semantically general' (Levinson 2000: 181). Much of this book, particularly its typological Part II, is devoted to reduced referential devices, as they figure in various human languages.

As has been shown in (2.5), reduced referential devices fall into two categories: pronouns (category 2a) and zero forms (category 2b). Zero forms display the ultimate reduction: nothing is expressed, although a referent is intended (see subsection 2.3.3 below). Pronouns, however, are reduced but overt referential devices.

Pronouns are of central relevance to the book. Traditionally pronouns have often been thought of as a marginal lexical class, far less important than major substantive parts of speech, such as nouns and verbs.[2] However, in recent years the truth has emerged that pronouns are central to a linguistic system.

---

[2] This approach is often implicit, but cf. the influential dictionary Trask (1993: 166) that explicitly lists four major lexical categories, including noun, verb, adjective, and preposition, as opposed to minor categories.

For example, Švedova (1998: 8) pointed out that 'the pronominal system ... is, by its nature, self-sufficient; but at the same time it is oriented toward all other word classes and interacts with them. ... This system stands above all other word classes: it conceptualizes their structure and mutual links. The class of pronouns is an array of semantic abstractions, contained in a language as a whole'. Pronouns are thus extremely important in language. A linguistic device's significance in language can be roughly assessed through its frequency in natural discourse. One can easily infer from the counts in Biber et al. (1999: 334), based on their 20-million-word corpus, that personal pronouns account for every seventh word in conversation and every eleventh word in fiction.

The category of pronouns is of a high internal complexity. In the first place, it includes personal pronouns; see Siewierska (2004) about the notion of person. Among the personal pronouns there is a fundamental difference between the first and second person pronouns, on the one hand, and the third person pronouns, on the other; see subsection 2.3.2. Many languages have more than one series of personal pronouns, such as strong and weak pronouns; see section 4.5. On top of that, as we will see in Chapter 3, pronouns do not have to be phrases or words, they can be affixes. So discussing referential expressions as types of NPs is a significant simplification (which will be allowed at some points for a while, in order not to overcomplicate this preliminary discussion).

Apart from personal pronouns, there are several other classes of pronouns used for specific definite reference. Among these minor classes, demonstrative pronouns probably constitute the most important class of pronouns functioning as a discourse-oriented device. To the extent that demonstratives are clearly distinct from third person pronouns (see subsection 4.2.1), they are far less central a referential device compared to personal pronouns. According to Biber et al. (1999: 237), in corpora of English discourses third person pronouns make up from 20% to 85% of all anaphoric expressions depending on discourse register, while nominal demonstratives from below 2.5% to 5%, that is ten to thirty times less frequent (17 times less frequent in conversation). Therefore much less attention will be given to demonstratives in the book, although they will be discussed focally in a number of sections as a referential device complementary to third person pronouns (or their equivalents). There also exist several other discourse-oriented but minor types of reduced referential devices, including classifiers (Chapter 4), logophoric pronouns (Chapter 8), and several others that will be mentioned in the relevant portions of the book.

Reflexives and reciprocals are reduced referential devices, typically used in a very narrow domain, that is, within one clause with their antecedents. From this perspective, in this book about reference in discourse they are not of central interest. In addition, they are a lot less frequent in discourse than personal pronouns. According to Biber et al. (1999: 334, 345, 347), compared to 64, 000 third person pronouns per million words in conversation and 56, 000 in fiction, third person reflexives (*himself, herself, itself, themselves*) rate 200 and 1700 occurrences, and reciprocals (*each other, one another*) 80 and 260, respectively. Thus from a discourse perspective third person pronouns are a couple of orders of magnitude more important than reflexives and reciprocals. As reflexives and reciprocals appear in the pragmatically marked situation of coreference between clause participants (see Levinson 1987), many languages treat this situation not as a referential phenomenon but rather as something from the domain of diathesis and voice; see e.g. Kemmer (1993). (On the other hand, other languages extend the use of reflexive pronouns beyond the limits of the clause – so-called long-distance reflexives; such instances will be given some attention in Chapter 8.) In addition, Ariel (2006) shows that among the English reflexive *self*-pronouns a very significant share is non-referring, intensificational uses, often in intransitive clauses (such as *He himself did not come*).

Yet other kinds of pronouns used for specific definite reference are relative pronouns. These are highly specialized for certain syntactic contexts and are thus outside the domain of discourse reference.

The theoretical range of referential options is huge and in fact unlimited. I propose to handle this difficult problem by partitioning it. The highest hiearchical node in the taxonomy of referential devices is the basic referential choice between full and reduced NPs. In order to understand all nuances of referential choice one needs to understand this hierarchically prime choice in the first place, and then proceed further on the basis of such understanding.

A number of well-known proposals exist that put forward much more complex scales of referential devices. In particular, Givón (1983b: 17) posited the so-called coding scale that comprised – besides zero anaphors, pronouns, and definite full NPs – items as diverse as right-dislocation, left-dislocation, contrastive topic, cleft constructions, and indefinite NPs. (See Givón 2001: Vol. I, 417ff. for a more recent and abbreviated version of this scale.) In the work of Ariel (1988, 1990: 73, 2001: 31) the so-called scale of accessibility was proposed containing about 18 positions beginning with a full name with a modifier and ending with a zero. The claim is that 'each referring expression codes a specific (and different) degree of mental accessibility' (Ariel 2001: 31). Some of the positions on the scale are as concrete as last name, first name, distal demonstrative+modifier, stressed pronoun+gesture, etc. A somewhat less bulky scale was proposed by Gundel et al. (1993), under the name of givenness hierarchy. The hierarchy comprises six positions, from maximal to minimal givenness: in focus (*it*) > activated (*that, this, this N*) > familiar (*that N*) > uniquely identifiable (*the N*) > referential (indefinite *this N*) > type identifiable (*a N*).

It is beyond my goal here to provide a detailed critique of these scales, but, in brief, my position is that they attempt to collapse too many different semantic dimensions within a one-dimensional scale. For example, in the hierarchy of Gundel et al. (1993) the difference between third person pronouns and full NPs is of the same nature as the difference between definite and indefinite NPs. However, it has been convincingly demonstrated already in Chafe (1976) (see also Chafe 1994) that these two distinctions rely on two different cognitive categories – givenness and identifiability, respectively. Givenness is a referent's status in the speaker's working, or short-term, memory, while identifiability relates to knowledge in long-term memory. In order to be cognitively realistic, one must recognize multiple dimensions of referential choice and, accordingly, more elementary coding choices, such as the basic referential choice between full and reduced devices.

Another problem with large and elaborate coding scales is that they are completely non-universal. As we will see in Part II of this book, it is not at all necessary that each language amply uses zero reference and plain pronouns. The only truly universal opposition is that between full and reduced referential devices. So in this book I mostly discuss this stark choice, only occasionally going into more fine-grained distinctions. It will be seen that the simple choice between a full and a reduced referential device is complex enough to begin with, without attempting to immediately bring into the picture all possible variations of referential options.

2.3.2 *Locutors vs. non-locutors*

Following A. E. Kibrik (1997), I will use the term 'locutor' for main communication participants, the speaker and the addressee, and, in accordance with that, the cumulative term 'locutor pronouns' instead of 'first and second person pronouns'. The locutor pronouns perhaps are the most specialized referential devices of all. The first reason for this is the fundamentally egocentric character of human cognition and language (see e.g. Dahl 2000). Every human being inherently views him/herself as the centre of orientation, or 'origo' in terms of Bühler (1934). Self-reference is distinct from reference to any other possible entity. In communication this exclusivity is extended to the second person, that is, the communicative partner, or the addressee. Locutor pronouns are almost universal; see Siewierska (2004). Probably the closest to being an exception to such universality is Riau Indonesian (Austronesian) as described by Gil (1999).

Distinction of the locutor persons from the third person (that is, all the rest) is well known; see e.g. Benveniste (1958). Unlike all other referents that can be brought to mind in the course of communication, the speaker and the addressee are permanently activated in each other's minds. It is for this reason that first and second person pronouns, unlike third person pronouns, normally do not interchange with coreferential full NPs (outside special contexts, such as reported speech); therefore, the problem of referential choice between a full and a reduced device does not arise for them. Locutor pronouns are not anaphoric: each mention of the speaker or the addressee relies on the prominence of the referents in communication rather than on prior mentions.

Locutor reference thus constitutes a very specialized type of reference. Locutor pronouns are included in reduced referential devices in (2.5), rather than listed as a separate type of referential device, because of the plural first and second person pronouns, such as *we* and *you guys*. Of course, these plural pronouns refer to sets of referents that potentially include individuals other than the speaker and the addressee(s), and this makes the locutor vs. non-locutor distinction somewhat blurred. An additional reason for such blurring is that the third person includes audience, or overhearers – that is, potential participants of communication; see Schober and Clark (1989).

The question of relative primacy of locutor vs. non-locutor personal pronouns is complex enough; see Helmbrecht (2004: Ch. 7). In terms of frequency, locutor and non-locutor pronouns are generally comparable; specific proportions depend on discourse type. For example, according to Biber et al. (1999: 334), in conversation there are 80 thousand locutor pronouns per million words vs. 64 thousand third person pronouns, whereas in fiction the proportion is 36 to 56, and in the news 12 to 23. So, overall the importance of locutor and non-locutor pronouns is comparable in language use. In this book I am primarily interested in non-locutor, that is, third person pronouns as the least referentially restricted. Locutor pronouns are discussed where necessary for systematic reasons.

2.3.3 *Overt vs. zero reduced referential devices*

Third person pronouns and zero reference are the anaphoric devices par excellence. Much of the discussion in this book will be centred on the distribution of third person pronouns or zeroes vs. full NPs in anaphoric contexts. Some languages, such as English, mostly use third person pronouns as the dominant reduced referential device. Other languages, such as Japanese, prefer zeroes as the main reduced referential device and lack dedicated third person pronouns; see Chapter 3. Still other languages use both in a certain proportion.

English is strongly committed to pronominal reference, but, in fact, not fully devoid of zero reference either. Previously we discussed example (1.5) with a gerundial clause. That is a typical gerundial clause – it does not have its own overt subject but shares the subject with the main clause it attaches to. In such cases it is theoretically possible to avoid positing a zero in a gerundial clause as there is at least an overt subject next door. Consider, however, the following example from an article about Sergei Ivanov, the supposed participant in the Russian presidential campaign of 2008 (The Sydney Morning Herald, 2 August 2007, http://www.smh.com.au/text/articles/2007/08/01/1185647976014.html):

(2.7) ... among a field of candidates, most of them friends of Mr Putin from the days he worked in the St Petersburg city administration, Mr Ivanov is now regarded as favourite. *Whether Ø attending a concert, Ø opening a gym or Ø touring a factory,* his daily routine is given lavish coverage on state TV, boosting his opinion poll ratings.

The italicized portion is a series of three gerundial clauses. In these clauses there is a clear mention of the referent 'Ivanov' in the subject role, but in the main clause this referent appears in a different syntactic position, namely a possessor. So subjects are not shared, and one cannot avoid positiong zeroes in these gerundial clauses. If so, one can extend this convention, by analogy, to more standard gerundial clauses as in (1.5). Further, and less obvious, examples of zero reference in English will be provided in the subsequent chapters.

As zero reference is invisible, there is a question: when is it necessary to postulate a zero, and when not? The practical solution I adopt is the following. Whenever there is no overt coding of a referent in a clause and, at the same time, natural comprehension of the clause suggests that the referent *is* mentioned in this clause, then posit a referring zero element. It is worth noting that zeroes are not a theoretical construct but rather a convention of representation. Practical issues related to this convention are addressed in section 3.4.

2.3.4 *Position of referential devices: clause participant vs. other*

Prototypically, referential devices assume in the linguistic structure positions of clause participants, including arguments [=actants] and adjuncts [=circumstants]. Most of the underlined examples of referential devices in

(2.1), (2.3), (2.4), (2.6), (2.7) above belong to this category, and most of the discussion of referential devices in this book is devoted to such occurrences. However, there are two major exceptions to this prototypical correspondence between referents and clause participant positions.

The first exception is the possessive position; cf. *Cheney's* and *his* in (2.6). There is evidence that the principles underlying the use of clause participant and possessive referential devices are not identical (Krasavina 2006: Ch. 5). In other words, revealing the rules for using *he* does not necessarily guarantee that one understands the use of *his*. This is particularly true with respect to a language such as English, having no difference between plain and reflexive possessive pronouns. (In Russian, for example, the occurrence of *his* in (2.6) would translate into a reflexive possessive pronoun *svoj*, but the occurrence of *his* in (2.7) into a plain third person possessive pronoun *ego*.)

The second major exception is noun phrases accompanying clauses but not belonging to clauses as such. In Kibrik and Podlesskaya (eds.) (2009: Ch. 5) such clause-accompanying units are classified into prospective (that is pre-clausal) and retrospective (post-clausal). Examples of both appear in the following excerpt of spontaneous speech – from a conversation about shoeing horses. (Refer to the publication Du Bois et al. 1992 for the conventions employed in Du Bois et al.'s discourse transcription.)

(2.8)   Du Bois et al. (2000), conversation SBC0001 'Actual Blacksmithing', seconds 434 to 442
   a.   a lot of people,
   b.   .. that have a lot of horses and stuff,
   c.   .. and that they're riding a lot,
   d.   they'll just,
   e.   (H)... let the college kids do em.
   f.   .. For em you know.

The main clausal structure appears in lines (d–e) of this excerpt. This structure is preceded by a prospective referential expression of a rather complex internal organization: a topic noun phrase in (a), followed by two relative clauses. Also, there is a retrospective supplement to the clause in line (f) – a benefactive participant (plus the discourse marker *you know*).

Possessive referential devices, as well as NP supplements to clauses (especially the retrospective ones) are highly frequent in natural discourse. Still they are secondary with respect to clause participant referential devices, and are not given special attention in this book. Of course, they do participate in discourse reference; in particular they can serve as antecedents of the clause participant referential devices that I will be mostly focusing on.

2.3.5 Reference, prosody, and gesture

Discourse consists of the vocal and the non-vocal channels. The vocal channel is further split into the segmental, or verbal, component, and the non-segmental, or prosodic, component. The non-vocal channel includes various components related to 'body language', in the first place gesture. Both prosody and gesture are quite relevant to discourse reference.

The phenomenon of reduction, or attenuation, found in referential devices expresses itself not only segmentally (e.g. pronouns are shorter than full NPs) but also prosodically. Activated information typically is coded by unaccented referential expressions, while non-activated information receives full prosodic coding, such as pitch accent (see e.g. Chafe 1994: 75–76, Arnold 2008). The bond between the lexical choice of referential expression and accent is so tight that some authors in fact propose that concrete types of referential expressions result from a combination of these two parameters. In particular, Givón (1983a, 2001: Vol. I, 417ff.) puts forward the suggestion that there are two different referential devices: unaccented pronouns and accented pronouns. Examples of prosodically marked pronouns appear in the following example from Givón (2001: Vol. I, 419):

(2.9) I talked to Joe and Sally. *HE* was agreeable. *SHE* wasn't.

As Givón himself remarks in his discussion of such examples, there is 'referential contrast' between two referents here. This is what is often discussed, e.g. in Chafe (1976), under the name of contrastiveness – emphatic selection of one candidate rather than the other from a predefined set. Contrastiveness is a separate semantic category and in example (2.8) it simply superposes over referents' activation. Activation is coded by pronominal forms and contrastiveness by contrastive accent; see e.g. Kameyama (1999). (For a review of various analyses of similar facts see Cornish (ed.) 2005.)

Givón's example demonstrates that, even though lexical and prosodic reduction prototypically coincide, they do not have to. A convincing argument that accent placement is a process in principle separable from the choice of referential form is found in Jasinskaja et al. (2007). These authors demonstrate that 'the decision to accent or deaccent a pronoun is not independent from the decision to accent or deaccent other constituents in the sentence. ... The dependence of pronoun resolution on accentuation is a by-product of the general functioning of prosodic focus as a contrast-signaling device'. (Jasinskaja et al. 2007: 2). So accentual reduction is distinct from lexical reduction and they can operate independently. Of course, full NPs can be both accented and unaccented as well.

Accentuation is not the only prosodic feature sensitive to referential processes. Another such feature is the tempo of pronunciation. There exists variation in how full NPs are uttered depending on the level of activation. Levy and Fowler (2000) demonstrate that references to familiar characters performed by full NPs are systematically pronounced in a more lengthened way at the beginning of episodes in narratives, and in a shortened way on a second or further mention. (It will be discussed in detail in Part IV that discourse boundaries are places of referent activation update; so beginnings of episodes are where the minimal referent activation is expected.) According to these authors' results, 'names that were first in an episode averaged 536 ms in duration. This compares with an average duration of 496 ms for words that occurred second in the same episode and 491 ms for words that occurred last in a previous episode' (Levy and Fowler 2000: 224). Essentially the same results were replicated by Robertson and Kirsner (2000). See also Arnold (2008) for a review of studies on phonemic reduction vs. prominence in its relation to reference.

In Levy and Fowler (2000) one more feature sensitive to referent activation was explored – not only non-verbal but also non-vocal: gesture. Pointing gestures are intimately connected to referential processes. In linguistics, this is usually mentioned in connection with deixis, but in fact the use of pointing goes far beyond that and is found in various referential contexts; see Chapter 15. According to Levy and Fowler (2000), full NP mentions that are first in an episode were accompanied by a gesture a lot more frequently than the subsequent mentions; in three samples of narratives first mentions in episodes were accompanied by gestures in 63 to 86% of all instances, and non-first mentions only in 19 to 27% of all instances (Levy and Fowler 2000: 222). Levy and Fowler subsume the presence of a gesture, lengthening, and lexical explicitness under a general category of 'greater expenditure of energy' in the act of reference.

While acknowledging the importance of prosody and gesture in referential processes I will only occasionally mention them in the main chapters of the book. The reason is that the data on which most of the book is based is not particularly associated with prosody and gesture. In Parts II and III I strongly rely on various descriptions of typologically diverse languages that rarely if at all contain this kind of information. Part IV is primarily based on the written mode of discourse. I will turn to the relationships between gesture and reference in Chapter 15. Throughout the other chapters of this book, my attention will be mostly restricted to the distinction between full and reduced referential devices.

2.4 Referential choice and alternative notions

Like other discourse phenomena, reference can be viewed from a range of perspectives. First, it can be approached from the speaker's perspective, as a process performed by the speaker in the course of discourse production. The second perspective is from the addressee's point of view, as a process of attributing referents to referential expressions. Finally, reference can be viewed as a property of discourse form as such, in particular as coreferential relations between linguistic expressions. In this book, I am taking the production-oriented speaker's perspective. The reason for taking this perspective is that it is the speaker who is responsible for shaping the actual form of discourse. Modelling and reconstructing cognitive processes in the speaker leading to observable discourse phenomena is the most efficient route to understanding why discourse is the way it is. In accordance with this approach, I use the notion of referential choice, already introduced in Chapter 1, subsection 1.4.3.

Referential choice is part of a broader process of reference. As a speaker produces discourse, he/she may decide to mention referent R at point P. When such a decision is in place, the problem of choice emerges: which referential option to use for coding the referent. As has been argued above, the basic choice is between full and reduced NPs. This choice is performed by the speaker constantly, as nearly any clause contains one or more referents that need to be mentioned in this or that way.

Referential choice is just one kind of choice facing a speaker or, actually, any acting subject; see Kibrik (2006). When speaking, we choose between the active and the passive voice (Tomlin 1995), the finite and the non-finite form of a predicate (Kibrik 2008b, in press b), etc. When acting in the physical world, we choose between braking or accelerating in driving, between the right and the left hand when reaching for an object, etc. Here I concentrate on just one kind of linguistic choice, but would like to point out that a more general theory of making fast, near-automatic choices in human linguistic and non-linguistic behaviour is required.

To the best of my knowledge, the term 'referential choice' was first used in the Pear Stories book (Chafe (ed.) 1980), specifically in the chapter Clancy (1980). This term or at least this idea is occasionally used by various authors (e.g. Matthews et al. 2006, Arnold and Griffin 2007, Greenbacker and McCoy 2009) but it is not very common. The notion of referential choice is an alternative to a number of more traditional terms used by linguists when talking about essentially the same phenomenon.

Among these terms the most common one is anaphora. There are several reasons why the notion 'anaphora' is of limited applicability to the conceptual framework of this book. First, it has certain connotations ultimately stemming from its etymological descent (<Greek 'carrying back'). It implicitly suggests that an anaphor sends the addressee back to the antecedent where the clue to reference is found, and that this clue presumably has a clearer and more straightforward reference. So the notion of anaphora: (i) is mostly addressee-oriented; (ii) suggests an idea of a search through the overt form of the preceding discourse, in order to find the antecedent and the referent. The former idea does not quite fit the adopted speaker-orientation,[3] and the latter one is psychologically implausible (see Garnham 2001): if a listener makes a search through anything when resolving an anaphor it is his/her cognitive system rather than the external form of previous discourse. I occasionally use the expressions 'anaphora' and 'anaphoric pronouns', understanding anaphora in such a cognitive fashion, when these terms are convenient in a certain context, especially when contrasting anaphora to alternative cognitive procedures, such as exophora.

A further problem with the notion of anaphora is that it captures a narrower range of instances than referential choice. It does not include introductory reference. And since the difference between introductory and repeated reference is not categorical, in many instances it is not immediately clear whether or not it is anaphora. Finally, the term anaphora is ambiguous with respect to those referential expressions it is applicable to. It is conventional to talk about anaphoric pronouns and zero anaphora. Sometimes anaphora is understood as confined to such reduced referential expressions, while sometimes it embraces anaphoric full NPs as well. The latter approach is more appropriate. As has been demonstrated by Vieira and Poesio (1999), in a corpus of English written texts full NPs with a definite article are split between entirely new (non-activated) referents and at least partly activated referents almost evenly. These authors found that full NPs with a definite article are clearly anaphoric and have an explicit antecedent in 30% of instances, have an indirect, associative antecedent (see section 2.4) in 20% of instances, and have no antecedent at all, that is are completely non-activated in 47% of instances. (The remaining 3% belong to idioms and doubtful cases.) This proportion 3:2:5 gives an approximate idea of how full NPs relate to anaphora. For somewhat different counts see Biber et al. (1999: 266).

---

[3] There is, however, a way to reconcile the notion of anaphora with the speaker-oriented approach: one can assume that it is not anaphors but the speaker who 'sends back' the addressee to an antecedent.

There are a number of further notions competing with 'referential choice'. According to one of them, the addressee keeps track of the referents mentioned in the discourse, and thus identifies the referents of incoming NPs. In this framework, linguists often speak about reference-tracking or referent-tracking (see e.g. Foley and Van Valin 1984: Ch. 7, Comrie 1989b). A similar approach assumes not the addressee's but the speaker's perspective. Here what is central is not the addressee's tracking procedures but the speaker's strategies ensuring that referent identity is properly expressed. Under this approach, one sometimes talks about maintenance of reference, or reference-maintenance (Marslen-Wilson et al. 1982; see also Kibrik 2001a). A number of other terms for the process of referent mentioning have been used in the literature, such as management of reference (Tomlin and Pu 1991, Staley 2007). Unlike all these notions, the notion of referential choice focuses on mentioning one individual referent on one individual occasion, rather than on the discourse-wide referential process as a whole.

The notion of referential choice is also an alternative to a variety of transformationally-minded approaches. There is a long-standing idea in linguistics that full NPs are in some way simpler, or more original, while the use of reduced devices is somehow secondary. In fact, even the term 'pronoun', by virtue of its inner form, suggests that it is a kind of a pro-form, somehow substituting for nouns. This idea, having deep historical roots, finds no support within the discourse-oriented approach to language. Clauses such as (2.10i, iii) are in no way secondary or derived with respect to clauses (2.10ii, iv):

(2.10)   i. She is jumping.
         ii. Sue is jumping.
         iii. He called her.
         iv. The teacher called Sue.

On the contrary, clauses like (2.10i, iii) are in fact more frequent and, therefore, typical and basic in natural discourse. Chafe (1994: 108ff.) formulated the 'one new idea constraint' – a powerful generalization governing the structure of elementary units of natural (spoken) discourse. According to this constraint, such units, typically of a clausal nature, rarely introduce more than one new piece of information. If we try to fit our constructed examples (2.10i, iii) into a likely discourse context, it will be clear that each of them already has one piece of new information, expressed by the verbal predicate. Therefore, it is only natural that arguments are expressed by pronouns – exemplary linguistic devices coding given information. In contrast, examples in (2.10ii, iv), especially the latter one, have much too much information formulated as new, and therefore are less likely to be found in natural discourse.

The proportion of pronouns to full NPs in actual discourse can vary greatly, depending on mode (spoken vs. written), genre, and register (Biber et al. 1999: 235), as well as other factors, but cf. the results of one count, performed by Givón (1983b: 352) on the basis of a spoken English story. In this count, the proportion of pronouns to full NPs (of various kinds) turned out to be 423 to 179, that is, roughly 7:3. There are thus good reasons to believe that clauses as in (2.10i, iii) are at least as central in linguistic architecture as clauses in (2.10ii, iv). Referential choice involves a consideration of comparable options, rather than something like transformation of an underlying full NP into a derivative pronoun.

The question is raised sometimes whether it is reduced or full referential devices that are easier to process. Gordon et al. (1993, esp. pp. 322–323), proposed the 'repeated name penalty' suggesting that using full NPs is the dispreferred option in discourse. In a number of experiments, they demonstrate that pronouns are easier and faster understood than full NPs (in the clause topic position).[4] They also argue against the Gernsbacher's (1990) opposite claim that more explicit referential devices are generally understood better and faster than less explicit pronouns. My view on these matters is that neither pronouns nor full NPs enjoy some inherent preference in discourse production or comprehension. There are different cognitive conditions, and each of the basic referential devices is preferred in appropriate conditions and dispreferred otherwise. Garrod et al. (1994) performed a reaction-time experiment demonstrating that reduced devices are better processed by language users when the referent is highly activated, while full NPs are more appropriate in cases of low activation. This suggestion is in line with the cognitive approach to referential choice, laid out in the following section.

During the last three decades or so reference and referential choice have been a subject of multiple studies, including many monographs and collections. A sampling of some of the important ones might include Kreiman and Ojeda (eds.) (1980), Hirst (1981), Givón (ed.) (1983), Paducheva (1985), Fox (1987a), Ariel (1988), Arutjunova (1988), Chafe (1994), Fox (ed.) (1996), Fretheim and Gundel (eds.) (1996), de Mulder and Tasmowski (eds.) (1996), Zribi-Hertz (ed.) (1997), Cornish (1999), Botley and McEnery (eds.) (1999), Huang (2000), Garnham (2001), Kehler (2002), Simon and Wiese (eds.) (2002), Branco et al. (eds.) (2005), Schwartz-Friesel et al. (eds.) (2007), Gundel and Hedberg (eds.) (2008), Abbott (2010), Gibson and Pearlmutter (eds.) (2011). In developing the

---

[4] See also the recent study Tily and Piantadosi (2009) that makes a similar point, relying on a web-based experiment and sophisticated statistical analysis.

approach proposed in this book, I rely on this rich literature, as well as on my own studies of reference, beginning from the early ones, such as Kibrik (1983, 1984, and 1988).

2.5 The cognitive approach to referential choice: activation in working memory

All languages employ reduced referential devices and offer a choice between them and lexically full expressions. Furthermore, in every single language reduced referential devices are used with extremely high frequency. These facts may seem strange, if looked at from a purely logical point of view. Reduced referential devices, such as pronouns, have a very broad range of possible referents. For example, any group of any referents (except for locutors) can be referred to by the English pronoun *they*: humans and animals, males and females, objects and abstract concepts, etc. Why would languages care to employ such obscure referential devices, instead of using full NPs such as *the Jones, these dogs*, or *linguistic theories*? Would not such a strategy be more efficient in ensuring unique reference?

In fact it would not. And the cognitive approach to reference explains why. Full NPs, based on proper names or common nouns, indeed have a narrower range of potential referents – what is called the extensional in logic. But such extension is still very broad. Too broad to serve as the sole basis for efficient reference. There are too many Jones families, various dogs (or groups of dogs), and a plethora of linguistic theories. In contrast, *they* picks a plural referent that the speaker and the addressee are currently thinking about. Such a referent is unique or nearly unique as the human mind is highly restrictive in the amount of information it can handle at one time. So the cognitive approach to reference explains the most basic facts about reference: the cross-linguistic universality of reduced referential devices, as well as their high frequency in discourse.

The idea that referential choice is motivated by certain processes in the human mind has been around for quite a while, beginning at least from the early studies of Chafe (1976) and Givón (1983a). There are a variety of cognitively oriented notions used to explain referential choice, including consciousness (Chafe 1994), attentional activation (Givón 1993), mental accessibility (Ariel 2001), knowledge and attention state (Gundel et al. 1993), focus of attention (I used to use this terminology in my early studies (Kibrik 1983, 1987b); also cf. Francik 1985 and more recently Arnold 2008), salience (Kaiser and Trueswell 2011), etc. It is quite usual that several or all of these cognitive notions are used interchangeably, without a clear distinction. For example, Arnold (2008) uses the terms such as accessibility, focus of attention, being in the discourse model, activation, givenness, prominence with a similar meaning; see also Cornish (1999: Ch. 6). It seems that many authors believe that choosing a precise and consistent cognitive terminology is not particularly important.

The listed cognitive terms are sometimes used somewhat impressionistically. The cognitive approach adopted in this book demands that we take cognitive notions seriously and coordinate an account of linguistic phenomena with what is known from other disciplines studying human cognition, in particular, cognitive psychology and cognitive neuroscience. The claim I am going to put forward here is that the cognitive domain responsible for referential choice is what is known in cognitive science as **working memory**. The degree of a referent's current activation in working memory is directly responsible for referential choice. It is not some metaphoric activation that governs referential choice, it is activation in working memory, which is a functional system of the brain.

In non-technical terms, what are activated in working memory are those referents that the speaker is currently thinking about. It is easy to see what this means with the help of a simple illustration. Full NPs vary in their complexity. A full NP consists of the nominal head and, optionally, one or more attributes. From the point of view of referential choice, attributes restrict reference of the full NP. For example, I say *the big box* if I cannot afford to simply say *the box*. The reference-restricting function of attributes manifests itself in the fact that reduced referential devices do not allow attributes. By their very nature, reduced referential devices such as *he* point to the most obvious referent that the speaker and the addressee are currently thinking about. Adding an attribute to restrict the most obvious referent would be discordant. This cognitive fact is grammaticalized in the refusal of many languages to use collocations such as *big he*. What is perceived as a grammatical constraint actually has a clear cognitive basis.

In fact, there exist two distinct, albeit closely related, cognitive processes involved in referential processes, of which the first one is attention, whereas activation in working memory is the second one. Each of these processes has a linguistic representation. The first process, **attention**, is represented in linguistic structure as reference, or mention. That is, the speaker's act of mentioning a referent at a certain point in discourse is a subcase of a more general phenomenon of attending to a referent.

Whenever the speaker's decision to mention a referent is in place, the second cognitive process comes into play: **activation** in working memory, on which referential choice immediately depends. Referential choice thus becomes relevant only after the decision to mention a referent has been made by a speaker. Activation can vary from high to null, and there is a threshold in this range of activation values that is decisive for referential choice: above this threshold, a reduced referential device is used, and below it, a full NP. This dependency is the main law of referential choice.[5]

As will be argued in detail in Chapter 10, attention and working memory are connected by a causal link. What is attended to at moment t_n becomes activated in working memory at moment t_{n+1}. In terms of linguistic structure, a speaker's mention of a referent affects referential choice on the next mention at the next moment of discourse. To make this discussion more concrete, consider a simple example from natural conversation:

(2.11) Du Bois et al. (2000), conversation SBC0001 'Actual Blacksmithing', seconds 459 to 464
 a. And so we have our instructor right there,
 b. and we asked a million questions,
 c. ..all the time I mean,
 d. (H) he e- --
 e. he just runs around.

The referent 'the instructor' is first mentioned in line (a); by this mention the speaker establishes attention to this referent. As a result, this referent gets activated in working memory, and this activation is maintained for a short while. If the speaker wants to sustain his/her attention to the referent, that is mention it again, referential choice is dependent on the referent's activation in the interlocutors' working memories. In lines (d) and (e) of example (2.11) the referent 'the instructor' still enjoys a high level of activation, and this is the reason why the third person pronouns *he* can be used. Attention to the instructor is not sustained after line (e), and the referent gets deactivated. If the speaker wants to mention the referent after it got deactivated, a full NP would be required, just as in the case of introductory reference.

Referent activation is not a dichotomy, as is implied by the traditional opposition given vs. new information. Chafe (1994: Ch. 6 and elsewhere) proposed a threefold distinction: active vs. semiactive vs. inactive information. The semiactive status results either from being associated with a currently activated concept (the notion of indirect anaphora, or bridging, is based on this kind of secondary activation; see e.g. Cornish 1999) or from deactivation of a previously fully activated concept. As will be argued in Part

---

[5] This is the first and rough formulation of this law. As is shown in Part IV, more than one threshold actually must be posited to account for referential choice.

IV, a threefold distinction is still insufficient, a continuum from maximal to null activation must be recognized, and the referent's current degree of activation can be numerically estimated. Further details of the cognitive theory of reference and referential choice will be elaborated in Chapter 10.

This cognitive approach suggests that it is the referent's current cognitive status which determines actual referential choice. What is the role of an antecedent then? In linguistics, it is often presumed that an antecedent directly affects referential choice. For example Simon and Wiese (2002: 5) say that 'it is via the link to this antecedent that the pronoun gets its meaning.' According to the cognitive theory of referential choice, antecedents are important, but only as tools that boost referents' activation. In Chapter 15 we will look at referential processes of deixis and exophora that are in principle insensitive to any discourse antecedents. Exophora, however, is very similar to anaphora in being based on the already available activation of a referent. Besides the source of referent activation (perceptual environment in case of exophora and prior discourse in anaphora) these two referential processes are nearly identical. Antecedents as discourse elements do not directly control referential expressions as discourse elements. Cognitively, existence of an antecedent means that attention was directed to the referent at a certain previous moment, and this results in the referent's current activation level. In other words, antecedents affect activation, and activation directly affects referential choice.

There is a well-known correlation between referential choice and the choice of clause topic or subject. The latter process was explored by Tomlin (1995) who suggested that assignment of topic/subject in a language like English is regulated by the cognitive status of focal attention. As will be argued in Chapter 10, it is not just that attention governs working memory but working memory in turn facilitates attention. Referents that are already activated are more likely to be mentioned in the next stretch of discourse than other referents. Apparently, focal attention is more easily allocated to activated referents. In different terms, this insight was captured in Chafe's (1994: Ch. 7) 'light subject constraint' stating that activated referents most easily turn out as clause topics/subjects, whereas non-activated referents get into this position only in very restricted circumstances. Therefore it is no surprise that reduced referential devices turn out most frequently in the subject position (in Biber et al.'s 1999: 334 corpus data, the proportion of nominative and accusative animate third person pronouns is nearly 10:1 in conversation and over 3:1 in fiction) and the subject position is most frequently filled by reduced referential devices (79% of subjects are pronouns in Chafe's 1994: 85 spoken data). The phenomenon of 'topic chains' (chains of clauses with coreferential topics/subjects coded by pronouns or zeroes), widely attested in discourses of many languages (see e.g. Li and Thompson 1979), is ultimately based upon the activation-based facilitation of focal attention.

2.6 The speaker's and the addressee's minds: referential strategies

So far when talking about activation in working memory I have avoided specifying who this working memory belongs to. Evidently, it is the speaker's working memory. But there is normally more than one participant in communication. Apart from the speaker, there is an addressee. (There can also be a third participant, an audience or an overhearer. But here I will presume a simpler model involving only two participants.) So, what about the addressee's mind and, specifically, his/her working memory? Is it relevant for the speaker when choosing a referential expression whether the referent is activated in the addressee?

Of course, it should be. The addressee's mind cannot directly influence the discourse that the speaker produces; but what matters is the speaker's assessment or model of what is in the addressee's mind. In cognitively-oriented discussions of referential choice it is often remarked that what actually determines referential choice is a referent's activation not in the speaker's mind but rather in the addressee's mind, according to the speaker's assessment. On the face of it, this claim seems incontestable: indeed, how can someone understand my *he* if I don't care whether the addressee knows who I am thinking and talking about? If so, it is not the speaker's working memory that matters in referential choice but rather the addressee's. We will see below that this view is somewhat overstated.

The speaker's ability to take into account the addressee's state of mind can be described in different terms. In linguistics, sometimes the notion 'the addressee factor' has been used (Arutjunova 1981). In psychology and other related disciplines the notion 'theory of mind' has become current during the last couple of decades (the term was originally coined by Premack and Woodruff 1978). This term (rather infelicitous by itself) refers to the characteristic, specifically human, ability to realize that another person is not simply a physical being but a cognitive agent, having his/her own intentions, beliefs, and other cognitive functions.

The theory of mind faculty plays a central role in language. A recent account of the role of understanding others for the evolution of language is offered by Givón (2005). Givón suggests that grammar is all about discourse production, which is immediately related to coding intentions. An original theory of human communication, using the understanding of others' intentions as a key element, is proposed in Tomasello (2008). Theory of mind was explicitly linked to reference in the paper Gundel et al. (2006).

2. Basics of reference in discourse 57

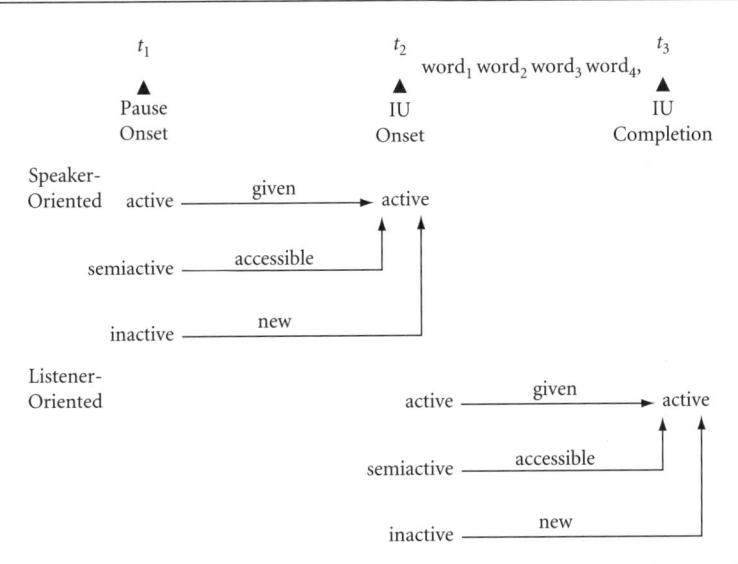

```
                t₁                    t₂                         t₃
                                           word₁ word₂ word₃ word₄,
                ▲                     ▲                         ▲
              Pause                   IU                        IU
              Onset                  Onset                   Completion

Speaker-
Oriented    active ────given────▶ active
                                      ▲
                                      │
          semiactive ──accessible─────┤
                                      │
            inactive ─────new─────────┘

Listener-
Oriented                           active ────given────▶ active
                                                             ▲
                                                             │
                                 semiactive ──accessible─────┤
                                                             │
                                   inactive ─────new─────────┘
```

FIGURE 2.1. The timing of activation costs with relation to speaker and listener (from Chafe 1994: 74) (IU = intonation unit)

An important aspect of theory of mind, directly relevant to referential choice, is that a human being X realizes that another human being Y does not automatically think at any given time about the same things as X does. So when performing referential choice, one needs to somehow coordinate what one has activated with the state of the addressee's mind. This was very well represented in Chafe's (1994: Ch. 6) account of the timing of activation in the speaker's and addressee's minds. On the basis on the triad 'active – semiactive – inactive' Chafe defines another triad 'given – accessible – new' that constitutes the category he calls activation cost. The rationale behind the latter term is that keeping active something that is already active is cognitively least costly, while activating a piece of inactive information is more effortful. Activation cost is thus, according to Chafe's idea, a dynamic notion embracing activation states before and at the time of reference. The speaker activates a referent for him/herself during the pause preceding a discourse segment (intonation unit), and for the addressee while uttering this discourse segment. This is clearly depicted in Figure 2.1.

Thus, according to Chafe's framework, the timing of activation is coordinated but different for the speaker and the addressee. When choosing a verbalization, the speaker relies on his/her assessment of the referent's status in the addressee. For example, a reduced referential device is used if the speaker believes the referent is already active in the addressee at moment t_2.

However, after presenting this quite coherent picture Chafe proceeds with a kind of a disclaimer saying that there is no categorical difference between the speaker- and addressee- oriented activation processes. 'Typically the speaker may assume that the processes in the listener's mind are in harmony with those in the speaker's own mind, allowing for the time lag occupied by the utterance of the intonation unit. ... As far as the speaker's production of language is concerned, there is no essential difference between, for example, a change from inactive to active in the speaker's mind during the pause and a predicted change from inactive to active in the listener's mind during the utterance of the intonation unit.' (Chafe 1994: 75). Chafe's point about 'the harmony of the minds' suggests that the speaker, when producing a referential expression, tries to keep both his/her own efforts and the addressee's effort in interpretation to the minimum. This resonates with the principle of 'Minimal Collaborative Effort' proposed by Clark and Wilkes-Gibbs (1986), as well as with what Pickering and Garrod (2004, Garrod 2011) call referential alignment.[6] As is discussed by Geluykens (1994) and Garnham (2006), interlocutors may gradually negotiate their ways of reference. I assume throughout this book that activation of referents in the speaker's working memory is aligned with timely activation in the addressee, and for the sake of brevity will continue to mention the speaker's working memory alone. The addressee's projected perspective is, however, central in the discussion of referential conflict; see section 2.8.

Despite this I would like to remark that the human capacity for understanding others, and even the human desire to understand others, should not be overestimated. In some recent psychological work it was demonstrated that adult humans have only a limited ability to understand others; see e.g. Keysar et al. (2003). These authors have shown that 'adults do not reliably consult this crucial knowledge about what others know when they interpret what others mean ... Adults and children consistently show an egocentric component to comprehension' (pp. 37–38). In the domain of referential choice, there is direct experimental evidence that speakers may crucially rely on their own, rather than the addressee's, discourse model, see Fukumura and van Gompel (2009). See also Arnold (2008) for a recent and useful review of psycholinguistic work, inquiring into speaker- and addressee-oriented strategies found in the processes of reference.

---

[6] The difference between Clark's and Garrod's theories is that the former suggests a more conscious effort on the part of the speaker in modelling the addressee's mind, while the latter presupposes more automatic alignment processes.

I suggest that speakers may use a variety of strategies of referential choice that can be tentatively grouped into three types: egocentric, optimal, and overprotective.[7]

The **egocentric**, or minimal, strategy may be used by young children. The very idea of egocentric language was originally proposed in connection with child language by Piaget (1923), although nowadays the age when a child develops a fully-fledged theory of mind is thought to be between two and three years of age, which is radically younger than what was believed by Piaget (see e.g. O'Neill 1996, Matthews et al. 2006, 2009). Furthermore, the egocentric strategy of reference is something that we may encounter in adults. In Chafe's words, 'we may all be familiar with cases in which someone said *he* or *she* under circumstances where we, as listeners, had no idea who the referent was, the speaker relying too much on his or her own mental processes and not enough on ours' (Chafe 1994: 75). In the egocentric strategy a speaker tacitly assumes that the addressee must have the same organization of working memory as he/she (the speaker), thus overestimating the addresee's ability to align his/her mental processes with those of the speaker.

Sometimes the opposite extreme is proposed as the norm of referential choice, in particular in computational linguistics contexts. For example, Paraboni et al. (2007) suggested that 'referring expressions tend to contain logically redundant information'; see also Koolen et al. (2009). I call this strategy **overprotective** because it rests on the premise that an addressee needs an overcareful treatment to have reference straight, so the more information given the better. However, redundancy may be good for reference resolution by computers, but probably not in normal human interaction. As was rightly remarked by Levy and Fowler (2000: 229), 'a pronoun referring to a focal referent fosters faster retrieval of information about the referent than does an explicit referring expression (Cloitre and Bever 1988). Accordingly, we can conclude that an appropriately opaque referring expression can help to pick out its referent better than an inappropriately explicit one'; see also Garrod et al. (1994), Tily and Piantadosi (2009). Someone who would use the overprotective, or solicitous, strategy, would presuppose less knowledge in the addressee and thus underestimate his/her ability to follow the speaker's mental processes.

In between lies the **optimal** referential strategy that fits the descriptions of Chafe's harmony, Clark's cooperative effort, and Garrod's alignment. It is this strategy that I presume throughout this book, although the alternating use of

---

[7] A similar suggestion is put forward in the paper Horton (2009) under the name of different degrees of 'consideration of the addressee' that can be used by a speaker.

different referential strategies is an intriguing research issue in itself. As was found in an early eye-tracking study of reading processes (Ehrlich 1983), regression to antecedents happens only about 10% of the time in interpreting pronouns. This suggests that addressees normally understand reduced referential devices quite easily, and, supposedly, speakers/writers are generally efficient in modelling their addressees' minds. In the study Savel'eva-Trofimova (2008), exploring a 14,000-word corpus of spoken Russian, 19 instances of the so-called antitopic (Lambrecht 1994) were found: contexts in which a pronoun is used in a clause, and a fuller NP is used subsequently to make reference more explicit. This indicates that, first, speakers may at times (rarely) fail modelling addressees' minds, and second, they may immediately discover such failures and repair them. The processes of online repairing of referential expressions in spontaneous discourse have been explored by Geluykens (1994) and Schiffrin (2006).

2.7 Multi-factorial approach

Apart from the variety of cognitive approaches to referential choice mentioned above, there is another train of thought, according to which certain properties of the discourse context directly influence referential choice. To pick just one example from dozens of studies, Arnold and Griffin (2007) discuss various approaches to referential choice in terms of direct mapping of the properties of the discourse context upon referential choice: 'speakers tend to use less specific forms to refer to referents that have recently been mentioned in a discourse. ... Likewise, speakers use pronouns more often when referring to a character that was the grammatical subject ... or first-mentioned entity ... in the preceding clause' (p. 522). There is thus a whole range of discourse factors that can potentially affect referential choice. In fact, the range of such factors proposed in the literature is much greater that in the above quotation; see Part IV. In addition, besides the factors of discourse context there are also factors of a referent's internal properties, such as animacy.

This kind of approach, suggesting a direct mapping from discourse factors onto referential choice, poses two major problems. The first problem deals directly with the multiplicity of factors: Do all of the factors affect referential choice individually or collectively? What if one of the factors 'votes' for a pronoun and another for a full NP? The second problem is related to the explanatory force of this approach: if properties of discourse context map directly upon referential options, there is no place for any kind of a cognitive account.

To solve both of these problems, I propose a **multi-factorial approach** to referential choice that complements the cognitive approach outlined in section 2.5. The main features of this approach can be summarized by the following four theses:

- Referential choice is immediately influenced by the referent's current degree of activation in working memory.
- The referent's current degree of activation depends on a wide range of factors, stemming from the discourse context and the referent's internal properties.
- These factors are dubbed activation factors.
- Each activation factor contributes a share to the referent's aggregate activation, and each factor's contribution can be estimated numerically.

The essentials of this approach appear in a flow chart in Figure 2.2.

This model allows one to combine the richness of activation factors, identified by various researchers, with the unified cognitive approach. The model will be worked out in detail and further elaborated in Part IV, in application to Russian and English discourse.

Referential choice is just one linguistic process of a multi-factorial nature. There are many other multi-factorial choices made by a speaker as discourse unfolds. For example, in Kibrik (2008a) I analysed another multi-factorial choice, ubiquitous in the discourse of many languages: the choice between the rising and falling pitch accents in non-final discourse units. As was pointed out in section 2.6, a theory of linguistic (and other behavioural) choices is indispensable, and such a theory must acknowledge and explore multi-factorial choices. Unlike more determined choices, such as those forced or prompted by a language's grammar, multi-factorial choices always involve an interaction and cumulative effect of several factors and are probabilistic in character.

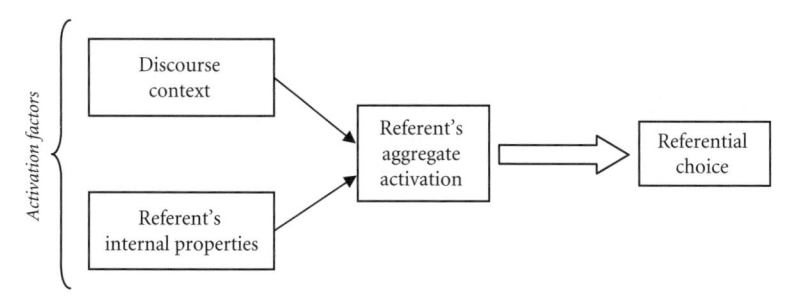

FIGURE 2.2. The cognitive multi-factorial model of referential choice (the first pass)

2.8 Referential conflict and referential aids

When referring, speakers use various referential devices – nominal expressions that link to concepts in the cognitive representation. Apart from that, another important kind of linguistic device is involved, although not performing the act of reference as such: various classifications helping to discriminate between referents. In order to see this, consider the following simple constructed example in which there are two referents mentioned by pronouns in the same clause:

(2.12) Uncle John$_J$ was sitting at the table. Suddenly a girl$_g$ approached him$_J$.
   i. He$_J$ yelled at her$_g$.
   ii. She$_g$ yelled at him$_J$.

In both continuations (i) and (ii) there are a pair of referents playing the roles of participants in a two-place event; in each case it is quite clear which referent plays which role. Apparently, in this particular context both referents are sufficiently activated for being referred to by a pronoun.

Now consider another example, minimally different from (2.12):

(2.13) Uncle John$_J$ was sitting at the table. Suddenly a boy$_b$ approached him$_J$.
   i. $^?$He$_J$ yelled at him$_b$.
   ii. $^?$He$_b$ yelled at him$_J$.

Here the structure in (2.13) presents significant difficulties for understanding and is much less likely to be used. Apparently the only difference from (2.12) is that both referents are of the same gender and the pronouns that can be used to refer to them are identical. Therefore, the category of gender is an intrinsic component of referential choice in English.

Although gender does participate in the process of referential choice, it cannot be a part of referent activation. It is quite obvious that activation of the two referents (John and the person who approached him) after the end of the second sentence in (2.13) is exactly the same as in (2.12). Thus we must conclude that gender belongs to a different component of the process of referential choice than activation. Specifically, it cannot possibly be among the activation factors. A referent's high activation is a necessary condition for reduced referential choice, and, in the case of an egocentric referential strategy, it may be a sufficient condition. In contrast, unambiguousness of reference can never be sufficient for using a reduced device. Suppose there is only one male referent mentioned in a discourse, then using *he* with respect to this referent would always be unambiguous. However, if the referent is of a low level of activation at a certain point in discourse, such a *he* would never be used.

The situation occurring in (2.13) (but not in (2.12)) is what is often called referential ambiguity; see Nieuwland and Van Berkum (2008) for a recent review of work in several fields. I, however, prefer the notion of **referential conflict** (originally proposed in Kibrik 1987a). A prerequisite for referential conflict, realized both in (2.12) and (2.13), is the simultaneous presence of more than one activated referent. Referential conflict as such occurs if nothing in the linguistic structure discriminates between the activated referents – this is the case in (2.13) but not in (2.12).

Referential conflict is a component of the speaker's discourse production system. In the process of making a referential choice, the speaker may judge that a reduced referential device, deemed appropriate on the basis of activation level, may create a referential conflict. This is what happens in contexts such as the above: there is more than one activated referent, and a further pronoun runs the risk of being attributed to a wrong referent by the addressee. This kind of a wrong referent can be called a competing referent (or distractor in terms of Dale and Reiter 1995).

Speakers normally anticipate referential conflicts and check if a classificatory device such as gender would help to preclude referential conflict. In (2.12i, ii) gender does preclude a referential conflict, as the given gender fits only the referent in question, and not the competing referent. In contrast, in (2.13i, ii) nothing precludes referential conflict, and a way out of this situation is to use something like this:

(2.13) i'. Uncle John$_j$ yelled at him$_b$.

It is very important to emphasize that the full NP is used in (2.13i') not for the reasons of insufficient activation but for a totally different reason: the threat of referential conflict filters out a pronoun that is perfectly appropriate on the grounds of activation in working memory. Thus I posit a revision of the model shown in Figure 2.2 above; see Figure 2.3. An additional component, the referential conflict filter, is added in this version of the model.

The referential conflict filter inherently embraces the speaker's assessment of the addressee's knowledge and perspective. The addressee does not know which referent the speaker has in mind, and referential expressions should preferably be uniquely interpretable. The speaker's caring about precluding referential conflicts is a part of his/her efforts in establishing the common ground (Clark and Brennan 1991, Clark and Bangerter 2004, Hanna et al. 2003) with the addressee. The position of the referential conflict filter as a separate component, as shown in Figure 2.3, reminds us of the suggestion by

64   I. Preliminaries

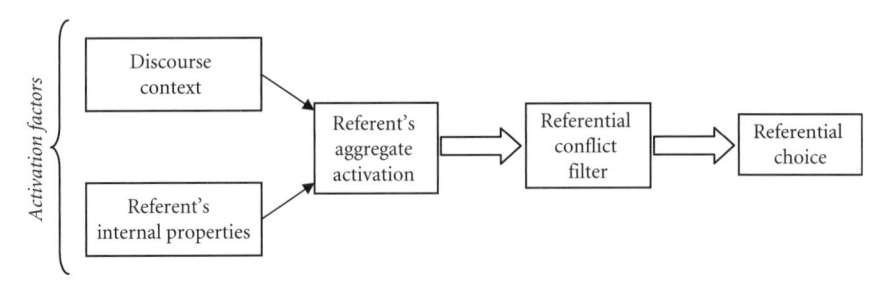

FIGURE 2.3. The cognitive multi-factorial model of referential choice (the second pass)

Keysar et al. (2000) that the common ground is used as a second-stage filter in the process of processing referential expressions, although this latter study looks into comprehension, not production.

Within the optimal referential strategy (see section 2.6 above) the process of referential choice comprises the following stages. When a referent is highly activated, the speaker projects a reduced mention; if it is the only highly activated referent, then a reduced mention can be produced. If not, a referential conflict is possible. Then the available referent sortings, such as gender, are monitored for whether they actually preclude the referential conflict. If they do, a reduced expression is still possible. If not, the projected reduced mention must be revised, and the speaker may resort to a full NP mention as the only way to remove the referential conflict, as in (2.13i′).

When saying that the speaker discovers, anticipates, and precludes a referential conflict, I do not imply that the speaker consciously and deliberately performs these cognitive operations in real time. Discourse production, at least in the spoken mode, proceeds at such a rate that this suggestion would be unrealistic. I believe that such choices made by the speaker operate in a quite automatic way and may be below the level of awareness.

When using the egocentric strategy of reference (see section 2.6), speakers may fail to take the addressee's interests into account, skip the referential conflict filter in his/her referential process, and produce an irresolvably ambiguous referential expression. Along with the failure to model the addressee's current working memory, mentioned in section 2.6, this is another common cause for producing infelicitous referential expressions. Conversely, under the overprotective referential strategy, speakers may produce fuller referential devices even where a more reduced device would suffice due to the operation of a classificatory device such as gender (see below).

English gender belongs to a broad class of diverse linguistic devices that help to discriminate between two or more concurrently activated referents.

These devices will be called **referential aids** and they must be clearly contrasted to referential devices that perform the act of reference as such.[8] Gender is a classificatory category, it cannot refer by itself. It just assists in the process of referential choice. There is a vast repertoire of referential aids in human languages, including conventional and ad hoc linguistic elements. A detailed typology and discussion of referential aids is provided in Part III of this book.

Of course, speakers do not always have to follow the optimal referential strategy. But even if a speaker employs an egocentric strategy, not caring about the addressee's needs at all and not monitoring potential referential conflicts, referential aids are still at work. Referential aids, such as gender, are certainly not used by speakers specifically in order to preclude referential conflicts. The dependency is quite the opposite: when two referents are distinguished due to the gender opposition or another property of the local discourse context, referential conflict is precluded by itself, without any additional effort on the part of the speaker. Referential aids tell concurrently activated referents apart more often than not. As is argued in Part III, referential aids are not necessarily inherent and dedicated disambiguation devices, they mostly exist in languages for other purposes, and their usefulness in the preclusion of referential conflicts is a by-product of their use with separate and specialized semantic functions.

The view of referential conflict and its role in discourse production laid out above contains two crucial elements: first, the recognition of referential conflict as an important component of the system of referential choice, and second, separateness of referential conflict from activation factors. Both of these points have been questioned in the literature, and brief comments on this are in order.

Chafe (1990a) suggested that ambiguity exists primarily in the imagination of 'exocultural' linguists, while for real speakers 'familiarity and context are likely to remove most problems of keeping third-person referents straight' (p. 315). But consider the above-cited examples (2.12) and (2.13). The difference in acceptability of (2.12i, ii) and (2.13i, ii) is due precisely to the fact that in the first case referential conflict is precluded by gender, and in the second case it is not. Therefore, gender does participate in the process of reference and can be given the status of a referential aid. Referential conflict is quite real in language users' everyday practice, as anyone can verify from his/her actual experience. A kind of view opposite to that of Chafe but also questioning the

---

[8] In a number of my previous publications, for example Kibrik (2001a), I used somewhat different terms for what I call here referential devices and referential aids: namely, primary referential devices and subsidiary referential devices, respectively. Here I reserve the term 'referential devices' specifically for those linguistic elements that perform the act of reference, such as full NPs or pronouns.

significance of referential conflict from another side was offered by Arnold et al. (2000), who reported that speakers do not always avoid ambiguities. I believe that this issue must be addressed with the idea of alternative referential strategies in mind: indeed, referential conflicts may be kept in language due to an egocentric strategy.

Another group of authors (Clancy 1980, Givón 1983a: 14, Ariel 1988: 28, Payne 1993: 89, Gernsbacher 1990) suggested (in their respective terminologies) that referential conflict is among the activation factors and that a mention of an intervening referent inhibits the previously activated referent. Once again, examples (2.12) and (2.13) may be useful to assess this judgement. Suppose that the use of the pronoun he_i in (2.13i) is unfavourable due to the fact that the intervening referent 'the boy' has inhibited the activation of the referent 'John'. Then in (2.12i) the intervening referent 'the girl' must equally inhibit 'John', but this apparently does not happen. Therefore, referential conflict is a component of the system of referential choice, separate from the operation of activation factors. Referential conflict can rule out reduced referential expressions that are perfectly acceptable from the viewpoint of activation. Furthermore, the number of simultaneously fully active referents is of course limited (see Chapter 13), but the human mind can operate with two and even three activated referents at a time. In natural discourse it is not a rarity to see a clause with two or three arguments, all marked by pronominal or zero forms. So overall it appears that referential conflict per se does not inhibit referent activation.

A particularly sophisticated argument against the role of referential conflict as a distinct component of referential choice was proposed in Arnold and Griffin (2007). In one of the experiments, these authors compared referential choice in three conditions: (i) when there was only one referent activated, (ii) when there were two activated referents of different genders, and (iii) when there were two of the same gender. The percentage of pronouns used by experiment participants turned out to be, respectively, 85%, 53%, and 23% (p. 523). Whereas there is a dramatic decrease in the use of pronouns in condition (iii) (with a genuine referential conflict), there is also a big difference between conditions (i) and (ii). That is, referential choice seems to be more explicit even when there is no danger of referential conflict, but there are simply more than one activated referents (condition ii). Arnold and Griffin suggest there exists a special 'Two-Character Effect', found in both conditions (ii) and (iii) and stemming from a competition for the speaker's own cognitive resources: 'the Two-Character Effect emerges out of the speaker's own attentional allocation, and not out of any consideration of whether the expression would be interpretable for the listener. ... The reduction in pronoun use for situations with more than one character is likely to result from competition between entities in the speaker's mental model, which results in a lower level of activation for each entity' (Arnold and Griffin 2007: 528). As for the difference between conditions (ii) and (iii), Arnold and Griffin go even further and consider the possibility that the 'Gender Effect' (condition iii) may also emerge 'out of competition within the speaker's own mental representation' (p. 533) rather than from the speaker's concern for the addressee's needs.

Whilst these authors' results are interesting and worth further consideration, I am not convinced that having two concurrently activated referents should be so devastating for speakers' cognitive resources. As I argue in Chapter 13, having even three fully activated referents is perfectly feasible for language users. I would like to point out that there may be a very different – and quite contrary – reason for Arnold and Griffin's results, namely the employment of an overprotective referential strategy by (some of) the experiment participants. When speakers deal with more than one activated referent, they may sometimes fail to check whether referential conflict is precluded and may end up using a more explicit referential device just to be on the safe side. Probably one should not expect by default that all experiment participants should use the same referential strategies; individual preferences can vary from egocentric to overprotective. An additional reason for believing that the overprotective strategy might have been involved is that Arnold and Griffin instructed the participants to produce discourse 'imagining that they were making up the story for a 5-year-old child' (p. 525). So there is an alternative explanation for having so many fewer pronouns in condition (ii) compared to condition (i).

I will proceed on the basis of the optimal referential strategy and keep assuming that referential conflict is a second-stage filter, quite separate from activation factors.

2.9 The structure of the subsequent parts of the book

The structure of the book has already been outlined in the Preface. I provide a more detailed outline here as the reader now has more background information.

The process of referential choice has two main aspects: (i) the options the speaker chooses from and (ii) how this choice is actually made. Parts II and III of this book are devoted to the first aspect. They review the cross-linguistic diversity of linguistic devices employed in the process of referential choice. Part II 'Typology of Reduced Referential Devices' addresses referential devices per se – those linguistic elements that perform the function of reference; this part consists of five chapters. Chapter 3 introduces the major cross-linguistic types of reduced referential devices, including free and bound pronouns and zero reference; languages vary in being disposed to one of these three types. Chapter 4 discusses several specific issues related to the referential functions of pronouns and some other functionally analogous devices. Chapter 5 is devoted to various language-internal inconsistencies in the use of reduced referential devices, such as using zero expression in one kind of argument position and pronouns in other argument positions. Chapter 6 inquires into the relationship between the pronouns' boundness and tenacity, the latter meaning copresence with another referential device in a single act of reference. Finally, Chapter 7 looks into the diachronic aspects of bound pronouns and their relationship to the phenomenon of agreement.

Part III 'Typology of Referential Aids' deals with those linguistic devices that do not refer themselves but assist the process of referential choice, disambiguating between concurrently activated referents. This part comprises two chapters. Chapter 8 provides a typology of referential aids, such as noun class, animacy hierarchy, switch-reference, etc. Chapter 9 discusses the degree of functionality of referential aids, that is the extent to which they actually contribute to referential choice. This chapter also includes a comparative account of two related languages with noun classes, one of which extensively uses noun class as a referential aid, whilst the other does not.

In contrast to Parts II and III, Part IV 'The Cognitive Multi-Factorial Approach to Referential Choice' is devoted to the second aspect of referential choice; it inquires into how specific referential choices are made the way they are. A much more detailed level of granularity is used in this part, with a focus on specific factors of referential choice. In Chapter 10 I outline the cognitive multi-factorial (CMF) approach to referential choice, recognizing the multiplicity of factors affecting a referent's activation in the speaker's working memory and, ultimately, referential choice itself. Chapters 11 and 12 present specific applications of the CMF approach to the data of two languages, Russian and English. Chapter 13 discusses cognitive inferences that can be drawn from these linguistic studies. Finally, Chapter 14 overviews a number of other studies, done by myself and by my colleagues, within the framework of the CMF approach.

Part V 'Broadening the Perspective' addresses certain important issues in discourse reference that have not been sufficiently elucidated in the previous parts, particularly those related to the visual aspects of discourse. Chapter 15, the only one in Part V, looks into the relationships between verbal and gestural reference and discusses pointing as a referential device – both in gesticulation accompanying speech and in a sign language.

Summary

Referents are concepts in language users' minds. The most prototypical kind of referents are specific definite ones. Specific definite reference strongly intersects with what is known as discourse anaphora. Referents are conveyed in linguistic structure by referential devices – various kinds of nominal expressions. There is a great variety of referential devices, but the basic division is between lexically full and reduced devices. Reduced referential devices are particularly important for this book. Other distinctions between referential devices are locutors vs. non-locutors, overt vs. zero devices, clause participants vs. other. Apart from nominal expressions, other devices involved in reference are prosodic features and pointing gestures.

Referential phenomena are approached in this book from a speaker's perspective. When a speaker intends to mention a referent, the problem of choosing between the available referential options becomes relevant. This process is called here referential choice, this term being preferred to other alternatives, including anaphora, reference-tracking, etc. Referential choice is a part of a broader process of reference. Reference is about whether a referent is mentioned, and referential choice about how it is mentioned. Referential choice becomes relevant only after the decision to mention a referent has been made by a speaker. Reference and referential choice are representations of two different cognitive processes – attention and activation in working memory, respectively. When making referential choice, a speaker may take the state of the addressee's mind into account to different degrees. Such degrees can be described as different referential strategies: egocentric, optimal, and overprotective.

While a referent's activation is the immediate predictor of referential choice, it depends, in turn, on multiple factors, here called activation factors. These are either properties of a discourse context, or of a referent itself. A multi-factorial approach is adopted in this book, allowing us to describe the integration of activation factors in each individual instance of referential choice. Apart from activation in working memory, there is one more significant component of referential choice: the referential conflict filter. By using this filter, a speaker may revise a projected reduced referential device if it creates a threat of ambiguity for the addressee. A variety of referential aids, both conventional and ad hoc, are used in languages to preclude possible referential conflicts.

Part II
Typology of Reduced Referential Devices

When a speaker needs to mention a referent, he/she chooses from a certain repertoire of available linguistic means. Part II of this book is about **what** the speaker chooses from, that is, about the kinds of referential devices available in human languages.

This part is primarily about **reduced referential devices**, while lexically full referential devices are only occasionally discussed and are generally beyond the scope of my attention here. The main reason for the focus on reduced devices is that they are most intimately related to a language's most foundational grammatical properties. Also, reduced referential devices are inherently designed for specific definite reference in discourse, whereas lexically full expressions occur in a variety of other referential statuses as well.

The primary goal of Chapters 3 to 7, comprising this part of the book, is to identify which linguistic units perform the referential function. I will begin with simpler cases and with more consistent languages that always perform reduced reference in one and the same way. Then I will gradually proceed with more complex cases and conclude this part with a discussion of very intricate systems, even though belonging to familiar languages.

In this part of the book I provide a **typological** account of referential devices. This means describing the diversity across human languages in what devices they use to refer, as well as the limits of such diversity. Thus the main intention is to further our empirical knowledge about referential devices and their use in natural languages. At the same time, when doing empirical typological work, one inevitably addresses theoretical issues.

As an example of a theoretical issue that occurs in many places in this part of the book, consider the problem of the number of a referent's representations on one individual mention. If language speakers know that in a certain clause, such as the English *He played*, an act of reference is contained, one expects, by default, that there is a linguistic element in the clause that performs this act of reference. Our example satisfies these expectations: the pronoun *he* apparently is the referring element. However, in the structure *He plays* there is an additional element, the agreement marker *-s* that is in a way analogous to the pronoun *he*, also conveying such semantic elements as third person, masculine, and singular. Does this agreement marker represent a second representation of the same referent in the same clause? This question may require different answers for English and for other related languages, such as Spanish or Russian.

Now, in the structure *He played and sang* there are two clauses, and the second one does not contain any overt element to which the referential function could possibly be ascribed. Apparently we face an instance when reference is performed by a 'zero' expression. So, a referent can be represented by at least three different numbers of potentially referring units in the linguistic structure: one, two, and none. These are very basic theoretical issues that must necessarily be addressed, if one strives for a sensible typological analysis.

Typologizing referential systems is not an easy task, as information about individual languages is not readily available. In descriptive studies, it is represented in an incommensurable way, or is scattered in different parts of the description, or is missing completely. Nevertheless, I attempt to collect as much information as possible about cross-linguistic frequency of the observed patterns, about their genealogical and areal representation.

3

Major types of reduced referential devices

Overview

In this chapter I outline the cross-linguistic diversity of reduced referential devices.[1] These devices are specifically employed in human languages to mention those referents that currently enjoy high activation in the speaker's and addressee's minds. Reduced referential devices are a central and integral part of any language's grammar and naturally lend themselves to a typological analysis. I will demonstrate that a language's preference for a certain kind of reduced referential device is a part of the language's typological profile and correlates with its other grammatical features. Among the reduced referential devices, I primarily focus on non-locutor (third person) referential devices, although much of what is said below applies to locutor reference as well.

I differentiate between three fundamental kinds of reduced referential devices found in the world's languages: free pronouns, bound pronouns, and zero reference (section 3.1). Each of the fundamental devices is discussed in turn (sections 3.2 to 3.4). In accordance with this threefold distinction, three groups of languages are identified, each predominantly inclined to using one of these devices. In section 3.5 I discuss the representation of such internally consistent languages of the world, and in section 3.6 the relation between the language's preferred referential device and morphological complexity.

3.1 Three major types of reduced referential devices

In the languages of the world, the following three most fundamental kinds of reduced referential devices are found:

---

[1] An early version of the typology proposed here, as well as in Part III of this book, appeared in a sketchy form in Kibrik (1991). I thank the publishing house Mouton de Gruyter for granting permission to include the ideas proposed in that publication in this book.

(3.1) (i) free personal pronouns, such as English *he*
(ii) bound personal pronouns: affixes attached to a head constituent (typically the verb)[2]
(iii) zero forms.

Consider examples from three languages, each of which is particularly prone to using one of the three types of devices. The first example is taken from an original Navajo tale, and the other two are its rather close English and Japanese translations:

(3.2) Navajo (Na-Dene, Southwest of the USA; from a story by Bernice Casaus, speaker)

a. ʔałk'idą́ą́ʔ shį́į́ ch'oshts'aaʔ ʔa-ji-łhosh   jin.
   long.ago   PTCL snail   PREF-he-sleep.IMPFV QUOT

b. nt'ééʔ shį́į́ ts'éé-<u>dz</u>-í-dzid-o,
   then   PTCL PREF-he-PFV-wake.up.PFV-SBRD

c. shį́į́   dichin   ho-ʔ-nii-lį́.
   PTCL   hunger   him-something-PREF-kill.PFV

(3.3) English[3]
a. A long time ago <u>a snail</u> was sleeping, they say.
b. Then, as <u>he</u> woke up,
c. hunger was killing <u>him</u>.

(3.4) Japanese[4]
a. mukashi-mukashi aru <u>katatsumuri ga</u>   nemut-te
   long.ago   one snail   NOM   sleep-CONV
   i-ta   soo   des-u.
   be-PAST   EVID   COP.ADDR-PRES

b. <u>Ø</u> mezame-ta   toki
       wake.up-PAST   when

---

[2] Apart from the verb, other head constituents to which bound pronouns may be attached include nouns (in possessive phrases) and adpositions.

[3] I do not indicate genealogical affiliation and area for the best known European languages, such as English, Spanish, or Russian, as well as for major language isolates, such as Japanese, and also omit this information where it is obvious from the context of a chapter or section.

[4] Japanese examples in this chapter and the subsequent chapters of Part II have been collected or checked with the assistance of Zoya Efimova, Wakana Kono, and Yoshiaki Koga. I am very grateful to all of them for their help.

c. <u>Ø</u>   gashi   shi-soo   desh-ita.
   starvation   VERBZR-EVID   COP.ADDR-PAST

Referential devices are underlined in all of these examples. The referent is invariably introduced in all three languages by a full NP, that is, a noun meaning 'snail'. However, after the referent is so introduced, its activation becomes high in the subsequent clauses, and reduced referential devices are employed. These, however, operate very differently in all three languages.

The most familiar among the reduced devices shown in the examples are **free**, or **separate, pronouns**, such as English *he* or *him* in (3.3). They are separate words, even though they are prosodically weak. The way in which English relates referents to referential devices is graphically represented in Figure 3.1. [Brackets in the plane of talk indicate clause boundaries.]

Navajo, in contrast, uses **bound pronouns** – they are affixes attached to the clause's verbal predicate; see Figure 3.2. Another important fact about Navajo is that it uses such bound pronouns irrespective of whether the referent is activated or not and, accordingly, whether a full NP is contained in the clause or not. The same bound pronoun[5] is used in (3.2a) and (3.2b), although the referent's activation is radically different in these two clauses. In (3.2a), therefore, we see a double representation of the referent in the clause. This phenomenon is discussed in detail below in this chapter and especially in Chapter 6 under the name of pronoun tenacity.

Japanese, unlike both English and Navajo, does not employ any overt referential device when a referent is highly activated. In other words, language users clearly know that a referent is mentioned in a clause, but there is nothing in the clause's formal structure to which such a function can be attributed, as shown in Figure. 3.3. This phenomenon is conventionally called **zero reference**, and I will use this term here.

Referents (plane of thought)

Referential devices (plane of talk)   [...   <u>he</u>   ...   ]

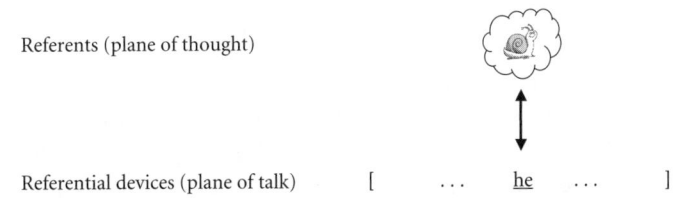

FIGURE 3.1. Linking of free pronouns, such as English *he* in (3.3b)

---

[5] The prefixes *ji-* and *dz-* are morphophonemic variants of the same bound pronoun, the so-called fourth person used in folk narratives to refer to a discourse protagonist; see Chapter 8, section 8.5.

76   *II. Typology of Reduced Referential Devices*

Referents (plane of thought)

Referential devices (plane of talk)   [... ts'éé-<u>dz</u>-í-   ...   ]

FIGURE 3.2. Linking of bound pronouns, such as Navajo *dz-* in (3.2b)

Referents (plane of thought)

Referential devices (plane of talk)   [...   Ø   ...   ]

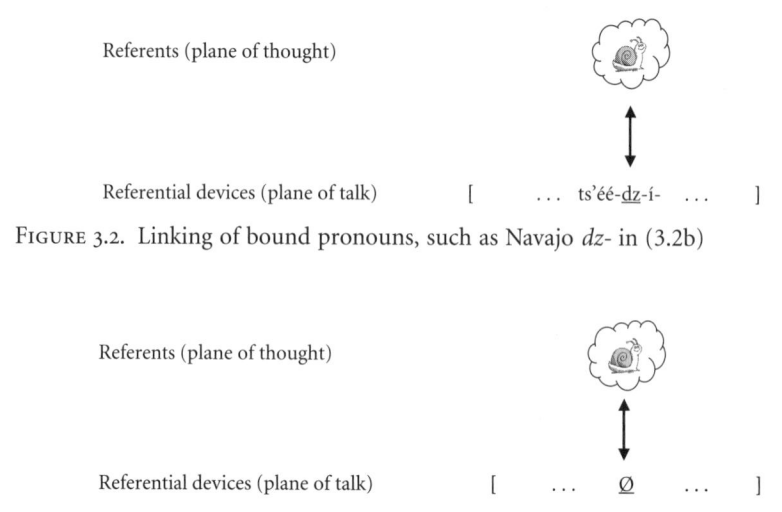

FIGURE 3.3. Linking of referential zeroes, such as Japanese Ø in (3.4b)

In grammar-centred linguistic traditions, a clause is thought to prototypically consist of a verbal predicate and one or more NPs, such as Sapir's famous *The farmer killed the duckling*. Semantically, this structure reflects an event and its argument(s). However, grammar is the system that evolved to serve discourse. In a typical clause in natural discourse, at least one referent, and often all referents, are highly activated, and therefore are coded by reduced referential devices. As a result, average clauses look quite different in the three kinds of languages outlined above. In languages inclined to using free pronouns, average clauses have the same structure as Sapir's decontextualized clause, with the difference that free pronouns stand in the slots where a grammarian expects a full NP (*He killed it*). By contrast, in both bound pronoun and zero reference languages a typical clause consists of a verb alone. The difference is that in a bound pronoun language, unlike a zero reference language, this verb contains morphological mentions of the referents (*He-it-killed* vs. *Killed*). Compare clauses (b) from the Navajo, English, and Japanese examples (3.2)–(3.4) above. These observations suggest that the threefold distinction discussed in the present chapter may be among the central typological parameters grouping human languages into broad types.

A note on the widely circulated term 'pro-drop' is in order here. This term opposes free pronoun languages such as English to other languages that favour other reduced referential devices. The category of 'pro-drop' languages includes zero reference languages, such as Japanese, and bound pronoun languages, such as Navajo. 'Pro-drop' originated in the writings of generative grammarians (see e.g. Rizzi 1982) and was with surprising ease picked up by some linguists belonging to other theoretical approaches. The term is very unfortunate, at least for two reasons. First, it suggests that something (apparently, a free pronoun) used to exist, but then somehow got dropped. However, nothing is dropped in a language like Japanese when zero reference is used, and nothing is dropped in Navajo under the high activation of a referent. These languages are simply organized so that free pronouns are not used, unless very special conditions apply (see Chapter 5).

The second drawback of the notion 'pro-drop' is that it throws all un-English languages into one wastebasket category, not differentiating between bound pronoun and zero reference languages. In addition to languages such as Japanese and Navajo, 'pro-drop' includes a wide range of less consistent languages that use free pronouns in some contexts and other referential devices in other contexts (see Chapter 5). Siewierska and Bakker (2005) have demonstrated that 96.2% of a sample of 428 languages are pro-drop. Non-pro-drop are only Germanic and a handful of other languages (see Chapter 6, subsection 6.7.1). It must be obvious that basing a typology on the 'English vs un-English' parameter is not very insightful. In addition, as will be seen towards the end of this chapter, the free pronoun type is very far from being a typological default.

Languages differ greatly in what referential devices they use. Moreover, languages are not always internally consistent in this respect. More than one of the major reduced referential devices, or even all three of them, can be often found within one language. In particular, different devices may be used in different clause participant positions, semantic contexts, or grammatical environments. For example, English is mostly inclined to using free pronouns but it does use zero reference in the subject position under clause coordination. A discussion of this and other kinds of language-internal inconsistencies is postponed until Chapter 5.

In this chapter the focus is on the working of referential devices as pure types. Accordingly, I will draw illustrations from languages that are consistent in this respect and mostly confine themselves to one of the major referential devices. Among the internally **consistent**, or **pure**, languages there are, evidently, three major types differing in what is their prevalent kind of reduced referential devices. Sometimes I informally use terms such as 'a free pronoun language', meaning a consistent language that is exclusively committed or at least strongly inclined to free pronouns rather than other reduced referential devices.

3.2 Free pronouns

Free, or separate, personal pronouns are the most familiar kind of pronouns. Much of widespread thinking about grammar has been based on languages employing this type of reduced referential expression as the default option. In grammatical theories, most of the time (a notable exception is Role and Reference grammar; see Van Valin and LaPolla 1997: 23ff.; see also Bresnan 2001b) free pronouns are tacitly presumed to be the neutral, or unmarked, kind of reduced referential device. As the discussion in the next sections of this chapter and in the subsequent chapters demonstrates, this view is untenable: free pronouns are but one among other widespread reduced referential devices.

Free personal pronouns feature in a number of well-studied languages, such as English, German, or Russian. (The use of English and Russian free pronouns is discussed in fine detail in Chapters 11 and 12 of this book.) However, using familiar European languages to give the first and clearest illustration of free personal pronouns is not very convenient, as they (particularly German and Russian, and English in a more vestigial way) also have another way of person marking – personal subject desinences on the verb. Later on I demonstrate that this phenomenon is not as foreign to matters of reference as it may seem (Chapters 6 and 7).

So let us begin with languages that perform reduced reference (and express person) almost exclusively by free pronouns. Numerous examples of such languages are found in West Africa, for example in Lyélé, clearly described by Showalter (1986):

(3.5) Lyélé (Southern Gur, Burkina Faso; Showalter 1986: 211–212, 208)
  i. gɔ   lìbí   zɛ̀ỹ   bè   yi   bè   zɛ   ya
     bush   people arise   they   arrive   they   take   him
     'The bush people came and captured him'

  ii. e   zɛ̀ỹ   e   k'   e   kwè   e   la   e   vò   e   pyà   gɔ
      he   arise he   again he   take   he   leave he   go   he   search bush
      lìbí   jaa-esho
      people   place
      'He went back and looked for the place where the bush people lived'

  iii. ń   pɔ   mɔ   se
       he[6] give   him   them
       'He gave them to him'

---

[6] Showalter (1986: 206) explains that the third person ń appearing in (3.5iii) is the singular human gender pronoun, while the pronoun e appearing in (3.5ii) is the singular diminutive gender pronoun. The same is the difference between object pronouns – human mɔ in (3.5iii) and diminutive ya in (3.5i). Lyélé third person pronouns distinguish 9 classes (genders).

These examples illustrate the following points about reference in Lyélé, as a representative of free pronoun languages:

- Free pronouns are used pervasively, even in contexts where most languages would use zero reference – that is, to express coreferential subjects of coordinate clauses (3.5i, ii)[7].
- There can be multiple distinct pronouns in a clause (3.5iii).
- Free pronouns alternate with full NPs in argumental positions, such as subject (3.5i) or object (compare 3.5ii and 3.5iii).

It appears that the Gur family is one of the language families that are particularly inclined towards this kind of referential device[8]. Consider examples from two other Gur languages, Sùpyíré and Dagbani (see also Naden 1986):

(3.6) Sùpyíré (Senufo[9] Gur, Mali; Carlson 1994: 573)
u ahá m̄-pyí u à pa náhá, u gú kù ɲyè
he COND INTRANS-be he PF come here he POT FUT.it see
'If he were to come here, he would see it'

(3.7) Dagbani (Northern Gur, Ghana; Olawsky 1999: 45, 46)
i. o zaŋ li ti o
he take it give her
'He gave it to her'

ii. doo maa ti paɣa maa sima
man DEF give woman DEF groundnuts
'The man gave groundnuts to the woman'

Even in these languages, predisposed to using free pronouns, there are certain contexts in which an alternative referential device, namely the zero, is used. In Lyélé, reference to an activated referent in the object position can be sometimes performed by zero (Showalter 1986: 208). Regarding Dagbani, Olawsky (1999: 21) remarks that pronouns 'are not generally omittable, except for a few particular contexts in clause coordination'. In Sùpyíré, again, there is substantial

---

[7] Showalter (1986: 211) treats these examples as a serialized construction forming one clause. The issue of whether it is one clause or several coordinate clauses does not affect my analysis. Under Showater's interpretation, the point about the preference for free pronouns can be made even more strongly, as languages typically avoid pronouns in serial verb constructions.

[8] This inclination is not general, however. For example, in Kabiyè, a Gur language of Togo, bound pronouns are used; see Lébikaza (1999: 454'ff.'). Naden (1986: 276) mentions that some Gur languages strongly rely on zero anaphora.

[9] Affiliation of the Senufo languages in the Gur family is questioned by some.

80   *II. Typology of Reduced Referential Devices*

use of zero reference in coordinate constructions, even though Carlson seems not to specifically discuss this in his grammar; see also Carlson (1987).

Like other referential devices, free pronouns not only refer but also fulfil another function: they indicate the clause participant's semantic role in a clause. There are two major ways in which this can be done: by means of segmental material (that is, by case marking) and by means of ordering. Both of these techniques can be illustrated by Lyélé examples. In this language third person singular pronouns have different case forms which Showalter (1986: 207) describes as 'subject' and 'object' forms. For example, compare the subject form *ń* and the object form *mɔ* of the same third person singular pronoun in (3.5iii). In contrast, plural third person pronouns do not distinguish between case forms. For example, the plural pronoun *bè*, as in (3.5i), may occur in both the subject and the object positions. Furthermore, Showalter (1986: 207–208) remarks that the subject position is the preverbal one, and the object position is postverbal. So in the case of third person plural pronouns semantic role in conveyed by the order of clause constituents alone, while in the singular pronouns it is conveyed by both order and by case forms.

3.2.1 *Free pronouns can be tenacious*

One of the properties of Lyélé free pronouns, emphasized above, is the fact they are in complementary distribution with full NPs: if a referent is activated enough, it is mentioned by a pronoun, if not by a full NP. However obvious this pattern may seem, it is not universal. In some languages certain pronouns may cooccur with coreferential full NPs in the same clause. One example of such a language is Hausa, a major language of West Africa, spoken in Nigeria and Niger and belonging to the Chadic subfamily of Afro-Asiatic. Principal (traditionally: subject; see section 1.9 where I introduced terminology associated with clause participants) pronouns are free, and they are expressed in a single word with the clause's tense, aspect, mood, focus, and polarity grammemes. In Chadic linguistics (see e.g. Jaggar 2001: 148ff.) these words are dubbed 'person-aspect markers' or 'person-aspect complexes'. Since they convey the referential function, it seems adequate to allow an interpretation according to which they are pronouns, inflected for clausal categories; see section 4.4. As the following discourse example demonstrates, Hausa Principal pronouns are found in a clause irrespective of whether there is a coreferential Principal full NP or not. (This is an extract from a story in which a lion killed some game, put it aside, and went off to look for some more.)

(3.8) Hausa (Chadic, Afro-Asiatic, West Africa; Jaggar 2001: 708-709[10])
    a. Sai damisa <u>ya</u> tafo, <u>ya</u> ishe nama, babu
       then leopard 3M.FOC.PFV come 3M.FOC.PFV find meat NEG.EXIST
       kowa.
       everyone

    b. Shi kuwa <u>ya</u> ji yunwa, sai <u>ya</u> tsuguna,
       3M and 3M.FOC.PFV feel hunger then 3M.FOC.PFV squat.down
       <u>shina</u> ci.
       3M.IMPFV eat.VN

    c. Sai zaki <u>ya</u> tarda shi, <u>shina</u> ci.
       then lion 3M.FOC.PFV find 3M 3M.IMPFV eat.VN

    'And the leopard came and found the meat, with no one near it. Now he felt hungry, so he squatted down and was eating. Then the lion came across him, as he was eating.'

In this extract, the Principal pronoun (underlined) is the sole representative of the referent in a number of clauses. When the Principal full NP is there, as in the first clauses of (3.8a) and (3.8c), the Principal pronouns are nevertheless in place. This is a very important typological property of pronouns that will be discussed in detail in further sections, as well as in Chapter 6, under the name of pronouns' tenacity. One may suggest that Hausa Principal pronouns are tenacious specifically because they are not just pronouns, but also markers of the clause's semantic categories. Even though this may be a contributing factor in this particular instance, in other languages tenacity is found in more classical pronouns that only contain marking for person and number (see Chapter 6). Note that the Hausa Patientive pronouns do not have this property – they are in complementary distribution with full NPs. When a Patientive referent is sufficiently activated, as in the first clause of (3.8c), an accusative pronoun occurs, and when it is not, just a full NP occurs, as 'the meat' in the second clause of (3.8a).

3.2.2 Free pronouns and pronominal clitics are one category

Descriptions of languages with free pronouns often indicate that these pronouns' behaviour is somewhat ambivalent. On the one hand, they are usually

---

[10] In the texts included in Jaggar's grammar the standard Hausa orthography is used, in which some phonemic distinctions, such as vowel length and tone, are not reflected. This is the reason why some homographic elements are glossed differently in different places. In the analytical part of the grammar these distinctions are marked. I follow the way in which the text is broken into sentences (lines) in the original source.

in complementary distribution with full NPs and are supposedly nominals themselves. On the other hand, they are often deprived of certain features of independent words, such as prosodic independence. Consider the authors' comments about the three Gur languages discussed above. About Lyélé: 'Subject pronouns function phonologically as pre-nuclear syllables. ... Verbs in Lyélé may be seen to be composed of a nucleus of one or two syllables, plus an optional pre-nuclear or post-nuclear syllable.' 'In fast speech, the vowel of the object pronoun is assimilated to the height of the vowel of the preceding verb.' (Showalter 1986: 207, 216, 208). About Sùpyíré: 'anaphoric pronouns are normally unstressed and cliticize on the following word' (Carlson 1994: 156). About Dagbani: both subject and object pronouns 'are very short in their phonological structure' (Olawsky 1999: 21).

In other words, free pronouns are what is known as clitics – grammatical words that are prosodically somewhat deficient. I propose that there is no principled distinction between free pronouns on the one hand and clitic pronouns on the other.

A caveat is in order here: the claim about the clitic status of free pronouns applies not to all but only to **weak** free pronouns. Many, if not all, languages exhibit strong free pronouns that are prosodically fully-fledged words. In languages like English, where discourse accentuation plays an important role, the weak vs. strong pronoun opposition is realized in the distinction of minus or plus accent. Accordingly, one distinguishes between unaccented and accented pronouns (but cf. the discussion below in this subsection on possible segmental differences between English weak and strong pronouns). Other languages display a segmental difference between weak and strong free pronouns, instead or in addition to the difference in accentuation. The issue of strong pronouns is discussed in more detail in Chapter 4, section 4.5. So the argument below concerns weak pronouns alone.

Some authors propose more complex classifications of free pronouns than the one put forward here. For example, Siewierska (2004: 16–40) differentiates between independent, weak, clitic, and bound person markers.[11] The first three types apparently correspond to my 'free' category, and the first type (independent) coincides or at least strongly intersects with the 'strong free' pronouns (see section 4.5). Furthermore, the second and the third of Siewierska's types (weak and clitic) both correspond to my 'weak free' pronouns. I propose that differences between weak and clitic pronouns are due more

---

[11] Various subgroupings within this range are found in the literature; in particular, Cardinaletti and Starke (1999) use the term 'deficient pronouns' for weak pronouns and pronominal clitics, taken together.

to descriptive traditions than to actual differences between languages. Before I present arguments to support this claim, a digression is required concerning the notion of clitic.

There is an extensive tradition in modern linguistics of opposing free forms to bound forms, the latter including clitics and affixes (for example, Haspelmath 2002: 148ff.). However, if one assumes that words and affixes are categories rather than values on the scale of 'wordness', this approach seems dubious. The term 'clitic' originally evolved, and still is used, to describe kinds of words that are restricted in their freedom, rather than kinds of affixes that are freer than other affixes. Clitics are as independent as other words, except for their prosodic behaviour. Prosodically, they need to lean to some host word but they are not firmly affiliated with any host word. The crucial difference between clitics and affixes is that clitics have at least some freedom in associating with a host, or anchor, word. 'Clitics are elements which share properties of fully fledged words, but which lack the independence usually associated with words' (Spencer 1998: 350). (For more on criteria helping to differentiate clitics from affixes see e.g. Spencer 1998: Ch. 9, Aikhenvald 2002, Haspelmath 2002: 148ff., Plungian 2003: 28–32.)

The first-order division is between words and affixes, while the distinction between prosodically fully-fledged words and clitics is of only a secondary importance. It is desirable to accord the terminology with this hierarchy of distinctions and use the 'free' category so that it embraces all kinds of words, including prosodically deficient words, and the 'bound' category so that it excludes partially free elements (that is, clitics). I thus deliberately diverge from the terminology in which bound forms include clitics and adopt that bound forms are equivalent to affixes, whereas clitics are free rather than bound. After all, freedom is always relative rather than absolute, and weak pronouns, that are generally clitic, can justifiably be characterized as free forms in comparison to affixal pronouns.

Of course, the boundary between word and affix, or between syntax and morphology is notoriously non-discrete. Since words often evolve into affixes in the course of linguistic evolution (grammaticalization), there must be numerous intermediate cases, difficult to interpret. This is similar to the wings of bats developing from the front legs of more typical mammals. In intermediate cases, it may be useful to avoid unnecessary specification and use overarching terms such as 'morphosyntax' or 'forelimbs'. But positing a separate grammatical level between syntax and morphology or a separate category qualitatively different from both words and morphemes hardly helps but rather makes the problem still more perplexing. The more categories one posits, the more boundaries must be drawn, so this tactic is not fruitful. For these or similar reasons some authors have proposed to drop the notion of clitic altogether, suggesting instead that it is better to think about typical and atypical words and affixes; see the discussion in Joseph (2002); Spencer and Luís (2009). I do, however, believe that clitic is a useful notion if understood as a subtype of word.

The final general point to make about clitics is that these elements vary with respect to their syntactic behaviour. There is a cline of clitics' mobility in terms of choosing a host, comprising at least the following kinds: (i) fully mobile clitic > (ii) clitic fixed to a certain syntactic position in the clause > (iii) clitic attached to a certain morphosyntactic unit, such as noun phrase or inflected verb. Nikolaeva (2008: 142) provides a still more detailed classification of clitics. In the studies of clitics, various terms are used for the kinds mentioned; in particular Zaliznjak (2008: 25) calls types (ii) and (iii) phrasal and local clitics, respectively. Type (iii) clitics are the ones that gradually develop into affixes. Distinctions between the three types are fluid, and it certainly makes sense to understand elements of all three kinds as belonging to the class of clitics. Concluding the digression about clitics, it is worth mentioning that in the course of further discussion we will encounter free pronouns belonging to all the three types of clitics.

Free pronouns are generally clitics rather than prosodically independent words. It is well known that given (activated) information is prosodically reduced, or attenuated (see Chafe 1994 inter alia). Pronouns are a conventional way to express given information, so, unless some special concerns are involved, they are expected to be prosodically reduced and therefore clitic. Special concerns would include factors such as contrastiveness. In such instances we would observe strong pronouns (see section 4.5) while weak pronouns are the default, are of high frequency, and are not associated with specialized semantic or grammatical contexts. I have counted unaccented and accented third person pronouns in the Russian spoken corpus 'Night dream stories' (Kibrik and Podlesskaya (eds.) 2009). For the nominative pronouns (masculine *on*, feminine *ona*, neuter *ono*, plural *oni*) the proportion of unaccented and accented usages is 75% to 25%, and for the accusative masculine *ego* 87% to 13%. Unaccented usages form a single prosodic complex with an adjacent accented word.

English pronouns are clitics as well, although this fact is rarely recognized in the theoretical literature. In this connection, Givón (1983b: 37) bluntly states: 'In English the writing system obscures the stress difference between stressed and unstressed pronouns, but a field linguist would easily identify the English unstressed pronouns as clitics.' One can go even further and suggest that English strong and weak pronouns are different not only in the presence

TABLE 3.1. A selection of English strong and weak pronouns from a list on p. 1613 of Palmer et al. (2002)

Graphic	he	him	his	she	her	them
Strong form	/hi:/	/hɪm/	/hɪz/	/ʃi:/	/hɜ:ʳ/	/ðem/
Weak form	/hi/, /i/	/ɪm/	/ɪz/	/ʃi/	/həʳ/, /ɜ:ʳ/, /əʳ/	/ðəm/

vs. absence of accent, they are segmentally quite different; cf. notorious examples of English phrases such as *saw him*, often pronounced as something like [sɔm]. Table 3.1, based on Palmer et al. (2002: 1613), shows the segmental differences between the weak and strong forms of some English pronouns. If not for the orthographic tradition, strong and weak pronouns could have been spelled differently in certain cases.

Facts such as these recur in many other languages; cf. Rhodes (1997). Lehmann (1995: 41), in his book on grammaticalization, mentioned a common clitic-type use of German pronouns, such as accusative *ne/se/s* 'him/her/it' (compare orthographic *ihn/sie/es*). See also the evidence of several unwritten Gur languages cited at the beginning of this subsection. The general cross-linguistic tendency is clear: there is no important difference between weak and clitic pronouns. It is one and the same category, dubbed here (weak) free pronouns, that is fundamentally distinct from bound pronouns (affixes). (Note that below the term 'free pronoun', unless otherwised specified, means 'weak free pronoun'.)

One of the main reasons for many authors' failure to see that English pronouns are most of the time clitic forms is the approach that can be called paradigmatically-oriented. The reasoning is this: since English pronouns, for example the pronoun spelled *him*, **can** be prosodically fully-fledged words on some occasions, they **are** such by their nature. However, according to the usage-, or discourse-based, approach, English pronouns are prosodically deficient most of the time, and only more rarely, under special conditions, function as strong pronouns. These two kinds of usages need not be treated uniformly. The basic pattern of English pronouns is their use as clitics.

It is useful to make a distinction between contextually clitic pronouns and inherently clitic pronouns. Examples of contextually clitic pronouns (that can be accented on certain occasions) are English *him* and Russian *ego*, while Spanish *lo* or Polish *go* are inherently clitic and have segmentally distinct counterparts that are used if the pronoun is prosodically prominent. This distinction is close to what Zwicky (1985) calls simple and special clitics; see also Nikolaeva (2008), especially p. 151. Zaliznjak (2008: 70) mentions the

86   II. *Typology of Reduced Referential Devices*

TABLE 3.2. Paradigmatically- and discourse-oriented approaches to free pronouns

	Lo viste.	*You sàw him.*	*You saw hìm.*
Ordinary paradigmatically-oriented approach	Clitic	Non-clitic	Non-clitic
Refined paradigmatically-oriented approach	Special clitic	Simple clitic	Non-clitic
Discourse-oriented approach	Clitic = weak pronoun	Clitic = weak pronoun	Non-clitic = strong pronoun

term 'semiclitic' for contextual clitics. In paradigmatically-oriented approaches, even if this distinction is appreciated, it is still pronominal forms rather than discourse usages that are classified. In a discourse-oriented approach, the difference between the two kinds of free pronouns, or pronominal clitics, is of only secondary relevance. What matters is the kind of discourse usage. Table 3.2 summarizes various terminologies associated with the term 'clitic' as applied to free pronouns; the Spanish structure *Lo viste* 'You saw him' and two English structures, with an unaccented and with an accented pronoun, are used as representatives of different kinds of pronouns.

To recapitulate, free pronouns typically:

- are prosodically reduced (in languages that use discourse-motivated accents they are unaccented).
- undergo segmental reduction.
- make a prosodic complex with some prosodically strong word (a host), often a verbal predicate.

3.2.3 *How to distinguish free pronouns from bound pronouns?*

As was pointed out above, orthographies of written languages may obscure the grammatical status of pronouns. The same applies to languages with little or no tradition of literacy: it is often hard to judge from descriptions the degree of pronouns' morphological freedom. Decisions to spell pronouns as separate words or as elements attached to other words may depend on many considerations, of both substantive and incidental character. Among the incidental considerations there can be grammatical tradition, existing practical orthography, or simply author's preferences.

Throughout Part II of this book I cite multiple examples from various language descriptions. Conventions used by different authors are quite variable. Cross-linguistically equivalent elements, such as clitics, can be spelled by different authors either as separate words (separated by blank spaces from other words), or can be marked as clitics relying on the modern convention with the equals symbol '=', or sometimes indistinctively from affixes, just hyphenated to host words.

Explicit marking of pronominal elements as clitics is relatively rare. For example, Atóyèbí (2007) is developing a linguistic transcription for Ọ̀kọ, a Benue-Congo language of Nigeria on which he is doing fieldwork. In this transcription he marked pronouns as clitics, for example[12]:

(3.9)　Ọ̀kọ (Benue-Congo, Nigeria; Atóyèbí 2007: 18)
ὲ=wὲ=ja
1SG.SUBJ=give=3SG.OBJ
'I gave him/her/it'

Atóyèbí (2007) treated pronouns as clitics in particular because they undergo a harmonic influence from the verb root.

According to Joseph Dele Atóyèbí (personal communication, February 2007), in Yoruba, the major language of the part of Nigeria where Ọ̀kọ is spoken, the status of pronouns is essentially the same, including phonological influence from the verb upon at least some pronouns. However, in standard orthography pronominal clitics are represented as separate words:

(3.10)　Yoruba (Benue-Congo, Nigeria; Atóyèbí 2007: 21)
mo　　fṹ　ú
1SG.SUBJ give 3SG.OBJ
'I gave him/her/it'

Such discrepancies, however, are not problematic, provided the discussion above of the clitic nature of weak pronouns. Some authors who spell pronouns as graphic words (separating them on both sides by blank spaces) state at the same time that they are clitics; see for instance the discussion of Sùpyíré above.

Much more problematic is the situation when it is difficult to distinguish affixal pronouns from clitic (that is, free) pronouns. Some authors indicate that what they transcribe as a part of a word can be a clitic. One example of such discrepancy between analytic description and spelling is found in the account of Chemehuevi, a language of the Southern Numic branch of Uto-Aztecan, by Press (1980). This discrepancy is resolved in favour of the analytic description. According to Press, the most common pattern of pronouns' use in Chemehuevi is that they cliticize to the first prosodically full word of a

---

[12] I thank Joseph Atóyèbí for useful discussions of his data in 2007 and 2010.

clause, less animate preceding more animate. This suggests that pronouns are free rather than bound. Chemehuevi third person pronouns, derived from demonstratives, have a two-way distinction in animacy, two-way distinction in number (animates only) and a three-way distinction in proximity (here at hand; visible; invisible; see Press 1980: 45):

(3.11) Chemehuevi (Uto-Aztecan, California; Press 1980: 75, 57, 65)
    i. nukwi-ji-aŋ
       run-PRES-DEM.SG.AN.VIS
       'He is running'
    ii. paʔa-ntɨ-m   aipac   nukwi-j
       tall-PARTIC-AN   boy   run-PRES
       'The tall boy is running'
    iii. maŋ   nukwi-j
       DEM.SG.AN.VIS   run-PRES
       'He is running'

(3.12) Chemehuevi (Uto-Aztecan, California; Press 1980: 102, 79)
    i. haita-uka-aŋ   tɨka-mpɨ
       then-DEM.INAN.INVIS-DEM.SG.AN.VIS eat-PAST
       'He ate it then'
    ii. nɨ   maka-j   wacɨ-mipɨ
       I   DEM.INAN.VIS-OBL   put-PAST
       'I placed it'

As these examples illustrate, clause participants in Chemehuevi can be expressed by either weak pronouns or full NPs or strong pronouns. Strong pronouns, such as in (3.11iii) and (3.12ii), are associated with a 'mild' emphasis (Press 1980: 47), do not cliticize, and can actually serve as a host for cliticizing a pronoun referring to another participant. Weak pronouns, such as in (3.11i) and (3.12i), are clitic, that is free, even though they are spelled together with host words.

This demonstrates that the morphological status of a pronoun should not be judged on the basis of spelling alone, and all available information about a language must be taken into account. A typical reason for authors' writing a clitic together with (or, more typically, hyphenating it to) a host word is that discourse segmentation into words is done on the basis of phonetic words while the identification of free and bound forms relies on grammatical criteria.

In deciding on which pronouns are free and which are bound, the most reliable strategy in cross-linguistic research is the default acceptance of the interpretation provided by the author specializing in the given language. This approach is pragmatic and it does not suggest that an author's current interpretation is the ultimate truth. For example, the analysis of Ọ̀kọ by Atóyèbí has changed since 2007, and in the dissertation Atóyèbí (2009) the former clitic pronouns got reinterpreted as affixes. This shows that the clitic vs. affix dilemma is complicated, but nevertheless at any time a typologist should rely on the best of the experts' knowledge. (But cf. Creissels's 2005 warning that actual treatment of pronominal elements in descriptive work may be misleading.) My interpretation of pronouns as either words (clitics) or affixes will be based primarily not on spelling but on the authors' explanations and argument.

3.2.4 Genealogical and geographical distribution

I am not aware of general surveys of the cross-linguistic spread of free pronouns, as opposed to bound pronouns and zero reference. However, useful information can be gained from the study by Dryer (2005a), looking at the patterning of subject (that is, Principal) pronouns in a sample of 674 languages. Of course, Dryer's study focuses only on one kind of argumental position and its result cannot be automatically extended to pronouns in general. Still Dryer's results are instructive and provide a significant part of the story, as the Principal position is inherently associated with activated information, and most reduced referential devices occur in this position (see e.g. Chafe 1994). According to Biber et al. (1999: 334), in their 20-million-word corpus of English discourse the proportion of nominative (*he*) and accusative (*him*) forms of the English masculine third person pronoun is 11:2 in conversation and 17:5 in fiction.

According to the understanding of free pronouns outlined in subsection 3.2.2 above, the category 'free pronouns' embraces three values of Dryer's typological parameter: 'obligatory pronouns in subject position', 'subject clitics on variable host', and 'subject pronouns in different position'. On Dryer's map, thus identified free pronoun languages primarily cluster in the following areas: West Africa, northern Europe, and western Oceania (Micronesia and Melanesia outside of New Guinea).[13] West Africa has been

---

[13] On Dryer's map, one more area, namely central-eastern North America, makes an impression as having quite numerous free pronoun languages of the type 'subject clitics on variable host'. This impression is partly due to the fact that Dryer has listed all Algonquian languages in his sample as belonging to this type. I find this decision surprising; see Wolfart (1996) portraying a typical Algonquian language as clearly belonging to the bound pronoun type. Apart from that, there are many scattered free pronoun languages and small families in western North America, but they do not define the overall picture of this continent.

illustrated above by the examples from Gur languages. Besides Gur languages, two other groups of West African languages also tend to use free Principal pronouns pervasively: languages of the Mande family and western Benue-Congo (roughly those of Nigeria and Cameroon).[14] Many West African languages have free pronouns combined with clausal categories, such as tense (see 4.4). The languages of northern Europe primarily belong to the Germanic and East Slavic groups. These languages actually are not pure free pronoun languages as they contain person marking on the verb; this problem is discussed in Chapter 7. Languages of western Oceania mostly have tenacious free pronouns; some examples are discussed in Chapter 6, section 6.2. About one half of Pama-Nyungan Australian languages in Dryer's sample are free pronoun languages – for example, Arrernte. Occasionally the free Principal pronoun pattern is found in other parts of the world, including the northern coast of New Guinea (for example, Namia of the Sepik family), the Himalayas (for example, Lepcha, Sino-Tibetan), western North America (for example, Pomoan languages), some parts of South America (for example, Kaingang, Macro-Ge, Brazil; Wiesemann 1986c) and several others. Overall, the free pronoun pattern is clearly minor on a worldwide scale. This conclusion may be surprising, provided that much of modern linguistic theorizing still regards free pronouns as the most typical, most common reduced referential device.

3.2.5 *Free pronouns and related typological features*

For many linguists, who are native users of free pronoun languages, free pronouns are unjustifiably considered the cross-linguistic default and are not perceived as something exotic. For this reason, by way of a kind of ethnocentric logic, free pronouns have rarely been viewed as worth attentive analysis, including searching for potential typological correlates, compared to other major referential devices (see subsections 3.3.5 and 3.4.4 below). Usually, free pronoun languages have been characterized as being an unmarked member of an opposition with other languages. For example, Li and Thompson (1976) opposed subject-prominent languages, such as English, to topic-prominent languages, mostly exemplified by languages of East and Southeast Asia. One of the key distinctions they indicated is the necessity of

---

[14] The interpretation of typical West African pronouns as free forms is questioned sometimes. For example, Creissels (2000: 235–238, 2005) suggests that this interpretation is often erroneous and many languages use affixal pronouns.

free pronouns to occupy argumental positions in subject-prominent languages.[15]

Hale (1983), Jelinek (1984), Austin and Bresnan (1996) and others have contrasted 'configurational' languages, such as English, to 'non-configurational' ones. The latter is a large and heteregenous class of un-English languages (see Pensalfini 2006 for a recent review) that do not display syntactic properties typical of familiar European languages. Among such missing properties are the fixed, role-coding word order, syntactic contrast between subject and object, and, what interests us most, inclination to use free pronouns. 'Non-configurational' languages include both bound pronoun and zero reference languages. I believe that a useful outcome of this research tradition is an understanding of what makes English-type languages peculiar and unlike other languages of the world. Languages of northern Europe and West Africa are more syntax-centred than most other languages. Any clause must have distinct argumental NPs, no matter whether referents are activated or not. This is one of the main reasons for which the modern grammatical tradition, based in the first place on free pronoun languages, has put so much emphasis on syntax and often equates syntax with grammar and even with language.

As the reader will see in typological discussions of bound pronouns and zero reference languages below, both of these language classes are substantially correlated with certain morphological features. To test hypotheses on such correlations, I will use pairwise combinations of WALS (Haspelmath et al. (eds.) 2005, 2008) features; see subsections 3.3.5 and 3.4.4 below.[16] But what can one find out about grammatical correlates of free pronouns?

If one combines the aforementioned study Dryer (2005a) and the study Bickel and Nichols (2005) on the degree of inflectional synthesis of the verb, the basic result is that there is no clear interaction between these two parameters: free pronoun languages make up a very similar share of languages of very different degrees of verb synthesis: for example, 35% of languages with 2 to 3 inflectional categories, 30% of languages with 4 to 5 inflectional categories, 33% of languages with 10 to 11 inflectional categories, etc. (See more on this in section 3.5.) It appears that free pronouns can cooccur with very different morphological systems. Free pronoun languages may display

---

[15] Li and Thompson actually spoke about English pronominal dummy subjects, as in *it rains*; but note that the Germanic languages' requirement of dummy subjects is a special case of a more general preference for free pronouns.

[16] This can be done by using the Composer function of the program in Haspelmath et al. (eds.) (2005), or by the combining function of the web version of WALS (Haspelmath et al.(eds.) 2008).

more correlations with certain syntactic features, but empirical large-scale typological surveys allowing this kind of research questions do not yet exist.

3.3 Bound (affixal) pronouns

Personal affixes have become widely recognized as bound pronouns, that is, genuinely referring units, relatively recently (Kumaxov 1974, Van Valin 1977, 1985, Van Valin and LaPolla 1997: 330–332, especially Jelinek 1984, 1985, Mithun 1986a, Kibrik 1992b), although Boas (1911: 646) and even von Humboldt (1836/1988: 130ff.) and Duponceau (1819: xxxi) already wrote about pronouns incorporated into the verb.

Consider the following examples from Abkhaz, a language with ergative alignment:

(3.13) Abkhaz[17] (Abkhaz-Adyghean, Abkhazia)
  i. i-rə-l-tejt'
     it-them-she-gave
     'She gave it to them'

  ii. i-l-z-i-c-sə-rgəlojt'
      it-her-for-him-with-I-build
      'I am building it [e.g. the house] for her together with him'

These are inflected verb forms that are also fully-fledged clauses. The verb-clause in (3.13i) has three participants: the agent, the patient, and the recipient. The verb-clause in (3.13ii) has four participants: the agent, the patient, the beneficiary, and the comitative; the roles of the latter two are indicated by special prefixes 'for' and 'with'.[18] Each participant is represented in the verb form by means of a prefixal person marker. Person markers are simultaneously:

- verbal affixes, that is, morphologically bound elements
- pronouns, analogous in their referential function to morphologically free pronouns such as English *she, it,* or *him*.

---

[17] Abkhaz examples come from my fieldwork conducted in 1987 in the village of Xuap, Abkhazia, as a part of the field expedition of Moscow State University, and later on in Moscow, with the assistance of Galija Kalimova. The Roman phonemic transcription employed was developed by Sandro V. Kodzasov and differs in details from the transcriptions of Hewitt (1979) and Spruit (1986); the recent transcription in Hewitt (2005), though, converges with the one used here in some respects, in particular in using *j* and not *y* for the palatal continuant.

[18] Besides benefactive and comitative, there are a variety of other non-core participants that can be likewise marked on the verb, including malefactive, instrumental, subject-matter (about what), locative, etc.; see Hewitt (1979: 208–209). As concerns the number of bound pronouns concurrently appearing on one verb, Hewitt (2005: 58) proposed that Abkhaz avoids quadripersonal verbs, but cf. (3.13ii).

In order to see how bound pronouns operate in discourse, consider an excerpt from an Abkhaz folk tale 'The father's will'[19] about an old man [=m] who had four sons [=S]. The lines in the example correspond to clauses.

(3.14) Abkhaz (Abkhaz-Adyghean, Abkhazia)
    a. i-kuraxy   d-nejxyan,
       his$_m$-old.age   he$_m$-was,
    b. apsra   d-analaga,
       die   he$_m$-when.started
    c. i-č'k$_o$'ənc°a   d-rə-pxyan,
       his$_m$-sons$_S$ he$_m$-to.them$_S$-called,
    d. j-aajn,
       they$_S$-came,
    e. adc'a   r-i-tejt'
       the.task   to.them$_S$-he$_m$-gave
    'He [=the old man] was in his old age, and when he started dying, he called his sons, and they came, and he gave them a task'

Apart from the fact that the pronouns in (3.14) are morphologically integrated into their respective verbal predicates, the basic discourse pattern of pronoun usage is quite familiar: whenever a referent is activated, a (bound) pronoun alone is used, and there is no full NP. In (3.14), there are multiple instances in which an argument of a clause is represented solely by a bound pronoun affixed to the verb. This is the same pattern as the one illustrated for Navajo in Figure 3.2. As (3.14a, c) demonstrate, Abkhaz possessive pronouns are also bound, but they are bound, of course, not to a verb but to a head noun. (The same applies to oblique clause participants; in this case pronouns are bound to adpositions.)

In Abkhaz, as in many other languages with old bound pronouns, they are very simple morphemes, often monophonemic. In some other languages bound pronouns are much more complex. For example, in Larike, a Central Moluccan language (Austronesian) non-singular bound pronouns are rather cumbersome, very similar in form to free pronouns of the language (Laidig and Laidig 1990: 91–95) and probably of recent origin:

(3.15) Larike (Central Moluccan, Austronesian, Maluku, Indonesia; Laidig and Laidig 1990: 96)
    karena   i-lou   rene   pehe-matua,   laku   matuai-loko
    because 3SG.NH.A-far very   tired-3DU.P   then   3DU.A-sit
    'Because it was very far the two of them were tired, so they sat down'

---

[19] This tale was published in the book: Аҧсуа Лакуқуа. Карҭ, 1976.

A characteristic feature of bound pronouns in a language such as Abkhaz is that they are so pervasive. In principle, bound pronouns may have a much more restricted distribution; such languages are discussed in Chapter 6, section 6.6. In this section we are concerned primarily with Abkhaz-type languages that use bound pronouns unrestrictedly and abundantly.

3.3.1 *Pronominal arguments*

Since bound pronouns in a language such as Abkhaz refer to event participants, they constitute clause arguments. This applies to all bound pronouns in (3.13i, ii) and includes both core and non-core arguments. There is simply nothing else in these clauses that could serve as possible arguments. We clearly deal here with arguments that are represented by affixes on the verb rather than by syntactic constituents. In order to capture the specificity of the Abkhaz-type structure, with arguments morphologically integrated into the verb form and expressed by bound pronouns, the term 'pronominal argument languages' is frequently used, after the seminal papers by Jelinek (1984, 1985). This notion implies two things: bound pronouns *are* arguments, and, therefore, noun phrases *are not*; the latter point is addressed in subsection 3.3.3. Pronominal argument languages are contrasted to nominal argument languages, such as English.[20]

In the context of this book, we are mostly interested in the referring function of bound pronouns. However, it is important to note that they fulfil a second function, separate from their referring function: namely, they code the referents' semantic roles. Like the referring function, this function is performed quite analogously to NPs bearing case markers. For core arguments, such as all participants in (3.13i) and the agent and the patient in (3.13ii), role coding devices are twofold: first, linear positions inside the verb word; second, the shape of an individual pronominal element (for example, the third person feminine in the ergative position in (3.13i) is *l-*, but it would be *d-* in the nominative position). The roles of other participants are encoded by separate morphemes – for example, the beneficiary by *z-* and the comitative by *c-* in (3.13ii); these preverbs, similar to oblique cases of other languages, follow their respective pronominal morphemes.

I believe that the role-coding technique found in Abkhaz is functionally parallel to case marking in languages with nominal cases. It is justified to think of this technique as of **verb-marked case**, and to use usual case terminology: nominative, ergative, accusative, etc. Throughout this book I

---

[20] Of course, the notion of nominal argument languages should not imply that in a language such as English only nouns can function as arguments – free pronouns are argumental as well.

primarily use this terminology to refer to verb-internal morphological positions in which bound pronouns are inserted. It is also acceptable to use the hyperrole-based terminology: Agentive, Principal, etc., but not terminology based on syntactic relations: subject, object, etc. For an extensive argument in favour of this approach to verbal role coding see Kibrik (in press a). This approach does not dominate in the analysis of Abkhaz-type languages but occasionally occurs in the literature; cf. Grinevald Craig (1977: 119ff.), Wichmann (2008); see also the discussion in Bossong 2003.

Henceforth in the glosses of Abkhaz-type language examples each core argument bound pronoun is glossed by a combination of two kinds of features, separated by a dot: first, reference-related properties of a pronoun are indicated, such as person, number, and gender, and after the dot its case feature. Example (3.13) is rewritten below in accordance with these conventions, with the addition of some other morphological details:

(3.13′)   Abkhaz (Abkhaz-Adyghean, Abkhazia)
   i. i-rə-l-te-jt'
      3NH.NOM-3PL.DAT-3F.ERG-give-DYN
      'She gave it to them'
   ii. i-l-z-i-c-sə-rgəlo-jt'
      3NH.NOM-3F.OBL-for-3M.OBL-with-1SG.ERG-build.PRES-DYN
      'I am building it [e.g. the house] for her together with him'

Note that in Abkhaz nouns do not inflect for case, so the entire burden of role marking rests on pronominal affixes.

Studies exploring reference and referential choice in languages with bound pronouns include, for example, Heath (1983), Kibrik (1988: Ch. 2), Thompson (1989), Chafe (1990a), Payne (1993), Chafe (1994: Ch. 12), Evans (2002), Mithun (2003), Amidu (2006). Kim et al. (2001) is an interesting example of a constrastive study comparing referential choice in a bound pronoun language (Mayali, Gunwinyguan, northern Australia) and a free pronoun language (Kala Lagaw Ya, Pama-Nyungan, Torres Strait Islands, Australia).

3.3.2 Tenacity

In example (3.14), clause (c) contains a full NP, namely 'his sons'. However, this does not affect the way in which the corresponding bound pronoun operates in the clause: the recipient third person plural bound pronoun r(ə)- works in exactly the same way in clauses (c) and (e), that is, irrespective of whether the coreferential NP is present in the clause or not. This omnipresence is a fundamental property of Abkhaz-type pronouns. I call this feature of Abkhaz-type pronouns **tenacity**, and pronouns themselves **tenacious**. Tenacious pronouns are found in a clause even if a referent is of low activation and a full NP is required. In the case of tenacious pronouns referential choice amounts to absence or presence of a full NP; the pronoun is there anyway. The opposite of tenacious is **alternating**, that is, the pronouns' ability to alternate with full NPs.[21] Tenacity and alternation, along with their relatedness to boundness vs. freeness of pronouns, are discussed in Chapter 6. In particular, it will be shown there that tenacity and boundness are two logically and factually independent parameters.

Linguists often intuitively presuppose (and sometimes formulate it explicitly in their theories) that one and the same instantiation of a referent cannot be reflected by more than a singleton expression in linguistic structure. This tacit assumption is common in both theoretical and descriptive literature. For example, the authors of a Persian (Iranian, Indo-European, Iran) grammar plainly state: 'Since subject agreement is marked on the verb ... the anaphoric pronoun is typically deleted' (Mahootian and Gebhardt 1997: 91). However, double (and more than double) representation does happen; see Chapter 6. Such a possibly uneconomical situation is found in Abkhaz, as shown in Figure 3.4.

The tenacious character of Abkhaz-type bound referential devices renders the term 'pronouns', as applied to them, somewhat paradoxical. The term 'pronoun' originally evolved to designate free pronouns that alternate with nouns (rather, full NPs) and take the same or similar syntactic positions, that is, metaphorically, are substituted for nouns. Even there 'pronoun' is a misnomer, as discussed in sections 2.4 and 4.1, because the metaphor of substitution is misleading. But in the case of bound tenacious referential devices the term 'pronoun' not merely evokes a wrong conceptual metaphor but is self-evidently inappropriate, if taken literally: first, affixes are not syntactic constituents and cannot possibly be substitutes for full NPs, and second, they actually cooccur with coreferential full NPs in the same clause. However, I do not attempt to alter such traditional terminology in this book. As will be discussed in section 4.1, I take the term 'pronoun' to imply only that

---

[21] It is important to emphasize that the term 'alternating' is used henceforth in the technical sense and means only alternation of pronouns and full referential devices. This is not to be confused with alternation of reduced referential devices, discussed under the name of 'sensitivity' in Chapter 5. This terminology is somewhat tricky. When looking for an antonym to 'tenacious', I considered the term 'recessive'. If this term were adopted, tenacious could be renamed 'excessive' (thus rhyming with the converse term), or 'dominant', thus replicating the opposition 'dominant vs. recessive', familiar from genetics. I opted, however, against 'recessive', as this term has unnecessary transformational overtones (cf. subsection 3.3.3).

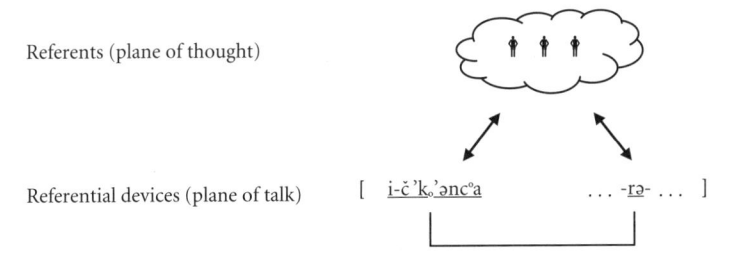

FIGURE 3.4. Linking of the coreferential full NP and bound pronoun, both referring to 'the sons', in Abkhaz, example (3.14c). The brace indicates coreference

the element in question is referential and that it is an overt reduced referential device, nothing else. On these counts bound personal affixes qualify as pronouns, and I will keep using this term henceforth. But it is useful to keep the terminological reservations in mind.

The tenacious character of Abkhaz-style personal affixes often leads linguists to treat them as agreement markers, and such treatment is sometimes even opposed to the pronominal analysis. The pronouns vs. agreement issue is quite controversial, and it is addressed specifically in Chapter 6.

It is noteworthy that in Abkhaz, as well as in many other bound pronoun languages, it is not only clause participant pronouns but also possessive pronouns that are tenacious. Consider the following Abkhaz possessive NP:

(3.16) Abkhaz (Abkhaz-Adyghean, Abkhazia)
a-č'k̥'ən i-la
DEF-boy 3M.POSS-dog
'the boy's dog'

Within this NP, reference to the boy is performed twice: by means of the full NP and by means of the possessive bound pronoun. Evidently, this is the same phenomenon as what we observe in the domain of clause participant marking.

3.3.3 Status of noun phrases

Provided that bound pronominal morphemes are arguments (or other clause participants), and they are tenaciously present in the clause, a question arises: what is the function of coreferential full NPs, such as 'his sons' in (3.14c), and in fact other kinds of coreferential NPs (including free pronouns, demonstratives, etc.)? It has often been argued, especially after the influential paper Jelinek (1984), that in Abkhaz-type languages coreferential NPs are in a loose 'adjunct' (or 'apposition') relation to pronominal morphemes on the verb, and may even be outside of the clause, resembling anticipatory topics or afterthought NPs; see e.g. Baker (1996). Syntactic interpretation is not the central concern in this book, but the issue is so important for Abkhaz-type languages that we need to briefly discuss it.[22]

Full NPs in clauses such as (3.14c) are relegated by some authors to the status of adjuncts for the reason that a coreferential bound pronoun has already been recognized as the argument, and supposedly there should not be more than one formal element per clause expressing a given argument. However, the latter supposition is not necessary – nothing prevents one from lifting it. If it is lifted, and double representation[23] of a referent in a clause is permitted, then the picture becomes much simpler.

Argumenthood does not necessarily have to be restricted to only one element in a clause. Bound pronouns do serve as sole representatives of arguments when no coreferential NPs are present, as in (3.14b), but if there is an NP, as in (3.14c), then the pair [pronoun, coreferential NP] as a whole constitutes the representation of the argument.[24] A similar suggestion was put forward by Mithun (2003): 'Pronominal affixes certainly function as core arguments, but their presence does not entail a specific syntactic status on the part of coreferential nominals in the same clause. ... Since they evoke the same entity, lexical nominals and coreferential pronominal affixes may simply share that status, and languages may differ in the extent to which the nominals are integrated formally into the clause.' (Mithun 2003: 275–276). So I will assume by default that NPs, associated with bound pronouns, can belong to the same clause and be considered argumental.

This kind of theoretical reasoning for the feasibility of distributed argumenthood and against the putative 'adjunct' status of free NPs can be further supported empirically by evidence from languages that, like Abkhaz, have tenacious bound pronouns, but, unlike Abkhaz, mark cases on nouns. Among such languages, are, for example Basque (isolate, Spain and France; see Hualde and Ortiz de Urbina (eds.) 2003) or Svan. Svan, a language of the Kartvelian family (Georgia), has a complex system of person markers on the verb, both prefixal and suffixal (see Kibrik 1996b). These markers are traditionally seen as agreement markers but can safely be considered bound

---

[22] An early version of this argument appeared in Kibrik (1988, 1992b). I am grateful to Matthew Dryer for a useful discussion of these issues in October 2000 that helped me to clarify some difficult points.

[23] Cf. the term 'multirepresentation', proposed by Corbett (2006: 106).

[24] The rendition in Figure 3.4 suggests that the full NP and the bound pronoun relate to the same referent independently. In fact, it may be more insightful to propose that they form an aggregate that performs reference en bloc.

pronouns.[25] They are organized in accordance with the accusative pattern. In the domain of third person arguments, there exist suffixal bound pronouns indicating the Principal's person-number (the nominative position), and prefixal bound pronouns indicating the recipient's person (the dative position). The third person bound pronouns that can appear on Svan verbs are summarized in Table 3.3.

TABLE 3.3 Third person nominative (referring to Principal) and dative (referring to recipient) bound pronouns appearing in Svan verbs

	No recipient	to him/to her/to them
he/she	-ø	x- ... -ø
they	-x	x- ... -x

In addition, Svan has nominal case markers used according to a complex, split alignment pattern. Consider the following excerpt – the beginning of a Svan tale[26] about three brothers [=B]:

(3.17) Svan (Kartvelian, Georgia)
    a. läs\<x\>w   semi   laxwba.
        COP.IMPF\<3PL.NOM$_B$\>   three   brothers.NOM$_B$

    b. aljär-s   x-or-da-x   semi   daqlīd.
        these$_B$-DAT   3.DAT$_B$-be-IMPF-3PL.NOM$_G$ three   goat.NOM$_G$

    c. atxe   čw-äd-īt-än-x   aljär.
        then   PV-PV-separate-AOR-3PL.NOM$_B$ these.NOM$_B$

    d. čw-er-äd-īt-än-x \<...\>
        PV-SBRD-PV-separate-AOR-3PL.NOM$_B$

'There were three brothers. They had three goats. They [=the brothers] parted. As they parted \<...\>'

---

[25] To be sure, Svan has a much more restricted system of bound pronouns than Abkhaz. But this system suffices to demonstrate the point.

[26] The Svan data come from fieldwork conducted in Mulakhi, Svanetia, in 1989 (in a field expedition of Moscow State University). The cited folk tale was originally collected by Mira Bergelson and subsequently checked and corrected by myself with the help of Nani Gujejiani in 1990 in Tbilisi and Saint-Petersburg. During the final stage of analysis, the assistance of Yakov Testelets was invaluable.

<three intervening clauses, telling that each brother took a goat, and then the oldest brother [=b] started for a marketplace in order to sell his goat>

h. <...>   sga-la-x-xwidda-ø   bap'.
           PV-PV-3.DAT_b-occur.AOR-3SG.NOM_p   priest.NOM_p

i. bap'-d   x-äkwin-ø   ere
   priest_p-NARR   3.DAT_b-say.AOR-3SG.NOM_p   SBRD

j. "mi   eser   a-m-äq'ädə   ala   daqlīd."
   1SG_p   QUOT   PV-1SG.DAT_p-sell.IMPER this goat.NOM

k. čw-ad-x-q'id-ø.
   PV-PV-3.DAT_p-sell.AOR-3SG.NOM_b

'<...> he [=the brother] met a priest. The priest told him: "As for me, sell me this goat". He [=the brother] sold it to him.'

This excerpt demonstrates that Svan personal affixes are bound pronouns, that is, they perform reference. They are the sole referential devices when a referent is highly activated, as for example -*x* referring to 'the three brothers' in (3.17d) or *x*- referring to 'the older brother' in (3.17h). However, when a referent is not so highly activated, full NPs are used along with bound pronouns, as is the case with 'three goats' in (3.17b), or sometimes along with demonstratives, e.g. *aljär-s* referring to 'the three brothers', again in (3.17b). Given that the language cares to encode cases on nominals (for example, the 'narrative'[27] case in (3.17i), or the dative case in (3.17b)) they are evidently argumental and cannot possibly be outside the clause in some kind of appositional function. So one must recognize that both bound pronouns and NPs are arguments.

Now, if this is possible in a language like Svan there is no reason to rule out such a possibility in Abkhaz, even though the latter does not have nominal case marking. The pattern of linking depicted in Figure 3.4 applies to both Svan and Abkhaz.

To recapitulate, when a referent is activated prior to the beginning of the current clause, a third person bound pronoun mentions this referent in the same way as free pronouns do. Under the conditions of a lesser degree of activation, a coreferential NP is employed in addition to the tenacious bound pronoun.

---

[27] 'Narrative' is the traditional term in Kartvelian studies referring to the case of an Agentive participant (in both transitive and intransitive clauses). In the tenses of the aorist series active alignment is used.

Since NPs share the argumental status in Abkhaz- and Svan-type languages, the opposition between pronominal argument languages and nominal argument languages is not a very fortunate terminology. The single distinction between two kinds of arguments classifying all languages into two gross types appears to oversimplify the actual picture. In the subsequent chapters I develop a more comprehensive typology in which several things matter, including boundness vs. freeness of arguments, their nominal vs. pronominal character, tenacity, and the possibility of internal inconsistencies within a language.

3.3.4 *Genealogical and geographical distribution*

Perhaps the most striking feature of the bound pronouns in Abkhaz, the language featured in this section, is that they are so abundant. As we have seen in the examples, every argument of a clause is marked by a bound pronoun, and when we have an *n*-place clause we observe *n* bound pronouns. In addition, there are bound possessive and adjunct pronouns, although they appear not on the verb but on other constituents. Most of the time Abkhaz bound pronouns are overt (not zero), which makes them very visible in the language. Although this degree of abundance and visibility is not always reached, there are many languages on earth that predominantly use bound pronouns. Interestingly, most such languages are found in parts of the world very distant from the western Caucasus where Abkhaz is spoken. Abkhaz, an exemplary bound pronoun language, together with its relatives from the Abkhaz-Adyghean family, are located amidst the language families of Europe and western Asia in which free pronouns predominate. (Abkhaz's neighbour, Svan, and other Kartvelian languages use both bound and free pronouns.)

The highest concentration of bound pronoun languages are found in the Americas, especially in North America. To this type belong all of the major families of the continent, including Eskimo-Aleut, Na-Dene, Salishan, Algonquian, Siouan, Iroquoian, Muskogean, Uto-Aztecan (partly), Mayan, and others. Some important South American families, including Arawakan and Cariban, often display this pattern. Other large areas prone to bound pronouns are New Guinea and some other parts of western Oceania, northern Australia (non-Pama-Nyungan languages of Arnhem Land), the central-eastern part of Africa (particularly the Bantu languages and various languages of the 'Nilo-Saharan' hypothetical macrostock), and also some restricted areas of Eurasia (certain parts of Siberia, the Himalayas). Generally, it can be concluded that the bound pronoun pattern is prominent in each of the continents, either in the whole continent (North America) or in some of its parts. Eurasia is the continent least prone to bound pronouns.

If one limits one's consideration to bound pronouns in the Principal position alone, then bound pronouns are by far the most frequent device among the world's languages. In Dryer's (2005a) typology of reduced Principal expression, out of 674 languages 409 use verbal affixes, that is bound pronouns. Languages of this kind are represented in all parts of the world, the exempt areas being only Southeast Asia and the Pama-Nyungan area in Australia.

3.3.5 *Bound pronouns and related typological features*

The predisposition to the use of bound pronouns is highly correlated with two established typological features, one of which is classic and the other more recent.

The phenomenon of bound pronouns incorporated into the verb form constitutes one of the hallmarks of the so-called polysynthetic languages (see Mithun 1999: 38–39, Kibrik 2001c, Evans and Sasse 2002). Polysynthesis means a high average number of morphemes per verb form compared to a cross-linguistic baseline. Many grammatical meanings that are often conveyed by nominal morphology or function words cross-linguistically are expressed by verb morphology in polysynthetic languages. Polysynthesis includes a wide range of meanings expressed by verb morphology (such as tense, aspect, mood, polarity, location, direction, etc.) and does not obligatorily entail extensive use of bound pronouns or even their existence in a language (see Mattissen 2002). However, presence of bound pronouns in polysynthetic languages is highly likely. Polysynthesis is essentially verb-centredness; such languages tend to express as much as possible in the verb, including the clause arguments. Polysynthesis is one of the values of the typological parameter 'inflectional synthesis (of the verb)'.

Nichols (1986, 1992), interested in different aspects of essentially the same phenomenon, proposed the typological parameter 'head-marking vs. dependent-marking' of predicate–argument relations. Nichols's consistently head-marking languages largely coincide with languages with bound pronouns. If a language preferably and massively marks predicate–argument relations on the head element, prototypically a verb, it is most likely that the way of such marking would be by means of personal morphemes, in other words, bound pronouns.

That said, it is no surprise that the geographical and genealogical distribution of both polysynthesis and head-marking is very similar to that of predisposition to bound pronouns. Languages of all these kinds – and typically they are the same languages – are particularly well represented in North

America. Let us compare three maps from WALS (Haspelmath et al. (eds.) 2005) plotting the following typological parameters: Verbal person marking (Siewierska 2005e), Locus of marking in the clause (Nichols and Bickel 2005b), and Inflectional synthesis of the verb (Bickel and Nichols 2005). We will look at certain individual values of each parameter, respectively 'both A and P',[28] 'head-marking', and '8 categories and up'.[29]

The graphs in Figure 3.5 are derived from the data in these three studies. As is conventional in WALS, six macro areas are compared. I have calculated percentages of the given parameter's value from the total amount of languages of the given area included in the study. For example, out of 68 North American languages included in the Siewierska's sample 54 languages (which makes 79%) have verbal person marking for both A and P. Then, out of 49 North American languages found in Nichols and Bickel's sample 28 languages (or 57%) are characterized as head-marking. Finally, among the 27 North American languages included in the Bickel and Nichols's sample 13 (or 48%) have 8 inflectional categories or more in their maximally inflected verb forms.

A visual comparison of the three graphs in Figure 3.5 demonstrates a striking resemblance. Although particular sets of languages are somewhat different in the three studies, this is mostly due to the differences between the samples.[30] Evidently, the sets of languages carved out by the given values of the three parameters are very close[31] and literally correlated. The peak of all three features is found in North America, and the percentages in South America and Australia – New Guinea are also high. There are some occasional exceptions to such correlations, in particular, in Africa there are very few polysynthetic languages, but nearly as many languages with bound pronouns as in South America. In general, the results of this comparison suggest that the three different phenomena are in fact the facets of one and the same typological realm.

---

[28] This value means that both the Agentive and the Patientive arguments are marked on the verb. This is the best approximation we can get from Haspelmath et al. (eds.) (2005) to the feature we are interested in, that is, 'predisposition to the use of bound pronouns'.

[29] This value includes languages that have eight or more inflectional categories in their maximally inflected verb forms. This value actually collapses several more detailed values in Bickel and Nichols (2005).

[30] There is a fringe where the Nichols and Bickel's map and the Siewierska's map contradict each other. For example, the WALS composer shows seven languages that simultaneously belong to the no-marking type, according to the first map, and have both Agentive and Patientive verbal person marking, according to the second map. Evidently, in this case the linguistic facts were susceptible to varying interpretation, and this became evident due to the procedure of composing several studies that was undertaken.

[31] If one includes double-marking languages (double-marking logically entails head-marking) in the comparison, then the graphs for 'Verbal person marking: both A and P' and for 'Locus of marking in the clause: head-marking, including double-marking' practically coincide.

104   II. Typology of Reduced Referential Devices

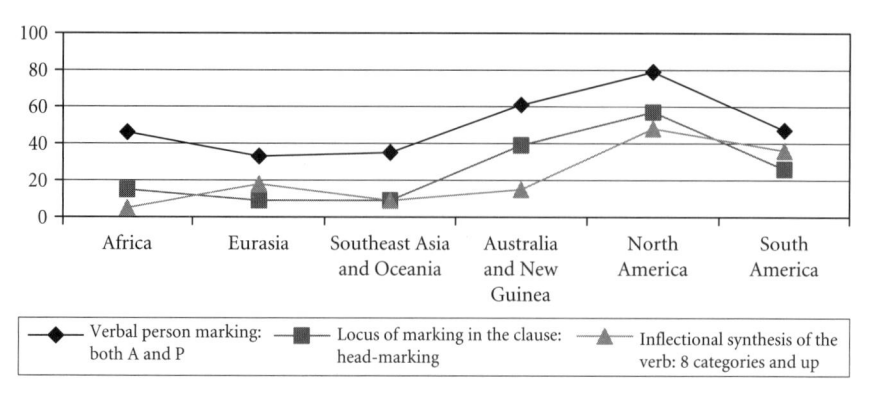

FIGURE 3.5. A comparison of global distribution of three typological features: predisposition to bound pronouns, head-marking, and polysynthesis (percentages derived from Siewierska 2005e, Nichols and Bickel 2005b, and Bickel and Nichols 2005)

Degree of synthesis and locus of marking are among the most fundamental typological parameters. Therefore, polysynthesis and head-marking, being respective values of these parameters, as well as the closely associated predisposition to bound pronouns, must be among the basic properties of a language and exert influence on its other characteristics, or at least demonstrate relationships with other such characteristics. Indeed, Nichols (1992) has proposed a number of morphosyntactic features that are strongly correlated with head-marking, for example the stative–active alignment or plurality neutralization. Mithun (1987) has suggested that employment of bound pronouns frequently entails grammatically unrestricted (that is, purely pragmatic) order of basic clause constituents, and may in fact be an important explanation for free word order phenomena.[32] There are also other specific consequences of the pervasive use of bound pronouns – for example, languages with bound pronouns typically tend not to use the headed strategy of relativization; see Kibrik (1992b).

3.4 Zero reference

Free and bound pronouns, taken in conjunction, are overt referential devices. Opposed to these is the third formal type of reduced referential device: the so-called zero, or null, reference. In the second and third clauses of the Japanese example (3.4) the specific referent 'the snail' is implied but not overtly

---

[32] But cf. Austin 2001a who used the example of Jiwarli (Australia) to argue that an equally free word order language may have no bound pronouns at all.

3. Major types of reduced referential devices   105

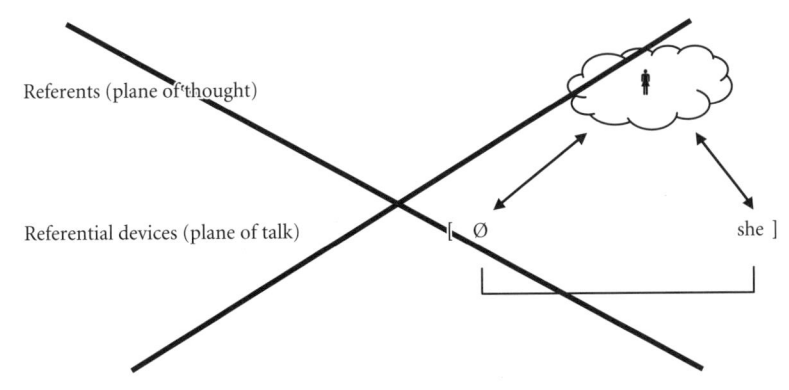

FIGURE 3.6. A disallowed use of the zero convention

expressed. It is in such instances that we conventionally talk about zero reference: a referent is mentioned within a clause, but there is no particular formal device, neither free nor bound, that performs this act of reference; see Figure 3.3.

A word of caution is necessary: linguists have become so used to positing zeroes that they sometimes treat them on a par with overt elements. Obviously, zeroes are not real linguistic elements but rather a conventional technique used as a shortcut to point to significant absence of form.

Also, it must be kept in mind that languages do not randomly opt for the absence of form, so it is no coincidence that certain functions are not overtly marked. I am going to be discriminating in positing zero elements. In particular, an important principle is: if a language systematically uses an overt element to which the referential function can be attributed, do not posit a zero. This principle is graphically represented in Figure 3.6.

With this caveat, I will be using zeroes and will even differentiate between several types of them (Chapter 11). In the present chapter only specific definite zeroes are discussed. There are many other kinds of significant absence in language; for a useful recent classification see Nariyama (2007).

Since zero is by definition invisible, a number of questions arise. First, how does one practically mark zeroes in discourse structure, where in a clause is the best location to mark a zero? Given that zero is a part of the system, there are more natural and less natural ways to place them in linguistic transcription. In the material below, zeroes are marked on the basis of available knowledge about a language's constituent order: to the extent possible, zeroes are marked in those spots where a non-zero element most likely might occur. For example, if in a language subjects appear preverbally, it makes sense to posit subject zeroes in the same preverbal position.

106   II. *Typology of Reduced Referential Devices*

Second, is there a difference between free and bound, or syntactic and morphological, zeroes? This question may be not as scholastic as it may seem. I will return to it in section 6.8. In this section, as well as in Chapters 4 and 5, I am discussing the material of languages that have no or almost no bound pronouns, and therefore zeroes are by default free.

Some languages are very much inclined to using zeroes. One example is provided by Yidiny, a language of northeastern Australia (Dixon 1977). Consider an extract from a story about two brothers, Damari and Guyala:

(3.18)   Yidiny (Pama-Nyungan, northeastern Australia; Dixon 1977: 514)[33]

a. Ø   gali:ɲ   Ø   wawa:liɲu   bulmba /
         go.PAST   look.GOING.PAST   place.ABS

b. "ɲundú / Ø   bama   binaŋ   yiɲu   gugu   ɲinaŋ /
    hey!   person.ABS   hear.PRES this.ABS noise.ABS   sit.PRES

c. gana Ø wawa /   gana   ŋaɲḍi   wawa:lina" /
    TRY   look.IMPER   TRY   we.NOM   look.GOING.PURP

d. Ø gali:ɲ/   Ø wawa:liɲu/   bama   ŋabi   ɲinaɲunda/
      go.PAST   look.GOING.PAST   person.ABS   many.ABS   sit.DAT.SBRD
   bulmba   ḍimu:r /
   camp.ABS   house.ABS

e. "bama   yiɲu   ŋabi   ɲinaŋ /
    person.ABS   this.ABS lots.ABS   sit.PRES

f. gana   ŋaɲḍi   gaymbar /   Ø   wawa" /
    TRY   we.NOM   sneak.up.IMPER   look.IMPER

g. Ø   Ø   wawa:liɲu /
               look.GOING.PAST

h. bama:l   Ø   wawa:l /
   person.ERG   see.PAST

'They [=Damari and Guyala] went, went looking for a [suitable] place. "Hey! We can hear this noise and the noise coming from some people sitting around" [Damari said]. "Let's try to have a look! We should try to go and have a look." They went, went and saw lots of people sitting there, and a large house. "A lot of these people are sitting there. Let us sneak up and have a look at them." They went up and looked at them. The people saw them.'

---

[33] Division into lines is kept as in the original. The slash indicates the end of an intonation group. Zeroes have been added by myself, guided by the details of the Dixon translation.

3. Major types of reduced referential devices   107

In this extract, there are multiple zero references. Most of the zeroes refer to the group 'Damari and Guyala', and there are two zeroes referring to 'the people' in lines (f) and (g). Zeroes in this example correspond to a variety of clause argument positions.

A better known language that also uses zero as a default form of reduced reference is Japanese. Consider this example:

(3.19) Japanese (Clancy and Downing 1987: 18)[34]
    a. ... de Yukichan$_Y$ ga, daidokoro no naka de
           and Y. NOM kitchen GEN middle INSTR
           issshookenmei onigiri o tsukut-te i-mas-u.
           busily onigiri ACC make-CONV be-ADDR-PRES

    b. ... de kondo Ø$_Y$ kore o ... nanka--... iremono ni
           and this.time this ACC sort.of container DAT
           tsume-mash-ite ne,
           pack-ADDR-CONV EX

    c. ... de ... Ø$_Y$ dekake-te ik-u wake des-u.
           and go.out-CONV go-PRES NMZR COP.ADDR-PRES

    d. ... Ø$_Y$ dekake-te ik-u wake des-u.
           go.out-CONV go-PRES NMZR COP.ADDR-PRES

    e. ... de Ø$_Y$ onigiri o tor- toridash-ite,
           and onigiri ACC FS take.out-CONV

    f. ... Ø$_Y$ hoobar-inagara
           cram.into.mouth-while

    g. ... Ø$_Y$ kooen ni ik-imas-u.
           park DAT go-ADDR-PRES

'Yukichan is busily making onigiri in the kitchen. And next she packs them and goes out. She goes out. And she takes out an onigiri and, cramming it into her mouth, goes to the park.'

There are numerous studies demonstrating how pervasive zero reference is in Japanese. For example, according to Hedberg (1996), zero reference constitutes 85% of all reduced forms of reference in Japanese discourse (percentage derived from her Table 4 on p. 187). Yamamoto (1999) provides separate data for written

---

[34] This example is taken from a transcript of spoken discourse, so it contains marking of pauses, false starts, and some other spoken language phenomena. Division into lines (elementary discourse units) and zero references have been added by myself [A.K.], with the kind assistance of Zoya Efimova. Referential indices are provided in the original line (rather than in the glosses line) because that is where zero elements are marked.

and spoken Japanese; zero reference constitutes 62% of all third person reduced forms of reference in written Japanese discourse (percentage derived from Yamamoto's tables on pp. 118 and 123) and 94% in spoken Japanese discourse (derived from Yamamoto's tables on pp. 121 and 125).[35] See also Podlesskaya (1990), Downing (1996a), Matsumoto (2003: 121ff.), Nariyama (2003: 26), Shimojo (2005), Efimova (2006). Note that the use of zeroes in Japanese is not restricted to third person reference. Locutors are very often marked by zeroes as well; one example can be seen in (3.20) and (3.22) below. This demonstrates that the concern for coding person is not as universal as it may seem from languages with the dominant use of free or bound pronouns.

It is often proposed (see e.g. Givón 1983a, Levinson 2000: 267) that zero reference, being formally weaker and semantically more general than pronouns, naturally corresponds to a greater degree of activation or givenness than pronouns. Languages that use both zeroes and pronouns and distribute them in accordance with the degree of activation do exist; see section 5.2. But zero reference does not have to be inherently or universally associated with a greater degree of activation than pronouns, as must be clear from the fact that some languages almost exclusively use either zero or overt referential devices. As far as third person reference is concerned, pronouns are as general as zero reference, even though they are formally more elaborate. Of course, various categories can be marked on pronouns, such as gender or obviation. But these categories are only indirectly related to the referential function of pronouns. As was briefly mentioned in Chapter 2 and is argued in detail in Chapter 8, these kinds of categories are not referential devices as such – they are referential aids, that is various ways to sort the presently activated referents. The fact of their cumulative expression with reduced referential devices should not prevent us from understanding that the act of reference and the sorting of referents are two distinct functions. So the qualitative difference between zero and pronouns is much less than between both of them together, on the one hand, and full NPs, on the other.

3.4.1 Zeroes can take various positions in a clause

In (3.19), zeroes refer to the main protagonist alone and all of them appear in the Principal position in the clause. This is indeed the most typical position for reduced referential devices – both cross-linguistically and in Japanese. However, Japanese zeroes are not restricted to this position. In Efimova's (2006: 92) sample of natural written discourse, out of 181 instances of zero

---

[35] Probably these numbers relate to animate referents only.

reference 31 instances (that is, 17%) were found in other argument positions. In the study of Nariyama (2003), looking at Japanese reference from a computational perspective, counts are provided in the opposite direction: from function to form. In Nariyama's data (see p. 26), subject vs. object (that is, Principal vs. Patientive) ellipsis is found with the following frequencies in various genres: in interviews – 64% vs. 42%; in written narratives – 56% vs. 11%; and in written expository discourse – 27% vs. 17%.

Let us consider several examples of zero reference in non-Principal positions.

(3.20) Japanese (Shimojo 2005: 132)
    A: dooyuu   tokoro no   daigaku   no?
        what.kind.of   place   GEN   university GEN
    B: reitakudaigaku   toka   yuu.
        Reitaku.University etc.   called
    A: aa   Ø   Ø   shit-te-ru.
        oh   know-CONV-AUX.PRES
    'A: "A university of which area?"[36] B: "The one called Reitaku University." A: "Oh, I know it."'

Of interest to us is the second zero in the last line of this conversational example corresponding to the referent 'the university'. If this referent were conveyed by a non-zero NP it would appear with the accusative postpositional case marker *o*. This demonstrates that zero reference can occur in the Patientive position. Furthermore, it can occur in positions of non-core arguments, in particular in the recipient role that, if overtly expressed, is marked with the dative postpositional case marker *ni*. This can be seen in the following example taken from a narrative whose protagonist, a woman [=w], suffers a shortage of water:

(3.21) Japanese[37]
    a. tonari   no   okusan$_n$ ga   kodobin o   sage-te   ki-ta.
       neighbour GEN lady/wife NOM teakettle ACC carry-CONV AUX-PAST
       <2 clauses of direct speech skipped>

---

[36] In fact, this is a question about something belonging to a university, so a more accurate translation would be: 'Of a university of which area?'.

[37] This example, as well as example (3.24) below, is taken from: Kawabata, Yasunari. Mizu. In: *Tenohira no shoosetsu*. Tokyo: Shincho: Bunko (1981), 366–367. I thank Zoya Efimova for providing these examples to me.

110　II. *Typology of Reduced Referential Devices*

```
     d. mizu    wa   nokot-te        i-na-i          ga.
        water   TOP  remain-CONV     be-NEG-PRES     though

     e. Øw Øn  ocha  no   wakash-ita     no    o    wake-te      age-ta.
              tea   GEN  boil-PAST      NMZR  ACC  share-CONV   give-PAST
```
'The neighbour lady came carrying teakettle. <...> Though no more water was left, she [=the protagonist] gave her [=the neighbour] some of the amount she had boiled for tea.'

Other non-core arguments can be coded by zero as well, for example:

(3.22)　Japanese (Shimojo 2005: 47)
```
        anoo   Ø   Ø   Ø   hanash-ita    kamoshirena-i   kedo <...>
        well                say-PAST      may.be-PRES     but
```
'I may have told you about this but <...>'

If participants of this clause were coded by overt NPs, the recipient participant would have the dative case marker *ni*, and the subject matter participant the postpositional marker *nitsuite* 'about'; the remaining zero corresponds to the position of Principal. Still more peripheral clause participants, such as starting points and goals with verb of movements, can also be expressed by zero:

(3.23)　Japanese[38]
```
        A: Kyooto   e    it-ta      koto    ga    ar-imas-u       ka?
           Kyoto    to   go-PAST    NMZR    NOM   be-ADDR-PRES    QU

        B: iie,  mada   des-u.            Ø  Ø   rainen       ik-u      tsumori
           no   still   COP.ADDR-PRES             next.year    go-PRES   plan
           des-u.
           COP.ADDR-PRES
```
'A: "Have you already been to Kyoto?" B: "No, not yet. I am planning to go there next year."'

The two zeroes in the last clause correspond to the Principal and to the goal ('to Kyoto'). Possessors also can be zero-coded as easily in Japanese as clause arguments, for example:

(3.24)　Japanese
```
        a. Ø  Ø   kata        made    hitat-te
                  shoulder    up.to   immerse-CONV
```

---

[38] This example was provided to me by Zoya Efimova.

b. yu   no   naka   ni   Ø teashi   no   utsukushi-ku
   hot.water GEN inside DAT   hands.and.feet GEN beautiful-ADV
   mie-ta
   be.seen-PAST

c. Ø   Ø   kokyoo   no   furo   ga   omoidas-are-ru
          home   GEN   bath   NOM   recall-PASS-PRES
   'She remembered the bath in her home, as she was immersing up to her shoulders and the beauty of her hands and feet could be seen through hot water.'

In this example, there are three instances of possessive zeroes referring to the discourse protagonist; such zeroes are italicized, to differentiate them from zeroes corresponding to the clause's Principal.

3.4.2 Role markers associated with zeroes

In Japanese, when a referent is conveyed by a zero, it is not only a referential device per se that is missing in the linguistic form but also the corresponding argument's role marker (as well as the topic marker): *wa* (topic) in most lines of (3.19), *o* (accusative) in (3.20), *ni* (dative) in (3.21), *no* (genitive) in (3.24), etc. In other languages, a different situation is registered, namely that zero reference is combined with non-zero role markers. An example of this kind comes from the Beledugu dialect of Bamana (Bambara). This dialect, unlike standard Bamana (Bergelson and Konate 1988), uses zero reference widely. The following examples are taken from the tale 'Rabbit, Hippo, and Elephant':

(3.25) Beledugu Bamana (Mande, Mali; Bergelson and Konate 1988: 97)[39]
        a. ní   í   yà   sòzán yé
           if   you   COMPL   rabbit see
        b. í   k'   á   fɔ́   Ø   yè
           you   SBJV   3   tell   to
        'If you see Rabbit, tell this to him'

(3.26) Beledugu Bamana (Mande, Mali; Bergelson and Konate 1988: 97)
        kó   dɔ̀   kún   mɛ̀   ɛ́ɛ   ní   Ø   cɛ̀
        business   some   PAST   be   3.EMPH   and   between
        'There was a business between him [=Elephant] and him [=Rabbit]'

---

[39] These examples were checked with the assistance of Mira B. Bergelson and with the use of Konate (1989: 130–131).

(3.27) Beledugu Bamana (Mande, Mali; Bergelson and Konate 1988: 97)
sàma táa-ra í kɛ́ Ø lá fùra lɔ́ myɛ̀n
elephant go-PFV REFL do GEN forest behind IDPH
'The elephant went to hide in his forest'

In (3.25a) the postposition 'to' is associated with the zero-coded referent 'Rabbit'. Still more remarkable is example (3.26) in which the postposition is attached to a coordinate NP, and the second member of this coordinate NP is zero, so the postposition 'between' immediately follows the conjunction 'and'. Example (3.27) demonstrates that this pattern is not limited to argument-marking postpositions but extends to the possessor-marking associative postposition: the sequence Ø *lá fùra* can be literally rendered in English as *'s forest* (instead of *his forest*). Given such a difference between Japanese and Beledugu Bamana, a study of cross-linguistic variation in the conduct of zero-associated adpositions is clearly desirable.

3.4.3 *Genealogical and geographical distribution*

Languages that pervasively use zero reference display a very clear geographic pattern. In the first place, unrestricted zero reference is characteristic of East and Southeast Asia. In this part of the world, zero reference predominates, and this is really an areal rather than a genealogical pattern. Languages that often display strong reliance on zero reference include many Sino-Tibetan languages, Tai-Kadai, and Austro-Asiatic. Japanese and Korean, though not belonging to any of these families and being typologically very different, also follow the zero reference pattern. The East and Southeast Asian zero reference pattern has outliers in a number of relatively close areas, including India, Indonesia, New Guinea, and especially in Australia (Pama-Nyungan languages only; see e.g. Austin 2001b). Outside this quite coherent part of the world, pervasive use of zero reference is found only occasionally. In Africa there are few languages that strongly rely on zero reference, while in most of Eurasia and in the Americas this pattern is almost absent.

Of course, this is true of only predominant zero reference pervading the whole linguistic system as is the case, for example, in Yidiny and Japanese. Restricted, or sensitive (see Chapter 5) zero reference is found all over the place. Some elements of it can be found in every language. English is among the languages that are very much anti-zero, but in certain syntactic contexts it does allow zero; see discussion in sections 5.4 and 6.7. So zero reference is universal, but its predominance is highly area-specific. Some sense of the geographical distribution of zero reference, though only in the Principal position, can be gained from the map in Dryer (2005a); about 9% of languages belong to this type in Dryer's sample.

3.4.4 *Zero reference and related typological features*

Besides predisposition to zero reference, languages of East and Southeast Asia are very well known for their peculiarity that can be generalized as scarcity of morphology. This scarcity is reflected in several basic typological features, including:

- isolation: separation between morphemes, frequent monomorphemic words.
- analytism: grammatical meanings are conveyed by function words rather than affixes.
- no-marking (or null-marking): relations between constituents are not marked on either head or dependent; these relations are mostly conveyed by linear order.

Naturally, a hypothesis may emerge: perhaps zero reference is favoured by morphologically impoverished languages. (This would be a converse of the fact that morphologically rich languages typically use bound pronouns; see subsection 3.3.5.) Zero reference, as well as morphological scarcity, can be subsumed under the general concept of a language's 'lesser complexity' (see Dahl 2002; Sampson et al. (eds.) 2009); note that the latter has been recently hypothesized to be connected with population size and a number of other social parameters (Lupyan and Dale 2010).

However, it is not so easy to prove a relationship between zero reference and morphological scarcity. First, West Africa also is an area of isolating, analytic, and no-marking languages, but zero reference is not typical there at all. Second, there are languages that are morphologically quite developed but still have zero reference. Both Yidiny and Japanese, languages featured in this section, exemplify this combination. In particular, Japanese is characterized by Bickel and Nichols (2005) as having between four and five grammatical categories per inflected verb, the most common type cross-linguistically.

In order to test if there is a correlation between the degree of synthesis and the inclination towards zero anaphora, we can combine two linguo-geographical studies from WALS: 'Inflectional synthesis of the verb' (Bickel and Nichols 2005) and 'Expression of pronominal subjects' (Dryer 2005a). This will provide us only with a partial picture, in particular because the latter study can only shed light on referential options used in the subject (Principal) position. If a language uses zero reference in the Principal position, one cannot infer from this that this is generally a zero reference language. But since Principal is the most frequent position for reduced referential devices, this partial picture is still informative.

In Dryer's typology, the closest approximation to the zero reference type is called 'Optional pronouns in subject position'. (This formulation includes both predominantly zero reference languages, such as Japanese, and languages in which free pronouns alternate with zero.) Among the 18 languages of this kind shared by the Bickel and Nichols's and the Dryer's studies, there are four languages like Japanese (four to five categories per inflected verb), nine less morphologically developed languages, and five more developed ones. This distribution shows that Principal zero reference is found in languages of varying morphological complexity; there is only a slight preference for less inflectionally developed languages.

Looking at the composition of features from the other end, there are 22 languages shared by both samples that are morphologically poorly developed (have three or fewer categories per inflected verb). Translating Dryer's types into the typology adopted in this chapter, out of these 22 languages nine use zero reference in the Principal position, six use free pronouns, and six use bound pronouns. (There is one language in the 'mixed' category.) Again, there is a slight preference for zero reference among the inflectionally undeveloped languages, but one cannot conclude that morphological scarcity entails zero reference.

If so, a cautious attitude would be to simply assume that zero reference is an areal trait of the same parts of the world that have many morphologically impoverished languages, and the impression of association between these features may be a result of this geographical bias. However, it may still be more than a mere accident that these two features more often coincide than not. This may result from the fact that zero reference is disfavoured by morphologically developed languages – quite naturally, they usually have bound pronouns. There exist some morphologically developed and even polysynthetic languages that use zero reference, but this is rather a typological exception.

In order to avoid triviality, let us look at the languages of average, rather than rich, synthesis, such as Japanese (four to five categories per inflected verb). There are forty such languages shared by the samples of Bickel and Nichols (2005) and Dryer (2005a), and among them only four (10%) are zero reference languages, while the majority (24, or 60%) predictably use Principal bound pronouns and 12 (30%) free pronouns. Of course, if one looks at languages of higher synthesis, the dispreference for zero reference will be much clearer still. So it may be that zero reference is found primarily in

East and Southeast Asia partly because it is ousted from the other parts of the world, where languages are overall morphologically richer.

To the best of my knowledge, little is known about correlates of predominant zero reference with other grammatical features. It is probably the case that this choice of a major reduced referential device a language can make does not imply as much as bound pronouns do. Gundel (1980) proposed a connection between zero reference and 'topic-prominence' (Li and Thompson 1976), arguably a typical feature of East and Southeast Asia.

3.5 Frequencies of pure language types among the languages of the world

There is a way to estimate the frequency of the pure, or internally consistent, language types on a worldwide scale, both with respect to the whole array of languages and with respect to each other, by using a composition of two WALS studies: Dryer (2005a) and Siewierska (2005e). As was pointed out above, Dryer looked only at the Principal position, but provided a fine-grained differentiation between the distinct kinds of reduced referential devices. His classification easily translates into the opposition between free pronominal (including clitic), bound pronominal, and zero Principal. Siewierska provides information on how many person markers are found on the transitive verb (Agentive, Patientive, or both, or none), although she does not distinguish between affixes and clitics. Combining the two studies allows one to use the advantages of both and to approximately figure out the frequency of pure languages.

I will be assuming that if a language has a bound Principal and it also has the Patientive person marker attached to the verb, then this Patientive marker also is affixal, that is bound. This assumption is somewhat too strong (see discussion in Siewierska 2004: 42–46), but probably not extremely strong: as Siewierska (2005e: 414) remarks, affixes are more frequent among her verbal person markers than clitics. Also, according to Dryer's (2005a) results for Principal referential devices, the proportion of affixes to clitics is 9:1. If it is of a similar order in the domain of Patientive devices, for the purposes of a rough estimation we can simply ignore this internal variation within Siewierska's data.

Out of the thirty combined values of the product of Dryer's and Siewierska's parameters 21 are actually attested, and three of these correspond to pure types. If a language has a bound pronominal Principal and verbal person marking for two arguments it is inferred to be a predominantly bound pronoun language. If a language has free pronouns[40] and no person marking on the verb, it counts as a free pronoun language. Finally, if a language uses zero in the Principal position and has no verbal person marking, it can be tentatively considered a zero reference language. Table 3.4 summarizes this kind of inference and provides quantitative data for each of the pure types.

Dryer's and Siewierska's language samples have an intersection of 248 languages. Among them, 158 belong to the three pure types. This constitutes 64% of the whole number of languages considered, that is, nearly two-thirds. The remaining one third are various mixed subtypes, corresponding to 18 other attested combinations of Dryer's and Siewierska's typologies. Some of these other subtypes will be mentioned in Chapter 5.

158 pure languages are broken into three types as shown in Table 3.4. Bound pronoun languages appear by far the most frequent among the pure types. In fact, this type predominates among the world's languages as a whole, as it accounts for 45% of all languages in the shared sample (111 out of 248).

The bound pronoun pattern prevails in the world not only in terms of the sheer quantity of languages or genealogical groups prone to this pattern, but also in terms of geographical coverage. All continents have at least some areas where the bound pronoun pattern dominates; see subsection 3.3.4. In contrast, both the free pronoun and the zero reference patterns are very much skewed towards particular geographic areas. Pure free pronoun systems are mostly

TABLE 3.4. Frequency of pure language types, as derived from the studies on the expression of reduced Principal (Dryer 2005a) and on the amount of arguments cross-referenced on the verb (Siewierska 2005e)

Expression of reduced Principal	Verbal person marking	Pure language type	Number of languages of pure types (158 in all)
bound pronoun	both Agentive and Patientive	predisposed to bound pronouns	111 (70.3%)
free pronoun	none	predisposed to free pronouns	21 (13.3%)
zero	none	predisposed to zero reference	26 (16.4%)

---

[40] As was pointed out in subsection 3.2.4, this option corresponds to either of Dryer's values 'obligatory pronouns in subject position', 'subject pronouns in different position', and 'subject clitics on variable host'; only the former two are found among the languages shared by the two samples that have the 'no person marking' according to Siewierska's study.

found in West Africa[41] and western Oceania, and zero reference systems in East and Southeast Asia; see subsections 3.2.4 and 3.4.3, respectively.

3.6 Type of dominant referential device and morphological complexity

Much attention has been given in this chapter to the relation between a language's dominant type of referential device and morphological complexity. We have seen that preference for bound pronouns strongly correlates with well-developed morphology, particularly verb morphology. In contrast, there are indications of a connection between zero reference and morphological impoverishment. But what about free pronouns, the best known kind of reduced referential devices? In order to compare three referential types vis-à-vis morphological complexity the studies by Dryer (2005a) and Bickel and Nichols (2005) can be composed. The two samples have an intersection of 121 languages. The results are shown in Figure 3.7.

In Bickel and Nichols's study (2005) languages are divided into seven groups according to the number of inflectional categories per inflected verb (see the horizontal axis in Figure 3.7). In Figure 3.7 the overall number of languages in the shared sample having the given level of morphological complexity (for example, six to seven categories) is taken for 100%, and

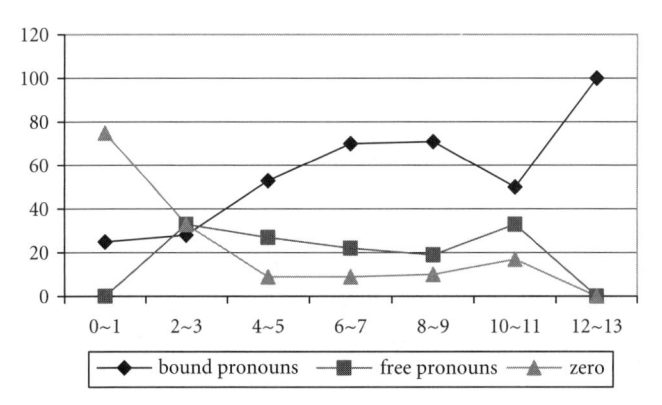

FIGURE 3.7. Frequency of the three types of dominant reduced referential devices (interpretation of Dryer 2005a), plotted against the degree of verb inflectional synthesis (Bickel and Nichols 2005)

---

[41] If Creissels (2005) is correct in claiming that in many African languages bound pronouns are traditionally misinterpreted for free pronouns, then the worldwide preference for bound pronouns is even greater.

these are further divided into three referential types. The graphs in Figure 3.7 suggest that the clearest relationship is found between the verb's inflectional synthesis and bound pronouns: there is a steady increase in bound pronoun languages as inflectional synthesis increases. Extreme morphological impoverishment correlates with zero reference; however, beyond that no dependency can be seen. As for free pronouns, there is no dependency at all: frequencies of free pronouns remain the same throughout the scale, except for the extreme values of inflectional synthesis (0 to 1 and 12 to 13) that are very rare anyway (four and two languages, respectively). This conclusion supports the hypothesis offered in subsection 3.2.4 that predisposition to free pronouns is characteristic of syntax-centred languages and should not be expected to display any clear correlation with morphological phenomena.

Overall, it appears that predisposition to bound pronouns is the strongest choice made by a language. More can be predicted about a bound pronoun language than about other language types. As we have seen in a number of case studies composing various WALS parameters, bound pronouns correlate with a number of other typological phenomena, while zero reference and especially free pronouns much less so. This observation probably suggests that morphology is the kernel part of grammar. Since referential choice is a fundamental linguistic phenomenon, using mophologically fixed reduced referential devices has many structural corollaries. In contrast, predisposition to other, non-morphological, types of referential devices does not impose as strong constraints on language structure.

Summary

In this chapter I have considered the three most fundamental types of reduced referential devices: free pronouns, bound pronouns, and zero reference. Free pronouns are syntactically independent words. Typically they are prosodically weak and have the status of clitics. Bound pronouns are affixes, most importantly on verbs, but they nevertheless function as clause arguments. Zero reference is a conventional representation of the following situation: a referent is referred to in a clause but no overt element can be taken to perform such an act of reference.

Bound pronouns often have the property of tenacity – they are present in a clause even when the referent is of low activation and a coreferential noun phrase is found in the same clause. In such instances a bound pronoun and a noun phrase share the argumental status. The property of tenacity is not exclusively associated with bound pronouns: free pronouns can be tenacious as well.

In this chapter, attention has been primarily restricted to those languages that are relatively pure, or internally consistent, in what referential devices they use, that is, are dominated by a single reduced referential device. The languages featured in this chapter as illustrating the pure types are: for free pronouns – Lyélé and other Gur languages, and also English; for bound pronouns – Abkhaz (Abkhaz-Adyghean) and Navajo (Na-Dene); for zero reference – Yidiny (Pama-Nyungan) and Japanese.

According to the information available to date, pure languages account for about two-thirds of all languages, and among them the bound pronoun languages are the most common type. The widely held assumption that free pronoun languages are the typological default thus turns out to be untenable. Pure free pronoun systems are particularly typical of West Africa and the western part of Oceania. Zero reference systems are found primarily in East and Southeast Asia. Bound pronoun systems are frequent in all continents, but are particularly abundant in North America.

The dominant type of reduced referential device is among a language's most important grammatical choices. This choice also relates to other typological properties. In particular, languages with the preference for bound pronouns typically have a higher degree of morphological complexity, and are polysynthetic and head-marking.

4

Pronouns and related devices

Overview

This chapter is devoted to pronouns, that is reduced but overt referential devices, both free and bound. The most basic parameters for a typology of pronominal systems, including the categories of person and number/membership, have been extensively studied in recent literature; a brief review is provided in section 4.1.

The main goal of this chapter is to address a variety of relatively complicated issues in the typology of pronouns. The first of these is the problem of the boundaries of the notion 'pronoun'. In section 4.2 I discuss those linguistic devices that cannot be considered canonical personal pronouns but function in a very similar way in certain languages. Three types of such devices, probably the most salient ones cross-linguistically, include demonstratives, classifiers, and social status nouns. Some languages use such devices along with personal pronouns, while other languages use them instead of pronouns.

Another problem associated with pronouns is that some overt reduced referential devices simultaneously evoke two referents. I discuss such double reference pronouns in section 4.3. Section 4.4 is devoted to a relatively widespread phenomenon: compounding of the referential function with the marking of clausal categories, such as tense or mode. The question is addressed of whether such forms can be reasonably considered pronouns, and the distinction between free and bound pronouns is recast in the light of this discussion. Finally, section 4.5 treats the marked kind of pronouns – the so-called strong pronouns. The character of strong pronouns is considered in relation to languages' preference for certain types of reduced referential devices. I also discuss the cross-linguistic range of discourse contexts in which strong pronouns occur.

4.1 Pronouns and pronominal categories

The term 'pronoun' is a fairly bad misnomer. There is a whole series of problems associated with this term. Lyons (1977: 636–637) pointed out that pronouns, first, must be contrasted not to nouns but rather to noun phrases and, second, cannot be taken to substitute for anything in the case of locutor reference. (Similar points were made on many occasions in the literature; for example, see the discussion in Mühlhäusler et al. 1990: 49ff.) Lyons's critique presupposes, however, that some pronouns – specifically, anaphoric pronouns – can properly be viewed as substitutes. As has been discussed in section 2.4, this finds no support within the discourse-oriented approach to language: anaphoric pronouns simply constitute one of the options available to a speaker in referential choice. Furthermore, there exist tenacious pronouns that happily coexist in one clause with coreferential NPs. So the term 'pronoun' is actually a misnomer on all counts. Given that the term has a very long tradition of use, I am not going to attempt to avoid or alter it in the book. But it should never be taken to imply any transformational-style connotation – the connotation very deeply entrenched in the thinking of many linguists, both theoretical and descriptive.

This book is primarily devoted to personal pronouns, so, unless otherwise indicated, 'pronoun' is to be understood as 'personal pronoun' and, most often, 'third person pronoun'. So understood, the term 'pronoun' implies only three things. First, a pronoun is a referential device, directly coding referents. Second, it is a reduced referential device, that is, it does not have lexical content. Third, pronouns are **overt** devices, and so are opposed to zero reference. Zero reference is excluded from the notion of 'pronoun' here, although some linguists actually use the collocation 'zero pronoun'.

In the literature, other properties of pronouns are often indicated, helping to tell them apart from other classes of forms, particularly from nouns. For example, Sugamoto (1989) proposed a list of seven features helping to differentiate pronouns from nouns. One of them, of course, is reduction (lack of lexical content). Other important features include closed class membership and inability to take modifiers. Sugamoto proposed a scale of pronominality, relying on this list of features. In this chapter I use a different approach: first I discuss prototypical pronouns and then proceed with other kinds of forms that resemble prototypical pronouns but differ from them in this or that respect.

Languages typically have at least some kind of personal pronouns. Even those languages that use zero as the preferred reduced referential device, still use personal pronouns in certain contexts, as does Japanese. An extremely unusual example of a language that gets along without personal pronouns most of the time (with the exception of first person singular) is Riau Indonesian (Austronesian), described in various papers by David Gil (e.g. 1999).

How are pronouns, as overt reduced referential devices, different from zero reference? Zero reference by definition does not explicitly distinguish any categories. In a language like Japanese, anything can be referred to by means of a zero: a human being, a thing, or an abstract concept; a singular or a plural referent; a locutor or a non-locutor. In other languages more discriminate zeroes exist, but they can be ascribed a certain significance only through opposition to non-zero elements (such as third person zero as opposed to overt locutor reference). Pronouns, however, normally distinguish certain categories simply by virtue of having material form. By far the most important category distinguished by pronouns is **person**. It is because of this category's paramount significance that pronouns themselves are called personal.

It is only very rarely that one encounters pronouns not distinguishing person. One example of this kind is the French pronoun *y* that, in one of its uses, refers to an oblique participant of a clause, as in *J'y réponds* 'I am responding to it (for example, to the letter)'. French grammars state that *y* refers mostly to inanimate referents (Gak 1979: 149–150). Lambrecht (1981: 34, 36), however, indicates that *y* extends to other classes of referents, including not just human referents but also locutors and including singular and plural, for example:

(4.1) Colloquial French (Lambrecht 1981: 36)
 Pierre y-pense jamais, {à sa voiture / à nous / à toi}
 P. REFDIR-think.PRES never to his car to us to you
 'Pierre never thinks {of his car/us/you}'

Another similar case is reported for Cirebon Javanese (Austronesian, Indonesia) by Ewing (2001: 32–33); in this dialect the erstwhile third person pronoun *di-* has generalized to all persons. To be sure, instances of this kind are rare and peripheral. There is no known language that would distinguish no person in pronouns at all, or, in other words, would have a single overt reduced referential device (=pronoun).[1] One of the most economical pronominal systems is found in Balante (Atlantic, Guinea-Bissau) that, according to Wiesemann (1986b: viii), only differentiates the first person from the other person (including second and third) in the singular, and no person in the plural; see also Siewierska (2004: 75–79), Cysouw (2003). Evidently, the need to differentiate between the two locutors and then between the locutors and everything else is very fundamental to human cognition (Benveniste 1958).

---

[1] But see the discussion of Russian Sign Language pronouns in section 15.2.

Underdifferentiation happens in the case of zero reference, but whenever a language employs an overt reduced referential device, the first thing it cares about is to indicate person. This pattern is observed in the vast majority of instances.

The second category that is almost universally marked on pronouns is **number** – or, in some languages, the category of minimal vs. augmented **membership**. (The latter category accounts for some languages much more adequately than number; it was originally proposed by Conklin 1962 and McKay 1978; see Cysouw 2003: 85–90.) Number/membership is almost universal, although there are rare languages that neglect this category in pronouns. For example, in Jarawa (South Andamanese; Kumar 2006: 9) there are single pronouns for the first, second, and third persons; see also Helmbrecht (2004: 117ff.). Person and number/membership are often so closely interwoven in a pronominal system that it may be difficult to separate them. Below, 'person' will sometimes informally stand for 'person and number/membership'.

Other classificatory categories expressed in pronouns, such as animacy, gender, and deference, will become relevant in Chapter 8. Of course, pronouns also bear semantic roles with respect to the predicate, and these are encoded by case markers or otherwise; see subsection 3.3.1.

A significant literature is devoted to the typology of pronominal systems – among the relevant publications see Majtinskaja (1969), Vol'f (1974), Krupa (1976), Ingram (1978), Sokolovskaja (1980), Jacobsen (1980), Seliverstova (1988), Kibrik (1990a), Mühlhäusler (2001). A particularly rich source of data on the topic is the collection Wiesemann (ed.) (1986), containing detailed accounts of exotic pronominal systems in many individual languages (especially of South America, Africa, and Oceania), as well as typological articles. In recent years, the typology of pronouns has become a fruitful field again; cf. fundamental monographs Cysouw (2003), Bhat (2004), Helmbrecht (2004), Siewierska (2004).

4.2 Functional analogues of personal pronouns

Linguistic elements that can be characterized as overt reduced referential devices most typically coincide with what are traditionally known as personal pronouns. In the context of referential choice between full and reduced referential devices, most often these are third person pronouns. English is a typical example of a language that uses third person pronouns when a reduced referential device is needed. However, in this kind of language other reduced devices may be used, such as demonstratives. Furthermore, not all languages have dedicated third person pronouns: some languages employ overt reduced referential devices that fall out of the scope of what traditionally counts as third person pronouns. Several kinds of linguistic elements that belong to other pronoun types or even different lexico-grammatical classes may effectively function in discourse as **analogues** of third person pronouns. Such analogues can be thought of as marginal overt reduced referential devices.

Among these, the most salient ones are: demonstratives, classifiers, and social status nouns. All of these devices are distinct from personal pronouns, in particular because they do not contain the category of person. Demonstratives and social status nouns are apparently universal and in most languages coexist with pronouns in a certain distribution. Classifiers are not universal but again their central functions are different from those of pronouns. However, in certain languages that lack genuine third person pronouns these devices play the pronominal role. In the three following subsections I briefly consider each of these three kinds of devices in turn. In each of these subsections I provide examples of the device in question and discuss how it can function in the role of a third person pronoun. I consider evidence both from languages without dedicated third person pronouns, in which alternative reduced devices are used instead of them, and from languages in which alternative reduced devices are used along with dedicated third person pronouns.

4.2.1 *Demonstratives*

Demonstratives are referential devices originally used for deictic or exophoric pointing to entities and loci in the physical environment of the speech situation; see Chapter 15. Demonstratives usually distinguish between two or more degrees of proximity between the anchoring point (typically the speaker) and a referent in question. Demonstratives appear to be a universal phenomenon (Diessel 1999, 2005b). They can be used in a variety of grammatical positions, including the nominal one (*That is my cat*), the adnominal one (as a part of a full NP: *This cat is funny*), and the adverbial one (*My cat is there*). Apart from the original use associated with pointing, demonstratives have a number of other uses, one of them anaphoric: mention of referents enjoying a certain degree of activation. The relevance of the anaphoric function in demonstratives is widely held to be universal; cf. Himmelmann (1996).

An obvious proof of the demonstratives' relatedness to third person pronouns is that the latter most often evolve from the former (Majtinskaja 1969, Helmbrecht 2004: 153ff.). This issue was recently explored in detail by Bhat (2004, 2005). According to these studies, about a half of the world's languages display a clear resemblance between third person pronouns and demonstratives. Note that the relatedness between the two categories is actually even higher, because third person pronouns may be derived from old demonstratives, while being distinct from modern demonstratives. For example, in Russian (not in Bhat's sample) the third person pronoun's stem *on-* is the old distal demonstrative that is not in use as such any more in the modern language except in several fixed collocations such as *vo vremja ono* 'in that (remote) time'. In fact, English third person pronouns also go back to erstwhile demonstratives.

In the study of Wichmann and Holman (2009), Bhat's (2005) typological feature (relatedness of third person pronouns to demonstratives) was shown to be genealogically unstable – this means that related languages often pattern differently on this feature. One reason why this may happen is that ex-demonstratives may specialize as dedicated third person pronouns, ousting erstwhile third person pronouns from this function.

Since demonstratives are so closely related to third person pronouns, it is not surprising that they are often difficult to tell apart. The main criteria that are most helpful are: whether a pronoun forms a single structural and distributional system with locutor pronouns (if yes, then it is more likely to be a third person pronoun); whether a pronoun can be used adnominally (if not, then it is more likely to be a third person pronoun); see also Helmbrecht (2004: 154ff.).

An example of a language that shows a clear synchronic difference between third person pronouns and demonstratives is English. Third person pronouns such as *he, they* form a coherent paradigm with locutor pronouns (in particular, in having case forms) and are not used adnominally, in contrast to demonstratives *this, that.*

Particularly obvious is the distinction between third person pronouns and demonstratives in bound pronoun languages. According to Diessel (1999: Ch. 2), demonstratives appearing in the nominal position are almost exclusively morphologically free[2]. Even in languages with the most extreme tendency for bound pronouns, one does not find bound demonstratives. For example, in Navajo, a profoundly bound pronoun language, demonstratives are free forms. Consider the following excerpt (from a story in which the mother eagle was breeding two eggs, and one of the eggs remained motionless):

---

[2] The fact that demonstratives are generally free is probably related to their inherent relationship with pointing gestures and the concomitant prosodic salience; see Chapter 15, section 15.1.

(4.2) Navajo (Na-Dene, Southwest of the USA; from a story by Bernice Casaus, speaker)
a. ʔayęęzhii ʔéí   t'óó   ø-siʔą́   jiń.
   egg   that   just   it-sit   QUOT
b. ʔéí   shį́į́   ch'ééh   kóń-ø-j-iilʔįįh.
   that PTCL   in.vain   PREF-it-she-push

'That egg is just sitting there, they say. In vain she was pushing it'

In this example one and the same distal demonstrative *ʔéí* is used in the adnominal position in the first line and in the nominal position in the second. Note the second usage – a free form occupying a nominal position. Generally this is highly marked for Navajo reduced reference: much more neutral is the use of bound pronouns, such as *j-* in line (b). Navajo, as well as English, constitutes an example of a language in which the distinction between dedicated third person pronouns on the one hand and demonstratives on the other is very clear.

The opposite to such languages are those without dedicated third person pronouns. In this kind of language the distinction between pronouns and demonstrative is blurred. For example, many Turkic languages use the same demonstrative form *ol~al~ul~o* in the adnominal and in the nominal position, and the latter is treated as either a third-person-style usage of the demonstrative or a homophonous third person pronoun. Another example of a language that uses demonstratives in the role of third person pronoun and does not have a clear distinction between third person pronouns and demonstratives is spoken Sinhala (Indo-Aryan, Indo-European, Sri Lanka; spoken Sinhala is quite different from written Sinhala). Chandrasena Premawardhena (2002: 69) plainly states: 'The demonstrative pronouns function as the third person pronouns in discourse'. There are about forty different demonstrative forms, varying in accordance with animacy, number, gender, proximity, and deference, that can be used in the anaphoric function (Chandrasena Premawardhena 2002: 70).

One of the best known examples of languages without dedicated third person pronouns (cf. subsection 4.2.3 below) is Japanese. As has been discussed in Chapter 3, Japanese is a fundamentally zero reference language. Occasionally anaphoric demonstratives occur, as in the following:

(4.3) Japanese (Clancy and Downing 1987: 21)
a. Yukichan ga   <...>   daidokoro de   onigiri o   tsukur-oo
   Y.   NOM   kitchen   INSTR onigiri ACC cook-HORT
   to   shi-te   i-mas-u.
   QUOT   do-CONV   be-ADDR-PRES
   <a sequence of seven intervening clauses describing how Yukichan was preparing onigiri>

i. Ø   sore o   bentoo ni   shi-te,
               that ACC   lunch DAT   do-CONV

j. Yukichan wa sassooto   kooen   ni   dekake-te   ik-imas-u.
   Y.   TOP breezily park DAT   go.out-CONV   go-ADDR-PRES
   'Yukichan <...> is trying to make onigiri in the kitchen <...>
   Taking them as her lunch, Yukichan breezily sets off for the park'

In this example the medial distance demonstrative *sore* is used to refer to onigiri that has a certain non-null level of activation at this point. Anaphoric use of demonstratives in Japanese discourse is very rare (Clancy 1980: 133, Efimova 2006: 18), but when the speaker needs a non-zero device for some reason a demonstrative may be employed.[3]

What is the function of demonstratives, particularly in languages like English that have dedicated third person pronouns? Widely known is the suggestion by Ariel (1988), Gundel et al. (1993) that nominally used demonstratives convey less activated (less accessible, less given) information than third person pronouns. I find this suggestion rather dubious. Maes (1996) has argued that demonstratives in fact appear in the circumstances of higher referent accessibility or givenness. Krasavina (2004) has shown that the patterns of demonstratives' use are not as directly dependent on referent activation as are full NPs and pronouns. Very promising appears the hypothesis that in languages with an extensive use of dedicated pronouns demonstratives fulfil a variety of referential functions, filling diverse functional gaps in referential choice (Himmelmann 1996: 227, Krasavina 2004, Byron et al. 2008). Likewise, in languages without dedicated pronouns demonstratives are drafted in situations when an overt referential device is necessary. It appears that anaphoric demonstratives are troubleshooters of referential choice.

4.2.2 *Classifiers*

Some languages use classifiers rather than third person pronouns as reduced referential devices. Classifiers are morphemes or words indicating membership of a referent in a certain category, in accordance with its animacy, sex, size, shape, and so forth. Cross-linguistically, the basis for categorization varies greatly in terms of its semantic transparency. Detailed typologies of classifiers have been presented by Aikhenvald (2000) and Clark (2002).

---

[3] Also there are languages that have dedicated third person pronouns, but these are minor compared to demonstratives in terms of frequency in discourse. Among such languages are Jiwarli (Pama-Nyungan, Australia; Austin 2001b) and Cirebon Javanese (Austronesian, Indonesia; Ewing 2001). Both of these languages are strongly inclined to zero reference.

Largely following Grinevald Craig (1992), Aikhenvald groups classifiers of the world's languages in the following types: noun classes, noun classifiers, numeral classifiers, possessive classifiers, verbal classifiers, and locative and deictic classifiers. (A similar classification is proposed by Clark (2002), but she uses 'noun classifiers' as a cover term.)

The first of Aikhenvald's types – noun classes, or genders – are beyond our concern in this subsection; see Chapter 8, subsection 8.3.1. According to the received view, noun class is a category copying class membership of a noun upon other constituents; the latter constituents agree with the noun controller (Corbett 1991: 136–137, Grinevald 2000: 55). Conversely, in the languages not predisposed to relatively automatic feature copying, or agreement, class-marked words or morphemes are treated as classifiers. Examples of classifiers discussed in this subsection belong to Aikhenvald's noun classifiers and numeral classifiers. According to Aikhenvald (2000: 96, 122), the main areas where classifiers (not including noun classes) are found are East and Southeast Asia, Oceania, Australia, and the Americas – collectively this is the macroarea of the Pacific Rim. (Other parts of the world – Africa and most of Eurasia – also emphasize noun classes.)

A good example of classifiers employed as reduced referential devices is provided by Jakaltek, a Mayan language of Guatemala (Grinevald Craig 1977). One type of use of Jakaltek classifiers is prepositionally to nouns. Such usages of classifiers are sometimes found when a referent is indefinite and are consistently found with definite usages. In fact, Grinevald Craig often glosses them as definite articles. Furthermore, when a referent is activated, a classifier alone suffices to mention it. The following extract is from a story about an older woman who was trying to get a lazy son to become more active[4]:

(4.4)   Jakaltek (Mayan, Guatemala; Grinevald Craig 1977: 405)[5]
    a. hactu'   xin   xu   sto ya'   comi' tu'   skambenoj
       that.is.how then   did go   CL_OLD   lady   that ask

    b. tzet   wal   yuten sba   ya'   b'oj   naj
       what then   does   self   CL_OLD   with   CL_M

---

[4] Here and henceforth, when glossing classifiers (as well as noun classes), I use the following convention: the gloss CL is followed by the underscore '_' and a specification of class (either semantic or formal).

[5] I follow Grinevald Craig in the way she divides this extract into lines. In her morphological analysis, she also posits personal absolutive and ergative morphemes on the verb (Grinevald Craig 1977: 100ff.). Third person absolutive is always zero and third person ergative sometimes surfaces as zero. No morphological analysis is provided in the representation of the texts, so this information is absent from my examples as well. Even though Jakaltek has bound pronouns it seems to use free referential devices (either full NPs or classifiers) almost universally.

c. xbabi   ya'   yatut tiyoẍ
   advanced CL_OLD   house God

d. ab   xilni ya'   naj   pale
   they.say   saw   CL_OLD   CL_M   priest

e. skamben ya'   tzet consejohal ch'a'laxoj tet ya'
   asked   CL_OLD what advice   is.given   to   CL_OLD

f. yu   naj   ni'an tu'
   about CL_M small that

'That is why the woman went to ask what she should do with him. She went to the church. They say that she saw the priest and she asked what advice he could give her about that child.'

In this extract, there are several instances of classifiers *naj* (for male persons) and *ya'* (for elderly persons), both in the adnominal and in the nominal usage. Most of the nominal usages appear in core argument positions, but in (4.4b, e) there are usages in an oblique position (after a preposition). Also consider a clause with two arguments coded by classifiers (this occurs after the boy was given two piglets to look after):

(4.5) Jakaltek (Mayan, Guatemala; Grinevald Craig 1977: 406)

Such uses of classifiers are so similar to third person pronouns that a question is raised: are they really different? The crucial difference is that the basic usage of classifiers is within an NP, adjoined to a noun. This is definitional for noun classifiers (Aikhenvald 2000: 80)[6] and differentiates them from usual third person pronouns. But then, could not Jakaltek classifiers be characterized as demonstratives marked for referent's class membership, sometimes used adnominally and sometimes in a nominal position? (Remember that Jakaltek classifiers are strongly associated with definiteness; Grinevald Craig sometimes even glosses them as 'the'.) This recalls the use of the German *der/die/das* that is both a definite article and a demonstrative, is specified for gender and number, and is frequently used in discourse as an anaphoric device (Bosch and Umbach 2006). However, this idea does not work for Jakaltek; see (4.4a) where an NP contains both a prenominal classifier and a postnominal demonstrative. Evidently, the language treats classifiers and demonstratives as

---

[6] This raises an interpretational problem regarding English. As English lacks any syntactic noun class (gender) agreement, its gender-marked pronouns *he, she, it* are a rather deviant instance of noun class. Furthermore, English has the Jakaltek-type usages such as 'she teacher'; if this pattern were generalized to a broad range of contexts, English would qualify as a language with noun classifiers rather than with gender-marked pronouns.

distinct. Thus Jakaltek classifiers must be recognized as a linguistic device, distinct from both third person pronouns and demonstratives.

A specialized study of the classifiers' referential behaviour is found in the book by Daley (1998) about Vietnamese (Austro-Asiatic). The Vietnamese pattern is typologically similar to that of Jakaltek. Traditionally, the basic usage of Vietnamese classifiers is thought to be within a complex NP, in a position preceding a noun and specifying membership of this noun (or rather its referent) within a particular category. This is the case with the classifier *người* 'person' in the following example:

(4.6) Vietnamese (Austro-Asiatic, Vietnam; Daley 1998: 8)
 người nông dân ngạc nhiên
 CL_PERSON farmer citizen choke so
 'The peasant was surprised'

Apart from this type of usage, Vietnamese classifiers are used as independent referential devices. (Daley terms this usage pronominal or anaphoric; the latter designation is not appropriate as classifiers can refer to locutors.) Vietnamese classifiers are traditionally (Thompson 1965) broken down into two types that Daley (1998: 5) terms general categorical classifiers and modifying classifiers. The former are used referentially much more often. According to corpus counts done by Daley, general categorical classifiers are used in this function (Daley 1998: 63) in 40% of all instances, and for all classifiers this figure is 34%. Daley also questions the validity of this dichotomy and posits an intermediate group, named kin classifiers (Daley 1998: 103). An example of the referential use of a classifier is found in the following example from a story. A young man is the story's protagonist, and he has been called before *chàng thang* 'YOUNG.MAN (kin classifier) youth' on multiple occasions. Solely the classifier constitutes the referential expression in the following clause:

(4.7) Vietnamese (Austro-Asiatic, Vietnam; Daley 1998: 131)
 vào khoáng nửa đêm, <u>chàng</u> bỗng nghe <...>
 enter interval half night CL_YOUNG.MAN suddenly hear
 'At about midnight, the young man suddenly heard <...>'

According to Daley (1998: 65), classifier constructions constitute the most frequent referential device in Vietnamese stories – 36% of all referential devices, as compared to 21% of zero reference or 21% of nouns (this count probably does not include introductory mentions). However, the number of plain classifiers used as referential devices is much lower – only about 8% (derived from two tables on pp. 64 and 65 of Daley 1998). Note that

Vietnamese human classifiers are notoriously difficult to distinguish from social status terms discussed in subsection 4.2.3; see Đình-Hoà (1997: 94ff., 123ff.), Daley (1998: 95ff.).

Another book-length study of discourse usage of classifiers is devoted to Japanese – Downing (1996a); see also Downing (1986). In Japanese, classifiers are used only in one specialized context, that is in numeral phrases. (In Vietnamese, classifiers occur in numeral constructions too, but there this usage is not exclusive or even dominant.) Consider an example from a story:

(4.8) Japanese (Downing 1996a: 163)[7]
 a. Shuuichi wa Shingo no musuko da keredomo,
  S.   TOP S.   GEN son   COP but
 b. Kikuko ga konoyoonishitemade Shuuichi to   musubare-te
  K.   NOM to.this.extent   S.   COMIT be.bound-CONV
  i-na-kereba   naranai   hodo,
  be-NEG-COND not.acceptable extent
 c. <u>futa-ri</u>   wa risoo no fuufu na no   ka,
  two-CL_PERSON TOP ideal GEN couple COP NMZR QU
 d. Shingo wa utagai-dasu to   kagiri ga   na-katta
  S.   TOP doubt-begin QUOT limit NOM be.NEG-PAST
  'Even though Shuuichi was his son, Shingo couldn't help wondering whether they were such an ideal couple that Kikuko should be linked to Shuuichi to this extent'

In line (c), the person classifier *-ri* appears in conjunction with the numeral base *futa-* 'two'. This composite form could literally be translated as 'the two of them'. Both of the referents 'Shuuichi' and 'Kikuko' are activated at this point, but they are not sufficiently activated as a group, and this must be the reason why the numeral classifier construction rather than zero reference is employed at this point. Downing formulates the main reasons for using classifiers in Japanese discourse as follows: 'Classifier phrases … occupy a unique slot in this system of anaphoric alternatives, for two reasons. First, like nouns, they are useful in that they may appear at a considerable distance from their antecedents, often at a remove which excludes the use of zero anaphora or pronouns. Second, they constitute a stylistic alternative for the speaker anxious to avoid the ponderous repetition of full nouns or the social overtones

---

[7] Japanese examples in this and further chapters have been normalized with respect to transliteration and glossing, so their appearance may differ in details from how they were presented in the original sources. I gratefully acknowledge Zoya Efimova's kind assistance in this task.

attendant on the use of third person pronouns'[8] (Downing 1996a: 159). Classifiers appear at an average referential distance of almost four clauses in spoken discourse and of about seven clauses in written discourse (see counts in Downing 1996a: 168–179, 282). They are a relatively infrequent device in Japanese discourse; their low frequency and small contribution to reference in discourse directly follow from the generally low frequency of numeral constructions. So numeral classifiers cannot be an important referential device whatsoever.

The Japanese example of numeral classifiers suggests a refinement of the opposition between free and bound reduced referential devices. Japanese numeral classifiers are certainly not bound to the verb and are free in this sense. But they are morphologically bound to a numeral. So it might be more precise to distinguish between adverbal and non-adverbal referential devices. However, I prefer to keep to the free vs. bound distinction, understanding the latter as morphological binding to the verb.

A discussion of referential functions of classifiers is found in Aikhenvald (2000: 329ff.). Aikhenvald concludes that 'all classifier types are used as anaphoric pronouns and as participant tracking devices' (Aikhenvald 2000: 333). As we will see in Chapter 8, section 8.3, the conjunction *and* in this formulation should be replaced by *or*, as many linguistic elements Aikhenvald calls classifiers, for example noun class morphemes/features and verbal classifiers, do not refer themselves but aid the referential process by telling concurrently activated referents apart, that is, qualify as 'participant tracking devices'.

Even though classifiers can be effectively used for referential purposes, an in-depth language-specific analysis makes it unlikely that this is what they exist for in the respective languages. An interesting insight into the functions of classifiers is offered by Grinevald Craig (1986). This is a study of the function of classifiers in Jakaltek – a language that, as we have seen, uses classifiers as referential devices extensively. The conclusion that Grinevald Craig arrives at, at the end of her ethnocultural analysis is that 'the Jacaltec noun classifier system encompasses all aspects of the traditional Jacaltec life. ... They are enough in number to produce together a very realistic picture of the Jacaltec culture as a whole' (Grinevald Craig 1986: 287). Wilkins (2000, esp. p. 159), discussing the data of Arrernte (Pama-Nyungan, central Australia), demonstrates that a language that possesses an elaborate system of classifiers may use them not for referential purposes but for expressing the language speakers' cultural worldview. Classifiers are thus not a dedicated referential device; they are rather

---

[8] By third person pronouns Downing means what is more cautiously treated as social status nouns; see subsection 4.2.3.

drafted for this role in languages that lack or have a limited use of third person pronouns.

Various researchers have pointed out that classifiers typically evolve from nouns that gradually undergo a generalization and bleaching of their lexical meaning. For example, Mithun (1986b: 388) stated that native American 'classificatory stems begin life as nouns' and demonstrated several stages in grammaticalization of American bound classifiers, beginning from noun incorporation and ending with a closed-class system of fully grammaticalized affixes in the verb of Cherokee (Iroquoian, Oklahoma and North Carolina, USA). Corbett (1991: 311), in his discussion of classifiers, concluded that 'there is ample evidence that they come from nouns'. This naturally brings us to the next and final category of marginal reduced referential devices.

4.2.3 Social status nouns

In some languages nouns can be used as reduced referential devices; 'reduced' in this case means that the lexical meaning of a noun is bleached rather than fully-fledged. Such usage is particularly typical of nouns denoting human beings, and the area where such phenomena are widely spread is East and Southeast Asia. An example of a language using this kind of device is Vietnamese. Consider the following example from a tale:

(4.9) Vietnamese (Austro-Asiatic, Vietnam; Daley 1998: 147–148)
    a. ông liền   cỡi ngựa về   triều-đình
       KIN act.immediately ride horse return royal.court
    b. tâu   lại   với   Vua về   cậu bé   nhà   quê
       address again toward King about KIN small dwelling countryside
       đó
       that
       'The gentleman immediately rode his horse back to the royal court and addressed the king again about that young country boy'

In this example two relevant nouns are used (glossed KIN, following the terminology of Daley) as reduced referential devices. These are originally kinship terms; when talking about relatives, *ông* means 'grandfather', *cậu* means 'maternal uncle' (see Đình-Hoà 1997: 127). However, in this example they function not as kinship terms but as more general social status words, indicating an older male person and someone from a younger generation. Therefore, a certain degree of semantic bleaching, or reduction, is clearly in place. However, lexical overtones in their semantics are still there, so semantically they are different from what are pronouns in most languages. In (4.9), both referents are highly activated by the beginning of this excerpt as it was immediately preceded by a description of the gentleman's conversation with the boy. According to counts of Daley (1998: 65), social status terms constitute 8% of referential expressions in a narrative sample.

This kind of quasi-pronominal usage of social status nouns is often discussed in the literature on pronouns and personal markers; see the discussion of East and Southeast Asian languages in Siewierska (2004: 12–13, 228'ff'.). This usage of social status nouns is closely related to the expression of politeness, or deference, typical of East and Southeast Asian languages; see 8.4.2.

Social status nouns in Vietnamese and other languages of the area are rather rich in their repertoire. Vietnamese has a couple of dozens social status nouns that can be used in a quasi-pronominal way. The choice is guided by social hierarchical relations between the speaker and the addressee or between the speaker and the intended referent. Social status nouns can be used to refer to various persons, including locutors; cf. the discussion of various kinds of 'substitutes' in the Vietnamese grammar by Đình-Hoà (1997: 124ff.).

Some languages of East and Southeast Asia have developed referential devices that are still more similar to pronouns of other languages than the Vietnamese social status terms. Examples of these are Japanese *kare* and *kanojo* that are often described simply as third person pronouns – 'he' and 'she' respectively. Some authors, however, argue that these two words are qualitatively different from English or Mandarin Chinese third person pronouns, cannot be used in anaphoric contexts, and should be treated as nouns (Takubo and Kinsui 1997). Such discrepancies and similar ones suggest that it is hardly possible to draw as clear a line between pronouns and social status terms as some authors suggest. Consider the following by Simon and Wiese (2002: 4): 'In contrast to a nominal like *a man*, a pronoun like *he* does not provide such a conceptual representation by virtue of its descriptive content, but contributes the respective conceptual distinctions via grammatical features that draw on a morpho-semantic paradigm'. As Siewierska (2004: 10) rightly points out, even English third person pronouns, often taken as token pronouns, display nominal usages as in *He who strives wins* or *That's a she*. Such usages, as well as the properties of the Japanese alleged third person pronouns, render Simon and Wiese's clear-cut paradigmatic distinction between descriptive content and grammatical features unviable. From my perspective, much more viable is another semantic distinction: the distinction between full and reduced referential devices that is not lexicon-based but rather discourse-use-based. In this sense, prototypical pronouns are prototypical reduced referential devices while social status nouns, when semantically reduced, are marginal reduced referential devices.

Of course, there are languages in which erstwhile social status terms have historically developed into normal pronouns. For discussions of such evolution refer to Siewierska (2004: 247–249), Bhat (2004: 30–31, 111–112). Examples are found not only in East and Southeast Asia but also in other parts of the world, mostly in the Americas but occasionally also in Africa and Europe (examples such as the Polish pronoun *pan*, originally the noun meaning 'lord, master').

In this subsection we have looked only at human reference. The reason is that social status nouns are by far the most common kinds of nouns that display a quasi-pronominal usage cross-linguistically. Albeit more rarely, other nouns occasionally display a quasi-pronominal usage or even develop into genuine third person pronouns. Examples include a range of nouns, from human to non-human, especially 'person', 'man', 'woman', 'body', 'hand', 'thing'; see Helmbrecht (2004: 237–239, 384–387, Siewierska 2004: 248).

4.2.4 *Pronouns vs. their functional analogues*

From this brief outline of marginal reduced referential devices – demonstratives, classifiers, and social status nouns – the reader may have noticed that the languages of the same macroarea (East and Southeast Asia and, to some extent, adjacent regions) and even specifically the same languages, occurred more than once during this discussion. In particular, Japanese figured in all three subsections. This fact needs to be explored systematically, but by way of a preliminary observation it appears this is not a mere coincidence. East and Southeast Asia has been discussed in Chapter 3 as the distinct zero reference area. Many languages in this part of the world lack dedicated personal pronouns. Evidently, in this situation languages tend to draft or recycle various cousin devices that can be used as pronouns' substitutes, as overt reduced referential devices. The absence of dedicated pronouns makes these marginal devices quite visible in the respective languages. They cannot compete in their significance in discourse with zero reference but can be useful in filling various functional gaps on certain occasions. The same marginal devices, especially demonstratives, are also used as referential troubleshooters in languages that do use genuine pronouns, but there they have a lesser visibility against the background of dedicated overt pronouns.

In addition to demonstratives, classifiers, and nouns, there also exist several kinds of referential devices that are typically distinguished from third person pronouns in language-specific traditions but in fact are inherently very similar to them. These devices, including logophoric pronouns, long-distance reflexives, fourth person pronouns and several others, are just like third person pronouns in that they are, first, overt and, second, lexically reduced; in fact, they can often be understood as subcategories within personal pronouns. They differ from third person pronouns in that they are more specialized, appear in more restricted ranges of contexts. They also function in a certain distribution with neutral third person pronouns. All of these specialized devices apply to only a part of possible referents, to the exclusion of others. In this sense they are based on some sorting of referents, can discriminate between two or more concurrently activated referents and can thus participate in preventing referential conflicts. For this reason they will be considered at some length in Chapter 8 as referential aids.

4.3 Double reference pronouns

In Chapter 3 (subsection 3.3.2), we have seen instances in which more than one referential device in a clause corresponds to one and the same referent; see Figure 3.4. The reverse situation occurs as well in several languages of the world. This happens when one and the same pronominal morpheme simultaneously encodes two referents; such forms are called fused, or compound, or portmanteau pronouns; cf. Cysouw (2003: Appendix A). Consider examples from Dan-Gwèètaa (Mande, Ivory Coast)[9]:

(4.10) Dan-Gwèètaa (Mande, Ivory Coast; Valentin Vydrine, personal communication)
Gbàtò yà   à̏   gó   Tīà gɔ̀.
Gbato 3SG.PF 3SG.NSUBJ sell Tia to
'Gbato sold it (for example, a goat) to Tia'

(4.11) Dan-Gwèètaa (Mande, Ivory Coast; Valentin Vydrine, personal communication)
dɛ̀ ɤ́   pā gbà̰ pɛ́pɛ́ nū   dēbʌ̀nʌ́ dɛ̀ <...>
that 3SG.CJT thing all every give.CJT woman in.front
'When he gave away all the things to the woman <...>'

(4.12) Dan-Gwèètaa (Mande, Ivory Coast; Valentin Vydrine, personal communication)
a. Zà̰ yáá   yɤ́ɤ̏ kā,
   Jean 3SG.NEG.PRES shame do

---

[9] I thank Valentin Vydrine for his indefatigable willingness to discuss Dan-Gwèètaa and other Mande languages with me over the years.

b. yɤ̋   blúù ɓɛ̄ dō tò   dɤ̋
   3SG.NEUT   bread loaf one keep.NEUT so

c. ɤ̰̋'   wò   ɤ̄   kò tà
   3SG.CJT:3SG.NSUBJ[10]   expose 3SG.REFL hand in

d. ɤ̰'   ɓɤ̋ <...>
   3SG.CJT:3SG.NSUBJ   eat
   'Jean is shameless, he sets out a whole bread keeping it in his hand and eats it <...>'

Dan-Gwèètaa has tenacious free subject pronouns; see (4.10) where the subject pronoun cooccurs with the subject full NP. In addition, subject pronouns are marked for clause aspectual construction type (see section 4.4); cf. the perfect form *yà* of the third person singular subject pronoun in (4.10) or the so-called conjoint form *ɤ́* in (4.11), etc. An example of a non-subject third person singular pronoun *à* appears in (4.10). When both the subject and the object referents are activated, the two corresponding pronouns fuse, giving rise to a portmanteau form. Two examples of this kind can be seen in (4.12c, d): instead of two separate pronouns – the joint subject pronoun *ɤ́* and the non-subject pronoun *à* – a single pronominal form *ɤ̰̋'* occurs, referring simultaneously to 'Jean' and 'the bread'. This situation of double reference of a single pronoun is graphically represented in Figure 4.1.

In Dan-Gwèètaa, the double-referring portmanteau pronouns, such as *ɤ̰̋'*, can theoretically be described as bimorphemic and explained by a

Referents (plane of thought)

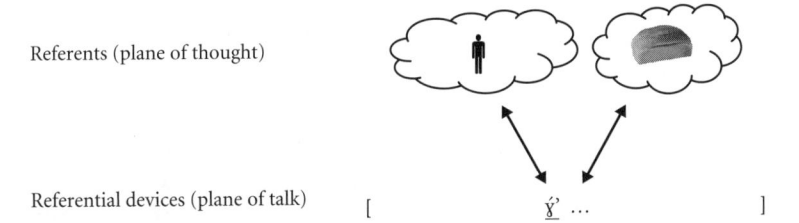

Referential devices (plane of talk)   [ɤ̰̋' ...   ]

FIGURE 4.1. Double linking of the portmanteau Dan-Gwèètaa pronoun, referring to both 'Jean' and 'the bread', examples (4.12c, d)

---

[10] In the glosses, I mark double reference by means of a colon.

morphophonemic rule. The vocalic base ɩ̀ actually is the subject pronoun (cf. (4.11)), and the ultralow tone, conveyed by the symbol `, is an allomorph of the object pronoun à (Valentin Vydrine, personal communication). In some other languages the specific morphemes corresponding to two distinct pronouns and, accordingly, to two distinct referents, are not so directly discernible. For example, in Yaouré, another Mande language of Ivory Coast, the first person singular subject pronoun is ā̄, the third person singular object pronoun is à, while the combination of these looks like mā̄à (Hopkins 1986: 196) see (4.13).

(4.13) Yaouré (Mande, Ivory Coast; Hopkins 1986: 199)
mā̄à   blù   jí
1SG.SUBJ:3SG.OBJ sister see.COMPL
'I saw his sister'

Note that in this example the non-subject pronoun refers not to a clause participant but to a clause participant's possessor. So even non-argumental referents can be involved in forming compound pronouns.

Still more idiosyncratic compound forms are found in bound pronoun languages. In a sketch of Seneca (Iroquoian, New York State, USA) Chafe (1996: 563) cites a table of pronominal prefixes in a reconstructed (abstract morphophonemic) form, and many of them display syncretism. For example, the Agentive third person singular feminine bound pronoun is ye-, and the Patientive third person singular feminine bound pronoun is (ya)ko-. The combination ('she her') looks like yǫtat(e)- which does not analyse clearly into two components. Another example of compound bound pronouns is provided by Alutor, a Chukchi-Koryakan language of Kamchatka, Russia. The Alutor verb contains Agentive and Patientive pronominal markers, and for certain person–number combinations portmanteau forms are used, in particular -tki (2PL.A:3.P) and -ni (3SG.A:3.P) (A. E. Kibrik et al. 2000: 217).

A somewhat more intricate instance, not easily lending itself to an obvious interpretation, is provided by Navajo. In this language, third person bound pronouns are most often zero, contrasting to non-zero affixes in locutor reference. Among the core argument third person pronouns,[11] the only non-zero ones appear in the accusative position, but only if the nominative argument is a third person as well. This is summarized in Table 4.1.
The three options shown in Table 4.1 are illustrated by the following examples.

---

[11] This extends only to those bound pronouns that are traditionally treated as third person as such. There exist more marked varieties of the third person, such as the so-called fourth person pronoun ji- that we saw in example (4.2) above.

TABLE 4.1. Navajo third person bound pronouns

Nominative	Accusative	
∅-	A first or second person pronoun appears in the nominative position	∅-
	A third person pronoun appears in the nominative position	yi-

(4.14) Navajo (Na-Dene, Southwest of the USA)
  i. shi-∅-ni-łk'eʳ
     1SG.ACC-3.NOM-PREF-cool
     'S/he is cooling me down'
  ii. ∅-ni-sh-k'eʳ   [sh-k'eʳ < sh-łk'eʳ]
      3.ACC-PREF-1SG.NOM-cool
      'I am cooling him/her down'
  iii. yi-∅-ni-łk'eʳ
       33.ACC-3.NOM-PREF-cool
       'S/he is cooling him/her down'

The example in (4.14iii) contains the bound pronoun *yi-* that appears in the accusative morphological position and thus belongs to the paradigm of accusative pronouns. Therefore, it should be considered on a par with the first person singular *shi-* as in (4.14i). On the other hand, this prefix does say something about the Principal of the clause, specifically that it is a third person; this fact is rendered by the '33.ACC' gloss[12] in (4.14iii). So one may argue that this is actually a compound pronoun referring simultaneously to two arguments. Interestingly, this pattern is extended to oblique participants. These are also coded by bound pronouns, prefixed to preverbs specifying a semantic relation and placed in front of the verb. When a first or second person appears in the nominative position, the oblique third person bound pronoun is *bi-*, and when a third person appears in the nominative position, the oblique pronoun is *yi-*.

(4.15) Navajo (Na-Dene, Southwest of the USA)

---

[12] This is an abbreviated gloss. The complete gloss could have looked as follows: 3.ACC:3.NOM.

i. bi-ch'į́ʔ   yá-sh-tiʔ   [sh-tiʔ < sh-łtiʔ]
3.OBL-toward   PREF-1SG.NOM-speak
'I am talking to him/her'

ii. yi-ch'į́ʔ   yá-ø-łtiʔ
33.OBL-toward   PREF-3.NOM-speak
'S/he is talking to him/her'

If we accept that the third person accusative pronoun is double-referring in (4.14iii), then we must accept the same thing for the formally identical oblique pronoun in (4.15ii). It seems a bit too far-reaching to suggest that a pronoun appearing as an affix on a preverb is the referential device evoking the clause's Principal. So, taking everything into account, a more moderate treatment is preferable, according to which Navajo accusative and oblique pronouns are chosen in accordance with the Principal's person, but do not refer to the Principal themselves. The Navajo example is the closest that I am familiar with to alleged compound pronouns involving oblique participants.

Bound double reference pronouns are not particularly frequent cross-linguistically, but they are not negligible either. In Siewierska's (2005c) study of verbal person 20 languages out of 379 in the sample have the Agentive and Patientive person markers fused[13]. The majority of these languages are found in the Americas, which is predictable in view of the fact that the Americas is the most bound-pronominal macroarea. No instances from Oceania or Asia are found in Siewierska's sample; but cf. the example of Alutor of Kamchatka cited above.

4.4 Pronouns marked for clausal categories

One particularly interesting aspect of pronominal systems that still awaits a comprehensive typological (and theoretical) study is the range of grammatical and/or semantic categories that can be expressed together with pronominal words or morphemes. Besides the obvious categories of person, number,

---

[13] Here is the full list of languages: North America – Achumawi (Palaihnihan, northern, USA), Acoma (Keresan, New Mexico, USA), Central Yup'ik (Eskimo-Aleut, Alaska, USA), Coos (=Hanis; Coosan, Oregon, USA), Karok (Karok-Shasta, northern California, USA), Makah (Wakashan, Washington, USA), Maricopa (Yuman, Arizona, USA), Tiipay (=Jamul; Yuman, northwestern Mexico), Yurok (Algic, northern California, USA); Mesoamerica – Copainalá Zoque (Mixe-Zoque, southern Mexico); South America – Aymara (Aymaran, Bolivia, Peru), Carib (Cariban, Venezuela), Guaraní (Tupian, Paraguay), Jaqaru (Aymaran, Peru); Australia – Gooniyandi (Bunaban, northwestern Australia), Nunggubuyu (Gunwinyguan, northern Australia), Wardaman (Gunwinyguan, northern Australia); Europe – Hungarian (Uralic, Hungary); Africa – Kunama (isolate, Eritrea), Maba (Maban, Chad) (both 'Nilo-Saharan').

gender (discussed in Chapter 8), and case, in some languages a range of clausal categories is expressed on free pronouns, such as aspect, tense, modality, and polarity. Examples of this kind were cited in examples (4.10)–(4.12) from Dan-Gwèètaa, a Mande language of Ivory Coast. In these examples four variants of the third person subject (Principal) pronoun appeared:

- yà – perfect (4.10)
- ɣ̀ – conjoint (a type of clause construction indicating that the given clause is closely related to another clause, Vydrine in preparation) (4.11), (4.12c, d)
- yáa – negative present (4.12a)
- yɣ̀ – neutral aspect (4.12b).

According to Vydrine (2006), there are five more types of personal subject pronouns in Dan-Gwèètaa, including subjunctive, prohibitive, negative past, imperative, and prospective. In Dan-Gwèètaa the expression of reference and clausal categories is fusional: it is not always possible to discern separate morphemes responsible for 'third person' and particular clausal categories. In other languages compounds of pronominal and clausal categories are more agglutinative; I do not here pursue this fusional vs. agglutinative distinction in any depth, although it is certainly of interest. The Dan-Gwèètaa system of compounding reference and clausal categories also displays the following two properties:

- expression of clausal categories is found on free pronouns.
- expression of clausal categories is attested on Principal pronouns only.

None of these properties is universal for the pronouns marked for clausal categories. As for the first property, there are enough examples of bound pronouns marked for clausal categories (provided in this section below). As for the second property, it is almost universal; a rare counterexample is provided by Nias, a western Malayo-Polynesian language of Sumatra. Nias uses reference plus realis mode compounds only in Agentive pronouns. A bound mode-marked Agentive pronoun and a free non-mode-marked Absolutive pronoun can be seen in the following examples:

(4.16)   Nias (Austronesian, islands west of Sumatra, Indonesia; Brown 2003: 5)
    i. la-tolo   ndrao
       3PL.REAL-help   1SG.ABS
       'They helped me'
    ii. mofanö   ira
       leave   3PL.ABS
       'They left'

At first sight, the systems compounding reference and clausal categories seem bizarre. Why would a language care to express clausal categories on Principal pronouns rather than on the verb, the clause's head? In the rest of this section I will demonstrate that the Dan-Gwèètaa system is not so rare and exotic, and similar facts are found in more familiar languages.

It is not self-evident that the above-cited Dan-Gwèètaa forms are pronouns inflected for clausal categories. An opposite interpretation can be entertained: they might be aspect/tense/modality/polarity auxiliaries inflected for person. However, Valentin Vydrine (personal communication, 2008) informed me that such treatment would be counterintuitive as it presupposes the existence of clauses with zero subjects, which goes against the very basics of Southern Mande grammar.[14]

Pronouns expressing clausal categories are widely attested not only in Mande languages (Vydrine 2006) but in other African families; cf. Bonhoff (1986) on Dii (Adamawa-Ubangi, Cameroon) and Burquest 1986 on Chadic; see also the Hausa (Chadic, Afro-Asiatic, West Africa) example (3.8). Similar facts are found in different parts of the world. For example, in Xerente (Macro-Ge, Brazil) nominative pronouns express evidentiality, aspect, and intensiveness (Popovich 1986: 366). A number of Oceanic languages (Austronesian) express tense and modality on nominative pronouns; see Hutchisson (1986) on Sursurunga (Meso-Melanesian Oceanic, Austronesian, New Ireland, Papua New Guinea), Crowley (2002) on Gela (Southeast Solomonic Oceanic, Austronesian, Solomon Islands). Similar phenomena are attested among Papuan languages; see Helmbrecht (2004: 421–422). For a preliminary cross-linguistic discussion see Nordlinger and Sadler (2000).

In other languages, however, quite similar facts are interpreted differently. For example, consider Spanish *ha comido* 'he/she has eaten'. Is the element *ha*, indicating simultaneously third person reference and tense-aspect, so different from the Dan-Gwèètaa pronouns cited above? Note that this element is contrasted to other elements, differing either in person, as in *has comido* 'you have eaten', or in tense-aspect, as in *había comido* 'he/she had eaten'. Despite obvious parallelism, elements *ha, has, había* etc. are treated not as pronouns expressing tense-aspect but as auxiliaries inflected for person. Indeed, the differences are real, as we see in forms such as *había* that they are structurally

---

[14] In fact, in a later personal communication (March 2010) Valentin Vydrine pointed out that he eventually changed his interpretation and now prefers to treat reference/clausal compounds as personal auxiliaries; see Vydrine (2010). The very fact of this change demonstrates that this interpretational problem is rather acute, and often probably irresolvable. Vydrine also pointed out that genuine pronouns, marked for clausal categories, are found in other Mande languages, closely related to Dan-Gwèètaa, including Guro (Vydrine 2005) and Tura (Vydrine 2010).

verbs and therefore should preferably be interpreted as being fundamentally verbal rather than pronominal. Still differences between Dan-Gwèètaa and Spanish are more of a matter of degree than a binary opposition, and the whole domain of coexpression of reference and clausal categories clearly calls for a thorough study.

Another language in which compounds of referential and clausal meanings are found is Warlpiri (Pama-Nyungan, central Australia). In Warlpiri clausal morphemes (treated as auxiliaries) occur in one morphological complex with pronominal morphemes; both core arguments can be represented in such complexes, for example:

(4.17) Warlpiri (Pama-Nyungan, central Australia; Hale 1983: 18)
maliki-jarra-rlu ka-pala-jana puluku-patu wajilipi-nyi
dog-DU-ERG PRES-3DU.NOM-3PL.ACC bullock-PL.NOM chase-NPAST
'The two dogs are chasing the several bullocks'

Warlpiri in fact is one of the most widely discussed languages with bound pronouns, largely due to the work of Kenneth Hale (particularly Hale 1983). For example, in Andrews (1985: 75) Warlpiri evidence was provided as the only illustration of 'cross-referencing' of arguments outside of NPs. But the fact is that the Warlpiri pattern is very different from typical bound pronoun languages such as Abkhaz, see section 3.3, in which bound pronouns are a part of the synthetic verb word. In contrast, in Warlpiri the lexical verb is separated from the auxiliary representing tense (as well as polarity), but the auxiliary is combined in one word with pronominal morphemes.

What are the reasons for treating Warlpiri pronoun-clausal compounds as auxiliaries inflected for two persons rather than pronominal compounds inflected for tense? Probably there are language-internal reasons for this interpretation. It should be noted, however, that the mere fact of having two pronominal morphemes in compounds (such as *ka-pala-jana*) does not automatically entail this interpretation. Recall bipronominal compounds of many Mande languages discussed in the previous section. They can be further complicated by a clausal meaning; cf. the Dan-Gwèètaa compound *ɏ̀* in (4.12c, d) that has three semantic components in it (third person singular subject; conjoint construction; third person object). Obviously, abstracting away from the fusion vs. agglutination distinction, this is very much like the Warlpiri example. So, once again, detection of the basic grammatical nature of pronominal-clausal compounds is an important interpretational problem. For the time being, Dan-Gwèètaa, Spanish, and Warlpiri pronominal-clausal compounds can be considered one broad category.

The case of Warlpiri raises a still more important interpretational problem. It calls into question the validity of the free vs. bound pronoun distinction elaborated in Chapter 3. Indeed, Warlpiri pronominal morphemes, such as -*jana* in (4.17), are free with respect to the verb. But they are bound with respect to the tense marker. In the discussion in Chapter 3 I implicitly presupposed that pronouns that stand free with respect to the verb stem must also be free with respect to categories such as tense that is a textbook example of a verb-marked category. However, languages may express some (as Spanish) or even all (Warlpiri) of the clausal meanings outside the verb. Out of 1,062 languages in Dryer's (2005c) sample 139, that is 13%, do not have any tense-aspect inflection.

In order to keep things sufficiently simple, I am not going to revise the free vs. bound pronoun distinction at this point. I will consider pronominal elements such as those in Dan-Gwèètaa and Warlpiri free, as they occur separately from the lexical verb. However, I offer a brief outline of a three-way typology that may turn out useful in future research. Let us consider three types of meanings typically expressed in a clause: verb lexical meaning conveyed by the root (with or without concomitant derivational affixes); clausal categories (tense in the first place, but also aspect, modality, evidentiality, polarity, etc.); and reference. Table 4.2 represents all five logically conceivable values of the following parameter: are these three kinds of meanings conveyed in a given language within one morphological word or separately? Accordingly, five theoretical language types are posited. In type 1, purely analytic, all three kinds of meanings are morphologically separate. In type 5, polysynthetic, all three are within the verb word, Types 2 to 4 represent three pairwise combinations of the meanings, and these correspond to languages of a moderate degree of synthesis.[15]

Type 1 analytic languages, such as Lyélé (see discussion in section 3.2; further examples in Showalter 1986) and Mandarin Chinese (see example (5.1) below) keep both reduced referential devices and tense markers morphologically separate from verb stems. Contrariwise, type 5 polysynthetic languages express all three kinds of meaning in morphological complexes – words; see the above discussions of Navajo (section 3.1) and Abkhaz (section 3.3). Among the three moderately synthetic types, type 3 has just been exemplified by the data from Dan-Gwèètaa and Warlpiri: in both languages referential devices are combined with clausal categories, notwithstanding differences in fusional vs. agglutinative morphological technique

---

[15] Note that the terms 'synthetic' and 'analytic' in this discussion are not intended to characterize respective languages in their entirety. I am talking about synthetic vs. analytic strategies employed by these language only vis-à-vis the three types of meaning under discussion.

Table 4.2. Freedom vs. boundness of referential devices and clausal categories with respect to the verb in the languages of the world

Type#	Verb lexical meaning	Clausal categories	Reference	Language examples	Degree of synthesis
1	separate	separate	separate	Lyélé Mandarin	analytic
2	combined		separate	Eastern Pomo Arrernte	moderately synthetic
3	separate	combined		Dan-Gwèètaa Warlpiri	
4	combined with reference	separate	combined with verb lexical meaning	Sm'algyax	
5	combined			Abkhaz Navajo	polysynthetic

and in the interpretation of compounds as fundamentally either pronouns or auxiliaries. The remaining two types call for some additional comment.

Type 2, keeping referential devices apart from verbs inflected for tense and other clausal categories, is very familiar from northern European languages, such as German, Russian (both Indo-European) or Finnish (Uralic). All of these languages, however, are not pure representatives of type 2 as they have one element of referential marking on the verb, namely subject agreement. (As will be discussed in Chapters 6 and 7, such agreement markers also partly count as referential devices.) Purer examples of type 2 come from Arrernte or Eastern Pomo:

(4.18) Arrernte (Pama-Nyungan, central Australia; Wilkins 1988: 161)
re ikwere lhwarrpe-le pwerte nthe-ke
3SG.NOM 3SG.DAT sad-ADV money give-PAST.COMPL
'She gave the money to him sadly'

(4.19) Eastern Pomo (Pomoan, northern California, USA; McLendon 1996: 527)
mí·p̓ mí·r-al šá·k̓-·hi
he.AG she-PAT one.kill-ANT
'He killed her'

Finally, in type 4 languages verbs contain bound pronouns but not marking of clausal categories. This type can be illustrated by Sm'algyax, or Coast Tsimshian:

(4.20) Sm'algyax (Tsimshianic, southern Alaska, USA, and northern British Columbia, Canada; Beck 2002, ex. 7b, quoting from Mulder 1994: 93)
dm=t næksg-u æmi=m dzi ænoχ-t
FUT=3.ERG marry-1SG.NOM if=2SG.ERG PTCL agree-3.NOM
'He will marry me, if you agree to it'

This example is not ideal as an illustration of type 4 as it is only nominative pronouns that appear on the verb while ergative pronouns are clitics attaching to clause-initial words. (By the criteria developed in Chapter 3, clitic pronouns are free.) The important aspects of the Sm'algyax example are that, first, some referential devices appear in the verb, and second, tense morphemes are free.

It is possible to estimate the worldwide frequency of some of these language types, composing certain studies from WALS (Haspelmath et al. (eds.) 2005). Two studies are useful to this end: Siewierska (2005e) on verbal person marking and Dryer (2005c) on position of tense-aspect affixes. By far the most common is type 5: out of the 312 languages shared by the two samples, 119 languages display the combination 'both the A and P arguments' person is marked on the verb' and 'tense-aspect suffixes/prefixes/tone'. 43 languages correspond to the combination 'no person marking' and 'tense-aspect suffixes/prefixes/tone' (type 2). Type 4 is noticeably less frequent: the combination 'both the A and P arguments' person is marked on the verb' and 'no tense-aspect inflection' is found in 17 languages. Types 1 and 3 cannot be discerned: both of them correspond to the combination 'no person marking' and 'no tense-aspect inflection', and only 21 languages display this combination. Obviously, this little inquiry into language type frequency is very rough, as the features and values of the two studies only partially match the research question we are targeting. For example, 'no person marking' embraces both languages with free pronouns and with zero reference. However, the comparison provided is still useful; in particular, it indicates that in moderately synthetic languages, expression of clausal categories on the verb occurs more frequently than the consistent use of bound pronouns.

A final remark about compounds involving referential devices and clausal categories is based on the data of very familiar languages, such as Latin or Spanish. For example, in Spanish reduced reference to subjects is performed (in clauses with synthetic verbal predicates) by means of verb inflection.[16] However, personal endings convey not just reference to the subject but also the clause's tense and mood. In some instances the tense/mood morpheme

---

[16] This applies to Spanish synthetic tenses; Spanish analytic tenses, such as perfect, have been discussed earlier in this section.

can be segmentally discerned (4.21iii, iv), but sometimes they are expressed as a complete portmanteau with referential morphemes (4.21i, ii, v)[17]:

(4.21) Inflected third person singular forms of the Spanish verb *hablar* 'speak'

    i. Present   habla-ø
                           speak-PRES.3SG

    ii. Past   habl-ó
                           speak-PAST.3SG

    iii. Future   habla-r-á
                            speak-FUT-3SG

    iv. Imperfect   habla-ba-ø
                            speak-IMPF-3SG

    v. Present of the subjunctive   habl-e
                            speak-PRES.SBJV.3SG

In Indo-European linguistics, it is often supposed that the person-tense desinences originally evolved from a linear combination of a pronominal element and a tense morpheme; see e.g. Shields (1992: 16). Clearly the Indo-European pattern is very similar to Dan-Gwèètaa and Warlpiri, the only significant difference being that the reference-tense compounds are not free but bound with respect to the verb. (Note that Spanish also employs free reference-tense compounds; see discussion of Spanish analytic forms above.) This analogy demonstrates that compounding of reference and clausal categories is not as exotic and bizarre as it may seem.

4.5 Strong pronouns

As has been argued in Chapter 3 (section 3.2), free pronouns as one of the major referential devices are prosodically weak and are hardly distinguishable from clitics. However, this property exempts strong pronouns that are found in many free pronoun languages. Strong pronouns are just like weak pronouns in being lexically reduced, but they differ from the prosodic point of view. Unlike weak pronouns, strong pronouns are prosodically fully-fledged words. Segmentally they may either be identical to or differ from weak pronouns. Some branches of Indo-European languages, in particular

---

[17] Note that in Spanish and other Indo-European languages, due to their fusional morphology, tense grammemes, such as PRES or PAST, are conveyed by both personal inflections and stem allomorphs. The tense-related stem allomorphy is ignored in glosses here and henceforth.

Romance and Slavic, are known for their morphological distinction between weak (clitical) and strong forms of pronouns; see Harris and Vincent (eds.) (1997) on Romance, Franks and King (2000) on Slavic, inter alia. For example, in Spanish the dative form of the masculine third person weak pronoun is *le*, while for the strong pronoun it is *a él*. In Lyélé, cited in section 3.2 as a typical free pronoun language, morphologically more complex pronouns are attested on some occasions:

(4.22) Lyélé (Southern Gur, Burkina Faso; Showalter 1986: 209)
    i. à-myɛ
       I-EMPH
       'Who, me?'

    ii. ò   dùr,   ò-myɛ   ǹdé   o   kɛỹ   ǹdé   ò   bya
        he   run   he-EMPH   CONR   he   wife   CONR   he   children
       'He ran, he and his wife and children'

    iii. wɔ   ń-myɛ̌   ń   ju   gɔ   min
         it's   he-EMPH   he   start   field   fire
       'It was him, he lit the field fire'

In these examples regular free third person pronouns occur in default contexts, for instance *ń* in (4.22iii) appearing in the clause subject position. Also, there are strong, or 'emphatic', pronouns that are formed by adding the morpheme *-myɛ̌* (or *-myɛ́*) to regular (weak) pronouns. The emphatic pronouns are used in a variety of special situations, such as one-pronoun utterances (4.22i), coordination with full NPs (4.22ii), or the 'highlighted' position, as Showalter puts it (4.22iii). Thus a neat iconic correspondence is observed between function and form: weak pronouns appear in standard contexts, strong pronouns in specialized contexts.

Such specialized contexts are apparently universal and should not depend on a language's preferred type of reduced referential device. What do other languages do in contexts such as those illustrated in (4.22)? Some free pronoun languages, including English, use prosodic prominence rather than morphological elaboration to distinguish strong pronouns from weak ones (but cf. Table 3.1 in Chapter 3, subsection 3.2.2, and discussion there). Bound pronoun languages typically have free strong pronouns. Zero reference languages may use free strong pronouns or other free devices. I consider these three kinds of languages in the following three subsections. In the subsequent two subsections I discuss formal and functional properties of strong pronouns.

4.5.1 *Free pronoun languages without morphologically specialized strong pronouns*

Most discussions of accented English pronouns are based on constructed examples, such as this oft-cited one from Lakoff (1976):

(4.23)   Paul called Jim a Republican. Then *HE* insulted *HIM*.

(For experimental studies of this kind of structure see, inter alia, Kameyama 1999, Venditty et al. 2001.) There are not many English natural discourse resources marked for accentuation. One of them is the body of examples in Chafe (1994). It is difficult to find instances of accented pronouns among them – the vast majority of pronouns are weak. One of the rare exceptions is this (Chafe 1994: 200):

(4.24)   a. ... And hé thought,
         b. maybe the mótor was just wèaring òut,
         c. it's got so màny hóurs on it,

Well-known is Givón's (Givón 1983b: 17; 2001: Vol. I, 417ff.) suggestion that accented pronouns constitute a separate position on the coding scale – between weak pronouns and full NPs. This implies that accented pronouns occur when referents are of a medium activation. Although this issue requires a thorough study based on natural discourse data, it is much more likely that accented pronouns can be explained not by a certain activation level but by a range of special factors of a various nature. Most probably, they appear in the same kinds of contexts as strong pronouns in other language types; see subsection 4.5.4.

Since discourse-based accents of the English kind are not necessarily universal, I use a more neutral expression 'prosodic prominence' from here on. Avoiding the notion of accent as the only distinction between strong and weak pronouns is further justified because, as has been shown in Chapter 3 (Table 3.1), these two kinds of English pronouns may be segmentally different.

Interestingly, English displays some symptoms of developing more morphologically elaborate strong pronouns. In some contexts, accusative rather than nominative forms of pronouns are used. This is well established in some contexts, such as topicalization (*as for him,* ...). But the accusative forms are spreading to other positions as well, such as the position within the clause predicate (*That is him*). This phenomenon is supposed to be marginal from the point of view of prescriptive grammar, but in fact prevails in actual language usage and is nearly universal in conversational language (Biber et al. 1999: 335–336). The same situation is observed in other contexts, such as inside a nominal coordinate phrase (*him and Ed*); see Biber et al. (1999: 337). Perhaps it can be argued that English is developing the category of morphologically specialized strong pronouns, building upon the morphology of the accusative forms.

Thus English is not the extreme in the absence of dedicated strong pronouns. Russian is an example of such a language – in all possible contexts where strong pronouns might be used, the same morphological forms are employed as in weak free pronouns, but of course differing in prosodic prominence and absence of reduction. An example of weak vs. strong Russian pronouns is provided in the following

(4.25) Russian (from a corpus of Russian spoken stories, Kibrik and Podlesskaya (eds.) 2009: 622–623; transcription is simplified)
a. .. ty .. podojdi čego-to samá k nemu _
   you approach DM self to him
b. ne ón dolžen sjuda perejti,
   not he must here cross
c. a tỳ dolžna tuda perejti.
   but you must there cross
'You yourself approach him! Not he must go over here, but you must go over there.'

In line (a) two regular weak pronouns are used. They are completely unaccented, even when separated from all neighbouring words by a pause, as *ty* at the beginning of line (a). On the other hand, lines (b) and (c) contain one strong pronoun each occurring in the situation of contrastiveness. These pronouns bear their respective lines' primary accents.

When describing languages such as English and Russian, people do not usually posit strong pronouns. The reason is that in these languages prosodically prominent pronouns do not contain extra morphology compared to regular weak pronouns (if one disregards the relatively peripheral facts of English discussed above). Similarity of these two kinds of usages is particularly complete if one is hypnotized by the orthographic identity of words. However, from a discourse-oriented perspective English and Russian prosodically prominent pronouns appear as good tokens of strong pronouns as do Lyélé pronouns with the *-myě* extension. So in these kinds of languages the class of free pronouns, even if looking homogeneous, is rather heterogeneous. Strong, prosodically prominent pronouns must be viewed as a phenomenon distinct from regular weak, unaccented pronouns.

This does not necessarily imply that accented pronouns are lexemes separate from the corresponding weak pronouns. I agree with Jasinskaja et al.'s

(2007) argument that discourse-based accentuation is a relatively independent phenomenon and should not be treated in firm association with any particular verbal element. But my point is that strong occurrences of free pronouns are governed by principles that are quite different from those that apply to weak occurrences. Whereas weak occurrences are a part of the basic referential choice, strong occurrences are highly specialized; see 4.5.4. In general, prosody is just as legitimate and important an aspect of linguistic form as segmental material, and the fact that regular (weak) pronouns are inherently devoid of prosodic prominence is very significant. Adding such prominence to a pronominal word is a highly marked phenomenon and must be treated as such, even when no segmental differences are found.

To conclude, two alternative situations are observed in free pronoun languages: some of them use morphologically specialized strong pronouns (e.g. Lyélé) while others use the forms that are segmentally identical to those in weak usages, but with extra prosodic prominence (e.g. English and Russian). This difference is clearly visible, but it is secondary compared to the difference between free pronoun languages and languages relying on bound pronouns or zero reference.

4.5.2 *Strong pronouns in bound pronoun languages*

One of the clearest illustrations of strong pronouns in a bound pronoun language was provided by Schwartz and Dunnigan (1986), based on the material of Southwestern Ojibwe (Algonquian, Algic, Midwestern USA). For regular reference, this polysynthetic language employs bound pronouns contained in the verb. Strong pronouns appear in specialized contexts, such as contrastiveness. This pattern is generally observed in languages disposed to bound pronouns.

For example, Navajo relies on bound pronouns most of the time. However, in certain contexts a free pronoun may be used, for example:

(4.26) Navajo (Na-Dene, Southwest of the USA; from a story by Bernice Casaus, speaker)
bí		t'éiyá	shi-ł			ø-deez-ʔáázh
he.EMPH	only	1SG.OBL-with	3.NOM-INC.PFV-two.go
'Only him I will take with me'

Here the third person pronoun *bí* 'he/she' is used in the context of the focus particle 'only'. The context of this example was that the speaker was pointing at the person in question. The act of gestural pointing is inherently connected to prosodic prominence (see Chapter 15), and attaching prosodic prominence probably encourages the use of a free strong pronoun rather than a bound pronominal prefix. For discussions of strong pronouns in bound pronoun languages see Schwartz (1986), Helmbrecht (2004: 216ff.).

As we have seen in the case of Lyélé, those free pronoun languages that do employ morphologically distinct strong pronouns typically form them as follows: they add a certain morphological element to the corresponding weak pronoun (see various studies in Wiesemann (ed.) 1986). In bound pronoun languages, material similarity between bound and strong pronouns is often observed as well. For example, Navajo *bí* is based on the third person accusative/oblique/possessive morpheme *b(i)-*; in the strong pronoun the element *-í* is added to this base. Note, however, that the bound pronoun *b(i)-* and the strong free pronoun *bí* are not identical. As Siewierska (2004: 251ff.) justly observes, bound pronouns are often of significant antiquity, and complete identity of free and bound pronouns is not to be expected, even if the modern bound pronouns developed from erstwhile free pronouns. In some languages bound and strong free pronouns do not bear any trace of resemblance – this is for example the case in Huallaga Quechua singular pronouns of all persons (Weber 1986: 334–335).

In bound pronoun languages, two major patterns are observed regarding the relationship between bound and strong free pronouns. In some languages bound pronouns appear as bleached, sometimes quite opaque, versions of erstwhile free pronouns. For example, consider personal desinences in conservative Indo-European languages that have been and still are effectively used as referential devices (see Chapter 7). In Indo-European studies it is taken for granted that the ancient first person singular verb desinence *-m*, still visible in English *am*, is the result of grammaticalization of free pronouns with the *m-* base; cf. English *me* (see Babaev 2008: 54ff. for a recent review; Nikolaeva 2008). Likewise, the Indo-European third person singular verb desinence *-t*, as in Latin *ama-t* or Russian *ljubi-t*, both meaning 'loves', is often connected (e.g. Brugmann and Delbrück 1916: 593, Greenberg 1986: xx, Gasparov 2001: 116–117, Nikolaeva 2008) to the distal demonstrative stem *t-* whose reflexes are found in many branches of Indo-European (including English *that*) and is used as the plain third person pronoun in some languages, for example in Bulgarian *toj* 'he'.

The second kind of similarity between bound and strong free pronouns in bound pronoun languages is of a very different, perhaps opposite, kind. In such languages, modern strong free pronouns use bound pronouns as a part of their own structure. For example, in Abkhaz, strong pronouns such as *sara* 'I', *jara* 'he' and others consist of the initial element identical to the corresponding bound pronoun (*s-* '1SG', *j-* '3SG.M', etc.) and the obscure element *-ara*. These kinds of formations, often based on stems meaning 'self', 'person' or 'body', are further discussed in Siewierska (2004: 254–255). Generally, it appears that bound pronoun languages typically have dedicated strong pronouns.

4.5.3 *Strong pronouns in zero reference languages?*

Unlike free pronoun and bound pronoun languages, zero reference languages do not have any readily available morphological material that could serve as the basis for strong pronouns. Accordingly, the typical pattern found in zero reference languages is to draft some other referential devices to be employed as strong pronouns. The two languages used in Chapter 3 as representatives of the zero reference type, Japanese and Yidiny, draft demonstratives in this function; see subsection 4.2.1 above for Japanese evidence. Consider a Yidiny example:

(4.27) Yidiny (Pama-Nyungan, northeastern Australia; Dixon 1977: 188)
yiɲu   biṛmbi:rḍi   ɲinaŋ   waɲḍu:ngu
this.NOM jealousy.COMIT.NOM sit.PRES QU.H.PURP
'He is sitting feeling jealous for whom?'

Dixon does not comment on when and how demonstratives are used, but their basic use is obviously adnominal (Dixon 1977: 180ff.), and they are occasionally used in nominal positions, as example (4.27) shows. Since Yidiny is an essentially zero third person reference language, it is likely that demonstratives are used in the contexts where other languages opt for strong pronouns.

4.5.4 *Functions of strong pronouns*

In an interesting article, Schwartz (1986) explored the use of strong pronouns in five genealogically diverse languages: Spanish, Temne (Atlantic, Sierra Leone), Southwestern Ojibwe (Algonquian, Algic, Midwestern USA), Inga (Quechuan, Colombia), and Egyptian Arabic (Semitic, Afro-Asiatic, Egypt). She concluded that strong pronouns, as opposed to free weak and bound pronouns, are used in a number of cross-linguistically typical contexts. She pinpoints several recurring functions of strong pronouns in the explored languages. The distinguishing function is relevant in situations where default, in particular bound, pronouns are underdifferentiated for person. For example, in Spanish strong subject pronouns are used more often in combination with verb forms that are ambiguous between first and third person (Schwartz 1986: 411). Another context of strong pronoun use is related to a syntactic pressure: when a speaker needs to express a conjunction of an activated and a non-activated referent, he/she often uses a marked strong pronoun as a member of the coordinate construction in order to ensure syntactic commensurability of two expressions being conjoined; cf. the Lyélé example (4.22ii) above. The following large group of contexts can be described with the cover term 'focus', including questions and answers to questions, clefting (or language-specific analogues), topicalization, contexts of focusing particles such as 'only'; see the Lyélé examples (4.22i, iii); Navajo example (4.26). Related to this is the contrastive use, such as in the Russian example (4.25). Other functions discussed by Schwartz are the so-called affective uses and switch-subject.

Markus (2007) has undertaken a systematic study of strong pronouns in Athabaskan languages of North America that are generally disposed to bound pronouns. Many functions she found actually coincide with those identified by Schwartz (1986). Several additions include: verbless clauses that do not provide a host for using a bound pronoun; elliptical clauses (see the strong first person pronoun in example (4.28) from the Hare dialect of Slave, an Athabaskan language of Canada); afterthoughts; second person pronouns used for address. See also Mithun (2007) for a discussion of strong pronoun uses in another bound pronoun, polysynthetic language – Mohawk (Iroquoian, Southeastern Canada, New York State, USA).

(4.28) Slave (Na-Dene, Canada; Rice 1989: 1071)
beka?uht'ée   yeniwę   seni   w'ila
3SG.OPT.cook   3.want   1SG.EMPH and
'He wants to cook and so do I'

It is important to stress that the contexts for the use of strong pronouns do not depend on the character of the major (weak) referential device. Languages with dominance of free (weak) pronouns employ strong pronouns in situations similar to those registered in bound pronoun languages. An interesting case is reported by Zaliznjak (1995: 150–153) who reported extensive lists of contexts in which Old Russian strong pronouns were used, first considering the object and then the subject position. Both lists have much in common, although the basic object pronouns were free and subject pronouns bound (person inflections).

Not all contexts of strong pronoun use are readily captured even by extended lists of functions. Authors of language descriptions often notice strong pronoun uses that can be accounted for neither by structural requirements (such as coordination) nor by semantic concerns, such as focus or contrastiveness. Various wordings are used to express this observation. For example, in Godié, a Kru language of Ivory Coast, strong pronouns rather than regular weak free pronouns are used not only under obvious emphasis but also in 'slightly emphatic' contexts (Marchese 1986: 225, 242–243). In his description of the bound pronoun language Abkhaz (Abkhaz-Adyghean, Abkhazia) Hewitt (1979) demonstrated that strong pronouns occur under emphasis (pp. 155–156), in answers to who-questions (p. 156), in 'pseudocleft' constructions 'It's me who ...' (p. 156), and for certain formal reasons (some postpositions require a free pronoun, p. 155). However, in reply to the Comrie-Smith questionnaire's question 'Do free pronouns occur in non-contrastive non-emphatic contexts?' Hewitt says 'they may do so' (p. 155) and provides an example. Mithun (2007) demonstrated that in Mohawk (Iroquoian) there is a significant number of strong pronouns in discourse that are not easily explained by emphasis or contrastiveness; she describes them as 'mildly contrastive' (personal communication, 28.12.2006). Chafe (1994: 87) remarks that in his corpus of conversational English there are fairly numerous instances of accented first person pronouns, such as this:

(4.29)   Í got to go to have a tálk with em.

Chafe finds no other way to explain such examples but to hypothesize that the speaker referent occasionally gets somewhat deactivated for the addressee, as the speaker assesses his/her state of mind, and the speakers, by using an accented pronoun, are 'bringing the ideas of themselves back into the active consciousness of the listeners' (Chafe 1994: 87). Turk (2007) explored the English first person singular accented pronouns and proposed that they may result from the process of disaggregation – the speaker's intention to separate him/herself from the other activated referents, including the addressee or third persons. Apparently, there are a great variety of discourse conditions leading to the use of strong pronouns.

4.5.5 *Frequency of strong pronouns*

Most of the information on strong pronouns is anecdotal; we know that they exist in languages, but how important are they in discourse? This can be assessed by looking into their frequency in discourse corpora. A good corpus to take advantage of is the Romance corpus of Cresti and Moneglia (eds.) (2005). Let us have a look at the frequency of Spanish strong third person singular subject pronouns *él* (masculine) and *ella* (feminine), as well as the first person singular *yo*. As Spanish uses bound subject pronouns (personal desinences on the verb) as the main reduced referential device, strong pronouns can be expected to occur only occasionally. It is important to know not merely sheer numbers but the proportion of strong subject pronouns to all subject pronouns, including personal desinences. However, it is difficult to extract morphological information from a relatively large body of discourse, so

TABLE 4.3. Number of strong subject pronouns in Spanish, as compared to weak subject pronouns in French. Conversational discourse samples are used (around 4,500 words each) from Cresti and Moneglia (eds.) (2005)

	Spanish	French[18]
Third person singular	1	147
First person singular	47	175

a different method is needed. In order to estimate the expected number of subject references, I use a comparable French discourse as a baseline.

In spoken French, subject pronouns *il* (third person singular masculine), *elle* (third person singular feminine), *je* (first person singular), even though cognate to the respective Spanish forms, are of a very different nature. In the dominant use, they are weak, tenacious, and arguably even bound; see discussion in Chapter 7, subsection 7.3.3. They are easily searchable, and their quantity can be used for an estimate of the expected number of subject references in a given amount of discourse. The Spanish and French discourses analysed comprise around 4,500 words each. Both belong to the 'family/private conversation' discourse type, as the corpus authors label them.

The most striking fact following from Table 4.3 is the conspicuous near-absence of strong third person pronouns in Spanish. Assuming that there is a comparable number of reduced third person subjects in Spanish conversation as in French, only once out of about 150 instances does a context occur that prompts the speaker to use a strong subject third person pronoun.[19] The single such context that was found is contrastive, or at least parallel, and it also contains another strong pronoun, second person singular:

(4.30) Spanish (spoken) (Cresti and Moneglia (eds.) 2005, conversation 'Las muelas', code efamcv06)
<u>ella</u> nos dij-o lo que <u>tú</u> nos ha-s dicho
she us tell-PAST.3SG it that you us AUX-2SG tell.PARTIC
'Shé told us what yòu have told us'

---

[18] Of course, non-referential usages of *il* in expressions such as *il y a* 'there is', *il faut* 'one should', etc., were excluded from the counts. Non-subject uses, such as *pour elle* 'for her' were also excluded. (The same policy would be applied to Spanish if such contexts were found.) For the first person singular, both *je* and *j'* were included.

[19] I have also tested spoken monologue discourses from the same multilingual corpus, and there the turnout of Spanish strong third person pronouns was more significant. In about the same amount of discourse (4,500 words) 11 instances of such pronouns occurred in Spanish, as compared to 37 pronouns in French.

The second important observation following from Table 4.3 is that strong first person singular pronouns occur vastly more often than third person pronouns. Again, if it is permissible to use the analogous French discourse as a baseline, about every fourth reference to the speaker is strong (47 constitutes about 27% of 175); see also the earlier similar results reported by Schwartz (1986: 407–414). In fact, a more accurate estimate is possible if one takes into account 31 usages of *moi*, the French first person singular strong pronoun. The overall number of French weak and strong subject pronouns is 175+31=206. 47 Spanish strong subject pronouns make about 23% of this overall number.

Similar observations can be made about Russian. As was mentioned in Chapter 3, subsection 3.2.2, in the Russian spoken corpus 'Night dream stories' (Kibrik and Podlesskaya (eds.) 2009), nominative third person pronouns are accented in one quarter of all occurrences, and accusative pronouns in 13% of all occurrences. As for the first person singular pronouns, the share of accented usages is significantly greater: 50% for the nominative form (*ja*) and 20% for the accusative form (*menja*). Overall, there is converging evidence that pronominal reference is strong more frequently in the first person than in the third person.

Hopefully, future research will tell us whether it is 'slight emphasis' or partial deactivation or both that is responsible for numerous strong first person pronouns, or, perhaps, the need to disambiguate between homophonous first and third person forms (Helmbrecht 2004: 226). In the domain of third person reference that is the main focus of this book it seems warranted to conclude that strong pronouns are a peripheral phenomenon in discourse reference.

Summary

In this chapter I have considered several issues in the typology of pronouns, that is overt reduced referential devices. Since the most basic parameters of this typology, such as the categories of person and number/membership have been subject to detailed study in recent literature, I concentrated on more complicated issues, including functional analogues of personal pronouns, double reference pronouns, marking of clausal categories on pronouns, and the structure and use of strong pronouns.

Languages employ several kinds of referential devices that are distinct from personal pronouns but are similar in function; these can be called marginal referential devices. Closely related to third person pronouns are demonstratives; they are a common diachronic source for third person pronouns. In languages without dedicated third person pronouns the demonstrative vs. pronoun distinction is blurred. Demonstratives can generally be characterized as troubleshooters of referential choice. The second kind of marginal reduced referential devices are classifiers – function words that canonically attach to nouns in noun phrases but are also used by themselves. The third kind are social status nouns, functioning in a pronominal fashion in languages without dedicated pronouns. All three kinds of marginal reduced referential devices are particularly common in the languages of East and Southeast Asia, which is quite predictable as many of these languages lack canonical pronouns.

Just as two referential devices in conjunction may perform one act of reference, it is also possible that one portmanteau pronominal form evokes two referents simultaneously. This kind of double reference pronoun can be both free and bound. The former are common in Africa, the latter in the Americas.

For a number of languages from Africa, South America, Australia, and Oceania a seemingly exotic pattern has been attested: marking of clausal categories, including tense, aspect, mode, polarity, etc., on pronominal words. Similar compounds are also attested as bound morphemes. This pattern is actually quite common cross-linguistically, and the familiar personal desinences of conservative Indo-European languages often also encode clausal categories, especially tense, and thus should be viewed as an instantiation of the same phenomenon. A typology of freedom vs. boundness of referential devices and clausal categories with respect to the verb has been proposed, and it has been shown that all five logically conceivable values of this complex typological parameter are actually attested.

Strong pronouns are different from plain (weak) personal pronouns both structurally and functionally. Structurally, they either contain additional morphology or involve prosodic prominence; in either case strong pronouns are derivative with respect to weak pronouns. Functionally, strong pronouns occur in a wide variety of marked contexts, such as conjoined constructions or contrastiveness. Among the free pronoun languages there is a difference between two subtypes: languages that have dedicated strong pronouns, morphologically distinct from weak pronouns (for example, Lyélé) and languages that only use prosodic prominence in contexts where a strong pronoun is needed. Bound pronoun languages universally use specialized strong free pronouns in appropriate contexts. Zero reference languages seem to employ demonstratives for this purpose.

5

Sensitivities of reduced referential devices

Overview

Many languages are consistent in using exclusively or primarily one kind of reduced referential device. In this chapter I consider those languages that are less consistent or altogether inconsistent in this respect, as they use more than one kind of reduced device. Those reduced referential devices that yield to different reduced devices in certain contexts can be called sensitive. In section 5.1 I introduce the theoretical basics of this chapter and review some better known kinds of referential sensitivity, in particular that related to the opposition between locutors and non-locutors.

It is often assumed that different reduced referential options may be appropriate at different levels of referent activation. This kind of putative sensitivity is very special since it is a part of the cognitive process of referential choice, outlined in Chapter 2. That is, the choice between two different reduced devices is allegedly based on the same grounds as the choice between reduced and lexically full devices: on the degree of referent activation. In section 5.2 I consider if this is actually the case and whether different reduced devices can be contrasted along this line.

In contrast, other kinds of sensitivities found in reduced referential devices are not immediately related to activation and activation factors. They result from various grammatical, semantic, or pragmatic environments in which referential devices occur. In most detail I consider the influence of clause participant position (section 5.3) and, more briefly, a number of other contexts (section 5.4).

5.1 Inconsistency and sensitivity in referential choice

In Chapter 3, the three fundamental kinds of reduced referential devices were introduced: free pronouns, bound pronouns, and zero reference. They were illustrated by the data of languages that are mostly committed to one referential device. Such languages can be termed referentially **pure**, or **consistent**. In these languages, when a speaker needs to mention an activated referent the single preferred type of reduced device is normally used. In other words, consistent languages have one highly preferred reduced option of referential choice.

Of course, even such pure languages cannot be expected to use their preferred device universally. There can be various factors that prompt language users to deviate from the major pattern in certain conditions. In addition, there are a significant number of languages, perhaps about one third (see section 3.5), that do not have one preferred reduced referential device and thus display what is sometimes called 'split' or 'mix' in typology. **Inconsistencies** of languages in referential choice can thus be of two kinds:

(i) the language is predisposed to referential device A, but in certain conditions concedes to device B;
(ii) the language is not predisposed to any particular reduced referential device but uses two of them to a comparable degree.

In this chapter I consider various inconsistencies in the use of referential devices, not attempting to systematically distinguish between situations (i) and (ii). Making such a distinction systematically would require too much of an in-depth analysis of individual languages.

These kinds of facts can be looked at not from the perspective of whole languages but from the perspective of particular referential devices. Those referential devices that interchange with others are here termed **sensitive**. To give a simple example, English is strongly committed to free pronouns, and it is among the highly consistent languages. But in clause coordination, if subjects of coordinate clauses are coreferential, all but the first one can be conveyed by the zero form. In this particular context the English language itself demonstrates an inconsistency, while English free pronouns yield to zero reference and thus prove sensitive with respect to this context.

Several types of sensitivity/inconsistency can be distinguished. The most obvious one is the one observed between the broad types of referents: locutor vs. the rest. As is well known at least since Benveniste (1958), locutors are ontologically very different from all third person referents. This profound difference is amply represented in languages. Consider the examples of Japanese and Yidiny that, as we have seen in section 3.4, are quite similar in terms of non-locutor reference. However, they are sharply different in terms of locutor reference. Japanese uses zero pervasively for all persons. According to counts in Yamamoto (1999: 95ff.), first person singular reference is zero 50% of the time in written discourse and 79% in spoken discourse, compared to 62% and

94% for reduced third person reference. Obviously, patterns of reference are quite close for locutor and non-locutor reference. In contrast, in Yidiny the patterning is very different. There are no counts for Yidiny analogous to those for Japanese, but an inspection of the texts published in Dixon (1977) reveals that, despite the very strong preference for zero reference in non-locutors, locutors are almost universally coded by free pronouns. Unlike the Japanese zero, the Yidiny zero is sensitive with respect to person.

There are multiple ways that locutors and non-locutors can be treated differently by languages. They are often conveyed by formally different devices, for instance bound pronouns associated with different morphological positions. Third person forms are often zero in paradigms, as opposed to overt locutor forms (see the discussion of Lakhota in section 6.8). Locutor and non-locutor pronouns may differ in number marking or alignment. These and other asymmetries have been extensively considered in the recent fundamental studies of Bhat (2004), Cysouw (2003), Helmbrecht (2004), and Siewierska (2004), so I will not discuss these kinds of inconsistencies any further. These and other studies also demonstrate that languages' tendency to treat locutor and non-locutor referents as members of a single class should not be underestimated. In particular, Siewierska (2005d) looked at the expression of third person bound person markers representing the Sole argument of intransitive verbs. Among the 284 languages in her sample that do have person marking on the verb only 103 have zero markers for certain third person occurrences. That is, 181, or 64%, of these languages treat third person referents on a par with locutors in this particular respect (presence of overt markers).

In this chapter I focus on several other ways in which referential choice can be sensitive. The main distinction is between those factors that can be subsumed under activation-based referential choice and those that cannot.

5.2 Different levels of activation

Widely known is Givón's suggestion that different reduced referential options correspond to different levels of activation (or degrees of referential continuity, in Givón's terms). In the formulation of this idea in Givón (2001: Vol. I, 417) the following referential options are mentioned:

(i) anaphoric zero
(ii) unstressed anaphoric pronouns[1]

---

[1] Recall that in Givón's conceptual system this category embraces both free and bound pronouns; this fully accords with the approach adopted in this book.

(iii)   stressed independent pronouns
(iv)   full NPs.

In my view, substantiated in section 4.5, strong pronouns (≈ Givón's stressed independent pronouns) are a specialized device that cannot be considered on a par with other members of this scale. Furthermore, the difference between items (i) and (ii) on the one hand and item (iv) on the other hand in terms of underlying referent activation is unquestionable and is, in fact, the main theme of this book. But what about the difference between items (i) and (ii)? Can they correspond to different activation levels in a single language?

Obviously, such situations must be sought among languages that use zero and pronouns with a comparable frequency. It appears that one such language is Mandarin Chinese. Mandarin is often cited as a zero reference language along with Japanese, but under closer examination it turns out that its pattern of referential choice is substantially different. Li and Thompson (1979) demonstrated that speakers of Mandarin sometimes prefer the third person pronoun *tā* to zero reference. In Li and Thompson's experimental study, third person pronouns were preferred by native speakers in less than 10% of all discourse contexts. Other studies indicate a greater proportion of pronouns. Consider an example including instances of both pronominal and zero reference:

(5.1)   Mandarin Chinese (Sino-Tibetan, China; Tao 1996: 491)
   a. tā$_c$ jiù   tiào-dào   dì-shàng-lái,
       3   then   jump-arrive   ground-on-come
   b. Ø$_m$ dào-dǐ   gěi   tā$_c$ zhuā-zhù   le
                till-end   by   3   catch-stop   PFV
       'It [=the cat] then jumped down. It [=the moth] finally was caught by it'

Assuming that this example is typical, it looks quite different from what we observed in the case of Japanese in section 3.4. This impressionistic assessment is corroborated by the counts of Hedberg (1996), comparing Mandarin and Japanese; see Table 5.1.

The counts in Table 5.1 reveal that Japanese relies on zero reference very heavily and does not have an overt form that can qualify as a third person pronoun, while in Mandarin (at least in the kinds of discourses analysed by Hedberg) third person pronouns are used with a frequency comparable to and even greater than that of zeroes. Moreover, they nearly always correspond to the cognitive status that Hedberg calls 'in focus' which means the maximal

TABLE 5.1. Proportion of various reduced referential devices in Japanese and Mandarin (percentages derived from data in tables 3 and 4 on p. 187 of Hedberg 1996)

	Japanese	Mandarin
zero	85%	38%
third person pronoun	n/a	60%
demonstratives	15%	2%

activation of a referent. However, Li and Thompson (1979), Giora and Lee (1996), and Pu (2001) suggest that weak free pronouns in Mandarin appear after certain boundaries in discourse structure. As will be discussed in Part IV, discourse boundary is among the important activation factors, and referents noticeably deactivate after such boundaries. So, taking into account the assessments of the mentioned authors, the most plausible hypothesis is that free pronouns appear under a slightly lower activation than zeroes. A particularly detailed discussion of Mandarin referential phenomena is found in Chu (1998: Ch. 8), which also suggests that the use of third person pronouns, as opposed to zero reference, occurs at topic boundaries or indicates an intermediate level of the referent's accessibility or activation (Chu 1998: 303).

More research is needed to prove that it is specifically the degree of activation that is responsible for the zero vs. pronoun choice in Mandarin. At the present state of our knowledge, it cannot be ruled out that either zero or pronouns constitute the dominant reduced referential device opposed to full NPs, and only this choice is immediately governed by difference in activation level, while the other reduced device is drafted in special situations, akin to those discussed in the next two sections. Deciding between these two competing theories is possible only on the basis of fine-grained analysis of the kind provided in Part IV of this book. However, from the available data it seems at least feasible that Mandarin does not have a single dominant reduced device and differs from Japanese in this respect. Zero is not as pervasive a reduced device in Mandarin as in Japanese, so it is probably accurate to characterize Mandarin zeroes as more sensitive vis-à-vis activation level.

Another point regarding Mandarin is that the third person pronoun tā mostly applies to animate referents.[2] As is discussed in Part IV of this book, in some languages animacy operates as one of the activation factors. However, if animacy operated in this manner in Mandarin, one would expect that

---

[2] I thank Ksenia Antonian for a helpful discussion of Mandarin.

animate or human referents would be more likely to be referred to by zero than inanimate referents. This is contrary to what is found in reality: in Mandarin, animacy increases the probability of using third person pronouns, as opposed to zero. Similar facts are attested in many languages, but here I only mention one. In Swahili (Bantu, East Africa) object bound pronouns appear on the verb when the referent is human and specific and/or activated (Bearth 2003: 123,) while otherwise no pronominal object marking appears in the clause. This situation is contrary to what is expected on the basis of Givón's generalization: a language likes to have an overt pronoun in case of higher activation. This phenomenon deserves a cross-linguistic exploration, but it is not pursued at any depth in this chapter.

Returning to the Givón-style distribution between reduced referential devices, another language strongly relying on zero reference but having a significant use of free pronouns is Eastern Kayah Li, a distant relative of Mandarin. Consider an extract from a story about several blind men who wanted to steal a gong[3]:

(5.2) Eastern Kayah Li (Karen, Sino-Tibetan, Myanmar and Thailand; Solnit 1997: 312)

a. ʔa cwá cwá cwá
   3 go go go

b. Ø ʔe   thɛ   bé   kʌ̄   ʔū   hi
     exploit ascend able COMIT 3.INDEF house

c. Ø thɛ   bé   kʌ̄   ʔū   hi   rʌ
     ascend able COMIT 3.INDEF house PTCL

d. Ø cwá mɛ́   ʔeho kʌ̄   nʌ
     go look steal COMIT PTCL

e. Ø thɛ   phjá nì   bé   kʌ̄   ʔū   mo   du <...>
     ascend take get able COMIT 3.INDEF gong big

'They went and went and went and managed to get up into somebody's house. They were able to get up into the house; they went looking to steal; they managed to get up and take their big gong <...>'

This example shows a heavy reliance on zero reference, at least in the cases when there is one major participant in a stretch of discourse, invariably appearing in the Principal position. More diversity is found in the following

---

[3] In the Eastern Kayah Li examples line breaks (in accordance with clause boundaries), as well as referential zeroes, have been added by myself [A.K.] to the original transcript.

extract, describing the events after the blind men stole a gong and decided to test how it sounds:

(5.3) Eastern Kayah Li (Karen, Sino-Tibetan, Myanmar and Thailand; Solnit 1997: 314)
    a. ʔa dɔ mɛ́ kʌ̄ rʌ́ Ø təphó
        3 beat look COMIT OBL   one.time
    b. hi bɛce nìhō sɛ́ phɛ́ Ø
        house owner hear in.reaction simply
    c. a: hi bɛce lɯ tā lɛ Ø
        HES house owner chase fall descend
    d. Ø phjá phe sɛ́ phɛ́ lū Ø rʌ
        take supplanting in.reaction simply 3.OBV   PTCL
    e. ʔa lɛ dʌ́ lū ʔíkwa təphre təphō rʌ <...>
        3 descend give 3.OBV stick one.CL_H one.CL_BLOOM PTCL
    'They beat it once to try it out, and the owner of the house heard that, the owner of the house came down after them and took it away from them, he came down and gave each one a stick <...>'

In this extract, one can see zero anaphors in the Patientive (5.3c, d) and in the Oblique (5.3a) positions. In the Principal position, there are two instances of the third person pronoun *ʔa* 'he/she/it/they' (5.3a, e). Probably these occur when activation is not sufficient for zero reference. Finally, the so-called obviative pronoun *lū* is used on certain occasions (5.3d, e). (The use of this pronoun will be discussed in Chapter 8, section 8.6.) All in all, there is significant competition with zero reference on the part of free pronouns. It seems probable that in Eastern Kayah Li zero and pronominal reference are distributed in accordance with the level of activation; at least the data available does not naturally lend itself to a simpler interpretation.

Among other languages that possibly use zero and free pronouns in accordance with different activation levels are Tuvan (Turkic, southern Siberia, Russia; see Kibrik 2002b) and Hindi (Indo-Aryan, Indo-European, India; Prasad 2003: 101, Kibrik 2009b). Also this is sometimes claimed about Russian; see Grenoble (2001) for a review. Whenever an activation-based distribution between zero and pronouns is suspected in a certain language, it is always the case that a higher degree of activation is attributed to zero and a lower degree to pronouns, and never vice versa. So the iconicity principle 'more material – more cognitive effort' proposed by Givón is not questioned by the available evidence.

Languages that are inclined to the use of zero reference can use two different strategies when it comes to referents of lowered activation. Some of them, such as Mandarin, draft free pronouns from the core cross-linguistic inventory of major reduced referential devices. Other languages, such as Japanese, draft some supplementary devices, for example demonstratives. This difference is reflected in discourse frequencies as shown in Table 5.1: Mandarin free pronouns, drafted in under lowered activation, are at least as frequent as zero, while the Japanese troubleshooter device, that is demonstratives, is significantly less frequent. Japanese thus is a radical zero reference language, while Mandarin uses two of the major reduced devices to a comparable degree.

The Givón-style scale 'Ø > pronoun > full NP' is thus possibly viable for some languages as reflecting a three-way distinction in activation levels. However, most languages manifest a simpler distinction between high activation and low activation, reflected in the opposition of reduced and full referential devices.

The examples of the three-way distinction we have considered so far are from languages that interchange zero reference and free pronouns. Are there instances where zero would be contrasted to bound pronouns, corresponding to a higher and a lower activation level? I am not aware of any convincing instances of this kind, but it cannot be ruled out that such examples may exist. Now, what about a distribution between bound and free pronouns as dependent on activation level? Here, again, I do not have a conclusive example, but one that may possibly be relevant is found in To'aba'ita (sometimes also spelled Toqabaqita), an Oceanic language of the Solomon Islands, as described by Lichtenberk (1996, 1997). Normally, To'aba'ita transitive verbs, if the Patientive is third person, contain a bound suffixal pronoun -*a* referring to the Patientive:

(5.4)   To'aba'ita (Southeast Solomonic Oceanic, Austronesian, Solomon Islands; Lichtenberk 1997: 302)
nau   ku   rongo-a
1SG   1SG.NOM.FACT   hear-3.ACC
'I hear him/her'

The -*a* pronoun is quite insensitive: it occurs when a referent is activated, as in (5.4), but also when a referent is not activated; then it cooccurs with a full NP within a clause (see 5.5i), that is, is tenacious.[4] Moreover, the bound

---

[4] To'aba'ita also has tenacious free pronouns in the Principal position; these pronouns are marked for tense; see Lichtenberk (1996: 383).

pronoun can cooccur with inanimate NPs, indefinite NPs (5.5ii), and even interrogative pronouns (5.5iii):

(5.5) To'aba'ita (Southeast Solomonic Oceanic, Austronesian, Solomon Islands; Lichtenberk 1997: 302, 305)
  i. 'adosi   e   thaungi-a   wela
     evil.spirit   3SG.NOM.FACT   hit-3.ACC   child
     'The adosi spirit has possessed the child'
  ii. nau   ku   mantai-a   te'e   si   mantaa
      1SG   1SG.NOM.FACT   think-3.ACC   one   CL   thought
      'I have had an idea'
  iii. taa   n-o   rofe-a?
       what   FOC-2SG.FACT   look.for-3.ACC
       'What are you looking for?'

However, this bound pronoun is missing when there is a free third person Patientive pronoun in the clause (free pronouns are nearly exclusively human in To'aba'ita):

(5.6) To'aba'ita (Southeast Solomonic Oceanic, Austronesian, Solomon Islands; Lichtenberk 1997: 304)[5]
  'o   riki   nia?
  2SG.FACT   see   3SG
  'Did you see him/her?'

As Lichtenberk (1997) indicated, To'aba'ita free pronouns are not necessarily contrastive, sometimes they are used in relatively neutral contexts, that is they can be used as weak, not strong pronouns. According to Lichtenberk (1996: 403), among all third person Patientive mentions free pronouns account for about 13% of all instances; in all other cases bound pronouns are used, with (42%) or without (45%) a full NP. The question of when exactly free pronouns are used remains obscure; Lichtenberk (1996: 407) only remarks that third person free pronouns provide 'availability for foregrounding in contrast to the dependent pronominals'. It is not clear whether this can be understood in terms of a distinct level of activation. However, a possible hypothesis regarding the To'aba'ita data is that free Patientive pronouns may be used under somewhat lowered activation, while bound pronouns are used

---

[5] This question can be otherwise formulated with a bound pronoun (rather than free); Lichtenberk does not comment on whether there is a semantic difference between these two variants.

in two situations: under high activation (no full NP) and with a full NP within the same clause (a sort of syntactic anaphora).

The kinds of referential sensitivities discussed in the following two sections cannot be easily subsumed under the general umbrella notion of distinct activation levels, so they are considered separately.

5.3 Different clause participant positions

Some languages use different reduced referential devices in different clause participant positions. For example, Spanish uses bound pronouns (traditionally, personal endings) for clause subject referents and free pronouns (traditionally, pronominal clitics) for clause object referents. This difference cannot possibly be attributed to difference in activation level, since the bound subject vs. free object pronoun in Spanish is categorical while the corresponding activation levels are not: even though subjects are more often activated than objects, they do not have to be activated, and objects do not have to be non-activated. Unlike the probabilistic process of referential choice, here we deal with a more conventionalized linguistic factor. One must recognize that the difference in Spanish bound vs. free pronouns is morphosyntactically based, and referential choice in this language is sensitive to clause participant positions. The research question of this section is: what kinds of such sensitivities are found in the languages of the world?

5.3.1 *Principal vs. Patientive as the optimal pair of contrastive clause participant positions*

Subject and object are not universal statuses; they are restricted to Spanish and some other languages. So, in order to discuss clause participant sensitivities one needs to rely on some universally applicable set of notions. Because of the natural limitations of space, we cannot test referential choice in all possible clause participant positions. We need to select a contrastive pair of positions that may most likely bring to light different patterns of referential choice. What would be the best candidate for such a contrastive pair?

Languages differ with respect to alignment, that is, coexpression of elementary core arguments' roles: intransitive agent, intransitive patient, transitive agent, and transitive patient (see e.g. A. E. Kibrik 1997). Cross-linguistically, the three most frequent alignments are neutral, accusative, and ergative; each of the latter two manifest an opposition between two hyperroles. Two recent studies by Comrie (2005) and Siewierska (2005a) allow us to assess how

TABLE 5.2. Frequencies of alignment types for different referential options, according to Comrie (2005) and Siewierska (2005a) [percentages added by this writer – A.K.][6]

	Neutral (No opposition)	Accusative (Principal vs. Patientive)	Ergative (Agentive vs. Absolutive)	Total
Alignment of full NPs	98 (52%)	52 (27%)	32 (17%)	190 (100%)
Alignment of free pronouns	79 (46%)	64 (37%)	20 (12%)	172 (100%)
Alignment of bound pronouns	84 (22%)	212 (56%)	19 (5%)	380 (100%)

patterning of the hyperroles differs vis-à-vis referential choice: full NPs vs. reduced NPs; see Table 5.2.

The two major trends we observe in Table 5.2 are the increase in accusativity in reduced referential devices (free and especially bound pronouns), as compared to full NPs, and the converse decrease in ergativity.[7] (A rather rare example of the ergative pattern in pronouns is provided by Jarawa (South Andamanese) where pronominal prefixes can only express Absolutives, whereas transitive Agentives can only be conveyed by free pronouns (Kumar 2006: 17–19). The converse pattern with the ergative alignment, in which Agentive pronouns are bound whereas Absolutive pronouns are free, is provided by the Austronesian language Nias; see example (4.16) in section 4.4.) The increase in accusativity is obviously due not only to the languages that have the ergative alignment in full NPs but also to the languages with neutral alignment in full NPs.

The increase of accusativity in reduced referential devices is in line with the well-known observation of Silverstein (1976) that the ergative pattern recedes as we move from full NPs to pronouns. In the context of this book, what interests us most is that reduced referential devices clearly favour the

---

[6] In Table 5.2, the rows 'Alignment of full NPs' and 'Alignment of free pronouns' are derived from Comrie (2005), and the row 'Alignment of bound pronouns' from Siewierska (2005a). I ignore some minor alignment types, so the sum of numbers in each row does not equal the number in the Total column. In fact, in bound pronouns the active alignment (agent-like vs. patient-like arguments, irrespective of transitivity) is slightly more frequent that the ergative one; see Siewierska (2005a). But since it is very rare on NPs (only three languages in each of Comrie's counts) I do not include the active alignment in this table.

[7] In fact, the mentioned trends must be more striking than Table 5.2 suggests, because many 'free pronouns' in this table are actually strong pronouns that behave in a more noun-like fashion than free weak pronouns.

accusative pattern. They highlight the distinction between the Principal and the Patientive hyperroles.

The most likely explanation for the reduced devices' propensity to accusativity is that referents' high activation is functionally and statistically correlated with the Principal hyperrole (as opposed to the Patientive hyperrole). Reduced referential devices typically figure in a clause in the Principal role. This is sometimes stated directly (e.g. Givón 1983a) but more often this association is established indirectly via the notions of subject or topic. In a language like English, the status of subject is widely held to be a grammaticalization of topic (cognitively, attention focus or starting point; see Tomlin 1995; Chafe 1994). At the same time, prototypical English subjects are instantiations of the Principal hyperrole. Subjects are known to be the preferred positions for reduced referential devices (or, vice versa, referential reduction is preferred for subject referents). Chafe (1994: 82ff.) has formulated a powerful and explanatory light subject constraint, according to which 81% of subjects in English conversation encode highly activated information. In terms of actual referential choice, it is useful to look at the data of Biber et al. (1999: 236) allowing us to compare subjects to objects and prepositional complements with respect to the patterning of free and reduced NPs. Table 5.3 contains data for three registers of written English, each represented by approximately 5 million words.

Although reduced reference is associated with the subject position to various degrees in various registers, the share of pronouns at least doubles

TABLE 5.3. Referential choice in various clause participant positions, in various registers of written English discourse; after Biber et al. (1999: 236)

		% use of nouns	% use of pronouns
Fiction	subject	35	65
	object	70	30
	prepositional complement	85	15
News	subject	75	25
	object	95	5
	prepositional complement	>97.5	<2.5
Academic texts	subject	80	20
	object	90	10
	prepositional complement	>97.5	<2.5

(and in the news rises five times) in the subject position compared to the object position. A comparison of the subject position with the prepositional complement position is even more striking. So the evidence considered so far converges on the hypothesis that the best universally applicable pair of clause participant positions that are likely to display different patterns of referential choice is the pair Principal vs. Patientive. Note that what is meant here is the following: this is the pair of positions in which one can expect conventionalized differences in preferred reduced referential devices.

5.3.2 *An alternative suggestion: Agentive vs. Absolutive*

A caveat is in order here: there is a well-known research tradition that makes a claim incompatible with what has just been said. Du Bois (1987), Du Bois et al. (2003) proposed a theory (the so-called Preferred Argument Structure framework) according to which the division between semantic hyperroles that is most crucial for discourse is the ergative-type division between Agentive and Absolutive.[8] Agentives pattern differently from both Soles and Patientives (that form Absolutives, if taken in conjunction) in terms of typical referential choice in discourse, while Soles and Patientives pattern similarly. Specifically, reduced referential expressions (which normally encode activated referents) tend to turn out as Agentives, while full NPs (which often encode non-activated referents) as Absolutives. Du Bois (2003: 37) presents quantitative data from several languages that is intended to support this point.

Available evidence, however, is not always conclusive. For example, in the case of English conversation full NPs are Agentives in 8% of all instances, Soles in 35%, and Patientives in 57%, that is, Soles pattern in an intermediate way rather than together with Patientives. Some other studies published in Du Bois et al. (2003) also do not provide clear support for Du Bois's theory. For example, in Nepali (Indo-Aryan, Indo-European, Nepal) full NPs turn out as Agentives, Soles, and Patientives in 20%, 29%, and 44% of all instances, respectively (Genetti and Crain 2003: 218[9]). For Roviana (Meso-Melanesian Oceanic, Austronesian, Solomon Islands) the corresponding percentages are 7%, 18%, and 26% (counted by myself relying on raw numbers given in Table 4 in Corston-Oliver 2003: 286). For Finnish (Uralic), new referents are coded in the three argumental positions in 8%, 12%, and 30% of all instances (counted

---

[8] I here translate Du Bois's terminology into the terms adopted in this book.
[9] These percentages, for reasons that are not clear, are based on overt referent mentions only, that is, do not take into account abundant zero mentions; cf. Genetti and Crain (2003: 215).

Table 5.4. Breakdown of occurrences of hyperroles in a spoken English corpus according to givenness; data derived from Kärkkäinen (1996: 684)

	% New	% Given	Total, N
Agentive	5	95	217 (100%)
Sole	8	92	253 (100%)
Patientive	48	52	164 (100%)
Oblique	61	39	70 (100%)
Other	31	69	70 (100%)

by myself relying on raw numbers given in Table 6 in Helasvuo 2003: 259), etc. This last quantitative result and several others are clearly in better concord with the 'activated Principal' hypothesis rather than the 'activated Agentive' hypothesis. Also consider the results of Kärkkäinen (1996) on spoken English; her article does not provide direct information on the relationship between hyperroles and referential choice, but cf. the percentages in terms of givenness in Table 5.4.

Here we observe a remarkably clear co-patterning of Agentive and Sole (that is, Principal) vis-à-vis givenness, and the Principal's distinction from the Patientive, as well as other clause participant positions.[10] So I will continue to assume that the alignment that has a discourse basis is the accusative alignment, while the functional basis of ergativity is of a different nature (discussion of which is beyond my goal here). (See also the study of Maslova and Nikitina 2007 that demonstrates conclusively the worldwide preference of the accusative alignment over the ergative one, which points to the probable discourse motivation.) Therefore, the two clause participant positions, or hyperroles, that I discuss in the rest of this section is the Principal and the Patientive. The issue to consider is whether different types of reduced referential devices may be distributed differently vis-à-vis these two hyperroles.

5.3.3 A typology of sensitivities based on clause participant position

A number of various sensitivities of referential choice with respect to the Principal vs. Patientive hyperroles are found in the languages of the world. As has already been discussed, Spanish uses bound Principal pronouns and free Patientive pronouns. An almost mirror-image pattern is found in Roviana (Meso-Melanesian Oceanic, Austronesian, Solomon Islands): according to

---

[10] Cf. the recent study of Everett (2009), also casting doubt on the Preferred Argument Structure framework.

Corston-Oliver (2003), reduced Principals are coded primarily by free pronouns[11], while reduced Patientives by bound pronouns[12], (the fact that they are affixes is emphasized by Corston-Oliver, p. 283). The same pattern is characteristic of the neighbouring and related language Gela. Both pronouns are tenacious; note that Gela subject pronouns also contain marking for tense:

(5.7) Gela (Southeast Solomonic Oceanic, Austronesian, Solomon Islands; Crowley 2002: 532–534)

    i. e   goti-a   na ɣai   na mane
      3SG.SUBJ.PAST break-3SG.OBJ ART firewood ART man
      'The man broke the firewood'

    ii. e   ɣani-a   na kake
       3SG.SUBJ.PAST eat-3SG.OBJ ART taro
       'S/he ate the taro'

    iii. ku   tate-a   vani-ɣo
       1SG.SUBJ.FUT show-3SG.OBJ DAT-2SG.OBJ
       'I will show it to you'

The frequency of this type (free Principal pronouns and bound Patientive pronouns) can be estimated by composing the studies by Siewierska (2005e) and Dryer (2005a): among the 248 languages shared by the two samples only eight languages (evenly distributed between Africa, Oceania, and South America) display this combination.

There are also similar sensitivities involving zero as the option appearing in one of the clause participant positions. Some languages limit the extensive use of zero reference to the Principal position. This is the case in Masa:

(5.8) Masa (Chadic, Afro-Asiatic, Chad and Cameroon; Caitucoli 1986: 82-85)[13]

    a. năʔ   mūʔ   īr-àʔ   góȳ   mūʔ / Ø cūk sīmī cūk //
       3SG.F turned eyes-3SG.F to.outside turned   shed tears shed

    b. "c-ūm-āwā-ñ   náy   dàf-áy-déyā"   //
      killed-3SG.M-EMPH-GENER 1PL.INCL cook-1PL.INCL-ANT

---

[11] In fact, zeroes are also used in this position, but the proportion of zeroes to free pronouns is 3:10 (Corston-Oliver 2003: 286).

[12] Sometimes free pronouns are used too, in addition to bound pronouns, but this happens only one time out of eleven on average (Corston-Oliver 2003: 286).

[13] I preserve the symbols used by Caitucoli to indicate prosodic boundaries: double slash (//) means the end of a phrase (Caitucoli 1986: 408), and in English translation it is effectively conveyed as the end of a sentence; single slash (/) indicates a pause in the middle of a phrase.

c. Ø slī dùwày-n-àwà //
   took pot-GENER-EMPH

d. Ø jág-ām   ják   //
   hung-3SG.M hung

e. Ø fiók   nìí   hāy-àmù //
   poured water in-3SG.M

f. nìí-n   fōg-óy   wīlīn wīlīn //
   water-GENER rise-ANT IDPH   IDPH

g. Ø gí   gòī   hāy-àm   wāŋ   //
     threw child in-3SG.M reclining

'She [=the lioness] turned her eyes to the side and shed tears. "Since he has been killed, we start cooking him." She took a pot. She hung it (over the fire). She poured water in it. The water boiled (*lit.* did plop plop). She put her son in it.'

As is clear from this excerpt, when a referent is highly activated it is coded by zero in the Principal (subject) position (lines c, d, e, g). A free pronoun may occur too if a referent is less than maximally activated or if there is a possible referential conflict; this is the case in line (a). In other clause participant positions highly activated referents are coded by bound pronouns, suffixing to the verb if it is the Patientive (direct object) (lines b, d) and otherwise to a preposition (lines e, g). In the intersection of the studies by Siewierska (2005e) and Dryer (2005a) only one language is found that has this profile, namely Nakanai (Western Oceanic, Austronesian, New Britain, Papua New Guinea).

An almost mirror-image system is found in Urarina, a Peruvian language with the accusative alignment (Olawsky 2006). Activated Principals are expressed by bound tenacious suffixal pronouns, similar to those of Spanish (Olawsky 2006: 487ff.). Activated Patientive referents are coded by zero (Olawsky 2006: 213ff.). Sufficient illustrative evidence is found in the following short extract from a story of how a girl was lost in the forest and her parents were looking for her:

(5.9) Urarina (isolate, Peru; Olawsky 2006: 902)[14]

a. Ø mɨkɨ-ɨrɨ-a=ne   hana=te   kuhjuri
   catch-PL-3.DEP=SBRD   when=FOC   scream:3

---

[14] Free zeroes in this extract were added by this writer [A.K.]; they were placed in accordance with the basic OVS word order of Urarina (Olawsky 2006: 654ff.). All zeroes marked refer to 'the girl'. Note that Urarina has different sets of Principal pronominal markers – one set for dependent clauses, and two sets for main clauses.

b. nii   hana=te   Ø muku-ĩ   Ø ra-e   raj   neba
   that   when=FOC   catch-PARTIC   receive-3   POSS mother
   'When they caught her, she screamed. Then her mother caught her and took her.'

A system similar to that of Masa seems to occur in Zuni, an isolate of western New Mexico (USA), with the difference that the Patientive pronouns are free, not bound. In a grammatical sketch of Zuni it is stated that the third person subject pronouns are missing, 'the third-person reference being indicated in context by the absence of a pronoun' (Newman 1996: 498–499), whereas the object third person pronoun is overt and has the shape *ʔa·wan*.

Theoretically there are nine ways for languages to select the major reduced referential devices for Principal and Patientive. Three of the nine ways are characteristic of pure, or consistent, languages (Chapter 3), and six are various kinds of inconsistencies/sensitivities. Eight types out of nine – those that I can exemplify with particular languages – are shown in Table 5.5.[15]

The upper three rows of Table 5.5 correspond to consistent languages, while the lower five rows to types of inconsistencies/sensitivities discussed above.

TABLE 5.5. Reduced reference to Principal and Patientive and the attested types of sensitivities. The rightmost column indicates, where applicable, the number of languages of the given type in the intersection of the samples of Siewierska (2005e) and Dryer (2005a)

	Principal	Patientive	Representative language	Number of languages in shared sample of Siewierska and Dryer
Consistent languages	free	free	Lyélé	26
	bound	bound	Abkhaz	111
	zero	zero	Japanese	21
Inconsistent languages	free	bound	Gela	8
	zero	bound	Masa	1
	zero	free	Zuni	n/a
	bound	free	Spanish	n/a
	bound	zero	Urarina	n/a

[15] The representation in the table is inevitably simplified, compared to the actual situations in individual languages. For example, it has been shown above that Masa allows not only zeroes but also free pronouns in the subject position, but this activation-related sensitivity is ignored in the table, as we concentrate here only on participant-position sensitivities.

176   II. Typology of Reduced Referential Devices

Where it is possible to estimate the frequency of a particular type, relying on the composition of Siewierska (2005e) and Dryer (2005a), I indicate this in the rightmost column. This figure shows the representation of the given type among the 248 languages shared by the samples of the two studies.

The remaining kind of sensitivity – free pronoun in the Principal position and zero Patientive – is not included in Table 5.5 as I cannot indicate a representative language. This type may seem improbable at first sight, but it still may be found in a language that has a tendency towards zero reference but has pronominal compounds involving clausal categories that are thus necessary in a clause (see section 4.4).

5.4 Various specific contexts

In this section I consider an internally diverse group of referential sensitivities. This group embraces various specific contexts where such sensitivities can show up.

One of the obvious contexts is the context of **imperative** clauses. Imperatives are often structurally simpler than other clause types – this extends to verb morphology and also to expression of the clause's Principal who is also the addressee of the speech act. In many, probably most, free pronoun languages, including English, the Principal is not expressed in imperatives (English *Run!* or *Give it to me!*). Cysouw (2003: 60), relying on a number of prior studies, states that 'in most languages, the imperative is a special construction, not marked for person at all'. This, however, may be a bit of an overstatement: languages with bound tenacious pronouns often include second person bound pronoun in imperatives; cf. Abkhaz (Hewitt 1979: 189) and Navajo (Young and Morgan: 204–205); see also the discussion in van der Auwera and Lejeune (2005) who demonstrate that imperatives quite often include marking for second person. Since this book is primarily about non-locutor reference, I will not dwell on the topic of imperatives any further.

A context that is more relevant here is that of **clause coordination**. Consider the case of Babungo, a language of Cameroon. It is essentially a free pronoun language. The following examples are quite characteristic:

(5.10)   Babungo (Bantoid, Benue-Congo, Cameroon; Schaub 1985: 96)
   i. Làmbí   jwì   bù'   làa   ŋwɔ́ kɔ̀ə   yé   ghɔ̀
      Lambi   come.PFV   because   that   he   want   see   you
      'Lambi came because he wants to see you'

ii. vɨ́i   vî   gàŋtə̀   mə̀. mə̀ kə́ə kɔ́ fá   tɨ́ věŋ.
    people those help.PFV   I   I   want   give thing to they
    'Those people helped me. I want to give them something.'

However, if a referent plays the same role in coordinate clauses, zero is used in the non-first clauses. This extends not only to subject coreference but also to coreference between direct objects and even between prepositional indirect objects. (There are some further differences in behaviour of reduced referential devices in these positions; see Schaub 1985: 54–55, 96ff. for details.) For example:

(5.11) Babungo (Bantoid, Benue-Congo, Cameroon; Schaub 1985: 55, 96)
    i. nshú   wī fì   yíkɨ́ŋ yî, Ø twàŋ   Ø Ø nùŋ
       mother her take.PFV   crab   that   roast.PFV   keep.PFV

       Ø   fúu   yìshwí
            on   fireplace.stone
       'Her mother took that crab, roasted it, and kept it on the stone of the fireplace'

    ii. à   kɔ́   ká   tɨ́ Làmbí mū, mū à   kɔ́   fá
        you give.PFV money to Lambi QU   QU you   give.PFV thing
        dày   Ø
        other
        'Did you give money to Lambi, or did you give him something else?'

In languages without a well-established tradition of literacy, such as Babungo, where it is often difficult to distinguish a coordinate construction from a sequence of syntactically unrelated clauses (sentences), the surrender of the usual pronoun to zero may actually be used as a diagnostic, indicating that we face a coordinate construction.

Compared to Babungo, English pronouns yield to zero in a narrower class of instances: not all pronouns do it in coordinate constructions, but only subject pronouns. In example (5.12)[16] there are six reduced subject mentions of the protagonist referent. Only one of them is zero, and this is exactly within a coordinate structure, in a non-first clause:

(5.12) Al Gore is truth. Think about it. <u>He</u> says what needs to be said without fear, without posturing. <u>He</u> leads. (*paragraph*) <u>He</u> succeeds in the

---

[16] From the website CubaNow.net, 25 January 2008, the very beginning of the article 'Why Al Gore is not president' by Rick Jacobs.

worlds of politics, business, and diplomacy. He reads and Ø writes history. He has access to the smartest people on the planet.

The offered account of zero use in coordinate constructions is reasonably accurate with respect to written English (but see fn. 18). According to an internet search, the sequence *he/she reads and writes* is found 8,030 times, while *he reads and he writes* and *she reads and she writes* together only 64 times, which makes only 0.8% of all instances. For comparison, Russian is even more extreme than English in requiring zero reference in non-first clauses: the sequence *on(a) čitaet i pišet* 'he/she reads and writes' is found 1,694 times while the structure with a repeated pronoun is not found at all.

In spoken English the relationship between clause coordination and subject zero reference is much less clear-cut. Biber et al. (1999: 156) have pointed out that in English 'ellipsis in coordinated clauses is common both in spoken and written registers'. However, a brief search through the corpus of spoken English (Du Bois et al. 2000) indicates that the use of subject pronouns in non-first coordinate clauses is not a rarity at all. In the following excerpt there are four instances of reduced subject reference, and all of these are performed by third person pronouns:

(5.13) Du Bois et al. (2000), conversation SBC0001 'Actual Blacksmithing', seconds 749 to 764
    a. (H) this girl's been .. in this f=errier,[17]
    b. ... uh,
    c. she's going to an actual .. ferrier college.
    d. (H) They have a lo=t of those around.
    e. .. a lo=t.
    f. (H) And she's going to one of em,
    g. and she's been going for,
    h. .. like nine months.
    i. .. to this one,
    j. and she's still got [a lot more=],

Three out of these four occurrences (in lines c, g, and j) can arguably be interpreted as belonging to non-first coordinate clauses. This is particularly obvious with respect to the uses in lines (g) and (j), due to two converging observations: first, the previous clause has non-sentence-final prosody

---

[17] In the original source the erroneous spelling *ferrier* appears, instead of *farrier*.

(marked by a comma in transcription) and second, the line begins with the coordinator *and*. Taking into account evidence of spoken language, English appears less sensitive to coordination contexts than it is usually thought to be: pronouns as the predominant reduced referential device do not always yield to zero even in coordinate constructions.[18]

At the same time, some authors picture English in a different way, emphasizing the spread of zero reference. In particular, Pu (2001) cites examples such as the following, from a conversation about Lily [=L] and the cat named Thomas [=T]:

(5.14) a. On your birthday it was,

b. and Lily$_L$ she$_L$ was all for it,

c. Thomas$_T$ must have a bow on.

d. Ø$_L$ Took one off the chocolate box,

e. and Thomas$_T$ was mad about it.

Such instances cannot be easily treated as an extension of the coordination pattern to independent sentences, as the zero in line (d) is not coreferential to the subject of the previous clause. Similar examples are occasionally found. Consider another illustration from a Christmas letter that I received (that has three instances of sentence-initial zero reference per one page of text, all of them representing first person singular). The author is telling us about a chain of trips she undertook during the year under report; the trip in question apparently happened in May or June[19]:

(5.15) Then came Hawaii and it was a nice interlude to just visit and relax. Still Ø had wonderful weather.

This pair of sentences constitutes a whole paragraph. So this example is even further away from the coordination prototype than Pu's example (5.14), as the referent is not even explicitly mentioned within the paragraph. Of course, the referent, that is the letter's author, is the whole discourse's protagonist and has a significant level of activation throughout. Interestingly, Pu (2001) treats

---

[18] In fact, examples such as in (5.13g, j) bring us back to the issue of referential sensitivity even in written English. As another internet search demonstrated, zero reference is far less prevalent in coordinate clauses, if the predicate is conveyed by analytic verb forms such as in (5.13g, j) (*has been going* or *has got*). For example, *and s/he has been going for* and *and s/he's been going for* were found 171,610 times, while *and has been going for* less frequently, namely 133,000 times. So even in written English there are additional factors that render referential choice less sensitive and more faithful to the preferred reduced device, namely pronouns.

[19] I thank Roly Sussex for a useful discussion of English zero reference.

English almost on a par with Mandarin Chinese with respect to the extent of zero use. I believe this is a strong overstatement; but the degree and character of sensitivities shown by English pronouns still need to be specified in further research. Biber et al. (1999: 156, 158, 1005) treat such examples not as zero reference but as 'initial ellipsis', involving just the subject pronoun or also an auxiliary operator. Biber et al. (1999: 1106) report about 3000 instances of both kinds of ellipsis per million words in their conversational corpus. The controversial issue of English zero reference is further discussed in Chapter 6, section 6.7.

A typologically interesting example of distribution between zero reference and free pronouns is found in Pulaar-Fulfulde (Atlantic); see discussion in Chapter 9 (subsection 9.4.3).

A grammatical context that creates an even stronger predisposition to zero reference, even in languages with pronouns, is the context of *verb serialization*, that is, a combination of verbs jointly forming a single clause and denoting a single event. As is pointed out in Durie (1997), verbs belonging to a series tend to have common arguments, and sometimes such commonality, especially with respect to the Principal, is even required. Serialization is particularly frequently associated with languages of one macroarea – from Southeast Asia to Oceania, especially New Guinea. However, comparable phenomena are common in other parts of the world, including West Africa and central Eurasia. For example, serialization is found in Russian, rarely figuring among the serializing languages. The following examples are borrowed from the corpus of Russian spoken stories explored in Kibrik and Podlesskaya (eds.) (2009) (see pp. 249–254):

(5.16) Russian (spoken)
    a. .. Tam u kogo-to krovát' slomalas',
        DM at somebody.GEN bed.NOM break.PAST.SG.F
    b. my vzjáli pomenjàli krováti,
        we.NOM take.PAST.PL replace.PAST.PL bed.PL.ACC
    'Then somebody's bed broke, we went ahead and replaced beds,'

(5.17) Russian (spoken)
    I ja ego pri ètom stojú i protiràju,
    and I.NOM 3M.ACC by this.LOC stand.PRES.1SG and wipe.PRES.1SG
    'And meanwhile I am standing and wiping it [=the motorcycle],'

Both of these examples illustrate constructions that display unmistakable symptoms of serialization. In example (5.16) the verb 'took' is delexicalized and, though inflected as a normal finite verb, has an aktionsart rather than a lexical meaning. Also, there is no coordinating conjunction between the two verbs. In (5.17), contrariwise, there is the conjunction 'and', but the direct object of the verb 'wipe' (the pronoun *ego*) appears on the left of the whole serial complex, that is, is separated from the verb it immediately belongs to by the other verb. And, again, the linearly first verb 'stand' is at least partly delexicalized. As was pointed out above, Russian strongly prefers to use zero subject, rather than a pronoun, in non-first coordinate clauses. The difference of serialized constructions from clause coordination is that using pronouns with non-first verbs is not simply dispreferred but ruled out: repeating the pronoun 'we' in (5.16) and 'I' in (5.17) is completely impossible. So I would be inclined not to posit zero reference with the second verbs in this kind of example, but rather consider that there is a single shared subject pronoun for both verbs, that is, per whole clause. Not having repeated mention of a Principal referent with non-first verbs in serialized constructions is highly common in the world's languages; see Aikhenvald and Dixon (eds.) (2006). Only particularly insensitive, or stubborn, languages, such as Lyélé, use free Principal pronouns with each verb in a serial verb construction (see example 3.5ii).

An example of a shared Patientive pronoun under serialization is provided by To'aba'ita. To begin with, this language uses free Principal pronouns (marked for tense); see examples (5.4)–(5.6) above; these pronouns are used almost universally in clauses (are highly tenacious) and are absent only in the instances of serialization (Lichtenberk 1996: 381). Also, as has been discussed in section 5.2, To'aba'ita has bound third person Patientive pronouns that are found in the vast majority of transitive clauses. One context in which they are not used is verb serialization, when two transitive verbs in a clause have a shared Patientive, marked by a bound pronoun on the final verb alone:

(5.18)   To'aba'ita (Southeast Solomonic Oceanic, Austronesian, Solomon Islands; Lichtenberk 1997: 309)
'asufa 'e   'ala muusi-a   taunamo
rat   3SG.NOM.FACT bite break-3.ACC mosquito.net
'The rat chewed up, and made holes in, the mosquito net'

Still another grammatical context often provoking a referential sensitivity is **clause subordination**. This can again be illustrated with Russian examples. The following three examples, again from the Night Dream Stories corpus described in Kibrik and Podlesskaya (eds.) (2009) (originals are found on pp. 676, 585, and 600), are ordered from the minimal to the maximal degree of preference for zero subject in subordinate clauses:

(5.19) Russian (spoken)
    a. a onâ po dèrevu streljála-streljàla,
       and she.NOM at tree.DAT shoot.PAST.SG.F-shoot.PAST.SG.F
    b. Ø dúmala,
       think.PAST.SG.F
    c. čto Ø menja ubìla.
       that me.ACC kill.PAST.SG.F
    'and she was shooting and shooting at the tree, she thought that she had killed me'

(5.20) Russian (spoken)
    a. ... i dóma .. ona mne pokăzyvaet,
       and at.home she.NOM me.DAT show.PRES.3SG
    b. ... to čto Ø umēet.
       that REL know.PRES.3SG
    'and at home she is showing me what she knows how to do'

(5.21) Russian (spoken)
    a. .... i my stáli kopàt' .. tam .. u sebja jàmu,
       and we.NOM begin.PAST.PL dig DM at self.GEN pit
    b. čtob Ø sdèlat' sebe šalàš,
       in.order.to make self.DAT wikiup
    'and at our home we started digging a pit, in order to make a wikiup for ourselves'

In (5.19), the zero subject in line (c) appears in a complement clause subordinate to a matrix verb of thinking. As the analysis of the Night Dream Stories data indicate, in such contexts pronouns and zeroes vary, both used with comparable frequency. In (5.20) the subject zero is found in a relative clause. Here the zero is strongly preferred, but a pronoun can possibly be used too. Finally, in (5.21) the purposive infinitival clause does not allow anything but a zero at all; this is a fully grammaticalized context for zero reference.

    Some kind of zero reference is found in almost any language, in some construction or under some circumstances. Even in the case of Lyélé that is remarkably faithful to pronominal reference there is one context where zero is used: one of the two activated objects of a ditransitive clause may be conveyed by a zero (Showalter 1986: 208). In Chapter 6 (section 6.7) I discuss instances in which English allows zero subject reference in independent, non-coordinate clauses. This is related to the vestiges of bound pronouns in English (third person singular verb agreement in the present), which again points to minor referential sensitivities in even the most consistent languages.

The common denominator of the kinds of phenomena reviewed in this section is that even quite referentially consistent languages yield to grammatical, semantic, or pragmatic properties of specific contexts and employ referential devices that are generally atypical for them. Of course, the list of contexts presented here that stimulate referential sensitivities is by no means exhaustive; I have indicated only the most obvious ones among such contexts. Some further contexts, of a more complex character, are mentioned in the subsequent chapters. In particular, in Chapter 7 (subsection 7.3.3) I discuss the French bound pronouns that are sensitive with respect to referential properties: while they are tenacious in the case of definite referents they are not if a referent is indefinite.[20]

Summary

There is a very limited set of reduced referential devices, available in human languages. Some languages are primarily inclined to one of these major devices, but still yield to a different device in certain specialized circumstances. For example, English mostly relies on free pronouns, but has some elements of zero reference – specifically, in clause coordination. Accordingly, English is a referentially consistent language, but it demonstrates a particular inconsistency; English free pronouns turn out to be sensitive to the context of clause coordination. Other languages are still more variable and use different reduced devices depending on cognitive, pragmatic, semantic, or grammatical factors.

Some kinds of referential inconsistencies/sensitivities are amply studied in the literature. This particularly concerns the ways languages treat locutors vs. non-locutors differently. In this chapter I have looked at several other kinds of referential inconsistencies/sensitivities. The first of these is a part of the general process of referential choice. Some languages seem to employ more than one reduced referential device in the major repertoire of referential choice, in particular, they use both zero reference and pronouns depending on the degree of referent activation. This pattern is attested among the world's languages, but it is relatively infrequent; most languages are inclined to one reduced referential device, usable under high referent activation.

---

[20] The phenomenon of referential sensitivity is also mentioned in Siewierska and Bakker (2005). In particular, they discuss the sensitivity related to verb's lexical properties. Referring to Frajzyngier and Shay (2000: 111), they cite examples from Hdi (Chadic, Afro-Asiatic, Northern Cameroon) where some verbs require free and some other bound object pronouns.

Other kinds of sensitivities considered in this chapter are not immediately related to activation levels. Particularly important is the difference between clause participant positions – such as the difference between Spanish subject bound pronouns (personal desinences) and object free pronouns. Such differences are of a rather categorical, conventionalized nature and are not a part of the probabilistic process of referential choice. The most clear and universally applicable pair of clause participant positions displaying different referential devices is the pair of hyperroles 'Principal vs. Patientive'. Reduced referential devices are cross-linguistically prone to highlighting the accusative opposition between these two hyperroles. A typology of sensitivities displayed by reduced devices with respect to the Principal vs. Patientive opposition is proposed. Some of the typological options are more frequent, such as the 'free Principal pronouns and bound Patientive pronouns', while other options are rare, such as the 'zero Principal and bound Patientive pronoun'.

A number of other contexts exist in which languages tend to display sensitivities of reduced referential devices, including imperatives, clause coordination and subordination, and verb serialization. Creation of a more comprehensive typological calculus of contexts stimulating referential sensitivities is an important task for future research. Language-specific referential sensitivity is an intricate field of research, because each language may have a great variety of particular sensitivities. Probably each of the major reduced referential devices can be found at least in some marginal situation in almost every language.

6

Challenges of bound pronouns

Overview

Linguistics is traditionally biased towards free pronouns. However, as has been shown in Chapter 3 (section 3.5), languages with bound pronouns are the most frequent type cross-linguistically. So understanding referential processes in language is unthinkable without a particular regard for these languages and bound pronouns as such. This chapter adresses several important issues related to bound pronouns.

Apart from the free vs. bound distinction, the second most fundamental parameter in the typology of pronouns is the tenacious vs. alternating distinction. We have seen in the previous chapters that these two parameters are in principle independent. The relationship between these two parameters is discussed in sections 6.1–6.5 of this chapter. In section 6.1 evidence of a well-known language, namely Spanish, is introduced that uses both bound and free tenacious pronouns. Section 6.2 treats the feature combination 'free tenacious' in a more general fashion. Section 6.3 is devoted to the converse unusual combination 'bound alternating'. In section 6.4 I discuss languages that are most unconventional in having both free tenacious and bound alternating pronouns. Languages are often inconsistent (see Chapter 5) in what kinds of pronouns they employ, so within each of the sections 6.2–6.4 discussion is based on particular clause participant positions, such as Principals or Patientives. Section 6.5 concludes the part of the chapter devoted to the relationship between boundness and tenacity. A typology of languages based on these two parameters is proposed.

Another issue always raised in connection with bound pronouns is the relationship between bound pronouns and agreement. For example, personal desinences in Latin verbs are typically treated as agreement with subject. But pronominal subject NPs in Latin are rare and reference may be performed by personal desinences that then can qualify as bound pronouns. Which of these two interpretations has more truth to it? These problems are addressed in sections 6.6 and 6.7. More specifically, in section 6.6 I discuss the putative agreement nature of personal markers in three types of languages: those with polypersonal verbs, those with bipersonal verbs, and those with monopersonal verbs (such as Latin), and an approach applicable to all of them is proposed.

Section 6.7 addresses the evidence of very familiar but nevertheless very intricate (in this respect) languages, namely Germanic. The Germanic pattern is special in employing agreement markers that are less than referential on most occasions. The question of cross-linguistic frequency of this pattern is discussed, as well as those peripheral uses where some referential force can be attributed to agreement markers.

The final issue related to bound pronouns and addressed in this chapter is concerned with referential zero. In those languages that do not have bound pronouns, such as Japanese, but have only free referential devices it is natural to think of zeroes as free forms. However, some languages with bound pronouns do not express certain person–number combinations by any overt affixes; this especially concerns third person singular. Should we think of bound zeroes in this case? Or perhaps the free vs. bound zero dilemma is inessential? These questions are discussed in section 6.8.

6.1 Boundness does not equal tenacity

As has been discussed in Chapter 3 (subsection 3.3.2), bound pronouns are often tenacious: they are present in a clause irrespective of whether the referent is activated or not, and whether a corresponding full NP is present or not. If both a bound pronoun and a full NP are present, we face the situation of **double expression**, or double representation, of the same referent in a clause by two distinct elements. It is important to emphasize that such double expression is not just about referring to the same entity more than once. Of course, the latter happens within a clause in case of reflexivity, and possessive pronouns can also corefer to another mention of the same referent. In such cases, a referent has multiple instantiations in a clause. One and the same referent has three instantiations within one clause – as the agent, the goal, and the possessor – in the following example[1]:

(6.1)   One day, Cosette chanced to look at herself in her mirror <...>

In contrast, double expression occurring with tenacious pronouns means having more than one linguistic element corresponding to *one and the same* instantiation of a referent. In other words, more than one of the elements cumulatively perform a single mention of a referent.

---

[1] From an English translation of Victor Hugo's 'Les Misérables' (Volume 4, Book Third, beginning of Chapter 5, http://en.wikisource.org/wiki/Les_Mis%C3%A9rables/Volume_4/Book_Third/Chapter_5).

In discussions of bound pronouns it is often presumed that they are inherently tenacious and, conversely, only bound pronouns can be tenacious. Likewise, it is commonly presumed that free pronouns are alternating,[2] that is, are in a complementary distribution with independent NPs. This is indeed the case in many languages, including English, where there is one subject and one object expression per referent. This, however, is not universally so. In Chapter 3 (subsection 3.2.1) we have already seen some evidence from Hausa, a language with free pronouns remaining in the clause even when there is a coreferential full NP in the clause. Other examples of free tenacious pronouns have also been occasionally mentioned in Chapters 4 and 5. So the features of boundness and tenacity are independent. But are they fully independent? Along with free tenacious pronouns, do there exist bound alternating pronouns, that is pronominal affixes that are in a complementary distribution with the referent's full NP mention in the clause? I approach these questions, starting with the analysis of a familiar language, namely Spanish.[3]

6.1.1 *The case of Spanish*

Like other Romance languages, Spanish displays ample evidence of pronouns' tenacity:

(6.2) Spanish (Halpern 1998: 107)
Le   pus-o   comida   al   canario
3SG.DAT put-PAST.3SG food   to.the   canary
'S/he gave food to the canary'

(6.3) Spanish (Bossong 2003: 34)
A Juan lo   ha-n   visto   los profesores
to J.   3SG.M.ACC AUX-3PL see.PARTIC the professors
'The professors have seen Juan'

(6.4) Spanish (Bentivoglio 1983: 273)
<...> y   una parte de este aceite lo   tom-ó
       and a   part of this oil   3SG.M.ACC take-PAST.3SG
'<...> and she drank a part of this oil'

---

[2] Recall from Chapter 3 that the term 'alternating' strictly applies to the alternation between lexically full and reduced referential devices, rather than, for example, alternations between different reduced devices; the latter phenomenon was discussed under the name of referential sensitivity in Chapter 5.
[3] I thank Susanne Michaelis and Søren Wichmann for a useful discussion of Spanish, as well as of other Romance languages as discussed in Chapter 7 below.

(6.5) Spanish (Fernández Soriano 2000: 1260)
Se   lo   di   a María
3SG.DAT 3SG.M.ACC give.PAST.1SG to M.
'I gave it to María'

These examples illustrate: (6.2) – the dative pronoun *le* cooccurring with the recipient full NP in the clause; (6.3) – the accusative pronoun *lo* cooccurring with the Patientive human full NP in the clause; (6.4) – the accusative pronoun *lo* cooccurring with the Patientive inanimate full NP in the clause; (6.5) – both the dative and the accusative pronouns in one clause, the former cooccurring with a human recipient full NP. These kinds of pronouns are usually referred to as clitics, that is grammatical words that phonetically attach to another word. However, in their phonetic behaviour Spanish clitics are not very different from unstressed free pronouns in other languages, since unstressed pronouns generally cliticize to host words; see discussion in 3.2.2.

So the term 'clitic' does not really tell us much about the specialty of Spanish pronouns. Their really remarkable feature is that they are tenacious, that is they can (and sometimes must) occur together with coreferential full NPs contained in the same clause (and without them, of course, too); see e.g. Butt and Benjamin (2000: 146). This phenomenon is sometimes referred to as 'clitic doubling' or 'redundancy', and certainly reminds one of the Abkhaz-type bound pronouns in terms of tenacity. The question to address, then, is whether Spanish pronouns are indeed free (like English pronouns) or bound (as Abkhaz pronouns).

Among the criteria used to differentiate between affixes and clitics one usually begins with the clitics' variable location in the clause, which is not typical of affixes (see e.g. Haspelmath 2002: 152). In modern Spanish, pronouns are proclitic with indicative finite verbs (cf. 6.5 above) and enclitic with imperatives and and non-finite forms (cf. the gerund form in 6.6c below); see Green (1997: 108); Butt and Benjamin (2000: 136). By this criterion pronouns are not affixes but free forms. An even clearer piece of evidence pointing to the free status of Spanish pronouns is the phenomenon sometimes described as 'clitic climbing'. This means that a pronoun semantically belonging to a subordinate clause formally turns out in the matrix clause: instead of the previously prescribed construction such as *voy a verlo* 'I'm going to see it' more and more often *lo voy a ver* is used (Green 1997: 109).

The free character of Spanish pronouns cannot prevent us from noticing that Spanish pronouns are gradually accruing certain properties of affixes and may develop into fully-fledged bound morphemes in the future. The most general indication of this tendency is the aforementioned pattern of pronouns stacking in front of the verb and forming a template, according to which the indirect object pronoun precedes the direct object.[4] Anyway, overall the contemporary Spanish pronouns are far from being affixes and should be viewed as free forms.

These free pronouns are tenacious. In fact, their tenacity comes in various degrees depending on a number of factors. Generalizing over multiple diverse analyses, these factors can be formulated as hierarchies,[5] including:

- indirect object > direct object (Bresnan 2001b: 114)
- human > animate > inanimate (Green 1997: 107–108; Butt and Benjamin 2000: 147)
- definite > indefinite (Butt and Benjamin 2000: 146; Fernández-Ordóñez 2000: 1345)
- coreferential NP is pronominal > nominal (Green 1997: 107)
- coreferential NP is preverbal (topicalized) > postverbal (Butt and Benjamin 2000: 148).

In each of these hierarchies, the upper member is associated with higher tenacity. There is also a sociolinguistic dimension to the tenacity of Spanish pronouns: they differ strongly across dialects and registers – this concerns even dialects of Spain (Klein-Andreu 1996), not to mention dialects of Latin America. But when the conditions of the upper parts of the hierarchies are met, Spanish pronouns are fully tenacious. This analysis demonstrates that tenacity is not an all or nothing feature; it is rather a scalar notion.

In order to see how the Spanish free tenacious pronouns operate in discourse, consider an extract from a spoken Pear film (Chafe (ed.) 1980) retelling:

---

[4] There are also more concrete facts pointing to the teething affixal properties of the pronouns, one of which is the *l*-replacement. In Spanish, two pronominal clitics with the stem *l*- cannot follow each other. When a dative clitic *le* (plural *les*) is to be followed by an accusative clitic *lo(s)/la(s)*, it is replaced by *se*. That is, *se* stands for both singular *le* and plural *les*. In some Spanish dialects, plurality is, however, marked, but distantly from *se*: it attaches to the stem of the accusative pronoun. As the authors of a reference grammar put it, 'there is a universal but grammatically illogical tendency in spontaneous Latin-American speech to show that *se* stands for *les* by pluralizing the direct object pronoun, i.e. ?*se los dije* "I told it to them"' (Butt and Benjamin 2000: 141); see also example (6.5) above; for natural discourse examples see e.g. Company (2003: 223). These kinds of phenomena suggest that the pronouns are forming a tighter morphological complex between themselves and with the verb.

[5] In fact, some authors formulate certain of these distinctions as absolute, but the available body of evidence suggests that they are relative and hierarchical.

(6.6) Spanish (spoken)[6] (Comajoan 2006: 73)
   a. y   la chica   pues le   da-ø   le
      and   the girl_g then 3SG.DAT_b   hit-PRES.3SG_g 3SG.DAT_b

      quita-ø   al   chico   al   niño   el   sombrero
      seize-PRES.3SG_g to.the   boy_b   to.the   boy_b the hat
   b. que lleva-ba-ø
      that wear-IMPF-3SG_b
   c. y   entonces en esto de que quitar estar mirá-ndo-le
      and then   in this of that seize   be   look-GER-3SG.DAT_g
      a   ella
      to she_g
   d. pues no   se   da-ø   cuenta   bien de la carretera
      then not 3.REFL_b   give-PRES.3SG_b   account   well of the road
   e. y   en una y   ah   tropieza-ø   eh   con   una piedra
      and in a   and HES collide-PRES.3SG_b HES with a   rock
      'and the girl then takes the hat from the boy, that he was wearing,
      and then while looking at her he does not realize about the road
      and hits a rock'

In this extract three instances of the tenacious pronoun *le* appear in lines (a) and (c), all combined in their respective clauses with a coreferential NP, either nominal or pronominal (strong pronoun). The occurrences in (a), referring to the boy, are proclitic with respect to finite verbs, and the occurrence in (c) is enclitic as it appears with a gerund. For comparison, this extract also contains several instances of reduced subject reference by means of bound pronouns (traditionally, personal desinences). Bound subject reference is found in lines (a), (b), (d), and (e) (cf. subsection 6.6.3). The last three refer to the boy and are sole representatives of the referent in their respective clauses, while the occurrence in (a), referring to the girl, cooccurs with a full NP. So in Spanish both Principal and Patientive pronouns are tenacious, but they differ in freeness/boundness.

6.1.2 *Boundness vs. tenacity*

Conclusions to be drawn from the prior discussion are the following. First, tenacity is in principle independent from boundness: both Hausa (Chapter 3, subsection 3.2.1) and Spanish display free tenacious pronouns. Second, as the case of Hausa suggests, pronouns' tenacity in a language does not have to be uniform across

---

[6] Note that there are multiple false starts, repairs, and hesitations (such as *eh*) in this extract. I thank Julen Manterola Agirre for kindly clarifying some details of this Spanish example to me.

different clause participant positions. Just as Principal and Patientive pronouns can be different in terms of freeness/boundness (section 5.3), they can be different in terms of tenacity. So the issue of tenacity, in a general case, must be considered separately for Principal and Patientive pronouns. Third, as the Spanish material indicates, tenacity is scalar: some pronouns are fully tenacious while others only partially, and lose this property in certain semantic or pragmatic contexts. This can also be formulated in terms of referential sensitivity; see Chapter 5.

The discussion in the three subsequent sections follows these lines. Sections 6.2 and 6.3 are devoted to two unusual combinations of the features free/bound and tenacious/alternating, that is 'free tenacious' and 'bound alternating', respectively. In section 6.4 I discuss languages that are most unusual in having both free tenacious and bound alternating pronouns. Within each section, different clause participant positions (Principal vs. Patientive or other oppositions in alternative alignments) are considered, and some attention is paid to different degrees of tenacity as observed in different languages.

It must be kept in mind that the features of boundness and tenacity, although logically and empirically distinct, are correlated across the world's languages. Table 6.1 points to the difference between frequent and rare combinations of these features' values.

TABLE 6.1. Frequent and rare types of pronouns

	Free	Bound
Alternating	*frequent*	*rare*
Tenacious	*rare*	*frequent*

In this chapter I address the comparatively rare kinds of pronouns: free tenacious and bound alternating. This affects how the terms 'tenacious' and 'alternating' are used. Being alternating is assumed to be default for free pronouns. So pronouns that remain along with a coreferential NP at least in some contexts already qualify as tenacious. Likewise, being tenacious is the expectation for bound pronouns. Those bound pronouns that are absent on at least some occasions are considered alternating.

6.2 Free tenacious pronouns

6.2.1 *Principal*

In this subsection I present evidence from several languages whose Principal free pronouns have a certain degree of tenacity, while Patientive pronouns pattern variously. Ebira, a language of Nigeria, is a language with free pronouns; Adive (1989: 119 and elsewhere) calls them preverbs and writes them as separate words to verbs. With respect to tenacity they behave differently in different argumental positions. Principal (subject) pronouns are tenacious,[7] and Patientive (object) pronouns alternating:

(6.7) Ebira (Nupoid, Benue-Congo, Nigeria; Adive 1989: 108, 109, 120)
    i. Ìzé ọ̀ ré ozí
       Ize she see child
       'Ize saw the child'

    ii. ọ̀ ré ozí
       he see child
       'He saw the child'

    iii. Ìzé ọ̀ hị́ ọ́
       Ize she call him
       'Ize called him'

In Ọ̀kọ, another Nigerian language, free Principal (subject) pronouns are used.[8] Interestingly, they are highly tenacious in negative clauses but alternating in clauses with positive polarity:

(6.8) Ọ̀kọ (Benue-Congo, Nigeria; Atóyèbí 2007: 12)
    i. è=jìre íkíbà àjɛ
       3SG.SUBJ=steal money DET
       'S/he stole the money'

    ii. e=mè-jìre íkíbà àjɛ
       3SG.SUBJ=NEG-steal money DET
       'S/he did not steal the money'

    iii. Ɛ̀bola wá ádɛ́
       Bola drink beer
       'Bola drank beer'

    iv. Ɛ̀bola a=mà-wá ádɛ́
       Bola 3SG.SUBJ=NEG-drink beer
       'Bola did not drink beer'

---

[7] In all constructed examples cited by Adive there is always a pronoun cooccurring with a Principal full NP. But in the texts published in the same book there are instances when Principal pronouns are absent, especially if the referent appears highly activated. So in this language the pronouns' tenacity is limited.

[8] As I became aware at the final stage of the preparation of this book, Atóyèbí (2009) changed the interpretation of Ọ̀kọ pronominal elements from clitics to affixes; see comments on this at the end of subsection 3.2.3.

Semelai, a language of Malaysia, uses Agentive pronominal morphemes attached to the verb that Kruspe convincingly characterizes as clitics rather than affixes (Kruspe 2004: 87ff.). The presence of an Agentive pronoun does not depend on the presence of the corresponding full NP:

(6.9) Semelai (Austro-Asiatic, Malaysia; Kruspe 2004: 157, 262)
    i. smaʔ   ki=gɒɲ   la=kubuŋ
      person 3SG.A=bite A=flying.lemur
      'The flying lemur bit the person'

    ii. ki=tarek   hn-jalaʔ
      3SG.A=pull P-casting.net
      'He pulled the casting net'

Semelai third person pronouns are still tenacious when the referent is indefinite or generic:

(6.10) Semelai (Austro-Asiatic), Malaysia; Kruspe 2004: 157)
    de=ʔye-iʔ   la=smaʔ
    3PL.A=see-ITER A=person
    'People will keep on seeing you'

But they are sensitive in other ways – they can only be used when the referent is inherently active, when the event is individuated, and when the clause is transitive (Kruspe 2004: 158–161). Patientive pronouns in Semelai are free and alternating.

A system typologically similar to that of Semelai is found in Hmar, a language of the Kuki-Chin group of Sino-Tibetan, spoken in northeastern India (Dutta Baruah and Bapui 1996: 141, 126, 146).

To'aba'ita and Gela (both Southeast Solomonic Oceanic, Austronesian, Solomon Islands) are similar to the above discussed languages in that their Principal pronouns are free and tenacious but different in that their Patientive pronouns are bound and tenacious. This pattern is, in a sense, a mirror-image of that of Spanish. Both To'aba'ita and Gela examples have been presented in Chapter 5, see (5.5), (5.7).

6.2.2 Patientive

Free tenacious Patientive pronouns have already been illustrated by Spanish which also has bound tenacious Principal pronouns. As has been pointed out above, the Spanish system of free tenacious Patientive (and recipient) pronouns is found in other Romance languages as well, of course with certain variations; see Wanner (1987) for a historical account of this phenomenon.

A similar system emerged in other Indo-European languages of southern Europe, especially in South Slavic; see discussion in section 7.4.

Another language belonging to the same broad type (but of course different in details) is Yagua (Peba-Yaguan, Peru), described by Payne and Payne (1990) and Payne (1993). This language has the active alignment, that is, distinguishes Actors and Undergoers rather than Principals and Patientives. Actor pronouns are bound (prefixal)[9]; see (6.11i) below. With respect to tenacity, they pattern differently depending on where in the clause the full NP appears: if it is preverbal, pronouns do not occur (6.11ii), and if it is postverbal, the pronoun must be present (6.11iii):

(6.11) Yagua (Peba-Yaguan, Peru; Payne 1993: 18)[10]

    i. sa-jųtú=rà
       3SG.ACT-carry=3INAN.UND
       'S/he carries it'

    ii. jíryoonú   sų́ų́y-janu=níí
        bushmaster bite-PAST3=3SG.UND
        'A bushmaster (snake) bit him'

    iii. sa-suvų́ų́y   Anita
        3SG.ACT-afraid A.
        'Anita is afraid'

Undergoer pronouns are free (clitics); as Payne and Payne (1990: 403) point out, they phonologically attach 'to whatever precedes them'; in (6.11i) above an Undergoer pronoun is attached to the verb. Undergoer free pronouns are again tenacious, while the limitations on their tenacity is still more complex compared to Actor pronouns. When there is a preverbal NP, again a pronoun is absent; see (6.12i) below. When there is a postverbal NP, an additional factor comes into play, namely the importance of the referent in question in discourse (Payne 1993: 71–72). The pronoun is absent in case of the 'arguments that do not persist on the discourse stage, i.e., they are not "destined", as it were, to figure prominently in the immediately ensuing discourse' (Payne 1993: 29); see (6.12ii). In contrast, the pronoun is present if the referent 'will persist for a greater span of text' (Ibid.); see (6.12iii):

---

[9] Payne and Payne (1990) call these pronouns clitics, but in the later publication Payne (1993) uses different phrasing: for Actor pronouns he uses the term 'prefixes', thus obviously contrasting them to Undergoer clitics. I follow the phrasing of the later source.

[10] Yagua examples are provided here in Payne's morphemic transcription that makes morpheme boundaries clear rather than in phonemic representation in which such boundaries are often blurred.

(6.12) Yagua (Peba-Yaguan, Peru; Payne 1993: 31, 27, 28)
  i. suvǫ́ǫ́ ri-jivaay
     string.bag 1SG.ACT-make
     'I am making a string bag'
  ii. sa-jatu buyąą
      3SG.ACT-drink manioc.beer
      'S/he drinks manioc beer'
  iii. sa-ruuy-yęęy=rà japatiy
       3SG.ACT-roast-DISTR=3INAN.UND coca
       'S/he is roasting coca'

Further subtler factors potentially affecting pronouns' tenacity include adjacency of a full NP and referent's animacy (Payne and Payne 1990: 254ff., 361ff.).

6.2.3 Both Principal and Patientive

As there are languages with free tenacious Principal pronouns, as well as languages with free tenacious Patientive pronouns, there is a chance that we can find languages with both. Indeed, such languages do exist. Bilua, a Papuan language of Solomon Islands (potentially Central Solomon family; see Obata 2003: 2–5), displays both Principal and Patientive free tenacious pronouns. This is made apparent by the following natural discourse examples:

(6.13) Bilua (Central Solomon, Solomon Islands; Obata 2003: 115)
  a. omadeu taku sike tamania ke=beta e=ke
     one time five brother&sister 3PL.NOM=CONT stay=HIST
  b. ke=beta e=ke inio <...>
     3PL.NOM=CONT stay=HIST and.then
     'Once upon a time, there were five brothers and sisters living. They were living, and <...>'

(6.14) Bilua (Central Solomon, Solomon Islands; Obata 2003: 30)
  sai vo=a ziolo ke=papue=v=e
  there 3SG.M.NOM=LIG devil 3PL.NOM=sit=3SG.M.ACC=REMPAST
  jari topi
  copra.house on.top
  'There, they sat the devil on the copra house'

(6.15) Bilua (Central Solomon, Solomon Islands; Obata 2003: 114)
  ke=v=a ina-inae=k=e <...>
  3PL.NOM=3SG.M.ACC=VALINCR REDUP-get.ready=3SG.F.ACC=REMPAST
  'And they got food ready for him <...>'

196   *II. Typology of Reduced Referential Devices*

In this set of examples, one can see that the Bilua pronouns are indeed free. They attach to various hosts – in particular, the third person plural Principal (nominative) pronoun is procliticized to the continuity analytic marker in (6.13a, b), to the valency-increasing marker in (6.15), and to a lexical verb in (6.14); Patientive (accusative) pronouns can be either enclitic or proclitic (6.14), (6.15). Principal (nominative) pronouns are tenacious – they appear as the sole referential device in (6.13b), (6.14), and (6.15) and along with a full NP in (6.13a). Patientive (accusative) pronouns are tenacious as well; they appear both by themselves in (6.15) and along with a full NP in (6.14). Finally, (6.15) demonstrates that ditransitive clauses can have three similar clitic pronouns: the one for the Patientive encliticized to the verb and the one for the recipient procliticized to the valency-increasing marker. This last example also suggests that the Patientive pronouns are referentially insensitive: the generic Patientive 'food' is referred to by a regular third person pronoun. Some examples provided by Obata (2003: 25) may suggest that Principal pronouns are more sensitive and are absent when the participant in question is indefinite or inanimate. However, they are kept in clause coordination (see e.g. Obata 2003: 255).

Another language also employing a full set of free tenacious pronouns is Dan-Gwèètaa (Mande, Ivory Coast). Dan-Gwèètaa Principal (subject) pronouns have been illustrated already in Chapter 4, examples (4.10)–(4.12). These Principal pronouns are compounded with clausal categories, and this fact possibly contributes to their tenacity. Principal pronouns are insensitive to lowered referential status, such as indefiniteness in the following example, formally marked by *dō* 'one, certain':

(6.16)   Dan-Gwèètaa (Mande, Ivory Coast; Valentin Vydrine, personal communication)

yɤ́	ń	nìmɔ́ɔ̀	ɓā	à̱		gbɤ̄	dō
CONS	1SG.NSUBJ	younger.inlaw	ART	3SG.NSUBJ		son	one
ɤ́	nū	Dōmōɗô					
3SG.CJT	come.CJT	Domoro					

'Then a son of my younger inlaw came to Domoro'

In general, the Dan-Gwèètaa Principal free pronouns are as tenacious as bound pronouns in polysynthetic languages, such as Navajo and Abkhaz. This is what Creissels (1991) apparently means by calling these kinds of elements in African languages pronominal indexes (*indices pronominaux*).

Patientive (object) pronouns in Dan-Gwèètaa are also tenacious; see the nonsubject pronoun à̱ in (6.17a):

(6.17) Dan-Gwèètaa (Mande, Ivory Coast; Valentin Vydrine, personal communication)
a. ɗɛ́ ɤ́   kwɛ́ɛ̀ ɓā à   ɗū,
   that 3SG.CJT load ART 3SG.NSUBJ pack.CJT
b. yɤ́   ɤ́   à   dà   gɔ̄   gúu
   CONS 3SG.CJT 3SG.NSUBJ go.up.CJT vehicle in
   'When he packed the luggage he put it into the car'

However, Patientive pronouns are not as fully tenacious as Principal pronouns: they are absent if the referent is marked with the indefiniteness marker *dō*; see example (4.12b) in Chapter 4 where the loaf of bread is indefinite and there is no subsequent pronoun.

Interestingly, these rules for 'nonsubject' pronouns are the same irrespective of whether they appear in the Patientive position, as in (6.17) and (4.12b), or in the possessor position. An example of the latter appears in (6.16), where in the possessive NP 'my younger inlaw's son' the 'younger inlaw' is marked with the definite article *ɓā*, and in accordance with that the nonsubject pronoun *à* follows. This means that the tenacity of free pronouns can extend to possessive NPs. A comparable phenomenon is well known in consistently head-marking, bound-pronominal languages that require the name of the possessed to contain a possessive pronominal affix referring to the possessor. In such languages the meaning 'the boy's dog' is literally conveyed as *the-boy his-dog* (see the Abkhaz example (3.16) in Chapter 3). The difference of the much less synthetic Dan-Gwèètaa pattern is that possessive pronouns are words, not affixes; otherwise the structure is isomorphic: *boy the his dog*. This pattern is noted in the typological study of Nichols and Bickel (2005a), and exemplified by the northern Australian isolate Tiwi.[11]

6.3 Bound alternating pronouns

In this section I discuss the pattern that is converse to the one just considered: the combination of the features 'bound' and 'alternating'. Just like the combination 'free' and 'tenacious', this combination is typologically rare, but it is attested.

---

[11] This pattern actually is not totally exotic, as can be seen by composing the two studies of Nichols and Bickel (2005a) and Dryer (2005b). The combination of features 'head-marking' and 'no possessive affixes' carves out the relevant subset of languages with this pattern. There are nine of them out of 164 languages shared by the two studies. Tiwi is not among these nine, since it was judged to use a different pattern as the main one by Nichols and Bickel (2005a).

6.3.1 Patientive

Upper Kuskokwim, an Athabaskan language of central Alaska,[12] uses bound pronominal affixes for Principals and Patientives. In particular, the accusative (Patientive) bound pronouns appear in the accusative position on the morphological template of Upper Kuskokwim verbs:

(6.18) Upper Kuskokwim (Na-Dene, Alaska, USA)
    i. si-ch'i-ne-ł'anh
       1SG.ACC-INDEF.NOM-PREF-look
       'Something (an animal) is looking at me'
    ii. yi-ø-ne-ł'anh
       33.ACC-3.NOM-PREF-look
       'S/he is looking at it/him/her'

In (6.18i) one can see both nominative and accusative overt pronouns. In (6.18ii) both participants are third person, and the only overt pronoun is the accusative one, as the third person nominative is zero. (The issue of zero person marking, and, in particular, reasons for postulating or not postulating a zero affix, will be discussed at some length in section 6.8.)

In contrast to (6.18ii), when there is a Patientive full NP in the clause, there is no accusative pronoun any longer:

(6.19) Upper Kuskokwim (Na-Dene, Alaska, USA)
    guga'   ø-ne-ł'anh
    baby   3.NOM-PREF-look
    'S/he is looking at the baby'

The accusative pronouns in (6.18) are certainly argumental, while in (6.19) argumental is the full NP. Theoretically, it is possible to suggest that there is a zero accusative pronoun in (6.19), but I believe this is exactly the case when 'zero is not there' (Mithun 1986c). Since there is a clear difference between the presence of bound pronouns in (6.18) and absence thereof in (6.19), and there already is an element that bears referentiality in (6.19) a zero referential device should not be posited; see discussion at the beginning of section 3.4. Therefore, the bound third person pronoun *yi-* (6.18ii) must be judged alternating.

The same pattern is discussed by Helmbrecht (2004: 228) for Warembori, a Papuan language (Papua, Indonesia), quoting from Donohue (1999a). An isolated element of a bound pronoun's alternation is found in Abkhaz.

---

[12] Upper Kuskokwim data come from my fieldwork on this language in Nikolai, Alaska, in 1996–97 and 2001.

Normally, all Abkhaz bound pronouns are fully tenacious. But there is one exception: the Absolutive pronoun *j-* (third person singular non-human and third person plural) is absent when a full NP is found in the clause. One such instance can be seen in example (3.14e) where the verb lacks a bound pronoun referring to 'the task'.

6.3.2 Both Principal and Patientive

The Upper Kuskokwim pattern extends to both core arguments in a number of languages with bound pronouns. The Kabba language (Central Sudanic) provides such an example. Moser (2004: 93–112) unequivocally describes pronominal elements of this language as affixes: subject pronouns are prefixes and object pronouns are suffixes. Both subject and object pronominal affixes appear to be present in a complementary distribution with the corresponding full NPs. Note the verb meaning 'throw, place, put' in the following two examples:

(6.20) Kabba (Central Sudanic, Chad and Central African Republic; Moser 2004: 230, 221)

    i. Lúbba ìla ji kàjì` là-á dɔ-jé tɔ́ kára kára tóyn
       God put hand heal GEN-3SG head-1PL LOC one one all
       'May God place his healing hands on each one of us'

    ii. n-íl-ɛ́ kɔr.ɔ́
       3SG.SUBJ-put-3S.OBJ bush.LOC
       'He threw it into the bush'

Another language of this kind is Macushi (Cariban; Guyana, Brazil, and Venezuela), described by Abbott (1991) and discussed in the recent books by Siewierska (2004: 123ff.) and Corbett (2006: 108). Examples relevant to the point appear on pp. 83–84 of Abbott (1991).

Siewierska (2004: 163) provides illustrative lists of languages that have alternating bound pronouns (pronominal agreement markers, in her terminology): eight languages for the agentive pronouns and 21 languages for the patientive pronouns. To her list I can add Larike (Indonesia), a language with active alignment. Although Larike bound pronouns are tenacious (Laidig and Laidig 1990: 96), they are actually absent when the referent is of a lowered referential status.[13] Consider the bound pronoun in (6.21i) vs. its absence (6.21ii), with a referentially lowered Undergoer:

---

[13] See also Laidig and Laidig's (1990: 106) suggestions on when bound pronouns are absent.

200 II. *Typology of Reduced Referential Devices*

(6.21) Larike (Central Moluccan, Austronesian, Maluku, Indonesia; Laidig and Laidig 1990: 97, 96)
  i. <...> la   itidu-na-ʔuna-ya
     then 1TRI.INCL.ACT-IRREAL-make-3SG.NH.UND
     '<...> then the three of us can make it'
  ii. ite siʔu ite-hala   weidu
      we   also 1PL.INCL.ACT-bring water
      'We also brought water'

6.4 Free tenacious and bound alternating pronouns

Both types of languages – those with free tenacious and those with bound alternating pronouns – are infrequent among the world's languages. Still more surprising are languages that display both of these kinds of pronouns. One of these, the Oceanic language South Efate, has free tenacious Principal pronouns and bound alternating Patientive pronouns. This is a rather unusual combination.

(6.22) South Efate (Southern Oceanic, Austronesian, Vanuatu; Thieberger 2006: 269)
  a. ra=pitlak   tesa   nmatu iskei.
     3DU.REAL.NOM=have   child girl   one
  b. i=skot-i-r   to.
     3SG.REAL.NOM=be.with-TRANS-3PL.ACC   stay
  'They had a daughter. She stayed with them.'

(6.23) South Efate (Southern Oceanic, Austronesian, Vanuatu; Thieberger 2006: 113–114)
  ale,   ntuam i=na   i=to <...>
  then   devil 3SG.REAL.NOM=want   3SG.REAL.NOM=stay
  'Then the devil stayed <...>'

(6.24) South Efate (Southern Oceanic, Austronesian, Vanuatu; Thieberger 2006: 294)
  u=mer   taos   apap   nigmam go
  1PL.EXCL.REAL.NOM=in.turn   follow father our   and
  mama   nigmam pak talm̃at
  mother our   to   garden
  'We then followed our father and our mother to the garden'

South Efate Principal (nominative) pronouns are free; they attach to verbs in most examples above, but to an adverbial in (6.24). At the same time, they are tenacious – one appears along with a full NP in (6.23). In contrast, Patientive (accusative) pronouns are bound (6.22b). When there is a full NP in a clause, the Patientive pronoun is absent. This concerns not only indefinite (6.22a) but also human definite referents (6.24).

A similar combined pattern is found in Godié, a Kru language. Marchese (1986) makes it clear that subject pronouns in this language are free and relatively tenacious, while object pronouns are bound[14] and alternating:

(6.25) Godié (Kru, Ivory Coast; Marchese 1986: 221, 223)
    i. ɔ lʌ̀-ɔ-ny-a
        3H brought-3H-EPENTH-3NH
        'He brought it to him'
    ii. Dali (ɔ) mʉ̀ Dakpadu
        D.   3H went Dakpadou
        'Dali went to Dakpadou'
    iii. ɔ   lʌ̀   kifi   pʉtʉ
        3H brought chief package
        'He brought the chief a package'

Both a free Principal pronoun and bound Patientive and recipient pronouns can be seen in (6.25i). The Principal pronoun optionally stays when a full NP is present (6.25ii), whereas the Patientive and the recipient pronouns are absent on such an occasion (6.25iii).

6.5 Boundness and tenacity

As we have seen, the two typological parameters 'free vs. bound' and 'alternating vs. tenacious' are in principle independent, and all possible combinations exist. The combinations 'free tenacious' and 'bound alternating' are clearly a typological minority. A precise specification of their frequency among the world's languages is a matter for future empirical research. To the extent that the typology of Dryer (2005a) can be translated into the notional system proposed here, it can be estimated that 10 to 15% of languages may use free tenacious Principal pronouns. No comparable quantitative evidence is available for bound alternating pronouns. Relying on the available partial evidence, my prediction is that the relative cross-linguistic frequencies of the four types of pronouns forms the following cline: bound tenacious > free alternating > free tenacious > bound alternating.

Unlike the distinction between free and bound forms that is notionally categorial (even though there are transitional cases), the tenacity feature is

---

[14] Marchese (1986: 222) uses the term 'clitics' to refer to object pronouns but he describes their behaviour so that they seem more like affixes; he also contrasts them quite sharply to subject pronouns, so my interpretation should not be too far from reality.

behavioural and, therefore, is a matter of degree. Various pronouns of various languages are sensitive to diverse context factors that lead, cumulatively, to various types of behaviour and, consequently, different degrees of tenacity. In the future, a thorough study of all factors, favouring the alternating pattern in bound pronouns, as well as the limits on free pronouns' tenacity, is in order. It appears that the typologically more frequent kinds of pronouns, such as in Lyélé (free alternating) and Navajo (bound tenacious) are relatively insensitive, whereas tenacity in free pronouns and alternation in bound pronouns are often subject to a variety of factors which renders the picture in the respective languages substantially more complex; cf., for example, the case of Yagua discussed above in detail.

Judging by the evidence analysed above (section 6.2), free pronouns are never as tenacious as the bound pronouns of languages such as Navajo. The tenacity of free pronouns is always amenable to various restrictions. This fact points to the qualitative difference between morphology and syntax: if something is morphologically expressed in a language, then it is really deeply engraved in its nature. Syntax, on the other hand, is always more fluid and prone to various context factors. It is morphology, in the first place, that forms the core of a language's grammar.

Although the feature tenacity vs. alternation is explicitly introduced in this book, other authors have addressed the issue in their own terms, partly intersecting with my approach. In particular, my alternating and tenacious pronouns are similar in their scope to Siewierska's (2004: 126) pronominal and ambiguous agreement markers, respectively. Also consonant to the idea of tenacity is the notion of multirepresentation proposed by Corbett (2006: 106).

The notion of tenacity is a theoretical replacement for the notion of 'argument type' (that is, nominal vs. pronominal arguments). As was demonstrated in 3.3.3, this latter notion oversimplifies things too much. There are not merely two classes of languages, each with its own argument type. When there is tenacity of pronouns, whether bound or free, argumenthood is distributed between pronouns and other NPs. Languages do not break up neatly along the tenacity distinction, as pronouns are variably tenacious in different circumstances.

The most obvious distinction between pronouns within individual languages is the distinction in terms of clause participant roles. For the sake of simplification I construe this distinction as Principal vs. Patientive, though in fact other alignments can be employed. Table 6.2 lists 16 theoretically imaginable language types, resulting from multiplication of two binary features (free/bound and alternating/tenacious) and their possible distributions to two clause participant positions. Where known, representative languages are

TABLE 6.2. A typology of languages in accordance with pronoun boundness, tenacity, and clause participant role

Type #	Principal	Patientive	Example languages
1	free alternating	free alternating	Lyélé, English
2	bound tenacious	bound tenacious	Abkhaz, Navajo
3	free alternating	free tenacious	Hoava[15]
4	free alternating	bound alternating	
5	free alternating	bound tenacious	
6	bound tenacious	free tenacious	Spanish, Yagua
7	bound tenacious	bound alternating	Upper Kuskokwim, Warembori
8	bound tenacious	free alternating	
9	free tenacious	free tenacious	Bilua, Dan-Gwèètaa
10	free tenacious	free alternating	Ebira, Semelai
11	free tenacious	bound tenacious	Gela, To'aba'ita
12	free tenacious	bound alternating	South Efate, Godié
13	bound alternating	bound alternating	Kabba, Larike
14	bound alternating	free alternating	
15	bound alternating	bound tenacious	
16	bound alternating	free tenacious	

cited corresponding to language types. The two purest types are located at the top of the table.

What do the empty boxes in Table 6.2 indicate? They may simply indicate that appropriate language examples have not been located. However, it may be more than mere chance that such languages were not found. If the emptiness of the boxes is not accidental, implicational regularities might be proposed, such as 'If the Principal pronoun is free alternating, the Patientive pronoun is free', and 'If the Principal pronoun is bound alternating, the Patientive pronoun is the same'. Such suggestions, however, are speculative at this point and much more cross-linguistic work is necessary to prove or falsify them.

---

[15] In Hoava (Meso-Melanesian Oceanic, Austronesian, Solomon Islands), as described by Palmer (2009), there is a clitic (therefore, free) accusative pronoun appearing with third and second singular objects which is highly tenacious; they are absent, however, if the object NP follows the verb, or, as Palmer puts it, is incorporated (word order is normally VSO). Subject pronouns, being phonologically heavier and less integrated with the verbal word, are alternating.

TABLE 6.3. Yagua system of pronouns: a summary

		Actor	Undergoer
1	Boundness	bound (prefix)	free (enclitic)
2	Tenacity	tenacious	tenacious
3	Factors favouring tenacity	• postverbal position of full NP	• postverbal position of full NP • referent's importance in discourse

Grasping a language's system of pronouns in terms of boundness and tenacity is important for a holistic understanding of the language's nature. This is because pronouns are at the very core of referential processes, and reference, in turn, is one of the most fundamental components of language production and comprehension. Extracting information on the system of pronouns from language description is not always easy. Thinking of future and better language grammars, it would be helpful if the systems of pronouns were concisely characterized according to the most central parameters, including boundness, tenacity, possible difference between clause participant roles, and specific sensitivities. By way of an exercise, in Table 6.3 I present a matrix comprising the main features of Yagua, a language that was accounted for above in detail.

Of course, a matrix such as in Table 6.3 must be adjusted to the properties of a given language. In particular, a language's alignment may be not active, as in Yagua, but accusative, ergative, or tripartite. Also, it is informative to ask about the patterning of pronouns in non-core argumental positions, as well as possessive pronouns. Potentially, there can be differences in the patterning of different third person pronouns and different persons as well. The number of factors in line 3 can be much greater; cf. the discussion of Spanish in subsection 6.1.1 above; Siewierska (2005e: 415) mentions a wide range of potential factors, including those as remote from reference as aspect and polarity.

6.6 Bound pronouns are not agreement markers

Languages with bound pronouns look very unusual from a Eurocentric perspective. This especially concerns polysynthetic Abkhaz-type languages that include multiple bound pronouns, corresponding to all arguments, in the inflected verb. This unusual appearance results in divergent views of the nature of verbal person markers among linguists.

On the one hand, specialists in polysynthetic languages usually have little doubt that personal affixes on the verb are of a pronominal nature, that they are direct analogues of free argumental pronouns in a language like English, and thus are referring units; see e.g. Boas (1911: 646) on Chinook (Chinookan, northwestern USA), Bloomfield (1946: 97–99) on Algonquian, Sapir and Hoijer (1967) on Navajo (Na-Dene, Southwest of the USA), Van Valin (1977: 3) on Lakhota (Siouan, South Dakota and North Dakota, USA), Chafe (1996: 563) on Seneca (Iroquoian, New York State, USA), Mithun (1991, 1999: 189ff.) on North America in general, Reed and Payne (1986: 325) on Asheninca (Arawakan, Peru), Heath (1984: 347ff.) on Nunggubuyu (Gunwinyguan, northern Australia), etc. For Abkhaz-Adyghean languages, a similar point has been made by Kumaxov (1974) on Circassian (Russia), Hewitt (1979: 101, 208ff.) and Spruit (1986: 108ff.) on Abkhaz (Abkhazia).

On the other hand, some linguists are reluctant to recognize the functional equivalence of bound pronouns of polysynthetic languages and free (weak) pronouns of more familiar languages and prefer to call the polysynthetic person markers agreement; see e.g. Baker (1996), Bresnan (2001a), Bickel and Nichols (2007). Within the agreement approach, the Abkhaz-type structure is often called polypersonal agreement,[16] in contrast to monopersonal agreement such as in Spanish. Some authors seem to use the bound pronoun and personal agreement terminology interchangeably; see e.g. Helmbrecht (2004: 223ff.).

The bound pronouns vs. agreement dilemma has been discussed on many occasions during the last decades, beginning with Givón (1976), Jelinek (1985), Bresnan and Mchombo (1987). Some more recent discussions need to be briefly assessed here. Evans (2002) argued against the generally pronominal character of person markers in the verb of Bininj Gun-wok (Gunwinyguan, northern Australia), a highly polysynthetic language, relying primarily on the observation that the person markers are not as referentially sensitive (or committal, in Evans's terms) as their counterparts in languages with free pronouns, and therefore should better be considered analogues of agreement markers in European languages. Mithun (2003) provided a detailed counterargument, based on the data of Central Yup'ik (Eskimo-Aleut, Alaska, USA) and Navajo (Na-Dene, Southwest of the USA), and suggested that the difference between bound and free (weak) pronouns is not that great: bound pronouns are referential most of the time, while free pronouns of European languages can be non-referential (this is well known about English *it, they,* and *you*). It can be added to Mithun's argument that, in fact, in certain instances bound pronouns are referentially more sensitive than free

---

[16] In fact, these are unfortunate terms since what is invariably 'poly' in an Abkhaz-type verb is not persons (all person markers can be third person) but rather coded participants. So 'poly-participant agreement' would probably be a more adequate term. However, below I stick to the traditional terminology.

pronouns. For example, the third person masculine free pronoun of standard French *il* is quite insensitive as it is used in all kinds of non-referential contexts, such as *il faut* 'it is necessary, one should', *il y a* 'there is/are'. At the same time, in colloquial French, where pronouns have largely become bound (see Chapter 7), non-referential *il* usually is absent:

(6.26) Colloquial French (Lambrecht 1981: 27)
    i. Y-en-a   qu'   pour lui
       there-REFPART-have except for him
       'He/she/they care(s) only for him'

    ii. La   maison est nue, pas habitée, faut   arriver, faut
        the   house is bare not inhabited should come should
        tout nettoyer
        all   clean
       'The house is empty, uninhabited, one should come, one should clean everything'

This suggests that bound pronouns of colloquial French have become more referentially sensitive than their free counterparts at an earlier stage of development, still preserved in standard French.

While both Evans and Mithun contrast pronouns and person agreement (though interpreting specific instances differently), other authors essentially lift an opposition between the two phenomena.[17] Siewierska (2004: 125) proposes that 'the attempts to distinguish person agreement markers from anaphoric pronouns so far have met with little success', and uses the 'person agreement' as a cover term embracing bound pronouns as well.[18] Corbett (2006: 100–112) enumerates five criteria that he finds particularly useful in telling apart free pronouns, pronominal affixes and agreement: number of case roles (agreement typically singles out one privileged participant); degree of referentiality (see the discussion of the Evans–Mithun debate above); descriptive content (agreement markers have little or no content, and free pronouns have the maximum); balance of information between full NPs and person markers (pronouns have more features than agreement); and multi- vs. unirepresentation (the idea of this criterion is close to my tenacity feature: how many copies of an entity is found in a clause). Having reviewed these criteria in detail, Corbett concludes that 'the relative nature of these differences shows why it is difficult to frame tests to distinguish agreement markers

---

[17] This approach was characteristic already of Givón (1976).
[18] Cf. the ideas of Bosch (1983) who equated syntactic anaphora with agreement.

from pronominal affixes ... the insistence on a rigid classification into languages with agreement or with pronominal affixes would limit rather than enhance future research' (Corbett 2006: 110–112).

Of course, as personal pronouns and person agreement are diachronically related (the latter emerges from the former), they cannot be strictly opposed in all instances. However, it is still useful to distinguish between these two phenomena as two different prototypes. Before I present arguments for this point, the question of what exactly agreement is needs to be addressed.[19]

6.6.1 What is agreement?

An oft-cited definition says: 'The term *agreement* [original emphasis – A.K.] commonly refers to some syntactic covariance between a semantic or formal property of one element and a formal property of another' (Steele 1978: 610). Similarly, according to A. E. Kibrik (1977c), agreement is observed when an independent or dependent feature A of word X implies a dependent feature B in word Y. Of course, these definitions require agreement markers to be tenacious.

It is important to specify: the target of alleged agreement in the relevant instances is the verb, and the relevant question is whether the verb agrees with external NPs. The assumed domain of agreement is the clause. If we conclude, after all, that the personal markers in question are bound pronouns, they may still agree with antecedents or referents, as free pronouns do. But in this case they would be referential items rather than mere copies of NP features on the verb. So the concept of the agreement of pronouns is irrelevant to this discussion. When talking about agreement, I only mean agreement with a syntactic controller.

Another reservation is that what interests us at this point is the potential person (and number) agreement of the verb. Instances of person agreement on non-verbs (for example, on possessed nouns) and of other categories that can possibly be involved in agreement, such as gender (e.g. in Daghestanian languages), are excluded from this discussion.

The bound pronoun vs. agreement dilemma is considered below, beginning with Abkhaz-type languages with polypersonal verbs and proceeding with Spanish-type ones with monopersonal verbs. Then I discuss the intermediate languages with bipersonal verbs.

---

[19] After this book was essentially completed, I became acquainted with the article Siewierska and Bakker (2005) devoted to the relationships between reference and agreement. Some ideas of that article are quite consonant with what is proposed below.

6.6.2 *Languages with polypersonal verbs*

In a polysynthetic language such as Abkhaz, when a clause argument is highly activated by the beginning of the given clause – because of being a locutor or an activated third person referent – then it gets coded normally only as a personal affix on the verb. This is a typical situation: the verb simply has nothing to agree with. The proportion in the Abkhaz discourse example (3.14) is representative: out of eight argumental mentions of referents, six are expressed by bound pronouns alone. If the referent was not activated before the given clause, a full NP appears along with the personal affix, as in (3.14c). Mithun (1987: 286), analysing three polysynthetic languages of North America and Australia, counted that transitive clauses have two overt nominal constituents only in 1 to 3% of all instances, and Principal NPs are found in 10 to 12% of all clauses. According to Du Bois (1987), in Sacapultec (Mayan, Guatemala), another polysynthetic language, only about a half of clause arguments are realized as full NPs.

If a full NP is absent in the clause, the agreement analysis is untenable by definition of agreement. Therefore, in such instances we must recognize that personal markers are referential, and thus they are pronouns (in accordance with the understanding of pronoun adopted in this book). But what about those instances when a full NP is present? In this case one can logically claim that this is agreement, since at least there is a potential agreement controller within the clause. However, it would be preferable to come up with a unified interpretation of person markers that would hold both for clauses with and without full NPs. Now, if we do recognize that they are always bound pronouns, what is the relationship between a bound pronoun and a full NP within the same clause? My suggestion, put forward in Kibrik (1988, 1992b), is that there is a kind of anaphoric relation between the full NP and a bound pronoun; this is a case of syntactic anaphora, that is, coreference in a local domain. This kind of syntactic anaphora is often referentially insensitive and may involve new, indefinite, negative-pronominal (such as 'nobody') full NP antecedents; cf. the discussion of the Evans–Mithun debate above. See also the following formulation: 'Yup'ik and Navajo differ from English and German simply in the absence of a restriction: pronominal reference can be established within the same clause as well' (Mithun 2003: 274). As was argued in section 3.3, a bound pronoun and a coreferential full NP can both safely be considered argumental.

In addition to this general reasoning, applicable to all polysynthetic languages with polypersonal verbs, languages often provide anecdotal evidence rendering the agreement approach particularly unsuitable. Such evidence is language-specific and therefore can hardly be generalized, so I would just provide an illustration here. Navajo[20] has several prefixal slots in its polysynthetic verb form for inserting pronominal elements. One of these slots is for accusative[21] bound pronouns, for example:

(6.27) Navajo (Na-Dene, Southwest of the USA)
　　　i. né-i-ø-ni-łts'in
　　　　ITER-33.ACC-3.NOM-PREF-beat
　　　　'S/he (3) beats him/her (3) repeatedly'
　　　ii. ná-ho-ø-ni-łts'in
　　　　ITER-4.ACC-3.NOM-PREF-beat
　　　　'S/he (3) beats him/her (4) repeatedly'

In (6.27i) the accusative-coded participant is expressed by the regular third person bound pronoun *yi-* (surfacing as *i-* in this particular case),[22] while in (6.27ii) it is the special pronoun *ho-*, traditionally called fourth person. To put it simply, Navajo fourth person is a deferential variant of the third, sometimes second, person pronoun; see Haile (1941: 17, 72, 114), Kibrik (1988: 81–96), Willie (1991: Ch. 4.) Any of these accusative pronouns can cooccur with a full NP indicating the patient of beating:

(6.28) Navajo (Na-Dene, Southwest of the USA)
　　　i. hastiin né-i-ø-ni-łts'in
　　　　man　　ITER-33.ACC-3.NOM-PREF-beat
　　　　'S/he (3) beats the man (3) repeatedly'
　　　ii. hastiin ná-ho-ø-ni-łts'in
　　　　man　　ITER-4.ACC-3.NOM-PREF-beat
　　　　'S/he (3) beats the man (4) repeatedly'

That is, the choice of an accusative pronoun remains variable, even when the full NP is present. Clearly this behaviour does not fit naturally into the notion of agreement, according to which a controller (in this case, presumably, the full NP 'the man') influences the properties of the target. In Navajo, this is an anecdotal piece of evidence showing that bound pronouns are referential devices and can hardly be viewed as agreement with free NPs. Also note that Navajo bound personal pronouns appear in the same morphological positions as other bound

---

[20] Navajo data comes from my fieldwork on this language conducted during the 1990s in Arizona, New Mexico, and Moscow.
[21] The traditional term is 'object pronouns'. In Kibrik (in press a) I provide an extended argument in favour of the case-based terminology for morphological positions in the verb of Navajo and other polysynthetic languages.
[22] As was discussed in Chapter 4 (section 4.3), this pronoun occurs when the nominative-coded argument is a third person as well, hence the gloss '33.ACC'.

pronouns, including reflexive, reciprocal, indefinite and areal pronouns; see Young and Morgan (1987: 64ff.) That is, different kinds of pronouns form a coherent paradigm. This makes the agreement interpretation even less likely.

Evidence from native speakers' intuitions also contributes to the pronominal interpretation of person markers in polysynthetic languages. As was pointed out by Mithun (1986a: 51, 1986c: 198), bilingual speakers report that person markers are akin to English free pronouns and would never surmise that something is omitted in a clause consisting of a verb with person affixes. Perhaps some day an experimental psycholinguistic (or neurolinguistic?) study can be performed, testing the claim about functional equivalence of bound pronouns and free pronouns.

6.6.3 Languages with monopersonal verbs

It is generally the case that the issue of bound pronouns is discussed in connection with polypersonal verbs. But do bound pronouns have to be multiple? Such a categorical requirement appears highly unlikely. Evidently, a language does not have to acquire the full set of bound pronouns in a flash, but rather one after another. In Chapter 7 we will look into the evolutionary rise of bound pronouns. Now let us consider an example of a well-known language that arguably has a single bound subject pronoun, namely Latin. Consider an elementary example:

(6.29) Latin
    i. Lūd-it
       play-PRES.3SG
       'S/he plays'
    ii. Puer   lūd-it
       boy.NOM play-PRES.3SG
       'The boy plays'
    iii. Is   lūd-it
       he.NOM play-PRES.3SG
       'Hé plays'

The intransitive verb 'play' is used in this example. In (6.29i) the sole argument of the verb is coded in the clause by the personal desinence -t, while in (6.29ii) reference is performed by the combination of the same desinence and a full NP. The situation is exactly as in Abkhaz or Navajo, with the difference that only one argument is represented in the verb by means of a personal affix. (Another difference, though irrelevant here, is that some of the Latin personal affixes are compounds, also involving clausal categories, particularly tense; see discussion at the end of section 4.4.) If a transitive verb were used, still only the Principal personal affix would be found on the verb.

The structure as in (6.29iii) contains a strong third person pronoun (or a demonstrative, on an alternative analysis) and can only be used in specialized contexts, such as contrastiveness (Wheelock 1995: 69).

The reasoning for the Latin Principal (subject) desinences should be the same as for Abkhaz multiple personal affixes. In (6.29i) there is nothing to agree with – for activated referents it is generally this way, both non-locutors and locutors. Clauses without Principal NPs are the default in discourse, and therefore it makes no sense to interpret personal desinences as agreement markers. They are referential bound pronouns. When there is a full NP in a clause the character of the person marker in Latin remains the same: it is a bound referential pronoun, just the antecedent is found in the same clause. To see how this works in discourse, consider the following excerpt from Horace's Satires, in which a playful altercation between two characters, Cicirrus [=C] and Sarmentus [=S], is reported:

(6.30) Latin (Quintus Horatius Flaccus, Satires, Book 1, Chapter 5, lines 65 to 70)[23]

a. Multa Cicirrus ad haec:
   much C.$_C$ to   these

b. donasse-t   iam-ne   catena-m   ex
   present.PLPF.CONJ-3SG$_S$ already-QU chain-ACC.SG from
   vot-o   Lar-ibus,
   wish-ABL.SG   L.-DAT.PL

c. quaereba-t
   ask.IMPF-3SG$_C$

d. scriba   quod esse-t,
   scribe.NOM   that be.IMPF.CONJ-3SG$_S$

e. nilo   deterius   domin-ae   ius   esse.
   nothing worse   mistress-GEN.SG right   be.INF

f. Roga-ba-t   denique cur umquam fugisse-t,
   ask-IMPF-3SG$_C$ finally why sometime flee.PLPF.CONJ-3SG$_S$

g. cui   satis   una farr-is   libra   fore-t,
   who.DAT   enough   one grain-GEN.SG pound   be.IMPF.CONJ-3SG

h. gracil-i   sic tam-que pusill-o.
   slender-DAT.SG so so-and tiny-DAT.SG

i. Prorsus iucunde   cena-m   produc-imus   ill-am.
   straight pleasantly dinner-ACC.SG prolong-PRES.1PL that-ACC.SG

---

[23] No vowel lengths are indicated in this excerpt. The material of the site http://latin-language.co.uk/text/horace/sermonum/1/ was useful in the analysis.

'Cicirrus said much to this: he asked whether he [=Sarmentus] had already devoted a chain to the Lares [household gods]; though he [=Sarmentus] was a scribe his mistress has no less rights over him. Finally he asked why he had ever fled, he, so slender and tiny, to whom one pound of grain would have been enough. So we prolong the dinner pleasantly.'

This example contains seven bound pronouns, only one of which (in line g) is accompanied by a subject full NP. Note particularly the fact that the second bound pronoun in line (f) serves as the head of a relative clause. This example suffices to demonstrate that Latin desinences are as pronominal and referential as Abkhaz prefixes. The decision to treat Latin person markers as bound pronouns entails the refusal to posit subject zero reference. If there is an overt element that carries out the referential function, then it would be notionally wrong to think that this function is formally unexpressed – which is the essence of the concept of zero reference.

There are several reasons why linguists are often reluctant to accept the referential status of Latin-style personal markers compared to the Abkhaz-style ones. Among these reasons are:

- tradition of grammatical thought: Abkhaz-type languages are perceived as exotic, in which nearly everything is conceivable, while Latin is familiar, in fact foundational for grammatical concepts, and more difficult to look at from a novel perspective.
- the cumulative effect: Abkhaz bound pronouns are so omnipresent that it is difficult to neglect them and their properties, while Latin bound pronouns are restricted to one clause participant and thus can more easily be dismissed as something more particular and restricted.
- the subject status: it is often presumed that subject, as the privileged clause participant, has a greater chance to be represented on the verb by way of agreement.

These considerations are not substantial enough to challenge the basic similarity between polypersonal and monopersonal languages. Only the last consideration calls for a brief comment. Indeed, unquestionable agreement is usually selective, that is restricted to one privileged participant; see Corbett (2006: 103). But the converse is not necessarily true: if something is selective, it still may be bound pronouns, not agreement.

The pronominal treatment of Latin personal desinences is in fact very old; at the dawn of modern linguistics Bopp (1833: 109) proposed that in ancient Indo-European languages verbal personal desinences 'show a strong similarity to isolated pronouns'; see also Shields (1992) and Nikolaeva (2008). Facts similar to those of Latin have been frequently discussed with respect to Spanish personal desinences, directly descending from those of Latin and functionally equivalent to them. The pronominal character of these desincences was recognized in the influential papers of Givón (1976: 168) and Jelinek (1984) that were instrumental in drawing attention to bound pronoun phenomena in modern linguistics. This idea is entertained not only by linguistic theorists but also by the authors of a reference grammar who state bluntly: 'The ordinary subject pronoun is expressed by the verb ending: *hablo* 'I speak', *habló* 'he/she/you/it spoke' ...' (Butt and Benjamin 2000: 128).

We have seen above that Navajo offers additional anecdotal evidence that renders the agreement approach particularly implausible. Similar pieces of evidence can be found in languages with a single bound pronoun. For example, in Spanish the third person bound pronouns can also be used as deferential second person, with or without the strong free pronoun *usted(es)*.

6.6.4 Languages with bipersonal verbs

What lies between the two poles – Latin with a single bound pronoun, restricted to the subject role, and Abkhaz with its multiple pronouns, as unrestricted as one can get? Of course, all intermediate systems are found in the world's languages. Very common are systems in which two arguments are represented by bound pronouns on the verb. An example from Huallaga Quechua can serve as an illustration:

(6.31) Huallaga Quechua (Quechuan, Peru; Weber 1986: 335)
allqo-yki-ta   qo-ma-ra-n
dog-2SG.POSS-OBJ give-1SG.OBJ-PAST-3.SUBJ
'He gave your dog to me'

In this Huallaga example two participants are marked by personal affixes on the verb, and these affixes are interpreted as bound pronouns by Weber. Similar examples from Svan (Kartvelian, Georgia) have been discussed in Chapter 3 (subsection 3.3.3), and it was argued there that verbal person markers are genuine bound pronouns.

In both Huallaga and Svan examples the participants expressed by bound pronouns are Principals and recipients. In other cases, both in Huallaga and in Svan, the second argument marked on the verb is the Patientive. For our current goals it makes no difference what the role of the second participant is: it is important that the verb is bipersonal. We can get an idea of how frequent bipersonalism is in the world's languages from a sample-based study of

Siewierska (2005e), inquiring into how many personal markers occur on the transitive verbs of 378 languages. What was specifically explored was whether the Agentive and the Patientive argument's person was expressed on the verb.[24] Among the possible typological options (none; only Agentive; only Patientive; either one or the other; both) the most frequent one turned out to be the option 'both': 193 languages, that is, a little over a half of the sample, use this pattern. Apparently, among the 193 languages there are those that have more than two bound pronouns, so this study actually shows the frequency of bipersonal and polypersonal languages in conjunction. Siewierska also found 103 monopersonal languages, including 73 with only the Agentive, 24 with only the Patientive, and 6 with either one or the other.

So far we have concluded that personal markers can function as bound pronouns in polypersonal, bipersonal, and monopersonal languages. A question then arises: does verbal person agreement exist at all, or should all instances of alleged agreement more accurately be treated as referential bound pronouns?

6.7 Verbal person agreement

The most obvious candidates for languages with person agreement are Germanic languages, for example German and English that use free pronouns along with verbal person markers.[25] Consider the following German examples, as well as their English counterparts. German examples are provided because English has much less agreement left, even though in these particular examples the structures are parallel.

(6.32) German
    i. Der   Junge spiel-t
       the.M boy   play-PRES.3SG
       'The boy plays'
    ii. Er spiel-t
       he play-PRES.3SG
       'He plays'

Like Abkhaz and Latin, German and English have person markers on the verb. They are as tenacious as are bound pronouns in Abkhaz and Latin. The similarity is complete in structures such as (6.32i), where the Principal

---

[24] In fact, not all of the verbal personal markers considered by Siewierska are bound: she also included clitics. So her results are only partially relevant to the issue. She remarks, though, (p. 414) that in most languages it was actually affixes that were counted as bound markers.

[25] Discussion in this section is restricted to English and German. Even though I am using the expression 'the Germanic pattern', no claim is made about the uniform character of all Germanic languages in the organization of their referential devices.

referent is, presumably, of low activation: there is a full NP and there is a person marker on the verb. However, there is a crucial difference, when the Principal referent is activated (6.32ii): German and English use a free (weak) pronoun along with the verbal person marker. The difference of the Germanic-type structure from everything that we have analysed so far is significant. We have discussed the instances of tenacious bound pronouns, remaining in their places when there is a coreferential full NP in the clause. But here we face verbal person markers staying together with a reduced referential device, a free pronoun.[26] So, if verbal person markers are referential, we have two reduced referential devices per a single instantiation of a referent. Can we accept this interpretation or, as is more conventional, should we assume that in structures such as (6.32ii) the real (and sole) bearer of referential function is the pronoun, while the person marker on the verb is an agreement marker copying features from NPs? Note that the compound character of the Germanic personal endings (similarly to other Indo-European; see discussion at the end of section 4.4) is irrelevant to this question: while partly carrying information about clausal categories, they may or may not have referential capacity.

Our goal in this section is to choose between the two alternative interpretations. It is highly desirable to come up with the same interpretation for verbal person markers in both (6.32i) and (6.32ii), rather than suppose that they are agreement in one kind of context and bound pronouns in the other.

Of course, German and English subject pronouns are sensitive with respect to certain grammatical contexts. In particular, they can be absent in non-first coordinate clauses. This was discussed in section 5.4 regarding English. Consider further examples:

(6.33) Zero pronominal anaphora occurs when the anaphoric pronoun is omitted but Ø is nevertheless understood.[27]

(6.34) German[28]
Kunst ist   schön, Ø mach-t   aber viel Arbeit
art   be.PRES.3SG nice   make-PRES.3SG but much work
'Art is beautiful, but creates much work'

---

[26] It is also relevant that German and English are committed to having something in the subject position, even when there is no Principal in the semantic structure. As a result of such commitment, non-referring pronouns are used in constructions such as *it rains* or German *es gibt* 'there is', literally 'it gives'. Evidently, such dummy subjects cooccur with person markers on the verb.

[27] From Mitkov (2002: 13); note that the theoretical notion of omission, figuring in the Mitkov's witty example relies on a transformational or processual idea of deriving linguistic structures from something underlying. This idea is not used in this book.

[28] Motto belonging to the Bavarian comedian and author Karl Valentin (1882–1948).

(6.35) German[29]
a. Daher hab-en   die Zoobesucher die Möglichkeit,
   thus have-PRES.3PL the zoo.visitors the possibility
b. die Menschenaffen nicht nur in den Außen- und
   the apes   not   only in the outdoor and
   Innengehegen zu beobachten,
   indoor.cages to observe
c. sondern Ø könn-en   darüber   hinaus einen Blick auf
   but   can-PRES.3PL   moreover away   a   glance upon
   die Durchführung der   wissenschaftlichen Studien werfen
   the execution   of.the scientific   studies cast
   'Zoo visitors may thus observe the apes in both their outdoor and indoor areas, and even observe some scientific studies as they take place'

In the second clauses of (6.33) and (6.34) and in clause (6.35c) the personal markers on the verb (underlined) are the only overt expressions of the subject referents. Such instances are usually described as zero reference or ellipsis; according to the agreement interpretation, zero reference in such contexts controls verbal person agreement.

Overall, English and German are strongly committed to the use of free pronouns. Bound person markers usually go along with NPs, either nominal or pronominal, and need not necessarily be interpreted as referential elements. In those specialized contexts where free pronouns are missing, zero reference can be postulated. So generally the agreement interpetation of verbal person markers seems credible. (In fact, as will be seen below, the situation is a bit more complex.)

Paradoxically, the German- and English-type languages with both free pronouns and verbal person markers, having been used as a point of departure by many modern linguistic theories, prove to be among the most difficult to understand with respect to the organization of referential devices.

6.7.1 How common is the Germanic pattern?

Apart from being difficult to interpret, the Germanic pattern appears to be exotic among the world's languages. In fact, it is very peripheral, however salient it may seem to many linguists. Siewierska (2004: 268) reports that in

---

[29] From the website of the Primate Research Center at Leipzig Zoo (http://wkprc.eva.mpg.de/deutsch/index.htm). The idiomatic English translation is taken from the English version of the same web site.

her extensive language sample Europe is the main location of languages exhibiting this pattern (in her terms, syntactic agreement markers). Most of the languages she mentions are Germanic, and there are several from other branches of Indo-European – Romance (written formal French, Rheto-Romance, both probably affected by Germanic) and East Slavic. Siewierska (2004: 272) cites the widely-held historical explanation for the rise of obligatory free subject pronouns in western European languages: the verb-second character of their word order that emerged at some point in the syntax of Germanic, as well as those Romance languages that were influenced by Germanic. (For Old French see also Harris 1997: 231–232.) For some discussion of the rise of free pronoun subjects in East Slavic see Chapter 7, subsection 7.4.4. Besides these European languages, Siewierska only found a handful (specifically, seven out of her sample of 402 languages) with a similar pattern in Oceania (both Austronesian and Papuan; Siewierska 2004: 268).

Another way to assess the frequency of the Germanic pattern is to look at the composition of the studies of Dryer (2005a) and Siewierska (2005e), specifically at the combination of values 'Obligatory pronouns in subject position' and 'Only the A marking on the verb'. The intersection of these values yields eleven languages, out of which six belong to the Germanic or neighbouring Indo-European groups (Dutch, English, French, German, Latvian (Baltic), Russian) and the remaining five are scattered in various parts of the world: Byansi (Western Himalayish, Sino-Tibetan, northern India), Dumo (Sko family, Papua New Guinea), Evenki (Tungusic, Russia), Khasi (AustroAsiatic, northeastern India), Taba (South Halmahera, Austronesian, North Maluku, Indonesia). Once again, this composition also suggests that the Germanic pattern is only sporadically found among the world's languages.

One of the Austronesian languages, cited by Siewierska as following the Germanic pattern, is Anejoñ, described by Lynch (1982, 2002). In Anejoñ, under high activation of a referent, two ways to refer to a clause's Principal are available: by means of a free pronoun[30] and by means of the so-called subject/tense/mood particles – in fact, another set of free pronouns that are synchronically analysed as portmanteau morphemes expressing not only reference but also tense and mood[31] (Lynch 1982: 116–118). As pointed out by

---

[30] Lynch (1982: 100) dubs these pronouns focal, but the text he provides on pp. 145–149 demonstrates that these pronouns occur in entirely unmarked situations and are most commonly used as weak pronouns; see examples below. In Lynch (2002: 726–727) they are simply described as personal pronouns.

[31] Note that in the past tense that is pervasively used in narrative (see the text on pp. 145–149 of Lynch 1982) the expression of subject person has become obsolete in the modern language; the original third person singular form *is* is now used irrespective of person (Lynch 1982: 117, 2002: 739). For this reason I have chosen below relatively rare examples in the 'aorist', which means 'present or unspecified past'.

Lynch (1982: 144–145), both referential devices can be present in a clause, but often one of them suffices. Therefore, each of these two devices can perform the referential function by itself and none of them can be relegated to the status of agreement. Below are natural discourse examples showing all three possibilities: when both referential devices are present (the most frequent situation; 6.36), when only a free pronoun is present (6.37),[32] and when the subject/tense/mood particle alone is found (the most rare situation; 6.38c):

(6.36) Anejom̃ (Southern Oceanic, Austronesian, Vanuatu; Lynch 1982: 147, 149)
<u>era</u>   apam <u>aarou</u> m-aji ehele-k m-ika <...>
NSG.AOR come they.DU ss-stand DAT-my ss-say
'The two of them came and stood beside me and said <...>'

(6.37) Anejom̃ (Southern Oceanic, Austronesian, Vanuatu; Lynch 1982: 147, 149)
rectidai <u>attaj</u> m-athut m-apan a-nlii-i   niom
get.up they.TRI ss-run ss-go LOC-inside-INAL house
'They got up and ran inside the house'

(6.38) Anejom̃ (Southern Oceanic, Austronesian, Vanuatu; Lynch 1982: 147, 149)
a. jai inpiñ <u>era</u> itiyi atou akaja
but today NSG.AOR NEG know we.INCL.PL

b. mika <u>et</u> invijic intas uwun aen
that 3SG.AOR true word POSS.his he

c. ka <u>et</u>   acil
or 3SG.AOR false
'But today we don't know whether his words are true or false'

This analysis of the Anejom̃ evidence suggests that this language does not actually follow the Germanic pattern: Anejom̃ reduced referential devices are all free and none of them really resembles agreement. And, most importantly, we see that two reduced and clearly referential devices, belonging to the same instantiation of a referent, can actually be found within one clause in a human language.

---

[32] Lynch (2002: 739) lists the limited range of instances when the subject/tense/mood markers may be absent, but this context – the context of an indicative, sentence-initial verbal predicate – is not mentioned by him.

The presence of more than one reduced device representing a referent is not limited to Anejoṁ. Two different forms of free subject pronouns (of any person) are reported to sometimes combine in the same clause in Berik, a Papuan language, for example:

(6.39) Berik (Tor-Kwerba, West Papua, Indonesia; Westrum and Wiesemann 1986: 38–40)
je jam aol-yan Somanente-wer
he he   go-not   S.-to
'He does not go to Somanente'

But this is not the limit. The Papuan language Skou, not in Siewierska's list but discussed in some detail by Corbett (2006: 75–77, 265–266), displays truly multiple marking of the same instantiation of a referent in a clause, for example:

(6.40) Skou (Sko, Papua, Indonesia; Donohue 1999b: 16)
pe   pe=p-o
she 3SG.F=3SG.F-go.seawards
'She goes towards the sea'

In this example we observe: a free pronoun, a clitic pronoun (also free, in my terms), and a personal prefix to the verb. Note that the three ways to express the participant are cognate. Consider a still more extreme example, in which one additional way to express the Principal's person (and gender) on the verb is found (not counting its triple expression as the possessor of the noun 'brother'):

(6.41) Skou (Sko, Papua, Indonesia; Donohue 1999b: 14)
pe   yu-pe-pè=pe
she brother-3SG.F.DAT-3SG.F.POSS=3SG.F.DAT
ta-ké=ke   pe=rúe
hair-3SG.NF.POSS=3SG.NF.DAT   3SG.F=3SG.F.shave.3SG.F
'She shaved her brother's hair'

As Donohue (1999b: 14) explains, in this example 'we see the subject referred to by four morphological means:

(1) the regular use of the free pronoun *pe*;
(2) the regular use of the subject proclitic *pe=*;
(3) the regular choice of the initial *r*, *p* or *n* on the verb and
(4) the use of the vowel *ue* or *u* (feminine backing), *i* (plural fronting).'

Donohue suggests (pp. 6–7) that free pronouns (such as *pe* in (6.41)) are preferably or even obligatorily present in the clause, and clitics (such as *pe=* in

(6.41)) are agreement markers, and not of pronominal nature. However, texts in his own draft grammar demonstrate that the elements he identifies as free pronouns occur very rarely and are evidently a marked device, that is strong pronouns. Probably Donohue's clitics are normally the main bearers of the referential function, as in this example from natural discourse:

(6.42) Skou (Sko, Papua, Indonesia; Donohue 2004: 572)
rahé   pe=w-á,
coconut.strainer 3SG.F=3SG.F-pound
'She beats a coconut strainer,'

The structure in (6.42) is quite similar to the Germanic pattern, as in *He plays*: it contains one bound representation and one free (weak, or clitic, pronoun) representation of the Principal. However, the system of Skou apparently goes one step further in the number of concurrent person markers belonging to the same instantiation of the same referent. As we have seen in (6.41), Skou weak pronouns are tenacious (see Donohue 2004: 237ff.); in particular, if a strong pronoun is found in a clause, the weak pronoun still remains there. The same occurs if a full NP is contained in a clause:

(6.43) Skou (Sko, Papua, Indonesia; Donohue 2004: 111)
áì   ya   ke=k-ang
father thing 3SG.NF=3SG.NF-eat
'Father ate'

In this kind of structure there are two clearly referential representations of the Principal referent (the full NP and the free pronoun *ke-*) plus one semi-referential one by means of the agreement prefix (*k-*).

In analysing the evidence from Skou, Corbett (2006: 75–76) suggests that clitics in this language may be targets of agreement. In the understanding of agreement adopted here, that does not hold because, according to my analysis above, Skou clitics are the primary bearers of referential function. However, Corbett's hypothesis raises an interesting question: can agreement markers, in principle, be free, or are they always bound? An answer has been proposed by Siewierska (2004: 162) who stated flatly that 'syntactic agreement markers are invariably affixes'. I find this generalization very likely.

Thus it appears that Skou and, perhaps, a handful of languages of the same area listed by Siewierska (2004: 268) (but not Anejoṁ), as well as several from other parts of the world, are the only representatives of the Germanic pattern that are not related to Germanic in either genealogical or areal terms. Clearly, the Germanic pattern is highly exotic, and it must occupy a relatively modest place in the typology of referential devices – incomparably more modest than is given to it in mainstream linguistic theory.[33]

6.7.2 Germanic person markers can occasionally be referential

Even though the agreement interpretation of Germanic verbal person markers is apt in most instances, there are some pieces of evidence hinting at these markers' possibly referential function. Some evidence of this kind, mostly from English, is presented in this subsection. Of course, English only has vestigial verbal person marking: it is maximally preserved in continuous tenses, is found in third person singular alone in simple and perfect present, and is altogether absent in simple and perfect past, in the future, and in modal verbs. Still the extant vestiges of person marking allow one to address the issue.

Modern English happens to display several contexts in which person markers still fulfil their erstwhile referential function.[34] One class of examples comes from perception verbs (such as *look, sound, smell, feel, seem*) that have an intransitive usage in which a feature is attributed to the perceptual stimulus: *Sounds good; Looks nice* etc. For instance, if I am checking how a new instrument, such as a guitar, resonates, I can say *Sounds good*. If I am listening to several guitars or, say, to an instrument that is a plurale tantum, such as castanets, it is not possible to say *Sound good. It is absolutely impossible to use this construction without the third person singular marker on the verb. (Also, the construction cannot be used in the past, where no agreement is preserved.) Therefore, the explicit third person singular person marker -*s* has a certain referential potential which disappears together with the marker. Note that we should not posit zero reference in the structures in question; if it were there in some sense, both singular and plural forms should have been equally appropriate.

These examples may be not totally convincing. Probably the case is that *Sounds good* refers not to a specific referent ('This guitar sounds good') but rather to a more abstract referent, something like 'The way in which this guitar resonates sounds good'. This may be the actual reason why only the

---

[33] The typological and areal distribution of the Germanic pattern makes the notion of 'pro-drop' rather comic. As was already discussed in section 3.1, this notion puts into one category all of the vast, internally heterogeneous, linguistic variety to the exclusion of a handful of highly unusual languages, mostly in Europe. The notion of 'pro-drop' is one of the most striking examples of extreme Anglocentrism.

[34] I am grateful to David Gil, Juliette Blevins, and Elena Lieven for discussing the English examples with me and for straining their native speakers' intuition.

singular form of the verb is usable. But even so, it is hardly a mere accident that English uses the conventional construction *Sounds good* but not **Sound good* or **Sounded good* where nothing can pick up any sort of referential function. (See also the discussion of English 'ellipsis' in Miller and Weinart 1998: 209–212.)

There are other kinds of examples, probably clearer ones, in which there is no subject NP and still there is an obvious reference to the subject. The following (inspired by a similar example in Stirling 2002: 1540) is a constructed, but quite possible English dialogue, presumably between the members of a sports team:

(6.44)   What's the new guy like? – Doesn't know how to play.

What is of interest here is the reply part: there is a clear subject reference to a specific individual introduced in the question, and there is nothing overt in the clause structure besides the person marker -s that can possibly bear the referential function. Another possibility would be to recognize zero reference in these contexts, but the following casts doubt on this treatment:

(6.45)   What're the new guys like? – *Don't know how to play.

Unlike (6.44), this structure is not used. Since (6.44) and (6.45) are a minimal pair, the only thing the difference can be attributed to is the presence vs. absence of the personal marker -s. Evidently, under some circumstances, the exact nature of which remains to be identified, the personal marker -s is able to operate as a referential unit, that is, as a bound pronoun. Even this kind of vestigial material can be occasionally recycled by language, returning to its original referential function that was there some centuries or even millennia ago. Interestingly, -s operates as an isolated referential device; its absence is not equivalent to a zero referential element (that is, an unmarked member of the pair), but rather is not functional at all.

A final piece of evidence I would like to cite comes from exophoric third person reference, often found on commercial products. This usage is exophoric because, as a consumer reads the text, he/she holds the product in his/her hands and the referential device points to this perceptually available entity (see Chapter 15). Consider a multilingual notice, found on a pack of cereals, the English version being *Note for allergy sufferers: May contain traces of milk, peanuts, and other nuts*. Of course, Spanish (as well as Italian) uses a bound pronoun as the sole reference to the product:

(6.46)   Spanish
      a. Advertencia   para   alérgicos:
          note   for   allergic.individuals

b. Puede-ø   contener trazas de leche, cacahuetes
may-PRES.3SG contain traces of milk peanuts
y   otros frutos secos.
and other fruits dry

This behaviour is not surprising; in an exophoric context Spanish employs what is expected of a language with prevalent use of subject bound pronouns.

English (the formulation is cited above) is less predictable: it does not use any overt reference to the product: no NP is used, and the modal verb *may* does not distinguish person forms. This must be interpreted as zero reference, due to the modal verbs' idiosyncrasy. Now consider the German variant – it uses the third person singular form of the verb, that is, in this context its behaviour is indistinguishable from that of Spanish:

(6.47)   German
        a. Hinweis für Allergiker:
           note   for allergic.individuals

        b. Kann   Spuren von   Milch, Erdnüssen und
           may.PRES.3SG traces of   milk peanuts   and
           anderen   Nüssen enthalten.
           other   nuts   contain

In both English and German a free pronoun would not be appropriate in this context.[35]

Interestingly, there is a language among those found on the package that is more insistent on having an overt subject, and it is French (in this case, of course, in its standard variety):

(6.48)   Standard French
        a. Avertissement pour allergiques:
           note   for   allergic.individuals

        b. Le produit peut   contenir des   traces de lait, de
           the product may.PRES.3SG contain INDEF.PL traces of milk of
           cacahouètes et   d'autres types de noix
           peanuts   and of.other types of nut

Evidently, the third person singular form *peut* cannot ensure reference to the product by itself, and an NP is required. In requiring a subject NP and thus keeping up to the verb-second principle standard French, in this case, outdoes

---

[35] I thank Jan Wohlgemuth for a useful discussion of German evidence.

German and English in 'Germanicness'. Some aspects of reference in French will be discussed in Chapter 7, section 7.3.

We have thus reviewed several distinct examples in which English and German display a deviant pattern: verbal person markers appear to be used referentially. How can this be reconciled with the above conclusion that Germanic verbal person markers are essentially of an agreement nature?

Occasional use of a contemporary agreement marker as a bound pronoun, apparently anomalous in modern language, is a manifestation of the continuous diachronic process known as grammaticalization: gradual transformation of free forms into more bound, more automatic, more compact, and less meaningful material. (Many volumes have been devoted to grammaticalization during the last couple of decades. Some relatively recent ones include Wischer and Diewald (eds.) 2002, Fischer et al. (eds.) 2004, and Van Linden et al. (eds.) 2010. The Germanic pattern historically arose from the Latin-style pattern which was still found in Gothic; see for example Weerman (1989: 209ff.)[36]. As free pronouns became common and then obligatory, and turned into the main reduced referential device (in other words, turned from strong to weak), bound pronouns were rendered less functional and eventually evolved into what is known as agreement markers. This is the path of grammaticalization often discussed in the literature; see e.g. Givón (1976), Lehmann (1995: 42), Siewierska (2004: 262–268).

Since grammaticalization is a process not a leap, various patterns of use, corresponding to different stages of the grammaticalization cline, can cohabit in a synchronic linguistic system. This is quite well known: for example, English *am/are/is going to* is an almost grammaticalized new future, but it can still be used in a fully lexical way, as in *I am going to the marketplace*. Diachrony is often partly alive in synchrony. Despite semantic and formal bleaching, characteristic of grammaticalization, grammaticalized elements can occasionally be recycled as fully-fledged meaningful forms. This is the case with agreement markers that trace back to referential pronouns and have the capacity of being recycled as reduced referential devices under certain conditions.[37]

---

[36] As Siewierska (1999) demonstrated, agreement develops from tenacious bound pronouns (in her terms, grammatical agreement from ambiguous agreement). This is very natural; it would be hard to imagine how tenacious agreement might develop from alternating pronouns in a flash. See also Creissels's (2005) evolutionary theory, according to which (in his respective terms) the stage of alternating pronouns precedes the tenacious stage, and the latter is followed by the agreement stage.

[37] An alternative explanation of the referential use of English agreement markers would be through the notion of degrammaticalization; see various studies in Fischer et al. (eds.) (2004).

6.7.3 *Germanic agreement participates in reference as an ancillary*

The general pattern of the Germanic referential system is very different from the Latin one. One way or another, we should offer a notional approach that would treat the two differently. The traditional agreement terminology naturally lends itself as a useful conceptualization of the Germanic pattern. Whereas Latin uses bound subject pronouns, in Germanic free pronouns are used as the dominant reduced referential device. On most occasions person agreement is not referential as such.

Note that the qualification of Germanic verbal person markers as agreement is not due to any a priori principles, such as disallowing more than one reduced referential device per a single instantiation of a referent in a clause. As we have seen from the Anejoм evidence, there can actually be two reduced mentions of the same referent in a clause. But in Anejoм two kinds of reduced devices are largely independent of each other, whereas German/English person markers, in the vast majority of cases, cooccur with NPs, either nominal or pronominal, either specific-referential or not, and therefore can be considered their agreement copies.

As was shown in the previous subsections, there are, however, certain instances in which agreement markers still have referential capacity. Such contexts of the glimmering erstwhile Latin-style use are too marginal to affect our understanding of the dominant pattern, but they still must be accounted for in a comprehensive picture. If agreement markers have referential capacity in those special instances, they may also have an ancillary referential status in common situations, such as *Der Junge spielt / The boy plays* and *Er spielt / He plays*. That is, at a first approximation, German and English are equivalent to such purely free pronoun languages as Lyélé (see discussion in Chapter 3, section 3.2). However, if one strives for a more exhaustive understanding of the Germanic pattern, it must be recognized that such equivalence is not complete. Whereas Lyélé represents a referent exactly once in a clause by means of a free pronoun, German and English, under certain circumstances (only subject referent; in English – only present and continuous tenses, etc.), represents it more than once – so to speak, one and a half times.

Figures 6.1 and 6.2 demonstrate how the Germanic system (as exemplified by German) can be schematically portrayed against the background of the Latin and Lyélé systems, with respect to the linking of Principal referential devices.

In Lyélé, a referent is always represented once in a clause, either by a full NP or by a free pronoun. In Latin, a referent is represented once (by a bound pronoun), if the referent is activated, and twice if it is not activated; the latter situation is shown by a solid arc uniting two representations. In German the basic pattern resembles that of Lyélé, but there is also an ancillary representation by means of the agreement marker, shown by a dotted arc. This ancillary representation is in place irrespective of whether the referent is activated or not.

226   II. Typology of Reduced Referential Devices

                    Lyélé: full NP   German: full NP   Latin: full NP plus bound
                                           plus agreement marker   pronoun

Referents
(plane of thought)

Referential devices
(plane of talk)   [líbí   ...]   [der Junge ...   -t]   [puer ...   -t]

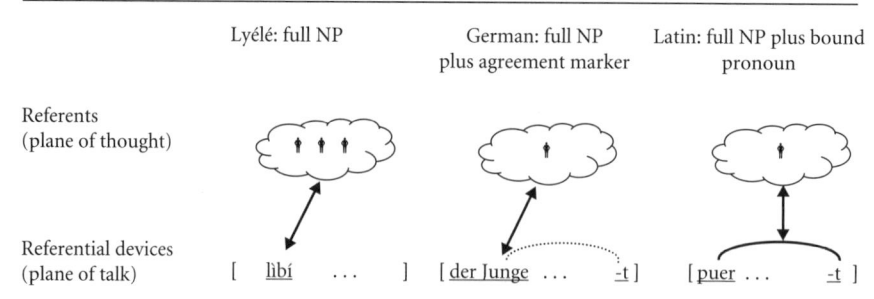

FIGURE 6.1. Linking of Principal referential devices in Lyélé (example 3.5i), German (6.32i), and Latin (6.29II): referent non-activated

                    Lyélé: free pronoun   German: free pronoun   Latin: bound pronoun
                                           plus agreement marker

Referents
(plane of thought)

Referential devices
(plane of talk)   [bè   ...]   [er   ...   -t]   [...   -t]

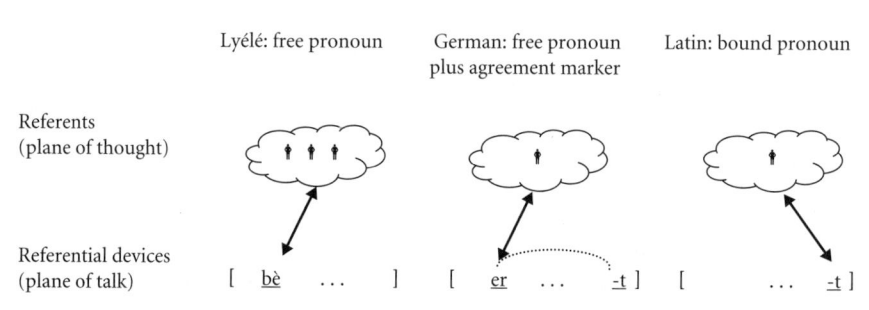

FIGURE 6.2. Linking of Principal referential devices in Lyélé (example 3.5i), German (6.32ii), and Latin (6.29I): referent activated

The character of the Germanic referential system, against the background of Latin and other languages emphasized in this and other chapters of this book, can be made clearer through the following simple quantitative technique. Let us consider each overt referential device, associated with a referent in a clause, to have the referential force of 1. This applies to full and reduced noun phrases, to free and bound pronouns. Zero reference has the force of 0. Agreement markers can then be assumed to be in between, that is having the force of 1/2. Table 6.4 shows the summary referential exponent (per referent per clause) in five languages, for each of them in two conditions: (i) the Principal referent is activated; (ii) the Principal referent is not activated. In condition (i) a candidate language scoring 2, that is having two fully-fledged overt devices, is Russian; see Chapter 7, subsection 7.4.4.

How can one tell the German and the Latin patterns apart in a random undescribed language? When a referent is activated and the two structures are distinct, they can be schematically represented as *He heplay* (German) and *Heplay* (Latin), where *he* stands for any person marker. But, as we know, both German and Latin occasionally use both *He heplay* and *Heplay*. What we need to be able to decide about a given language is what is the main carrier of referential function. If the structure *He heplay* is more common in a language,

TABLE 6.4. Referential devices employed in German and four other languages for activated and non-activated Principal referents, and summary referential exponents

Condition	Referent is activated	Referent is not activated
Meaning of an exemplary clause:	'He plays'	'The boy plays'
Japanese	0 (zero reference)	1 (full NP)
Lyélé	1 (free pronoun)	1 (full NP)
German	1½ (free pronoun plus agr. marker)	1½ (full NP plus agr. marker)
Latin	1 (bound pronoun)	2 (full NP plus tenacious bound pronoun)
Skou	1½ (free pronoun plus agr. marker)	2½ (full NP plus tenacious free pronoun plus agr. marker)

while *Heplay* occurs only in special contexts, such as (6.47), then we face a German-type language where free pronouns are the main carriers of referential function while the bound *he-* is an ancillary device, that is agreement. Conversely, if *Heplay* is more common and *He heplay* is reserved for special contexts, such as (6.29iii), then it is a Latin-type language with a bound pronoun, while the free element is a strong pronoun.

In those instances in which a free pronoun is not used for some reason, as in non-first coordinate clauses, zero reference must be recognized in Germanic. In connection with this claim, recall from Chapter 3 (section 3.4) the zero reference convention, according to which zeroes should not be postulated if a language systematically uses non-zero referential devices. This applies to zero as the preferred referential device of a language. In a language such as Latin that systematically uses subject bound pronouns as the main reduced referential device, it would be ridiculous to posit a subject zero on top of that. The situation is different in Germanic. Clauses without a subject NP are a marked phenomenon, and it is quite reasonable to posit a 'free' zero occupying the NP slot in such instances. Among other things, this approach allows us to treat all instances of verbal person marking uniformly as agreement.[38]

---

[38] An alternative would be to grant the Germanic agreement markers the status of referential devices in coordinate clauses. This seems a rather unnatural solution, especially with respect to English where agreement is found in very few inflected forms.

There are also more specialized usages in Germanic where agreement markers regain their original referential function. These usages are peripheral and must be treated as such.

To summarize, the proposed interpretation of the Germanic referential system is:

- Free pronouns are the main reduced referential device.
- Agreement markers are erstwhile bound pronouns.
- They are not equivalent to bound pronouns synchronically.
- But their referential function is occasionally revived on demand.

The Germanic system is thus quite entangled. Clearly, theories of reduced referential devices, assuming this system as the typological point of departure, can hardly be successful.

6.7.4 Is agreement functional?

Formal linguistic phenomena rarely exist for no particular reason. Verbs denote events, nouns and pronouns referents, tense markers orient events with respect to the moment of speech, etc. But what about agreement? Does it have a function, or is it simply a remnant of what used to be functional but is no longer? The latter position was expressed, for example, by Haiman (1985: 164). Epithets such as 'redundant' are often associated with agreement in the literature. A rather opposite view is taken by Barlow (1999) who offers a view of agreement as a discourse-oriented, functional phenomenon. In the recent fundamental monograph 'Agreement' by Corbett (2006) only a little over one page (274–275) is devoted to functions of agreement. Among these, Corbett mentions redundancy, which in this case means not afunctionality, as usual, but, quite the contrary, helpful exuberance facilitating referential processing. Also Corbett mentions that agreement may provide alternative perspectives in reference to groups as either indivisible entities (*the committee was ...*) or as sets of individual entities (*the committee were ...*). Such facts suggest that agreement is not as automatic as it may seem. Biber et al. (1999: 180–190) demonstrate, for English, that there are many situations in which the supposedly automatic agreement rule is not so easy to formulate – for example, in cases of coordinate subjects or indefinite pronouns.

Here I would like to focus on one potential function of agreement, related to the differential disposition of clause pariticipants to being controllers of agreement. The instances of verbal person agreement we have reviewed were invariably associated with control from a single clause participant, namely Principal. Is this an artefact created by the range of consulted languages, or is it a regularity? Can there be clear verbal agreement with other hyperroles, either belonging to the accusative (Patientive) or other alignments (Agentive, Absolutive, Actor, Undergoer)? Can agreement be polypersonal?

There exists an intuition that the number of participants is a criterion when deciding whether the given person marker in the given language is a pronoun or an agreement marker. Corbett (2006: 103) mentions the number of participants as the first criterion in his list of five: 'In the indisputable instances of verb agreement, normally we find that just one case role can be indexed'. It is often claimed that verbal person agreement is a selective mechanism oriented to one prestigious type of argument (cf. Mithun 1986c: 197). More specifically, agreement is not just monopersonal, it takes up Principal as the controller in those scarce languages that do have verbal agreement. As Siewierska (1999, 2004: 268) has demonstrated, all languages (European and non-European) that happen to have a clear person agreement pattern show agreement with the Principal (S and A, in her terminology).

This points to a possible function of agreement: highlighting the grammatically privileged participant. Control of verbal person agreement is usually mentioned as one of the constituting properties of subjecthood (beginning from Keenan 1976: 316). Probably preference for Principal agreement is related to the cross-linguistic preference for Principal-based subjects and for accusative syntactic patterns.

The only exception to the Principal preference of agreement I am aware of comes from Daghestanian languages. Most Daghestanian languages only have verbal gender agreement, but several have also developed person agreement, in particular Dargi and Lak (Russia). In the Chirag dialect of Dargi, person agreement is split in transitive clauses: it is agent-oriented when the agent is first or second person, but patient-oriented if the agent is third person. Compare the patterning of person agreement in intransitive (6.49i, ii) and transitive (6.49iii, iv) clauses:

(6.49) Chirag Dargi (Nakh-Daghestanian, Russia; A. E. Kibrik 2003: 483–484)
    i. du   čerk<r>ibli-da
       I.F.NOM sit<F>-1
       'I (female) am sitting'

    ii. ʕu   čerk<r>ibli-de
       you.F.NOM sit<F>-2SG
       'You (female) are sitting'

    iii. ʕiče   du   r-iqan-de
       you.M.ERG I.F.NOM F-lead-2SG
       'You(male) lead me (female)'

iv. it-e ʕu r-iqan-de
he-ERG you.F.NOM F-lead-2SG
'He leads you (female)'

Taking together transitive clauses with third person agents (6.49iv) and instransitive clauses (6.49i, ii), we can conclude that in this class of instances Chirag Dargi agreement operates on the ergative basis. It is important to note that free pronouns are the preferred referential device in Chirag Dargi discourse, whereas person markers on the verb can, with a high degree of certainty, be indeed considered agreement, not bound pronouns (A. E. Kibrik, personal communication). This assessment is further corroborated by the analysis of discourse evidence of Dargi in van den Berg (2004). Chirag Dargi thus presents an example, however limited, of the ergative-based person agreement.

Another language also displaying partial verbal person agreement with the Absolutive is Lak; in this language it is found in some tenses (aorist and future) in the second and third persons (A. E. Kibrik 2003: 468). These rare examples do not disprove the cross-linguistic tendency for agreement to be Principal-oriented. Interestingly, there is still another Daghestanian language, namely Tabassaran (Russia), that has developed verbal person markers; in this case, the markers are polypersonal. However, judging by the clearly pronominal form of affixes and the optional character of free pronouns (A. E. Kibrik 2003: 507), Tabassaran has bound pronouns. So the monopersonal character of agreement is not questioned by Daghestanian languages.

The facts of those sparse languages that do have clear verbal person agreement suggest that agreement is characterized by decreasing functionality. Siewierska (2004: 268ff.) has demonstrated that in those few languages (in her terminology, languages with syntactic agreement, as opposed to pronominal agreement) there is a visible trend towards erosion of these markers. Obviously, in English and French this has been pushed to the extreme, each language having only one distinct personal desinence in the present: English in the third person singular,[39] French in the second plural.[40] Similar development was found by Siewierska (2004) in the languages of Oceania that share the Germanic pattern.

---

[39] An interesting research question is whether the reduction of agreement in English, as compared to German, can be shown to be related to other changes in its core grammar.

[40] See Chapter 7, subsection 7.3.2, on the replacement of the first person plural pattern *nous V-ons* by the alternative *on V-e*.

Indeed, English agreement opposes (in the present) third person singular to all other person–number combinations. This points to the vestigial, semi-functional character of English agreement. In the domain of genuine referential devices no language can afford to distinguish only between a third person singular pronoun and a pronoun serving all other person–numbers. Furthermore, in contrast to agreement, there is no evidence of erosion of bound pronouns in those languages that rely on them as the main reduced referential device. Quite the contrary, a rise in their extent is often observed; see Chapter 7, subsection 7.5.4.

English verbal person agreement is apparently simple. Nevertheless, the share of instances when speakers use non-standard forms even with prototypical subjects is very high: according to Biber et al. (1999: 191), in their conversational corpus, the combination *I says* occurs 50% of the time, and *he don't* 40% of the time; *you was* and *she were* are found in 10% of instances each, and *they was* in 5% of all instances. These facts may be due partly to errors, partly to existence (or formation) of various dialects in which the actual agreement rules are different from what is usually presupposed for English (this is fairly well known for those English dialects that lack agreement altogether and systematically use *he don't*).

Overall, it can be concluded that agreement is not as fully functional as referential devices. However, it is semi-functional and can occasionally participate in referential processes in various subtle ways. One can liken agreement, in terms of the degree of its functionality, to biological vestiges, such as wisdom teeth, or third molars, in humans. In modern people, the job of chewing is done by other molars and premolars, but wisdom teeth still erupt in most people. They are inherited from our ancestors who had larger jaws and needed them. We normally do not use them and their extraction is even believed by some to be beneficial for the organism. Still wisdom teeth can turn out helpful if, say, a person lost other molars. In this case a third molar is called into service in a way that echoes its erstwhile evolutionary function.

6.8 Bound zeroes

In Chapter 3 and subsequently zero reference has been considered as one of the three alternatives among the major reduced referential devices, along with free and bound pronouns. The question I address in this section is the following: does it make sense to differentiate between free (syntactic) and bound (morphological) zeroes?

Zero reference is a linguist's convention, utilized when reference is clearly performed in a piece of language, but not by any overt device. Even though it is a mere convention, it is still a good idea to use it in a thoughtful way when deciding whether to posit a zero, and if so, where specifically in linguistic structure. Many linguists who are native speakers of free pronoun languages are quick to posit zeroes in languages without free pronouns. But what about those contexts in which no overt referential device occurs in European languages, while other languages use them? Consider the structure of possessive NPs. In English the possessive relation is marked on the possessor, as in *the boy's head*. There are numerous languages that mark this relation on the head noun, that is, the possessed. Let us take a language that is double-marking (Nichols 1986) and thus minimally differs from English in simply having one extra device:

(6.50)　Tuvan (Turkic, southern Siberia, Russia)
　　　　ool-duŋ　　　baž-i
　　　　boy-GEN　　　head-3
　　　　'the boy's head', *lit.* 'boy's head-his'

The person marker on the possessed can be used in Tuvan as the sole carrier of referential function if the possessor referent is activated (*baži* 'his head'), so, at least putatively, can be considered a bound possessive pronoun. This pronoun is tenacious: it is there irrespective of whether a full possessor NP is present. There are also languages that use free tenacious possessive pronouns; this has already been discussed above in connection with example (6.16) from Dan-Gwèètaa. If major linguistic traditions were founded by native speakers of Tuvan or Dan-Gwèètaa they might have proposed that in the English phrase *the boy's head* there is a zero possessive pronoun referring to the possessor and morphologically or syntactically attached to the possessed. This interpretation may be strikingly unsatisfactory, but it serves to illustrate the point that the ways one posits zeroes must be coordinated with a language's basic properties.

We have previously discussed those languages that are generally committed to free pronouns but occasionally use zero reference. Here we will discuss a parallel group of instances: languages that use bound pronouns as the dominant reduced referential device but occasionally display zero reference. This is the case of Athabaskan languages, for example Upper Kuskokwim:

(6.51)　Upper Kuskokwim (Na-Dene, Alaska, USA)
　　　　i. zi-s-do
　　　　　 PFV-1SG.NOM-stay
　　　　　 'I am sitting'
　　　　ii. z-e-do
　　　　　 PFV-2SG.NOM-stay
　　　　　 'You are sitting'

iii. zi-do
PFV-stay
'S/he/it is sitting'

In the third person form, there is simply no overt counterpart for the bound pronouns found in the first and second person singular. These kinds of phenomena are very common in languages. In the study by Siewierska (2005d) the zero marking of the third person (as opposed to other persons) on intransitive verbs was explored on a sample of 380 languages. Out of 284 languages that do mark the person of the Sole participant on the verb, 103 (that is, 36%) have zero third person marking in at least some cases, and 36 of them (13%) have zero marking of all third persons. Cysouw (2003: 61–62) and Helmbrecht (2004: 376ff.) also note that zero third person markers are widespread in the world's languages and are contrasted to non-zero locutor markers.

It would certainly be wrong to think that the inflected verb in (6.51iii) is unmarked for person in terms of semantics. It is simply that third person is negatively defined with respect to the locutor persons. The form in (6.51iii) unequivocally contains third person reference. Cysouw (2003: 64) formulates the criterion for positing vs. not positing morphological zeroes as follows: 'The crucial argument for the existence of a zero is that the counterpart (here: speaker and addressee marking) is obligatorily marked in a certain "slot" of the linguistic structure. The emptiness of this slot can then be interpreted as having a meaning.'

Since zero units are by definition invisible, one may wonder in some cases whether it is a 'free' or a 'bound' zero. Is it a zero affix in (6.51iii), in parallel to non-zero affixes, or is it rather a zero free NP, analogous to free pronouns? Of course, if something is not there, one can only wonder where it would be if it were present. From one perspective, it may not matter where we posit zero, and whether we posit it at all. But still it is useful to distinguish between syntactic, 'free', zeroes and morphological, 'bound', zeroes. In practical terms, in studies of reference linguists usually try to mark zero forms, at least to be able to attach a referential index to something. And if so, it is a good idea to posit these zero forms not randomly but on some systematic grounds. If a language has no bound pronouns, and only uses free referential devices, then it by all means makes sense to think of a syntactic zero, and this is what we have been doing with respect to Japanese (Chapter 3). In contrast, if a language has a full paradigm of bound pronouns (for example, for locutors) but does not express a third person pronoun, it is reasonable to posit a morphological zero referring to a non-locutor participant.

In this book, decisions about syntactic (=free) vs. morphological (=bound) zeroes are made on the basis of such or similar systematic considerations. In particular, it makes more sense to think of Upper Kuskokwim as having a zero third person affix, while of Japanese and English as having a 'free' zero. This is just a way of representation, but, other things being equal, it is preferable to have a representation that is more faithful to the nature of the language we are dealing with. In some intermediate cases a decision may be a matter of personal taste, but in more polar situations there is a better and a worse way to interpret things. For such reasons, I distinguish between the two types of theoretical referring expressions: I posit a bound, lower-case zero (ø) and a free, upper-case zero (Ø). In those cases when it is difficult to decide I give preference to the free zero simply because it is more visible.

In the case of bound zeroes, systematic concerns often lead us to a further question: to deciding where in the verb form to posit the bound zero morpheme. In fact, the evidence of Upper Kuskokwim suggests that the zero third person pronoun appears in a position different from the one of first and second person singular pronouns. The reason is that Athabaskan languages have several non-locutor bound pronouns, and of these only the plain third person is zero, while others are overt. For example, the indefinite pronoun *ch'i-* appears on the left of the perfective prefix *z-*, unlike the locutor pronouns that appear on the right of it (see 6.51i, ii):

(6.51) Upper Kuskokwim (Na-Dene, Alaska, USA)
  iv. ch'i-z-do
    INDEF.NOM-PFV-stay
    'Something (such as an animal) is sitting'

By analogy with all non-locutor pronouns, I posit the third person nominative zero in the same position:

(6.51) Upper Kuskokwim (Na-Dene, Alaska, USA)
  iii'. ø-zi-do
    3.NOM-PFV-stay
    'S/he/it is sitting'

Mithun (1986c) has argued that some languages that have obvious bound pronouns for locutors are more tricky with respect to third person arguments. One such language is Lakhota (Siouan). In Lakhota, a verb inflected only for locutor persons constitutes a fully-fledged clause, while for third person arguments speakers tend to offer demonstratives or even full NPs when translating from English:

(6.52) Lakhota (Siouan, South Dakota and North Dakota, USA; Mithun 1986c: 202)
- i. špamáyaye
  burn.2SG.ACT.1SG.UND
  'You burned me'
- ii. hé špayáye
  that burn.2SG.ACT
  'You burned him'
- iii. hé španíye
  that burn.2SG.UND
  'He burned you'
- iv. hé wíya hé špáye
  that woman that burn
  'He burned her'

This behaviour is actually very different from a language like Upper Kuskokwim where third person zero bound pronouns should be posited on systematic grounds, in particular because verbs constitute full clauses irrespective of which person the arguments belong to. Probably it is accurate to believe that Lakhota does not have an inherent third person bound affix and uses free referential devices instead. If we encounter a context in Lakhota discourse where a free device would be absent, we would then have to posit a free zero.

If a language uses bound zeroes, does it make sense to discuss whether such zeroes are tenacious or not? Evidently, such a question is paradoxical with respect to zeroes as invisible elements, just as with respect to Japanese-style free zeroes. Decision on a language's degree of referential device tenacity must be made on the basis of overt forms alone. For example, in Navajo, although it often has zero third person bound pronouns, it still makes sense to say that this language's pronouns are tenacious: whenever there is an overt bound pronominal form it acts tenaciously. So in this case again one should interpret zero forms on the basis of the dominant patterns explicitly displayed by explicit forms.

The adopted conventions of zero use can be recapitulated as follows. The first convention states:

- If a language normally does not use any overt reduced referential devices, then posit (free) zero as the language's dominant reduced referential device.

The subsequent conventions apply to languages that use either full or bound pronouns as dominant reduced referential devices, and zero is restricted in some way (third person as opposed to locutors, Principals of coordinate clauses, etc.):

- Do not posit zero whenever an overt referential device is present that can possibly carry referential function.
- When no overt referential device is present, posit a free or bound zero in accordance with the language's dominant pattern.

From these conventions it follows that, for example, in Latin-type languages (using bound tenacious pronouns) no free subject zeroes should be posited. In contrast, in German they can be posited even if agreement markers are present, because agreement markers are not fully-fledged referential devices.

Summary

Cross-linguistically, bound pronouns are the most common among the major reduced referential devices. However, they are strongly underrepresented in theoretical and typological accounts of referential processes. In this chapter I have discussed several issues concerned with bound pronouns.

The first of these is the question of the relationship between the typological parameters 'free vs. bound' and 'tenacious vs. alternating'. The boundness of pronouns does not equal tenacity and freedom of pronouns does not equal alternation, even though the combinations 'bound tenacious' and 'free alternating' are more frequent across the languages of the world.

I have considered in some detail examples of languages exhibiting less common combinations 'free tenacious' and 'bound alternating'. Also, some languages exist that employ both free tenacious and bound alternating pronouns. Languages are often inconsistent in what types of pronouns they use in different clause participant positions. For example, Spanish uses strongly tenacious bound pronouns in the Principal (subject) position and relatively tenacious free pronouns in the Patientive and recipient positions.

In accordance with the two binary parameters, as well as the opposition between two major clause participant roles, a 16-way typology of languages has been proposed, with exemplary languages for many of its values.

The following important issue associated with bound pronouns is more of a matter of theoretical interpretation. Bound pronouns are sometimes treated as non-referential, rather automatic, agreement markers. This especially concerns languages that have just one personal marker per verb, such as Latin or Spanish, but sometimes this kind of argument extends to polypersonal languages, such as Navajo or Abkhaz. I have attempted to demonstrate that most of the instances of personal markers, irrespective of how many of these are found on the verb, are of a truly referential character and can hardly be dismissed as 'mere agreement'. This view becomes particularly appropriate if one recognizes the widespread phenomenon of the tenacity of pronouns: presence of more than one representation of a referent in a clause does not entail the agreement-based interpretation.

The phenomenon of verbal agreement does still exist in some languages, even though it is quite exotic. The 'exotic' languages displaying this pattern are, in the first place, the Germanic languages, such as German and English. They are highly unusual in their near-obligatory requirement for an overt subject NP in a clause. This pattern seems to be found, apart from in Europe, only in some languages in Oceania (and perhaps a few languages in Asia). One of the Papuan languages, Skou, seems to exceed Germanic in how many representations of the Principal referent per clause it requires or allows.

Even in Germanic, agreement markers are occasionally referential. However, the peripheral character of such contexts makes one recognize that, under normal circumstances, they do not constitute fully-fledged referential devices and rather participate in the referential process as an ancillary to truly referential elements. A hypothesis on the function of agreement markers is proposed, associated with highlighting one privileged clause participant. This function is probably not absolutely essential, judging by the common diachronic process of agreement markers' erosion.

The final issue, related to bound pronouns and considered in this chapter, is the question of zero reference in those languages that are generally disposed to bound pronouns. In these kinds of languages it may be natural to posit bound, rather than free zeroes. Does the discussion of the free vs. bound character of non-existent elements make sense? I do not attribute a principled status to this discussion. But, at least in the aspect of technical notation, it makes sense to treat zeroes in accordance with a given language's general properties. For example, if a language uses a full set of bound pronouns, and the third person forms are analogous to other forms except for having no overt person marker, it is sensible to consider such a zero bound and technically posit it in the same location within the verb form as the overt pronouns.

7

The rise and fall of bound tenacious pronouns

Overview

This chapter is devoted to diachronic aspects of referential systems, particularly those involving bound pronouns. It is of interest how languages change their referential systems over time (section 7.1). Three case studies are presented in this chapter, each concerned with a certain genealogical group of languages: Athabaskan (section 7.2), Romance (7.3), and Slavic (7.4). In each case I restrict my main attention to one or several languages of the group. In the course of this discussion we will see different routes of how referential systems can change over time, including the processes of developing and losing bound and/or tenacious pronouns. There is sufficient evidence of the accretion of bound pronouns in a language, but a converse evolution, that is loss of bound pronouns, is possible as well. In section 7.5 I offer a wider typological picture of possible evolutionary pathways in the domain of reduced referential devices.

7.1 The diachrony of referential systems

Each language has a system of referential devices, and such a system does not have to be stable over time. In fact, closely related languages may have very different referential systems. An important question arising in this connection is: how do such changes occur, and what directions of development are attested? Particularly interesting are changes involving bound pronouns, since morphological devices are most profoundly connected to languages' basic features.

In a well-known article, Givón (1976) demonstrated that bound pronouns[1] diachronically develop from free pronouns. A similar point was made by

---

[1] Givón actually discussed them in terms of agreement markers, but since he pointed out that they 'retain their original anaphoric-pronoun function' (p. 168) he was obviously discussing the phenomenon named bound pronouns here.

Mithun (1991) for North American languages among which bound pronouns are particularly widespread. For a review of the rise of bound pronouns see Siewierska (2004: 261–268) and also Helmbrecht (2004: 400ff.).

In the context of this book, what is relevant is not the evolution of specific morphemes but rather **historical shifts between language types**, that is changes in languages' preferred reduced referential devices. For example, in the previous chapter we have looked in some detail at the referential system of Germanic languages. It evolved historically from a system similar to that of Latin, in which an activated Principal referent is coded by a bound pronoun. In the history of Germanic, the syntactic principle of verb second position is thought to be responsible for the spread of free pronouns (see e.g. Weerman 1989). Once this principle came into operation, free strong pronouns became obligatory in the clause-initial position and, accordingly, were reanalysed as free weak pronouns. They became the main carriers of the referential function, simultaneously depriving the bound pronouns (personal desinences) of this function. As a result, personal desinences turned into less than fully functional agreement markers and underwent the process of gradual erosion. Compared to the common Indo-European stage of development, modern Germanic languages have changed the dominant reduced referential device for Principal referents: from bound pronouns to free pronouns.

In the three subsequent sections we will look at evolutionary processes in three other genealogical language groups – two of them also Indo-European and one from a totally different part of the world. Various directions of development are considered – in particular, some languages accrue bound and tenacious pronouns, while other languages (including Germanic) lose them. Specific causes of evolutionary changes, such as the verb-second principle in Germanic, will also be examined.

7.2 Athabaskan, with focus on Navajo

Athabaskan languages (forming the main part of the Na-Dene family, to which also the more distantly related languages Eyak and Tlingit belong) are spread throughout much of the western part of North America. There are three separate areas where Athabaskan languages are (or were) spoken: Alaska and the western part of Canada (the northern area); northern California and Oregon (the Pacific area); American Southwest (the southern, or Apachean, area). Like many other North American languages, Athabaskan languages are generally polysynthetic (see Rice 2000 for an overview; Kibrik 2002a for a typological characterization of Athabaskan) and, as is usual for polysynthetic languages, their verb contains pronominal affixes.

Unlike most other North American languages, the Athabaskan are almost exclusively prefixing languages; in fact, they are among the most prefixing languages on earth. Prefixes are arranged in front of the verb root in a certain sequence, and prefixes of different classes occupy fixed positions in this sequence. Among the pronominal prefixes, the closest to the stem (and presumably the earliest to fuse with it historically) are nominative (traditionally: subject) pronouns. Locutor nominative pronouns appear very close to the root, while non-locutor nominative pronouns are expressed further away.

7.2.1 Northern Athabaskan

Consider examples from Upper Kuskokwim, a typical representative of the northern group of Athabaskan:

(7.1) Upper Kuskokwim (Na-Dene, Alaska, USA; ii – from a story by Bobby Esai, speaker)
  i. tighi-s-kał
     FUT-1SG.NOM-paddle
     'I will paddle'
  ii. jiles   hi-to-łtse
      cross   3PL.NOM-FUT-MAKE
      'They will cross themselves', *lit.* 'They will make a cross'

The difference in the location of locutor and non-locutor pronouns is highly visible in (7.1): the first person and the third person pronouns are found on different sides of the future tense marker *tighi-* (or its morphophonemic variant *to-*). Nominative pronouns are tenacious. All these features of nominative pronouns are shared by other Athabaskan languages as well.

Accusative pronouns (of all persons) occur one step further away from the stem than the non-locutor nominative, for example:

(7.2) Upper Kuskokwim (Na-Dene, Alaska, USA)
   ts'a-s-hi-na-ne-yut
   PREF-1SG.ACC-3PL.NOM-PREF-PFV-wake
   'They woke me up'

Upper Kuskokwim third person accusative pronouns, however, are not tenacious; see Chapter 6, subsection 6.3.1. Examples in (7.3i, ii) repeat (6.18ii) and (6.19) and show the accusative pronouns' alternating character. In the examples, arguments and other clause participants are underlined; sometimes they are NPs, sometimes bound pronouns, but not both in each instantiation of a referent.

(7.3) Upper Kuskokwim (Na-Dene, Alaska, USA)
  i. yi-ø-ne-łʼanh
     33.ACC²-3.NOM-PREF-look
     'S/he is looking at it/him/her'
  ii. gugaʔ   ø-ne-łʼanh
      baby   3.NOM-PREF-look
      'S/he is looking at the baby'

The alternating pattern extends in Upper Kuskokwim not only to accusative pronouns referring to Patientives but also to the coding of other non-Principal participants, including non-core arguments and adjuncts. Such participants are connected to the verb semantically by means of postpositions[3]. As is often the case in polysynthetic languages, postpositions can be inflected for person by affixal bound pronouns. I call this clause participant position oblique. As the following example shows, oblique third person pronouns are in a complementary distribution with full NPs:

(7.4) Upper Kuskokwim (Na-Dene, Alaska, USA)
  i. DAMIAN[4] mo   hwtł   ʔi-łtsenh
     D.   for   sled   3.NOM.PFV-made
     'S/he made a sled for Damian'
  ii. hwtł   yi-mo   ʔi-łtsenh
      sled   33.ACC-for 3.NOM.PFV-made
      'S/he made a sled for him/her'

The following two extracts from stories demonstrate how reference in the accusative and oblique positions operates in natural discourse:

(7.5) Upper Kuskokwim (Na-Dene, Alaska, USA; from a Holikachuk story told by Hannah Maillelle, translated into Upper Kuskokwim by Irene Dennis and Betty Petruska)
  a. dinaʔena hi-ti-łʼey   tsʼeʔ.
     people   3PL.NOM-PREF-see.NEG   PTCL

---

[2] As was pointed out in Chapters 4 and 6, the Athabaskan accusative third person pronoun *y(i)-* appears when the nominative is third person too, so this morpheme is glossed '33.ACC'. The discussion in this section relates only to these situations. When the nominative pronoun is other than plain third person, the accusative pronoun is always zero.

[3] There exists the dative position in the Upper Kuskokwim verb that does not involve a postposition, but demonstrating how it is different from the accusative involves too many technical details. The same concerns the Navajo language discussed below; on the Navajo dative, see Kibrik (2001d).

[4] English names in Upper Kuskokwim discourse, as well as in some other languages, are a kind of code switching, and for this reason they are spelled with capital letters.

b. ts'iyozra hi-t'anh.
   canoe   3PL.NOM-had
c. hwlek'it deno ts'ima dzagha? ?ił   no-hi-yi-dzah.
   it.is.crusty when spruce pitch   with ITER-3PL.NOM-33.ACC[5]-pitch
d. ts'ima   dzagha? eko srito-no-hi-didił.
   spruce   pitch   for in.the.woods-back-3PL.NOM-they.go
e. no-hi-yi-łgheh.
   ITER-3PL.NOM-33.ACC-melt
   'They [=the girl and her mother] did not see any people. They had a canoe. Every spring they smeared it with spruce pitch. They went back into the woods for the spruce pitch. They melted it.'

(7.6) Upper Kuskokwim (Na-Dene, Alaska, USA; from a story by Lena Petruska, speaker)
a. hwye?ił chu   mich'imidin?anh mi-?ił   ø-ghi-yoł.
   and.then PTCL her.husband   3.OBL[6]-with 3.NOM-PROG-walk
b. yet   hi-de-ghi-lts'e?   hidonh   ?ił.
   there 3PL.NOM-PREF-PFV-lived   their.mother with
   'And then her husband was walking with her. They lived there with their mother.'

This system of alternating bound pronouns in the accusative and oblique positions is characteristic of other northern Athabaskan languages as well, for example Chipewyan (=Dëne Sųłiné; northern Canada); see Cook (2004: 284–85); on some other northern Athabaskan languages see Thompson (1996). Among the modern Athabaskan languages (see below), this system is apparently conservative. However, in a deeper historical perspective this system is of a much lesser antiquity than the nominative pronouns. At the Proto-Athabaskan stage, it is likely that bound accusative pronouns developed from free pronouns; in Tlingit (Alaska, USA, British Columbia and Yukon Territory, Canada), a distant relative of Athabaskan, the transition from the free (proclitic) to the prefixal status is of a relatively recent descent; see Leer (1991: 122).

---

[5] The combination '3PL.NOM + 33.ACC' is realized in the reverse morpheme order of what is expected: *hi-yi-* instead of *yi-hi-*.

[6] Difference of third person *mi-* from the more conventional *yi-* is complex and irrelevant here; both pattern the same way with respect to tenacity.

7.2.2 Navajo

A different system has evolved in Navajo, a related language spoken in New Mexico, Arizona, and the adjacent areas. Navajo has generally developed a noticeably greater degree of polysynthesis compared to the northern languages (Kibrik 2002a). The third person accusative pronoun became tenacious: it is always present in the verb irrespective of the presence or absence of the corresponding full NP in the clause; compare (7.7i, ii). Moreover, Navajo third person pronouns are quite insensitive with respect to referential properties. As (7.7iii, iv) show, they can corefer with indefinite NPs and interrogative pronouns.

(7.7) Navajo (Na-Dene, Southwest of the USA; from a story by Bernice Casaus, speaker)

   i. yi-ø-ní-ł'í
      33.ACC-3.NOM-PREF-look
      'S/he is looking at it/him/her'

   ii. ʔawééʔ yi-ø-ní-ł'í
       baby   33.ACC-3.NOM-PREF-look
       'S/he is looking at the baby'

   iii. naadą́ą́ʔ de-i-ø-łtązh
        corn   DISTR-33.ACC-3.NOM-peck
        'They are pecking corn'

   iv. ni-má   héí   yi-ø-yii-łtsą́?
       your-mother$_m$ who$_i$ 33.ACC$_i$-3.NOM$_m$-PFV-saw
       'Who did your mother see?'

The same development as with accusative pronouns happened in Navajo with the oblique pronouns attached to postpositions: they are tenacious as well. Several instances of Navajo tenacious accusative, dative (see fn. 3), and oblique pronouns can be seen in the following excerpts from a spoken story, used both as sole referential devices in their clauses and alongside with full NPs:

(7.8) Navajo (Na-Dene, Southwest of the USA; from a story by Bernice Casaus, speaker)

   a. t'áá   shį́į́ ʔayóo neeʔ yi-ø-ní-dí-lchiʔ-go
      PTCL PTCL very   PTCL 33.DAT-3.NOM-ITER-PREF-touched-SBRD

   b. ná-ø-hidi-ltsiʔ-go
      ITER-3.NOM-PREF-moved.around-SBRD

   c. ʔayęęzhii   yi-k'i   ø-si-dá.
      egg   33.OBL-on   3.NOM-PFV-sat
      'Slightly touching them and moving around, she sat on the eggs.'

(7.9) Navajo (Na-Dene, Southwest of the USA; from a story by Bernice Casaus, speaker)
a. nah-déé⁷   na⁷ahóóhai yighan   yi-yi⁷-déé⁷
   behind-from   chicken   their.house 33.OBL-inside-from
   ch'é-ø-lwod   ńt'éé⁷,
   out-3.NOM-ran   then
         <two intervening clauses>
d. na⁷ahóóhai yę́ę́   ła⁷   yi-ł=ø-yi-lwoł   jiń.
   chicken   that   one   33.OBL-with=3.NOM-PROG-run   QUOT
e. ⁷áádóó shį́į́ yi-k'ee   ń-ø-dínii-dzood.
   then   PTCL 33.OBL-because   PREF-3.NOM-PREF-fled
f. hááhgóshį́į́   ⁷atsá yáázh   yę́ę́ ⁷a-tah   bit'a⁷
   strongly   eagle little that INDEF.OBL-among   his.wings
   yi-ø-łhal-go
   33.ACC-3.NOM-flapped-SBRD
g. ø-yi-lwoł   jiń.
   3.NOM-PROG-run   QUOT
h. ńléí   náwóne⁷   wóne⁷   y-ah
   over there inside of   inside   33.OBL-into
   ⁷a-ná-ø-níí-chą́ą́⁷.
   away-back-3.NOM-PREF-escaped
i. mą⁷ii   ⁷éí na⁷ahóóhai yę́ę́ yi-ł=⁷ee-lwod.
   coyote that chicken   that 33.OBL-with=away.3.NOM.PFV-ran
   'From behind, from inside the chickens' house he [=the coyote] ran out, <...> with that chicken he was running, they say. Then because of that they [=the chickens] started running. The little eagle among others was flapping his wings and running, they say. Into over there, into it [=the chicken house] he ran back in. The coyote ran away with that chicken.'

As is already familiar from the previous chapters, Navajo arguments and other clause participants can be expressed in two different ways. When a referent is judged by the speaker as activated, then just a bound pronoun, either on a verb or on a postposition, is used. When a referent is not activated, both a full NP and a tenacious pronoun are used, and the two in conjunction constitute the mention of the referent.

The change of bound pronouns from alternating to tenacious in Navajo is clearly a sign of the expansion of bound pronouns and of the growth of polysynthesis. In addition to this, Navajo has made one further step in increasing its polysynthesis and reliance on bound pronouns, compared to northern Athabaskan. As is clear from the examples above, an Athabaskan postposition is generally found between the NP it relates to and the inflected verb. As was demonstrated in Kibrik (1990b), in Navajo many erstwhile postpositions have become attached to the verb and reinterpreted as preverbs, that is, verbal markers of the clause's oblique participants' roles (such as locative, directional, comitative, etc.). (See also Young et al. 1992: 922. Cf. a discussion of a different grammaticalization path for adpositions, characteristic of dependent-marking languages – their transformation into case affixes, as discussed by Lehmann 1995: 77ff.)

(7.10) Navajo (Na-Dene, Southwest of the USA; from a story by Bernice Casaus, speaker)
ts'ídá shį́į́   naʔahóóhai   b-a-ʔ-í-ltsood
just   PTCL   chicken   3.OBL-to-INDEF.ACC-PFV-were.fed
'Probably at that time the chickens were fed'

The preverb -a(a) 'to', here functioning as a benefactive, has changed its host from a noun, as is usual for postpositions, to the verb. A still clearer example of a preverb's affiliation in the verb form is found here:

(7.11) Navajo (Na-Dene, Southwest of the USA; from a story by Bernice Casaus, speaker)
wónáásóó   shį́į́   bimá   hadah
finally   PTCL   his.mother   down
ha-b-í-ʔ-ch'-íí-yil
up.out-3.OBL-against-PREF-4.NOM-PFV-push
'Finally, it appears, his mother pushed him out (of the nest)'

Here the combination of the pronominal morpheme b- and the preverb -í- 'against' occurs between the outright derivational prefix ha- and the rest of the verb form. Having a wide range of such preverbs is not unique among native American languages; Craig and Hale (1988) have provided a useful survey of similar phenomena in a number of other languages of the continent.

The change from alternating to tenacious bound pronouns in Navajo, shared by all Apachean languages, is an obvious innovation. Apachean is a group of very closely related languages, quite distinct from all the other Athabaskan that are rather diverse. The difference between the northern pattern, exemplified here by Upper Kuskokwim, and the southern pattern, exemplified by Navajo, appears abrupt: in the northern pattern accusative and oblique pronouns are fully alternating, in the southern pattern completely tenacious. This kind of change could not have happened in a flash, and it is interesting to ask: through which intermediate stage or stages did the original Athabaskan pattern, represented in the northern languages, evolve into the Navajo pattern? An empirical answer to this question would be possible if we could find some languages that represent an intermediate pattern, in which tenacious, but not completely tenacious pronouns could be found.

7.2.3 The rise of the Navajo pattern

A priori, the most obvious language to look into is Sarcee (=Tsúùt'ínà), the southernmost outlier of the northern Athabaskan area, spoken in Alberta (USA). This language is geographically the closest among the northern Athabaskan to Navajo and the other Apachean and it has sometimes been suggested that it is the closest relative of the Apachean among the northern languages. However, it turns out that Sarcee demonstrates the same pattern as Upper Kuskokwim and the northern languages in general; see Cook (2004: 404–406).

Still the missing link exists. It is found in another southern outlier of the northern Athabaskan area, a language of British Columbia known as Babine-Witsuwit'en. In this language the neat complementary distribution between nominal and (bound) pronominal third person accusative arguments has been disrupted, as has been shown by Gunlogson (2001). According to the general Athabaskan pattern, shared by Upper Kuskokwim and Navajo, in Babine-Witsuwit'en accusative pronouns are obligatory when the referent is highly activated before the given clause, that is, when there is no full NP. Now, when a Patientive full NP is there, the accusative pronoun may be present or absent in Babine-Witsuwit'en. Gunlogson presents examples showing that the accusative pronoun is there when the referent is definite and absent when it is indefinite:

(7.12)   Babine-Witsuwit'en (Na-Dene, British Columbia, Canada; Gunlogson 2001: 374)
   i. hida   dinï   yi-ø-nïlh'ën
       moose   man   33.ACC-3.NOM-look.at
       'The moose looks at the man'
   ii. sis   dinï   ø-sëlhghï
       bear   man   3.NOM-killed
       'The bear killed a man'

Thus Babine-Witsuwit'en accusative pronouns are tenacious but sensitive: they are absent when a referent is indefinite. The same pattern is observed in oblique pronouns used with postpositions and preverbs, for example:

(7.13) Babine-Witsuwit'en (Na-Dene, British Columbia, Canada; Gunlogson 2001: 391, 375)
 i. PAT <u>bitsë</u>   <u>yi</u>-be   c'otakiih   wika'nïnzin
    P. his.daughter   33.OBL-to INDEF.ACC.3.NOM.buy   3.NOM.want
    'Pat wants to buy something for his daughter'
 ii. <u>kikh</u>   ha'it'ah   khït
     rabbit   3.NOM.hunt.for wintertime
     'He hunts rabbits in the winter'

(7.13i) illustrates the definite NP 'his daughter' accompanied by a tenacious pronoun on the postposition, whereas (7.13ii) shows that there is no pronoun on the preverb 'for'[7] in the context of the indefinite NP 'rabbits'.

Gunlogson (pp. 389ff.) emphasizes that the referential distinction marked by the presence or absence of $y(i)$- is not givenness: definite, but discourse-new referents are introduced by a combination of a full NP and a bound pronoun. In fact, it is not clear whether it is exactly definiteness that triggers presence vs. absence of Babine-Witsuwit'en accusative and oblique pronouns. Gunlogson mentions that in some instances it is rather the difference between specific and non-specific referents that is crucial (p. 390), and several of her examples (pp. 374, 390ff.) actually incline one to this interpretation. In some other examples it appears that the status of discourse importance may be relevant (pp. 389–390). Apparently some combination of these referential statuses is responsible for the sensitivity of Babine-Witsuwit'en pronouns. In any case, we observe a pattern that is intermediate between the Upper Kuskokwim and the Navajo patterns. A similar system is cursorily reported for Dena'ina, an Alaskan language of the Cook Inlet area (USA), by Müller (2004: 105), and analogous phenomena are reported for Slave of northern Canada (Rice 2003).

Evidently, the Navajo strongly tenacious pattern could have evolved from the general Athabaskan pattern, still kept by most northern languages, only through the Babine-Witsuwit'en stage. A more general historical hypothesis can be derived from this evidence. Some languages diachronically accrue the number of bound pronouns on the verb and increase polypersonalism. The two differences between Navajo and northern Athabaskan – Navajo's use of strongly tenacious bound pronouns and its centripetal evolution of postpositions into preverbs (together with associated pronouns) – are related and are a part of the same tendency: accretion of bound pronouns. Of course, no language is programmed to this kind of evolution. But it seems that as soon as

---

[7] Gunlogson does not provide morpheme-by-morpheme glossing but makes it clear (p. 374) that a preverb is present in the verb form in (7.13ii).

languages of a certain family develop bound pronouns, at least to a limited degree, some languages of this family are likely to further this tendency, potentially to the extreme.

7.3 Romance, with focus on French

Evolution of the Romance referential systems is intricate. In most general terms it can be characterized as similar to the Navajo case: gradual accretion of polypersonalism, culminating in modern spoken French. Romance languages have a well-documented history, which makes it possible to explore some diachronic pathways in a more factual way than can be done with only recently documented languages, such as Athabaskan. So it seems appropriate to discuss the Romance data within the framework of a typology of referential systems.

Of course, the Romance facts are quite well known. A detailed study of the development of Romance pronouns from Classical Latin and through the Old Romance period can be found in Wanner (1987); another useful reference source is Harris and Vincent (eds.) (1997). There has also been a great deal of theoretical interest in Romance, especially in the abundant literature on pronominal clitics during the 1980s and 1990s (a useful summary can be found in Halpern 1998; see also a large bibliography in Nevis et al. 1994; among the more recent publications, see Monachesi 2005). Still it makes sense to put Romance in a typological context. It seems that despite the existence of the vast literature the facts of Romance are still not sufficiently appreciated. Also note that the phenomena laid out here are often mentioned only cursorily in language-specific discussions, as for example in the historical chapter of Fagyal et al. (2006).

7.3.1 *Spanish and general Romance*

We have discussed the use of both subject and object reduced referential devices of Spanish in sections 6.6 and 6.1, respectively. Subject pronouns are bound and strongly tenacious, object pronouns are free and partly tenacious (sensitive). This system was formed in its main traits about one thousand years ago: 'cliticisation[8] of pronouns to the verb is by no means a recent process in Spanish; it appears well established at the time of earliest texts'

---

[8] The terms 'clitics' and 'cliticization' are used by Romance linguists in the sense that pronouns have become fixed in terms of their position in a clause, having attached to the verb. Of course, according to the approach adopted in this book, all weak pronouns are clitics, irrespective of whether they have a fixed position or not.

(Green 1997: 108). Evolution during the ensuing centuries is characterized by the two main processes: gradual rise of object pronouns' tenacity and relocation of these pronouns from the postverbal to the preverbal position in finite clauses. See example (6.6) for an illustration of how the Spanish referential system operates in discourse.

In the most general terms, the Spanish pattern is very representative of the situation in most other Romance languages. The Romance system has been summarized as follows:

... Most varieties [of Romance – A.K.] have kept the original Latin grammemes (verb endings) marking the first actant. ... In addition to this verbal subject marking, most if not all Romance languages have developed a new verbal object marking, also from original pronouns which have become cliticized. These object clitics may be more or less bound, or obligatory, depending on the individual languages, and even registers within individual languages. In general, these clitics are more frequent in spoken than in written language. In some varieties, such as Modern Spanish, Sardinian, and especially Rumanian, the degree of boundedness and obligatoriness is such that these grammemes can be considered already as a fully-fledged 'object conjugation'. (Bossong 2003: 38).

The general vector of Romance development, as compared to the Latin archetype, is towards an increasing parallelism between the subject and object pronouns. Object pronouns are becoming more like subject pronouns, gaining in tenacity and even boundness. Such similarity has been discussed by Duranti and Ochs (1979) with respect to Italian. This parallelism, however, is formally and functionally limited: subject pronouns are fully bound, strongly tenacious, and postpositive with respect to the verb stem, while object pronouns are, at best, only incipiently bound, tenacious but sensitive, and prepositive.

The situation is very different in another Romance language, namely French, that probably went further towards developing a fully-fledged and consistent bound (or almost bound) tenacious pronominal system than any other Romance language.

7.3.2 *French: from medieval to modern standard*

Like Latin and most Romance, medieval French used personal desinences as bound subject pronouns and, in connection with that, rarely used free pronominal subjects. Deriving from the counts in Ashby and Bentivoglio (2003: 66, Table 4a), in the *Chanson de Roland* (late 11th century) 70% of all reduced subject referential devices were represented by pronominal desinences alone. Examples can be seen in the last line of the following:

250   II. *Typology of Reduced Referential Devices*

(7.14)   Old French, around 1090 (Chanson de Roland, XXIX, after Ashby and Bentivoglio 2003: 75–76)
Mult grant mal fu-<u>nt</u>   e   [cil] duc e   cil cunte
much great bad do-PRES.3PL and these dukes and these counts
A lur   seignur, <u>ki</u> tel   cunseill li   dune-<u>nt</u>:
to their lord   who   such counsel   him   give-PRES.3PL
Lui e   altrui   travaille-<u>nt</u>   e   cunfunde-<u>nt</u>.
him and others torment-PRES.3PL and overwhelm-PRES.3PL
'A great wrong do these dukes and these counts
Unto their lord, giving him such counsel;
Him and others they harry and confound.'[9]

Note the recipient pronoun *li* in the second line of this example, operating, in terms of its position, similarly to object pronouns of Spanish and other Romance.

During the following centuries there was a gradual increase in the amount of free subject pronouns, and a parallel steady decrease in the amount of reference performed by personal desinences alone. For example Vance (1997: 322) provides the following percentages of null subjects (in fact, bound pronominal subjects) for a number of texts: *Erec* (1167) – 55%, *Villehardouin* (1212) – 33%, *Froissart* (1375) – 26%, *Les Cent Nouvelles Nouvelles* (1505) – 23%.[10] The main force that contributed to making free pronouns obligatory is the same as in Germanic: the verb-second syntactic principle; see e.g. Harris (1997: 231). This principle became dominant during the Middle French period (14th to 16th centuries). Of course, the wide-scale free subject pronouns can only be weak pronouns, used when a referent is activated, that is, in complementary distribution with full NPs; free strong pronouns (of low frequency) were used at all periods.

Referring to Fontaine (1985), Vance (1997: 323) reports that by the year 1600 the number of 'null free subjects' decreased to less than 1%, thus giving rise to the system well known from modern standard French. Compare the structure of the 11th century Old French with that of modern standard written French:

---

[9] Translation by Charles Scott Moncrief (London, 1919), from The Online Medieval and Classical Library (www.omacl.org/Roland/), slightly modified and made more literal by myself [A.K.]. The same source was used for the next example.

[10] As for the 16th century, Vance argues in detail that there was a temporary rise in the number of 'null subjects' in that period, but that is difficult to assess as her numbers for the text *Saintré* (1456) in the tables on pp. 294 and 322 contradict each other.

(7.15) Old French, around 1090 (Chanson de Roland, CLXVIII), and standard French[11]

De	ses	pers	prie-t	Deu	ques	apel-t,
Pour	ses	pairs,	il prie	Dieu	qu'	il les appelle,
E	pois	de	lui	a	l'angle	Gabriel.
Et	puis	pour	lui-même	à	l'ange	Gabriel.

Pris-t l'olifan <...>
Il prend l'olifant <...>
'He prays to God that He will call the peers,
To Gabriel, the angel, for himself.
Takes the olifant[12] <...>'

So what happened between the 11th and the 17th centuries is that French changed its system of subject reference from bound pronouns to free pronouns, thus diverging radically from the common Romance pattern (as exemplified by Latin and Spanish). Former bound pronouns are recast into verbal agreement. This is the system familiar from standard French, as it is taught in schools. The same system is found in Rheto-Romance (Switzerland) and in most dialects of northern Italy (Bossong 2003: 38). In its adherence to free subject pronouns French became for a while like the Germanic languages. In fact, standard written French even surpasses written English in the range of contexts where it requires free subject pronouns; this has already been mentioned in Chapter 6, subsection 6.7.2. In particular, free subject pronouns are most likely to appear even in a coordinate construction such as the following (see also Lambrecht 1981: 24):

(7.16) Standard French
Il lit et puis il écrit
He reads and then he writes

In (7.16), using a zero subject in the second clause is nearly impossible, unlike the parallel English structure *He reads and then writes*. An internet search has found no instances of the sequence *lit et puis écrit*, but 9,700 instances of *reads and then writes*. It is very likely, however, that the discourse marker of temporal boundary *puis/then* may contribute to the disfavour towards zero subjects in this case. So let us make a comparison of simpler structures without this marker. In another internet search, the English sequence *reads and writes* was found 641,000 times, while the phrase *reads and s/he writes*

---

[11] Modern standard French translation composed on the basis of the variant provided by Fernando Martinho at http://sweet.ua.pt/~fmart/rolan.htm.
[12] Olifant is a medieval wind instrument made from elephants' tusks.

7,776 times, which makes 1.2% of the instances with the zero subject. In contrast, the sequence *lit et écrit* is found 17,400 times, while *lit et il/elle écrit* 2,366 times. This is 13.6% of instances with zero subject, that is one order of magnitude more frequently than in English.

As concerns tenacity, in standard French subject pronouns are clearly alternating. Authors of a modern reference grammar prescribe:

> The pronouns *il* or *elle* should not be used in formal written French where another noun is already the subject, even if it no longer immediately precedes the verb:
> **Pierre, mon voisin de l'étage du dessous, il m'a dit que ...* [13]
> Such constructions are however typical of spontaneous spoken French. ... Similarly, repetition of the object is considered poor style, although such repetition is common in the spoken language and acceptable in that context. (Judge and Healey 1990: 72).

Due to the prestige of literacy, French is still often portrayed as a language with alternating pronouns in linguistic studies – this view is reflected in how French is categorized in the WALS studies (Nichols and Bickel 2005b, Comrie 2005, Dryer 2005a, and Siewierska 2005e). This approach also presupposes that French still marks subject person on the verb by means of personal desinences. In fact, in its oral form, French has mostly lost its personal suffixal inflection. As a result of this process, in modern spoken French in the present tense only the second person plural form is phonologically distinct (provided the firm establishment of the first person plural form *on V-e* instead of the erstwhile *nous V-ons* in modern French; see e.g. Lambrecht 1981: 41, 47; Mühlhäusler et al. 1990: 179ff.);[14] on the degree to which original subject person markers are kept in other tenses see Lambrecht (1981: 48).

As has been pointed out on many occasions, there is a huge difference between the two varieties of modern French: the prescribed, written, formal French on the one hand, and the colloquial, popular, spoken, and informal French, on the other. Different authors on different occasions emphasize at least two different distinctions between these varieties: sometimes the mode (spoken vs. written), sometimes the degree of formality (formal vs. informal, standard vs. non-standard). It is likely that both variables can contribute to differences, so, to be on the safe side, I will presume both of them. Terminologically, I will contrast standard French and colloquial French. One of the best known and forceful demonstrations of what colloquial

---

[13] *Lit.* 'Pierre, my neighbour from the downstairs floor, he has told me that ...'.
[14] According to Mühlhäusler, this transition essentially occurred during the 1960s and 1970s. However, evidence from some spoken corpora, such as Beeching (2001), demonstrates that the *nous V-ons* form is still in active use, along with the *on V-e* form.

French really is belongs to Lambrecht (1981). (For another early analysis see Galambos 1980). My further discussion mostly concerns colloquial French, as this variety clearly demonstrates the vector of the French language's development.

7.3.3 *Colloquial French*

The difference of colloquial French from standard French is that in the former subject pronouns have become both bound and tenacious. These two properties are sometimes described as one and the same property, for example:

The appropriate conjunctive pronouns, ... have become steadily more tightly bound to the verb of which they are subject, to the extent that they are found ... in popular speech, increasingly even when there is an overt nominal subject (*mon père il dit que* ... literally 'my father he says that ...'). ... Put at its simplest, we may regard French *ils aiment* /izɛm/ 'they love' as one polymorphemic word (subject-prefix + stem) in exactly the same way as one regards Latin AMANT or OFr. *aiment* as one polymorphemic word (stem + subject-suffix). (Harris 1997: 231–232).

... The synchronic data of ISF [informal spoken French – A.K.] suggest that colloquial French is approaching a stage where ALL verb stems (except imperatives) will attach preverbal P/N [person/number – A.K.] markers, and that these morphemes will occur *obligatorily* in the appropriate context. Should such tightness between P/N morphemes and the verb indeed be reached, the currently still clitic *je, tu, il,* etc. would then fit the definition of *inflections* (Schwegler 1990: 105).

However, as we know, boundness and tenacity are two separate features, both logically and empirically, so they must be considered separately. Before that, however, another remarkable difference of French from other Romance languages must be pointed out. Unlike Spanish, in French all pronouns have formed a homogeneous class. Erstwhile pronominal subject suffixes have been replaced by preverbal elements, similar to object pronouns. Different pronominal elements line up in a colloquial French clause in front of (or at the beginning of) the verb:

(7.17)   Colloquial French (Lambrecht 1981: 77)[15]
   i. I-la-voit
      3SG.M.NOM-3SG.F.ACC-see.PRES
      'He sees her'

---

[15] I follow Lambrecht's transcription of colloquial French that is a compromise between conventional orthography and the phonetic facts – for example pronouns *il* 'he' and *ils* 'they' (masculine) often appear as *i-*. See Lambrecht (1981: 19, 34).

ii. Pierre i-la-voit, Marie
P. 3SG.M.NOM-3SG.F.ACC-see.PRES M.
'Pierre sees Marie'

Lambrecht (1981: 17–22, 32ff.) enumerated a number of formal properties of colloquial French pronominal elements, including:

- phonological: liaison, elision of the final element, erosion of the initial element, inability to bear stress (except some special circumstances)
- morphosyntactic: do not separate from the verb, stack in a stable order in front of the verb.

Taken together, these features amount to recognition of pronouns as affixes. (Compare, for example, with the criteria for the clitic vs. affix distinction in Haspelmath 2002: 151–154.) Lambrecht himself arrives at the same conclusion, despite his usage of the term 'clitic': after having mentioned several criteria, he concluded that 'NSF [=non-standard French – A.K.] clitics clearly satisfy these criteria for (bound) morpheme status' (Lambrecht 1981: 103); see also the quote from Harris (1997) above and Fagyal et al. (2006: 115). One aspect of pronominal syntax that clearly differentiates French from Spanish is the absence of 'clitic climbing' – one of the main diagnostics we used in 6.1.1. to conclude that Spanish object pronouns are still free. In French, 'clitic climbing' disappeared in the 18th century (even though it is still used under certain stylistic circumstances in written French); cf. *Je peux le voir* 'I can see it', *Je le peux voir (Heap 2000: 12; see also Fagyal et al. 2006: 114–115).[16]

There is a tradition in French studies of comparing the structure of colloquial French to that of polysynthetic languages of North America that have multiple bound pronouns (Lambrecht 1981: 8ff.). To appreciate the actual similarity to North American languages (or to Abkhaz), one needs to see a phonological transcription of a French verb, for example this one that is usually conceived as a four-word clause *Je te le donne*:

(7.18)   Colloquial French (Lambrecht 1981: 20)
š-t-lə-dɔn
1SG.NOM-2SG.DAT-3.M.ACC-give.PRES
'I am giving it to you'

---

[16] The analysis of French pronouns as affixes is also customary in some formal linguistic literature, for example Miller and Sag (1997) (although other aspects of their analysis are different from the ones adopted here).

Still I would like to suggest that French pronouns must be tested more carefully for their complete boundness, as we understand it from Navajo and Abkhaz. Since grammaticalization of free forms into bound forms is an inherently continuous process it may well be that we are catching it in the present-day colloquial French at a stage that is not fully conclusive. Informal inspections of extended corpora of colloquial French, such as Beeching (2001), give an impression that hesitation pauses between pronouns and the rest of the verb occur more frequently than one might expect if these were whole morphological verbs.

Besides being bound (or almost bound), colloquial French pronouns are also tenacious. As Lambrecht (1981: 25) puts it, 'whenever a verb *can* have a clitic, it *must* have a clitic'. An example of tenacity has been already given in (7.17ii). However, as follows from the evidence cited by Lambrecht, colloquial French pronouns are not fully tenacious. First, there is some variation in the presence/absence of a pronoun under the presence of a full NP:

(7.19) Colloquial French (Lambrecht 1981: 51)
    i. Pierre   i-vient
       P.   3SG.M.NOM-come.PRES
       'Pierre comes'
    ii. Pierre vient
       P.   come.PRES
       'Pierre comes'

See also the natural discourse examples in (7.24) below.

Second, bound pronouns are consistently absent when the referent is indefinite – therefore, they are sensitive to certain referential properties (recall the discussion of Babine-Witsuwit'en above):

(7.20) Colloquial French (Lambrecht 1981: 61)
    i. Le   garçon il-attend   devant   la   porte
       the boy   3SG.M.NOM-wait.PRES in.front.of the door
       'The boy is waiting in front of the door'
    ii. *Un garçon il-attend   devant   la   porte
       a   boy   3SG.M.NOM-wait.PRES in.front.of the door
       'A boy is waiting in front of the door'

As example (7.18) has already demonstrated, colloquial French bound pronouns are not limited to two arguments. Consider the following example showing that the dative pronoun is also tenacious (while the accusative pronoun is missing from the verb form in this case):

(7.21) Colloquial French (Lambrecht 1981: 59)
Pierre j-ui-ai-donné le livre hier
P. 1SG.NOM-3SG.DAT-1SG.have-give.PARTIC the book yesterday
'I've given Pierre the book yesterday'

In addition to nominative, accusative, and dative bound pronouns, colloquial French allows two more case forms of bound tenacious pronouns that can be dubbed directive and partitive (see Lambrecht 1981: 34). These are pronouns *y-* and *en-*, respectively. Interestingly, they do not differentiate either person or number (Lambrecht 1981: 34ff.), that is, they constitute an example of bound pronouns of a generalized referential capacity:

(7.22) Colloquial French (Lambrecht 1981: 36, 32)
 i. Pierre y-pense jamais, à sa voiture
    P. REFDIR-think.PRES never to his car
    'Pierre never thinks of his car'
 ii. tu-leur-en-donnes
    2SG.NOM-3PL.DAT-REFPART-give.PRES
    'You are giving them some of that'

Finally, like other highly polysynthetic languages with bound pronouns, French displays some integration of still more peripheral clause participants into the verb. 'The prepositions *après, devant, contre* are reanalysed as adverbial affixes loosely attached to the verb' (Lambrecht 1981: 39). Each of these postpositive oblique role markers is accompanied by a corresponding referential prefixal pronoun:

(7.23) Colloquial French (Lambrecht 1981: 39)
Pierre y-passe-devant, à son frère
P. REFDIR-pass-ahead to his brother
'Pierre goes ahead of his brother'

As in other languages with bound pronouns, the status of these reduced referential devices is related to the status of full NPs. Lambrecht (1981) has made a strong claim that full NPs are outside the clause, while Harris is less inclined to exclude them from the clause saying that 'spoken French has a highly flexible word order of the kind often called "free", and that the device which all such languages necessarily have to avoid ambiguity is in the case of French not a set of nominal case affixes as in Latin but a complex system of preverbal affixes derived from earlier conjunctive personal pronouns' (Harris 1997: 236). I think the latter position has more truth to it, and, as in other languages with bound pronouns, the assumption should be taken that argumental properties are shared between bound pronouns and coreferential full NPs.

To see how the colloquial French system of referential devices operates, consider a natural discourse example from the French spoken corpus published on a DVD attached to Cresti and Moneglia (eds.) (2005). This is an extract from a dialogue between two young women, one of whom is telling a story to the other. This dialogue is characterized in the corpus as informal (as opposed to formal) and family/private (as opposed to public). The preceding context is that the narrator was going to buy a chinchilla (at a chinchilla sale), and the man called Fred who was helping her has just been introduced.

(7.24) Colloquial French (Cresti and Moneglia (eds.) 2005, dialogue 'Allumage', code ffamdlo1, units 99 through 110)[17]

a. donc   **on**   a   acheté une   toute petite   cage
   so   we   have   bought a   very small   cage
   pour   **le** [/] **l'**   amener &euh # là-bas //
   for   him   him   carry   HES   there

b. **nous**   **on** **en**   a   déjà   une grande // #
   we.EMPH   we   REFPART have   already   a   big

c. **c'**   est   une   grande   puis   **c'** est   notre grande
   it   is   a   big   then   it   is   our   big
   pour [/] &euh #   voilà // #
   for   HES   OK

d. et   Fred rentre / #
   and   F.   returns

e. donc **il** y   avait **l'**   autre chinchilla qui   **nous** attendait / #
   so   it   there had   the   other chinchilla who   us   waited

   <four intervening lines, including a backchannel cue from the interlocutor>

---

[17] The following transcription conventions (Moneglia 2005) are used in this extract:
  // conclusive prosodic break
  / non-conclusive prosodic break
(Both these kinds of breaks have been used as the basis for dividing discourse into numbered lines.)
  [/] non-conclusive prosodic break caused by a false start
  # significant pause
  & false start.
I thank Céline Mounole Hiriart-Urruty for her kind assistance with the spoken French examples.

j. donc l'   autre / **elle** a   réussi   à   se   barrer / #
    so   the   other   she   has managed   to   self   escape

k. et   &euh Fred / **il** a   fait   toute la   maison /
    and   HES   F.   he has searched all   the house

l. parce que   faut   voir /
    because   one.should   see

m. c' est un étage   et   tout quoi /
    it is   a   storey and all   OK

n. donc c' est assez   grand // #
    so   it is   rather   big

o. eh   ben   il   l'   a   retrouvée /
    PTCL well he   her   has   found

p. **elle** dormait sur notre lit // #
    she   slept   on   our   bed

'So we have bought a very small cage to carry him. We already had a big one. It is a big one, for our big one. And Fred returns, and there was another chinchilla who was waiting for us <...> But the other one managed to escape and Fred has searched all the house because one needs to see it, it is a whole storey and all that, so it is rather big. Well he found her, she was sleeping on our bed.'

In this excerpt multiple instances of bound pronouns are found, and there is at least one in each line of discourse. Bound pronouns are boldfaced in the example. Sometimes occurrences of pronouns stacking at the beginning of the verb form can be seen; such instances appear in lines (b), (o). In most instances, whenever there is a full NP (or a strong pronoun) in the clause, the corresponding weak pronouns display tenacity. Such instances are underlined: three tenacious subject pronouns are found in lines (b), (j), (k). But tenacity is not always observed: in line (d) a full NP alone constitutes the clause subject. Also note that dummy subject pronouns behave variously: *il* is present in *il y avait* 'there was' in line (e), but absent from *(il) faut* in line (l).

No tenacious object pronouns have been observed in this example. Consider the one in the following, in line (c):

(7.25) Colloquial French (Cresti and Moneglia (eds.) 2005, dialogue 'Allumage', code ffamdlo1, unit 480)

a. # surtout   que   j' ai   appelé mon père /
       the.more.so   that I   have called my   father

b. il   m'   a   dit   qu'   effectivement /
   he   me has told that actually

c. l'   allumage/ il l' avait &ja [/] il l' avait jamais changé // #
   the ignition he it had   FS   he it had never changed
   'On top of that I called my father and he told me that he had actually never changed the ignition'

7.3.4 *The French story*

The convoluted history of the French referential system can be summarized as follows. Old French was typologically quite similar to Spanish and other Romance: it kept the original bound subject pronouns and was also developing partly tenacious preverbal object pronouns. During the Middle French period, the verb-second principle, probably resulting from Germanic influence, engendered the expansion of free subject pronouns, turning from necessarily strong to mostly weak. Since the referential function was picked up by free subject pronouns the former suffixal subject pronouns were relegated to the status of agreement and began undergoing erosion. The Middle French period can be characterized as the Germanic stage in the history of the language. During this period French got temporarily sidetracked from the Romance route. Modern standard French still conserves the Middle French pattern in a petrified form.

However, during the modern period French has regained the Romance vector of its evolution in a strongly amplified manner. Free nominative pronouns have become tenacious and formed a tight preverbal complex with dative and accusative pronouns. Lining up at the beginning of the verb, these pronouns are being transformed into bound elements. Colloquial French has reached a stage in the development of bound tenacious pronouns that is unavailable to other Romance languages, in which subject and object pronouns are too different in terms of descent, structure, and location with respect to the verb stem. So the general Romance tendency of the increase in boundness and tenacity has approached its peak in French. This became possible due to the temporary Germanic-influenced zigzag in the history of French. Modern colloquial French can be characterized as a polypersonal, strongly head-marking language. As in the case of Athabaskan, we see that seminal features of a language family are furthered to the extreme in a subpart of this family.

Germanic languages, to which French became typologically similar for a while, generally do not demonstrate a drive for pronoun boundness and tenacity. They do not exhibit this vector that manifested itself so strongly in colloquial French. One cannot guarantee, though, that a Germanic language never undergoes a similar evolution. Givón (1976: 155–156, 168–170) demonstrated that these kinds of developments, involving formation of bound and tenacious pronouns, are happening in a wide range of varieties of English, including English-based creoles and some American English dialects.

7.4 Slavic, with focus on Russian

Slavic languages display a substantial variety of referential systems. The original system, found in the oldest written Slavic languages, is quite similar to that of other old Indo-European languages, such as Latin. Later on, a development remarkably similar to mainstream Romance happened in South Slavic. In contrast, East Slavic followed a very different evolutionary route, resulting in systems more similar to the Germanic type.

7.4.1 *Old Slavic*

The original Slavic pattern, found in the oldest written Slavic languages (Old Church Slavonic, early Old Russian) amounts to the following:

- Reduced primary referential devices in the subject position are bound, fully tenacious pronouns, that is, verbal personal desinences.
- Reduced referential devices corresponding to other clause participant positions are free alternating pronouns.

Consider the following examples:

(7.26) Old Church Slavonic, Luke 19: 12–15 (Gasparov 2001: 165)
a. člověk-ъ edin-ъ dobr-a rod-a id-e na
   man-NOM one-NOM good-GEN family-GEN go-AOR.3SG to
   stran-ǫ daleče
   country-ACC far
b. <...> prizva-vъ že i desętь rab-ъ
   call-PARTIC.M.SG PTCL and ten servant-GEN.PL
   svo-ixъ
   REFL.POSS-GEN.PL
c. i das-tъ i-mъ desętь mъnas i
   and give-AOR.3SG 3-DAT.PL ten pounds and
   reč-e kъ ni-mъ
   say-AOR.3SG to 3-DAT.PL

d. <...> i   bys-tъ   egda sę   vъzvrati-ø
          and be-AOR.3SG   when REFL return-AOR.3SG

e. <...> i   reč-e   a   priglas-ętъ   e-mu
          and say-AOR.3SG   PTCL invite-PRES.3PL   3-M.DAT.SG
   rab-y   t-y
   servant-ACC.PL that-ACC.PL

f. i-mъ   že   das-tъ   sъrebr-o
   3-DAT.PL   REL   give-AOR.3SG   money-ACC

'A certain nobleman went into a far country <...> and he called his ten servants, and delivered them ten pounds, and said unto them: <...> And it came to pass, that when he was returned <...> then he commanded these servants to be called unto him, to whom he had given the money.'

There are multiple examples of tenacious subject pronouns and alternating object (direct and indirect) and oblique pronouns in this extract. The third person plural ending in line (e) indicates indefinite reference that could be conveyed in English also by a third person plural pronoun: *said that they should invite*.

In a recent study, Efimova (2004) investigated the use of first person singular subject pronouns in Old Church Slavonic, including a comparison of different versions of New Testament texts and a comparison to the Greek original. The main conclusion is that subject pronouns of Old Church Slavonic appear in specialized semantic contexts, such as contrastiveness. Clearly, the Old Church Slavonic pattern is equivalent to the pattern of Latin in its main traits. The same pattern is shared by the early Old Russian system (till the end of the 12th century); see Borkovskij and Kuznecov (1979: 376ff.). At the beginning of the second millennium Slavic languages still kept the conservative Indo-European referential system.

Similarly to Romance, non-subject pronouns of old Slavic languages have inherently weak (clitic) and inherently strong forms, such as 1Sg dative *mi* and *mъně*, or 3Sg masculine accusative *i* and *ego*. This division is assumed to go back to the common Slavic stage (Zaliznjak 2008: 270). There is substantial literature devoted to Slavic pronominal clitics; see e.g. Jakobson (1935/1971), Cyxun (1968), Franks and King (2000), Nikolaeva (2008).

7.4.2 *South Slavic*

Some modern languages of the South Slavic branch (to which Old Church Slavonic also belongs), keeping the subject pronoun pattern generally intact, developed the Spanish-type pattern in which weak object pronouns became tenacious. This is the case in Bulgarian (see Cyxun 1968, Guentchéva 1993, Rubadeau 1996, Legendre 2000, Franks and King 2000: 51ff., Leafgren 2002):

(7.27) Bulgarian (Franks and King 2000: 52, 63, 53)
    i. Vze-x   mu   gi
       take-AOR.1SG   3SG.M.DAT 3PL.ACC
       'I took them from him'
    ii. Vera mi   go   dad-e   včera
       V.   1SG.DAT 3SG.M.ACC give-AOR.3SG yesterday
       'Vera gave it to me yesterday'
    iii. Ivan   go   tărs-jat
       I.   3SG.M.ACC seek-PRES.3PL
       'They are looking for Ivan'

Examples in (7.27i, ii) show that the subject reference pattern in Bulgarian is still the same as in Old Church Slavonic, while (7.27iii) demonstrates that object pronouns have become tenacious. They are, however, not strongly tenacious and are often absent in the presence of a full NP or an emphatic pronoun:

(7.28) Bulgarian (Rubadeau 1996: 52, 66)
    i. Stefan   li   čaka-š?
       S.   QU   wait-PRES.2SG
       'Are you waiting for Stefan?'
    ii. Nego   čaka-m
       3SG.M.ACC.EMPH wait-PRES.1SG
       'I am waiting for him'

Leafgren (2002: 114) provides natural discourse examples, both from written and from spoken corpora, and demonstrates that direct as well as indirect object pronouns can be tenacious, and coreferential full NPs may be preverbal or postverbal. Consider the following two examples:

(7.29) Bulgarian (written) (Leafgren 2002: 114)
    a. <u>Na Ralčev</u>   mu   se   struva-še   stranno
       to Ralchev   3SG.M.DAT REFL seem-IMPF.3SG strange
    b. ubita-ta   da   otid-e   na rabota v naj-novija kostjum
       killed-DEF.F INF go-PRES.3SG to work   in most-new outfit
       'It seemed strange to Ralchev that the slain woman had gone to work in her newest outfit'

(7.30) Bulgarian (spoken) (Leafgren 2002: 114)
Viž kak săm gi măkna-l-a tija cvetja
look how COP.PRES.1SG 3PL.ACC carry-PARTIC-F.SG these flowers
v edin kašon ot Zimnica do tuka
in one cardboard from Z. to here
'Look how I carried these flowers from Zimnica to here in a cardboard box'

Dative and accusative pronouns such as in examples (7.27), (7.29), and (7.30) (*mu, gi, mi, go*, etc.) are inherently clitic; when a prosodically prominent, strong pronoun is needed, a different form is used, such as *nego* in (7.28ii).

In Macedonian, a language closely related to Bulgarian, object pronouns became more strongly tenacious. According to Usikova (2005), the accusative pronoun always accompanies a full NP if the referent is definite (7.31i) and is usually absent with an indefinite NP (7.31ii), while the dative pronoun is present with either definite or indefinite referents (7.31iii, iv), that is, qualifies as an insensitive tenacious referential device. This is a rather rare feature for a free pronoun; cf. section 6.2.

(7.31) Macedonian (Usikova 2005: 133)
  i. Go vido-v dete-to
     3SG.N.ACC see-AOR.1SG child-DEF.N
     'I saw the child'
  ii. Vido-v edn-o dete
      see-AOR.1SG one-N child
      'I saw a child'
  iii. Mu ja dado-v na dete-to kniga-ta
       3SG.N.DAT 3SG.F.ACC give-AOR.1SG to child-DEF.N book-DEF.F
       'I gave the book to the child'
  iv. Mu ja dado-v na edn-o dete
      3SG.N.DAT 3SG.F.ACC give-AOR.1SG to one-N child
      kniga-ta
      book-DEF.F
      'I gave the book to a child'

So the modern Bulgarian and Macedonian pattern is the same as the original Slavic one in the domain of subject reference but quite different in the domain of reference in other clause participant positions: these languages have extended the distinction between weak and strong object pronouns to the third person and developed the property of tenacity. Like the Romance languages, South Slavic languages have extended the tenacity of bound subject pronouns to free object pronouns.

7.4.3 *Russian*

A very different development took place in another branch of Slavic, namely East Slavic, here represented by Russian. Contrary to Bulgarian and Macedonian, Russian has lost the original Slavic distinction between the inherently accented and inherently unaccented object pronouns (Zaliznjak 2008), while preserving the object pronouns' alternating pattern. But what is more central to this section, Russian has altered the use of subject pronouns. On the face of it, modern Russian generally follows the Germanic pattern in having both subject agreement and free pronominal subjects. Default Russian translations of the German examples in (6.32i, ii) and the Latin examples in (6.29ii, i) would be:

(7.32) Russian
    i. Mal'čik   igra-et
       boy   play-PRES.3SG
       'The boy plays'
    ii. On igra-et
       he play-PRES.3SG
       'He plays'

Apparently there is a direct isomorphism between the Russian and German structures. The same point can be illustrated by some discourse pattern comparisons. The data in Table 7.1 demonstrate the difference between Russian and another Slavic language, Polish, in the dominant patterns of subject reference, and the equivalence of the Russian pattern to that of English. (Parallel texts, excerpted from Hans Christian Andersen's fairy tale 'The tinder box', were taken from Wordtheque, the internet site of multilingual literature.[18]) Polish (one of the major languages of the West Slavic branch) can serve as an approximation to the system from which Russian evolved, as it has largely preserved the original Slavic pattern, including bound subject pronouns and the lack of weak free subject pronouns. In Table 7.1 all instances of reference to the protagonist, the soldier, are underlined. Lines 3 to 10 contain reduced reference to the clause subject, in all cases being 'the soldier'. Seven lines, 3 to 6 and 8 to 10, are of primary interest to us now; in line 7 translators have used different diatheses in different languages, which prevents a direct comparison.[19]

---

[18] Later renamed www.logoslibrary.eu.
[19] The Russian variant can be literally conveyed as 'and was right in doing that', and the Polish one as 'which was very nice on his part'.

TABLE 7.1. Comparison of the patterns of subject reference in English, Russian, and Polish

	English	Russian	Polish
1.	'I should like very much to see her,'	'Èx, kak by na nee pogljadet'',	'Chciałbym ją zobaczyć'
2.	thought the soldier <...>	– dumal soldat <...>	– pomyślał-ø żołnierz <...>
3.	However, he passed a very pleasant time;	Žil on teper' kuda kak veselo:	Tymczasem więc pędził-ø wesołe życie,
4.	Ø went to the theatre,	Ø xodil v teatry,	chadzał-ø do teatru,
5.	Ø drove in the king's garden,	Ø vyezžal na progulki v korolevskij sad	zwiedzał-ø ogród królewski,
6.	and Ø gave a great deal of money to the poor,	i Ø mnogo deneg razdaval bednjakam,	a biednym dawał-ø zawsze dużo pieniędzy,
7.	which was very good of him;	i Ø xorošo delal!	co było bardzo ładnie z jego strony:
8.	he remembered what it had been in olden times to be without a shilling.	Ved' on po sebe znal, kakovo sidet' bez groša v karmane.	pamiętał-ø bowiem z dawnych czasów, jak to niedobrze być bez grosza!
9.	Now he was rich,	Nu, a teper' on byl bogat,	Teraz był-ø bogaty,
10.	Ø had fine clothes <...>	Ø razodet v pux i prax <...>	miał-ø piękne ubrania, <...>

In English, free pronouns are used if the referent is activated – see lines 3, 8, and 9. (According to the well-known sensitivity in the context of clause coordination, English subjects surrender to zeroes in non-first coordinate clauses, cf. lines 4, 5, 6, and 10.) Polish patterns in a very different way. No free pronouns are used. Whenever the referent is activated, a bound pronominal reference suffices, irrespective of anything like coordination context. Specifically, this is the third person singular masculine form of the past tense; this form has the zero ending, in contrast to all other person–number forms.[20]

Russian referential choices are different from those of Polish and similar to the English ones. In fact, third person pronouns are used in exactly the same three lines as in English (3, 8, and 9), in contrast to Polish. How are we to

---

[20] This treatment may be questioned as third person forms are contrasted to the forms with non-zero enclitics in locutor persons. I prefer the simpler interpretation here, as Polish is only used here for comparison. In fact, the Polish system is quite similar to Old Russian, as discussed in subsection 7.4.4.

interpret Russian verb forms? Morphologically, they are identical to the Polish past tense with the *-l* suffix. However, functionally they are different: the Russian past does not distinguish person, although it does distinguish gender and number. This is different from the other major synthetic tense, the present, that distinguishes person and number (but not gender); see (7.32) above. As is discussed in the next subsection, the lack of person marking in the past tense may be intimately related to the rise of the modern Russian referential system. As of now, I adopt the interpretation, according to which subject zero reference is recognized, irrespective of the clause's tense (see below).

More extensive discourse studies confirm that it is indeed the case that the presence of a pronominal subject is the default option in Russian. This seems similar to the Germanic pattern. However, zero reference is more widespread in Russian than in Germanic. Consider the quantitative data for the expression of referentially reduced subjects in the discourse sample investigated in Kibrik (1996a) and in Chapter 11 of this book. If we filter out all instances of syntactically conditioned zero reference, that are very similar indeed to the Germanic pattern, and take into consideration only contexts with third person reduced subjects, we actually see the third person pronoun in 80% of all instances and zeroes in the remaining 20% of instances. Pronouns constitute the dominant pattern, but one fifth of instances is not a negligible minority. In the following excerpt pronouns are found in lines (c) and (d), and a discourse-conditioned subject zero in (e). In addition, a direct object zero is used in (f):

(7.33) Russian (from Boris Zhitkov's story 'Over the water')
    a. <u>Mexanik</u> sunulsja,
       mechanic started,
    b. no   <u>Ø</u> sejčas že vernulsja –
       but   now PTCL returned
    c. <u>on</u> stal ryt'sja v jaščike s <u>instrumentami</u>,
       he began dig in box with instruments;
    d. a <u>oni</u> ležali v svoix gnëzdax, v strogom porjadke.
       but they lay in their slots in strict order.
    e. <u>Ø</u> Xvatal <u>odin ključ</u>,
       he grabbed one wrench,
    f. <u>Ø</u> brosal <u>Ø</u>, <...>
         dropped
       'The mechanic started, but immediately returned – he started digging in the box of instruments, while they were sitting in their slots, in full order. He was grabbing one wrench, dropped it <...>'

Quantitative results similar to those just mentioned were obtained by other researchers. Seo (2001: 167) reports 22% of zero subjects in a larger sample of Russian prose. Essentially the same figure (23%) can be derived from Grenoble's (2001: 8) counts, although they are based on Russian conversational data. See also the discussions in Nichols (1985), Grenoble (1998: 189–193), Miller and Weinart (1998: 212–229), Timberlake (2004: 223–227). The study of Fougeron and Breillard (2004), specifically devoted to the use of the first person singular subject pronoun, indicates a wide variety of factors involved in the choice between presence and absence of the pronoun in Russian.

This evidence indicates that the Russian system is not exactly equivalent to the Germanic one. Whereas Russian has made a significant step in the Germanic direction compared to the old Slavic system, it has not reached the same condition. The range of instances where subject zeroes are used in Russian is wider than in English or German. This relates to a more referential character of Russian verbal person markers, compared to their Germanic counterparts; see below. There are also instances of object zeroes in Russian, as in (7.33f.), which is utterly unGermanic, but this phenomenon will remain beyond my consideration here.

The question of how users of Russian choose between pronominal and zero subject reference is not sufficiently understood and requires further study. There may be similarity between Russian and Mandarin Chinese (see section 5.2), but it is more likely that a more complex kind of referential sensitivity is at play here. See Grenoble (2001) for a review; some comments can be found in Chapter 11 below (subsection 11.6.2).

7.4.4 *The rise of the Russian pattern*

How has the Russian pattern evolved from the original Slavic pattern, known from Old Church Slavonic and Old Russian and largely retained in Polish? In Kibrik (2004) I proposed that one of the reasons may have been the disappearance of person marking in the past tense in the history of Russian.[21]

Slavic languages originally had several past tenses that were conjugated for person just like the present; cf. the aorist forms in the Old Church Slavonic example (7.26). (In this kind of conjugation, personal desinences are compounds conveying both reference and tense.) Among the old Slavic past tenses, along with the synthetic aorist and imperfect, the analytic perfect was found, consisting of the participle in -*l*, inflected for number and gender

---

[21] I am grateful to Andrej A. Zaliznjak, Sergej S. Skorwid, Vadim B. Krys'ko, and Peter Arkadiev for the useful discussions of the phenomena considered in this subsection.

plus the person- and number- inflected present tense copular verb 'be'. (The actual order of the participle and the copula was quite variable; see Zaliznjak 2008.) For an illustration of this analytic form cf. *săm măkna-l-a* 'I (have) carried' (COP.PRES.1SG carry-PARTIC-F.SG) in (7.30) from Bulgarian, where it has been preserved intact.[22]

In a number of Slavic languages, the perfect quite early started expanding and ousting synthetic past tenses, gradually losing its obligatory perfect (or resultative) semantics and becoming the exclusive past tense. (See e.g. Borkovskij and Kuznecov 1979: 283ff., Ivanov 1982: 92ff., Townsend and Janda 1996: 221ff., Sussex and Cubberley 2006: 242.) In Old Russian vernacular, documented particularly by Novgorod birchbark letters (see www.gramoty.ru), the perfect was dominant already from the beginning of the written period, that is the 11th century, whereas in more official and religious documents more ancient synthetic forms were used for a few more centuries; see Zaliznjak (1995: 154ff.). Consider a relatively early example of the analytic perfect, used in a semantic context typical of the former aorist (a punctual event in the past, a part of a narrative sequence):

(7.34) Old Novgorod Russian, between 1100 and 1120 (Birchbark letter #109)
koupi-l-ъ   esi   rob-ou   plъskov-e
buy-PF-M.SG COP.PRES.2SG ancilla-ACC Pskov-LOC
'You bought an ancilla in Pskov'

As is demonstrated by Zaliznjak (2008: 223ff.), the person-marked copulae, such as *esi* in (7.34), were inherently clitic in Old Russian. They were among the phrasal enclitics, that is typically occupied the so-called Wackernagel position after the first prosodically independent word in a prosodic group. In the third person, perfect forms were lacking a copula already in the earliest documents of vernacular Old Russian (Zaliznjak 2008: 236). That is, where in Old Church Slavonic and official Old Russian forms such as *da-l-ъ es-tь* (give-PF-M.SG COP-PRES.3SG) 'he gave' were used, in vernacular Old Russian it was simply *dalъ*. Since the locutor forms required a copula, as in (7.34), third person forms were semiotically identified as such. It is, however, a zero-marked form, not containing a person marker. The lack of copulae in the

---

[22] These kinds of analytic forms pose an interesting question: what is the actual device here that performs reference? It is not easy to pinpoint an individual carrier of the referential function. Both the person–number morpheme in the copula and the gender–number morpheme in the participle contribute to reference. A number of different interpretations can be considered here, such as having two distinct referential devices, or positing a single but interrupted referential device, or attributing the referential function to the analytic form as a whole rather than to individual morphemes. Below I assume that it is the person inflection that is the main carrier of referential function.

third person suggests that the erstwhile *l*-participle was firmly reanalysed in Old Russian as a finite form (perfect, later past).

A similar development was happening in some other languages, for example Polish (West Slavic). In modern Polish the old perfect is used as the major past tense and is still specified for person, as well as number and gender. The original participle has been reinterpreted as a finite form, and the original copulae have been reinterpreted as person markers, usually cliticizing to the verb (and more rarely to other hosts). In the third person no overt person markers are found, but they are still negatively specified for person in opposition to other persons. Illustrations of third person past tense have been demonstrated in the Polish part of Table 7.1. For example, the Polish past tense verb *pamiętał* 'he remembered' in line 8 unequivocally indicates that its subject must be third person singular masculine, since other persons (as well as third person plural and other genders) would require overt inflectional markers.

According to Zaliznjak (2008: 246–262), throughout the Old Russian period (11th to 15th century) the old pattern was dominant: in locutor persons copulae with attached bound pronouns were used (such as *da-l-ъ es-mь* give-PF-M.SG COP-PRES.1SG 'I gave'), in contrast to the third person form with a zero copula (*da-l-ъ* give-PF-M.SG 'he gave'). During this period, the pattern with free pronouns (*ja da-l-ъ* 'I gave') was also attested, constituting about 15% of all instances in vernacular documents (Zaliznjak 2008: 248). Many of these instances are due to the use of strong pronouns.

Reference to activated subjects can be illustrated by an example from the Novgorod birchbark letter #605. This is a personal letter in which a monk named Efrem is trying to sort out his relationships with another monk, Isuxija. This letter, 62 words long, contains 14 clauses, out of which four are nominal clauses, five have a verbal predicate in one of the synthetic forms, and five have a verbal predicate that is perfect-marked. Four perfect clauses can be seen in the following excerpt:

(7.35) Old Novgorod Russian, between 1100 and 1120 (Birchbark letter #605)[23]
    a. ne   raspraša-vъ   rozgněva-ø-sja
       not inquire-CONV anger-AOR.3SG-REFL
    b. mene   igoumene   ne   pousti-l-e
       me.ACC prior.NOM not let-PF-M.SG

---

[23] See the website www.gramoty.ru. Additional comments on this letter are available in Zaliznjak (1995: 246–248). The original text is given in direct transliteration; note that some features of Old Novgorod graphics may seem peculiar to someone who is not familiar with this tradition.

c. a   ja   praša-l-ъ-sja
   and I.NOM   ask-PF-M.SG-REFL

d. nъ   posъla-l-ъ   ∅   s   asaf-ъmъ   kъ posadnik-ou
   but send-PF-M.SG   with   A.-INSTR   to mayor-DAT
   medou   dělja
   honey-GEN   for

e. a   prišь-l-a   es-vě <...>
   and come-PF-M.DU   COP-PRES.1DU

'You grew angry without inquiring: the prior had not let me go. Though I was asking, he sent me together with Asaf to the mayor to get honey. The two of us arrived <...>'

Clause (b) has a nominal subject, as the referent is not activated. Three other instances are directly relevant to the issue of reduced subject expression. Clauses (e) and (d) are formed in accordance with the Old Russian pattern described above: *l*-form plus the copula in locutor persons; just the *l*-form in the third person. Clause (c), in contrast, represents the modern Russian pattern: subject pronoun plus the former *l*-participle, reanalysed as a finite verb. As is pointed out by Zaliznjak (2008: 242), the use of the free pronoun in this case is perhaps due to contrast with the subject of the previous clause, so this may be a strong pronoun. But this example is nevertheless instructive: it is exactly in these kinds of contexts that the modern pattern was first introduced, albeit with strong pronouns.

As we have seen throughout the previous chapters, languages differ in how much they care to encode activated referents. Some languages, such as Japanese, favour zero reference and, accordingly, activated referents (and the category of person) remain overtly unexpressed most of the time. Other languages, such as Anejom̃, can express the same activated referent twice in a clause. In Germanic a similar pattern is found: although the verbal marking is not fully referential anymore, there still is double encoding of subject person. While being attested, the systems underrepresenting and overrepresenting person are in the minority. Most languages encode the person of activated referents just once.[24] Old Russian evidence suggests a commitment to a single encoding of reduced subjects and their person. Where free (and perhaps strong) pronouns needed to be used in the subject position (due to contrastiveness, emphasis or other concerns), copulae with bound pronouns are

---

[24] This tendency is sometimes formulated as a universal rule; this is what the generative 'null subject parameter' is about. Formulated in such a way, it is clearly untenable; see Huang (2000: 50–77) for a discussion.

almost invariably absent (Zaliznjak 2008: 248) in vernacular documents. The construction as in (7.34c) apparently paved the way for the modern Russian pattern.

In the 16th century a transition to the modern pattern with free pronouns occurred, and in the 17th century the modern system, different from both Old Russian and modern Polish, was firmly established (Zaliznjak 2008: 255). All present tense copulae, participating in the perfect tense analytic forms, have disappeared in modern Russian,[25] along with the bound pronouns that were attached to them. Russian past tense forms, such as *znal* 'knew' in line 8 of Table 7.1, are not inherently specified for person and can equally refer to first, second, or third person. (They are, however, specified for number and gender – masculine singular in this case.) The equivalent of the Old Russian example (7.34) is:

(7.36) Russian
ty kupi-l-ø rabynj-u vo Pskov-e
you buy-PAST-M.SG ancilla-ACC in P.-LOC
'You bought an ancilla in Pskov'

What was the cause of this change? The view sometimes implied by Slavicists (Ivanov 1982: 100ff., Zaliznjak 1995: 153) is: subject pronouns gradually expanded beyond their original limited usage (namely, the contexts of emphasis, contrast, etc.; see Zaliznjak 2008: 241–245), which rendered person-marked copulas redundant and thus caused their gradual decay. An alternative (or a complementary) hypothesis may be the pressure of third person forms, lacking a copula. By analogical levelling, copulae in locutor person forms also started being ousted, and free pronouns were called into service.

If the latter is true, the change of referential pattern must have started in the perfect and only later extended to the other major tense, synthetic and person-marked present. A preliminary analysis suggests that this is what indeed happened. I have analysed the first fifty present and perfect tense clauses with locutor person subjects in the catalogue in Zaliznjak (1995: 223ff.), thus covering the Novgorod birchbark letters of the 11th and the first half of the 12th century. Among these, the perfect constructions of the type *dalъ естъ*

---

[25] The loss of present tense copulae was not restricted to perfect/past verbal clauses alone but also applies to clauses with nominal/adjectival predicates; the meaning 'he is a prince' was expressed first as, literally, *Prince is*, then as *Prince*, and later on as *He prince*, as in modern Russian. The dynamics of the loss of copula depending on (i) clause type and (ii) locutor vs. third person was rather complex, and the evolution of different forms towards the modern pattern proceeded at a different pace; see Zaliznjak (2008: 239–262).

'I gave' occurred 18 times, and the type *ja dalъ* five times. In contrast, in the present tense clauses the proportion of usages without and with a free subject pronoun is 21 to 1. The latter unusual occurrence is found in the relatively late letter #380 of the mid-12th century (Zaliznjak 1995: 260). These differing figures support the hypothesis that the pattern with free pronouns originated in the perfect and spread to the present only later.

In addition, five usages were found that are contextually first or second person but grammatically are unmarked for person, that is consist of the *l*-form alone. Among these, three usages are found in non-first coordinate clauses where the lack of person marking can be explained away by this special syntactic context. But two usages do not lend themselves to this kind of explanation: letter #752 of the late 11th century (Zaliznjak 1995: 229)[26] and letter #736 of the early 12th century (Zaliznjak 1995: 241). These facts suggest that copulae were sometimes lost in locutor persons, thus rendering person entirely unmarked. If this was so, there must have been strong additional pressure to introduce free subject pronouns (Kibrik 2004). See also Borkovskij and Kuznecov's (1979: 379–380) opinion that as late as the 17th century free personal pronouns occurred primarily in perfect clauses and were unusual in present clauses, with the exception of semantically specialized contexts such as emphasis. According to the results from the corpus-based study by Pavlova (2010), even modern Russian still demonstrates a difference in the frequency of subject pronouns depending on tense: the share of clauses without a subject pronoun is higher in the present tense (44%), compared to the past tense (33%), and the difference is statistically significant.

Of course, there might have been other factors contributing to the change from the Old Russian to the modern Russian pattern. Cf. Jakobson (1935/1971) and Zaliznjak (2008: 267) about the role of changing prosodic properties in the history of Russian in the evolution of the Russian referential system.

Table 7.2 summarizes the development of subject reference in the history of Russian. Referential devices are underlined. A locutor and a non-locutor kind of reference are separately indicated in the perfect/past tense, as they formally differed in Old Russian. A synthetic form, third person singular present, is also shown for comparison.

---

[26] In this example the verb form is in fact not perfect but subjunctive; Old Russian subjunctive is morphologically very similar to perfect, just the particle *by* is used instead of the copula.

TABLE 7.2. Dominant patterns of subject reference in the history of Russian, following the treatment by Zaliznjak (2008: 246–262). The verb *da-* 'give' is used as a schematic representative; *(j)es-* is the copular stem, *ja* 'I', *on* 'he'

	Common Slavic	Old Russian (11th–15th century)	Modern Russian (starting from 17th century)
Perfect/past, 1SG.M	*dalъ jesmь*	*dalъ jesmь*, more rarely *ja dalъ*	*ja dal*
Perfect/past, 3SG.M	*dalъ jestь*	*dalъ ∅*	*on dal*
Present, 3SG	*daetь*	*daetь*	*on daët*

To recapitulate, in the original Slavic system, bound subject pronouns were used, and this pattern remained intact in South and West Slavic. In East Slavic, the following change took place in the past tense:

- person-marked (analytic) verb → free pronominal subject + person-unmarked verb.

This process consists of two components: bound pronouns were (partly) lost, and the extensive use of subject pronouns spread. Both of these phenomena are found in East Slavic, in contrast to most other Slavic languages. These two changes cannot be unrelated, and it is likely that the former caused the latter. Russian (and generally East Slavic) is an outlier within Slavic, just as French is within Romance. But in a very different direction: whereas French has developed a full set of near-bound pronouns, Russian has lost a part of those that were originally found in Indo-European. Unlike the two case studies reported above (Navajo and French), in Russian we face not the rise but rather the fall of bound pronouns.

How are we to interpret the modern Russian referential system? What type of reduced referential devices are employed in this language? It appears that the Russian system is among the most complex and entangled ones, especially with respect to the role of verb inflections. There are at least two problems here.

First, in the present tense the characteristics of the subject referent represented in the verb are person and number, and in the past tense gender and number. So, if verb inflections are referential, they are differently referential depending on the tense. In particular, if we conclude that the present tense personal desinences have kept their referential force and are bound pronouns, it is not immediately clear what interpretation should be applied to the past tense clauses. Postulating bound pronouns in the past tense would imply pronouns that are unmarked for person. Although such a possibility is not entirely excluded, it would be a rather exotic solution.

Second, Russian displays a referential behaviour that is intermediate between the Latin/Romance and the Germanic patterns. In Latin and Romance, subject personal desinences are so clearly referential that they must be unequivocally characterized as bound pronouns. In contrast, in German and English the referential potential of personal desinences is so limited that they clearly have the status of agreement markers, participating in the referential process at best as ancillaries. The Russian system lies in between: free pronouns obviously prevail as the dominant reduced referential device, but the role of verb inflections is also far from being negligible.[27] (Note that there are no indications of erosion of present tense person markers in Russian.)

A thorough characterization of this highly typologically unusual system must become the subject of a separate study. In the rest of this book, I primarily rely on the incontestable fact that free pronouns are the most important referential device in Russian. While acknowledging the contribution of verb inflections to reference, I still allow that, when a free pronoun is missing, a subject referential zero is posited. Such a zero is free, and this provision enables a parallelism between the structures with and without subject noun phrases; compare, for example subject elements in lines 3 and 4 of the Russian text in Table 7.1.

In addition, positing free subject zeroes allows us to avoid in this book, which is not specifically devoted to Russian, the above-mentioned dilemma of person vs. gender inflection depending on tense and its potentially differing interpretation. The question of whether Russian verbal desinences are bound pronouns or agreement markers is inherently complicated, because of their intermediate status, and does not have to be unequivocally solved in this book.

7.4.5 Slavic and Germanic

The Russian referential system differs from the Germanic one primarily in one respect: the greater referential potential of verb inflections. There are a number of consequences that flow from this difference, in the first place the use of zero reference at a significantly larger scale than in Germanic. Another consequence is that Russian, unlike Germanic, does not use dummy free pronoun subjects. For example, in clauses with an impersonal subject, conveyed in English by impersonal *they* and in German by *man*, Russian uses third person plural verb forms and does not allow any free NP subjects. In general, the Russian system can be characterized as a near-Germanic system with a rather strong old Slavic accent (or Latin, which is the same

---

[27] If Russian verb inflections are considered fully-fledged referential devices, Russian structures such as *On igraet* 'He plays' would have a summary referential exponent of 2, calculated in accordance with the principles implemented in Table 6.4.

in this case); cf. Nikolaeva's (2004) suggestion that the patterns of use of Russian first person singular pronouns still bear traces of its Indo-European etymology.

Apart from the mentioned differences, the Russian and the Germanic systems are strikingly similar. An interesting direction of research would be to explore if the rise of the Russian pattern (also shared by other East Slavic languages, Ukrainian and Belorussian) might have been at least partially due to Germanic influence, for example through the Circum-Baltic area (Dahl and Koptjevskaja-Tamm (eds.) 2001).

It is worth noting that some westernmost West Slavic languages – Sorbian (Germany) and especially Kaszubian (=Cassubian; Poland) – demonstrate a development that is parallel to East Slavic: unlike their immediate neighbour Polish, they do not always require person marking in the past tense and, in concordance with that, have developed a wider use of subject pronouns (Stone 1993b, Sergej Skorwid p.c. on Sorbian, Stone 1993a, Dulichenko 2005 on Kaszubian). Dulichenko (2005) emphasizes that in Kaszubian the past (that is, *l*-perfect) clauses without a copula, marking person exclusively on subject pronouns, have an unrestricted range of uses. In the case of Sorbian and Kaszubian, this development is usually attributed to a massive influence of German (e.g. Stone 1993b: 668).

It is not readily obvious how the Germanic pattern could have permeated into East Slavic leaving the geographically intervening Polish out of such influence. At the same time, given the cross-linguistic rarity of the Germanic referential system (see Chapter 6, section 6.7), it seems unlikely that the East Slavic pattern evolved in a relative vicinity to the quite similar Germanic pattern by mere chance. Much remains to be explored in order to explain this areal picture. Apart from Germanic, other potential areal influences upon East Slavic that need to be considered are Uralic and Turkic languages.

7.5 Evolutionary paths of gaining and losing bound tenacious pronouns

There is substantial variation among genealogically related languages in what kind of reduced referential devices they use. In Dryer's (2005a) typology of the expression of reduced Principals it is often the case that related languages belong to different types. Wichmann and Holman (2009) have assessed the stability, or rate of change, of typological parameters included in WALS (Haspelmath et al. (eds.) 2005). According to their classification, Dryer's parameter is characterized as unstable, that is changing over time at a significant rate. What kind of changes are found among the types of reduced referential devices? Siewierska (2004: 262) has proposed a universal cline of person markers' diachronic development. In a somewhat simplified way, and with terminological adaptation, this cline can be represented as follows:

- Free pronouns > bound pronouns > zero.

In this section I discuss diachronic changes between several kinds of reduced devices, taking into account not only these three major kinds but also the distinction in tenacity. The difference of my perspective from that of Siewierska is that I am looking at changes in a language's dominant referential device rather than at the history of specific morphemes. These two perspectives often yield the same results, but not always. For example, for Siewierska the major change between Old French and modern French is the erosion of erstwhile bound subject person markers into zero, while I am more interested in the shift from the original subject personal endings to new subject pronouns.

Before discussing particular evolutionary paths, it is useful to summarize the main types of reduced referential devices, as introduced in the previous chapters.

7.5.1 *Major types of reduced referential devices*

In accordance with the typology offered in Chapter 3, the major distinction between reduced referential devices is threefold: free pronouns, bound pronouns, and zero reference. Pronouns can be tenacious or alternating. Cross-linguistically more frequent combinations between boundness and tenacity are: free alternating and bound tenacious. So I consider the three types of referential devices (and linguistic systems favouring such devices) to be the most prototypical ones and attribute numbers to them as follows: free alternating pronouns – type 1; bound tenacious pronouns – type 2; zero reference – type 0. These three types of referential devices and corresponding systems are widespread, and large areas of the world are fairly consistently committed to these systems. As has been shown in the previous chapters, system 0 is typical of East and Southeast Asia, system 1 is common in West Africa and Europe, while system 2 is the hallmark of native American languages and is also found in many other parts of the world (eastern part of Africa, New Guinea, western Oceania, northern Australia, and some limited areas of Eurasia).

In addition to these three, less prototypical and intermediate types must be posited. There are languages that use both zeroes and free pronouns (type 1−). There are free tenacious (1+) and bound alternating (2−) pronouns. Finally, there are bound strongly tenacious pronouns (2+) – those that are present in any, or almost any, circumstances.[28] All seven types of devices and the corresponding systems are represented in Table 7.3. Each type is illustrated by schematic structures, consisting of the English morphemes *play*, *boy*, and *he*, the latter used as either a free or a bound pronoun. [In square brackets I indicate structures that occur when tenacious pronouns are absent as a result of a certain sensitivity.] Examples of languages representing each type are provided, relying on the evidence discussed in the previous chapters. Each type is illustrated both by languages fully committed to it and by languages using it only in restricted clause participant positions.

Like any broad typological scheme, the scheme in Table 7.3 contains several simplifications. First, various kinds of sensitivities displayed by referential devices (vis-à-vis the degree of activation and vis-à-vis various semantic and other contexts) are not differentiated. For instance, Mandarin, Babungo, and Russian distribute free pronouns and zero reference on the basis of different principles and in different proportions, but still fit within one box of the table. The phenomenon of sensitivity, however, is acknowledged: there are different language examples for systems that are insensitive or sensitive to argumental position; differences between types 1 and 1– and between 2 and 2+ are due to various sensitivities.

Second, some sensitivities are plainly ignored. For example, English subject pronouns often yield to zero in non-first coordinate clauses. However, English is portrayed as a pronouns-only language because it needs to be contrasted in this scheme to Russian that allows the use of zeroes on a much wider scale.

Third, the typologically interesting phenomenon of two fully-fledged reduced devices per referent instantiation, such as in Russian, is ignored. Russian is classified as a type 1– language although it also contains inflectional person marking.

Fourth, it might be possible to posit one more type, 'free strongly tenacious pronouns', by analogy with bound strongly tenacious pronouns. I have opted not to include it as evidence is too scant. As has been mentioned above, Macedonian recipient pronouns seem to meet this description, unlike their Bulgarian counterparts. However, more research is required in order to substantiate this type of reduced referential device (it might be coded 1++).

On the basis of this typology we can now address diachronic changes between the types posited in Table 7.3, looking primarily at language families discussed in the previous sections of this chapter. I will have little to say about type 0, as

---

[28] Pluses and minuses in these designations are informally intended to mean a higher degree of the feature expressed by the number. For example, if '1' means free (alternating) pronouns, '1+' means more pronouns than in type 1.

TABLE 7.3. Language classes according to the typological parameter 'type of preferred reduced referential device'

Type #	0	1−	1	1+	2−	2	2+
Characterization	zero reference	free alternating pronouns varying with zero reference	free alternating pronouns	free tenacious pronouns	bound alternating pronouns	bound tenacious pronouns	bound strongly tenacious pronouns
High referent activation	zero reference	zero or free pronoun	free pronoun	free pronoun	bound pronoun	bound pronoun	bound pronoun
Schematic structure	*Play*	*Play* / *He play*	*He play*	*He play*	*Heplay*	*Heplay*	*Heplay*
Low referent activation	full NP	full NP	full NP	full NP + sometimes free pronoun	full NP	full NP + sometimes bound pronoun	full NP + bound pronoun
Schematic structure	*Boy play*	*Boy play*	*Boy play*	*Boy he play [Boy play]*	*Boy play*	*Boy heplay [Boy play]*	*Boy heplay*
Language examples — In various argumental positions	Japanese Yidiny	Mandarin Babungo Russian	Lyélé English	Bilua	Kabba	colloquial French	Abkhaz Navajo
Language examples — In a specific argumental position	Urarina (Patientive)	Masa (Principal)	Ebira (Patientive)	Ebira (Principal) Spanish (Patientive, recipient)	Upper Kuskokwim (non-Principal)	To'aba'ita (Patientive)	Latin (Principal)

only processes involving overt pronouns have been discussed in this chapter; but see subsection 7.5.4. Table 7.3 is generally organized so that more robust reduced referential devices appear more on the right, culminating in bound strongly tenacious pronouns, while more fluid devices, such as alternating free pronouns, are found on the left. In accordance with this dimension of the table, I differentiate between rightward and leftward evolutionary changes.

7.5.2 Increase in boundness and tenacity (rightward evolution)

The evolutionary rise of bound tenacious pronouns can go by different routes. Latin, the ancestor of all Romance languages, had bound tenacious Principal pronouns and free alternating Patientive pronouns. Modern Romance languages still have bound tenacious Principal pronouns (although, in the case of French, they are materially different from and not as strongly tenancious as the original ones) and tenacious Patientive pronouns, in particular bound tenacious in French. The Athabaskan evolution is somewhat similar as far as the starting point and the endpoint are concerned. Proto-Athabaskan also clearly had bound tenacious Principal pronouns and, probably, free alternating Patientive pronouns, while modern Navajo has a full set of bound tenacious pronouns, resembling colloquial French. However, the routes from the starting point to the endpoint were quite different in these two cases. In Romance, pronouns came to cooccur with full NPs while they were still free, and only thereafter are developing into affixes, as in modern colloquial French. In Athabaskan, contrariwise, Patientive and oblique pronouns first became bound, as in Upper Kuskokwim, and only at a later stage became compatible with full NPs, as in Navajo.

In Table 7.4 various diachronic changes towards greater boundness and tenacity are listed, along with illustrative languages.

TABLE 7.4. Increase in boundness and tenacity in Athabaskan, Romance, and Slavic

1 → 1+	Latin → Spanish: recipient and Patientive pronouns Old Slavic (preserved in Polish) → Bulgarian: recipient and Patientive pronouns
1 → 2−	Proto-Athabaskan → Upper Kuskokwim: Patientive and oblique pronouns
1 → 2	17th century French (preserved in modern standard French) → modern colloquial French (probably via stage 1+): all argumental pronouns
2− → 2	general Athabaskan (preserved in Upper Kuskokwim) → Babine-Witsuwit'en: Patientive and oblique pronouns
2 → 2+	pre-Apachean (preserved in Babine-Witsuwit'en) → Navajo: Patientive and oblique pronouns

There is substantial literature on the discourse mechanisms of the widespread transformation of free pronouns into bound pronouns. See Givón (1976), Ariel (2000), Creissels (2005), and two recent reviews in Siewierska (2004: 263–268) and Corbett (2006: 264–269).

Although free pronouns are by far the most common source of bound pronouns, it is not the only possible one. In particular, Babaev (2007) has reviewed much evidence from a number of Old World families (Indo-European, Turkic, Uralic, Afro-Asiatic) showing that former possessed deverbal nouns were on many occasions reanalysed as finite verb forms (roughly, 'my bringing' > 'I brought'), thus converting former bound personal possessive pronouns into bound argumental pronouns. This shows that bound pronouns can descend from other bound pronouns. Siewierska (2004: 247–262) has discussed a number of other diachronic sources of person markers, but most of her examples have free rather than bound pronouns as targets of development.

7.5.3 Decrease in boundness and tenacity (leftward evolution)

We have observed instances of leftward evolution, shifting from bound tenacious pronouns to free alternating pronouns, in a number of European languages from several branches of Indo-European. These instances, listed in Table 7.5, are confined to reduced reference to the Principal. In all of these instances the original reduced reference to the Principal was by means of bound pronouns. Subsequently, these erstwhile pronouns stopped being the sole bearers of reduced reference to the Principal, and new linguistic material was drafted as reduced referential devices, namely free pronouns. In the case of Germanic and French, former bound pronouns were relegated to the status of agreement markers and underwent partial erosion. In Russian they partly disappeared and partly are kept as additional referential devices. The driving forces were different: in Germanic and Middle French it was primarily the verb-second syntactic principle and in East Slavic the loss of old synthetic past tenses.

Table 7.5. Decrease in boundness and tenacity in Germanic, French, and East Slavic

2+ → 1	Proto-Germanic → German/English: Principal pronouns Old French → 17th century French: Principal pronouns
2+ → 1–	Old Russian → modern Russian: Principal pronouns

The discussed routes of historical development between the preferred types of reduced referential devices are depicted in Figure 7.1.

7. The rise and fall of bound tenacious pronouns 281

1–	1	1+	2–	2	2+
free alternating pronouns varying with zero reference	free alternating pronouns	free tenacious pronouns	bound alternating pronouns	bound tenacious pronouns	bound strongly tenacious pronouns

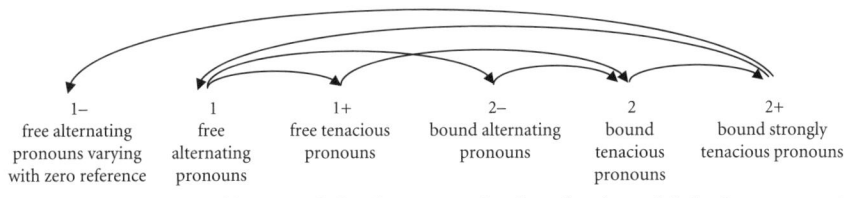

FIGURE 7.1. Routes of historical development of reduced referential devices, attested in Athabaskan, Germanic, Romance, and Slavic

7.5.4 Do bound pronouns give way to zero reference?

The evidence of the analysed languages demonstrates that the first step of Siewierska's (2004) evolutionary cline (see the beginning of section 7.5), that is the development of free pronouns into bound pronouns, is indeed a common evolutionary path in reduced referential devices. The following step, from bound pronouns to zero, is more problematic. What Siewierska means is the English-style development, in which former bound pronouns turn into agreement markers that are not fully functional and, as a result, gradually erode. However, as far as English is concerned, this does not imply that such languages become zero reference languages. Quite the contrary, English became a free pronoun language, of course using different material as referential devices. Moreover, a prerequisite for this kind of evolution is that erstwhile bound pronouns are reanalysed as agreement markers, which is by no means a necessary or even typical development.

In fact, the English development is not usual among the Indo-European languages of Europe. Most Romance and most Slavic languages have kept the original Principal bound pronouns and still use them as such. No substantial degree of erosion can be observed in languages such as Polish or Spanish. Furthermore, the development that is common among the languages with bound pronouns is the gradual accretion of bound pronouns. Proto-Athabaskan, Latin, and old Slavic each had a single set of bound tenacious pronouns, corresponding to the Principal role. In all Athabaskan and Romance and in some Slavic this feature was gradually extended to non-Principal pronouns, leading to an increase in overall boundness, or tenacity, or both. In some languages, such as Navajo and colloquial French, this trend was carried to an extreme, leading to a full set of bound tenacious pronouns. It is an empirical question how widely this pattern is spread among the world's languages, but the scenario of bound pronoun accretion and movement toward polysynthesis and polypersonalism is anything but exotic. As has been already pointed out, Givón's (1976: 155–156, 168–170) analysis of English-based creoles suggests that a Germanic language is not exempt from such evolution either.

It seems highly likely that languages expanding the use of bound tenacious pronouns are not expected to lose them. This is an empirical question again, but a preliminary survey of language families inclined to polypersonalism display an increase in this property rather than its decay. The fact that bound pronouns are the most cross-linguistically frequent type of reduced referential devices (see Chapter 3, subsection 3.3.4) also suggests that languages more easily accrue them than lose them.

Summary

In the previous chapters typological features of reduced referential devices have been discussed, as they are distributed across genealogical and areal language groupings. In this chapter a different aspect in the typology of reference was examined, namely diachronic changes of the languages' preferred reduced referential devices. The case study approach has been chosen, in order to look in some detail at the history of the referential systems of several groups of closely related languages.

The Athabaskan language family is one of major families of North America. The majority of the Athabaskan languages are spoken in the northern area, embracing Alaska and western Canada. One of the typical languages of this areal grouping, Upper Kuskokwim, was used for illustrative purposes. This language employs bound tenacious Principal pronouns and free alternating pronouns in other clause participant positions (Patientive and oblique). However, languages of the southern group, here exemplified by Navajo, have developed a rather different system. Principal pronouns remain intact but Patientive and oblique pronouns have become strongly tenacious. A specific evolutionary pathway of how this has happened can be uncovered, due to one of the relatively southern among the northern languages, Babine-Witsuwit'en, that uses an intermediate system.

Romance languages, Spanish being a typical example, preserve the system of Principal referential devices, inherited from Latin: bound tenacious pronouns (personal desinences). They have also developed a partial tenacity of object pronouns. Among the Romance languages, French stands out as having a very different and peculiar system of referential devices. About 1,000 years ago the Old French system was quite similar to the Romance standard just described. During the following half-millennium French underwent serious Germanic influence, including borrowing the syntactic verb-second principle. As a result, free subject pronouns became more and more obligatory, and strong pronouns got reanalysed as regular weak pronouns. Former bound pronouns became agreement markers. Modern colloquial French is strikingly different from standard (written) French in at least two respects: agreement markers have largely eroded, and both subject and object pronouns have become nearly bound and strongly tenacious. Modern colloquial French is structurally like polysynthetic languages, such as Navajo. Both in Navajo and in French the use of bound tenacious pronouns, represented in the respective proto-languages, was amplified and brought to the extreme. An interesting twist in the history of French is that this development was preceded by the opposite trend – the rise of free subject pronouns and the decay of the original bound pronouns.

The Slavic group is very heterogeneous in terms of referential systems employed. The original system, quite similar to that of Latin, was found in Old Church Slavonic and early Old Russian. Some languages, such as Polish (West Slavic) still keep this system with minor innovations. Some languages of the South Slavic branch, such as Bulgarian and especially Macedonian, have followed the Romance path, developing tenacity in object pronouns. Languages of the East Slavic branch, in particular Russian, have evolved a system that is very different from the original. In a first approximation, it is similar to the Germanic system: free alternating pronouns plus personal desinences on the verb. The analogy, however, is incomplete: free zero reference is much less restricted in Russian than in Germanic, and therefore chances are that verb inflections are in fact referential devices rather than pure agreement markers. The Russian system is difficult for unequivocal interpretation, as the status of verb inflections is intermediate between the general Romance and the Germanic patterns. The main historical cause that led to the formation of the modern Russian system is the increasing omission of person-marked copulae in the analytic perfect/past (between the 15th and the 17th centuries). As a result, free weak pronouns became common, seizing the main referential load.

Various referential systems can be tentatively represented along an axis of pronominal salience: beginning from zero reference (no overt marking at all) and ending with bound, strongly tenacious pronouns (maximal and grammatically salient marking). All changes in languages' preferred referential devices can be demonstrated as either increasing or decreasing such pronominal salience. The increase, or the rightward movement along the typological axis, is represented in various branches of Athabaskan, in South Slavic, in early Romance, and in modern French. The decrease, or the leftward movement, is found in Germanic, in Middle French, and in East Slavic. Of course, these observations are only the very beginning of a comprehensive diachronic typology of referential devices that may hopefully emerge in the future.

Concluding remarks to Part II

Summarizing over Chapters 3 to 7, comprising Part II of this book, it is useful to recapitulate the main findings. This part is a typology of reduced referential devices – those linguistic elements that, first, perform an act of reference and, second, are lexically lean or general. There exist three most fundamental types of reduced referential devices: free pronouns, bound (affixal) pronouns, and zero reference. There exist pure, or consistent, languages, more or less firmly committed to one of these devices. Other languages are less consistent and use two or more of the major devices in a certain distribution; such referential devices, appearing only in certain circumstances, are said to be sensitive. There exists a whole gamut of bases for sensitivities, including the degree of referent activation, clause participant position, as well as various more concrete contexts, such as the context of clause coordination.

Free and bound pronouns are two kinds of overt reduced devices. A number of complexities are associated with pronouns, including double reference pronouns, pronominal compounds involving the marking of clausal categories, and the distinction between weak and strong pronouns. There exist several classes of linguistic elements that are not identical with pronouns but are often cofunctional, such as demonstratives or classifiers.

Typologically very important, although underestimated, are bound pronouns – the most cross-linguistically frequent type of reduced referential device. Bound pronouns are often tenacious – that is, cooccur within a clause with another mention of the same referent, typically by means of a full NP. The parameters of freedom vs. boundness and tenacity vs. alternation are correlated but distinct. There exist free tenacious and bound alternating pronouns. Bound pronouns are not equivalent to agreement markers – affixes that participate in the referential process as ancillaries but do not refer by themselves. Languages' preferred reduced referential devices do not have to remain the same over time. In a number of relatively well-studied language families, diachronic changes of the preferred referential device are attested, including shifts from free pronouns to bound pronouns and vice versa.

In my early study of linguistic diversity in the realm of reference (Kibrik 1988) I proposed detailed accounts of referential systems belonging to three genealogically, areally, and typologically diverse languages (Navajo, Tuvan, and Pulaar); see also Kibrik (in preparation). In Kibrik (2009b) I attempted a concise characterization of several major languages of the world, including English, German, Spanish, French, Russian, Japanese, Mandarin Chinese, and Hindi in terms of their referential systems, including the preferred reduced referential devices, tenacity, and sensitivities. My hope is that the results of this Part II will prove useful for further descriptive work on individual languages. Appendix 1 at the end of this book contains a list of suggested questions, useful for someone who wants to create a coherent account of referential devices in a given language.

Part III
Typology of Referential Aids

Apart from referential devices, considered in Part II, other kinds of linguistic elements, crucially involved in the referential process, are **referential aids**. Referential aids, the subject of Part III, are those devices that help to tell apart two or more referents. This is particularly relevant in the case of reduced referential devices that have a broad reference domain. When a third person pronoun or zero reference occurs, and two or more referents happen to be activated, chances are high that an addressee may think of a referent different from the one that was originally intended by the speaker – this is the situation that can be called **referential conflict**. Referential aids help to distinguish between such concurrently activated referents. Referential aids are highly diverse, from ad hoc match to the semantic context to very specific grammatical devices, such as gender or switch-reference.

The goal of Part III is to propose a **typology** of languages from the point of view of the referential aids that they employ. It is interesting to ascertain what types of referential aids are found in languages and on what bases they can be classified. It is also important to discover the attested sites of expression of these aids in linguistic structure.

Preclusion of referential conflicts is clearly secondary in the process of referential choice in comparison to the activation-related factors. Thus I will examine the degree of functionality of referential aids. In particular, the questions to address are how many referential aids may operate in one language and whether referential aids are dedicated linguistic resources, having evolved specifically for the purpose of precluding referential conflicts.

8

Referential aids

Overview

In addition to referential devices, the second important type of linguistic resources involved in the referential process is referential aids. Referential aids help to discriminate between two or more concurrently activated referents and preclude a possible ambiguity, or referential conflict (section 8.1). The goal of this chapter is to propose a comprehensive typology of referential aids.

The highest-level distinction between the types of referential aids is the distinction between the ad hoc and conventional aids (section 8.2). Ad hoc referential aids discriminate between referents in terms of their match to the semantic context of a clause. Conventional aids are lexico-grammatical in their nature and sort referents according to a certain feature; hence they can be called referent sortings.

Referent sortings fall into stable and current ones, depending on the kind of referent feature they rely on: a permanent and inherent feature vs. a current and discourse-related feature. There exist absolute and relative stable sortings. Absolute stable sortings categorize referents into fixed classes (section 8.3), while relative stable sortings compare them along a certain dimension or hierarchy (section 8.4).

Current sortings are classified in accordance with the discourse domain to which the given referent's feature belongs. Broad domain current sortings are based on those features that are associated with a whole discourse, such as the status of protagonist (section 8.5). Narrow domain current sortings rely on very local characteristics, such as subjecthood or degree of activation (section 8.6). An additional parameter of the typology of referential aids, considered for all of their types, is the site of marking, such as pronouns vs. verbal categories.

8.1 Referential aids as deconflicters

When a speaker performs an act of reference, he/she employs a certain referential device. Referential devices do not link to referents tightly and uniquely, and an act of reference may be accompanied by a referential conflict. The notion of referential conflict, introduced in Chapter 2 (section 2.8), means that an addressee may attribute to a referential device a referent that is different from the one intended by the speaker. Referential conflicts are quite common in our everyday communication – this is evidently the case when we check back with our interlocutors, asking *Who are you talking about?* or simply *Who?*

Referential conflict can be associated with any referential device. If my interlocutor says *Jim* I may think of a different Jim than he/she intended. But of course referential conflict is much more probable with reduced referential devices that have a very broad domain of potential reference. When more than one referent is activated and the speaker uses a reduced device, the addressee has a chance of making a wrong referential attribution.

If a referential conflict has actually occurred, so that the verifying question *Who?* is appropriate or, even worse, a wrong referent was assigned by the addressee, that means that nothing in the speaker's discourse has precluded it. My concern in this chapter is not materialized referential conflicts but the ways speakers can **preclude** them. One obvious way is to use a more explicit referential device, such as *our neighbour from downstairs* rather than *he*. However, if a referent's activation is high, speakers tend to keep to reduced reference. Can a reduced device, such as *he*, be used, if there is more than one activated referent at the same time? Yes, it can, as there are many ways to guarantee that, despite a potential referential conflict, a reduced device would not cause one. The goal of this chapter is to review linguistic resources that can furnish such a guarantee. Such linguistic resources are here called referential aids, or deconflicters (I used to use the term 'subsidiary referential devices' in some of my prior work, e.g. Kibrik 2001a). Natural languages possess a broad repertoire of referential aids allowing one to stick to a reduced referential expression and still guarantee that the referent is recovered correctly.

In a well-known article, Heath (1975) observed that very different lexico-grammatical devices can be employed for the same purpose of discriminating between two or more confusable referents. He further illustrated this point with data from Nunggubuyu (Gunwinyguan, northern Australia; see Heath 1983), a language that uses a fairly complex noun class system for the purpose of 'referential tracking' for which other languages use the morphosyntactic device of switch-reference (see subsection 8.6.2 below). A more comprehensive typology of referential aids was proposed by Foley and Van Valin (1984: Ch. 7) and Van Valin (1987). Comrie (1989b, 1994) and Kibrik (1988, 1991, 2001a) further developed the typology or lexico-grammatical devices contributing to the preclusion of referential conflicts. Since the latter two papers provide a detailed account of referential aids, in this chapter I skip some minor details that are available there.

Opinions on the role of referential conflict and the deconflicting referential aids in discourse vary greatly (cf. Chapter 2, section 2.8). Some authors, in discussing referential processes in discourse, confine their attention to referential aids alone, and pay little attention to the referring function per se (Foley and Van Valin 1984: Ch. 7, Comrie 1989b). This approach implies that the major problem associated with reference in discourse is the problem of referential conflict and how it can be resolved. Some other authors, to the contrary, suggest that the problem of referential conflict, or ambiguity, is grossly overestimated in linguistics: 'Ambiguities may be more salient to the exocultural linguist than to the endocultural narrator or audience, for whom familiarity and context are likely to remove most problems of keeping third-person referents straight' (Chafe 1990a: 315).

My view, reflected in both the terminology used and in the relative amount of attention given to referential devices and referential aids in this book, can be summarized as follows. The heart of reference in discourse is the choice between full and reduced referential devices on the grounds of referent activation. Now, reduced referential devices, by their very nature, are the source of potential referential conflicts. Referential conflicts are a complication associated with reduced reference. Most instances of referential conflict are precluded due to referential aids. Referential conflict should not be overstated, but it is real.

8.2 Ad hoc vs. conventional referential aids

In the English examples (2.12) and (2.13), repeated as (8.1) and (8.2) below, a potential referential conflict is created due to the concurrent activation of two referents. In (8.1), however, referential conflict is precluded due to the grammatical category of gender, inherent in English third person singular pronouns. In (8.2), on the contrary, referential conflict is not removed, since both referents are masculine, and the pronominal references turn out to be confusing.

(8.1) Uncle John_J was sitting at the table. Suddenly a girl_g approached him_J.
  i. He_J yelled at her_g.
  ii. She_g yelled at him_J.

(8.2) Uncle John_J was sitting at the table. Suddenly a boy_b approached him_J.
  i. ?He_J yelled at him_b.
  ii. ?He_b yelled at him_J.

Compare these examples with the following where both referents are again masculine:

(8.3) Uncle John_J was sitting at the table. Suddenly a baby boy_b crawled up to him_J.
  i. He_J lifted him_b.
  ii. ??He_b lifted him_J.

In (8.3) referential conflict is again removed, but due to a totally different mechanism: semantic **compatibility** with the context of the clause, in conjunction with encyclopedic knowledge. The verb *lifted* has certain selective restrictions on its arguments. A speaker of English knows that this action can be done by a heavier agent upon a smaller and lighter patient. Therefore the reference as in (8.3ii) is ruled out. Referential aids fall into two main types: **conventional**, or lexico-grammatical, aids, such as gender, and **ad hoc** aids, based on semantic compatibility with the clause context. Conventional aids are treated in the subsequent sections, while ad hoc aids are briefly discussed here.

For what I call ad hoc referential aids Foley and Van Valin (1984: Ch. 7) and Van Valin (1987) used the term 'inference system' or 'pragmatic system', thus emphasizing that not only semantics but a wider array of encyclopedic, including cultural, information is important for this type of referential deconfliction. However, all this kind of information is ultimately actualized via the mediation of the semantics of the clause in which the reduced referential device occurs. So it is justified to claim that the common denominator of all ad hoc aids is the match of the intended referent to the semantic context of the clause, as contrasted to the mismatch of the competing referent.

Van Valin (1987) pointed out that the ad hoc deconflicting system is used in any language but is particularly important in the languages of East and Southeast Asia, including Mandarin Chinese (Sino-Tibetan), Thai (Tai-Kadai), and Japanese. Van Valin also suggested that this phenomenon typically cooccurs with zero reference. (This hypothesis appears plausible as languages inclined to zero reference typically have little morphology, see section 3.6, and therefore may very well be short of conventional referential aids.) Two notes of caution are in order, however. First, Nariyama (2001) (see especially p. 127) argues against Van Valin's claim as applied to such zero reference languages as Japanese and demonstrates a wide range of grammatical devices that are used to deconflict reference. Second, extensive use of ad hoc referential deconflicting is reported for some languages that use overt pronouns, at least in some clause argument positions; see e.g. Olawsky (2006: 852ff.) on Urarina (isolate, Peru).

Ample deployment of ad hoc referential aids can be illustrated by Ewing's (2001) discussion of reference in Cirebon Javanese. Ewing analyses a story about the rivalry of two gangs, named Gunungjati and Jatiwangi. Consider the following excerpt:

(8.4) Cirebon Javanese (Austronesian, Java, Indonesia; Ewing 2001: 44)
 a. Ø kewedien.
    scared
 b. yong Ø digolok Ø je´,
    because PASS.slashed EX
 c. Ø beli apa-apa.
    NEG anything
 d. Ø beli mempan.
    NEG vulnerable

'They [=Jatiwangi] were scared. Even though they [=Gunungjati] were slashed by them [=Jatiwangi], they [=Gunungjati] were not affected. They [=Gunungjati] were invulnerable.'

In this excerpt there are numerous zero references to both Gunungjati and Jatiwangi that are hardly intelligible for an addressee who is not familiar with the cultural context. For a Cirebon addressee, however, reference is straightforward. As Ewing comments, it is known from prior discourse that Jatiwangi attacked Gunungjati, hence the clarity of zero reference in (b). More interesting are other instances of zero reference. Gunungjati are known to be spiritually powerful and magically invulnerable, so, even though someone who was attacked may be expected to be scared, in reality it is only Jatiwangi that are unequivocally compatible with the context of (a). Likewise, only Gunungjati, to the exclusion of the competing referent, are compatible with the context of (c) and (d). Clearly, the conjunction of cultural and other external information with clause semantics makes it possible to discriminate between two activated referents in each individual instance.

A rather special subcase within the ad hoc referential aids is the situation that could be called the **engagement** factor. It becomes relevant when more than one referent (typically, two referents) are mentioned by reduced referential devices within a single clause. If the identity of one of these referents is guaranteed by some referential aid, the identity of the other one is guaranteed as well by way of elimination. Consider the following modification of (8.3):

(8.3′) Uncle John$_J$ was sitting at my table. Suddenly a baby boy$_b$ crawled up to him$_J$.
    i. He$_b$ pulled him$_J$ by the beard.
    ii. $^{??}$He$_J$ pulled him$_b$ by the beard.
    iii. $^{??}$He$_{J/b}$ pulled me by the beard.

Variant (i) is smooth, in contrast to the improbable (ii), as only one of the referents is likely to have a beard, that is 'uncle John'. This referent is therefore engaged by the pronoun *him*, and so of the two activated referents only 'the baby boy' is reserved for the pronoun *he*. The continuation (iii) demonstrates that there is no other semantic factor, except for the engagement, that would ensure the identity of *he*: each of the activated referents might correspond to this pronoun if only one of them is mentioned in the clause. So it is certainly the engagement factor that makes the use of *he* smooth in continuation (i).

Let us turn now to convential referential aids. They are all based on one general principle: they somehow **sort** referents that are currently activated according to a certain distinctive feature. In the case of gender, such sorting is based on **stable**, or permanent, properties of the referent and/or the corresponding NP. Stable sortings fall, in turn, into two main kinds: absolute and relative (i.e. hierarchies). Absolute sortings, or taxonomies (section 8.3), pigeonhole referents relying merely on their membership in certain categories, while in relative sortings, or hierarchies (section 8.4), referents' categories are compared along a certain dimension, such as the degree of inherent activity.

The other major kind of sorting is based on the **current**, or variable, properties of the referent (such as e.g. being the subject of the preceding clause). Among the current sortings, two kinds of domains are distinguished (broad and narrow), to which sections 8.5 and 8.6 are devoted.

Within each type of sorting I consider, where appropriate, an additional typological parameter, namely the site at which the sorting is expressed. Among such sites three major options must be distinguished: (a) free pronouns; (b) bound pronouns (attached to the verb); (c) other verb affixes or verb stem. Occasionally we will also see a fourth option: (d) expression on some specialized constituent, such as a function word.

8.3 Absolute stable sortings

Stable referent sortings rest on the notion of categorization. Categorization is a cognitive process that puts entities in ontologically different groups, such as flat vs. round objects, humans vs. animals vs. inanimates, males vs. females, etc. (See Zelinsky-Wibbelt 2000 on one view of the relationship between reference and categorization.) Stable sortings help to tell apart referents that belong to different ontological categories. Of course, the fine-grained categorization is realized through full NPs, especially with modifiers, such as *the red button, the house that Jack built,* or *dream caused by the flight of a bee around a pomegranate a second before awakening*. The range of grammaticalized ontologies that can function as conventional referential aids is, of course, much more restricted.

Absolute sortings, or taxonomies, represented on pronouns are widely known as **noun classes**, or genders; for an overview see Corbett (1991). As other classificatory systems, noun classes differentiate between referents along the lines of animacy, sex, shape, consistence, size, quantity, as well as less semantic and non-semantic features of nouns. In distinction to other classificatory systems (see Chapter 4, subsection 4.2.2), noun class is generally understood as a category copying class membership of a noun on various other constituents connected to this noun by some syntactic relation (Corbett 1991: 136–137, Grinevald 2000: 55).

Classification systems of languages displaying this kind of copying, or agreement, in syntactic domains are typically treated as noun class systems. Such languages often (but not always; see section 9.4 and Aikhenvald 2000: 68–70) display the same classification on pronouns; this is termed 'anaphoric agreement' by Corbett (2006: 10, 41, 227ff.), relying on the concept that noun class can be copied onto a pronoun from a nominal controller. Since such controllers are often found beyond a reasonable syntactic domain, the question of whether this is actually agreement with a noun or a more direct encoding of the referent's properties is not resolved. But if a language has syntactic agreement then its class-sensitive pronouns are interpreted as marked for noun class, for systematic reasons.

Noun classes are typical of Europe, the northern Caucasus, the Near East, much of Africa, non-Pama-Nyungan languages of northern Australia, Amazonia, and to a lesser extent New Guinea, and are relatively rare in Asia and North America.

8.3.1 *Marking on free pronouns*

According to Siewierska (2005b), one third of languages express gender in free pronouns. The operation of the noun class distinctions marked on free pronouns is well known from English; see examples (8.1) and (8.2). The number of classes found in English (three) is modest by cross-linguistic standards. One extensive noun class system marked on free pronouns is found in Pulaar-Fulfulde (=Fula; Atlantic, West Africa), displaying over twenty noun classes (Koval 1997). In Chapter 9 Pulaar-Fulfulde will be used as an exemplary language to illustrate how noun classes function in discourse and help to preclude referential conflicts; see also Kibrik (1991, 1992a). Seifart (2005) describes the noun class system of Miraña (Bora-Witotoan, Colombia) whose third person pronouns distinguish over sixty noun classes. In the Papuan language Nasioi (East Bougainville family, Bougainville, Papua New Guinea) no less than 115 noun classes are attested, according to Dixon (1982: 167–168).

The structure of class-marked pronouns can be quite diverse. Sometimes a third person pronoun may consist exclusively of a class morpheme; this is the case of Pulaar-Fulfulde; see section 9.4; in this case we must recognize that it is the class morpheme that performs reference. In other cases the class element is fused with the pronominal stem, as in English third person pronouns. In other languages still class elements may be agglutinatively added to pronominal stems; for example, Siewierska (2005b) cites the pronominal system of Korana (Central Khoisan; South Africa) that uses the stem //'ãi- in all third person pronouns but adds various affixes to mark gender and number, such as feminine singular //'ãi-s, feminine dual //'ãi-sara, masculine plural //'ãi-ku, etc.; a similar structure is displayed by Miraña (Seifart 2005). Notwithstanding these differences in formal structure, it must be understood that the referential function and the classificatory function are clearly distinct.

According to the received view (Corbett 1991: 136–137, Grinevald 2000: 55), classificatory systems other than noun classes, that is various subtypes of the so-called classifiers, are not expected to display regular copying of features from the controller noun upon other constituents. Classifiers are usually more transparently semantically based than noun classes; their use is less automatic and more open to alternative interpretations of the same referent as far as its class membership is concerned. Despite these differences, in the domain of referential devices the functioning of classifiers is quite similar to that of noun classes. In Chapter 4 (subsection 4.2.2) we have seen examples of Jakaltek classifiers that, when used as independent referential devices, perform simultaneously two functions: they not only sort referents as belonging to certain classes, but they also refer. As was argued in subsection 4.2.2, although classifiers are not pronouns, they function similarly to pronouns. Functionally they resemble English and especially Pulaar-Fulfulde class-specified pronouns.

Classifiers can also be used in the agglutinative Korana-style fashion – in this case the referring and the sorting morphemes are kept distinct. This can be exemplified with the case of Tariana, a northern Arawakan language. In Tariana, the use of classifiers is pervasive:

(8.5) Tariana (Arawakan, Amazonas, Brazil; Aikhenvald 2000: 204)
ha-dapana   pa-dapana   na-tape-dapana
DEM.INAN-CL_HOUSE one-CL_HOUSE   3PL-medicine-CL_HOUSE
na-ya-dapana   hanu-dapana   heku
3PL-POSS-CL_HOUSE big-CL_HOUSE   wood
na-ni-ni-dapana-mahka
3PL-make-TOPADV-CL_HOUSE-RECPAST.NVIS
'This one big hospital of theirs has been made of wood'

In this example the classifier -*dapana* is used in every word but one. Tariana pronouns that Aikhenvald glosses as 'he' or 'it' are not exempt from containing classifiers either, as the following demonstrates:

(8.6) Tariana (Arawakan, Amazonas, Brazil; Aikhenvald 2000: 332)
a. diha   yaɾu-maka-si-nuku   di-sōle <...>
   he   thing-CL_CLOTH-NPOSS-TOPP   3SG.NF-take.off
b. iɾa-mha   pa-pe-niki
   need-PRES.NVIS   IMP-throw-COMPL
   ha-ne-maka-nuku
   DEM.INAN-DIST-CL_CLOTH-TOPP
c. na-pidana
   3PL.say-REMPAST.INFR
d. nu-kesini   hau   piha   pi-a   pi-pe-niki
   1SG-friend   yes   2SG   2SG-go   2SG-throw-COMPL
   ha-ne-maka-nuku
   DEM.INAN-DIST-CL_CLOTH-TOPP
e. ha-ne-maka-naka   kaɾuna-naka   wa-na
   DEM.INAN-DIST-CL_CLOTH-EYEWPRES   be.afraid-EYEWPRES   1PL-OBJ
f. haiku-na   dhita   di-na-tha-pidana
   tree-CL_VERT 3SG.NF.take   3SG.NF-OBJ-FRUST-REMPAST.INFR

g. di-ni-thepi di-pe-niki
3SG.NF-make-TO.WATER 3SG.NF-throw-COMPL
di-na-pidana
3SG.NF-OBJ-REMPAST.INFR

h. diha-maka dhe-kha di-a-hna.
he-CL_CLOTH 3SG.NF.enter-away 3SG.NF-go-PAUS

'He [=the evil spirit] took off the shirt <...> "It is necessary to throw that [=the shirt] away," they [=the men] said, "my friend, yes, you go and throw that [=the shirt] away. That [=the shirt] is dangerous for us." He [=one of the men] took a tree-trunk and, in vain, tried to throw it away. It [=the shirt] came upon the man'

In this extract, the classifier -*maka* 'cloth' occurs in (8.6a) as a suffix on a noun designating the shirt. Within the direct speech, in (b), (d), and (e), it occurs three times suffixed to a distal demonstrative. Finally, in (h) it appears with the pronoun *diha* that also can be seen in (a). Note that in (h) three referents are activated, including 'the man', 'the tree-trunk', and 'the shirt'. Probably the classifier attached to the pronoun is thus instrumental in removing a possible referential conflict. This kind of 'classifier' use is hardly distinguishable from class-marking in pronouns, but is quite different from the usage of classifiers as independent referential devices described in subsection 4.2.2.

8.3.2 *Marking on bound pronouns*

Noun classes can be marked not only on free but also on bound pronouns. This is the case in Abkhaz, where masculine, feminine, and nonhuman are distinguished in the singular. To see the operation of class-marked bound pronouns consider the following discourse example[1]:

(8.7) Abkhaz (Abkhaz-Adyghean, Abkhazia)
a. Amra akəta də-ntala,
A.$_A$ village she$_A$-when.entered

b. aȝ°ə i-maxč i-c°əznə də-qan,
one$_m$ his$_m$-camel$_c$ he$_m$-having.lost he$_m$-was

c. d-š-e-jmdoz,
he$_m$-as-it$_c$-was.seeking

d. d-lə-k₀s°ejt'
he$_m$-her$_A$-met

---

[1] This is an excerpt from a tale published in the book: *Аҧсуа Лакуҟуа. Карт*, 1976.

'When Amra entered the village, there was one who had lost his camel, and as he was looking for it, he met her.'

By the beginning of clause (c) three referents ('Amra', 'the man', and 'the camel') are activated, and despite the potential referential conflicts in (c) and (d) bound pronouns alone suffice for reduced reference. Evidently, this is due to the effective discriminating function of noun class marking in bound pronouns, as all three activated referents belong to different classes: feminine, masculine, and neuter. Similar systems with noun class-marked bound pronouns are found, for example, in Nunggubuyu (Gunwinyguan, northern Australia; Heath 1983) and Seneca (Iroquoian, New York State, USA; Chafe 1996).

8.3.3 Number and person as absolute stable sortings?

As the case of Abkhaz indicates, gender is often tightly interwoven with number; see the discourse example (3.14) in Chapter 3. The category of number as such can also be judged a referent-discriminating, deconflicting referential aid. An illustration can be taken from the Peruvian language Urarina. Recall that this language marks Principals by bound pronouns on the verb. (Activated Patientives are coded by zeroes, but these are left unmarked in the example below since we are here primarily interested in Principal reference.) In (8.8) we see a narrative chain of clauses, each of which is morphosyntactically dependent on the following one. There are two activated referents, one of which is singular and the other plural (a group of people):

(8.8) Urarina (isolate, Peru; Olawsky 2006: 852)
    a. nitoaneĩ ni-a=ne hãʉ
       like.that be-3.DEP=SBRD because
    b. kwara-he-ʉrʉ-a=ne hãʉ,
       see-CONTIN-PL-3.DEP=SBRD because
    c. kʉ niriheĩ laʉlaʉelaʉ-he-ĩ,
       there like.that go.by.canoe-CONTIN-PARTIC
    d. ate taba-j mukuk-a hãʉ
       fish be.big-NMZR catch-3.DEP because
    e. kwara-hi-a hãʉ
       see-CONTIN-3.DEP because
    f. kwara-ʉrʉ-a hãʉ <...>
       see-PL-3.DEP because
    'As it was like that, as they were watching him, as he was going in a canoe like that, as he caught big fish, as they were watching, as they saw him <...>.'

The Principals of clauses switch between the singular and the plural referents, and the reference is kept straight due to the fact that the Principal's plurality in marked on the verb by means of the dedicated morpheme *-иrи*, distinct from the third person morpheme. Thus the Principal of clause (d) pertains to the single participant, while Principals of (b) and (f) to the group of people. This does not always help, though, since in (c), a participial clause, there can't be a bound pronoun on the verb. In (e) plural is not indicated on the verb even though the referent in question is the group of people – this is further 'corrected/specified' (Olawsky 2006: 852) in the next clause with the same verb.

Of course, the category of number is tightly connected not only to noun class but also to person. This raises the next question. If number can be considered among the sorting, deconflicting devices, can this perspective be extended to person as well? Usually we tend to think of the category of person as so inherent to pronouns that some authors even refuse to differentiate between these two notions (Siewierska 2004: 13). However, as has been pointed out in section 4.1, occasionally we come across referential pronouns that do not distinguish person. This is the case of the colloquial French oblique bound pronoun *y-* that has generalized to all persons. So logically the person distinction in pronouns can also be taken to be a sorting device, helping to tell apart the concurrently activated referents, such as the speaker and some third person referent. This approach, although fully logical, may be somewhat far-fetched as the distinction between locutors and non-locutors is too profound in cognition and precedes any concerns about distinction among third person referents. Still in Chapter 9, subsection 9.3.2 we will see some examples showing that person distinctions may preclude referential conflict in exactly the same way as noun class and number.

8.3.4 *Verbal marking*

Returning to the canonical idea of classification (according to animacy, shape, etc.), so far we have considered classifications marked directly on referential devices, including free and bound pronouns. Some languages have a kind of noun/referent classification system that is not directly associated with referential devices but is built into verb lexical semantics. (Aikhenvald 2000 calls this phenomenon 'verbal classifiers'.) The best known example is the Athabaskan languages of North America; see also Fortescue (2006) on a number of other North American languages. Athabaskan languages have several series of so-called classificatory verb stems with the same meaning, differing only in which class the Absolutive referent belongs to (animate, round, flat, multiple

TABLE 8.1. Upper Kuskokwim (Na-Dene, Alaska, USA) classificatory verbs; the verb stem that bears the classificatory meaning is underlined

	Class of Absolutive	Translation of the Absolutive Participant
1 mega ʔi<u>ł</u>chut	food	a slice of bread
2 mega ʔisdi<u>tł</u>ak'	wet stuff	dough
3 mega ʔisdi<u>nił</u>	multiple tiny objects	flour or bread crumbs
4 mega zid<u>lo</u>	set of objects	several slices of bread
5 mega ʔi<u>łt</u>onh	object in an enclosed container	flour or dough in a sack
6 mega zi<u>k</u>onh	object in an open container	bread on a plate
7 mega ziʔ<u>onh</u>	roundish object	a loaf of bread

count, etc.). For example, all of the Upper Kuskokwim clauses in Table 8.1 mean '*mega* lies, sits, is in a position', where *mega* means 'bread, flour, dough'.

As must be clear from this example, the noun only designates that the referent is a flour-based product, and further features of the referent, such as its shape, texture, quantity, etc. are encoded by the verb stem semantics. If a referent is activated, the verb meaning provides important clues to its identity. Consider a discourse example from another Athabaskan language, Navajo:

(8.9) Navajo (Na-Dene, Southwest of the USA; from a story by Bernice Casaus, speaker)
    a. shidą́ą́dii   yi-nííʔį.
       for.some.time   33.ACC-3.NOM.looked.at
    b. ńt'ééʔ   ʔayęęzhii yę́ę łaʔ   nááhidees'nááʔ   jiní.
       then   egg   that one   again.3.NOM.moved they.say
    c. łaʔ ʔéí t'óó t'áákǫ́ǫ́   t'óó doonaha'náóó,
       one that just right.there just without.moving
    d. t'óó   siʔą́   jiní.
       just   3.NOM.sit.ROUNDISH they.say
    e. ʔáádóó   shįį   t'óó   yi-k'i   nááneezdá.
       then   probably just   33.OBL-upon again.3.NOM.sat.AN
    'For some time she [=the female eagle] was watching. Then that egg moved again, they say. The other one was not moving, it was just sitting there. Then she sat upon them again.'

In this extract two classificatory verb stems are used: -ʔą́ in line (d), referring to Absolutives of roundish shape (it is cognate to the last of the Upper Kuskokwim verbs in Table 8.1), and -dá in line (e), applicable only to animate referents. In each of these lines reduced reference is performed: no full NP is present. Furthermore, in each of these lines both referents, 'the eagle' and 'the egg' are apparently activated. Since both verbs roughly mean 'sit', it is clear that the verb stems' classificatory semantics contributes to precluding referential conflict in both lines.

Interestingly, some Athabaskan languages have another verbal classificatory system apart from the verb stem, that is specialized classifier affixes (specifically, prefixes). These classifier[2] prefixes qualify as referential aids (rather than referential devices per se) as they are entirely distinct from bound pronominal morphemes. Recall from Chapter 7 (subsection 7.2.1) that Upper Kuskokwim has alternating bound third person accusative[3] pronouns – a pronoun is present if the referent is activated and there is no full NP, whereas in the presence of a Patientive NP no pronoun occurs; the latter is the case in all examples in (8.10):

(8.10) Upper Kuskokwim (Na-Dene, Alaska, USA)
    i. si-kaʔ   ti-no-zi-s-ʔonh
       1SG.POSS-foot   PREF-PREF-PFV-1SG.NOM-handled.ROUNDISH
       'I washed my foot'

    ii. tsasja   ti-no-da-zi-s-ʔonh
       cup   PREF-PREF-CL_WOODEN-PFV-1SG.NOM-handled.ROUNDISH
       'I washed the cup'

    iii. tsa   ti-no-na-zi-s-ʔonh
       rock   PREF-PREF-CL_ROUNDISH-PFV-1SG.NOM-handled.ROUNDISH
       'I washed the rock'

The lexical meaning 'wash' is conveyed in Upper Kuskokwim by the combination of two derivational prefixes (*ti-no-*) with the word-final classificatory root morpheme. In this set of examples the stem presupposing a roundish Absolutive is used (the same as in the last line in Table 8.1). So verb forms

---

[2] To prevent possible confusion, I must remark that in traditional Athabaskan studies the term 'classifier' is used for an entirely different class of morphemes, having nothing to do with noun or referent classification (see Kibrik 1996c), while what I call prefixal classifiers here is often dubbed gender in Athabaskan studies.

[3] In Athabaskan, the alignment of semantic roles as expressed by bound pronouns is arranged in accordance with the accusative pattern. However, the use of classificatory devices (both verb stems and prefixal classifiers) follows the ergative principle: they encode class membership of Soles and Patientives – in other words, Absolutives.

based on this stem can indicate washing roundish or compact three-dimensional objects, such as a foot, a cup, or a rock. Many Absolutives, such as 'the foot', are not accompanied by any verbal prefixal classifier; see (8.10i). In contrast, the Absolutives in (8.10ii, iii) require the appearance of a classifier prefix on the verb: *d-* (surfacing as *da-*) indicating a wooden or a phytogenic Absolutive and *n-* (surfacing as *na-*) indicating (once again) a roundish Absolutive, respectively. Prefixal classifiers may thus be added on top of classificatory verbs and even duplicate the classificatory categorization, as in (8.10iii).

Prefixal classifiers appear on the verb irrespective of whether an Absolutive full NP is found in the clause. When there is no Absolutive full NP in the clause, prefixal classifiers may participate in discriminating between activated referents that can possibly assume the Absolutive role. Consider such an example in which, once again, a classificatory verb stem (elongated) and a prefixal classifier (wooden) are combined and, in conjunction, carve out the set of possible Absolutives:

(8.11) Upper Kuskokwim (Na-Dene, Alaska, USA)
 no-di-ø-ghe-ghił
 down-CL_WOODEN-3.NOM-PFV-fell.ELONGATED
 'It fell down [for example, a stick]'

Bound classifiers in several Native American languages, as well as in Ngandi (Gunwinyguan, northern Australia), are discussed by Mithun (1986b).

The general property of all classificatory devices is that they provide an absolute stable sorting of referents and thus can participate in precluding referential conflicts. They are referential aids, but not referential devices, that is, they do not refer by themselves. This is particularly clear in the case of verbal classificatory devices, including both classificatory verb stem and classificatory affixes, as these elements are very clearly contrasted to referential devices. The distinction between the referential function and the classificatory function is also clear in those systems where classifiers or noun class markers are attached to referential devices in an agglutinative way, as in Korana or Tariana. But this distinction is much more blurred in those languages where class or classifier morphemes are fused with pronominal morphemes, as in English or Abkhaz. And it is still more blurred when a noun class or classifier morpheme alone can be used as a referential device, as in Pulaar-Fulfulde (see Chapter 9, section 9.4) or in Jakaltek and Vietnamese (see Chapter 4, subsection 4.2.2). However, these differences ought not to prevent one from having a clear understanding: reference and sorting are two independent functions, even though they are sometimes performed by one and the same device.

8.4 Relative stable sortings

Relative stable sortings are different from absolute stable sortings in that they compare referents along a certain semantic or pragmatic dimension rather than put them into rigid classes. It is usual in linguistics to call such dimensions, serving as a the basis of comparison, **hierarchies**.

8.4.1 *The animacy hierarchy*

One kind of hierarchy is the **animacy**, or activity, or inherent agentivity, hierarchy, such as the one discovered in Navajo by Hale (1973). This Navajo hierarchy has the form 'human > animal > inanimate'. It is a hierarchy rather than a taxonomy because what matters is not just affiliation of a noun/referent in a class but a relation between two nouns/referents along the animacy scale. The relation between 'man' and 'deer' is of the same type as between 'deer' and 'rock', or 'man' and 'rock'. In two-place clauses, the relation between the Principal and the non-Principal referents in inherent agentivity is one of the factors that influence the choice of a non-Principal (accusative, dative, or oblique) third person pronoun. Other things being equal, if the Principal outranks the non-Principal in animacy, it is more likely that the pronoun *y(i)-* would be used, while the opposite ranking favours the use of the *b(i)-* pronoun. The use of the *b(i)-* pronoun is often interpreted as the inverse form of the clause, as opposed to the direct form with *y(i)-*.

As Navajo pronouns are strongly tenacious, their presence does not depend on referent activation and on the presence of a coreferential full NP in the clause. A simple example of how the animacy hierarchy operates can be seen in (8.12):

(8.12)   Navajo (Na-Dene, Southwest of the USA; Martha Austin, speaker)
    a. shimásání   tł'ízí   yi-ł=deezdéel-go
        my.grandmother$_m$ goat$_g$ 33.OBL$_g$-with=3.NOM$_m$.caught-SBRD
    b. bi-yaa=haalwod
        3.OBL.INV$_m$-under=3.NOM$_g$.raced.away
    'When my grandmother caught the goat, it raced away from her'

In this example, the first clause has overt NPs indicating the participants. The *y(i)-* third person pronoun[4] is attached to the preverb (the oblique position)

---

[4] As has been discussed in the previous chapters, this pronoun indicates that not just its referent but also the clause's Principal are both third person, so it is glossed '33'.

and indicates, to put it most simply, that a more inherently agentive referent (human) acts upon a less inherently agentive referent (animal). This helps to identify 'my grandmother' with the clause's Principal and 'the goat' with the second participant. (Recall from subsection 6.6.2 that the relationship between bound pronouns and coreferential full NPs in the same clause can be viewed as a kind of an anaphoric relationship.) The second clause is again two-place, but has no overt NPs. Here the third person inverse prefix *b(i)-* is used (again in the oblique position). The prefix *b(i)-* suggests that the Principal is less inherently agentive than the second participant. Thus the reference of the two pronominal elements in the clause is established: among the two activated referents it is the goat that races away from the grandmother rather than vice versa.

The two alternative non-Principal third person pronouns are amply employed in Navajo discourse to discriminate between concurrently activated referents. It is important to note that the hierarchical difference in animacy is not the only factor that affects the choice between *y(i)-* and *b(i)-*. The other major factor is the referent's topicality, which is among the current, rather than stable, sortings of referents. So the Navajo sorting is actually of a mixed nature. (There are also other factors affecting this choice; see Kibrik 1988: Ch. 2, Thompson 1989, Willie 1991.)

After the animacy hierarchy was discovered in Navajo by Hale, similar phenomena have been identified in many other languages; see e.g. Kibrik (2002b) on Tuvan (Turkic, Russia). Whereas in Navajo the animacy hierarchy is instantiated in bound pronouns, in Tuvan it affects the choice between a free pronoun and zero reference. Apart from marking the hierarchical animacy distinctions in referential devices as such, some other languages have dedicated elements that serve this function. For example, in Kutenai (an isolate of British Columbia, Canada; Idaho and Montana, USA) there is a specialized overt suffix *-(n)aps* appearing on the verb in a variety of situations, in particular when a less animate referent acts upon a more animate one; see Dryer (1992a, especially pp. 124–125). This suffix, called the inverse marker, is entirely independent of referential devices. The Kutenai direct vs. inverse system, in which this distinction is marked by dedicated morphology, is more canonical than that of Navajo, where it is integrated with referential devices.

In Kutenai, as well as in Navajo, the system of direct vs. inverse marking is only partially conditioned by an animacy hierarchy and is also dependent on current distinctions between referents. In other languages the direct vs. inverse opposition includes not only distinctions between third person referents but also between and among locutors; see, inter alia, Givón (1994) and the useful recent study by Zúñiga (2006) focusing on the languages of the New

306   *III. Typology of Referential Aids*

World. The accounts of the direct vs. inverse systems rarely connect this phenomenon to issues in referential conflict and reference, although a connection is usually there, as it is in Navajo.

8.4.2 *The honorific hierarchy*

A totally different kind of hierarchy is based on the pragmatic status of relative social position. Such hierarchies concern human referents only and are known as **honorific**. Honorific hierarchies are most frequently materialized in free referential devices that are functionally similar to pronouns but are interpreted as partly delexicalized social status nouns; see Chapter 4, subsection 4.2.3. For example, in Vietnamese (Austro-Asiatic; Lý Toàn Thang, personal communication) referents that are comparable to or lower than the speaker in social status can be referred to by means of the third person pronoun *nó* whereas the polite way to mention referents such as e.g. the speaker's father in an anaphoric context is, literally, 'my father' or 'that old man'. Therefore, if there is a potential referential conflict between two referents with different social status with respect to the speaker, using the plain third person pronoun can rule out one of those referents.

A similar system is found in Sinhala, a South Asian language. In the following example referential options are arranged in accordance with decreasing deference:

(8.13)   Sinhala (Indo-Aryan, Indo-European, Sri Lanka; Chandrasena Premawardhena 2002: 73)
  i. maṇ   gihin   səːr-tə   kiyan-naṇ
      I   go.FUT   boss-DAT   say-FUT
      'I will tell him (about it)' [respectful, referring to boss/teacher]
  ii. maṇ   gihin   ∅   kiyan-naṇ
      I   go.FUT   say-FUT
      'I will tell him (about it)' [neutral]
  iii. maṇ   gihin   undœ-tə   kiyan-naṇ
      I   go.FUT   fellow-DAT   say-FUT
      'I will tell him (about it)' [familiar]
  iv. maṇ   gihin   {ōka-tə   ~   ū-tə}   kiyan-naṇ
      I   go.FUT   PROX.H-DAT   ANAPH.AN-DAT say-FUT
      'I will tell him (about it)' [derogatory, treating one as a scoundrel]

The options shown in these examples include social status nouns (i, iii; cf. 4.2.3), pronouns (iv), and zero (ii). Using nouns (especially proper names and kinship terms) in cases of high activation is quite common in Sinhala as all pronouns are generally disrespectful to a certain degree. Interestingly, zero reference can be helpful in such elaborate systems to avoid explicit marking of honorific distinctions. 'When elderly relatives are being referred to in discourse, mostly kinship terms are used. ... The occurrence of zero anaphora is also a common feature' (Chandrasena Premawardhena 2002: 74). Use of pronouns in reference to parents is impossible, and repeating full NPs feels redundant, so zero anaphora is a useful resort (Chandrasena Premawardhena 2002: 75):

(8.14) Sinhala (Indo-Aryan, Indo-European, Sri Lanka; Chandrasena Premawardhena 2002: 74)
tātta-ṭə sanīpə nœ:. ēnisā {tātta ~ Ø} bēt gannə
father-DAT well NEG therefore father medicine take.INF
giyā.
go.PAST
'Father is not well. So he went to the doctor.'

For some further information on honorific distinctions in pronouns see Head (1979), Levinson (2004) (section on the so-called social deixis), Helmbrecht (2004: 179ff.). According to Helmbrecht (2004: 263), honorific distinctions in pronouns are unattested only in Australia and South America. The continent most inclined to honorific distinctions is Eurasia; another important area where such distinctions are common is Mesoamerica. Complex honorific hierarchies are particularly typical of the languages of East, Southeast, and South Asia; for a detailed account of several languages of that area see Cooke (1968). Outside this area more limited honorific hierarchies are found. For instance, in the Russian language of the 19th and early 20th century a third person plural pronoun could have been applied to an individual referent if that referent was a person ranking high with respect to the speaker. An illustration can be seen in the following example from Mikhail Bulgakov's story 'Heart of a dog' (1925), excerpted from a doorkeeper's direct speech:

(8.15) Russian
Graždanin Šarikov kamnjami švyrjal <...> v
citizen Sharikov stones.PL.INSTR tossed in
xozjaina kvartiry. <...> Kuxarku Šarikov ixnjuju
owner.ACC flat.GEN lady.cook.ACC Sharikov 3PL.POSS.ACC
obnjal <...>
embraced
'Citizen Sharikov was throwing stones <...> at the flat owner. <...> Sharikov embraced his lady cook <...>'

The possessive pronoun *ixnjuju* is grammatically plural. But as there is no activated plural referent at this point in discourse, this plural marking is unequivocally due not to referent plurality but to its honorific status: the speaker (the doorkeeper) indicates that the referent (the flat owner) has a high social status with respect to the speaker. This eliminates a potential referential conflict, as the competing referents do not rank as high on the honorific hierarchy.

Most often honorific distinctions are typical in free pronouns and their functional analogues, but they can also be found in bound pronouns; such instances are found in Mesoamerica; see Helmbrecht (2005).

Apart from marking honorific hierarchies in pronouns, in some languages such hierarchies are built into verb lexical meaning. For example, Van Valin (1987), referring to Hinds (ed.) (1978), reports that in Japanese Ø *irasshaima-shita* 'X went' the zero reference most likely corresponds to a third person referent, specifically one not being close to the speaker. If there is a referential conflict involving, say, the speaker's wife and some foreign person, the zero would most likely refer to the latter due to the verb semantics.

To conclude, the hierarchies are relative sortings as they imply a comparison of referents' ranks, rather than specific membership, but they are also stable sortings as a referent's position on the hierarchy does not change through discourse.

8.5 Current sortings: broad domain

In natural discourse, it is often the case that simultaneously activated referents are ontologically equivalent, such as two plates on a table, two dogs, or two girls. In this kind of situation stable referent sortings cannot possibly help as the categorization of potentially conflicting referents is the same. In fact, referential conflicts occur more frequently between referents of comparable inherent properties, especially humans. Such referents can nevertheless be distinguished if they have a different status in the speaker's and addressee's processual cognitive representations. It is this kind of status that serves as the basis for current referent sortings.

Current sortings are based on various transient, fluid, contextual properties of referents, such as: being the subject or non-subject of the previous clause, being more or less activated at the present moment in discourse, being the protagonist or non-protagonist of the present discourse, etc. The range of such current properties is so great that it can only be partially illustrated. I divide the current properties of referents that can serve as a basis of sorting into two kinds: broad domain (such as a whole discourse) and narrow domain (such as a discourse fragment or a local discourse context); this is reminiscent of the division between global and local reference-tracking devices introduced by Comrie (1989b). This division is helpful in understanding differences between various kinds of current sortings, but of course it is not strict as there is no firm boundary between global and local discourse structure. The two kinds of current sortings are treated in this section and in the next section 8.6. Also, as in the previous sections, I pay attention to another important typological parameter, namely the site of expression.

A good example of a broad domain current sorting is provided by the so-called **fourth person** in Navajo. Like other Navajo pronouns, the fourth person is primarily used in the form of pronominal prefixes on the verb. Its underlying shape is *ji-* for the Principal and *hwi-* for other roles, although morphophonemic variants are diverse. The fourth person has a variety of uses, including indefinite reference (as in *jiní* 'they say', the verb form serving as a quotative marker), deferential reference (applicable to both addressees and other persons) and narrative reference to protagonists of discourses or their parts; see Haile (1941: 17, 72, 77, 114–116, Kibrik 1988: 81–96, Willie 1991: 108ff.). Here I concentrate on the latter usage alone, relying largely on the interpretation in Kibrik (1988: 81–96).

In its narrative usage, the fourth person invariably applies to specific human (or personified) referents. If there are two or more central referents in a recounted story, at some point 'person assignment' can occur. That means that the fourth person is attributed to a certain referent as its discourse-internal but quite persistent qualification. Hypotheses on the basis underlying such assignment vary (Reichard 1951: 81, Kibrik 1988: 88), but in any event only a protagonist can be assigned fourth person; for an example see (3.2) in Chapter 3. After such assignment has taken place, the fourth person pronoun alone suffices to mention this referent, without a danger of referential conflict, as long as is necessary. The fourth person effectively operates as a temporary proper name of the referent. The point of assignment and several ensuing mentions can be seen in the following:

(8.16) Navajo (Na-Dene, Southwest of the USA; Sapir and Hoijer 1942: 16–17)
a. ʔałk'idą́ą́ʔ naʔashóʔizhii k'i-ʔ-ø-díílá jiní.
long.ago horned.toad$_{ht}$ PREF-INDEF.ACC-3.NOM$_{ht}$-planted QUOT

b. ʔáádóó shį́į́ ná-ʔ-neest'ą́ą-go,
thereafter PTCL PREF-INDEF.NOM-ripened-SBRD

c. maʔii b-aa-ø-yílghod.
coyote$_c$ 3.OBL$_{ht}$-to-3.NOM$_c$-ran

d. naadą́ą́ʔ   b-á-ø-dzi-stʼé   jiní.
   corn   3.OBL_c-for-3.ACC-4.NOM_ht-roasted   QUOT

e. ńtʼééʔ   "ø-łikan   lá"   ø-ní   jiní.
   then   3.NOM-is.tasty   EX   3.NOM_c-said   QUOT

f. ʔa-ø-naalghod   jiní.
   PREF-3.NOM_c-ran.off   QUOT

g. ʔáádóó   náá-ø-nálghod   jiní.
   thereafter   again-3.NOM_c-ran   QUOT

h. b-á-náá-ø-ji-stʼé   jiní.
   3.OBL_c-for-again-3.ACC-4.NOM_ht-roasted   QUOT

i. ńtʼééʔ   jóhódah   ʔa-h-ø-ólnaʔ   jiní.
   then   unexpectedly   PREF-4.ACC_ht-3.NOM_c-swallowed   QUOT

j. ʔáádóó   shį́į́   dah-ø-diilghod.
   thereafter   PTCL   PREF-3.NOM_c-began.running

k. ńtʼééʔ   bi-ghiʔ-déę́ʔ   ha-dz-oodzííʔ.
   then   3.OBL_c-inside-from   PREF-4.NOM_ht-spoke

l. "díi-sh   xaʔátʼíí   ʔátʼé"   ji-ní-o,
   this-QU   what   is   4.NOM_ht-said-SBRD

m. bi-jéi   b-í-zh-dílnih.
   3.POSS_c-heart   3.OBL-on-4.NOM_ht-touched

'Long ago Horned Toad_ht planted, they say. Then, it seems, when things had ripened, Coyote_c came running to him_ht, they say. He_ht roasted corn for him_c, they say. And "It is indeed sweet!" he_c said, they say. He_c ran off back, they say.

Later, he_c came running again, they say. He_ht again roasted (corn) for him_c, they say. Then, unexpectedly, he_c swallowed him_ht, they say. Then, it seems, he_c began to run.

Then, from inside of him_c, he_ht spoke. "This, what is it?" he_ht said as he_ht touched his_c heart.'

In this story, the two protagonists, Horned Toad [=ht] and Coyote [=c], are initially mentioned by plain third person bound pronouns – see especially line (c). However, in line (d) the fourth person is assigned to 'Horned Toad', and this assignment is kept all the way through this excerpt and further in the story. Given that it is just these two referents that are activated in most of this discourse, the distinction between the fourth person (Horned Toad) and the third person (Coyote) proves to be a very efficient way to discriminate between them. Notice that the fourth person pronoun occurs as the sole reference to the protagonist at rather long distances, for example in line (h), whereas the previous mention was in line (d). Incidentally, this occurs across the boundary of an episode, marked by Sapir and Hoijer by a paragraph. This demonstrates that the third vs. fourth person distinction in Navajo is indeed of a broad domain, as a referent that is clearly less activated at the moment may be referred to by the fourth person pronoun.

Still more extreme examples can be encountered in Navajo narrative discourses. In another, rather lengthy, story published in Sapir and Hoijer (1942: 20–25) there are again two protagonists, Coyote and Skunk. At the end of the story, one mention of Skunk is by means of the fourth person pronoun alone, even though he was last mentioned eleven clauses and two paragraphs back. As has been demonstrated in Kibrik (1988), consistency in the use of fourth person is higher when there is actual referential conflict in the discourse.

Much more widely known is a somewhat similar current distinction between the so-called **proximate** and **obviative**, found in the Algonquian languages of North America (see Zúñiga 2006: 69–128 for a recent review). Various terms have been used to define the function of the proximate, such as 'discourse topic', 'focalized object', 'point of view', etc. (see Russell 1996 for a discussion). Overall, it appears that the Algonquian proximate is a less long-lived status than the Navajo fourth person, but it still qualifies as a broad domain sorting. Assignment of referents to the proximate vs. obviative status is usually done by explicit suffixes on the corresponding nouns; thereafter, reference is performed by pronominal suffixes on the verb. Consider an example from Nishnaabemwin, a dialect of Ojibwe spoken along the northern shores of lakes Huron and Ontario in Canada. This extract is from a story of a young man who was attacked by enemies.

(8.17)   Nishnaabemwin Ojibwe (Algonquian, Algic, Canada; Valentine 2001: 638)[5]
   a. mii   dash   gaa-aazhoo-ggizhebaawgak
      and   then   when.the.next.morning.came
   b. maaba   nini   gii-noondwaad   aazhi go
      this.3SG.PROX   man.3SG.PROX   heard.3SG.PROX>3.OBV   now   ASSERT
      bi-yaanid
      3.OBV.come

---

[5] In Valentine's transcription, hyphens in the original do not correspond to any boundaries in glosses. The > symbol in the glosses indicates the relationship between the Agentive and the Patientive participants of a transitive clause along the animacy hierarchy.

c. niw   waa-nsigjin
that.3.OBV   who.wanted.to.kill.3.OBV>3SG.PROX.INV
'When the next morning came, this man heard them coming, those who wanted to kill him'

In line (b) the full NP mentioning the young man (*maaba nini*) is explicitly marked as the proximate referent. The other referent having a certain degree of activation, 'the enemies', automatically receives the obviative status. The one-place verb *bi-yaanid* in line (b) contains the element *-nid* that refers to an animate obviative referent. Furthermore, the morphology of the transitive participle in line (c) indicates that the agent is obviative and the patient proximate. The participle also contains the inverse grammeme indicating that a referent lower on the animacy hierarchy (in this case, obviative) acts upon a higher referent (proximate). Note that the obviative marking also occurs on the demonstrative pronoun that refers to the enemies. A bit later on in the story the enemies arrive:

(8.18) Nishnaabemwin Ojibwe (Algonquian, Algic, Canada; Valentine 2001: 638)
a. mii   dash   aazhi   go   gii-bi-dgoshninid
   and   then   now   ASSERT   arrived.here.3.OBV
b. niw   waa-miigaan'gojin
   that.3.OBV   who.will.fight.3.OBV>3SG.PROX
'Now they arrived who were going to fight him'

In this passage it is clear that the attribution of the proximate and obviative statuses to particular activated referents remains intact, which allows one to tell referents apart effectively.

The consistency of the attribution of the proximate status to a particular referent is variable. If one looks at texts in Saulteaux (Logan 2001), another dialect of Ojibwe (or a closely related language), spoken in southern Manitoba and Saskatchewan, it appears that the proximate status is shifted between different referents quite easily. Since Logan's glossing is not detailed enough, I provide a schematic representation of several clauses from a story:

(8.19) Saulteaux Ojibwe (Algonquian, Algic, Canada; schematic representation; Logan 2001: 166, 170)
a. Again, pondering, she[OBV]-eats blueberries.
b. Soon she[PROX]-sees-it[OBV] a.truck coming.beside.
c. It.stops nearby.
d. A.man[PROX] he[PROX]-drives,
e. he[PROX]-is.going.to.laugh.at-her[OBV] the.girl[OBV].

In this extract, 'the girl' was obviative at first, then the speaker switched to proximate for a moment, and then, as 'the man' became strongly activated, the speaker made 'the girl' obviative again. Perhaps Saulteaux proximate vs. obviative distinction must be better interpreted as a narrow domain current sorting; see section 8.6 below. See also Goddard (1990) on Fox (=Mesquakie; Midwestern USA), another Algonquian language.

Among the North American languages that are generally inclined toward using bound pronouns, there are also other languages encoding current systems of a broad domain on pronominal affixes. Kutenai (an isolate of British Columbia, Canada; Idaho and Montana, USA) has a proximate vs. obviative distinction that is quite similar to Algonquian (Dryer 1992a); see also Zúñiga (2006) on a number of other native American languages.

Broad domain current sortings can also be encoded on free pronouns. An example of this is found in Bamana (Mande, Mali), as described by Bergelson (1988). In Bamana, there are two third person pronouns, *a* and *o*. In narrative discourse, the referent that is the discourse's protagonist is coded by *a*, while other referents by *o*. There are also other factors leading to the use of *a*, such as the referent being the author or addressee of quoted speech or being the topic of the preceding clause. These observations suggest that broad domain current sortings can occasionally operate on a more narrow basis; this is also true of the other systems discussed above.

In Nootka, a broad domain current sorting is marked not on pronouns but by means of the verbal category of inversion. Referents are implicitly sorted in accordance with the degree of their themehood (Whistler 1985: 244–246). The following three clauses are excerpted from a folk story whose protagonist, the folk hero Kwatyat [=K] is activated along with another character, the wolf [=w]:

(8.20) Nootka (Wakashan, British Columbia, Canada; Whistler 1985: 251)
 a. ʔaʔa·tu·-ʔat-weʔin <...>
  ask-INV-QUOT.he
 b. wa·-ʔaλ-weʔin <...>
  say-now-QUOT.he
 c. t'a·qukʷi-ʔat-weʔin <...>
  believe-INV-QUOT.he
  'He$_w$ asked him$_K$ <...> He$_K$ said to him$_w$ <...> He$_w$ believed him$_K$ <...>'

In clause (b) the protagonist, Kwatyat, acts upon the other activated referent, and this situation, supposedly the unmarked one, is not indicated on the verb by any special morphology. Conversely, in (a) and (c) the non-protagonist acts upon the protagonist, and this is signalled by the inverse inflection, which thus serves as a referential aid.

Finally, a broad domain current sorting can be marked on a special clause constituent. In Pirahã, a language of Brazil, there is a special particle *xagía* that attaches to a pronoun if it refers to the discourse protagonist:

(8.21)   Pirahã (Mura, Brazil; Everett 1986: 306)
         hi   xagía   gáxaisai <...>
         3   PROTAG   say.NMZR
         'He [=the one we are talking about] said: <...>'

We have thus discussed broad domain current sortings marked on four kinds of constituents: free pronouns, bound pronouns, verbal categories, and special constituents.

8.6 Current sortings: narrow domain

The narrowest domain in which current sortings may come up is the domain of a single clause. Reflexive and reciprocal pronouns typically corefer to certain antecedents inside the same clause, thus providing a basis for the distinction from other potentially activated referents. Since this book is about reference in discourse, I do not discuss this kind of narrowest domain; but see Wiesemann (1986a), Comrie (1989b, 1999), where reflexive reference is discussed in the context of and in comparison with discourse-wide sortings. However, I would like to briefly mention another likewise supernarrow domain system, for the reason that it is far less known than the reflexive.

In Eastern Kayah Li of Myanmar and Thailand there are two free third personal pronouns, not distinguishing number or gender: *ʔa* and *lū* (as well as zero reference; see Chapter 5, section 5.2). Solnit (1997: 149ff.) remarks that both pronouns refer to specific and foregrounded characters, but *lū*, termed obviative by Solnit, occurs only after *ʔa* or some other third person referential device (also including zero reference) has already been used in the clause. Therefore, *lū* can never be in the subject position (Eastern Kayah Li has the stable SVO word order). Thus the sorting operating in this case differentiates whether the referent is the same as the one that appeared earlier in the same clause or not.

(8.22)   Eastern Kayah Li (Karen, Sino-Tibetan, Myanmar and Thailand; Solnit 1997: 150)
         a. ʔa$_i$ ʔé   ʔojwā   lū$_j$ bý   tē
            3   call   wait   3.OBV   at   what

b. Ø_j　ʔojwā　kʌ̄　lū_i　to　bōʌ
　　 wait　 COMIT　3.OBV　NEG　then

c. ʔa_i　khrwā　ʔíchɔ̄　kʌ　lū_j
　 3　 follow　 curse　 COMIT　3.OBV

'Whenever he [=i] called them [=j] to wait, they did not wait for him; then he followed cursing them'

Apparently, this sorting is as supernarrow as the reflexive; since the dedicated form appears in a case of non-coreference, this device might be called anti-reflexive. It is important to note, however, that the use of *lū* operates on the linear, and not on the participant role basis; the previous third person participant does not have to be the Principal (although it most frequently is):

(8.23)　Eastern Kayah Li (Karen, Sino-Tibetan, Myanmar and Thailand; Solnit 1997: 151)

vē　dʌ́　pè　kó　kʌ̄　ʔa_i　lū_j-te
1SG　give　TRPOSS　temporarily　COMIT　3　3.OBV-thing

'I lent him [=i] his [=j]'

Eastern Kayah Li is not unique in having this system. A typologically identical current distinction is found in Teop (Meso-Melanesian Oceanic, Austronesian, Bougainville, Papua New Guinea) (Mosel 2010).

In the rest of this section I survey narrow (but not supernarrow) domain current sortings. In all instances narrow domain is a local discourse context, such as a pair or a group of clauses. Several bases for sorting are discussed, including logophoricity, topicality, and the degree of activation. Within each type I identify a variety of constituents on which the sorting is marked.

8.6.1 *Logophoricity, or perspective taking*

A well-known kind of a narrow domain current sorting is so-called **logophoric** pronouns, first identified in Africa by Hagège (1974). According to the keen formulation by Helmbrecht (2004: 153), 'logophoric pronouns are special third person pronouns that indicate the referent whose discourse or cognitive perspective is reported'. In other words, in a case of indirect reportive contexts (indirect quotation of speech/thought) typical logophoric pronouns appear in those spots where first person pronouns would appear in direct quotation.[6]

---

[6] Evans (2009) proposed that logophoric pronouns actually represent the combined perspectives of two subjects at once – the actual speaker and the quoted speaker. This appears to be true and logophoric pronouns are indeed biperspectival: they are different both from locutor pronouns in direct speech (quoted speaker's perspective) and from third person pronouns, used in indirect speech in languages like English (actual speaker's perspective).

For referents other than the author of quoted speech/thought (or 'mental source', in terms of Kemmer 1993: 82ff.) plain third person pronouns are used. In both of the following two examples from different African languages the first referential option in the complement clause is a logophoric pronoun and the second one a plain third person pronoun:

(8.24) Angas (Western Chadic, Afro-Asiatic, Nigeria; Burquest 1986: 92)
Músá lə̀ tèné {ɗyí / kɔ́ }
Musa_M say that LOG.SG.M.NPRES_M 3SG.NPRES_i
mét kàsúwá
go market
'Musa_M said that {he_M / he_i} will go to the market'

(8.25) Dan-Gwèètaa (Mande, Ivory Coast; Vydrine in preparation: 21)
yɤ̀ kʌ̀ Zâ̰ gṹ ɗɛ̀ {yá / yà̰}
3SG.NEUT become.NEUT Jean_J in that LOG.SG.PF_J 3SG.PF_i
kʌ̄ klɤ̌ɤ̌klɤ̀
become healthy
'Jean_J thinks that {he_J / he_i} has recovered'

Example (8.24) is a typical illustration of the kind usually cited to demonstrate what logophoric pronouns are; it is typical in the following respects:

  (i) the logophoric pronoun is precisely coreferential to the antecedent;
  (ii) the referent's antecedent is the subject of its clause;
  (iii) the antecedent designates the speaker/thinker (mental source);
  (iv) the antecedent is found in the main clause of the same complement construction.

All of these properties are not necessary attributes of the usage of logophoric pronouns. As for property (i), Dimmendaal (2001: 133) shows that partial coreference, such as $he_i - they_{i+j}$, can qualify as coreference. As for (ii), the Dan-Gwèètaa example (8.25) demonstrates that the antecedent does not have to necessarily be the subject of its clause: the referent 'Jean' is not a core argument in the matrix clause; this matrix clause can be more literally conveyed as 'it occurred on Jean'. As concerns (iii), in some logophoric systems not only speakers/thinkers but also hearers can be referred to by special logophoric pronouns. This is the case in Angas (Burquest 1986), where different logophoric pronouns are used to express coreference to speakers vs. hearers:

(8.26) Angas (Western Chadic, Afro-Asiatic, Nigeria; Burquest 1986: 92)
Músá lɔ́ m-Búlùs tènè mwā né gwár
Musa say to-Bulus_B that 3PL.INCOMPL see LOGHR.SG.M_B
'Musa told Bulus that they saw him [=Bulus]'

Note that in Angas logophoric pronouns can occur in various syntactic positions in a complement clause, including its subject, as in (8.24), direct object (8.26), indirect object, and even possessor.

The most interesting extension of the pattern found in (8.24) and concerning property (iv) is that a logophoric pronoun's antecedent does not have to be situated in the matrix clause, syntactically superordinate to the pronoun's clause. As has been convincingly argued by Dimmendaal (2001), the use of logophoric pronouns is not confined to complement clauses but can extend through sizeable stretches of discourse, such as paragraph or episode, provided that a single person's perspective keeps being reported. (See also Kemmer 1993: 86.) Dimmendaal demonstrates that evidence for the paragraph-, rather than sentence-size, scope of logophoricity is found in the very first influential publications about logophoric pronouns: Hagège (1974) about Tuburi and Mundange (both Adamawa-Ubangi, Cameroon and Chad) and Clements (1975: 170–171) about Ewe (Kwa, Ghana and Togo). Dimmendaal also provides the following discourse example from Ewe, in which a specific speaker's perspective is framed at the beginning of an episode and is further exploited below:

(8.27) Ewe (Kwa, Ghana and Togo; Dimmendaal 2001: 139)
a. nya lá-é nyé
   word DEF-FOC be

b. bé afétɔ́ gblɔ ná-m nyitsɔ ádé
   that boss say to-1SG earlier certain

c. bé ye-dí bé ye-a-ɖo-m ɖé ye-wo
   that LOG-want that LOG-SBJV-send-1SG ALL LOG-PL
   ɖé Ámérika.
   hometown America

   <four intervening clauses>

h. háfi ye-a-dzó lá,
   before LOG-SBJV-leave TERM

i. e-le bé ye-a-di ame ádé á-da
   3SG-be that LOG-SBJV-look.for person certain POT-put
   ɖé ye tefé.
   ALL LOG place

j. éyata   né   me-trɔ   gbɔ   lá
   therefore when   1SG-return   arrive TERM
k. ye-a-tsɔ-m   á-da   ɖé   tefé   má.
   LOG-SBJV-take-1SG   POT-put   ALL   place that

'The news is that my boss told me a few days ago that he wants to send me to his country America. <...> Before he leaves, he has to find someone to replace him. Therefore when I return, he will put me in his place.'

This example makes it clear that Ewe logophoric pronouns are used irrespective of sentence boundaries and are a discourse-based rather than a syntactically-based system. Still they must be characterized as a current sorting device of a relatively narrow domain, as they are dependent on the local discourse structure. All clauses where logophoric pronouns occur convey the content of what the boss said, that is are semantically related to clause (b) where the boss's talk is introduced.[7]

The Ewe example also demonstrates another relevant fact: logophoric pronouns can be not only free but also bound. The same it true, for example, of Lango (Western Nilotic, Eastern Sudanic, Uganda; Noonan 1992). Furthermore, logophoricity can be marked independently of referential devices, by means of an independent category on the verb. Such a system is found in Gokana, a Benue-Congo language:

(8.28)   Gokana (Cross River, Benue-Congo, Nigeria; Comrie 1983: 31-32)
   i. aè   kɔ   aè   dɔ-è
      he   said   he   fell-LOG
      'He_i said that he_i fell'
   ii. aè   kɔ   oò   ziv-èè   a   gíá
       he   said   you   stole-LOG   his   yams
       'He_i said that you stole his_i yams'
   iii. aè   dá   ḿ   gá   kɔ   aè   dɔ-è
        he   heard   me   mouth   that   he   fell-LOG
        'He_i heard from me that he_i fell'

In Gokana the logophoric character of reference in the dependent clause is indicated by a special suffix on the verb, while the referential devices

---

[7] In terms of Rhetorical Structure Theory (Mann and Thompson 1988; see Chapters 11 and 12), the whole reported speech is a satellite with respect to the introductory clause, which is the nucleus; at least this is a possible interpretation. In a rhetorical net of discourse units, reported speech is thus subordinate to an introductory clause, no matter whether there is syntactic subordination or not.

themselves are the same third person pronouns as those used in other instances. The logophoric suffix indicates that the referent is indentical to one of the participants of the communicative event, either the speaker (8.28i, ii) or the hearer (8.28iii). The referent's role in the dependent clause is not necessarily the subject; it can be another clause participant and even a possessor, as in (8.28ii).

Logophoricity is an areal feature of West and Central Africa; see various articles in Wiesemann (ed.) (1986). Dimmendaal (2001) argues that logophoric pronouns are characteristic of many branches of the putative 'Niger-Congo' macrophylum, a number of 'Nilo-Saharan' families (in particular, Western Nilotic), and some groups within Afro-Asiatic, specifically Chadic and Omotic. Dimmendaal further suggests that the common historical source for logophoric pronouns is demonstratives.

Outside Africa, logophoric pronouns are occasionally attested in the Americas; see Mithun (1990: 365ff.) on Central Pomo (Pomoan, California, USA) and Wiesemann (1986a: 444–445) on Maxakalí (Macro-Ge, Brazil). They are also attested in a number of Nakh-Daghestanian languages in the Caucasus (Russia); see A. E. Kibrik (1977a: 316–317) on Archi, and Lyutikova (2001: 651–658) on Bagvalal. In particular, Bagvalal has a dedicated pronoun appearing only in logophoric contexts. In Central Pomo and Bagvalal, as Mithun and Lyutikova point out, they not only can be controlled within a complement construction but can also represent the mental source in less restricted discourse contexts.

A wider range of languages use so-called long-distance reflexives, that is referential devices that are used to convey clause-internal coreference, but also extend to cross-clause coreference, particularly in logophoric contexts; see Huang (2000: 90–130). Long-distance reflexives are attested, among others, in a number of European languages, for example Latin (Clements 1975), in Nakh-Daghestanian languages (Testelets and Toldova 1998), in East Asian languages (Huang 2000: 190–199), and in South Asian languages (Lust et al. (eds.) 2002). For example:

(8.29) Gujarati (Indo-Aryan, Indo-European, India; Gair et al. 2000: 17)
Raaj Kišor kamiTimāā potaane nimše em lakhe che
Raj Kishor committee self.OBJ will.appoint thus write AUX
'Raj$_R$ writes that Kishor$_K$ will appoint self$_{R,K}$ on the committee'

In contrast, other languages have dedicated devices that can be called anti-logophoric. Leger (2005) reports that in several Western Chadic languages, in addition to or instead of logophoric pronouns, dedicated third person pronouns exist that convey non-coreference to the subject of speech. The same feature is found in some other West African families. For example, in the Kwa language Attié the so-called fourth person free pronouns are found that can be interpreted as anti-logophoric:

(8.30) Attié (Kwa, Ivory Coast; Heine and Claudi 1986: 40)
i. ò dʒwí kɔ́ ò bə̀
    3 say   that 3 come
    'He$_i$ said that he$_i$ had come'
ii. ò dʒwí kɔ́ kɛ̀ bə̀
    3 say   that 4 come
    'He$_i$ said that he$_j$ had come'

As is clear from this example, the plain third person pronoun is used, in particular, in logophoric contexts, while the dedicated form, the fourth person, in contexts that are expressly non-logophoric.

Still more exotic current classifications are attested, related to reporting speech but not to the properties of referents themselves. For example, Helmbrecht (2004: 184) mentions Diuxi-Tilantongo Mixtec (Oto-Manguean, Mexico; Kuiper and Oram 1991: 342) where third person masculine pronouns differ depending on the sex of the speaker. One can imagine that in this language in quoted speech this distinction may be helpful in conveying the identity of the quoted person: it is possible to identify whether the quoted person is male or female depending on what form of 'he' is used.

Dickinson (2009) has reported a sophisticated system in Tsafiki (Barbacoan, Ecuador), where the verb-marked categories of evidentiality, epistemic modality, and mirativity (plus or minus congruence to addressee's expectations) help to keep zero reference straight. This system allows us to distinguish between different perspectives on the reported events, including the original narrator's perspective, the current narrator's perspective, and the main character's perspective. 'While these markers do not code person, they do code the speaker's relationship to the event and the perspective from which the event is being narrated. This coding of participation can in turn function as a strategy for tracking reference' (Dickinson 2009: 9).

8.6.2 *Topicality and subjecthood*

Apart from logophoric pronouns, another well-known current sorting of a narrow domain is **switch-reference**. Switch-reference was originally defined in several North American languages by Jacobsen (1967). A canonical switch-reference system is based on a verbal inflectional category consisting of two morphemes: same-subject (ss) and different-subject (ds). The subject of the clause in question is compared to the subject of a controlling clause (normally, preceding and/or being the main clause with respect to the given clause) as being either coreferential or not. Once the subject of the controlling clause is known, the ss marker on the verb of the current clause helps to identify the referent. Furthermore, even the ds marker can be enough to identify the referent of the clause subject: if there are two activated referents, and one of them is the subject of the controlling clause, then only the other one can be the referent in question. The use of switch-reference can be illustrated by the following two examples, the first one constructed and the second from natural discourse:

(8.31) Bafut (Bantoid, Benue-Congo, Cameroon; Wiesemann 1982: 53)
  i. á-ghɛ́ɛ̀   ndá   ŋ́-kwérɔ́   fórɔ́
      3SG-go   house   SS-take   rat
      'He then went to the house and took a rat'
  ii. á-ghɛ́ɛ̀   ndá   ŋgwà   á-kwérɔ́   fōrɔ̄
      3SG-go   house   Ngwa   3SG-take   rat
      'He then went to Ngwa's house and then he [=Ngwa] took a rat'

(8.32) Kolyma Yukaghir (Yukaghir, eastern Siberia, Russia; Maslova 2003: 370–371)
  a. irk-id'e   tāt   Ø$_i$ Ø$_j$ qaŋī-t
     one-ITER   CONN   pursue-SS.IMPFV
  b. Ø$_i$ Ø$_j$ šar-din   l'e-de-ge
             catch-SUP   be-3SG-DS
  c. Ø$_j$ mottuškā   johurče   molho   šøk-telle
             gull   flock   in   enter-SS.PFV
  d. Ø$_j$ titte-n'e   Morotaja   monut   jalhil   budie-n
           they-COMIT   M.   called   lake   super-PROL
     mere-ŋi-de-ge
     fly-PL-3-DS
  e. Ø$_i$ aŋdilā-ŋōt   gude-delle
             hawk-TRANSF   become-SS.PFV
  f. Ø$_i$ Ø$_j$ qaŋī-nu-t
                    pursue-IMPFV-SS.IMPFV
  g. tā   Ø$_i$ mon-te-m   mottuškā   johurče-gele
     there   sit-CAUS-TRANS.3SG   gull   flock-ACC
     'Once he$_i$ pursued him$_j$ and was just about to catch him$_j$, he$_j$ entered a flock of gulls, flew together with them above a lake called Morotaja, but he$_i$ turned into a hawk, continued to pursue him$_j$ and made the flock of gulls land there'

The system of Bafut is relatively simple as it has only a dedicated same-subject (ss) marker (8.31i), whereas in the case of non-coreference the plain third person is used (8.31ii). The Yukaghir system, in contrast, includes both a same-subject and a different-subject (DS) marker. Example (8.32) demonstrates how this system is simultaneously economical and efficient, helping to discriminate between the two concurrently activated referents. In each clause zero reference can be unequivocally identified, provided that the previous clause's subject referent is known. For example, in clause (8.32b) the subject referent is signalled to be coreferential to the previous clause's subject by the ss marker in the previous clause, and the object zero is inferred to refer to the second activated referent. In clause (8.32e), the zero subject is signalled to be distinct from the previous clause's subject by the DS marker in the previous clause, so the second protagonist is inferred to be the referent in question.

In many languages where switch-reference is found, referents are thought to be sorted in accordance with the subject vs. non-subject distinction (Haiman and Munro 1983: x–xi). This treatment, however, may be problematic, given that the notion of grammatical subject is often used indiscriminately in language descriptions, without adequate demonstration of the necessity and adequacy of this rather complex notion in a language's grammar (A. E. Kibrik 1997). It may well be that some switch-reference languages sort referents in accordance with a more elementary semantic distinction, such as topic vs. non-topic or Principal vs. non-Principal. Roberts (1997: 161ff.), in his survey of Papuan languages with switch-reference, has proposed that languages differ in being oriented to subjecthood, or topicality, or a semantic role. In particular, he demonstrates that Amele (Madang family, Papua New Guinea) has a topic-oriented switch-reference system, while the Alamblak (Sepik family, Papua New Guinea) switch-reference is based on the Actor vs. non-Actor distinction. The question of the subject- vs. topic orientation is discussed by Comrie (1998: 423) with respect to another Papuan language, Haruai (Piawi family, Papua New Guinea), and he concludes that this language's switch-reference can safely be considered subject-oriented. In fact, it may be that the existence of switch-reference by itself increases a language's likelihood to have a grammatically defined subject status: after all, subject is nothing more than a grammaticalized cluster of role- and topicality-related properties used by languages as the basis for organizing inter-clausal relations (as well as clause-internal syntax). In the rest of this section, I continue using the terms 'subject', 'same-subject', and 'different-subject', without implying the universal grammatical status of subject.

In some languages, switch-reference signals coreference of clause participants other than the subject. For example, according to Jacobsen (1967: 257), in Capanahua (Panoan, Peru) a variety of switch-reference markers exist that signal (non)coreference of subjects and objects of the clause in question to subject and objects of the controlling clause.

Another parameter, characterizing switch-reference systems, is how far the target and the controlling clauses can be from one another. Most frequently, switch-reference marks the identity of the subjects of adjacent clauses; see examples above. However, the controlling clause may be further away from the marked clause. Consider the following example:

(8.33) Haruai (Piawi family, Papua New Guinea; Comrie 1998: 429)
a. wöñ'-as   ñŋ-ör   hölb   mgan   md-mön
   puppy   they-EMPH   house   inside stay-DS
b. nwö   h-b-a   md-m
   father.3.POSS   come-NMZR-SUFF   stay-DS
c. hömlö   wödö   mö   glk   pn-öŋ-a
   banana dry   some   break   descend-PAST.3SG-DECL
'The puppies were inside the house, they were waiting for their master to come, and the banana fell down'

As Comrie comments on the same page, both the first and the second clause are dependent on the third, and there is no immediate relationship between the first and the second clauses, so in the selection of the switch-reference marker in the first clause the second clause is skipped over. It appears that the Haruai switch-reference system (as well as the systems of many other languages) operates on the basis of discourse relations rather than syntactic dependency; clearly, the syntactic relations between the clauses in (8.33) are very loose. What is relevant in (8.33) is that both the first and the second clauses are connected to the third clause in a hierarchical discourse network (in the sense of Rhetorical Structure Theory, Mann and Thompson 1988). Of course, what is hierarchically adjacent most often also turns out linearly adjacent, and for this reason neat structures as in the Yukaghir example (8.32) are frequently observed. The discourse-based sorting of referents still qualifies as a narrow domain, as adjacency in discourse structure, either linear or hierarchical, suggests a comparatively tight discourse context. (See also Oswalt 1983 on Kashaya (Pomoan, California, USA) and a more general discussion in Stirling 1993: Ch. 1.)

Switch-reference morphemes may be agglutinative, or may fusionally express some additional clausal category, such as absolute or relative tense, aspect, realis, semantic type of adverbial clause, etc. (See Roberts 1997: 138–161 for a review.) In the Yukaghir example (8.32) above, the DS marker is agglutinative, while the SS marker combines a switch-reference meaning with imperfective. Comrie (1983: 23) has pointed out that switch-reference is a clausal category in itself, so the cross-linguistically frequent verbal marking of switch-reference is due simply to the fact that the verb is the nucleus of a clause.

However, switch-reference does not have to be marked on verbs; quite a few languages have analytic switch-reference markers or have them attached to auxiliary constituents. This can be illustrated by Sùpyíré (Senufo Gur, Mali; Carlson 1994: 602) or Kayapó (Macro-Ge, Brazil; Wiesemann 1986c: 377). In particular, switch-reference can be marked on interclausal linkers. Lungstrum (1995) analyses an extensive corpus of texts in the Siouan language Lakhota. The corpus consists of 63 texts originally published by Deloria (1931). Lungstrum has identified several (mostly clause-final) conjunctions, including $yu^n khá^n$ 'and so', 'and then', $cha^{nk}é$ 'therefore', $k'éyash$ 'but', $tkhá(sh)$ 'however', $waná$ 'now', 'next', etc., and suggests that their appearance signals 'noncoreference of grammatical subject or spatiotemporal location between sequential clauses' (Lungstrum 1995: 1).[8] As an example, consider the following word-by-word translation of the Lakhota original, as offered by Lungstrum (1995: 111):

(8.34) Lakhota (Siouan, South Dakota and North Dakota, USA; schematic representation)
   a. then they gathered him together and there set him afire $cha^{nk}é$
   b. $waná$ he really burned $yu^n khá^n$
   c. from the fire property all of the finest kind came jumping out $k'éyash$
   d. Iktó however commanded them not to take a single thing and commanded them <...>

Lungstrum's analysis includes 4,394 occurrences of conjunctions in corpus. He reports that his hypothesis on the correlation between the use of conjunctions and a switch of subject or spatiotemporal location accounts for about 85% of all instances, while there are about 13% of occurrences not predicted by his hypothesis and less than 2% in which the predicted conjunctions are missing (Lungstrum 1995: 141). He further provides several types of explanations for these counterexamples and connects the use of conjunctions with the ethnopoetic structure of traditional Lakhota discourse.

Switch-reference can also be marked on reduced referential devices themselves. For example, in the Brazilian language Kaingang there is a special

---

[8] Lungstrum does not specify what he means by grammatical subject; this presents a problem as Lakhota is a language with active alignment in which identifying grammatical subjects is notoriously problematic; see e.g. Van Valin (1985).

same-subject free pronoun, while different-subject is indicated by the plain third person pronoun:

(8.35) Kaingang (Macro-Ge, Brazil; Wiesemann 1982: 44)
    i. ã   tỹ   ti   ve   kỹ   tóg   fỹ
       SS   by   3SG see when 3SG.SUBJ cry
      'When he$_i$ saw him he$_i$ cried'
    ii. ti   tỹ   ti   ve   kỹ   tóg   fỹ
       3SG by 3SG see when 3SG.SUBJ cry
      'When he$_i$ saw him he$_j$ cried'

For a very similar system in Sereer (Atlantic, Senegal and Gambia) see Chapter 9, section 9.5. A parallel structure, but with same-subject marked on a bound pronoun, is found in the Oceanic language Lenakel. Lenakel also differs from Kaingang in that the controlling clause follows rather than precedes the switch-reference-marked clause; the same-subject pronoun is called 'echo-subject':

(8.36) Lenakel (Southern Oceanic, Austronesian, Vanuatu; Lynch 1983: 212)
    i. r-im-va   m-im-augin
      3SG-PAST-come SS-PAST-eat
      'He came and ate'
    ii. r-im-va   r-im-augin
      3SG-PAST-come 3SG-PAST-eat
      'He$_i$ came and he$_j$ ate'

A very similar structure has been demonstrated above, in example (8.31) from Bafut. Another analogous system is decribed for Central Yup'ik (Eskimo-Aleut, Alaska, USA) by Woodbury 1983; this language distinguishes between plain third person bound pronouns and reflexive, or coreferential, third person bound pronouns conveying coreference to the Principal of a superordinate clause.

Another example of a language encoding something quite similar to plus or minus topicality in bound pronouns is Caddo (Caddoan, Oklahoma, USA). According to Chafe's (1990b) description, Caddo has specialized 'defocusing'-bound pronouns used to mention referents that currently fall out of the focus of attention, in contrast to regular third person bound pronouns referring to focused participants. Chafe terms the cognitive status of such referents 'non-protagonist', but from his discussion it is clear that generally this is a narrow, rather than a broad, domain characteristic, as the statuses of protagonist and non-protagonist can shift back and forth between referents on a local basis (pp. 60–61).

We can thus conclude that the difference of switch-reference to logophoricity is not in the site of expression (verb inflection vs. pronouns), as is sometimes assumed. Rather the difference is in the character of the current sorting employed: subjecthood (or topicality) vs. being a mental source. In accordance with that, switch-reference and logophoricity are primarily observed in different types of constructions: clause chains and complement constructions, respectively. As has been argued above, both sortings are discourse, rather than syntactically, based. For both kinds of sorting a wide range of possible sites of marking are attested, although it is true that logophoricity most often is realized on pronouns and switch-reference as a verbal category.

Once thought to be an attribute of exotic languages, switch-reference in a basic form can be seen in European languages. Verb forms such as converbs, or adverbial participles, or gerunds, are nothing other than ss-marked verbs. An English structure such as *Having written the letter, John went to the post office* is a same-subject construction. Of course, English does not have a specialized different-subject form.

Originally identified in some North American languages (Jacobsen 1967), switch-reference turned out to be among the most widespread referential aids. Switch-reference systems are often found in languages of all continents. They are widely attested in the languages of North America (Jacobsen 1983, Mithun 1993, Watkins 1993) and Australia (Austin 1981). An exceptionally thorough study of switch-reference phenomena in Papuan (non-Austronesian) languages of Papua New Guinea (that is, the eastern part of New Guinea) is provided in Roberts (1997). Roberts suggests that the subset of Papuan languages displaying switch-reference correlates with the extent of the putative Trans-New Guinea phylum. Switch-reference is rare among the Austronesian languages, but see Lynch (1983). Some examples of switch-reference are found in South America; see Cole (1983), Longacre (1983b), Wiesemann (1986a). Similar phenomena are widely reported in Africa; see Wiesemann (1982, 1986a).

Switch-reference systems are widespread among the languages of the putative Altaic phylum; see Čeremisina (1977, 1978) and Bergelson and Kibrik (1995). This concerns all major language families included in Altaic: Tungusic – see Gorelova (1980), Brodskaja (1988), Malchukov (2006); Mongolic – see Skribnik (1980, 1988); Turkic – see Efremov (1980), Bergelson and Kibrik (1987, 1995),[9] Nevskaja (1993). Rarer discussions of switch-reference-type phenomena in other languages of Eurasia include studies on Nakh-Daghestanian (Nichols

---

[9] The Russian-language publications by Bergelson and Kibrik (1987) and the English translation in Bergelson and Kibrik (1995) contain a detailed typologically-oriented account of a developed switch-reference system in Tuvan, a Turkic language of southern Siberia; see also Kibrik (2002b).

1983), Himalayish (Genetti 1994), Japanese (Myhill and Hibiya 1988, Iwasaki 1992: Ch. 4).

A variety of typological and language-specific studies of switch-reference and related phenomena are found in Munro (1980), Haiman and Munro (ed.) (1983), Austin (1988), Wiesemann (ed.) (1986), Stirling (1993).[10]

8.6.3 *Degree of activation*

In Chapter 5, section 5.2, we have considered the case of Mandarin Chinese that chooses between zero reference and third person pronouns on the basis of differing levels of referent activation. Within the framework introduced in this chapter this can be interpreted as a current sorting of a narrow domain. This kind of current sorting is attested in a number of other languages as well. One example, involving an opposition between two overt referential devices, is found in Russian, where the distal demonstrative *tot* (masculine; feminine *ta*, plural *te*) 'that', in its nominal (rather than adnominal) usage is applied to referents of relatively low activation, whereas the third person pronoun *on* applies to referents that have higher activation. Consider two typical examples of *tot* from Russian newspapers:

(8.37) Russian (from a search in Russian National Corpus, ruscorpora.yandex.ru)
    a. Los'   napal   na   vos'miletn-ego   mal'čik-a,
       moose.NOM$_m$ attacked upon eight.year.old-ACC boy-ACC$_b$
    b. kogda   tot   igral   v   sad-u   svo-ego
       when   that.NOM$_b$ played in garden-LOC REFL-GEN$_b$
       dom-a <...>
       house-GEN
       'The moose attacked an eight-year-old boy when he played in the garden of his house <...>'

---

[10] In the typological accounts of referential aids the notion 'switch-function', echoing 'switch-reference', also figures (Foley and Van Valin 1984: 354ff., Comrie 1989b). Foley and Van Valin, who introduced this term, apply it primarily to grammatical ways of indicating what is the role of the most activated referent in the current clause, such as voice. As I argued in Kibrik (1991: 74–75), 'switch-function' should not be considered among referential aids, such as switch-reference and obviation, because it does not help to distinguish between two concurrently activated referents but rather is oriented to one referent, maintained as the most activated one through a stretch of clauses. A similar point was made by Comrie (1989b: 42) who nevertheless chose to keep switch-function among his referent-tracking systems (=referential aids), but in a reinterpreted fashion. Comrie illustrates switch-function with a Dyirbal morpheme that indicates whether the given zero is coreferential to the pivot or to the non-pivot of the preceding clause. In this understanding switch-function certainly qualifies as a referential aid, but it is not notionally different from switch-reference, so I am not sure a special term is required.

(8.38) Russian (from a search in Russian National Corpus, ruscorpora.yandex.ru)
a. Bylo by kuda čestnee neizvestn-omu zloumyšlennik-u
were SBJV much more.honest unknown-DAT malefactor-DAT_m
razbirat'sja naprjamuju s prokuror-om_p,
sort.out directly with prosecutor-INSTR
b. koli tot ego čem obidel
if that.NOM_p he.ACC_m what.INSTR insulted
'It would be a lot more honest for the unknown malefactor to sort out things directly with the prosecutor, if he [=the prosecutor] insulted him with something'

Antecedents of *tot* in both of these examples occupy a less privileged position in their clauses (in terms of semantic and syntactic roles, as well as topicality) and presumably have lower activation by the beginning of the second clause compared to the competing referents that appeared in the subject, Principal, and topic positions. Note that this more activated referent is mentioned by the third person pronoun in (8.38b). (See Chapters 10, 11 on antecedents' syntactic and semantic roles, as activation factors.) Thus the uses of *tot* in the above examples can be explained on the basis of **lesser activation**. However, there is another interpretation of the usages of *tot* in examples (8.37) and (8.38), not necessarily incompatible with the first one. In both examples the antecedent appears towards the end of its clause, and at the moment of reference in the second clause the referent's activation is not only lesser but also recent or **fresh**.

In fact, the use of *tot* is regulated by the inclusive disjunction of two compatible but distinct properties: *tot* applies to a referent that is of lesser and/or fresh activation. Particular instances of *tot* occur on the basis of any or both of these properties. In addition to these current referents' properties, there is also a stable element in the usage of *tot*: its referent must be animate and is usually human; some instances of personified reference, for example to institutions, are attested. For more on the discourse functions of *tot* as a special device see Kibrik (1987a), Krejdlin and Chekhov (1988), and (Kresin 1998).

In order to verify the basis of referent sorting instantiated in the *tot* vs. *on* opposition I have run a pilot corpus-based study in which I analysed the first fifty occurrences of nominal *tot*, produced by a search[11] in the Russian

---

[11] I have searched only for the word form *tot* which is the nominative masculine singular form. The feminine and the plural forms are likely to yield similar results. Other case forms are rare for the usage of *tot* that interests us now. The distal demonstrative *tot* has a range of other usages, including

National Corpus (ruscorpora.yandex.ru). The great majority (90%) of these occurrences are characterized by the following combination of properties:

- The antecedent of *tot* appears in the immediately preceding clause.
- The antecedent plays a secondary semantic and syntactic role in its clause (non-Principal, non-subject).
- The antecedent appears at the end of its clause, that is, assumes a non-topic position (see e.g. Yokoyama (1986) on Russian word order).

Among these 90% that can be called the canonical usage, 70% of all occurrences have an additional set of properties associated with the competing referent (such as 'the moose' and 'the malefactor' in the examples above). This competing referent, also animate, appears in the same clause as the antecedent of *tot* and functions there as Principal and/or subject and topic. In other words, the dominant context of the use of *tot* can be described by the scheme *X verbed Y and Y (→tot) verbed*. The remaining 20% of instances differ in having more than one potentially competing referent, or having a competing referent further away, or having no obvious competing referent (for example because of the impersonal character of the antecedent clause).

Ten percent of all usages in the sample (that is, five in absolute numbers) deviate from the canonical pattern in various ways: in two instances the antecedent is a non-subject and a non-Principal, but is more topical (appears more to the left) than the competing referent; in one instance the antecedent is non-topical but is the subject and the Principal; in one instance an inessential clause intrudes between the antecedent clause and the *tot* clause. These exceptions do not alter the prototype. Finally, in one case the antecedent of *tot* and the competing referent appear in different clauses:

(8.39) Russian (spoken) (from a search in Russian National Corpus, ruscorpora.yandex.ru)
 a. Opjat' že kogda nas ministr sobiral
  again PTCL when we.ACC minister.NOM$_r$ assembled
 b. indijskij ministr informatik-i priezžal
  Indian minister.NOM$_i$ informatics-GEN visited
 c. nas rossijskij ministr sobiral.
  we.ACC Russian minister.NOM$_r$ assembled

---

adnominal usages, usages in relative constructions, collocations with particles, etc. According to the corpus search, the nominal usage that is relevant to this discussion accounts for 22% of all occurrences.

d. <u>Tot</u>   skazal <...>
   that.NOM_i   said

'Once again, when the minister assembled us (the Indian minister of informatics was visiting), the Russian minister assembled us. He [=the Indian minister] said: <...>'

It is noteworthy that this is the only example in the sample that comes from spontaneous spoken discourse. What happens here is that the referent of *tot* ('the Indian minister') is introduced in the parenthetical clause conveying background information that the speaker failed to verbalize in due time. This parenthetical clause is separated from the *tot* clause by another clause where the competing referent ('the Russian minister') is mentioned. By the beginning of clause (8.39d) 'the Russian minister' is clearly more activated than 'the Indian minister', and simultaneously the activation of 'the Indian minister' is fresher. Outside of the present sample, I have more examples of this kind.

This spontaneous spoken occurrence indicates that a rather general cognitive formulation, such as 'lesser and/or fresh activation' proposed above, is necessary for an adequate description of the function of *tot*. A much more concrete formulation, such as 'non-Principal and/or non-topic of the preceding clause' would be adequate if only canonical usages existed. Note that the canonical usage constitutes a particular, even though frequent, case within the cognitive formulation 'lesser and/or fresh activation', and is fully accountable in terms of this more general formulation.

An additional piece of evidence for the lesser activation character of *tot* comes from the following fact. *Tot* almost never has a third person pronoun as its antecedent. This means that highly activated referents are not mentioned by *tot*. In some rare instances third person antecedents are encountered, but then the competing referent invariably is also mentioned by a reduced referential device (pronoun or zero) in the same antecedent clause. In such instances both referents are quite highly activated, but still the competing referent exceeds the referent of *tot* in activation.

Before concluding the discussion of *tot* it is worth mentioning that in many discourse contexts both *on* and *tot* are applicable to the same referent. Ranges of activation that are appropriate for *on* and *tot* are not mutually exclusive but intersect. This can tentatively be depicted as shown in Figure 8.1. (Refer to Chapters 10–12 for a more detailed discussion of the notion of range of activation.)

So the activation requirements for *tot* are, first, that the minimal threshold where it becomes usable is lower than it is for *on* (this will be discussed in Chapter 9) and, second, *tot* is not applicable to highly activated referents.

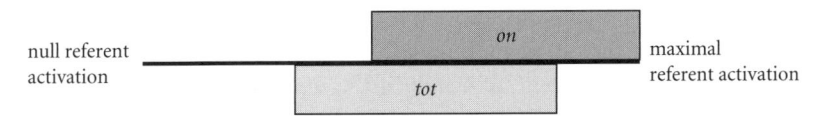

FIGURE 8.1. Ranges of activation appropriate for the Russian third person pronoun *on* and the lesser activation demonstrative *tot*

Interestingly, phenomena quite similar to Russian *tot* are found in other languages of northern Europe, including Slavic (Polish, see Wiemer 1997: 179–183), Germanic (German, see Wiemer 1997: 173–179, Bosch and Umbach 2006; Dutch, see Comrie 1994: 3–5), and Uralic (Finnish and Estonian, see Kaiser and Hiietam 2003). In all of these languages a demonstrative is used to refer to a lesser activated referent. There is clearly an areal pattern visible in this set of languages; it is likely that this shared pattern can be added to those found in the languages of the Circum-Baltic area (Dahl and Koptjevskaja-Tamm (eds.) 2001).

Degree of activation can also be encoded in bound pronouns. In the Mexican language Azoyú Tlapanec, discussed by Wichmann (2007), there is a system that he evaluates as intermediate between obviation and switch-reference. In this language, one pivotal referent of a clause (most often the Principal; see p. 804) can be assessed as being given vs. new by means of special morphology, primarily on bound pronouns attached to the verb, but also on other constituents. If the pivotal referent is mentioned by a full NP in the clause, it must be assessed as new. If a referent has been introduced in the preceding discourse and has some degree of activation, it is encoded by a bound pronoun alone. Most often, such referents are assessed as given. But if more than one referent has been mentioned in prior discourse, one of them can be assessed as less activated, that is new. In such instances this system can be functional in removing a referential conflict. In the following example the newly introduced referent 'Martín' is assessed as new in contrast to the discourse protagonist. The category 'given vs. new' is encoded primarily by tones (indicated by superscript numbers).

(8.40) Azoyú Tlapanec (Subtiaba-Tlapanec, Mexico; Wichmann 2007: 815)
 a. ne^2-hke^1 ga^2-^{ʔ}y-un^1 bisi^{2}ta^1 Ma^{3}rtiŋ^1
  PFV-go.3SG.GIVEN SBRD-do-PEG.3SG.GIVEN>3SG visit Martín
 b. ma^{1}ski^2 na-ya^{2}h-un^{ʔ3}
  although PROG-work-ERG.3SG.NEW
  'S/he went to visit Martín although he [=Martín] was working'

Wichmann (2007: 817–819) also shows evidence that in natural discourse the assessment 'given' is sometimes attributed to a discourse protagonist rather than another referent activated in the immediately preceding clause. This raises the question of whether the Tlapanec sorting is of a narrow or broad domain. I am inclined to believe that it is a narrow domain sorting, sensitive to the current referent's activation. A referent's protagonisthood is among the factors affecting a referent's activation at any moment in discourse; see Chapters 11 and 12. Overall, it appears that the Tlapanec system operates on the basis of quite short-lived referents' properties, even though protagonisthood can contribute to current activation.

Summary

Reference in discourse, in particular when it comes to reduced referential devices, may involve the situation of referential conflict: a referent different from the one intended by the speaker may be attributed to a referential device by an addressee. There is a wide range of linguistic resources that help to preclude referential conflicts. These are not referential devices per se but rather supplementary linguistic devices that help to tell potentially conflicting referents apart. In this chapter we have reviewed the cross-linguistically attested types of referential aids, or deconflicters.

The classification of referential aids is fairly complex, and it is summarized in an arboreal representation in Figure 8.2.

The highest level distinction is between the ad hoc and conventional referential aids. Ad hoc referential aids are based on highly specific semantic contexts provided by clauses, in conjunction with all available encyclopedic

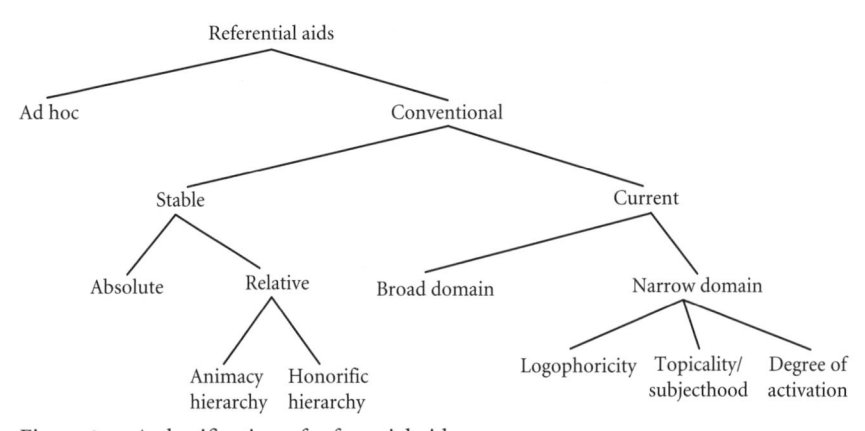

Figure 8.2. A classification of referential aids

information. It is often the case that, among the activated referents, only one matches the meaning of the clause it belongs to, whereas other activated referents are incompatible with this context. Many instances of theoretically possible referential conflicts are precluded due to ad hoc referential aids.

Conversely, conventional referential aids are lexico-grammatical devices that sort referents in one way or another, and can thus be called referent sortings. Among the conventional sortings, the major division is between stable and current ones.

Stable sortings are based on the cognitive process of categorization – ontological attribution of referents on the basis of their permanent features. Stable sortings are divided into absolute and relative ones. Absolute stable sortings treat referents on the basis of their membership in fixed categories. The primary grammatical system implementing this kind of sorting is noun class, or gender. Relative stable sortings are also based on categories, but what matters here is not just membership but a hierarchical relation between different categories. In particular, referents can be assessed as being higher or lower on an animacy or an honorific hierarchy.

Unlike the stable sortings, current sortings rely on the fact that concurrently activated referents may have different statuses in the interlocutors' current cognitive representation. I propose to tentatively classify current sortings on the basis of the discourse domain to which a given status pertains: broad vs. narrow. Broad domain current sortings are those related to discourse-wide referent characteristics, such as being a discourse protagonist. Narrow domain current sortings are based on more short-lived features, such as being or not being the mental source of a proposition; being or not being the subject or topic of an adjacent clause; having a higher or lower activation.

Apart from the type of referent sorting, another typological parameter is useful in describing particular referential aids: the site of marking, that is the type of constituent where the sorting is expressed. These are two independent typological parameters. In every type of sorting a variety of sites of marking are attested, including free pronouns, bound pronouns, verb base and verbal categories, and function words.

The fact that specific referent sortings contribute to referential choice does not automatically entail that this is what they exist for in languages. It may very well be that their contribution to reference is a side effect of their use for some other, inherent, purpose. For each of the conventional aids, what its basic function is must be explored specifically. In the following chapter the question of referential aids' functionality is discussed.

9

How functional are referential aids?

Overview

How functional are referential aids? It must be a priori obvious that the functional contribution of referential aids to referential choice is relatively modest in comparison to the activation-based choice between full and reduced referential devices. This is obvious since much of reference in discourse proceeds independently of referential conflict, for example if just one referent is currently activated. But it should not be nought either, as instances of referential conflict do occur in natural discourse.

The goal of this chapter is to assess several aspects of how conventional referential aids function in discourse. First, all languages have a functional need to preclude referential conflicts. How many conventional referential aids must a language have to satisfy this need? Do some languages put most of the load on one device, and other languages split it evenly between several? These questions are addressed in section 9.1. Section 9.2 deals with the varying placement of referent sortings in a clause, introduced as a typological parameter in Chapter 8. The question here is whether the site of expression chosen by the given referent sorting affects its functioning in discourse. In section 9.3 I address the functional bases of several kinds of referent sortings, both stable and current. Specifically, the question explored is: do referent sortings evolve in languages for the relieving of referential conflict, or, alternatively, do they evolve for other reasons such that their use as referential aids is a rather opportunistic one?

Sections 9.4 and 9.5 are case studies devoted to two related West African languages belonging to the Atlantic family: Pulaar and Sereer. Both of these languages have rather extensive noun class systems, but are very different in whether they use noun class as a referential aid. These case studies indicate that connections between referent sortings available in a language and their referential implementation are not rigid and deterministic.

9.1 How many referent sortings in one language?

As has already been noted in Chapter 8, Heath (1975) proposed that linguistic devices as diverse as switch-reference and noun classes are cofunctional in some way: they conspire at the cross-linguistic scene and within individual languages in the general task of ambiguity avoidance. It is worth noting that this idea, in a more general vein, circulated in linguistics even earlier. In particular, Nikolaeva (2000: 192ff.) discusses the so-called 'compensatory law of Peškovskij–Makaev', attributed to the works of two Russian scholars, A. M. Peškovskij and E. A. Makaev, both published in 1956. This law suggests that diverse linguistic devices may cooperate in fulfilling a certain function, as for example conjunctions, word order, and intonation all contribute to encoding interclausal relations.

Heath (1975) went even further and suggested (p. 103) that the amount of switch-reference-type phenomena in a language is inversely proportional to the amount of noun-class-type taxonomy. This suggestion may implicitly mean that there is a certain universal constant – a need for referential conflict preclusion. The main question of this section is whether the existence of such a constant is supported by the facts. Further questions include: How many conventional referential aids may languages use? How homogeneous are languages in this respect? Do some languages highlight one conventional aid while other languages engage several, giving each a certain load?

Some languages have been claimed to have little or none of the conventional referential aids; specifically, this has been proposed with respect to languages of East and Southeast Asia, such as Mandarin and Japanese, by Van Valin (1987). According to Van Valin, these languages rely on pragmatic inference alone to avoid referential conflicts, that is, in my terms, use only ad hoc referential aids. In fact, the situation in these languages may be a bit less extreme. As has been discussed above, Mandarin does use some conventional referential aids: the opposition between zero and third person pronominal reference is based on a current sorting between more and less activated referents (see sections 5.1 and 8.6.3), as well as long-distance reflexives (Huang 2000: 90–130, 190–199). Nariyama (2003) argues in detail that Japanese has a variety of conventional referential aids, contrary to Van Valin's suggestions. Nevertheless, Van Valin's observation still holds, if couched in a more conservative way: some languages make an apparently lesser use of conventional referential aids compared to other languages. If the tentative universal constant need for deconflicting devices is real, then the referential aids between which it is split must include not only conventional but also ad hoc referential aids.

In contrast to Mandarin-type languages, relatively impoverished in the use of conventional referential aids, other languages display a wide range of conventional aids. For example, a Western Grassfields Bantoid language Mundani has been shown by Parker (1986) to possess at least three kinds of token conventional referential aids: noun class-marked pronouns, logophoric pronouns, and switch-reference marked on free and bound pronouns. In addition, all these kinds of pronouns are in a certain distribution with classless pronouns, zero reference, and long-distance reflexives. Instances of classless, class-marked, logophoric, different-subject and same-subject pronouns are all found in the following short excerpt from a folk story:

(9.1) Mundani (Bantoid, Benue-Congo, Cameroon; Parker 1986: 157–158)
a. etsə́'   é   tsī   bɔ́   kɨ'ɨ.
   night CL.3.SUBJ POSS.no.longer they POSS.come

b. tá   nè̂   tsí' yé   bɨ-à   ń-tsáà   ábū
   he.DS that wait LOG be.first-IMPFV HORT.SS-send   arm
   ází   ábèm.
   ASSOC.REFL   inside

'The next day they arrived. He [=Tortoise] said that he will put his hand inside first.'

Such a spectacular gamut of conventional aids within one language casts doubt on the hypothesis that languages are somehow internally harmonized with respect to the number and relative load of various aids. Rather the Mundani case hints that these various devices may have other functions and they simply happen to all be occasionally useful for the preclusion of referential conflicts. Mandarin-type languages, in contrast, do get along without multiple conventional aids, resorting to ad hoc aids. It appears that languages may respond very differently to the same pragmatic need, and such response is hardly deterministic.

The existence of something like a universal constant need for disambiguation is further put into doubt by the fact that various languages rely on referential aids to a varying extent. Languages such as Navajo (Chapter 8) or Sereer (section 9.5 below) are strongly inclined to the use of reduced referential devices and exploit referential aids at their disposal vigorously. If we use English as a cross-linguistic baseline, those languages use a lot more reduced devices and fewer full NPs. In contrast, other languages are much less prone to reduced devices. For example, the Nakh-Daghestanian language Archi (Russia) (A. E. Kibrik 1977b: 274ff.), though having more than one current referent sorting, including noun classes, tends to repeat full NPs where reduced devices might be expected in a language like English (Kibrik 1991: 82). In a related train of thought, Bickel (2003) suggests that some languages (or cultures) are more tolerant to referents' underdifferentiation than others; Stoll and Bickel (2009) compare two languages, Belhare (Kiranti, Sino-Tibetan, Nepal) and Russian and conclude that the speakers of the former much more frequently leave referents unidentified.[1] On a more general note, Gil (2005) argues that languages may have a different degree of complexity or, conversely, simplicity; if a language lacks a certain structural domain, it does not have to necessarily compensate for it in other domains.

All these considerations bring us to the conclusion that universalist claims about something like a constant concern for disambiguation that must be divided between several major conventional referential aids make a strong overstatement. Whereas Heath's ideas about cofunctionality of various linguistic devices for the sake of referential conflict preclusion proved very fruitful and led to a typology of referential aids, languages possess significant freedom in how many referential aids they use and how much they rely on conventional aids.

9.2 Site of expression and the functioning of referential aids

As we have seen in Chapter 8, one of the major parameters useful for a typology of referential aids is their site of expression. They can be expressed on referential devices as such (including free and bound pronouns) or on different constituents. Some aids, such as English gender, are structurally so much integrated with the referential device that some analysts fail to notice the distinction between the referring force of a pronoun and the sorting force of gender – a category that is marked on the pronoun. Other conventional aids, such as switch-reference marked by verb inflection, are structurally separate from referential devices. As for ad hoc aids, they are dispersed in a still larger domain – they are 'somewhere' in the clause and even beyond the clause, as encyclopedic information is also relevant for their functioning. This provokes a question: are various referential aids, differently placed vis-à-vis referential devices, equivalent or not in how they help to fight referential conflicts?

On the one hand, clause is an important unit of processing (Chafe 1994, Thompson and Couper-Kuhlen 2005, Kibrik and Podlesskaya 2006). In the course of referential choice, a speaker may assume that the addressee will integrate all information available in a clause and will resolve reference

---

[1] It appears though that the zero representation of referents, as described for Belhare by Stoll and Bickel, is of a different character than specific definite zero reference discussed in Chapter 3, section 3.4.

thereupon. If discourse production had only one level of granularity, all referent sortings would be fully equivalent. However, it is well known that processing is incremental (Levelt 1989) and various levels of granularity may be relevant. The temporal structure of processing can proceed at increments smaller than the clause. In this sense referent sortings expressed directly on pronouns are more efficient as they provide a referential clue immediately. In contrast, sortings that are stationed elsewhere in a clause and require the understanding of the whole clause before they can be put to use are less efficient.

The following research programme can be envisaged in this perspective. Cross-linguistic experiments, psycholinguistic or neurolinguistic, can be devised that would address the question: do referential aids expressed directly on referential devices provide a more rapid support to a listener or reader under referential conflict, or do they operate on a par with referential aids stationed elsewhere in a clause? A more fine-grained difference may be sought between languages expressing referent sortings on free vs. bound pronouns, the former being detached from the verb as the focal spot of clausal information, and the latter being verb affixes.

9.3 Functions of referent sortings

The research tradition stemming from Heath (1975) assumes that preclusion of referential conflicts is the functional basis for conventional aids such as noun class or switch-reference. In other words, noun class and switch-reference exist in languages because language users need to sort referents involved in referential conflicts. However, this belief is not obviously true. Provided that ad hoc referential aids often suffice to preclude referential conflicts, then many uses of conventional aids are evidently afunctional, at least with respect to referential conflict. Consider a mini-text such as the following: *John ordered a soup. He ate it very quickly.* Even though the context of the verb *ate* makes it clear which of the two activated referents is the subject and which the object (people eat soups, rather than vice versa), speakers of English keep using gender-specified pronouns in such instances. This raises the following question: is the preclusion of referential conflict the basic function of noun class, switch-reference, etc., or do they perhaps exist in languages for other reasons and are simply conveniently employed by speakers to preclude referential conflict, when needed?

There is some evidence suggesting that the functional need for referential deconflicting enhances the employment of referential aids. Helmbrecht (2004: 372–373) discusses the cross-linguistic implicational hierarchy 3<2<1 that summarizes the facts of how widely switch-reference, logophoric pronouns, and noun classes are spread in different persons. (Helmbrecht refers to Haiman and Munro 1983, Wiesemann 1986a, and Greenberg 1963 as the original sources where the generalizations were proposed.) This hierarchy means that referent sortings are most widely spread in the third person, less so in the second, and are most rare in the first. In a more detailed recent study, Siewierska (2005b) shows that out of 124 languages in her sample displaying noun class on free personal pronouns, only two languages have it in the first or second person but not in the third.

Such facts prove that the threat of referential conflict (being an issue in the third person but, normally, not in locutor persons) is an environment stimulating the applicability of referent sortings. However, they do not prove that preclusion of referential conflicts is the prime cause for the existence of referent sortings in languages. It is this last issue that I discuss in this section, looking in turn at several types of conventional referential aids. I examine whether switch-reference, degree-of-activation-based systems, and noun classes are dedicated referential aids or rather serve some other underlying function.

9.3.1 *Switch-reference*

Switch-reference was originally believed to be a purely coreference-oriented device, serving the role of 'reference-tracking', or preclusion of referential conflicts: 'The function of switch-reference systems is to avoid ambiguity of reference' (Haiman and Munro 1983: xi). However, during the last couple of decades a substantial amount of evidence has accumulated that calls this interpretation into question. Some authors have noted complications with the requirement of strict coreference underlying the original definition of switch-reference. Franklin (1983), Bergelson and Kibrik (1987, 1995), and Wilkins (1988), inter alia, pointed to deviations from precise identity between referents. (See also Carlson 1987: 16.)

In other studies more direct arguments against the traditional interpretation of switch-reference were raised, showing that in some languages the alleged switch-reference serves a more general function – presence or absence of discourse continuity, or, rather, degrees of continuity: high or low. Mithun (1993) suggested that in many cases it may be clause connectedness rather than coreference that is coded by same-subject markers. A particularly detailed argument towards this end is found in Stirling (1993). After reviewing a large body of literature on switch-reference from the 1960s through the early 1990s, Stirling concludes that 'it can be difficult to distinguish between grammatical devices whose primary role is to indicate reference relations, and those which have some other major function but which may incidentally also fill this role. This is not surprising given that ... there is an intimate association between anaphoric interpretations and other aspects of clause linkage' (p. 153).

One of the particularly detailed arguments of this sort belongs to Rising (1992) who describes the switch-reference system of Koasati, a Muskogean language. Morphologically, the core of the Koasati switch-reference system consists of two suffixes, -k (same-subject) and -n (different-subject), that can appear on inflected verbs. The final verb of a chain serves as a reference point, and non-final verbs get a switch-reference marking. Canonical examples of switch-reference usage can be illustrated by the following constructed sentences:

(9.2)   Koasati (Muskogean, Louisiana and Texas, USA; Rising 1992: 4)
   i. Joeka-k   roomkā   itcokhalihko-k Edkā   hihco-k   cokko:lit
      Joe-GIVEN   room.NEW   enter-SS   Ed.NEW   see-SS   sat.down
      'Joe came into the room, saw Ed, and sat down'
   ii. Joeka-k   roomkā   itcokhali:ko-n Edka-k   hihca-n   cokko:lit
       Joe-GIVEN room.NEW   enter-DS   Ed-GIVEN see-DS   sat.down
       'Joe came into the room, Ed saw him, and Joe sat down'

In (9.2i), the same-subject marker on both non-final verbs indicates that all three clauses have one and the same subject. In (9.2ii), both non-final verbs bear the different-subject marker, and in accordance with that subjects switch twice through this sequence of three clauses. Looking at a corpus of texts in which the -k and -n suffixes occurred 393 times altogether, Rising identified twenty instances (which makes 5%) when a non-canonical usage is found (Rising 1992: 12). The following is a natural discourse example of the putative same-subject marker in the context of a clear distinction between the two subjects:

(9.3)   Koasati (Muskogean, Louisiana and Texas, USA; Rising 1992: 53)[2]
   a. miita mo-k   ilma:ka-t   itcokkahka-k   fayahko-k
      other 3-GIVEN   come.PL-CONN[3]   ILL.enter.PL-SS   quit.PL.3.NEG-SS
   b. alotkaahosi-t   ano:ka-k
      be.fully.very-CONN   be.done-SS
   c. roomkasi-k   coki:boshcooli-skan
      room.DIM-GIVEN   be.big.3.NEG.DIM-CAUS
      'Other people did not stop coming and entering until the room was completely full since it was quite small'

---

[2] Rising provides different degrees of glossing detail for different examples.
[3] The suffix -t, glossed by Rising as CONN (connective), belongs to the same set as -k and -n and indicates 'the highest degree of continuity' between clauses, connects clauses 'in a very close relationship', and only appears in the situation of subject coreference (Rising 1992: 11, fn. 20).

What is crucial in this example is the putative same-subject marker on the verb 'quit' in (9.3a): this clause's subject is 'other people', and the next clause's 'the room'. Examples of the putative different-subject marker occur under subject coreference as well (Rising 1992: 55). Rising's explanation of these phenomena is that the -*k* and -*n* markers fundamentally designate thematic continuity, and referential continuity is but one instantiation of this more encompassing and general phenomenon. The other instantiation is found in exactly the same suffixes on nominals – there are actually multiple occurrences in examples (9.2) and (9.3). I have glossed these nominal uses of -*k* and -*n* as GIVEN and NEW, following the lead of Rising on p. 56.[4] Rising suggests that the SS and DS markers should better be understood as +continuity and −continuity, and glossed accordingly. In particular, the +continuity marker in (9.3a) conveys the idea that there is a close causal relationship between the clauses.

To recapitulate, +continuity is realized as action continuity, or inertia, when marked on verbs and as old, continuous, predictable information when marked on nouns; −continuity is realized as an unexpected, surprising course of events when marked on verbs, and as new, surprising, disruptive information when marked on nouns. In terms of frequency, +continuity verbal marking most of the time is realized in same-subject environments, and nominal marking appears on subjects; −continuity verbal marking usually occurs in different-subject contexts, and nominal marking appears on objects or obliques (Rising 1992: 56–58).[5]

Thus many systems interpreted as switch-reference have in fact a broader function related to event linkage, and identity vs. non-identity of subjects or other privileged participants across the clauses is just one facet of such linkage. Probably it is accurate to say that what is known as switch-reference has evolved and is kept in many languages for encoding event linkage rather then specifically for marking coreference vs. non-coreference. This, however, does not negate the observation that switch-reference markers are often instrumental as a referent sorting. Hands, as an anatomical feature of hominids, have evolved for handling tools and food, and this fact is not invalidated by the observation that we so often use them for gesturing or typing. Likewise,

---

[4] Rising glosses -*k* and -*n* as K and N which is not very illuminating.
[5] These formulations, sufficing for the present discussion, probably could better be rephrased in terms of semantic roles or pragmatic functions, as Rising has strong reservations regarding the applicability of the notion of subject to Koasati (pp. 26–27).

9.3.2 The current sorting based on the degree of activation

In subsection 8.6.3 of the preceding chapter we looked in some detail at a current sorting instantiated in the Russian nominal demonstrative *tot*, opposed to the third person pronoun *on* on the basis of degree of activation (and also freshness of activation). *Tot* is used for mentioning referents that are less and/or freshly activated. Like other referent sortings, *tot* constitutes a referential aid and can effectively contribute to the preclusion of referential conflicts. However, as in the cases of switch-reference, the following question emerges: is the deconflicting function the primary one for *tot*, or is it a concomitant effect of its use, which is based simply on differing activation levels?

One way to approach this question is to look at a body of occurrences and see how often *tot* actually contributes to deconflicting. By way of a pilot study, I am using the same sample of fifty occurrences from the Russian National Corpus as was used in subsection 8.6.3. The crucial question that I assess, relying on my native speaker's intuition, was whether substituting an appropriate form of the third person pronoun *on* instead of *tot* leads to a satisfactory (on all counts) or non-satisfactory structure. If the structure is satisfactory, that testifies that *tot* does not aid in precluding a referential conflict, and if not, then *tot* probably is instrumental as a referential aid. The fifty occurrences broke down into several types as follows:

(1) in 9 instances *on* is inappropriate (and thus *tot* was necessary) for the clear reason that the referent had too low an activation[6];
(2) in 7 instances no referential conflict could be envisaged as there is no competing referent in the reasonable vicinity in prior discourse;
(3) in 27 instances referent activation is sufficient for using *on*, and *on* actually could be used, while referential conflict remained precluded due to the operation of various referential aids, including:

---

[6] Identifying instances when activation is too low for using a third person pronoun is actually quite straightforward. For example, if a referent is an inanimate that has just occurred for the first time at the end of the previous clause, or if a totally new referent occurred in a peripheral syntactic role, such as the possessor of an object, after a minimal training of one's intuition it becomes immediately obvious that such contexts make the use of *on* ruled out on the basis of low activation. When this was not obvious the corresponding examples were attributed to type 3 or 4.

a. conventional – 11, including:
   i. gender – 2
   ii. number – 7
   iii. person – 2
b. ad hoc – 16, including:
   i. 9 instances when the clause context easily precludes referential conflict, and thus using *on* is perfectly satisfactory;
   ii. 7 instances when the clause context could preclude referential conflict, but rather difficult reasoning was required, and thus *tot* is judged the preferred referential device, compared to *on*;
(4) in 7 instances referential conflict is precluded specifically with the help of *tot*.

In type 1 and 2 occurrences (16 altogether), there is no point in asking the question of the suitability of *on*, as it is immediately clear that in all these instances *tot* is used irrespective of the issue of referential conflict. The experimental substitution of *on* is relevant in types 3 and 4, together making up 34 occurrences. These 34 occurrences form the set of diagnostic instances in which the suitability of *on* would tell us if *tot* is related or unrelated to the preclusion of referential conflicts. In all of these examples referents mentioned by *tot* are in fact sufficiently activated for being referred to by *on*, so if *on* is inappropriate this must be due to an otherwise preserved referential conflict.

Type 4, including seven instances, are those cases when *tot* is clearly functional with respect to deconflicting. Consider an example of this type:

(9.4) Russian (from a search in Russian National Corpus, ruscorpora.yandex.ru)
a. Barmen   povël   glaz-ami   vlevo,
   barman.NOM   moved   eye-INSTR.PL   to.left
b. i   my   ponjali,
   and   we.NOM   understood
c. čto   nas   ugoščaet   neznakomyj   zdorovennyj   nemec.
   that   we.ACC   treats   unfamiliar   bulky   German
d. Tot   ulybalsja
   that.NOM   smiled
e. i,   pripodnja-v   rjumk-u,   smotrel   otkryto   i   po-dobromu.
   and   lift-CONV   glass-ACC   watched   openly   and   kindly
   'The barman pointed with his eyes to the left and we understood that we were being treated by an unfamiliar bulky German. He [=the German] was smiling and, having lifted his glass, was watching openly and kindly.'

In this example, using *on* instead of *tot* would preserve the referential conflict between the intended referent 'the German' and the competing referent 'the barman'. In contrast, using *tot* unequivocally singles out 'the German' as the less and freshly activated referent.

In type 3b-ii, containing another seven usages, *tot* also contributes to deconflicting; without it processing becomes noticeably more complicated, even though still possible; example (8.38) cited in Chapter 8 belongs to this type. In this type of usage *tot* can be judged to be used at least partly due to its function as a deconflicting device.

The remaining types 3a and 3b-i are those in which referential conflict is happily precluded irrespective of *tot*, and one may suppose that in these instances *tot* is used regardless of its deconflicting potential. Type 3b-i can be illustrated by example (8.37) in Chapter 8; in this case referent activation suffices for using *on*, and referential conflict is easily precluded due to the clausal context, so this use of *tot* is afunctional with respect to referential conflict. In order to see the role of conventional referent sortings (type 3a) consider the following set of constructed examples:

(9.5) Russian
    i. Ivan sobiralsja pogovorit' v sredu s Aleksandrom.
       Ivan$_I$ was.going to.talk on Wednesday to Alexander$_A$.
       No {tot ~ $^?$on} neožidanno zabolel.
       But {that$_A$ ~ he$_{I?A?}$} unexpectedly fell.ill.
    ii. Marija sobiralas' pogovorit' v sredu s Aleksandrom.
       Mary was.going to.talk on Wednesday to Alexander$_A$.
       No {tot ~ on} neožidanno zabolel.
       But {that$_A$ ~ he$_A$} unexpectedly fell.ill.
    iii. Kollegi sobiralis' pogovorit' v sredu s Aleksandrom.
       Colleagues were.going to.talk on Wednesday to Alexander$_A$.
       No {tot ~ on} neožidanno zabolel.
       But {that$_A$ ~ he$_A$} unexpectedly fell.ill.
    iv. Ja sobiralsja pogovorit' v sredu s Aleksandrom.
       I was.going to.talk on Wednesday to Alexander$_A$.
       No {tot ~ on} neožidanno zabolel.
       But {that$_A$ ~ he$_A$} unexpectedly fell.ill.

In all of these experimental examples what matters is the reference in the second clause to 'Alexander', which is the lesser and more freshly activated referent. In all examples using *tot* is perfectly okay, as the referent exactly qualifies for being mentioned by this specialized device. What differs is the suitability of the third person pronoun *on*. In (9.5i), where the competing referent is, as well as 'Alexander', a third person singular masculine, using *on* is questionable as it can correspond to either referent with an approximately equal likelihood. In contrast, in (9.5ii–iv) the competing referent differs from 'Alexander' in one of the stable sorting features: in (9.5ii) in gender, in (9.5iii) in number, and in (9.5iv) in person. As a result, in all three situations referential conflict is precluded, and this leads to one and the same result: *on* is as felicitous as is *tot*. This indicates that the unsuitability of *on* in (9.5i) is due not to insufficient referent activation but precisely to the retention of referential conflict.

The conclusion from this pilot study is that *tot* was used functionally with respect to the preclusion of referential conflicts in maximally 14 instances out of fifty, which makes 28%. Most uses of *tot* are simply based on the properties of a referent in question. If a referent meets the requirements of lesser and/or fresh activation, then *tot* may be used by the speaker. In these instances the speaker's decision to use *tot* or *on* is driven by subtle factors, such as willingness to highlight the referent's lesser activation. However, if there is a referential conflict, not precluded by other referential aids, between the intended referent and another referent, then the sutuation is totally different: the use of *tot* becomes not optional but indispensable for getting rid of the otherwise preserved referential conflict.

Analogous observations have been made by researchers regarding other similar current sortings. For example, despite the active use of the proximate vs. obviative distinction for referential conflict preclusion, experts in Algonquian languages usually judge it unlikely that deconflicting is the prime reason why this distinction has emerged. As is pointed out by Valentine (2001: 637), the proximate vs. obviative distinction essentially serves as 'a powerful foregrounding and backgrounding device, allowing storytellers to align their perspective and empathy with particular characters in a narrative'.

9.3.3 *Noun classes*

Given that noun class distinctions can be so handy in aiding referential processes, one can suspect that this is why they have evolved in many human languages. Corbett (1991: 320–322), in his brief discussion of the functions of noun classes, gives most attention to the referential disambiguation function. Contribution to referential processes is also indicated among the functions of noun classes by Aikhenvald (2000: 329). Seifart (2005: 281–283, 289) remarks that speakers of Miraña, a heavily noun class-marking language, may use specific markers in the cases of ambiguity and general class markers when there is no ambiguity. This suggests that noun classes are indeed functional with respect to referential processes. But this does not prove that preclusion of referential conflict is the leading motivation for the existence of noun classes.

In chapter 12 of her book, Aikhenvald (2000) surveys a much broader range of functions served by noun classes (as well as of other kinds of classificatory systems), among which the referential function is only one out of many. From Aikhenvald's survey a general conclusion emerges that noun classes (and other stable classifications) are primarily related in their function to categorization of reality. See also the related suggestions by Grinevald Craig (1986) (on Jakaltek) and by Wilkins (2000) (on Arrernte), mentioned in Chapter 4 (subsection 4.2.2), that classifiers in these languages have ethnoculturally-oriented categorization as their prime function.

One way to assess how important the deconflicting function is for noun classes is to see how often languages with noun classes express them in pronouns. Indeed, languages that have noun classes typically do distinguish them in pronouns, in particular in third person pronouns. In some languages, such as English, third person pronouns are the only site where noun class (gender) is marked; this kind of system, however, is very rare (Corbett 2005a: 126). Much more common is a converse type: languages that do possess noun class but do not use it in free pronouns. To see this, let us combine the WALS studies by Corbett (2005a) and Siewierska (2005b). Among the 188 languages shared by the samples of the two studies, there are 109 languages that have no noun class whatsoever and 74 languages that do have a noun class distinction.[7] Only the latter group is relevant for us at this point. Out of these 74 languages, 16 (that is, about 22%) do have noun class but do not express it in free pronouns. This may be partly due to some of these languages using bound pronouns or zero reference rather than free pronouns, or perhaps to some languages having noun class-marked demonstratives that are not considered third person pronouns. Still the sizeable character of this group cannot be neglected. In section 9.5 we will look at Sereer, a language that does have an extensive system of noun classes but fails to employ it for referential purposes.

As for the languages that do express noun class on reduced referential devices, it is not necessarily the case that this feature is very often helpful in the preclusion of referential conflicts. In section 9.4 I analyse Pulaar, a language with a large system of noun classes that are expressed on pronouns but often fail to contribute to fighting referential conflicts. The main reason for

---

[7] There are also five languages that were evidently interpreted differently by Corbett and Siewierska, as Corbett lists them among languages without gender while Siewierska characterizes them as having some kind of gender in free pronouns.

this is that Pulaar does not provide any class distinctions between human referents. As human referents are the ones most often mentioned by reduced referential devices and hence most prone to creating referential conflicts, even a sophisticated noun classification proves idle as a deconflicting device if it does not distinguish between subtypes of human referents. This situation is not rare among the world's languages. According to Corbett (2005b), out of the 112 languages with noun class in his sample one quarter (28) of the systems are non-sex-based. Among these, there is usually a human class but sometimes there is a single class for all animates or even all living beings, including plants.

Overall, it appears that the prime function of noun classification is some kind of categorization of reality, an ethnocultural taxonomy. (Of course this is less easily demonstrable for languages with 'formal' systems in which grounds for classification are less transparent or intransparent; see Corbett 1991: Ch. 3.) When such categorization is in place, most languages use it as a handy referential aid. But this use is not fundamental to noun classes, it is rather an opportunistic device that languages tend to employ to fight referential conflict but do not have to.

The analysis of several stable and current referent sortings offered above provides converging evidence that all referent sortings, usable as deconflicting devices, have different and in each individual case quite specific functions, and are not dedicated referential aids. Each of these devices plays a role in the respective languages that applies more generally than in the contexts of referential conflicts. Whenever the speaker needs to preclude a referential conflict an appropriate sorting can be opportunistically used as a deconflicting device.

9.4 Noun class and reference in Pulaar

This section is a case study in Pulaar-Fulfulde, a language with a ramified noun class system, used as a referential aid. Pulaar-Fulfulde belongs to the Senegalese, or Senegambian, branch of the Atlantic language family; for general treatments see Arnott (1970), Koval and Zubko (1986). Pulaar-Fulfulde is spoken in many countries of Sub-Saharan Africa, from Senegal and Guinea in the west to Sudan in the east. The Pulaar dialect, alternately called Fuuta-Tooro, is spoken by more than three million people in Senegal and the adjacent parts of Mauritania, Mali, Gambia, Guinea, and Guinea-Bissau. Pulaar-Fulfulde dialects, including Pulaar, are quite divergent and are sometimes considered separate languages.

Pulaar is a multi-noun-class language. There are 21 classes (Sylla 1982), 17 singular and 4 plural, and the class membership of a noun (and of the corresponding referent) determines its morphological, syntactic, and discourse properties. Each noun class is characterized by a specific noun class

348   III. Typology of Referential Aids

TABLE 9.1. Examples of Pulaar class-marked pronouns and related forms (classes O and NDI)

Class	O	NDI
Nominative pronoun	o	ndi
Accusative pronoun	mo	
Oblique (including possessive) pronoun	makko	mayri
Emphatic pronoun	kanko	kayri
Simple demonstrative (postpositive article)	oo	ndii
Extended demonstrative	oon	ndiin

marker, such as O, NDI, NGE,[8] and so forth. Markers appear in a variety of morphological and syntactic positions: one of their allomorphs typically appears as the suffix of the noun itself; they appear in attributes agreeing with the noun; they form the basis of definite articles, demonstratives, and various pronouns belonging to the given class, etc. Most centrally for the present discussion, nominative and accusative third person pronouns are based on noun class markers and most often coincide with them. Table 9.1 illustrates the most important pronominal and related forms, as exemplified by two singular classes: the human class O and the class NDI which includes, in particular, many terms for animals (Koval 1997: 178–180).

Illustrations in Table 9.1 give an idea of the morphology of class-marked pronouns. Most of the forms found in Table 9.1 will appear in certain examples below.

Reference in Pulaar discourse has been examined in several prior studies of mine, including Kibrik (1988: Ch. 4, 1991, 1992a). Only the information immediately relevant to the topic of this chapter is provided below; refer to the mentioned studies for further details.

9.4.1 Strength of noun classes as a referential aid

As is usually the case in the languages with noun classes (see Chapter 8, section 8.3), Pulaar noun classes are instrumental in discourse reference as a referential aid. Compare the following two constructed sentences[9]:

---

[8] Pulaar class markers are given in capitals, both in running text and in glosses. In examples, glosses indicate class attribution of pronouns, definite articles, and demonstratives.
[9] Unless otherwise indicated, Pulaar examples come from the work with my consultants, Usman Ka and Abdoulaye Ba.

(9.6) Pulaar (Atlantic, West Africa)
    i. nde   debbo   riiwi   nagge   to   galle   ndee, doktoor safri
       when woman_w drove cow_c to house when doctor treated
       {mo   /   nge}
       PRO_O.ACC_w   PRO_NGE_c
       'When the woman drove the cow home, the doctor treated {her / it}'
    ii. nde   baabiraaɗo oo   addi   suka   oo   ndee,
        when father_f   DEF_O brought child DEF_O_c when
        yummiraaɗo oo   noddi {mo   / oon ~ ɗum}
        mother   DEF_O called PRO_O.ACC_f EXDEM_O_c LOCAL.ACC_c
        'When the father brought the child home, the mother called {him_f / him_c}'

The difference between these two structures amounts to the following. When the two referents activated in the antecedent clause are distinct in their class membership, as in (9.6i), simple class (third person) pronouns are used in the second clause to perform reference. (Note that the human O class, unlike all other classes, has the dedicated accusative pronoun *mo*.) In contrast, when the two activated referents belong to the same class (O), as in (9.6ii), referential choice grows more complicated: if it is the subject of the antecedent clause that is intended, a simple pronoun still suffices to perform reference, but if the antecedent was a non-subject, then more peculiar forms need to be used to preclude referential conflict, such as the 'local' pronoun *ɗum* or the extended nominal demonstrative *oon* (see subsection 9.4.3 below on these referential devices).

Consider a natural discourse example illustrating the functioning of noun class as a referential aid. In this excerpt from a story two referents are activated, the man and the lion:

(9.7) Pulaar (Atlantic, West Africa; Gaden 1913: 174)
    a. ñannde kala   mbaroodi yaha,
       day   every   lion   go
    b. Ø wara   lella,
         kill   gazelle
    c. Ø addana   mo   o   ñaama.
         bring.to PRO_O.ACC PRO_O.NOM eat
    d. so   weeti[i],
       when   dawn
    e. ndi   yaha kadi,
       PRO_NDI go   again

f.	ndi	jagga	lella	walla	njawa,
	pro_NDI	grab	gazelle	or	red.antelope
g.	ndi	hela	koyɗe	mum,	
	pro_NDI	break	legs	its	
h.	ndi	roondoo,			
	pro_NDI	load.upon.one's.head			
i.	ndi	addana	mo.		
	pro_NDI	bring.to	pro_O.acc		

'Every day the lion goes, kills a gazelle, brings it to him [=the man] for he could eat. When it dawns, he goes again, he grabs a gazelle or a red antelope, he breaks its legs, he loads it upon his head, he brings it to him.'

This excerpt shows that, when two referents associated with different classes are activated through a substantially long stretch of discourse, class-marked pronouns suffice to perform reference and avoid referential conflicts. Much more extreme instances of class variability are found in Pulaar folk texts, especially those where various animals interact. In Kibrik (1991: 76–77) a discourse example is cited, where seven animals act in a series of events, coming into scene one after another, and in each case, except for one, class membership differs: NDI – BA – NDI – NGU – NDU – O – NGAL. A number of particularly striking examples of the referent-identifying force of noun classes in the Malian version of Pulaar-Fulfulde have been demonstrated by Koval (1999) who remarked (p. 235) that 'the diversity of class markers in each specific case assists the listener in successfully identifying the coreferential noun'.

9.4.2 *Weakness of noun classes as a referential aid*

Despite the strong potential of the jumbo noun class system of Pulaar, in many instances this system proves insufficient or irrelevant in terms of preclusion of referential conflicts. Of course, discourse often centres on the interaction of people. As has been already shown in example (9.6ii), when two or more activated referents are human, noun classes provide no clue to telling them apart, as all humans belong to the same class O. The following is an excerpt from an oral saga, told by a griot – a professional storyteller accompanying his speech by playing a lute. Before the beginning of this excerpt the most activated referent was the marabout (a Muslim sage and scholar) who was asked to settle a contention between the main characters.

(9.8) Pulaar (Atlantic, West Africa; Kibrik et al. 2005: 466–467)[10]

a. ♪(4.3) ↦o   wii   mawdo   guurdo   oo=/:
          PRO_O.NOM_m said   old   hale   DEF_O_o

b. ♪↘ "aan   suddi   suka   debbo   oo\?"
       you.EMPH   married young   woman   DEF_O_w

c. o   wii – "aha".
   PRO_O.NOM_o said   yes

d. ... o   wii – "mbate on   ɓooydaani/?"
        PRO_O.NOM_m said   what   you.folks   stay.long.NEG

e. ... o   wii – "min mbaddii   duuɓi jeedidi".
        PRO_O.NOM_o said we   spent.together years seven

f. ♪(2.7) o   wii – "ko   ceerdon   no   foti\?"
          PRO_O.NOM_m said since you.folks.parted   what equal

g. o   wii – >> "e   jooni   no   foti\?"
   PRO_O.NOM_m said   and   now   what equal

h. o   wii – "duuɓi jeedidi".
   PRO_O.NOM_o said   years   seven

i. ♪ o   wii – "nde   cuddataa   mo+
     PRO_O.NOM_m   said   when   you.were.marrying   PRO_O.ACC_w

j. hol   duuɓi   o   yaarata/?"
   how.many   years   PRO_O.NOM_w   reaches

k. o   wii – "duuɓi sappo e   joy."
   PRO_O.NOM_o said   years   ten   and   five

l. ♪(2.9) o   ƴeewi/ <···>
          PRO_O.NOM_m looked

'He [=the marabout] told the hale old man: "Is it you who married this young woman?" He said: "Yes." He said: "You folks [=the old man and the young woman] did not spend a long time together, did you?" He said: "We stayed together for seven years." He said: "How long ago did you folks part?", he [=the marabout] said: "Until now — how long is it?" He said: "It has been seven years."

---

[10] This example (as well as the following example) is taken from a study of spoken Pulaar that involved the construction of a fairly detailed discourse transcription. In this transcription system, boldface and arrows (↘, ↦) indicate tonal registers, italics the high tempo, the symbol ♪ a pause filled with music, etc.; refer to the original source for further details.

He said: "When you were marrying her, how old was she?" He said: "Fifteen years old." He made an estimate < ... >.'

In this excerpt a conversational exchange is recounted, in which the role of the speaker shifts from one character to the other ten times: the marabout and the old man are holding a dialogue. Every time the introductory phrase *o wii* 'he/she said' is used to introduce quoted speech. Obviously, the only kind of referential aids available here are ad hoc aids: in order to understand reference, the listener of the story is expected to very carefully match each entry of *o wii* to the context of the present and the preceding cue. Apart from the two characters involved in the conversation, the third one, 'the young woman' is also mentioned by the same class pronoun within the quoted speech.[11] This example clearly demonstrates that a large noun class system is not a cure-all solution for fighting referential conflicts.

Interestingly, in Pulaar folk texts, talking about the interaction of animals, personification sometimes takes place, resulting in non-differentiation of referents in terms of noun class. That is, even where two referents might be differentiated due to distinct class membership, they are still mentioned by pronouns of the same human class O.[12] (For an example see Kibrik 1992a: 8.) Thus language speakers sometimes waste the supposedly precious sorting resource.

Such facts challenge the hypothesis that deconflicting is the main function or is even among the central functions of noun classes. It is much more likely that noun classes exist in Pulaar for a different reason: they reify the folk taxonomy of the universe which is an important component of the sociocultural world view. The meticulous analysis of the semantics of one noun class after another, provided in Koval (1997), supports this point. Of course, this does not mean that noun classes cannot be used as a handy sorting device, when possible and when needed. We have seen this in example (9.7) above. But this is an improvised kind of use, and it is misleading to believe that fighting referential conflict is the prime function of noun classes.

---

[11] See also the example in Kibrik (1992a: 9) in which a conversation of three persons is reported, and each is introduced simply by the *o wii* phrase. This suggests that Pulaar speakers rely very heavily on ad hoc referential aids: resolving pronouns in case of three conversationalists is only possible if each of them can be identified from the content of quoted speech.

[12] According to Antonina Koval (personal communication), Pulaar (as well as other Pulaar-Fulfulde dialects) storytellers pronounce speech belonging to different animals in different voices (for example, low and hoarse voice for the hyena), and such alternation of voices is obligatory, almost as a grammatical rule; this apparently helps to ensure the identity of reported speakers.

9.4.3 Other conventional referential aids in Pulaar

Among the Pulaar noun classes, there is one that has a very special usage (along with other usages). This is the neuter class ƊUM. Pronouns of this class, in particular the accusative pronoun *ɗum* and the possessive (oblique) pronoun *muuɗum* (or *mum*), have a specialized usage that can be characterized as **local**. The nominative equivalent of *ɗum* and *muuɗum* is zero reference. Local referential devices are associated with referents that got activated within the given discourse passage (and, accordingly, were not activated immediately before it). In accordance with that, the first mention of a referent within a discourse passage is by means of a full NP, and subsequently by local devices (zero, *ɗum* and *muuɗum*). Within a given discourse passage, local devices cannot corefer to plain class pronouns, reserved for referents that were already activated by the beginning of the passage and thus operate across passages, non-locally.

Within a passage, reference by means of local referential devices sticks to the referent and is used throughout the passage, whereas plain class pronouns steadily apply to the referent that was already activated at the beginning of the passage. The two types of pronouns – plain class pronouns and local pronouns – thus have disjoint reference within a passage; we face here a peculiar current sorting on the basis of getting activated within vs. across discourse passages. Examples of local pronouns appeared above in (9.6ii) and (9.7b, c, g).

Within discourse passages, both plain class pronouns and local pronouns have the property of steadiness: once the speaker has started using one or the other kind of pronoun with respect to a given referent, he/she must go on, not switching to the other kind.[13] The steadiness of reference was first noted in another Pulaar-Fulfulde dialect by Arnott (1970: 153). Arnott defined the domain within which the principle of steadiness is observed as the sentence. However, the following spoken example demonstrates that a looser and larger domain, here defined as 'discourse passage', is relevant:

(9.9) Pulaar (Atlantic, West Africa; Kibrik et al. 2005: 446)
    a. ... yimɓe   (ɓee)   pokkitii,
         people   DEF_BEp departed

---

[13] The principle of steadiness is observed strictly in one direction and less so in the other. Sometimes a referent mentioned by several local pronouns is then judged as being more than locally important and shifts to plain pronominal reference. In contrast, a referent mentioned by plain class pronouns never shifts to local pronominal reference within a stretch of discourse in which it is continuously activated; to state this simply, a local pronoun never has a plain class pronoun as the immediate antecedent.

354   III. Typology of Referential Aids

b. Ø   na   njaha+
   LOCAL.NOMp COP   go

c. ↓kanko   o   ubbiti >>... suka   debbo   oo.
   PRO_O.EMPHm PRO_O.NOMm dug.out   young woman DEF_Ow

d. ♪ nde   o   heɓata   ɗum+
   when   PRO_O.NOMm reached   LOCAL.ACCw

e. Ø   seeɗa   maaya alla   e   leydi   ndii
   LOCAL.NOMw a.little   die   such   in ground   DEF_NDI
   wulde   e   teddude,
   heat   and   burden

f. ... o   watti   ngaska kaa,
       PRO_O.NOMm restored   pit   DEF_KA

g. no   wonnoo,
   as   had.been

h. ... ɓee-gaa   mbaali   e   janayse   tan+
        DEM_BEp-there   passed.night   in   remembrance   just

i. kamɓe   ɓe   mbaaloyi   koy
   PRO_BE.EMPHm+w PRO_BE.NOMm+w   passed.night.here PTCL
   dambordu.
   matrimony

j. ♪(10.7) o   soodani   ɗum   duufa-ñaafa <...>
            PRO_O.NOMm bought.for   LOCAL.ACCw   pound-munch

'They [=the people] left, they are walking, and as for him [=the young man], he dug out the young woman. When he reached her she was nearly dying, because of heat and burden in the ground, he restored the grave, as it had been before, those [=the people] spent the night in a remembrance ceremony, and as for them [=the young people], they spent the night here in a matrimonial ceremony. He bought for her "pound-and-munch" [=cola nuts] <...>.'

In this passage, 'the young man', the main participant, is steadily referred to by plain class pronouns (lines c, d, f, j). The less central referent, 'the young woman', first occurs in line (c) and is subsequently referred to by local devices alone (lines d, e, j). Still another referent, 'the people', is referred to by a full NP and a local device in lines (a) and (b), and by another device, a demonstrative, in line (h). (Also note the emphatic class pronouns, occurring with a subsequent plain pronoun, in lines (c) and (i).) As there is a sentence boundary[14] between lines (c) and (d), example (9.9) makes it clear that the domain of the steadiness principle is larger than a sentence and is kept through something like a discourse passage or an episode.

Apart from local pronouns, another current sorting device found in Pulaar is extended class-marked nominal demonstratives. They generally apply to referents that are less than fully activated; for an illustration see (9.6ii) above, see also Kibrik (1991: 78–79). This device is interesting in being a mixture of stable and current sortings: it is stable as it is class-marked and current in being oriented to less activated referents.

The phenomena discussed in this subsection further corroborate the point that a jumbo noun class system does not have to be the sole conventional referential aid in a language; other aids may have their own place as well. There is no determinism in the contribution of a noun class system to the preclusion of referential conflicts.

9.5 Noun class and reference in Sereer

In this section we look at Sereer, a language that also has a rather large noun class system, but does not use it as a referential aid. Sereer (alternatively Seereer, or Serer-Sine) belongs to the same Senegalese, or Senegambian, group of the Atlantic family as Pulaar, but the relationship between the two languages is not very close. Sereer is spoken in Senegal and Gambia by approximately 1.2 million people. On some aspects of Sereer that will be relevant here see Faye (1982, 1985), Crétois (1973), Mous (2007).

Sereer has 15 noun classes; see Diop-Fal (n.d.: ch. VIII), Pichl (1963). Noun classes are expressed in nominal constituents by a combination of a prepositive[15] (which is null in some classes) and a postpositive cliticial formant, and to the latter a definite or demonstrative morpheme may be attached. For example, for the classes O...OX and A...AL[16]:

---

[14] Establishing sentence boundaries in spoken language is notoriously problematic; see e.g. Kibrik (2008a). In the sample of spoken discourse cited here, sentence boundaries have been identified on the basis of systematic prosodic criteria and constitute a part of the Pulaar discourse transcription developed in Kibrik et al. 2005.

[15] The prepositive formant is variously interpreted as a prefix or a proclitic in different descriptions.

[16] Unlike Pulaar, in Sereer examples I do not indicate individual classes in glosses but rather use the generic gloss CL for all class-marked morphemes.

(9.10) Sereer (Atlantic, Senegal and Gambia)
　　　i. o　　　　koor　　　ox-e
　　　　PRECL　　man　　　POSTCL-DEF
　　　　'the man'
　　　ii. a　　　　cek　　　　al-eene
　　　　PRECL　　chicken　　POSTCL-DEM
　　　　'this chicken'

The prepositive formant is copied in agreeing adjectives and the postpositive formant is used in demonstratives. The crucial difference of the Sereer noun class system from that of Pulaar is that third person pronouns are not distinguished for class. The account of the Sereer referential system below is based on my previous studies in Kibrik (1988: Ch. 4, 1991, 1995).

There are two third person nominative pronouns that are not dependent on noun class in their use: *a* and *ta* (plural *da*). The accusative form, unlike the nominative, is not free but bound: it is the verb suffix -*(i)n*. The oblique third person pronoun is *ten* (plural *den*). Examples of nominative pronouns can be seen in (9.11), while the accusative and oblique pronouns will be illustrated below in (9.13).[17]

(9.11) Sereer (Atlantic, Senegal and Gambia)
　　　i. {a ~ ta}　moof　　no　　dek　　l-e
　　　　3　3　　　sat　　on　　chair　POSTCL-DEF
　　　　'He sat on the chair'
　　　ii. Ngoor　(a)　　moof　　no　　dek　　l-e
　　　　N.　　　3　　　sat　　　on　　chair　POSTCL-DEF
　　　　'Ngoor sat on the chair'

As (9.11ii) demonstrates, the third person nominative pronoun *a* is tenacious, although not fully. According to Crétois (1973: 3), when the clause subject is expressed by a full NP the pronoun *a* is normally present as well. This is also confirmed by the available discourse materials.

The distribution between the *a* and *ta* (*da*) pronouns is based on a current referent sorting. The pronoun *a* marks coreference to the subject of the preceding clause, and the pronoun *ta* (*da*) non-coreference. This can be seen in the following constructed examples:

---

[17] Unless otherwise indicated, Sereer examples come from the work with my consultant Saliu Dieng.

(9.12)   Sereer (Atlantic, Senegal and Gambia)
  i. Ngoor a   fad o   njac̓ onq-e,   a   y̓uf
     N.$_N$ 3.SS$_N$ hit PRECL boy   POSTCL-DEF$_b$ 3.SS$_N$ ran
     'Ngoor hit the boy and ran away'
  ii. Ngoor a   fad o   njac̓ onq-e,   ta   y̓uf
     N.$_N$ 3.SS$_N$ hit PRECL boy   POSTCL-DEF$_b$ 3.DS$_b$ ran
     'Ngoor hit the boy and he [=the boy] ran away'

Sereer thus uses a switch-reference-type current sorting, encoded on pronouns. To see the remarkable consistency with which this system operates in discourse, consider the following excerpt (somewhat abbreviated) from a story about a goat [=g] that was doing a hajj to Mecca and met a lion [=l] on the way.

(9.13)   Sereer (Atlantic, Senegal and Gambia; Diop-Fal n.d.: 216–218)
  a. a   cooxa   suk-fambe,
     3.SS$_l$ gave   goat$_g$
  b. ta   laq o   bay   ol-e <…> no ndog   onq-e,
     3.DS$_g$ hid PRECL hand POSTCL-DEF in calabash POSTCL-DEF
  c. a   soob   teen   soob   teen,
     3.SS$_g$ dipped   there   dipped   there
  d. boo   kiin   waagiran   o   jektir   fo   suum,
     for   someone   could.not   to   distinguish   from   honey
  e. ta   lay-n-ee:
     3.DS$_g$ said-3.ACC$_l$-that
  f. "ox-ene   koy <…> koo   ɗuudkan   rek!"
     POSTCL-DEM   PTCL   PTCL.you$_l$ swallow.it at.once
  g. ta   dal   fo   yaβat,
     3.DS$_l$ began   to   gape
  h. ta   naangam   no   ten   sabuux!
     3.DS$_g$ did   in   3.OBL$_l$ IDPH
  i. ta   ɗuudin <…>
     3.DS$_l$ swallowed.it
  j. a   lay: <…>
     3.SS$_l$ said
  k. ta   lay-n-ee   boo   "o   ɓat'u   sax".
     3.DS$_g$ said-3.ACC$_l$-that for   you$_l$ take.more   same

l. ta   dakwo   naang   wereet! <...>,
   3.DS₁   returned do   IDPH

m. a   cood-in,
   3.SS₁   passed-3.ACC_g

n. ta   soob   no   tiganam   k-e.
   3.DS_g dipped   in   thing   POSTCL-DEF

o. ta   nologilin,
   3.DS₁   gulped

p. a   nologilin <...>
   3.SS₁   gulped

'He [=the lion] gave the goat (a piece of skin), he [=the goat] hid his hand <...> in the calabash, he dipped it there repeatedly so that anyone could not distinguish it from honey, and told him: "This <...> you swallow in one go!" He [=the lion] started gaping, and he [=the goat] crammed it into him. He swallowed it <...> and said: <...> He [=the goat] told him that he should take more of the same thing. He [=the lion] went back to tear one more piece (of skin) <...>, passed it to him, he [=the goat] dipped it into that thing [=the calabash]. He [=the lion] gulped, he gulped <...>.'

The extent to which the Sereer current referent sorting is efficient as a deconflicting device can be appreciated due to the number of times one has to add a referential elucidation in the free English translation of (9.13). In the whole excerpt 'the lion' is not mentioned by a full NP at all, and 'the goat' only once in the first line. The current sorting largely operates on the linear basis: in line (e) 'the goat' is referred to by the different-subject pronoun *ta* because the previous clause (d), even though being subordinate to (c), had the non-referential subject 'someone, anyone'. Still quoted speech is skipped over when the choice between *a* and *ta* is made. In particular, in clause (g) 'the lion' is referred to by the different-subject pronoun *ta*, even though the same referent was the subject of quoted speech in line (f). The reason for the use of different-subject is that in (e) another referent, 'the goat', occurs as the subject.

The case of Sereer, especially in comparison to its relative Pulaar, again supports the lack of determinism in what referential aids are preferred in a language. Sereer possesses a noun class system that is comparable to that of Pulaar in its elaboration, but this system is entirely irrelevant for referential processes (beside the use of class-marked demonstratives). Contrary to possible expectations, Sereer strongly relies on a very different referential aid, the current sorting on the basis of subject (non-)coreference.

Is the Sereer opposition between two pronouns a dedicated referential aid, or, as other sortings considered above in this chapter, has it some other underlying function? This system has a higher chance of being a truly dedicated deconflicting device, compared to other widespread systems, such as noun classes or usual switch-reference. This suggestion is based on the fact that, first, this sorting is marked on referential devices (pronouns), and, second, the basis for sorting is referential in its nature (plus or minus coreference). This combination suggests that the basic function of this device is somehow connected to reference. However, this question remains for further research, both for this particular language and, cross-linguistically, for other comparable systems.

Summary

The evidence and reasoning presented in this chapter suggest that conventional referential aids play a visible but subsidiary role in referential processes as a whole. Languages are quite diverse in whether they have conventional referential aids, and if so, how many of them exist. Conventional referential aids (referent sortings), even though instrumental in precluding referential conflicts, evolve in languages for other reasons. Each sorting has its peculiar prime function. In particular, switch-reference systems appear to be primarily oriented towards encoding general connectedness between clauses, and their disambiguating force is a frequent but secondary employment. Noun classes are inherently designed to encode the ethnocultural system of categorization, and are used as deconflicters in an opportunistic way. None of the best studied referent sortings are dedicated referential aids, even though it cannot be excluded that such dedicated aids may be found.

Language users have the freedom to employ conventional referential aids for precluding referential conflicts to the extent needed, but often fail to use them even when they are available. This is apparently possible because the deconflicting function can easily be taken up by ad hoc aids. Conversely, referent sortings are often used in discourse where no need for deconflicting is observed.

Languages are not homogeneous in whether they employ a given referent sorting as a referential aid. Pulaar and Sereer are two related languages with comparable noun class systems, but whereas the former does use noun class as a significant referential aid, the latter does not: Sereer pronouns are not marked for noun class at all.

Overall, the concern for the preclusion of referential conflicts is of clearly secondary importance compared to the activation-related aspects of reduced referential devices, both in grammatical systems and in discourse use. At the same time, there is evidence that preclusion of referential conflict is among the forces that do influence referential choice on certain occasions.

Concluding remarks to Part III

Summarizing the two chapters comprising Part III, the main results are the following. Apart from the activation-based component of referential choice, there is another relevant component, here called referential conflict. When a referent is activated, and a speaker plans to use a reduced referential device, there is often a threat that a referent different from the intended one may be attributed to this reduced device by the addressee. A variety of linguistic resources are employed to preclude referential conflicts. A fairly complex classification of such resources, called referential aids, has been proposed. There is a difference between ad hoc and conventional (lexico-grammatical) aids, and the latter fall into many different types, according to the features stable vs. current, absolute vs. relative, broad vs. narrow domain. Conventional aids also differ with respect to the clause constituent where they are marked.

Preclusion of referential conflict is a subsidiary component of referential choice and, accordingly, referential aids play a more modest role in the referential process than referential devices. There is a great diversity across languages in how many referential aids they use and how they divide labour between them. There appear to be no or few dedicated referential aids – generally the linguistic resources functioning as conventional aids have other primary functions.

The chapters of this part supplement the typology of referential devices, provided in Part II. Appendix 1 contains a number of questions related to referential aids that should be elucidated in a complete descriptive account of any language.

Part IV
The Cognitive Multi-Factorial Approach to Referential Choice

Compared to Parts II and III, this part of the book zooms in on specific acts of referential choice that language speakers make in discourse. Whereas in the previous parts we were concerned with the question of what speakers choose from, in this part the research issue is **how** a certain choice is made. This part is based on the analysis of specific discourse samples containing numerous occurrences of referential devices.

I propose a cognitive multi-factorial (CMF) approach to referential choice, the main tenets of which are the following. Referential choice in discourse is **cognitively** motivated. If a referent enjoys a high level of activation in the speaker's working memory, a reduced referential device is used. Conversely, under a low activation a full device is used. Where does a referent's activation come from? Much of this part is devoted to **activation factors**, contributing to referents' current activation. Activation factors are **multiple**, and we are going to explore how they interact with each other in producing the aggregate activation score. Calculative and statistical methods will be presented that assess the factors' quantitative interaction.

The cognitive character of the proposed approach is not merely declarative, an attempt is made to ground it in the modern views of human cognitive processes, in the first place attention and working memory. Issues to be discussed include the relationships between attention and working memory and the linguistic manifestations of these processes. The functioning of attention and working memory in natural discourse can be illuminating with respect to these cognitive phenomena's basic features, so the cooperation between linguistics and cognitive science is mutually beneficial.

Studies reported in this part of the book primarily look into evidence from two languages, Russian and English. These studies can be regarded as a first attempt at an in-depth characterization of particular languages regarding their referential systems. In fact, the fine-grained analysis of the kind proposed here is possible only in regard to languages that are sufficiently well-studied and well-understood. Both of the languages under investigation have an extensive record of inquiry into the specifics of their referential choice. So the set of initial hypotheses regarding the factors that can be involved in referential choice is, in a sense, predefined. However, the CMF approach can easily be applied to other languages, provided that referential options are known and discourse data is available. One study of this kind, with respect to Japanese, has already been performed. A future typology of languages, involving sets of activation factors and their interactions, can thus be envisaged.

The CMF approach has accumulated a number of factual results and techniques, applicable to novel data sets. In accordance with these, the CMF approach is being elaborated in several directions, including the development of large-scale corpus data, machine learning-based modelling, and experimental testing.

10

The cognitive multi-factorial approach

Overview

Referential choice in discourse is generally believed to be a cognitively motivated process. However, the consensus is essentially limited to this very broad formulation, and there are many problems one needs to solve in order to propose a specific cognitively-based theory of referential choice. Among the most burning issues are: the specific character of the cognitive domain responsible for referential choice; the problem of circular reasoning; the multiplicity of factors affecting referential choice that need to be somehow reconciled (section 10.1).

There are many diverse ideas on what could be the specific cognitive domain responsible for referential choice. A linguistic theory of referential choice needs to be aware of the current views on such particularly relevant cognitive functions as attention and working memory; so a review of relevant psychological and neurophysiological literature is in order (section 10.2).

Section 10.3 presents my suggestions on linguistic implementations of attention and working memory, specifically their relatedness to reference and referential choice. Also I discuss some alternative cognitively-oriented treatments of referential choice.

Section 10.4 addresses the problem of circularity, recurrent in studies of discourse reference: one often infers the underlying cognitive status, explaining referential choice, on the basis of the actual choice made by a speaker. This problem can be solved by establishing factors of referential choice, entirely independent from the choice per se.

A great variety of factors affecting referential choice have been proposed in the literature. It is not clear which ones are really relevant and how they interact. A multi-factorial approach is proposed, bringing all potentially relevant factors within one picture (section 10.5). Finally, section 10.6 lists the main properties of the proposed Cognitive Multi-Factorial (CMF) approach to referential choice.

10.1 Cognitive analyses of reference: achievements and stumbling blocks

In a wide variety of linguistic, psycholinguistic, and computational approaches dealing with reference in discourse (Chafe 1974, 1994, Givón 1983a, 1993, Ariel 1988, Gundel et al. 1993, Cornish 1999, Garnham 2001, Gordon et al. 1993, Walker et al. (eds.) 1998, Poesio et al. 2004, Arnold 2008 inter alia) there is a common consensus that referential choice is fundamentally dependent on the referent's status in the cognitive system. The general idea is that a referent that is in some way more active in the speaker's (and addressee's) mind gets a more economical coding – in particular, by means of reduced referential devices, such as anaphoric pronouns and zeroes. The range of cognitive or quasi-cognitive notions recruited to specify this status is very broad: activation, memory, attention, focusing, consciousness, salience, prominence, accessibility, and so forth.

Most of these theories are cognitive in a general sense: they turn to some kind of mental phenomena in explaining linguistic phenomena. Such an approach is certainly better than trying to avoid mental explanations in linguistics, but still it is not literally cognitive in the sense of the 'cognitive commitment' (see Chapter 1, section 1.5; Lakoff 1990: 40) because the actual state of knowledge about relevant mental phenomena in the neighbouring disciplines (primarily cognitive psychology and cognitive neuroscience) is not consulted. In fact, uninformed use of cognitive terms (such as memory, attention, or consciousness) is rather vacuous. This presents the first stumbling block in the studies of reference: on the one hand, the need for a cognitive explanation is undeniable, on the other hand, a 'soft' cognitive explanation is not worth much. In order to avoid this stumbling block I attempt to ground my cognitive approach to reference on the positive knowledge about the relevant cognitive domains, available from **psychology** and **neuroscience**.

The second major stumbling block in the accounts of reference is that referential choice is explained in terms of referent activation (salience, accessibility, etc.), whereas the judgement on the relevant cognitive status is often based on the actual referential choices. Evidently, this approach is circular, and as a result the explanatory force of cognitive explanations is greatly decreased. One needs a way to establish referent activation independently of the actual referential choices. The approach proposed here satisfies this requirement. It is based on a set of factors, pertaining either to discourse context or to a referent's properties. These factors contribute to a referent's activation and are entirely **independent** of actual referential choices.

Individual factors of referential choice have been subject to analyses in various studies. In many of these studies quantitative relationships between a certain factor (such as distance to the antecedent) and referential choice have been noticed. The problem is that each factor accounts for only a part of the evidence, and remains silent with respect to the other part. To overcome this third stumbling block in reference-related research, I propose a **multi-factorial** approach. This approach not only acknowledges the existence of multiple activation factors but also incorporates a system of factors' interaction, so that their cumulative effect could be modelled.

My goal in this chapter is to present the essentials of a cognitive theory of reference and referential choice that is further elaborated and specified in the subsequent chapters of this part of the book.

10.2 Attention and working memory in cognitive psychology and cognitive neuroscience

As is argued below in detail, reference and referential choice are driven by general cognitive processes of attention and working memory. Therefore, a survey of these cognitive phenomena is in order.

Both attention and working memory belong to the most basic cognitive functions in humans and other species. Both of these notions have a long history of study in psychology. However, being complex and elusive, they still remain (and will certainly be for the foreseeable future) a matter of debate. During the early period of cognitive psychology, models of cognitive architectures were general enough to involve both attentional and memorial processes (Broadbent 1958, Atkinson and Shiffrin 1968). Later on, with specialization of different branches of cognitive psychology, the tendency was to consider these two processes independently of each other. Even though there is now a new tendency of synthesis, it makes sense to start off by separate accounts of attention and working memory. This is what subsections 10.2.1 and 10.2.2 look into, providing a concise review of attention and working memory research in cognitive psychology and specifically addressing varieties of each phenomenon, the question of capacity, and relationship to language. Working memory is discussed in somewhat greater detail, as it is more important for this book. In subsection 10.2.3 I discuss the mutual relations between attention and working memory, as conceived of by psychologists, and offer my cumulative understanding of the attention–working memory interface. In subsection 10.2.4 I proceed with a review of neural mechanisms of attention and working memory, as seen in modern cognitive neuroscience.

10.2.1 Attention

Defining attention is a notoriously difficult task. Perhaps the best way to get a feeling of what attention is is to consider several definitions, both classic and modern.

'Every one knows what attention is. It is the taking possession by the mind, in clear and vivid form, of one out of what seem several simultaneously possible objects or trains of thought. Focalization, concentration of consciousness are of its essence. It implies withdrawal from some things in order to deal effectively with others' (James 1890: 403–404). 'Attention can be seen both as an early sensory bottleneck and as a system for providing priority for motor acts, consciousness, and memory' (Faw 2003: 112). Attention is 'selection of stimuli for higher-level processing' (Cavanagh 2004: 16). 'Attention is not a unitary phenomenon. ... Attention is the emergent property of the cognitive system that allows it to successfully process some sources of information to the exclusion of others, in the service of achieving some goals to the exclusion of others' (Cohen et al. 2004: 71). Several reviews of attention studies appear in Parasuraman (eds.) (1984), Posner and Petersen (1990), Pashler (1998), Posner (ed.) (2004), Falikman (2006).

Psychological research in attention has become very compartmentalized. A number of attentional systems or functions have been found that are only remotely related to each other; see e.g. Posner and Petersen (1990). I mention but a few relevant parameters. First, Kahneman and Treisman (1984) classified attention studies into issues in divided attention and in focused, or selective, attention. It is the latter kind of attention that is relevant here. The most central idea about this relevant kind of attention is that it is a **limited capacity**, a selective process. Second, there is a well-known distinction between two kinds of attention: involuntary (triggered by external stimuli) and voluntary (driven by internal processes, such as intentions), introduced by James (1890). The kind of attention relevant in the subsequent discussion is **voluntary** attention resulting from motivational shifts in human online processing. Neurologically, this is Posner and Petersen's (1990) anterior attentional system (anterior cingulate cortex in the brain). Third, some authors make a distinction between object-based and space- or location-based attention (Levelt 1989, Carr 2004, Awh et al. 2006: 205). It is the **object** attention that will interest us here.

Since attention to objects is limited, the question of its capacity emerges: to how many items can attention be directed at one and the same time? It seems this issue has not been discussed as much as the working memory capacity (see below), but some authors mention the number of about four items (beginning with Wundt 1911 and recently by Cowan 2001, Cavanagh 2004: 24,

Treisman 2008); however, this assessment was questioned by some authors (McElree et al. 2003: 87). Among the set of selectively attended items there may be one that is superselective; this is what is called the **focus of attention** (attention focus, focal attention). This notion is equivalent to focal attention in vision research, that is opposed to ambient attention; see Velichkovsky et al. (2005).

Attention has been connected to linguistic functions in a variety of ways; for reviews see Logan (1995), Tomlin (1997), Myachykov and Posner (2005), Myachykov et al. (2005). A connection that is particularly relevant in the present context was proposed by Tomlin (1995) and suggests that the focus of attention is mapped onto the selection of clause subject in a number of languages. This idea will be discussed in detail in Chapter 13, section 13.3. Another hypothesis, namely that clefting (as in *It was his toothbrush that the traveller forgot to pack in the suitcase*) is a linguistic representation of attention focus, is critically evaluated in Foraker and McElree (2007).

10.2.2 *Working memory*

The notion of working memory (WM) is of a relatively recent descent in psychological science. Earlier terms, used in a very similar sense, include primary memory, short-term memory/store, and immediate memory (but see Cowan 2008 for a discussion of some distinctions between these terms). The term 'working memory' was originally proposed by Miller et al. (1960: 65) who introduced it in the following way: 'When we have decided to execute some particular Plan, it is probably put into some special state or place where it can be remembered while it is being executed. We would like to speak of the memory we use for the execution of our Plans as a kind of quick-access, "working memory".' In modern psychology, it is conventional to presume a distinction between WM and long-term memory. Glenberg (1997: 9ff.) is an example of a sceptical view of this distinction, but further comments by other experts in the same issue of the journal suggest that the distinction is being maintained by most researchers. The question of whether WM is a separate cognitive and neural structure or an activated substructure within the long-term memory (see e.g. Cowan 1995) remains debatable but does not bear on the discussion below.

The notion of WM was elaborated in the work of Atkinson and Shiffrin (1968)[1] and especially Baddeley and Hitch (1974) and Baddeley (1986). I would like to quote several definitions of WM borrowed from cognitive-psychological

---

[1] These authors actually used the term 'short-term memory'.

and neurophysiological literature. These definitions, taken in conjunction, probably would best characterize the rationale behind the notion of WM.

'Working memory is the theoretical construct that has come to be used in cognitive psychology to refer to the system or mechanism underlying the maintenance of task-relevant information during the performance of a cognitive task' (Shah and Miyake 1999: 1). 'The items in working memory are defined by a high level of activation, which enables reliable and rapid access to them' (Anderson 1990: 156). 'Any kind of information processing system that manipulates, integrates or analyzes information needs to have the ability to store the relevant information, the intermediate products and the results of manipulation at hand. Any kind of a system that needs to flexibly choose and execute behavioral plans needs to have the ability to hold that information online' (Repovš and Bresjanac 2006). 'Working memory allows individuals to maintain and manipulate a limited amount of information in an active state for a brief period of time. It can operate on a variety of cognitive representations, such as tastes, sounds, images, phonemes, concepts, locations, patterns, and colors' (Woodward et al. 2006: 317). 'Working memory is defined as a system that allows for temporary storage and maintenance of information. As working memory supports the interface between perception, action, and long-term memory it is an essential component of the cognitive system in humans as well as in animals. Much work has been done in order to identify the different sub-components of the working memory system' (Jensen 2006). 'WM is thought to be a limited-capacity system that enables a small number of items outside of focal attention to be maintained in a more accessible state than LTM [long-term memory – A.K.] representations, either because they are maintained in specialized storage structures ... or simply because that have residual activation from recent processing' (McElree 2001: 818). Several collections devoted to WM include Gathercole (ed.) (1996), Miyake and Shah (eds.) (1999), Schröger et al. (eds.) (2000), and issue 139.1 of the journal *Neuroscience* edited by Repovš and Bresjanac (2006).

The most influential model of WM, belonging to Baddeley (1986, 2007), distinguishes one master system, the so-called central executive that controls WM, two or more subordinate systems, responsible for maintenance of visuo-spatial and auditory information, and the episodic buffer that integrates information from different modalities. Subordinate systems are thought to each consist of a passive store and active rehearsal mechanism; information contained in the stores fades away quickly, unless being rehearsed. Views on the question of WM unity differ greatly – from unitary to very fractionated; this parallels the situation in attention studies.

The widely circulated assessment of the WM capacity, originally proposed by Miller (1956), is seven plus or minus two items. In more recent literature a more modest number, about four items, is usually cited; see e.g. Cowan (2001); as will be seen below, this hypothesis is more in line with linguistic evidence.

Despite the torrent of publications on WM, many aspects of it still remain hypothetical. Shah and Miyake (1999) enumerate the main research questions in WM. Among these, the most relevant to the further discussion are the following:

- How is WM related to attention?
- How does information enter (or, as psychologists often put it, get encoded into) WM?
- How is information in WM maintained?
- What is the capacity of WM, that is, how much information can it hold at one time?
- What causes forgetting from WM – simple decay or interference from newly incoming information?
- How is WM related to complex cognitive activities, such as language?

I will address these issues, in relation to referential processes, in subsection 10.3.2 and in Chapter 13. Here a comment is due about studies relating WM to language.

Much psychological work on WM is traditionally centred on verbal material. In many experiments the participants were asked to learn a list of words, and it was tested subsequently if they still have the list in their WM depending on additional loads on their WM, such as reading sequences of numbers out loud. The usual conclusion is that when a person is prevented from rehearsing words they get forgotten rapidly. In an influential psycholinguistic study, Daneman and Carpenter (1980) measured the verbal WM span by asking people to memorize and then repeat the last words of several unrelated sentences, heard one after another. These kinds of studies, even though they are based on verbal material, hardly shed any light on the relation between WM and language as they exploit verbal material in highly unnatural situations – not the situations that language is designed for. (In fact, psychological experiments with visual material seem to be more directly related to substantial linguistic questions about WM.) This does not mean, however, that studies playing with linguistic elements cannot tell us something important about the general properties of WM.

There is also a plentiful psycholinguistic literature, more directly targeting the relations between WM and language. Reviewing this literature is beyond my goals here, but see McElree et al. (2003), Hartsuiker and Barkhuysen (2006), Fedorova and Pechenkova (2007) for recent reviews. The main focus of this trend of research is inquiry into which operations in language production (or comprehension) place a load on WM. In the course of production or comprehension, experiment participants are asked to perform another verbal task, such as rehearsing a list of words, and it is tested whether this causes errors during concurrent language production. In this paradigm no specific claims are made regarding the relation between WM and certain linguistic choices, which is my main concern in this chapter. So the perspectives of this paradigm and of the theory proposed here are largely complementary with respect to each other.

10.2.3 *Attention and working memory*

In Atkinson and Shiffrin's (1968) once influential model of cognitive processing, both attention and WM were accounted for. According to that model, selective attention transfers, or encodes, information into a short-term store. Rehearsal, crucial for the maintenance of information in WM, also involves attention. Thus attention regulates the amount of information entering or staying in WM.

In later psychological approaches, the distinction between attention and WM became somewhat blurred. For example, in Baddeley's (1986) model the central executive, an essentially attentional mechanism, is considered a part of WM. In Cowan's work (Cowan 1988, 1995) an attempt was undertaken to explicitly integrate attention and WM into one model, but the relationship still remained unclear, in particular because the focus of attention was a zone inside WM. In both Baddeley's and Cowan's theories attention is somehow dissolved in WM.

During the last decade or so, a new trend is noticeable in cognitive psychology and neuroscience: attention and WM are being treated as simultaneously **distinct** and **related** processes, and their relationship is being explored in both behavioural and neuroimaging studies (see Repovš and Bresjanac 2006). According to Awh et al. (2006: 202), 'attention can serve as a kind of "gatekeeper" for working memory, by biasing the encoding of information toward the items that are most relevant to the current processing goal.' Awh et al. (1995: 115) and Awh and Jonides (2001) have argued that the same attentional mechanisms are responsible for both bringing information into WM and its active maintenance therein; also cf. Norman (1968). A similar treatment is discussed by Posner (1994) and Ivanitsky et al. (2008). Items in WM, unless attended to, get quickly forgotten. Attention thus exerts multifaceted control over WM. It is often pointed out that information can get activated in WM bypassing attentional control (see e.g. Cowan 1999: 63), but this stipulation probably is not very relevant for linguistic processes.

The question of the reverse influence of WM upon attention has also been discussed. Some have proposed that WM controls attention (Kastner and Ungerleider 2000, de Fockert et al. 2001). In this book, however, I join those authors (see above) who understand attention as a more deliberate, volitional, and controlling process, and WM as a more predictable and subservient process. Awh et al. (2006: 205–206) explain convincingly that items currently in WM can capture attention, but this is by no means obligatory; cf. Soto et al. (2008). That is, a kind of backward influence of WM upon attention does exist, but it is limited: activation in WM facilitates attention, but does not predict it.

The current understanding of the interplay between attention and WM is strongly based on neurophysiological evidence. Before discussing this, I summarize my vision of attention and WM that rests upon current theoretical views in this domain. I do this again in a series of theses.

- Attention and WM are two related but distinct cognitive systems.
- WM is the cognitive component for short-term storage of information.
- Information in WM is highly activated; information outside of WM is non-activated.
- Attention is the volitional mechanism that brings information into WM: when a piece of previously non-activated information is attended to, it enters WM at the next moment of time.
- Attention can be directed not only at previously non-activated items but also at those that are already in WM; in this case attention serves to maintain information in WM.
- Activation of information in WM facilitates sustained attention to a piece of information, but attention does not depend on WM.
- If not attended to, items in WM quickly deactivate.
- Both attention and WM are severely limited in capacity: attention can be directed only to several items at a time, and WM can hold only several items at a time; both capacities are limited to about four items, although this parity may be coincidental.

On the basis of these theses, derived from the current psychological and neurophysiological literature, I formulate my own and more linguistically oriented approach to attention and WM activation in section 10.3.

This set of theses presupposes two tenets that were not previously discussed but that will be important for further discussion. First, attention can be directed to two major kinds of targets: those outside of the cognitive system (perception of external stimuli) and those within it (long-term memory); see e.g. the classical model by Norman (1968). Both kinds of attention can bring information into WM.

The second point relates to the fact that in psychology activation in WM is often implied to be an all or nothing matter. This is implicitly presupposed when a certain number of items are discussed as either being or not being in the WM memory span; see e.g. Baddeley (2000). However, realistically this cannot be the case since deactivation (forgetting) is a gradual process. The latter immediately follows from how deactivation is measured: as slowing down of access to items as they decay from WM; see e.g. Anderson (1990: 150–156). So WM must have a centre and a periphery. In the centre items that are maximally activated are located, while the periphery contains items that are only partially activated. This point will become particularly important in the discussion in Chapter 13.

10.2.4 *The neural grounds of attention and working memory*

With the rise of cognitive neuroscience in the 1980s, the reality of WM was substantiated by an array of neuroimaging evidence, beginning with the studies of Goldman-Rakic (e.g. Goldman-Rakic 1987). This led to the formation of a neurocognitive model of WM that is considered 'standard' (Postle 2006). WM is thought to be based in the brain area known as the '(dorsolateral) prefrontal cortex'; see e.g. a review in Funahashi (2006). The idea of the association of WM with the prefrontal cortex comes not only from neuroimaging but also from other sources (Deco and Rolls 2003). In particular, recordings of individual neurons' activity (in monkeys) point to activation in this area when a subject is performing a task related to WM. Evidence from lesions in the prefrontal cortex also indicates deficit in WM-related tasks.

Awh et al. (1995) and Smith and Jonides (1997), in an unusually clear theoretical framework, suggested that in both verbal and spatial processing the prefrontal cortex is the locus of executive or control (that is, attentional) processes, while activation in the posterior parietal area of the brain is associated with the WM storage. A number of other authors, such as Lebedev et al. (2004), also support the suggestion that the prefrontal cortex plays a major role in attentional selection rather than memory maintenance. The problem of localization of attention and WM is far from being settled. In a recent review, Awh et al. (2006) seem to be less definitive on the distribution of WM and attention to two brain areas than in earlier studies; rather they say that there is a singificant overlap of the two processes. The picture is further complicated by the 'mushrooming working memory systems' (Postle 2006: 25), characteristic of the current research.

Many authors propose models that are different in approach from simple localization. For example, Schlösser et al. (2006: 101) review a number of studies that 'reveal a picture of distributed, hierarchically organized networks subserving WM functions. ... Due to its plasticity, the network has the potential for a flexible compensatory recruitment of pathways in case of disease-related partial disruptions of structural and functional integrity'. Hazy et al. (2006: 106) propose that 'instead of thinking about the moving of information from long-term memory into and out of working memory buffers, we think that information is distributed in a relatively stable configuration throughout the cortex, and that working memory amounts to the controlled activation of these representations'. Faw (2003) proposed a broad model involving an interaction of six cognitive domains (perception, working memory, attention, long-term memory, motor control, and thinking) as being served by a network of prefrontal (as well as other) areas of the brain. For some other publications containing extended discussions of brain systems subserving working memory and attention see Kastner and Ungerleider (2000), Engle and Kane (2004), Deco and Rolls (2003), McElree (2001).

Generalizing over the available range of views, it seems accurate to say that most specialists in the field believe that WM and attention are related but distinct systems. Neuroscientists are in an active search for specialized brain networks responsible for these two processes. It appears that in accordance with the bilateral functional connectedness of attention and WM there is a significant anatomic overlap of the two neural systems.

10.3 Attention and working memory as the basis for reference in discourse

On the basis of the presented ideas, especially the set of theses in subsection 10.2.3, I can now propose a theory that links attention and WM as cognitive constructs with reference and referential choice. In accordance with the topic of this book, I will discuss only attention to and activation of referents. Other concepts that can also get attended to and activated in discourse will remain out of the picture for now.

For the sake of concreteness of discussion, I cite an example of the simplest discourse type, natural face-to-face conversation, that contains several typical instances of reference and referential choice:

(10.1) Du Bois et al. (2000), conversation SBC0001 'Actual Blacksmithing', seconds 792 to 804

		LYNNE:	<...>
a.			...you know a guy,
b.			they've had a guy= being a horseshoer for,
c.			a long time you know?
d.			(H) And they,
e.			are um,
f.			... (TSK) (H) there's this girl,
g.			that's working with him,
h.			for the summer?
i.		DORIS:	Unhunh.
j.		LYNNE:	And she's gonna be a farrier.
k.		DORIS:	... Yeah.
l.		LYNNE:	... I couldn't believe it.
m.			<HI And she's just little HI>.
n.			... She's a tiny girl,
o.			but,
p.			boy I tell you,
q.			she's got ar=ms the size of --
r.			... (H) they're hu=ge.

In the theoretical discussion below I use this example to illustrate my claims.

10.3.1 *Attention determines mention*

The linguistic representation of attention to referents is **mention**, or **reference**. Linguistically, attending to a referent is equivalent to mentioning it. Within (10.1), the referent 'the guy' is mentioned (=attended to) in lines (10.1a, b, g); the referent 'the girl' in lines (10.1f, g, j, m, n, q); and the referent 'the girl's arms' in lines (10.1q, r). Repeated mention of a referent is the natural discourse equivalent of rehearsal, so much used in psychological experiments.

The selective character of attention is directly represented in the linguistic structure by how many referents can be attended to simultaneously. As is well known, discourse is not like a continuous current, it moves forward in chunks, or segments. In spoken discourse, these segments are termed variously, for example intonation units (Chafe 1994); they are represented as graphic lines in (10.1). I use the term 'elementary discourse unit' (EDU) (Kibrik 2001b, Kibrik and Podlesskaya 2006) as it provides a general framework for spoken and written discourse and underscores the functional role of discourse chunks. EDUs are quanta, or moments, of discourse time: discourse progresses in steps equalling EDUs. While uttering a current EDU, the speaker plans the next one. In terms of semantic and grammatical content, EDUs often coincide with clauses (Chafe 1994, Kibrik and Podlesskaya 2006). That is, a prototypical EDU is a clause, as lines (10.1b, f, g, j, l, m, n, p, q, r), and a number of other lines in this excerpt obviously result from unsuccessful attempts to build a clause. Speakers thus strive to organize their discourse as a chain of clauses (Thompson and Couper-Kuhlen 2005). Clauses are centred around predicates, typically verbs. Each verb denotes an event or a state and has arguments. The vast majority of verbs have one (see e.g. line (10.1m)) or two arguments (e.g. line (10.1b)). Few verbs have three arguments, and four-place verbs are rather an exception. Clauses can also contain adjuncts (circumstants), such as *with him* in line (10.1g). At any discourse moment, a speaker thus mentions (=attends to) from one to about three or four referents. The limitation on the number of concurrently mentioned referents is the linguistic analogue of attention span. This is how many individual referents the human mind can attend to simultaneously.[2] Language is designed in accordance with the limited attentional capacity.

Since this book is devoted primarily to referential choice, I do not elaborate on the connection between attention and reference any further and proceed with working memory; see also Chapter 13, section 13.3.

10.3.2 *Activation in working memory determines referential choice*

As has been argued from the beginning of this book (see Chapter 2, section 2.4), reference and referential choice are not identical processes. Reference is a more general phenomenon; it relates to a speaker's decision to mention a certain referent at a certain moment in discourse. Once such a decision is in place, the question of referential choice becomes relevant: which referential device to employ for the given referent. Whereas the decision to refer, or mention, is the linguistic representation of attention, the process of referential choice is the linguistic representation of the cognitive process of activation in WM. For example, the referent 'the girl' is differently verbalized in lines (10.1f)

---

[2] Of course, humans are able to handle a greater number of referents, if they treat several of them as a group. This is well known in psychology (Wundt 1911); in the linguistic structure grouped referents of a similar kind are encoded by plural referential expressions.

and (10.1j) because of the different statuses of this referent in the speaker's WM at these two distinct discourse moments.

Activation of referents in WM is not an all or nothing matter. Null activation means that a referent is outside of WM, maximal activation means being in the centre of WM, but there are intermediate degrees between these extremities. Chafe (1994) introduced the threefold distinction in the activation scale: active, semiactive, inactive. Chafe's intermediate semiactive category comes from two sources: (i) information that is secondarily activated because of being associated with highly activated information; (ii) information that was fully activated but decayed into the semiactive state. The referent 'the guy' can probably be said to have become semiactive around line (l) or (m) in (10.1). Once we admit semiactivation, the next logical step is to recognize that the three-way distinction between active, semiactive, and inactive is again an interpretational simplification, and there should be all possible intermediate degrees between fully activated and fully non-activated bits of information. Information scurries back and forth between the statuses of activated and non-activated, and at a certain moment a piece of information can be caught at any point on this scale. Activated information that is not being attended to decays into the non-activated state (see below) not abruptly but gradually; at least the burden of proof should be with someone who suggests the contrary. We should thus conclude that WM does not have discrete boundaries. Necessarily at any given moment there are items in WM that are fully activated and items that are at the periphery of WM.

Since the degree of referents' activation can be very different, the practice of measuring the WM span in terms of the number of items is questionable. So my assessment of the WM capacity will not be in the number of items but rather in conditional units, the value '1' equalling the maximal referent activation and allowing all fraction values between '0' and '1'.

The main law of referential choice is the following. If activation is **above a certain threshold**, the speaker chooses a reduced referential device, such as *him* in line (10.1g), *she* in line (10.1n), or *they* in line (10.1r). If activation is **below such a threshold**, a full NP is used. This is the case for each introductory mention of 'the guy', 'the girl', and 'the girl's arms' in (10.1), but this does not have to necessarily be a discourse-introductory mention. In the conversation which was partly cited in (10.1), almost immediately after line (10.1r) the interlocutors' attention was caught by an external stimulus – the dust blowing out of the air conditioner. The following 43 seconds of conversation concentrated on how to fix the conditioner, and after that Lynne continued, using a full NP again, since the referent 'the girl' got deactivated, see (10.2). Note that the full NP *this girl* in (10.2y) is identical to the very first mention of the referent in line (10.1f).

(10.2) Du Bois et al. (2000), conversation SBC0001 'Actual Blacksmithing', seconds 853 to 859
x. Anyway,
y. this girl must only weigh like,
z. a hundred and ten pou=nds.

Two caveats are in order regarding the main law of referential choice. Its formulation above suggests that there is a single fixed threshold that discretely separates two intervals of the activation scale, and that referential choice is a categorical and fully deterministic process. Of course, this is not exactly right, and the suggested formulation is overly strict. To be sure, there are intervals on the activation scale that make referential choice nearly deterministic. If a referent has a very low activation, reduced referential devices are excluded, and conversely, under a very high activation they may be required (see Chapters 11 and 12 for more concrete and empirical discussion). However, there are other intervals on the activation scale that only suggest a preference of one referential option over the other, or even a free variation between them.

A simple thought experiment on several instances of actual referential choices demonstrates that some of these are more categorical than others. For example, some reduced referential devices in natural discourse can hardly be replaced by a full NP (cf. the pronoun *she* pertaining to the referent 'the girl' in (10.1q)), while for some others there is a marginal or even a perfect full alternative (cf. the pronoun *him* in (10.1g) that could very well be replaced by a full NP, such as *this guy*). If so, two such uses of a pronoun certainly cannot correspond to the same level of activation. There are several thresholds between different intervals on the activation scale. Specifically, four thresholds (and, accordingly, five activation intervals) can be tentatively posited:

- Threshold A: below it only a full NP must be used.
- Threshold B: between A and B full NPs are preferred, but a reduced device is marginally possible.
- Threshold C: between B and C both full and reduced devices are equally appropriate.
- Threshold D: between C and D reduced referential devices are preferred, while above D they are required.

In the graph in Figure 10.1 the dependency between referent activation and referential choice is interpreted in terms of probabilities: probability of a

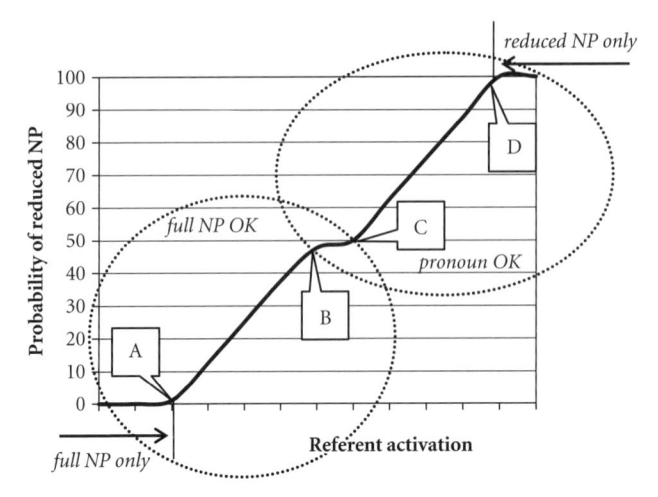

380   IV. Cognitive Multi-Factorial Approach to Referential Choice

FIGURE 10.1. Dependency of the probability of a reduced referential form upon the degree of referent's activation in WM: four thresholds

reduced referential device ranges between zero and 1. This dependency is not linear, and the graph has four curvings corresponding to the thresholds just listed.[3]

Thus there are instances when more than one referential device can be used, and the choice may be dependent on what were called referential strategies in Chapter 2, section 2.6. A speaker may adopt a more egocentric strategy, and this might result in more numerous reduced devices. If a speaker prefers the overprotective strategy, more full NPs would be found. So, in order to be realistic, one must recognize a substantial degree of flexibility of referential choice. Even though the basic referential choice is categorical at the level of realization (either a full NP or a reduced device must be eventually used) it is much more multivariate at the stage of planning.

The second caveat to the main law of referential choice concerns the role of referential filters – components of referential choice that are independent of activation and check the felicity of projected referential devices, primarily reduced referential devices. The most important filter is referential conflict; as was argued in Chapter 2, section 2.8, as well as in Chapter 8, referential conflict is a separate component of the referential choice, distinct from the operation

---

[3] Specific locations of thresholds in Figure 10.1 should not be taken literally; they are given here for illustrative purposes. The graph in Figure 10.1 is simplified in comparison to the threshold formulations above in that it does not take marginally appropriate referential devices into account.

of activation factors.[4] The typical function of referential conflict is to filter out a reduced referential device when it can be assigned a wrong referent by the addressee. So a full device may be used under a high activation because of the operation of the filters. A model of referential choice that includes referential filters is provided in section 10.6.

10.3.3 Interaction of attention and WM activation

In this subsection I formulate my own theory of the relationship between attention and WM activation, relying on the review of psychological and neurophysiological literature in section 10.2 (see especially the list of theses in subsection 10.2.3).

As has been argued in subsections 10.2.3 and 10.2.4 above, attention and WM activation are two distinct but related processes. In accordance with that, reference (=mention) and referential choice are also distinct but related. Attention and activation, as well as reference and referential choice, are distinct because the issues of a referent being attended to and activated at a certain moment in discourse are two independent issues. Referential choice (the linguistic representation of activation), of course, becomes relevant only if the speaker decides to mention a referent at the given point in discourse. But referential choice (based on WM activation) is in no way predicted by the speaker's current decision to perform the act of reference (attention). First, a referent to be mentioned may be of a high or low activation. In particular, if a referent may be attended to but not activated, then such referent is mentioned by a full NP. Second, a referent that is not going to be mentioned (no attention), may still maintain a certain degree of activation for a while; there are important consequences from this latter point; see Chapter 13, section 13.2.

In order to make clear how attention and WM activation can be simultaneously distinct and related, let me give a simplistic physical analogy. The motor and the wheels in a car are distinct but related mechanisms. They are clearly distinct in the architecture of a car, but the motor makes the wheels rotate. To make the analogy more complete, wheels may rotate for a while after the motor is turned off.

Even though activation is not predicted by current attention to a referent, it is dependent on whether the referent was attended to at the previous moment. It is in this sense that attention and activation are related: attending to a

---

[4] I believe that the failure to recognize the separateness of referential conflict from activation-related processes presents the fourth major stumbling block in the studies of reference (see seciton 10.1 for the other three).

TABLE 10.1. Possible combinations of attention and activation in cognition and in discourse

Cognitive structure	−attention −activation	+attention −activation	+attention +activation	−attention +activation
Linguistic structure	Referent is not mentioned	Referent is mentioned by a full NP	Referent is mentioned by a reduced referential device	Referent is not mentioned (even though being activated)
Example: referent 'the girl' in one of the lines in (10.1) or (10.2)	(10.1a)	(10.2y)	(10.1n)	(10.1p)
Referential device in (10.1) or (10.2)	n/a	*this girl*	*she*	n/a

referent at moment t_n leads to the referent's activation at moment t_{n+1}. Four possible combinations of plus or minus attention and activation are schematically represented and illustrated in Table 10.1.

After a referent gets activated in WM, it can be kept there for a while. However, the default life of a referent in WM is very short – it fades away quickly; this is what obviously happens to 'the guy', last mentioned in (10.1g), by the end of (10.1). There are different hypotheses on how and why this happens (see discussion in Chapter 13, section 13.4), but anyway rapid decay is the foundational property of information in WM. In accordance with that, distance to a prior mention of the referent (in other words, to the last time the referent was attended to) is among the best predictors of referential choice. Each occurrence of *she* in (10.1) is very close to the immediate antecedent, while the full NP *this girl* in line (10.2y) occurs at a long distance from its antecedent. Distance measured in clauses or EDUs is a measurement of discourse time.

There is a way to prevent referent deactivation: to mention it. In other words, sustained attention to a referent entails its sustained activation in WM. Once again, repeated mention is the natural analogue of rehearsal and, vice versa, explicit rehearsal is a very rough experimental analogue of normal sustained attention. Sustained activation is represented in the linguistic structure as the repeated use of reduced referential devices, such as four uses of *she* in (10.1). It must be made very clear that there are two aspects in a repeated mention of a referent: the fact of a repeated mention indicates that attention is sustained to this referent; while the repeated choice of a reduced referential device is due to the referent's high activation. Once again, reference and referential choice are two distinct phenomena and they are regulated by two distinct cognitive systems.

The primary relationship between attention and activation is that the former causes the latter at the next discourse moment. However, there is also a backward influence of WM activation upon attention; cf. Soto et al. (2008). Attention to referents that are already activated is facilitated (just like the rotation of the wheels in a car, ultimately caused by the motor, in turn helps to run the motor). Of course, having a referent activated does not predict that this referent will be mentioned again, but it makes such a chance higher. This fact relates to referential coherence – the much higher than chance frequency of mentions of the same referent in adjacent portions of discourse. In example (10.1), Lynne was intending to keep talking about the tiny girl with big arms. This referent's activation was evidently useful for keeping attention on 'the girl' within the following stretch of discourse. However, it so happened that attention was intercepted by a different stimulus (the air conditioner in the room where the conversation took place), so 'the girl' was not attended to for a while. Later on in the conversation, when the story about the girl eventually ended, Lynne dropped the referent out of her own and her addressee's attention, this time intentionally. So activation facilitates but does not regulate attention. Once the speaker decides to mention a referent, its current degree of activation is readily available.

Tomlin (1995) initiated a very unusual and fruitful research programme in which a direct mapping between cognitive statuses and linguistic form was tested. The cognitive status he explored was focal attention, or focus of attention. This status can be given to a single current referent. That is, among the very few simultaneously attended referents one can be focally attended to. According to Tomlin, focal attention is the cognitive reinterpretation of the traditionally vague linguistic notion of topic or theme. By experimental manipulation of participants' visual attention Tomlin demonstrated that in English, as well as in a number of other languages, focal attention is reflected in the linguistic structure as the clause subject, which is the grammaticalization of topic. In my understanding, attention is represented in the linguistic structure by any mention of a referent, while focal attention by a mention in the priviledged subject position.

Among other things, this approach points to an interesting congruence between different attentional systems: visual attention and what Michael Posner once called 'attention to meaning' (Posner 1989: 7). One can expect that a mention of a referent in the subject position, that is, focal attention given to the referent, can contribute more to referent activation in WM than does plain attention. I will return to this hypothesis and the relationship between focal attention and WM in Chapter 13, section 13.3. As was pointed out above, activation in WM facilitates attention. Likewise does it facilitate focal attention. As was convincingly demonstrated by Chafe (1994: Ch. 7), there is an overwhelming tendency to select activated referents for subjects in English conversation.

It appears that attention (let alone focal attention) is a much more volitional and deliberate process compared to activation in WM, which is a rather automatic consequence of prior attention. In order to predict which referents will be mentioned in a given clause one would need to model the speaker's cognitive plan and see how individual referent mentions can be derived from it. Fortunately, activation in WM is a much more automatic and predictable process, and that gives us a chance to explain much of actual referential choice in discourse.

In the following chapters of Part IV the cognitive theory of reference and referential choice is further elaborated. I make very specific suggestions regarding the crucial elements of this theory. In particular, in Chapter 13 I address issues such as the relationship between attention and WM, the capacity of WM, the mechanisms of forgetting from WM, etc.

10.3.4 *Alternative hypotheses on the cognitive basis of referential choice*

As was pointed out by Shah and Miyake (1999: 16ff.), in psychology the notions of working memory, attention, and consciousness are often merged in all possible combinations. William James (1890) referred to consciousness in his definitions of both primary memory and attention; Atkinson and Shiffrin (1971) equated short-term memory with consciousness; Baddeley (1993) once suggested that one could replace the term 'working memory' with 'working attention'; in Cowan's (1995) model attention is understood as a subset of activated memory; Baars (1997) almost identifies attention with consciousness. All of these traditional terms are maintained in modern science, and probably represent distinct, even though closely interacting, cognitive systems.

Provided this rather irregular use of terms in psychology, centrally involved in the study of cognitive processes, it is no surprise that linguists have a hard time trying to understand what memory, attention and consciousness mean and how they are different. All of these terms have been occasionally used as candidates for the cognitive controllers of referential choice.

One of the popular suggestions for the cognitive correlate of referential choice is (focal) attention. I myself proposed this hypothesis in a number of early publications (Kibrik 1987b, 1992a). In these papers I argued that focal attention gets coded in the linguistic structure by means of anaphoric pronouns and other reduced referential devices. However, the ingenious and profound studies by Tomlin (Tomlin and Pu 1991, Tomlin 1995) convinced me that my cognitive interpretation of referential choice was on the wrong track. Tomlin demonstrated that, first, focal attention is responsible for the choice of clause topic or subject, and, second, that referential choice is related to memory activation. This caused me to reinstate the notion of activation that was already present in my first published article about reference (Kibrik 1983) and explicitly connect it to the cognitive mechanism known as working memory, beginning from Kibrik (1994).

Relating referential choice to attention focusing used to be quite popular in research by Barbara Grosz and her associates (Grosz 1977, Grosz and Sidner 1986). Later on, this line of research turned into the so-called Centering Theory (Gordon et al. 1993, Walker et al. (eds.) 1998, Poesio et al. 2004, Beaver 2004) that tends to avoid explicit cognitive notions. One of the main concepts of Centering Theory is the so-called 'backward-looking center' (Cb). Cb is a replacement for the traditional notion of clause topic, and this is the basis for the claim that there is a singleton Cb per utterance. At the same time Cb is considered the main factor of referential choice. The so-called 'pronoun rule' states that the Cb is the preferred candidate for pronominalization. From the cognitive perspective we face here a confusion of topic selection (which is an attention-based process) and referential choice (which is WM-based).

Other studies that used the attention or attention focusing terminology as an explanatory cognitive notion for referential choice include Linde (1979), Tomlin (1987), Givón (1990: Ch. 20), Stevenson et al. (2000), Campbell (2002), Holler and Irmen (2007: 16). Even in the psycholinguistic literature the notions of attention and activation are sometimes used interchangeably, as synonyms (e.g. Garnham 2006). As I attempted to demonstrate above, the non-differentiation of attention and WM activation is highly undesirable. Attention and activation in WM are distinct cognitive phenomena; both have certain linguistic reflections, and referential choice directly relates to activation in WM.

A different conceptual tradition is associated with the studies by Wallace Chafe. Chafe is among the founders of the cognitive approach in linguistics; he made the first explicit suggestions on the direct links between language and cognition long before the enterprise officially known as 'Cognitive Linguistics' emerged. In a number of publications Chafe emphasized the role of consciousness in discourse production, in particular, in referential choice (Chafe 1974, 1976, Chafe (ed.) 1980, Chafe 1987, 1994). Chafe uses the notion of referent activation, but attributes it to the cognitive domain of consciousness rather than working memory. Some may think that this is a terminological quibble, but from my perspective having cognitive notions straight is important. I believe that explaining referential choice in terms of consciousness actually attributes to consciousness too passive a task. Consciousness is rather much more of a controlling, regulatory process, and in this sense it is more akin to attention than to activation in WM. (Cf. a book-long argument that consciousness does not equal WM – Baars 1997, an analysis in Cowan 1999, and an authoritative discussion of the relatedness of attention and consciousness in Posner 1994.) Referential choice, directly linked to activation in WM, is much more automatic and should not be at the centre of what consciousness is concerned with. Rather than doing such local things as referential choice, consciousness must concern itself with higher-level tasks, in particular discourse planning.

In addition to the notions referring to whole cognitive systems, a number of other designations are used, such as accessibility, recoverability, givenness, salience, prominence, and the like. From my perspective, all of these terms are exceedingly metaphorical and, partly for this reason, present a significant threat when used as explanatory theoretical notions. Indeed, one cannot avoid using metaphors even in scientific cognition (Lakoff and Núñez 2000), but metaphors must be thoroughly thought-through to be productive. The term activation that I prefer is much more straightforward and less metaphorical than accessibility, salience, etc., as it provides a direct link to the conceptual system of cognitive psychology and cognitive neuroscience.

It is beyond my goal to discuss and evaluate all approaches that employ the mentioned quasi-cognitive terms to explain reference and referential choice. I will only make several comments about two terms of the above-mentioned sequence, namely salience and recoverability.

The notion of **salience** has been around in linguistic studies of reference at least since Bosch (1983: 57). This widely circulated notion, apart from being overly metaphorical, is also dangerous in expressly non-differentiating the cognitive domains responsible for referent mention and for referential choice. An interesting example of a study showing that the overarching notion of salience is less than productive comes from within the tradition that emphasizes salience as a primitive concept. This is the study by Miltsakaki (2007) who challenges the view that there is a single functional or cognitive domain of salience, responsible for the use of referential expressions. Miltsakaki has run a sentence continuation experiment in Greek and discovered that (i) speakers of Greek reserve the weak form of reference (in particular, subject zero) for antecedents that are subjects in their clauses; and (ii) when semantics suggests that the first clause's object is referentially continued in the second clause (and is thus supposedly more salient than the first clause's subject), speakers choose not a zero but a demonstrative to convey this kind of coreference. From this Miltsakaki infers that the Greek zero anaphor is sensitive not to salience but to the antecedent's subject role.

I believe this conclusion is correct, but a more comprehensive explanation is in order. There is no problem here, if one differentiates between two cognitive processes: attention and activation in WM. The expectation for a certain referent to be mentioned in a given clause, as derived from semantic context (cf. the notions of focusing and implicit causality in Stevenson et al. 1994, 2000), is an attentional phenomenon. The fact that a referent is expected in a clause is not directly related to the referent's activation. Activation, on the other hand, regulates referential choice. In an experimental context such as the one used by Miltsakaki the referent that was the first clause's subject is certainly more activated that the object referent (see Chapters 11 and 12). In accordance with that, the primary reduced referential device, that is the zero, is used for subject coreference, while a more specialized device, the demonstrative, is drafted in the opposite case, including those instances when the object referent was expectable on semantic grounds. So Miltsakaki is correct in arguing against this kind of notion of salience, but in addition to that it must be recognized that two distinct cognitive processes are involved here: one responsible for the preference of what is mentioned in a given clause (attention) and the other responsible for referential form (activation). There is no use for the overarching notion of salience embracing both attention and high activation in WM, and the expectation of a referent mention should not be confused with how the referent is actually encoded.

A further notion in the same class, recoverability, is also quite often used instead or in addition to activation – in particular in computational literature (see e.g. O'Donnell 1994). This notion presupposes, with respect to discourse production, that speakers evaluate possible referential expressions as being recoverable for an addressee. Whereas I do believe that such evaluation actually takes place in some speakers' referential strategies (see Chapter 2, section 2.6), the activation-based selection of referential devices is a much more basic process. Quite a few recoverable referential expressions may be nevertheless infelicitous or impossible because of referents being insufficiently activated. One illustration is associated with the experiment described in detail in Chapter 12, section 12.3. In this experiment, I manipulated the form of natural written English discourse and changed certain referential devices for alternative ones. Then I showed the discourses thus manipulated to native speakers and asked them to see if there was anything wrong anywhere in the text. There were a number of instances where an original full NP was replaced by a pronoun, and experiment participants were pointing out that the pronoun was no good, even though there was no problem in identifying the pronoun's referent. The reason was that the referent was recoverable but not activated enough to produce a pronoun. Apparently, in human interaction recoverability (or decipherability) is not the optimal explanatory notion for the use of reduced referential devices.

Another illustration showing how the notion of recoverability can be insufficient or no good comes from this actual and quite unfortunate usage in a Russian magazine:

(10.3) Russian (magazine 'Bol'šoj gorod', 14.02.2007)
    a. Problemu   probok   v   Vene   popytalis'   rešit'
       problem.ACC jams.GEN in   Vienna.LOC   tried.IMP   solve
       s   pomošč'ju   ograničenija   na   parkovku.
       with help.INSTR restriction.GEN on   parking.ACC
    b. Vlasti   posčitali,
       authorities.NOM decided.PL
    c. čto, ubrav   mašiny   s   obočin   ulic,
       that remove.PAST.CONV cars.ACC from sides.GEN   streets.GEN
    d. oni   zametno   uveličat   ix   propusknuju
       they.NOM noticeably will.increase.3PL their throughput.ACC
       sposobnost'
       capacity.ACC

'In Vienna, an attempt was made to solve the problem of traffic jams with the help of parking restrictions. The authorities decided that, having removed cars from the sides of the streets, they would significantly increase their throughput capacity.'

What a native Russian reader stumbles upon in this excerpt is one particular instance of referential choice. The case in point is the possessive pronoun *ix* 'their' in line (10.3d). The pronoun is evidently intended to refer to the streets, as the throughput capacity is a characteristic of streets or roads. Upon a certain amount of reflection, everyone arrives at this conclusion. So reference is recoverable, but still it is not felicitous as it presents a difficulty to a reader. There are at least three other competing referents here: 'the authorities', 'roadsides', and 'cars'. None of them is compatible with the semantic context, as these referents cannot have a throughput capacity. So the correct referent can actually be computed. But the situation is that it is not referential conflict that makes this occurrence infelicitous. The intended referent 'streets' is not activated enough for pronominal reference, in particular because of the antecedent's very low syntactic status (see Chapters 11 and 12): the antecedent *ulic* 'of the streets' in line (10.3c) is a possessor inside an adjunct phrase. The referent that occurred as the previous clause's direct object, that is 'the cars', is clearly more – and sufficiently – activated here, and this referent is the reader's first guess, after which he/she gets confused. (I leave it for native English speakers to judge whether the rather parallel English rendering of this example creates the same effect.) So, once again, the notion of recoverability makes a wrong prediction regarding the appropriateness of a reduced referential device. With respect to the referent 'the streets' the pronominal form *ix* is inappropriate, even though the referent is recoverable for a standard reader.

10.4 The problem of circularity

As was pointed out in section 10.1, there are several common stumbling blocks in the studies of reference. The first one is the probable theoretical vacuity of those cognitive explanations that are not connected to what is known about memory and attention in psychology and neuroscience; I have attempted to address this problem in some detail in the previous sections. In this section I discuss the following stumbling block, also quite serious. It is the problem of circularity: referential choice is explained by the level of activation (or another similar status), and the judgement on the level of activation is inferred from the actual referential form employed.

Unfortunately, this problem is characteristic of many cognitively-oriented approaches to reference, including such influential approaches as Chafe (1994) or Gundel et al. (1993). Of course, the approaches suffering this problem do not recognize that they infer referent activation from the form of reference. They rather assume that the assessment of a referent as activated or non-activated is based on introspective expert judgement. But the thing is that linguistic form affects our expert judgement, and if we observe a *he* we are inclined to believe that it was used because the referent was highly activated.

Thus the problem here is the lack of an independent motivation for certain cognitive statuses. If such an independent motivation were found, then we could safely and uncontroversially use cognitive statuses as motivations for referential choice.

A solution to this problem that I propose is the following. The referent's current degree of activation is a dependent variable. As has been argued in section 10.3, activation in WM primarily results from the attention given to the referent at the immediately preceding moment in discourse. Attention is manifested in linguistic structure by means of referent mentions. So the current activation of a referent comes from its previous mentions. There are various ways previous mentions can possibly be characterized – for example, by asking how far back the nearest mention is, in terms of local or global discourse structure, or by asking what was the referent's attentional and activational status on its prior mention. These characterizations of the prior mentions can be subsumed under the general label of discourse context factors of referential choice. I interpret these factors as **activation factors**. They contribute directly to a referent's activation at any given moment in discourse. (As I discuss below, there also exist activation factors related to a referent's inherent properties.) Activation factors are enumerated and explored in the next section and in the subsequent chapters.

So we are able to overcome the stumbling block of circularity. The current referent's level of activation, which is the immediate determiner of referential choice, can be established entirely independently of the actual referential choice. There are a range of activation factors that are at work at all times in discourse, and at any given moment they determine every referent's activation. Once the speaker needs to mention a referent, the activation level is always at hand, and referential choice can be performed on this basis.

10.5 Multiplicity of factors and their interaction

A host of various factors have been claimed in the literature to affect referential choice. Many of those factors are discussed in Chapters 11 and 12, so let me just give several illustrative examples. Givón (1983b) proposed the so-called referential distance measurement: distance in clauses back to the nearest antecedent, which proved to correlate quite well with referential choices. Tomlin (1987) and Fox (1987b), among others, argued that episodic boundaries are a good predictor of referential choice. Grimes (ed.) (1978) emphasized the role of a referent's centrality in discourse, and Dahl and Fraurud (1996) demonstrated the influence of animacy. This list can be prolonged ad infinitum, but the main point should be clear. There are many factors that have been demonstrated to affect referential choice, or at least correlate with referential choice. Of course, the relevance of a given factor is always based on some partial evidence. Suppose each of these hypotheses is correct. Factor A is of primary importance in instance X, while factor B in instance Y. What is unclear is how these two factors can be brought into one picture. In other words, what is the role of factor A in instance Y and of factor B in instance X? For example, what happens if one factor (e.g. short distance to antecedent) favours the use of a reduced referential device, while another factor (e.g. existence of an episodic boundary) favours the use of a full device? The multiplicity of factors affecting referential choice is the third stumbling block, firmly entrenched in this research field.

In fact, the common practice in the studies of referential choice is to pinpoint a factor and attach a great significance to it, thus making an impression that the nature of reference has finally been found. Even though each such individual factor does have a value, it is very difficult to demonstrate that it has decisive power.

Some authors recognize the existence of several factors affecting referential choice; see e.g. Clancy (1980), Givón (1983a, 1990), van Dijk and Kintsch (1983), Lord and Dahlgren (1997), Kameyama (1998), Arnold and Griffin (2007), Kaiser and Trueswell (2011); external observers, such as the author of a cognitive psychology textbook (Barsalou 1992) sometimes also acknowledge of a wide range of factors proposed by linguists.

Unfortunately, the simple recognition of a variety of factors does not help to solve the above-mentioned difficulty. In order to address this difficulty, I propose the following. We must recognize the multiplicity and interaction[5] of factors affecting referential choice. This means that all factors work in all instances, pool together, and give rise to a cumulative variable that will predict referential choice.

What is the nature of this cumulative variable? As must already be clear by now, it is the referent's activation level in the speaker's working memory. That is, there are many factors that contribute to a referent's current aggregate activation which is immediately responsible for referential choice. As has been already pointed out, I construe these factors as activation factors. This is an important difference of my approach from many other approaches to referential choice. Activation factors influence referential choice not directly but through the mediation of the cognitive component, namely working memory. In contrast, other authors have often proposed a direct mapping between factors and referential choice. For example, Fox (1987b) argued that referential choice is directly influenced by the global structure of discourse.

For the proposed solution to be practical rather than declarative, one needs a way to evaluate the factors' relative strength and their specific contribution to aggregate activation. Although the details of the multi-factorial model will be expounded in the next two chapters, devoted to Russian and English data respectively, a brief account is due here.

Activation factors, numbering about a dozen, are formulated as properties of previous discourse (or of the referent itself; see below) open to public objective verification. For a hypothetical factor to be recognized as an actual

---

[5] Interaction is understood in a non-technical way here. I do not suggest that each factor must necessarily affect other factors, although such technically understood interaction may take place and will be discussed below. What is implied is simply that all factors are involved at all times.

activation factor it must display a significant covariation with referential choice. Each factor has a number of values; for example, for the factor of distance to antecedent, measured in clauses, it could be 1, 2, 3, etc. I propose a calculative model in which each value of each factor is assigned a certain numerical weight.

For any point of discourse, the values of all factors can be identified, and their corresponding weights are summed up, producing the current referent's activation score – the chief predictor of referential choice. Numerical weights are selected so that the activation score varies within the numerical limits between zero and 1. This range is not continuous, in the sense that there are certain important thresholds in it. If an activation score is above a certain threshold, then a semantically reduced (pronoun or zero) reference is possible, and if not, a full NP is used (see subsection 10.3.2 above).

The largest group of activation factors are those related to discourse context. Among these, there are two subgroups: various measurements of distance to the nearest antecedent (along the local vs. global discourse structure; along the linear vs. hierarchical discourse structure) and roles of the antecedent (syntactic and semantic). In addition to discourse context factors, there is another important group: activation factors related to the referent's properties. Among them there are more permanent factors, such as animacy, and less permanent but still quite stable factors, such as the status of the protagonist of a current discourse. Specifics of activation factors, along with their values and numerical weights, are explained in Chapters 11 and 12.

The CMF model of referential choice was originally proposed in Kibrik (1994, 1996a) and developed in Kibrik (1999, 2000), and Grüning and Kibrik (2005). Kibrik (2006) indicated a range of other linguistic phenomena that naturally lend themselves to multi-factorial description. The idea of multi-factorial modelling seems very important. So far it is not particularly widespread in linguistics,[6] although it has been entertained by a number of authors. In particular, Gries (2001) and Diessel and Tomasello (2005) use

---

[6] A very well-known framework that also recognizes a multiplicity of factors in linguistic phenomena is Optimality Theory (see e.g. McCarthy 2002). The general idea of Optimality Theory somewhat resembles my multi-factorial approach: it recognizes the fact that linguistic phenomena often depend on more than one factor, and these factors may influence the output variable in different directions. However, the Optimality Theory approach appears too simplistic: it assumes that each factor (constraint) is either satisfied or violated. In the CMF approach weaker factors are not simply violated (cancelled); rather they still make a contribution, even if not a decisive one. I propose that the human mind operates not in terms of violable constraints but rather in terms of contributing factors. Another difference between the CMF approach and Optimality Theory is that the latter has generally been applied not to online decisions in language use but rather to offline linguistic structures. See also Nesset (2008: 16–18) on a comparison of Optimality and Cognitive Linguistics.

this idea in connection with the placement of particles in English discourse; a similar approach has also been used by Geeraerts (2006). A congenial psycholinguistic model is proposed in Myachykov et al. (2007). In the realm of referential studies, cf. the study Kaiser (2008) pointing to several factors in the process of reference resolution; in that study, however, different factors compete rather than contribute to one single end. To the best of my knowledge, the closest analogue of the multi-factorial approach described in this part of the book is the computational linguistic study by Strube and Wolters (2000), discussed in Chapter 14, subsection 14.1.8. As for anaphora resolution, a weighted model acknowledging several concurrently relevant factors was developed in Balogh (2003).

10.6 Properties of the cognitive multi-factorial approach to referential choice

Thus the CMF approach to referential choice, most crucially, is:

(1) cognitively plausible: the model relies on what is known about attention and working memory in cognitive studies; factors of referential choice are interpreted as activation factors; all these factors in conjunction determine the current activation of the referent in working memory, which in turn determines referential choice;
(2) multi-factorial: potential multiplicity of activation factors is recognized; each factor is monitored in each case, rather than in an impromptu manner, and the issue of interaction between various relevant factors is addressed.

Further properties of the proposed approach include:

(3) explanatory: it is claimed that this approach models the actual cognitive processes, rather than relies on a 'black box' approach in which the processes between input and output remain mysterious;
(4) non-circular: factors must be identified independently of the actual referential choice;
(5) calculative: contributions of activation factors are numerically characterized;
(6) sample-based: the data for the study is a sample of natural discourse (see Chapters 11 and 12);
(7) general: all occurrences of referential devices in a sample must be accounted for;

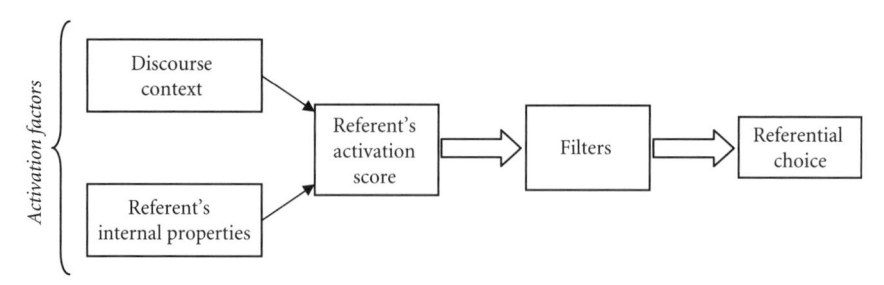

FIGURE 10.2. The cognitive multi-factorial model of referential choice (the third pass)

(8) closed: the proposed list of factors must be sufficient to account for all occurrences of referential devices;
(9) predictive: the proposed list of factors aims at predicting referential choice with maximally attainable certainty;
(10) testable: all components of this approach are subject to verification.

I repeat in Figure 10.2 the flow chart of the CMF model that already appeared as Figure 2.3 in Chapter 2, with a slight modification. After the referent's activation score is determined by the set of activation factors, the projected referential choice is checked by certain filters. One of these filters, the referential conflict, is already very familiar to the reader. One more filter, the world boundary, will be introduced in Chapter 11. In anticipation of that, I mention plural filters in the chart in Figure 10.2.

In the following two chapters of Part IV I am going to demonstrate that one can construct a consistent and empirical account of referential choice in natural discourse relying on the assumptions set out above.

Summary

In this chapter I have developed the CMF approach to discourse reference. Referential choice in discourse is fundamentally dependent on the referent's status in the speaker's and addressee's cognitive systems. There are a great variety of hypotheses about the concrete nature of the relevant cognitive domain. The two domains that are particularly obvious candidates for this role are working memory and attention.

A cognitively realistic theory of referential choice must be informed with respect to the knowledge about attention and memory, available from psychology and neuroscience. It was therefore necessary to review the specialized literature on these cognitive domains.

Attention is a selective process singling out those stimuli that are currently most important for cognitive processing. Working memory (WM) is a small and rapidly updating store of highly activated information, most relevant to the current goals. Attention and WM are two distinct but closely related cognitive systems; the relationship is both functional and neuroanatomical. Attention governs WM and brings information to WM. In order for information to be kept in WM, it needs to remain attended to.

Attention and WM are both relevant for referential processes in discourse and play different roles. In linguistic structure, attention is represented as a mention of a referent. Once the speaker has made the decision to mention a referent, the referent's level of activation in WM becomes relevant. Activation level maps onto referential choice. The main law of referential choice states: if activation is above a certain threshold, a reduced device is used; if it is below the threshold, a full device is selected.

Attention and WM are thus two distinct but related cognitive processes, both involved in reference in discourse. They are distinct because they are responsible for two different choices: attention for mentioning or not mentioning a referent, and WM for the choice between various referential expressions. At the same time, attention and WM are related because attention governs WM: it brings referents into WM, and what is attended to at moment t_n becomes activated in WM at moment t_{n+1}.

A number of alternative cognitive or quasi-cognitive concepts have been proposed in the literature as controllers of referential choice, including focal attention, consciouness, salience, etc. However, the available knowledge suggests that the component known as working memory is directly responsible for referential choice.

A recurring problem of cognitively-oriented studies of referential choice has been circular reasoning: a cognitive phenomenon, such as activation, is proposed to predict referential choice, while the degree of activation is inferred on the basis of actual referential choices. To avoid this problem, referents' activations must be assessed on independent grounds, such as properties of discourse context. I interpret such properties as activation factors, cumulatively determining a referent's current activation score.

There are a great variety of activation factors, that is, referential choice is a multi-factorial process. Activation factors, including properties of the discourse context and a referent's inherent features, interact with each other and give rise to an activation score. The gist of the proposed approach is the simultaneous recognition of the cognitive basis and the multi-factorial nature of referential choice.

11

Referential choice in Russian narrative prose

Overview

In this chapter[1] I apply the cognitive multi-factorial (CMF) approach, outlined in Chapter 10, to a sample of Russian narrative prose; this sample is characterized in section 11.1. My goal is to set up a system that would allow us to explain the attested referential choices in the data set. Russian possesses a number of referential devices, discussed in section 11.2. As the quantitative analysis (section 11.3) demonstrates, the basic options of referential choice are full NPs and third person pronouns. Minor options include referential zeroes and demonstratives.

The proposed system consists of a number of activation factors contributing to a referent's activation, rules for calculating a referent's current activation score, and a mapping from activation score onto referential options. In section 11.4 I identify the relevant activation factors and analyse their internal structure, including their values and the corresponding numerical weights. Section 11.5 suggests a mapping between activation levels and basic referential options and illustrates how activation scores are actually calculated. Minor referential devices are examined in section 11.6.

Apart from the activation component, additional filters affecting referential choice are identified: the world boundary filter (section 11.7) and the referential conflict filter (section 11.8).

---

[1] This chapter is based on the article Kibrik (1996a). I thank the publishing house John Benjamins for their permission to reproduce that article here in a somewhat revised form. I would like to thank Barbara Fox, Tom Payne, Alan Cienki, Russ Tomlin, Jean Newman, Immanuel Barshi, and especially Amy Crutchfield who provided useful comments on the original article.

11.1 The discourse sample

In this chapter I investigate a single sample of narrative prose – a short story by the Russian writer Boris Zhitkov 'Nad vodoj' ('Over the water'), written around 1923.[2] This particular sample of discourse was selected for this study for the following reasons:

(1) The genre of story was selected since it is one of the most basic discourse genres (see Chapter 1, subsection 1.4.1); it seems reasonable to apply a novel model of a discourse process first to a basic genre, and only thereafter consider how it is manifested in less basic genres.
(2) Written prose was selected because it is a well-controlled mode in the sense that previous discourse is the only source for the referents that appear; a convenience of written language is that we can fully control the processes of activation by fairly objective discourse data.
(3) Boris Zhitkov was selected as an excellent stylist, with a very simple and clear language, well-motivated lexical choices, and at the same time with a neutral, non-exotic way of writing.
(4) This specific story was selected since it is again a prototypical narrative primarily describing basic events – physical actions, interactions of people, people's reflections, sentiments, and speech. The story is written in the third person, so there is no locutor reference outside of quoted speech/thought.

The story describes dramatic events during one of the first civil aviation flights in the early 1920s. The main participants are the crew members (the pilot, the mechanic, and the trainee named Fedorchuk) and several passengers. About 80% of the original story was used for analysis; the beginning 20% of the text was excluded from consideration for technical reasons. The full text of the discourse sample, with an idiomatic translation, as well as word-by-word English glosses where necessary, can be found in an appendix to Kibrik (1996a). In that publication, as well as in the examples cited here, the discourse is broken into elementary discourse units (EDUs) that are kept as close to clauses as possible. (In some cases, however, a clause is broken by another clause, and then discourse units can happen to be smaller than clauses.) In both the above-mentioned publication and in the examples below, each EDU is represented as a graphic line. In the four-digit number of each line the first two digits indicate the number of the paragraph in text, and the last two digits the number of the EDU within the given paragraph.

---

[2] One of the publications of the story is found in: Boris Zhitkov. *Izbrannoe*. Moscow: Izdatel'stvo 'Pravda', 1988, pp. 36–42.

TABLE 11.1. The list of animate and inanimate characters and the corresponding referential subscript indices

pilot	p	aircraft	
mechanic	m	engine	e
Fedorchuk	F	carburetor	
fat passenger		nut	
lanky passenger	l	instruments	i
woman		altimeter	a
serviceman		door	
young passenger		handle	
elderly passenger		wing	
all passengers	P	book	
a subset of passengers		fog	
all aboard		snow	
		clouds	
		sea	

The discourse sample comprises about 300 EDUs. There are about 500 mentions of various referents in the sample, and there are some 70 different referents figuring in it. However, only a minority of them occur more than once. There are 26 referents appearing at least once in an anaphoric context, that is in a situation where at least a certain degree of activation can be expected. Table 11.1 contains the list of these referents. For those referents that appear in the examples cited in this chapter mnemonic referential subscript indices are indicated.

11.2 Referential devices in Russian

The basic distinction among the Russian referential devices is the distinction between full NPs and semantically reduced NPs. Full NPs can appear with adnominal demonstratives; such occurrences in principle present an interesting subject (see Krasavina 2004) but they appear only twice in the discourse sample so I do not discuss them any further.

The reduced NPs fall into personal pronouns, zeroes, demonstratives, and several minor types of pronouns. Among the pronouns, by far the most

TABLE 11.2. The paradigm of the Russian third person pronoun *on*

	Masculine	Neuter	Feminine	Plural
Nominative	on	ono	ona	oni
Accusative	(n)ego		(n)eë	(n)ix
Dative	(n)emu		(n)ej	(n)im
Instrumental	(n)im		(n)ej	(n)imi
Locative	nëm		nej	nix
Genitive	(n)ego		(n)eë	(n)ix

frequent kind is the third person pronoun *on*. It is the most neutral reduced referential device in the sample, as well as in Russian in general. The pronoun *on* has distinct singular and plural forms, and in the singular three genders are distinguished: masculine, neuter, and feminine. Pronouns inflect for case. Table 11.2 shows the paradigm of *on*.

Another important overt reduced referential device is the demonstrative *tot* 'that' (masc. *tot*, fem. *ta*, pl. *te*). The demonstrative *tot* is used both in an adnominal and in a nominal position, but only the latter usage will interest us here; this is exactly the kind of usage of *tot* that was discussed at some length in Chapters 8 (subsection 8.6.3) and 9 (subsection 9.3.2). This referential device is quite rare in the discourse sample, but some comments will be provided in subsection 11.6.1. Other moderately common Russian pronouns that can be used with specific definite reference include the relative pronoun *kotoryj*, the reflexive pronoun *sebja* (accusative), the possessive reflexive *svoj*, the reciprocal pronoun *drug druga*. None of these will be an object of special attention in this chapter. This also concerns locutor pronouns that appear in the sample discourse only within quoted speech/thought.

Zeroes are a convention used to indicate those argument, adjunct, or possessor positions in a clause that appear unfilled but still are understood as evoking a certain referent.[3] There exist a number of distinct discourse and syntactic contexts in which zeroes appear, and in accordance with that it makes sense to posit several different zeroes. For a comprehensive list of these refer to Kibrik (1996a); here I provide an abridged version of zero classification.

---

[3] See Chapter 7, subsection 7.4.3 for a justification of this interpretational decision for Russian, notwithstanding the fact that Russian person/gender-marked inflections participate in the referential processes. In the context of this chapter it is particularly convenient to consider zeroes the carriers of the referential function; personal inflections should then be seen as ancillary referential devices and will be largely ignored.

400   IV. Cognitive Multi-Factorial Approach to Referential Choice

TABLE 11.3. A classification of referentially specific zeroes attested in the discourse sample

Subject zeroes
$\emptyset^{ind}$ – zero subject of an independent non-coordinate clause (e.g. line 2310 in example (11.1))
$\emptyset^{co}$ – zero subject of a coordinate clause (e.g. line 2307 in example (11.1))
$\emptyset^{co\sim}$ – zero subject of a coordinate clause that can alternate with a pronoun
$\emptyset^{sbd}$ – zero subject of a subordinate clause
$\emptyset^{inf}$ – zero subject of an infinitive (occurring but left unmarked in a number of examples below, e.g. line 2308 in example (11.1); line 2704 in example (11.3); line 1402 in example (11.5), etc.)
$\emptyset^{conv}$ – zero subject of a converbal clause (e.g. line 2704 in example (11.3))
$\emptyset^{imper}$ – zero subject of an imperative clause

Other zeroes
$\emptyset^{dat}$ – zero Principal of the 'state predicates', normally requiring the dative case
$\emptyset^{obj}$ – zero object (e.g. line 2311 in example (11.1))
$\emptyset^{pos}$ – zero possessor (e.g. line 2312 in example (11.6))
$\emptyset^{nom}$ – zero nominal with a non-zero adjectival modifier (e.g. line 1305, example (11.5))
@ – a zero mention of the speaker in implicit introduction of quoted speech/thought (e.g. line 2706, example (11.3))

First, there are inherently non-specific zeroes like the indefinite-personal zero and the natural force impersonal zero. In the context of referential choice, more relevant are referentially specific zeroes. These can be broken into those firmly associated with the clause subject position and the rest; see Table 11.3.

Below I do not discuss those zeroes that appear in very special syntactic positions ($\emptyset^{co}$, $\emptyset^{inf}$, $\emptyset^{conv}$, $\emptyset^{imper}$). Those zeroes that are discourse-based are in principle of interest in the present context, but those of them that are exceedingly rare ($\emptyset^{co\sim}$, $\emptyset^{sbd}$, $\emptyset^{pos}$) are also ignored. Zeroes of the types $\emptyset^{nom}$ and @ are more frequent but they are quite specialized in their distribution and require a separate study. At any considerable length only $\emptyset^{ind}$, $\emptyset^{dat}$, and $\emptyset^{obj}$ will be discussed. All referentially specific zeroes, however, can serve as antecedents of other referential devices, so it is important to always recognize them as a virtual reality that can affect subsequent referential choice.

11.3 Distribution of referential devices in the sample discourse

Table 11.4 contains a classification of relevant referential devices, along with their frequencies in the sample. The basic division is that between a full NP and a reduced NP mention. Clearly, the central type of reduced referential device in Russian is the *on* pronoun, both because it is the most unmarked anaphoric device in Russian and because it is most amply represented in the discourse sample.

TABLE 11.4. Frequencies of referential devices in the discourse sample (an asterisk * marks those types of devices that will be relevant to the discussion below)

Reduced NPs	58	
on pronouns	33	*
without a full NP alternative	20	
with a full NP alternative	13	
tot pronouns	4	*
∅^{ind}	4	*
∅$^{co\sim}$	2	
∅^{sbd}	2	
∅^{dat}	7	*
∅^{obj}	3	*
∅^{pos}	3	
∅^{nom}	12	
@	7	
Full NPs	94	*
with a reduced alternative	23	
with an *on* pronominal alternative	8	
with a questionable *on* pronominal alternative	8	
with a *tot* pronominal alternative	3	
with a questionable *tot* pronominal alternative	2	
with another alternative	2	
without a reduced alternative	71	

In Table 11.4, a number of referential devices are subdivided into those allowing and not allowing a referential alternative. This is an important distinction because referential choice is not always categorical. One and the same referential device on some occasions may be used without an alternative, while on others it does allow a referential alternative.[4] These two different situations can be expected to correspond to different activation levels. When

---

[4] Note that the notion of referential alternative used here has nothing in common with the notion of alternating pronouns, as developed in Part II of this book. The notion of referential alternatives, or alterable referential devices, is discussed in greater detail in Chapter 12.

judging on which occurrences of referential devices allow an alternative and those which do not I relied initially on my own intuition as a native speaker. To check my intuition I ran a series of experiments aimed at collecting other speakers' opinions on what is an appropriate device and what is not. A detailed report of these experiments is beyond the scope of this chapter, but basically they were conducted as follows.

I would offer the text of the discourse sample to an experiment participant and ask him/her to read it through. The next day I would offer the participant a modified text where certain original mentions of referents were replaced by alternative ones, and this was done both when my intuition regarding the acceptability of a replacement was negative and when it was positive. I asked the participant to indicate such points in discourse that seemed not quite properly worded to him/her and that called for rewording. In the course of these experiments I found out that my intuitions mostly coincided with those of other native speakers of Russian. In all cases of divergence my intuitions were more conservative than those of the experiment participants: some modifications I had expected to be on the verge of acceptability were in fact recognized by the participants as quite appropriate. From this I inferred that my intuitive estimates, with a certain caution, can be taken as working hypotheses for referential device alternation.

The output of this procedure is that all instances of a certain referential device, for example a full NP, are divided into types, such as: (a) categorical full NPs that allow no referential alternative; (b) full NPs that do allow a questionable pronominal alternative; (c) full NPs that do allow a fully appropriate pronominal alternative. This is the method I propose in order to take account of the flexible and fluid character or referential choice. The methodology of obtaining judgements on referential alternatives will be further elaborated in Chapter 12.

11.4 Activation factors

A wide range of different factors have been suggested in the literature as affecting the choice of referential device. In this section I briefly introduce the groups of potentially relevant factors, test them for significant correlation with referential choice, thus detecting the actual activation factors, and then provide an extended characterization of these significant factors.

11.4.1 *The diversity of activation factors*

The largest class of factors capture certain properties of the discourse context, in particular, properties of the nearest antecedent. This makes perfect sense as we know that activation in WM is driven by attention: if a referent was mentioned, that is given attention, at some previous moment, this raises the chance that this referent is currently activated, and therefore is referred to in a reduced way.

Among the factors of discourse context, a salient place belongs to the factors of distance to the antecedent. The most obvious intuition is that the closer the antecedent is to the current point in discourse, the more likely is the use of a reduced referential device. Again, this is quite natural from the cognitive point of view. If a referent was attended to a while ago, and subsequently activated, the level of such activation can remain high only for a certain period of time, and decays subsequently. Distance factors are measurements of discourse time: the shorter the distance, the higher the level of activation upsurge that is due to recent attention; the longer the distance, the greater the impact of the time-related decay.

Best known is the suggestion by Givón (1983b, 1990) that linear distance from an anaphor to the antecedent, measured in clauses, is a good predictor of referential choice. (Other early discussions of this and similar distance factors include Chafe 1976, Clark and Sengul 1979, and especially Clancy 1980.) This measurement often figures in the literature as 'referential distance', but since this is not the only distance measurement I am using, the term 'linear distance' will be used instead. Measuring distance in clauses is psychologically plausible, particularly because clauses are units of discourse processing; as has been known for a long time (see e.g. Dell et al. 1983), the activation of referents is inherently connected with the activation of other elements that appear in the same clause.

Fox (1987a: Ch. 5) argued convincingly that it is hierarchical structure of discourse rather than plain linear structure that affects selection of referential devices. In this argument, she used Mann and Thompson's Rhetorical Structure Theory; see Mann and Thompson (1988), Mann et al. (1992), Taboada and Mann (2006). Rhetorical Structure Theory appears to be among the most powerful frameworks for discourse structure. Its main advantage is that it provides a common approach accounting for both local and global discourse structure. Rhetorical Structure Theory claims that every discourse unit is connected to at least one other discourse unit by certain rhetorical relations, such as sequence, cause, result, concession, etc. There is a crucial difference between two types of relations: mononuclear, or asymmetric, (connecting a nucleus and a satellite) and multinuclear, or symmetric (connecting two or more nuclei).

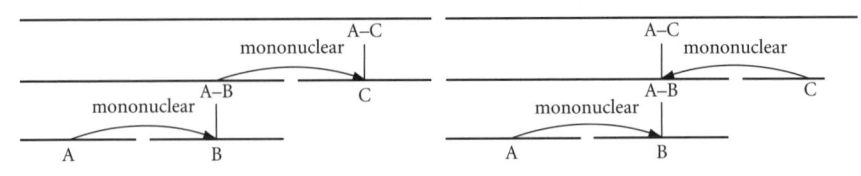

FIGURE 11.1. Examples of rhetorical tree fragments

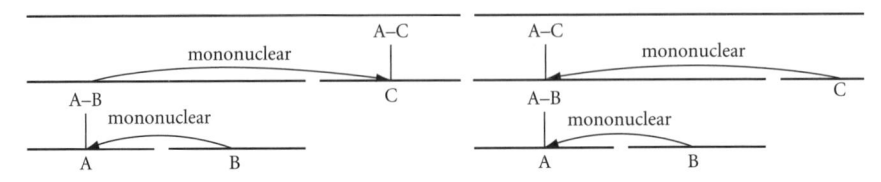

FIGURE 11.2. Examples of rhetorical tree fragments

Relying on Fox's insight, I introduced (Kibrik 1994, 1996a) the hierarchical, or rhetorical, distance measurement that is calculated as a number of steps along the hierarchical structure of discourse.[5] In many cases rhetorical distance (RhD) does not differ from plain linear distance (LinD); see e.g. the graphs in Figure 11.1 in which both RhD and LinD from C to A are 2.

Now, there are many instances in which RhD does differ from LinD. For example, linear and rhetorical distances from C to A and B in both configurations shown in Figure 11.2 are different, as shown in Table 11.5.

Rhetorical distance thus captures the closeness of nodes that are immediately connected in the hierarchical discourse structure but separated linearly, like C and A in both configurations in Figure 11.2. It also captures the hierarchical separation of linearly adjacent nodes, such as C and B in Figure 11.2. As will be seen below, the rhetorical distance measurement is a much more powerful tool for modelling reference than linear distance. However, linear distance also plays its role, though a more modest one. Some authors

TABLE 11.5. Linear and rhetorical distances in the trees in Figure 11.2

	From C to B	From C to A
LinD	1	2
RhD	2	1

---

[5] A parallel approach, also derived from Fox's work and bearing significant resemblance to mine, is the so-called Veins Theory of Cristea et al. (1998) and Ide and Cristea (2000). See also the research in the so-called right frontier constraint – Webber (1991), Holler and Irmen (2007).

(Clancy 1980, Ariel 1990, Streb et al. 2004) measure distance to the antecedent in sentences (as opposed to clauses).

Besides the distance along the local discourse structure (either linear or hierarchical), there is also a measurement along the global discourse structure. Paducheva (1965), Hinds (ed.) (1978), Marslen-Wilson et al. (1982), Tomlin (1987), Fox (1987b), Vonk et al. (1992), and Stirling (2001) all demonstrated, though using very different methodologies, that an episode/paragraph boundary is a borderline after which speakers tend to use full NPs even if the referent was recently mentioned. In accordance with these observations, the measurement of paragraph distance should be tested for written discourse.

Antecedent-related factors other than distance capture the properties of the antecedent, particularly its role in its own clause: syntactic and semantic. The influence of the antecedent's syntactic role, particularly subjecthood, upon subsequent referential choice has been proposed on many occasions, for example in Chafe (1976), Kibrik (1984), Gernsbacher (1990), Arnold (2001), Kaiser (2008). This factor is attributed an extraordinary significance in Centering Theory; see e.g. Brennan et al. (1987) and Gordon et al. (1993). According to all these studies, subjects make particularly good antecedents. In fact, what matters is not so much subjecthood but topicality (which is a linguistic rendering of focal attention; see Tomlin 1995), strongly associated with subjecthood. As has been discussed in Chapter 10, any prior mention of a referent potentially contributes to the current referent's activation, but a mention in the privileged subject position, instantiating focal attention, may contribute significantly stronger. In a language like English, syntactic subject in fact is grammaticalization of topic (Chafe 1994), but in Russian subject assignment is partly dependent on the semantic hyperrole of Principal, so the antecedent's semantic (hyper)role should also be tested as a possible activation factor (cf. Gernsbacher and Hargreaves 1992).

One might also suspect that the referential form of the antecedent may be a factor of referential choice: if a referent was pronominalized on its prior mention, that means it was activated, and activation at the previous moment may increase the chance that it is still there at the current moment in discourse (Kibrik 1984, 1988, Givón 1990: 916, Ariel 1990, Kameyama 1999, Strube and Wolters 2000, Beaver 2004). Furthermore, the syntactic and the semantic roles of the referential device in question may also correlate with referential choice.

All of these potential factors are subsumed under the label of discourse context because they are highly fluid: distance to the antecedent, as well as syntactic, semantic, and activation-related properties of referents are very unsteady. Apart from the factors of discourse context, there are factors related to the internal properties of the referent. One such factor was emphasized in Grimes (ed.) (1978) and Downing (1996b) – centrality of a referent in a discourse, which I call protagonisthood below. For a discussion of various ways to measure protagonisthood see Givón (1990: 907–909).

Protagonisthood is a property that is much more stable than the factors of discourse context, as it is established for a whole discourse. A still more stable internal referent's property is animacy. The role of animacy in language is pervasive; see Dahl and Fraurud (1996), Yamamoto (1999), Foraker and McElree (2007: 376–377). The reason is that human cognition is generally anthropocentric: we tend to attach significance to humans above all other entities. There is neuropsychological and neurophysiological evidence that animate and inanimate entities are stored and accessed differently in the brain (Mel'nik and Mnacakanjan 2010). This general fact applies to attention as well: it is known that human faces strongly capture people's attention (see e.g. Theeuwes and van der Stigchel 2006). Therefore, what is permanently attended to is permanently more activated, and one can expect animacy to be a factor of referential choice.

11.4.2 *Correlations between candidate activation factors and referential options*

All of the mentioned candidate factors were tested for the presence or the lack of correlation with the basic referential choice: the choice between the *on* pronoun and a full NP. The quantitative results of this test appear in Table 11.6 below. These calculations will serve as preliminary data for singling out those factors that really prove to be factors of referential choice. The counts in Table 11.6 use referential devices as the starting point, that is, they show, for example, how frequently *on* has an animate referent.

Various degrees of statistical sophistication can be used at this stage, when identifying which factors correlate with referential choice significantly and which do not. From my perspective, a rule of thumb suffices in this case, according to which a correlation between a value of a candidate factor and the usage of *on* is considered significant if it is observed in at least two-thirds of all cases (66%). Note that the term 'correlation' is used here in a non-technical sense.

By the adopted criterion, the following candidate factors (marked with an asterisk in Table 11.6) and their values significantly correlate with *on* pronominalization and are thus judged to be actual activation factors: animacy (value 'human'), protagonisthood ('yes'), linear distance ('1'), rhetorical distance ('1'), paragraph distance ('0'), syntactic ('subject') and semantic ('Principal') roles of the antecedent. There is no significant correlation between the syntactic/semantic role of the NP/referent in its own clause and referential choice. Also recent pronominalization of a referent does not correlate with its current pronominalization, and sentence distance appears irrelevant as well.

This way of positing the set of activation factors is further corroborated by the fact that the factors starred in Table 11.6 display very different patterns vis-a-vis full NPs, as compared to the pronoun. For example, the percentages of subjects vs. non-subjects and Principals vs. non-Principals are not significantly divergent when they are antecedents of full NPs, whereas there is a sharp contrast in the *on* column. In the full NP column, the distribution of animacy and protagonisthood is the mirror-image of that found in *on* pronouns. The percentages of different values of all distance factors are scattered across the scale in the full NP column, unlike the unipolar pattern found in *on* pronouns, and sentence distance appears irrelevant as well.

Thus, out of the candidate factors explored in Table 11.6, we will further discuss only those that appear to be actual factors of referential choice.

11.4.3 Structure of individual activation factors

Upon the identification of the list of actual activation factors, a trial-and-error heuristic procedure was undertaken, in order to explain all instances of referential choice in the data set. The basic referential choice was addressed, that is the choice between a full NP and a third person pronoun. The trial-and-error heuristic procedure was a search for optimal values of activation factors and the corresponding numerical weights that would allow such explanation. The general parameters of the target system are as follows:

- Referential choice is assumed to be fourfold: a categorical full NP; a full NP with a marginal pronominal alternative; equal allowability of a full NP and a pronoun; a categorical pronoun.
- These four types correspond to four intervals on the scale of activation score.
- The scale of activation score is intended to vary between 0 and 1.
- At every point in discourse, numerical weights corresponding to all activation factors are summed up and thus determine the current activation score.

As a result of the heuristic procedure, the set of activation factors' values and the corresponding numerical weights were selected, as shown in Table 11.7. Each numerical weight is measured in tenths of 1. The order of factors in

TABLE 11.6. Percentage of candidate activation factors' correlation with referential options[6]

Candidate factors and their values	Percentage of correlation		
	on	full NP	
Animacy			*
human	78	48	
inanimate	22	52	
Protagonisthood			*
Yes	66	46	
No	34	54	
Syntactic role of the referential device in its own clause			
subject	53	56	
non-subject	47	44	
Semantic role of the referential device in its own clause			
Principal	54	66	
non-Principal	46	34	
Linear distance to the antecedent			*
1	78	10	
2	13	21	
3	3	13	
4	–	9	
5	–	10	
>5	–	37	
no antecedent	6		
Rhetorical distance to the antecedent			*
1	91	21	
2	3	18	
3	–	11	
4	–	11	
5	–	11	
>5	–	28	
no antecedent	6		
Sentence distance to the antecedent			*
0	44	6	
1	50	27	

[6] In this table, all zeroes that at least once turned out immediate antecedents of other relevant devices were included in the section 'Antecedent's referential type'.

2	–	21	
3	–	17	
>3	–	29	
no antecedent	6		
Paragraph distance to the antecedent			*
0	91	44	
1	3	32	
2	–	10	
3	–	4	
>3	–	10	
no antecedent	6		
Antecedent's referential type			
full NP	53	62	
reduced NP, including:	47	38	
relative pronoun	3	2	
on	10	13	
tot	–	–	
Zero, including:	34	20	
$\emptyset^{ind}$	–	1	
$\emptyset^{co}$	19	11	
$\emptyset^{sbd}$	3	–	
$\emptyset^{inf}$	6	–	
$\emptyset^{dat}$	3	2	
$\emptyset^{obj}$	–	1	
$\emptyset^{pos}$	–	2	
$\emptyset^{nom}$	3	3	
Uncertain	–	3	
Syntactic role of the antecedent			*
subject	78	50	
non-subject	22	50	
Semantic role of the antecedent			*
Principal	81	63	
non-Principal	19	37	

410   IV. Cognitive Multi-Factorial Approach to Referential Choice

Table 11.7 is of no particular significance. The identified activation factors turned out to be almost sufficient for the explanation of referents' activation in the data set. However, I had to include one additional factor that was not anticipated at the previous stage. This factor (sloppy identity) will be explained below.

Factors in Table 11.7 vary in their logical structure. Comments on their structure, values, and the corresponding numerical weights are due. Activation factors will be considered in the order of their relative significance, from the strongest to the weakest.

Rhetorical distance to the antecedent. As was explained in subsection 11.4.1 above, this factor is a distance measured in EDUs from the current unit back to the rhetorically closest one containing an antecedent. This measurement captures the intuition that, as a discourse unit is produced, an important question is to which other unit it adds new content.

For figuring out rhetorical distance the quality of particular rhetorical relations is considered inessential (but see Chapter 14, subsection 14.2.5); what matters is where a given EDU connects. To see a simplified version of the rhetorical graph, consider the following example[7]:

(11.1)
2306   Mexanik$_m$ sunulsja,
        The mechanic   started,

2307   no   Ø$^{co}_m$ sejčas že   vernulsja –
        but   immediately returned –

2308   on$_m$ stal   ryt'sja   v   jaščike s   instrumentami$_i$,
        he   started   digging   in   the box of   instruments,

2309   a   oni$_i$ ležali   v   svoix gnëzdax, v strogom porjadke.
        while   they   were sitting   in   their slots,   in full   order.

2310   Ø$^{ind}_m$ Xvatal   odin   ključ,
        He   was grabbing   one   wrench,

2311   Ø$^{co}_m$ brosal   Ø^{obj}, <...>
                       dropped   it, <...>

---

[7] This example repeats (7.33) used in Chapter 7. Unlike the detailed glosses in Parts II and III of this book, in this part I use simplified glossing – a compromise between a word-by-word and free translation. Elements of the English translation that do not correspond to anything in the Russian original (such as articles) are located against blank spaces in the original. Likewise a blank space is found in the glosses line where nothing corresponds in English to a Russian word, for example a preposition. Most of the time it turned out to be possible to organize the English translation in such a compromise way. In those cases where that was not possible, two lines correspond to the original: word-by-word glosses and free translation in single quotes; this is the case, for example, in line 3502 of example (11.2).

Table 11.7. Structure of activation factors as identified for Russian narrative prose

Factor	Value	Numerical weight
Rhetorical distance to the antecedent (RhD)	1	0.7
	2	0.4
	3	0
	>3	−0.3
Linear distance to the antecedent (LinD)	1	0
	2	−0.1
	3	−0.2
	4	−0.3
	>4	−0.5
Paragraph distance to the antecedent (ParaD)	0	0
	1	−0.2
	>1	−0.4
Syntactic and semantic role of the antecedent	The closest linear antecedent is:	
	subject and Principal, and the rhet. antecedent is:	
	subject and Principal	0.4
	not subject and Principal	0.3
	either subject or Principal	0.2
	non-subject and non-Principal	0
Protagonisthood	Yes, and the current mention is:	
	the first mention in a series	0.3
	the second mention in a series	0.1
	more that the second mention in a series	0
	No	0
Animacy	Human, and the rhetorical distance to the antecedent is:	
	>2	0.2
	2	0.1
	1	0
	Inanimate	0
Sloppy identity	No	0
	Yes	−0.2

The extract in (11.1) is a typical narrative passage, most EDUs connected to the preceding ones by the rhetorical relation 'sequence'. As long as this pattern is observed, there is no difference between the rhetorical and the linear distance. For example, the pronoun *on* in line 2308 has both its linear and rhetorical antecedents in line 2307, therefore both distances are 1. However, occasionally there are deviations from this pattern, e.g. between lines 2308 and 2310. The zero anaphor in line 2310 has its nearest antecedent in line 2308. The linear distance is 2, but the rhetorical distance is 1: 2310 is immediately connected to 2308 by the sequence relation, while 2309 is an elaboration of 2308, falling out of the narrative sequence. In other instances rhetorical distance turns out to be greater than linear distance. I distinguish between the linear antecedent (the linearly closest antecedent) and the rhetorical antecedent (the antecedent that is closest according to the rhetorical structure). The two antecedents do not have to always coincide. In the cases of coincidence I merely say 'antecedent'. As rhetorical antecedents I counted all kinds of mentions, even the most implicit ones, such as e.g. the unexpressed author of quoted speech/thought. Measurements of rhetorical distance are further discussed in Chapter 14, subsection 14.2.2.

A fourfold distinction appears to be sufficient in the factor of rhetorical distance: its relevant values are 1, 2, 3, and above three. Rhetorical distance turns out to be the most powerful source of activation: it adds up to 0.7 to the overall activation score. Cognitively, this finding should be interpreted as follows. For activation, the most important thing is how long ago the referent was attended to; 'how long ago' is best modelled by the hierarchical, that is semantic discourse structure. The base level of rhetorical distance is 3: in that case its contribution to the activation score is null. When rhetorical distance is over 3, this penalizes activation. So this factor works both ways: as an activation-increasing and as an activation-decreasing factor.

Syntactic and semantic role of the antecedent. This is the second strongest activation factor. It captures the observation that those referents that were focally attended to on the last mention get activated more strongly than those referents that were 'simply' attended to. The role factor was primarily identified for linear antecedents, but see below. I have opted to merge the syntactic and the semantic role into one factor, with a certain degree of logical complexity. Most commonly the properties of subject and Principal coincide, but the combinations 'subject and non-Principal' (e.g. in passive clauses) and 'Principal and non-subject' (e.g. with state predicates requiring the dative case in Russian, such as *emu bylo udivitel'no* 'he was surprised', lit. 'to him was surprising') are also quite usual. I found it useful to distinguish between three situations: when the antecedent is both subject and Principal, when it is either of these two, and when it is neither. In the first case, the rhetorical antecedent is also taken into account, and there is a subtle distinction between the situations when it is also subject and Principal, and the case when it is not. Thus in some cases both the linear and the rhetorical antecedents affect the activation score.

Protagonisthood. This factor is different from the previous two in its operation. It can be called a correction factor. It comes into play when a referent had not been mentioned for a while, that is, in the situation of referent reintroduction (reactivation). Protagonist referents are easier to reactivate than referents that are peripheral to the story. When a referent is already active anyway, there is not much difference whether it is a protagonist or a peripheral referent. To capture this observation, I have applied the following technique. Protagonisthood counts only at the beginning of what I call a series. A series is a sequence of at least three consecutive elementary discourse units, such that: (1) all of these units mention the referent in question; (2) this sequence is preceded by a gap of at least three consecutive units without mentioning the referent in question. At the beginning of a series, that is, in the situation of reactivation, protagonisthood helps a referent to regain activation. In the explored sample of discourse I treated as protagonists the referents 'the pilot', 'the mechanic', 'Fedorchuk', and 'the passengers' (as a set). For a discussion of how to measure a referent's centrality (protagonisthood) see Givón (1990: 907–909).

Animacy is represented in the present corpus by two values: human and inanimate. Humanness, an inherent property of a referent, can increase a referent's activation. Dahl and Fraurud (1996: 56) discuss this in terms of the propensity of animate referents to pronominalization. In their data, 36% of animate NPs are pronouns, while among inanimates the pronouns' share is only 8%. However, it is not always that animacy increases activation. Much like protagonisthood, the influence of animacy is dependent on whether the referent is currently activated or it has become deactivated. Animacy is modelled as dependent on rhetorical distance. With longer distances, humanness demonstrably helps to keep activation higher, while with shorter distances human and inanimate referents are hardly distinguishable in this respect. I found out that with a rhetorical distance of 3 or more the influence of animacy is relatively high, with 2 it is slight, and with 1 it is none.

Linear distance might seem to be an unnecessary factor, given that we assume rhetorical distance as the most powerful factor. However, an analysis of the data suggests that a short rhetorical distance with a short linear distance is not the same as a short rhetorical distance with a long linear distance. In particular with the rhetorical distance of 1, long linear distance can considerably decrease the activation score. So linear distance operates differently from all factors discussed so far: it is an exclusively penalizing factor. It cannot add activation, but it subtracts it somewhat when the distance is long. I found it sufficient to distinguish between five possible linear distances: 1, 2, 3, 4, and above 4. Whereas rhetorical antecedents include all kinds of antecedents, even the most implicit ones, from linear antecedents I exclude the syntactically unidentifiable ones, particularly unexpressed authors of quoted speech.

An example of the influence of linear distance can be seen in the following:

(11.2) 3501 A Fedorčuk$_F$ smelo lez po krylu nazad k
And Fedorchuk bravely crawled along the wing back to the
upravleniju.
control unit.

3502 U nego$_F$ bylo veselo na serdce.
at him was happy on heart
'He felt happy.'

3503   Poryvy   štormovogo vetra brosali
The blows of the gale   wind were throwing
apparat.
the craft about.

3504 Fedorčuk$_F$ vzjalsja za ručku dvercy, <...>
Fedorchuk grabbed the handle of the door, <...>

For the mention of 'Fedorchuk' in line 3504, the rhetorical distance is 1. The rhetorical antecedent is in line 3501, as this is where 3504 is directly connected by the sequence relation. However, the linear distance is 2; the linear antecedent is in line 3502. This somewhat decreases the referent's activation score in 3504, and this is the chief reason why a full NP *Fedorčuk* could be used.

Paragraph distance is a factor reflecting the importance of the global discourse structure. Normally, within a paragraph activation is preserved relatively well, while a paragraph's boundary is reflected cognitively as an activation update. I distinguish between the zero paragraph distance (antecedent within the current paragraph), 1, and above 1. Like linear distance, paragraph distance is a penalizing factor. A clear example of the influence of paragraph boundary is found in the following:

(11.3) 2704 Ø$^{conv}_F$ Riskuja každuju sekundu sletet' vniz,
risking at any second fly down
Risking a fall at any second,

2705 dobralsja Fedorčuk_F do motora_e.
     reached Fedorchuk   to engine
     Fedorchuk reached the engine.

2706 @_F: Ø^{ind}_e Tëplyj eščë.
                     warm   still
     'It's still warm.'

2801 Fedorčuk_F slyšal   voj   iz   passažirskoj
     Fedorchuk   heard the howling from the passengers'
     kajuty <...>
     cabin <...>

If not for a paragraph boundary in front of line 2801, a full NP would hardly be appropriate.

Sloppy identity is the last factor on this list. 'Sloppy identity' has been used sometimes (see e.g. Dahl 1973) to convey incomplete referential identity of an anaphor with its antecedent. There are several sources for sloppy identity, such as different referential statuses of the antecedent and the anaphor, or identity of kind rather than of token (see line 1305 in example (11.5) below; for some further examples refer to Kibrik 1996a: 272). Sloppy identity is a weak penalizing factor.

The procedure for calculating activation scores can be described as a method of prizes and penalties. Points are added when a value increasing activation appears, and they are subtracted, when a decreasing value occurs. Some factors, as one can see from Table 11.7, are increasing-only – specifically, animacy, protagonisthood, and antecedent role: some values of these factors add something to the activation score, while other factors simply exert no influence. Another kind of factor, namely rhetorical distance, works both ways: short distances increase activation, long distances decrease it. Finally, the factors of linear distance, paragraph distance, and sloppy identity are decreasing-only: their unmarked value does not affect activation, while other values decrease activation.

The specific numerical weights for each factor value were found empirically, in several successive adjusting trials, to account for the occurrences of the *on* pronouns. When this was finally achieved, it turned out that all other occurrences of referential devices are properly explained by this set of numerical weights without any further adjustment. I interpret this fact as evidence supporting the adequacy of the system developed.

How can one be confident that this set of seven activation factors is necessary and sufficient for accounting for all evidence in the discourse sample? Below I discuss the activation counts for the data in the sample and demonstrate that these counts really do explain the observed evidence.

11.5 Referential mapping. Calculations of activation scores

Following the outlined methodology, the activation score was calculated for each referent mention. The system of numerical weights was designed with the intention that resultant activation scores fit within the limit between 0 and 1. It became clear, however, that this is mathematically impossible, given the purely additive character of interaction between factors. Keeping the mathematical side of the model as simple as possible was a priority, so the decision was made to allow activation scores to occasionally go beyond the range between 0 and 1. Cognitively, the activation score exceeding 1 must be interpreted as super-high activation, while all negative scores should be read as rounded to 0.

The **mapping** between the intervals of the activation scale and the basic referential devices appears as shown in Table 11.8. 'Basic referential devices' here means full NPs and *on* pronouns in the first place, but also zeroes of the type $\emptyset^{ind}$. Special comments about this and other kinds of zeroes, as well as about demonstratives, are provided in the following section.

Evidently, the mapping in Table 11.8 is between activation score and **potential** referential devices, while a speaker needs to choose an **actual** referential device. The reason for putting potential devices in the mapping is the above-mentioned flexibility of referential choice. As more than one referential device is often appropriate in the given circumstances, there must be certain intervals on the activation scale corresponding to such variability. So in the mapping shown in Table 11.8 there is a significant overlap between activations for actual full NPs and reduced referential devices. Full NPs can be used with the activation score from the minimum of the scale to up to 0.9, while pronouns are used with the activation score from the maximum down to 0.7 and, though unlikely, down to 0.4.

TABLE 11.8. Mapping between activation score intervals and potential referential devices

Referential device	Full NP only	Full NP most likely, pronoun/zero unlikely	Either full NP or pronoun/zero	Pronoun/ zero only
Activation score	0–0.3 or less than 0	0.4–0.6	0.7–0.9	1 or more

The mapping shown in Table 11.8 thus attributes significant liberty to a speaker. Recall from Chapter 2 (section 2.6) that there is a variety of referential strategies speakers can adopt, from egocentric to optimal to overprotective. This dimension of referential choice is addressed by the proposed design of referential mapping. For example, under the activation of 0.8 speakers more inclined to an egocentric strategy would use more pronouns, and perhaps extend this tendency to the interval down to 0.4. On the other hand, more apprehensive speakers would rather use full NPs with the activation score of up to 0.9. Of course, these are hypothetical scenarios, and the interaction between individual preferences and referential choice needs to be thoroughly explored.

The whole set of referent mentions that are of interest for us here includes 131 items (94 full NPs, 33 *on* pronouns, and 4 zeroes of the type $\emptyset^{ind}$; see Table 11.4). For each of these referent mentions activation scores have been calculated by simply adding the numerical weights corresponding to the activation factors' values, both positive and negative. Let us consider some examples.

(11.4)   0902   Passažiry_P   bespokojno   peregljanulis'.
                   The passengers   worriedly   exchanged glances.
         0903   Dolgovjazyj_1   poblednel
                   The lanky man   grew pale
         0904   i $\emptyset^{co}_1$ v   pervyj   raz   vzgljanul   v
                   and   for the   first   time   glanced   at   the
                   okno:
                   window:
         0905   ottuda   na   nego_1   gljanula   pustaja   temnota, <...>
                   from there at   him   looked   empty   darkness
                   'empty darkness looked at him from there', <...>

Let us examine the third person pronoun nego_1 in line 0905. This usage of the *on* pronoun is judged to have no full NP alternative. So, in accordance with the mapping in Table 11.8, the predicted referent's activation score must be '1 or more'. The factual calculation of activation score for this referent at this point goes as follows (see Table 11.7):

0.7 (RhD = 1) + 0.4 (Antecedent's role: subject and Principal) = 1.1

That is, only two factors make a tangible contribution here. Numerical weights for all other factors are simply zero. The result matches the prediction made on the basis of the referential mapping in Table 11.8.

An example of a slightly more complex calculation is presented by the following:

(11.5) 1302 Pilot$_p$ povernul   rul'
               The   pilot turned   the steering wheel

        1303 i   Ø$^{co}_p$ vyključil   levyj motor$_{e1}$.
               and   turned off   the left engine.

        1304 Fedorčuk$_F$ ponjal,
               Fedorchuk   understood

        1305 čto   pravyj Ø$^{nom}_{e2}$ stal   sam.
               that   the right one   had stopped   by itself.

        1401   Mexanik$_m$ poblednel
               The   mechanic   grew pale

        1402 i   Ø$^{co}_m$ stal kačat'   ručnoj pompoj vozdux v
               and   started pump with hand pump air   into
               benzinnyj   bak.
               gas   tank
               'and started pumping air into the gas tank with a hand pump.'

        1403 Fedorčuk$_F$ soobrazil,
               Fedorchuk   guessed

        1404 čto   on$_m$ xočet   naporom   benzina pročistit'
               that   he   wants   with   pressure of gas   clean out
               zasorivšijsja   karbjurator, <...>
               clogged   carburetor
               'that he intended to clean out the clogged carburetor with the pressure of the gas,' <...>

Consider the full NP Fedorčuk$_F$ in line 1403. This is a categorical usage of a full NP, allowing no pronominal alternative. Therefore, in accordance with the referential mapping, the predicted activation score must be 0.3 or less. The calculation of activation score for this referent mention goes as follows:

−0.3 (RhD = 4) + 0.4 (Antecedent's role: subject and Principal) + 0.3 (protagonisthood: yes, first mention in series) + 0.2 (Animacy: human, RhD > 3) −0.3 (LinD = 4) −0.2 (ParaD = 1) = 0.1

Again, the calculation matches the prediction derived from the referential mapping in Table 11.8. Finally, consider a more extensive set of examples. The following excerpt includes the portion of text already cited in (11.1) plus a few more EDUs:

11. Referential choice in Russian narrative prose 419

(11.6) 2306   Mexanik$_m$ sunulsja,
                The   mechanic   started,

2307   no   Ø$^{co}_m$ sejčas že   vernulsja –
       but   immediately   returned –

2308   on$_m$ stal   ryt'sja   v   jaščike   s   instrumentami$_i$,
       he   started digging   in   the box   of   instruments,

2309   a   oni$_i$ ležali   v svoix gnëzdax, v strogom porjadke.
       while they   were sitting in their slots, in full order.

2310   Ø$^{ind}_m$ Xvatal   odin   ključ,
       He   was grabbing   one   wrench,

2311   Ø$^{co}_m$ brosal   Ø^{obj},
                     dropped   it,

2312   Ø$^{co}_m$ motal   Ø$^{pos}_m$ golovoj,
                     shook   his   head,

2313   Ø$^{co}_m$ čto-to   šeptal
                     something   whispered
       'whispered something'

2314   i   Ø$^{co}_m$ snova   rylsja.
       and   again   dug
       'and reached in again.'

2315   Fedorčuk$_F$ teper'   jasno   videl,
       Fedorchuk   now   clearly   saw

2316   čto   mexanik$_m$ strusil
       that the mechanic   had chickened out

2317   i   Ø$^{co}_m$ ni za čto už ne vyjdet na   krylo.
       and   would never   go out to the wing.

2318   Pilot$_p$ razdražënno tolknul   mexanika$_m$
       The pilot crossly   pushed the   mechanic   with
       Ø$^{pos}_p$ kulakom   v   Ø$^{pos}_m$ šlem
       his   fist   at   his   helmet

2319   i   Ø$^{co}_p$ tknul   Ø$^{pos}_p$ pal'cem   na   al'timetr$_a$:
       and   poked   his   finger   at the altimeter:

2320   on$_a$ pokazyval   150.
       it   showed   150.

Table 11.9 contains a detailed analysis of nine referential devices found in excerpt (11.6). These nine devices include five full NPs used in anaphoric contexts; three *on* pronouns; one occurrence of zero of the type $\emptyset^{ind}$. The upper part of Table 11.9 contains a description of each referential device, including the activation score (AS) interval, predicted on the basis of the referential mapping (Table 11.8). The lower portion of Table 11.9 details the calculation of activation scores for each referential device based on six activation factors (with the exclusion of sloppy identity that was irrelevant for all nine devices).

As can be seen from Table 11.9, in eight instances out of nine the calculated activation score matches the prediction about the activation interval. One instance, the full NP *mexanika* from EDU 2318 for which the unpredictable activation score of 1.1 was calculated, involves an additional component of referential choice – referential conflict; see discussion in section 11.8.

In Kibrik (1996a: 275–277) I presented tables with the results of calculation for all referential devices in the discourse sample (except those full NPs that are obviously categorical and can only have very low activation scores). The full text of the sample is also presented there. An interested reader can verify that the system of activation factors, coupled with the mappings in Table 11.8, actually describes the full data set.

11.6 Minor referential devices

At this point brief comments are due about the minor, or relatively infrequent, referential devices attested in the sample discourse.

11.6.1 Tot *pronouns*

Demonstrative *tot* pronouns are an interesting device in the Russian referential system, designed specifically to refer to a referent second in activation (see Kibrik 1987a, 1988, and also Chapter 8, subsection 8.6.3 and Chapter 9, subsection 9.3.2). The most typical pattern of the use of *tot* is coreference with a non-subject of the preceding clause. All four occurrences of *tot* pronouns in the discourse sample follow this pattern, for example:

(11.7) 3601 Čerez   minutu   pilot$_p$ zlobno   vzgljanul na
            In   a   minute the   pilot viciously glanced   at the
            mexanika$_m$.
            mechanic.
       3602 Tot$_m$,   blednyj, vsë ešcë   perebiral
            That one,   pale,   was still pawing through the
            instrumenty   v   jaščike.
            instruments   in   the   box.

Referential device	full NP	on	on	full NP	∅ⁱⁿᵈ	full NP	full NP	full NP	full NP	on
Alternative device	?on, tot	∅	full NP	oblique	on	–	on	–	?on	full NP
Form	mexanik	on	oni	∅	Fedorčuk	mexanik	pilot	mexanika	on
Referent	m	m	i	m	F	m	p	m	a
Line number	2306	2308	2309	2310	2315	2316	2318	2318	2320
Predicted AS interval	0.4–0.6	≥1.0	0.7–0.9	≥1.0	≤0.3	0.7–0.9	≤0.3	0.4–0.6	0.7–0.9
Activation factors, their values, and the corresponding numerical weights (in boldface)										
Rhetorical distance	2	1	1	1	>3	2	>3	1	1
	0.4	**0.7**	**0.7**	**0.7**	**−0.3**	**0.4**	**−0.3**	**0.7**	**0.7**
Linear distance	2	1	1	2	>4	2	>4	1	1
	−0.1	**0**	**0**	**−0.1**	**−0.5**	**−0.1**	**−0.5**	**0**	**0**
Paragraph distance	0	0	0	0	>1	0	0	0	0
	0	**0**	**0**	**0**	**−0.4**	**0**	**0**	**0**	**0**
Antecedent's syntactic and semantic role	dir. object Patientive	subject Principal	oblique non-core	subject Principal	subject Principal	subject Principal	subject Principal	subject Principal	indir. object non-core
	0	**0.4**	**0**	**0.4**	**0.4**	**0.4**	**0.4**	**0.4**	**0**
Animacy	+	+	–	+	+	+	+	+	–
	0.1	**0**	**0**	**0**	**0.2**	**0.1**	**0.2**	**0**	**0**
Protagonisthood	+	+	–	+	+	+	+	+	–
	0	**0**	**0**	**0**	**0.3**	**0**	**0.3**	**0**	**0**
Calculated AS	0.4	1.1	0.7	1.0	−0.3	0.8	0.1	1.1	0.7
Fit within the predicted AS interval	Yes	Yes	Yes	Yes	Yes	Yes	Yes	No	Yes

The activation score of the four occurrences of *tot* varies between 0.7 and 0.8 while there is always a competing referent with the score of 1.0 through 1.2. So *tot* is actually used in the context of referential conflict.

11.6.2 *Zeroes*

Among the kinds of zeroes distinguished in section 11.2, one kind is particularly relevant in this discussion: the zero subject of an independent (non-coordinate) clause $\emptyset^{ind}$. This kind of zero can be called discourse-based, since it can obviously in no way be explained by syntactic rules. The discourse-based zero is clearly less dominant in Russian than third person pronouns, and may not even belong to the basic referential choice. (For some discussion see Nichols 1985; Grenoble 2001; Chapter 7, subsection 7.4.3.) This kind of discourse-based subject zero is a relatively rare phenomenon in the discourse under analysis; for an illustration see line 2310 in examples (11.1) and (11.6) above. There are four occurrences of this zero in the sample, out of which three could perfectly well be replaced by a third person pronoun. In addition, among the occurrences of the *on* pronoun there is one that could easily alternate with zero. This quantitative data suggests that, functionally, the discourse-based subject zero is a near equivalent of the third person pronoun that can be used under special circumstances.

It might be supposed, following Givón (1983b, 1990) and Ariel (1990), that zero reference appears in the situation of higher activation (topic continuity in Givón's terms, accessibility in Ariel's terms) compared to third person pronouns. However, in fact Russian discourse-based subject zeroes occur in the sample discourse under the same activation conditions as the *on* pronouns; see Table 11.8. It appears that for a discourse-based zero to take place some additional criteria must be met. There are too few examples in the sample, but, as a first approximation, these additional requirements are the following: rhetorical distance must be 1, the antecedent must be a subject, and paragraph distance must be 0. Furthermore, the current unit and the antecedent unit must be connected by a symmetric rhetorical relation, maybe even belong to the discourse mainline.

These preliminary generalizations suggest that the Russian referentially specific subject zero, occuring in independent non-coordinate clauses (what is called here $\emptyset^{ind}$), is based on the same principles as the zero subject of coordinate clauses ($\emptyset^{co}$). (The usages of the latter were ignored in this study because they can in principle be explained by syntactic rules, although all zeroes of this type, numbering 19 in the sample, were counted as antecedents.)

So it may be that in this domain the distinction between the discourse and the syntactic patterns is as exaggerated as it is elsewhere (see Chapter 2, section 2.2). It is very likely that common principles for Russian subject zeroes exist, and their use in coordinate clauses is simply a derivative grammaticalized version of the more general discourse pattern.

Other types of zeroes are also quite rare in the data, so it is difficult to make any specific conclusions. One could suggest that the object zero $\emptyset^{obj}$ (three occurrences, one of them in line 2311; see examples (11.1) and (11.6)) tends to be used with a mid-high activation score (between 0.5 and 1.0). The dative zero $\emptyset^{dat}$ accompanying stative predicates (seven occurrences) has very diverse activation scores ranging from −0.5 to 1.1 and varies greatly referentially (from specific to indefinite reference). Other discourse-based zeroes ($\emptyset^{co\sim}$, $\emptyset^{sbd}$, etc.) are still rarer. Much additional research is necessary to understand the functioning of zeroes in Russian discourse.

11.7 World boundary filter

Consider the following excerpt, describing the rise of the aircraft:

(11.8) 0309 Al'timetr pokazyval 800 metrov
              The altimeter showed 800 metres
        0310 i $\emptyset^{co}$ šël vverx.
              and was going up.
        0311 Uže blizko oblaka.
              already close clouds
              Clouds were already close.
        0312 'A kak v oblakax?' –
              and how in clouds
              'What's it like in the clouds?' –
        0313 pisal Fedorčuk$_F$.
              wrote Fedorchuk.

The case in point is the full NP *oblakax* in line 0312. By the rules of activation score calculation, the referent 'the clouds' fares very high at this point: 1.1. According to the standard referential choice principles, an anaphoric pronoun must be chosen. However, it is not just not chosen by the writer but absolutely impossible here. The reason is that the high activation and this referent mention are in different 'worlds': the former in the world of physical events that were happening in and around the aircraft and are being recounted to us by the writer, and the latter inside the world of Fedorchuk's speech. Evidently, there is a boundary between the two worlds that referential choice cannot trespass. Even if a referent is highly activated in the given area of a discourse, this activation does not count inside the world different from the one in which this activation has been accrued. Activation and referential choice work independently in two concurrently relevant worlds.

The 'world boundary filter' filters out certain reduced referential devices that can be projected on the basis of activation factors. The influence of 'world shifts' on referential choice has been discussed by Clancy (1980: 146ff.), Hinds (1984), Grenoble (1998); cf. Gavins (2006) on a general theory of worlds in discourse and Fauconnier's (1994) theory of mental spaces. This phenomenon certainly requires further study. One point to mention is that impenetrability of the world boundary is not exactly the same in different directions. In the example above the referent got activated in the external world, and its activation got completely depreciated in the world of quoted speech. In reverse situations, that is when a referent is activated inside quoted speech, its depreciation in the external world may be less extreme. The 'world boundary filter' must thus be considered a distinct component of the general model of referential choice; it is among the filters shown in Figure 10.2 in Chapter 10.

11.8 Referential conflict filter

Recall that one referential device listed in Table 11.9 has not received a satisfactory explanation. It is the full NP *mexanika* in line 2318 of example (11.6). This full NP represents of the referent 'the mechanic' that is so highly activated at this point that a full NP is not expected on the basis of the activation component of referential choice. The reason for this full NP occurrence is that a reduced referential device is filtered out by referential conflict, an additional component of referential choice (see Chapter 2, section 2.8, as well as Part III of this book).

By the beginning of EDU 2318, one more referent, apart from 'the mechanic', is highly activated: it is 'Fedorchuk', activation score 0.9.[8] This activation score is high enough for granting a possibility that a third person pronoun could refer to Fedorchuk. When producing discourse, speakers tend to preclude the usage of such referential devices that might be attributed a wrong referent by the addressee. At any time a speaker knows the activation scores for each referent, and if there is more than one significantly activated

---

[8] This referent is not actually mentioned in line 2318, but that does not matter. As has been argued in Chapter 10, activation factors operate at all times and provide an activation score for each referent irrespective of whether the given referent is mentioned or not at this point in discourse.

referent, the speaker can employ a referential aid – a linguistic device distinguishing the referent in question from the competing referent. In Russian, the most common lexico-grammatical means eliminating a potential referential conflict (that is, referential aids) include: number, gender, the demonstrative *tot*, and same-subject converbs (adverbial participles). None of these would work in 2318 if the speaker were to use a reduced referential device. In particular, number and gender would not help as both referents are singular and masculine. The demonstrative *tot* would not work as it is reserved for referents that are second in activation, and the converbal form of the predicate would be completely inappropriate in 2318. In addition to lexico-grammatical devices, there are less conventionalized, ad hoc ways to eliminate a potential referential conflict – those connected with the context of a particular clause; see Chapter 8. These are not helpful in 2318 either. If none of the deconflicting devices helps to distinguish the referents, then reduced forms of reference are blocked, and a full NP must be used. This is what apparently happened in line 2318. Note that there is a difference, however small, in the activation scores of the two referents; this might be the reason why the referent 'the mechanic' still is marginally pronominalizable, according to one native speaker's intuition.

It can easily be demonstrated that in all cases where a pronoun or a zero is used despite a threat of referential conflict the latter is removed by some readily available referential aid. For example, consider the pronoun *on* in line 1404, example (11.5). There are two highly activated referents here, 'the mechanic' and 'Fedorchuk', but only the former is compatible with the meaning of this complex sentence: a person normally makes guesses about somebody else's, not one's own intentions. Here an ad hoc referential aid operates, that is the factor of selective compatibility with clause semantics.

To conclude, the referential conflict filter is another component potentially blocking the usage of reduced referential devices. Its operation is much more frequently visible in discourse than that of the world boundary filter. Both of these are cumulatively represented as 'filters' in Figure 10.2 in Chapter 10.

Summary

This chapter is a focused study of discourse reference in one language, namely Russian. The key notion underlying the phenomenon of referential choice is that of referent activation in the speaker's working memory. In the type of discourse explored in this chapter – narrative written prose – all the referents' activations come only from previous discourse and/or internal properties of the referents, so the processes of activation and deactivation can be fairly effectively controlled. I have proposed a set of activation factors that can either increase or decrease activation of a particular referent. To each value of every factor corresponds a certain numerical weight, so for each referent an activation score – a cognitive and at the same time a numerical predictor of referential choice – can be calculated. The activation score of every referent at any given time emerges naturally from the previous discourse and the properties of the referent itself, and is always readily available without any special effort.

Among the activation factors that appeared crucial for the sample of Russian narrative prose are: rhetorical distance to the antecedent, syntactic and semantic role played by the antecedent, protagonisthood, animacy, linear and paragraph distances to the antecedent, and sloppy identity of referents. Among the candidate factors that appeared likely to be relevant but did not prove so are the antecedent's referential form, the referential and role properties of the current mention, and distance in sentences.

The set and internal structure of factors may be different for different languages, different registers and genres within one language, and possibly even for different speakers. It is worth noting that the developed system of activation factors was tested on another sample of Russian narrative prose (authored by the contemporary writer Fazil Iskander) and proved to be fully functional.

Aggregate activation score maps onto certain referential options. In some intervals of the activation scale this mapping is categorical, while some other values of activation score allow for a more or less free choice between a full and a reduced referential device.

Language speakers, when they are in the process of choosing a referential device, must rely on a single and cognitively simple mechanism. At the same time, it is clear that no single activation factor can fully explain all instances of referential choice. The proposed model happily combines the holistic nature of activation (a single activation score for every referent at any given time) with its multi-factorial origin. As activation factors operate in the mind irrespective of the prospects for any referent's mention, as soon as a speaker decides to mention a referent he/she has the relevant activation score available and makes the choice with a minimal effort.

The calculative technique employed to compute activation score is supposed to model the cognitive interplay of activation factors. Of course, cognitive processes cannot be that simplistic; they probably do not consist of the arithmetic operation of addition alone. I view this technique as a first approximation to a truly explanatory model of activation processes, perhaps employing a more sophisticated mathematical apparatus (see Chapter 14).

Activation is the central but not the sole component of referential choice. Two filters that can further affect referential choice have been identified. The world boundary filter prohibits a reduced mention of a referent activated in an alternative 'world'. The referential conflict filter blocks such reduced devices that can be ascribed a wrong referent by an addressee, primarily because this competing referent has a comparable activation score.

12

Referential choice in English narrative prose

Overview

This chapter[1] is another exercise in applying the CMF approach to a sample of natural discourse. This time I focus on English data. As in the previous chapter, I propose a system of activation factors, methods for calculating the aggregate activation score, and a mapping from activation score to referential options. In general, the design of this chapter is similar to that of Chapter 11 on Russian. In section 12.1 I characterize the discourse sample and the distribution of attested referential devices. Sections 12.2 and 12.3 address the difference between categorical and alterable referential devices and describe the experimental procedure of identifying potential referential options. In section 12.4 these potential options are connected to intervals of the activation scale via referential mapping. An account of activation factors, with their values and numerical weights, is provided in section 12.5. In section 12.6 specific illustrations of activation score calculations are presented. Finally, section 12.7 recapitulates the main steps one must go through when constructing a similar model for a random language.

The background of Chapter 11 allows me to be more concise in many parts of the discussion. In some details, however, the procedure in this chapter and its design differ from those of Chapter 11.

---

[1] This chapter (as well as the subsequent Chapter 13) is based on the article Kibrik (1999). I thank the publishing house John Benjamins for their permission to reproduce that article here in a somewhat revised form. A number of people provided important assistance, consulting, or comments that helped me to carry out this investigation and complete the original article, in particular Russ Tomlin, Gwen Frishkoff, Amy Crutchfield, Michael Tomasello, Leo Noordman, Wietske Vonk, Anatolij Baranov, Dmitrij Dobrovol'skij, Olga Fedorova, Karen van Hoek, Michael Posner, and Michael Anderson. This study was also reported at a number of conferences, and I would like to thank all who attended my talks and provided helpful comments, in particular António Branco.

12.1 The discourse sample. Distribution of referential devices

This chapter examines referential choice in a sample of English narrative prose. This sample was the entire children's story 'The Maggie B.' by Irene Haas.[2] The brief plot of the story is as follows:

A young girl called Margaret, or Maggie, daydreams of sailing her own ship. After she goes to sleep, she finds herself in a ship with her little brother James. There are a number of animals on board, and several trees. Margaret cleans the deck, cooks, feeds James, teaches him. Then a storm starts, and she fixes everything on the ship. After the dinner, Margaret plays the fiddle to James, and the day is over.

There are 117 elementary discourse units in the story. 76 different referents are mentioned in it, not counting 13 more mentioned in the quoted songs. There are 225 referent mentions in the discourse (not counting those in quoted text). There are 14 different referents mentioned in discourse that are important for this study, i.e. those mentioned at least once in a context where any degree of activation can possibly be expected. Among the important referents, there are three protagonist referents: 'Margaret' (72 mentions altogether, including 6 in collective references and 4 mentions by first person pronouns in quoted speech), 'James' (28 mentions, including 6 in collective references), and 'the ship' (12 mentions).

Any referent, including an important referent, can be mentioned in different ways, some of which (for example, first person pronouns in quoted speech) are irrelevant for this study. Referential occurrences that are relevant for this study fall into two large formal classes: references by full NPs (39) and references by third person pronouns (63).

Among the occurrences of third person pronouns there is a subgroup that can be called syntactic. These necessarily appear within a certain syntactic domain with the antecedent, are arguably controlled by the antecedent, and are obligatory and almost automatic. For example[3]:

(12.1) 1903 But <u>the sturdy little Maggie B.</u> kept <u>her</u> balance

(12.2) 1601 <u>She</u> took in <u>the sail</u>
       1602 and <u>Ø</u> tied <u>it</u> tight.

---

[2] One of the editions of this book is: Haas, Irene. *The Maggie B.* New York: Atheneum, 1977.
[3] As in Chapter 11, the sample discourse has been divided into elementary discourse units. EDUs are represented as lines. In the four-digit number of each line the first two digits indicate the number of the paragraph in the text, and the last two digits the number of the EDU within the given paragraph.

The possessive pronoun *her* in (12.1) is syntactically controlled by the same clause's subject; in some other languages, for example Russian, a reflexive rather than a third person possessive would appear in this position.

The zero subject in the second line of (12.2) is almost automatic in the context of clause coordination, that is, it can be accounted for as syntactically controlled. As has been discussed in the previous chapters, in certain English registers pronouns can actually occur in this context (Chapter 5, section 5.4), and at the same time marginal instances of discourse-based subject zeroes may take place in non-coordinate clauses (Chapter 6, section 6.7). In the present discourse sample neither of these phenomena is attested, and there is one-to-one correspondence between the subject position in non-first coordinate clauses, on the one hand, and zero reference, on the other. So all occurrences of zero reference can safely be considered syntactic.

The pronoun *it* in (12.2) is controlled by the antecedent in the preceding coordinate clause found in the same syntactic position. The object pronoun *it* in line 1602 is probably as automatic as the subject zero in the context of clause coordination.

So all of these three reduced referential devices (*her*, Ø, and *it*) can be treated as syntactically induced. They appear in such tight and stereotypical contexts with their antecedents that trying to explain them through the sophisticated apparatus of activation factors would be an overcomplication. This is an instance of grammaticalization: a discourse pattern is grammaticalized into a syntactic pattern.

In principle, nothing prevents one from including syntactic occurrences into the larger category of pronouns participating in referential choice. If they were included, they would perfectly well fit within the category 'pronoun with no referential alternative'; see below. The system of activation factors and activation mapping would remain the same. So the decision to exclude the syntactic occurrences of pronouns from the data set in no way affects the model developed below. There are 23 syntactic occurrences of pronouns in the sample. The discussion below is limited to 40 occurrences of pronouns that cannot possibly be accounted for by syntactic rules. For example:

(12.3) 1607 Lightning split the sky
       1608 as <u>she</u> ran into the cabin
       1609 and slammed the door against the wet wind.
       1610 Now everything was safe and secure.
       1701 When <u>she</u> lit the lamps,
       1702 the cabin was bright and warm.

The two occurrences of *she* in lines 1608 and 1701 are obviously discourse-based as they appear in different sentences from their antecedents. (In fact, also in different paragraphs.)

12.2 Categorical vs. alterable referential devices

The focus of this study is thus restricted to 39 full NP references and 40 discourse-based pronominal references. Note that the basic referential options are the same as in the Russian study in Chapter 11, even though the quantitative distribution is different.

As was discussed in Chapter 11, within each of the basic referential types – full NPs and pronouns – there is a crucial difference: whether the referential form in question has an alternative. For example, there is a big difference between an **alterable** pronoun that can be possibly replaced by a full NP, on the one hand, and a pronoun that is **categorical** (=allows no referential alternative), on the other. These two kinds of pronouns would correspond to different levels of activation. In (12.4) below an illustration of a pronoun usage is given that can vary with a full NP: in unit 1601 the full NP *Margaret* could well be used (especially provided that there is a paragraph boundary in front of unit 1601):

(12.4) 1502 A storm was coming!
        1503 Margaret must make the boat ready at once.
        1601 She took in the sail
        1602 and tied it tight.

On the contrary, there are occurrences of categorical pronouns. Consider an example which is an immediate continuation of (12.4):

(12.5) 1603 She dropped the anchor
        1604 and stowed all the gear <...>

In 1603, it is impossible to use the full NP *Margaret;* only a pronoun is appropriate.

In this study I accept that referential forms of each type (both full NPs and pronouns) fall into three categories: those allowing no alternative (=categorical), those allowing a questionable alternative, and those allowing a clear alternative (=alterable). Thus there are five **potential** referential options instead of two **actual**, or **attested**, options, and six possible correspondences between the five potential types and two attested realizations; see Table 12.1.

432 IV. Cognitive Multi-Factorial Approach to Referential Choice

TABLE 12.1. Attested and potential referential forms and correspondences between them

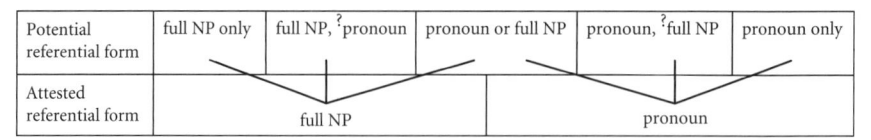

Potential referential form	full NP only	full NP, ?pronoun	pronoun or full NP	pronoun, ?full NP	pronoun only
Attested referential form	full NP	full NP		pronoun	pronoun

The information about referential alternatives is crucial for establishing a referential mapping, as different potential referential forms correspond to different intervals of the activation scale (see section 11.5). Of course, attribution of particular cases to one of the categories is not a straightforward matter. In this study, a more rigorous procedure for identifying potential forms has been applied, compared to the Russian study in Chapter 11.

12.3 Judgements on referential alternatives

The procedure of attributing each actual referential device to one of the five classes of potential forms consisted of several stages. At the preliminary stage, all instances of referential choice with the slightest chance of a referential alternative were identified. At the following stage a native speaker of English who was a linguist and had a full understanding of the problem and the research method was requested to supply her intuitive judgements on all thinkable referential alternatives in all relevant points of discourse. Each referential alternative was considered independently, under the assumption that the rest of the discourse is intact. Each referential alternative was subject to a four-way judgement: (i) appropriate; (ii) slightly awkward; (iii) questionable or significantly awkward; (iv) clearly inappropriate. Those referential alternatives that were attributed to category (iv) – clearly inappropriate – were excluded from further consideration and the corresponding referential choices were considered to be 'pronoun only' or 'full NP only' (that is, having no referential alternative).

Of course, fully relying on the intuitions of one person is undesirable, so in order to objectivize the attribution of referential devices to particular potential types, an experiment of the following design was conducted (the main stage of the identification procedure). The idea of the experiment was to modify the original referential forms, present such a modified form to an experiment participant, and see whether he/she identifies the modification as a linguistic (or 'stylistic') error. Of course, in order to keep the general well-formedness of the discourse one cannot make too many modifications at a time, because there is a threat of interference between modifications in the adjacent parts of the discourse. For this reason seven modified discourses were produced from the original discourse, and in each version modifications were kept far apart: adjacent changes never appeared closer than across a paragraph boundary, and usually had at least two paragraph boundaries between them. All relevant references were subject to modification in this or that modified discourse. On average there were ten changes of referential devices per modified version of the text. Consider an example of how modification was done. The following is an excerpt from the Margaret story in which three original referential devices are striken out and replacements are shown with underlining:

(12.6)   When she woke up, she was in the cabin of her own ship. ~~It~~ The ship was named *The Maggie B.* after her, and the nice company was her brother, James, who was a dear baby.
   A rooster crowed on deck, so Margaret knew the day was about to begin. She took ~~James~~ him out to welcome the sun. It warmed them up and brightened the sky.
   On the poop deck was a tiny farm. There was a goat and some chickens, an apple tree and a peach tree and an orange tree with a toucan perched on a branch. They picked an orange for breakfast.
   Since it was ~~her~~ Margaret's own little cabin, in her own little ship, Margaret worked hard and tidied it up with a joyful hustle-bustle.

There were thus eight different versions of the discourse (one original and seven modified ones). They were presented to twelve students of the University of Oregon, native speakers of English, who did the job of assessing the felicity of the discourse 20 times altogether.[4] Most of the participants did the assessment job twice (with the time interval of two days), but some only once. Those who did the assessment twice were presented distinct variants of the discourse. No dependency of the assessment on the number of the trial (first vs. second) was discovered. Each of the eight variants of the discourse was assessed either two or three times (2.5 times on average).

The next task was to bring all the linguist expert's and the students' judgements together and build an integral judgement of each referential

---

[4] The experiment participants were given a formal instruction, the crucial part of which is as follows: 'If you think that some of the character/object mentions in this text are not successful or appropriate, and you would prefer to edit or change them, please strike through the expression you do not like and clearly print your suggestion immediately above.'

434 IV. Cognitive Multi-Factorial Approach to Referential Choice

	−3/4	0	3/4	
	inappropriate	questionable		appropriate

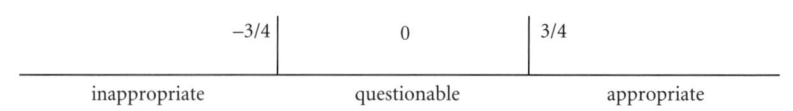

FIGURE 12.1. Averaged judgements on referential alternatives

alternative. A system of weights was set up for this purpose. The linguist expert's judgements were attributed the following weights: (i) appropriate: 2; (ii) slightly awkward: 0; (iii) questionable or significantly awkward: −2.

The student participants normally used only two options – they either did not notice a referential replacement or pinpointed it in the discourse and rejected it by reverting to the original referential option. The silent acceptance of a referential alternative was attributed the weight of 1. The rejection of an alternative was attributed the weight of −2. The difference in the absolute values is due to the fact that pinpointing an 'error' and rejecting it is a much more conscious and volitional act than default acceptance. I would even be inclined to attribute the weight of −3 to the rejection, except that it is not always clear to what degree a referential alternative is awkward.

At the final stage, all weights of judgements (including those of the linguist expert and the student participants) were totalled up and averaged. The integral judgements on referential alternatives were obtained through the numerical scale shown in Figure 12.1.

Referential alternatives with the value of −3/4 or less are considered inappropriate. Alternatives falling in the range between −3/4 and 3/4 are judged questionable. And referential alternatives with the value of 3/4 or more are considered as appropriate as the actual referential options in the original discourse. After this procedure was completed, each referential device in the discourse sample was attributed to one of the five classes of potential referential forms.

12.4 Referential mapping

The five categories of potential referential devices correspond to certain intervals on the referent activation scale. As in the Russian study (Chapter 11), here the system of activation factors was set up with the goal that activation scores mostly fit within the interval between zero and 1. However, as in the Russian study, the arithmetic nature of factor interaction sometimes pushes the activation score beyond this range. In this study I arrived at the mappings between the intervals of the activation scale and referential options, as indicated in Table 12.2.

TABLE 12.2. Mapping between activation score intervals and potential referential devices

Referential device	Full NP only	Full NP, ?pronoun	Either full NP or pronoun	Pronoun, ?full NP	Pronoun only
Activation score	0–0.2 or less than 0	0.3–0.5	0.6–0.7	0.8–1.0	1.1 or more

TABLE 12.3. Frequencies of potential referential forms in the sample

Full NP only	Full NP, ?pronoun	Either full NP or pronoun	Pronoun, ?full NP	Pronoun only[5]
15	17	22, including: 7 attested full NPs 15 attested pronouns	18	7

Total: attested full NPs – 39, attested pronouns – 40

Therefore, we here have four thresholds on the activation scale, as was first proposed in subsection 10.3.2 above. The way in which five categories of potential referential forms are numerically represented in the data set is shown in Table 12.3.

12.5 Activation factors

The set of activation factors obtained in the Russian study (Chapter 11) was originally taken as a working hypothesis for the English data. In the course of the heuristic procedure of factor analysis I arrived at a somewhat different, but quite similar set of factors. The system of activation factors that was eventually developed in this study is presented in Table 12.4.

The first three activation factors listed in Table 12.4 are distances from the point in question to the antecedent. This distance can be measured in three different ways. The simplest of the measurements is **linear distance** to the antecedent, and it is measured in the number of clauses (Givón 1983b).

Very powerful as a source of activation is the factor of **rhetorical, or hierarchical, distance**. This factor was first introduced in Kibrik (1994,

---

[5] Recall from section 12.1 that 23 occurrences of syntactic pronouns could be added to this category.

TABLE 12.4. Structure of activation factors, as identified for English narrative discourse

Factor	Value	Numerical weight
Rhetorical distance to the antecedent (RhD)	1	0.7
	2	0.5
	>2	0
Linear distance to the antecedent (LinD)	1	0
	2	−0.1
	3	−0.2
	>3	−0.3
Paragraph distance to the antecedent (ParaD)	0	0
	1	−0.3
	>1	−0.5
Linear antecedent role	Linear distance >3	0
	Linear distance ≤ 3:	
	subject of the main clause	0.4
	other active subject	0.3
	direct object, passive subject, predicate	0.2
	suppressed NP	−0.3
	other	0
Protagonisthood	RhD+ParaD ≤ 2	0
	RhD+ParaD ≥ 3:	0
	−	0.2 (first in series)
	+	0.1 (second in series)
Animacy	LinD ≤ 2	0
	LinD ≥ 3:	
	inanimate	0
	animate non-human	0.1
	human	0.2
Supercontiguity	−	0
	+	0.2
Temporal/spatial shift	−	0
	+	−0.2
Weak referent	−	0
	+	−0.2
Predictability	−	0
	+	0.1
Antecedent is introductory	−	0
	+	−0.1

12. Referential choice in English narrative prose   437

1996a); see details in Chapter 11, subsection 11.4.3. The measurement of rhetorical distance captures the idea that the hierarchical structure of discourse is highly relevant for the relationship between the point in question and the antecedent. Rhetorical distance is measured along a rhetorical graph, via a path from the current EDU to the EDU containing the antecedent. In order to conceive of this procedure more specifically, consider excerpt (12.7) and its rhetorical representation in Figure 12.2.

(12.7) 1801 James was given a splashy bath in the sink.
       1802 Margaret dried him in a big, warm towel,
       1803 and then supper was ready.
       1901 Outside, the wind howled like a pack of hungry wolves.
       1902 Rain lashed the windowpanes.
       1903 But the sturdy little Maggie B. kept her balance
       1904 and only rocked the nicest little bit.
       2001 <u>Margaret and James</u> ate the beautiful sea stew
       2002 and <u>Ø</u> dunked <u>their</u> muffins in the broth,
       2003 which tasted of all the good things that had cooked in it.
       2004 For dessert <u>they</u> had the peaches with cinnamon and honey, and glasses of warm goat's milk.
       2101 When supper was over,
       2102 Margaret played old tunes on her fiddle.
       2103 Then she rocked James in his cradle
       2104 and sang him his favourite song.

Detailed explanations why the graph in Figure 12.2 is the way it is are beyond my goals here; see accounts of Rhetorical Structure Theory in Mann

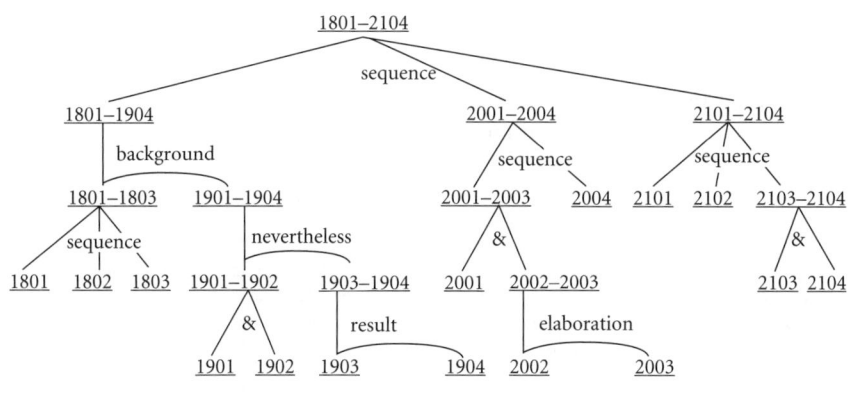

FIGURE 12.2. Rhetorical graph representing excerpt (12.7)

and Thompson (1988), Mann et al. (1992), Taboada and Mann (2006). Specific rhetorical relations between nodes of this graph are irrelevant in the current version of the CMF approach. The only thing that matters is the number of steps along the graph between the EDU where a referential device in question is contained and the EDU containing the antecedent. Rhetorical distance is measured as the number of horizontal steps from the former to the latter.[6] For example, consider the pronoun *they* in line 2004 of (12.7). The nearest previous mention is found in line 2002 – it is the zero subject of the clause (as well as the possessive pronoun). In order to get from 2004 to 2002 along the rhetorical graph, one needs to make a single horizontal leap, while other parts of the trajectory are vertical.[7] Note that the linear distance from 2004 to 2002 is 2.

Perhaps the most conclusive examples of the power of rhetorical distance as a factor in referential choice, and of its distinction from linear distance, are the instances of long quotations: it is often the case that in a clause following a long quotation one can use a pronoun, with the nearest antecedent occurring before the quotation. This is possible in spite of the very high linear distance, and due to the short rhetorical distance: the pronoun's clause and the antecedent's clause in such a case are directly connected in the rhetorical structure.[8] One such example is this:

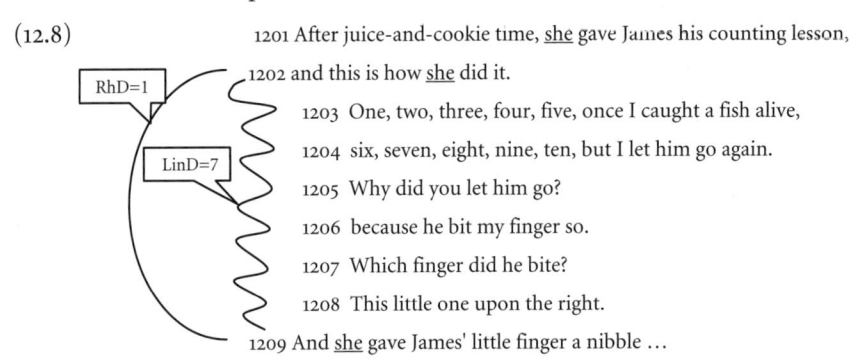

(12.8)

RhD=1

LinD=7

1201 After juice-and-cookie time, <u>she</u> gave James his counting lesson,
1202 and this is how <u>she</u> did it.
1203 One, two, three, four, five, once I caught a fish alive,
1204 six, seven, eight, nine, ten, but I let him go again.
1205 Why did you let him go?
1206 because he bit my finger so.
1207 Which finger did he bite?
1208 This little one upon the right.
1209 And <u>she</u> gave James' little finger a nibble ...

For further discussion of rhetorical distance measurement refer to Kibrik and Krasavina (2005) and to Chapter 14, subsection 14.2.2.

---

[6] Some technical difficulties arising in association with this method of measurement and not particularly relevant for this chapter will be addressed in Chapter 14, subsection 14.2.2.

[7] In this logic, one slanting line in multinuclear constructions counts as a vertical step and thus does not affect the RhD. Only going along a pair of slanting lines, such as from 2004 to 2001–2003, constitutes a horizontal step.

[8] The converse situation, that is long rhetorical distance with a short linear distance, does occur as well.

The third distance factor is **paragraph distance**; it was emphasized by Marslen-Wilson et al. (1982), Tomlin (1987), and Fox (1987b), inter alia. Paragraph distance is measured as the number of paragraph boundaries between the point in question and the antecedent.

Rhetorical distance is by far the most influential among the distance factors, and in fact among all activation factors: it can add up to 0.7 to the activation score of the referent. Linear and paragraph distance can be called penalizing factors, since they can only deduct something from the aggregate activation if the distance is too high.

The next factor indicated in Table 12.4 is that of **syntactic role of the linear antecedent** (note that because of the different principles of identifying rhetorical distance and linear distance one referent mention can have two distinct antecedents: a rhetorical and a linear one). The logical structure of this factor is rather complex. First, it applies only when the linear distance is short enough: after about four EDUs what the role of the antecedent was gets forgotten; only the fact of its presence may still be relevant. (This finding, not implemented in the Russian study, provides an interesting insight into the durability of the effect of focal attention.) Second, this factor has a fairly diverse set of features. Different subtypes of subjects have different weights, ranging from 0.4 to 0.2. Other relevant features of the factor include direct object, nominal part of the predicate, and 'suppressed NP' – a non-mention of a referent that is however semantically implied in the discourse unit, while not being syntactically identifiable;[9] an example of such a suppressed mention of 'the peaches' appears (or rather does not appear) in discourse unit 1707:

(12.9)   1706   She sliced some peaches
         1707   and put cinnamon and honey on top,
         1708   and they went into the oven too.

The antecedent role factor is the second most powerful source of referent activation after rhetorical distance.

The next couple of factors are related not to the previous discourse but to the relatively stable properties of the referent in question. **Animacy** (Dahl and Fraurud 1996) specifies the permanent characterization of the referent on the scale of the 'great chain of being', comprising at least three positions: human,

---

[9] This characterization of suppressed NPs does not include zero subjects in coordinate constructions, as they lend themselves to a very clear syntactic identification as subjects.

animal, inanimate. **Protagonisthood** specifies whether the referent is the main character of the discourse (Givón 1990: 907–909). Protagonisthood and animacy can be called rate-of-deactivation correction factors. They capture the observation that important discourse referents and human referents deactivate more slowly than those referents that are neither important nor human. In the formulation presented in Table 12.4, protagonisthood is connected with the rhetorical and paragraph distance: when these two together are high enough, a protagonist referent gains some extra activation; when they are not, protagonisthood does not matter; 'series' is a group of clauses all containing mentions of a referent preceded by a group of at least three clauses containing no mentions of the referent. Animacy is connected in this model with the linear structure of discourse: under high linear distance human referents deactivate not as much as other referents.

The final group is second-order, or 'exotic', factors, including the following ones. **Supercontiguity** comes into play when the antecedent and the discourse point in question are in some way especially close (are contiguous words or belong to the same clause). **Temporal** or **spatial shift** is similar to paragraph boundary but is a weaker episodic boundary; for example, occurrence of the clause-initial *then* frequently implies that the moments of time reported in two consecutive clauses are distinct, in some way separated from each other rather than flow from one to the other. **Weak referents** are those that are not likely to be maintained; they are mentioned only occasionally. Such referents often appear without articles (typical examples from the Margaret story are NPs such as *rain, cinnamon and honey, supper,* or parts of stable collocations designating stereotypical activities, such as *slam the door, light the lamps, give a bath, go off to bed*). **Predictability** is a relation of the current elementary discourse unit to the preceding, such that it is highly probable that a certain referent must be mentioned at this point; predictability is similar to what is sometimes dubbed implicit causality (Garvey and Caramazza 1974, Stevenson et al. 1994[10]). This is what happens with the referent 'Margaret' in discourse unit 1202:

(12.10)　　1201　　After juice-and-cookie time, she gave James his counting lesson,
　　　　　　1202　　and this is how she did it.

---

[10] As I have argued in Chapter 10, subsection 10.3.4, implicit causality is a process belonging to the class of attentional processes (rather than immediately related to activation in working memory). Still in this study of English referential choice I found it useful to include predictability as an activation factor. It may very well be the case that attentional projection of a referent from the prior context into the current EDU induces a slight but visible upsurge in the referent's activation.

Finally, **introductory antecedent** means that when a referent is first introduced into discourse it takes no less than two mentions to fully activate it.

Supercontiguity and predictability are factors potentially increasing a referent's activation, while temporal/spatial shift, weak referent, and introductory antecedent are penalizing-only factors.

12.6 Examples of activation score calculations

Numerical weights of each factor value cited in Table 12.4 were obtained through a heuristic 'trial-and-error' procedure, performed in cycles until the whole array of data was explained. There is no space here to demonstrate in detail how the system of activation factors works and predicts/explains particular referential choices in accordance with the referential mapping (Table 12.2). However, consider several examples of the system's operation. As was argued above, it makes sense to distinguish between five potential referential devices. One of them, full NP without alternative, is found in situations of null or near-null activation and is fairly straightforward. Each of the other four potential devices is illustrated in Table 12.5. The upper portion of the table gives a descriptive account of each of the four mentions and indicates a predicted activation score interval. The lower portion of the table shows the step-by-step calculation of activation score.

In contrast to the Russian study (Chapter 11), necessity for referential filters in this chapter, in particular the referential conflict, has been minimal (but cf. Chapter 14, subsection 14.1.3). This may be due to the fact that the discourse sample consisted of a children's story, and children's writers avoid situations of even a potential referential conflict.[11] This question calls for further research.

12.7 Constructing a cognitive multi-factorial model

In Chapter 11 and in this chapter I have demonstrated two examples from different languages of how the CMF approach can be used to model referential choice in a discourse sample. Perhaps it is useful to recapitulate the main steps that one must go through if one wants to build an analogous model for another discourse sample in a random language.

Step 1: Identify basic referential options. This is the choice between the most neutral and frequent referential devices. Most likely, such a choice is

---

[11] Due to the employment of the overprotective strategy; see Chapter 2, section 2.8.

TABLE 12.5. Different potential referential devices and activation score (AS) calculations

Potential referential device	Full NP, ?pronoun	Full NP or pronoun	Pronoun, ?full NP	Pronoun only
Actual referential device	full NP	pronoun	pronoun	pronoun
Alternative referential device	?pronoun	full NP	?full NP	–
Form	Margaret	she	him	she
Referent	'Margaret'	'Margaret'	'James'	'Margaret'
Example in which mention occurs	(12.7)	(12.3)	(12.7)	(12.5)
Line number	1802	1701	1802	1603
Predicted AS interval	*0.3–0.5*	*0.6–0.7*	*0.8–1.0*	*≥1.0*
Activation factors, their values, and the corresponding numerical weights (in boldface)					
Rhetorical distance	3 **0**	2 **0.5**	1 **0.7**	1 **0.7**
Linear distance	3 **−0.2**	2 **−0.1**	1 **0**	1 **0**
Paragraph distance	1 **−0.3**	1 **−0.3**	0 **0**	0 **0**
Antecedent's syntactic role	S **0.4**	S **0.4**	passive S **0.2**	S **0.4**
Animacy	Human, LinD ≥ 3 **0.2**	Human, LinD ≤ 2 **0**	Human, LinD ≤ 2 **0**	Human, LinD ≤ 2 **0**
Protagonisthood	Yes, RhD +ParaD ≥ 3 **0.2**	Yes, RhD +ParaD ≥ 3 **0.2**	Yes, RhD +ParaD ≤ 2 **0**	Yes, RhD +ParaD ≤ 2 **0**
Calculated AS	*0.3*	*0.7*	*0.9*	*1.1*
Fit within the predicted AS interval	*Yes*	*Yes*	*Yes*	*Yes*

twofold: between a full and a reduced referential device. Among the latter the most likely candidates are third person pronouns and zeroes. Besides the major referential devices, identify additional, or minor, referential devices in the sample as they are of interest too.

Step 2: Identify alterable vs. categorical referential devices. This must preferably be done through an experimental procedure, involving modification of referential options in natural discourses and using the intuitions of multiple native speakers. Categorical full NPs and reduced devices correspond to different activation levels than the alterable ones.

Step 3: Identify the significant activation factors, as opposed to insignificant. For example, in Russian discourse third person pronouns have subject antecedents in 78% of occurrences, while full NPs have subject antecedents only in 50% of occurrences; thus two different devices pattern very differently, and there is a high degree of correlation of subjecthood with one of the devices, so this candidate factor should be considered a genuine activation factor.

Step 4: Heuristically find an optimal combination of the following:

- activation factors' logical structure, that is, their values
- numerical weights corresponding to each value
- mapping between activation scores and potential referential options.

Step 5: Identify the role of additional components of referential choice, such as the referential conflict filter.

In section 14.3 the material of an additional language (Japanese) will be introduced, to which the CMF approach has been extended, essentially according to the steps just enumerated.

The CMF model developed and applied in Chapters 11 and 12 is not just formulated in a declarative way; there is also a mathematical, or at least quantitative, or calculative component to it. Both of the studies presented are based on small data sets, and there is a reason for this. As must have become clear from the exposition of the calculative component of this approach, it is extremely time- and effort-consuming, and initially must be restricted to small data sets. I believe this does not call into question the theoretical result: a system of interacting activation factors can indeed be constructed. It must be made clear that the original purport of these studies was of a theoretical character: to overcome the major stumbling blocks common in the studies of reference, including the lack of a real cognitive interpretation, circularity of argument, and inability to account for the multi-factorial character of referential choice. In Chapter 14 I present some extensions of this approach that are computationally and mathematically more sophisticated.

Summary

In this chapter I have demonstrated a CMF model of referential choice in a sample of English narrative prose. The design of this model is fundamentally the same as in Chapter 11 devoted to Russian. English referential choice is immediately determined by a referent's activation score – a numerical measurement indicating the level of a referent's current activation in working memory. Activation score, in turn, is derived from an interaction of relevant activation factors. At each point in discourse, values of all activation factors are easily identifiable, and to each value a fixed numerical weight corresponds. Activation score is calculated as a sum of all relevant numerical weights.

It is useful to point out the differences between the model developed in this chapter and the model proposed for Russian in Chapter 11. These differences may be partly due to the differences between the languages and between the particular discourses. However, the study reported in this chapter is more advanced than the Russian study on several counts.

Compared to the Russian study in Chapter 11, a more sophisticated procedure of judgement on referential alternatives was undertaken in this study. An experimental procedure was implemented, involving modification of referential options in the original discourse and collecting native speakers' judgements on such modifications. This procedure led to identifying, for each referential device, the type of potential device, such as 'pronoun only' or 'pronoun, questionable full NP'.

The system of activation factors developed for English is very similar in its main traits to that developed for Russian but has some important differences. The logical structure of activation factors is somewhat simpler, which is an asset. More factors were found necessary for accounting for all of the data set. In particular, several second-order factors have been added. In all, eleven activation factors have been posited.

The mapping between the intervals of the activation scale and the potential referential options also is organized similarly to the Russian study, but one more potential option is added. All data in the discourse sample are accounted for by the proposed system of activation factors, their values and weights, and the referential mapping.

The general model of referential choice is supposed to be universal but the set of activation factors, their relative numerical weights, and thresholds in the AS range are language-specific. A comparison of the referential systems of the two languages described here (Russian and English) may serve as a proto-typology in this domain. More extensive exploration in language typology from the viewpoint of the CMF approach is a matter of future research.

13

Cognitive inferences from the linguistic study of reference in discourse

Overview

Cognitive linguistics can boast a very moderate contribution to the general agenda of cognitive science. In this chapter I address several traditional issues in the theory of working memory (section 13.1) and attempt to demonstrate that linguistic evidence can be illuminating for these issues.

The first issue to address is the capacity of working memory. Provided that we have a framework for calculating every referent's activation at any given time, can it be used for estimating how much information working memory holds? In section 13.2 I argue that it can and present the numerical measurement of grand activation serving as an estimate.

The second issue is the control of working memory. Information is brought to working memory by the cognitive process known as attention. The linguistic manifestations of attention (in particular, focal attention) and working memory allow us to propose a coherent theory of the interplay between these two cognitive processes (section 13.3).

The third question is forgetting from working memory. Linguistic evidence sheds light on the traditional psychological debate on the leading mechanisms of forgetting – through simple decay or through interference (section 13.4).

In section 13.5 the relationships between cognitive linguistics and the more general interdisciplinary field of cognitive science are discussed.

13.1 Three classic puzzles of working memory

In Chapter 10 (section 10.2) I reviewed the main theoretical questions about working memory and attention, as perceived by contemporary cognitive psychologists and neuroscientists. These questions and the extant tentative answers helped to formulate the explanatory approach to reference, as exposed in Chapters 11 and 12. This approach, relying on and grounded in cognitive-psychological work, is still purely linguistic as it aims at explaining phenomena observed in natural discourse. Now, the question is: can this approach, in turn, shed some light on the general properties of working memory (and perhaps attention)? Can the linguistic results be significant for a broader field of cognitive science, specifically for research in working memory?

In Chapter 10, subsection 10.2.2 I listed the main traditional but still unresolved puzzles in working memory (WM) research, relying on a more extensive list in Shah and Miyake (1999). In this chapter I propose that this linguistic approach indeed can offer specific contributions to several classic problems in WM, especially the following:

- capacity: how much information WM can hold at one time?
- control: how information enters WM?
- forgetting: how information quits WM?

These three questions are addressed in some detail in this chapter. I attempt to demonstrate that linguistic data and analyses can contribute to these problems in general cognition. The linguistic model developed in Chapters 10 to 12 to explain and predict discourse phenomena has implications for more general cognitive issues. From observing reference in natural discourse one can make certain inferences about the human ability of working memory.

13.2 Working memory capacity

The question of the capacity of WM is the following: how much information can there be in WM at one time? In the context of the discussion of discourse reference, this question can be rephrased as follows: how many discourse referents can be activated in WM at one time? Before delving into this problem two preliminary issues must be settled. First, whether it is reasonable to discuss a specialized WM for referents; second, what could be the units in which the content (and capacity) of WM is measured.

13.2.1 *Working memory for specific referents*

There are multiple kinds of information processed in WM at any given time. When I am telling someone a story, the kinds of information passing through my WM include the characters I am talking about, the events these characters were involved in, the relationships of these events to my addressee's prior experience, meanings as opposed to sounds, processes of monitoring the flow of my discourse and the addressee's alertness with respect to my discourse, etc. Besides these kinds of information immediately related to my discourse production, my WM is possibly processing the physical environment, as perceived by my vision, hearing, and other senses.

The multiplicity of various concurrent tasks for WM is addressed in modern psychology and neuroscience, beginning with the early distinction between verbal and visuo-spatial WM (see e.g. Baddeley and Hitch 1974, Baddeley 2000: 83–85, Shah and Miyake 1999). Smith and Jonides (1997), relying on psychological and neurophysiological experimentation, suggested that there are multiple working memories, devoted to different types of information: spatial, verbal, and information related to visual objects. Still more numerous functional and corresponding anatomical distinctions were proposed within WM in more recent research; see Postle (2006) for a review. While recognizing the danger of an extreme compartmentalization of WM subsystems, in the current discussion I follow the logic of many prior researchers and postulate one specific kind of WM: WM for specific referents. This is probably very close to what is sometimes called 'object WM' in psychology and neuroscience; see Schacter et al. (2000: 631) for a review. Within the domain of discourse, referring is among the most central and effort-consuming cognitive tasks, so such a postulation seems plausible. If so, the question of the maximal capacity of such a portion of WM can be legitimately raised.

13.2.2 *The content of working memory: items or standard units?*

As was discussed in Chapter 10, psychologists traditionally measure the capacity of WM in terms of the number of items. In a famous paper, Miller (1956) estimated this capacity as seven plus or minus two items. More recently, a number of studies appeared that revised this number in the downward direction; most notably, Cowan (2001, 2005), carrying out various behavioural tests, observed a uniform limit of four items. (Cowan sometimes attributes this limit to the focus attention, but in his model focus of attention and working memory are not clearly delineated.) In language-related tasks, Daneman and Carpenter (1980) and their followers also describe the working memory span in terms of number of words an experiment participant can memorize.

Measuring WM capacity in items presupposes, explicitly or implicitly, a theory that residence in WM is a yes–no issue; see a review of many studies in Cowan et al. (2008). This tenet, however, is highly unlikely. As was argued in Chapter 10 (subsection 10.3.2), items in WM can enjoy various degrees of activation, and the process of deactivation is inherently gradual. At any given moment, WM can hold some fully activated referents and some partially activated referents. Therefore, actual volumes of WM cannot always be integers. So, in order to be realistic, one must recognize that WM capacity should be measured in some standard units rather than as the number of items.

The standard unit I propose is the maximal activation of an individual referent. Suppose that in a certain numerical system such maximal activation is 1. If at a certain point in discourse there are two activated referents, and one of them is maximally activated while the other enjoys a half activation, then the overall volume of WM for specific referents will be 1.5 at this moment of time.

13.2.3 *Grand activation*

The system of activation factors, their values, and corresponding numerical weights (Chapters 11 and 12) was developed in order to explain the observed instances of referential choice in discourse. In addition, this system accounts for potential referential alternatives, that is referential expressions that might be used instead of those actually attested. Originally this system was designed to address mentions of only those referents that were actually referred to by the speaker at certain points in discourse. However, when the system was already in place it was discovered to have an important advantage: it operates independently of whether a particular referent is actually mentioned at the present point in discourse. That is, the system identifies any referent's activation at any point in discourse. For example, the activation score of the referent 'Margaret' is identified for every EDU no matter whether the author chose to mention 'Margaret' in it. Consider EDU 1608 in the following excerpt of the story we analysed in Chapter 12:

(13.1) 1601 She took in the sail
        1602 and tied it tight.
        1603 She dropped the anchor
        1604 and stowed all the gear,
        1605 while rain drummed on the deck
        1606 and thunder rumbled above her.
        1607 Lightning split the sky
        1608 as she ran into the cabin
        1609 and slammed the door against the wet wind.

Only two referents are mentioned in 1608: 'Margaret' and 'the cabin'. However, a number of other referents have an activation score greater than zero at this point, including: 'the anchor', 'the gear', 'rain', 'the deck', 'thunder', 'lightning', and 'the sky'. The sum of activation scores of all relevant referents gives rise to a measurement that can be called **grand activation** – the summary activation of all referents at the given point in discourse. In 1608, for example, grand activation is 3.7.

To make this notion clearer, consider an analogy of referents spoken of in a discourse with a set of electric bulbs. At certain moments of time, individual bulbs can be fully lit, partially lit, or not lit at all. At any given moment, there is a certain cumulative amount of light produced by all bulbs, irrespective of which bulb(s) in particular we are interested in at this time. Likewise, at different times in discourse referents become more or less active, and grand activation is their cumulative effect in WM. A referent can contribute in a substantial way to grand activation, even if it is not currently attended to (that is, mentioned) by the speaker.

What are the standard units that grand activation is measured in? Recall from Chapters 11 and 12 that the value of 1 was initially intended as the maximal activation of a single referent, but the arithmetic specifics of the numerical systems worked so that a referent's activation could rate a little higher, 1.1 or 1.2. These levels of activation being super-high, it can be said that grand activation is measured in units defined as normal high activation of an individual referent (that is, 1). If so, grand activation can be used as an estimate of the current overall volume of the specific-referents portion of WM. Of course, since current activation of a specific referent is measured in decimals, grand activation does not have to be an integer either but can have various decimal values.

The question is what are the limits of variation of grand activation. Figure 13.1 below depicts the dynamics of activation processes in a portion of the English discourse analysed in Chapter 12.[1] There are three curves in Figure 13.1: two pertaining to the activation of the protagonists 'Margaret' and 'James', and the third representing the changes in grand activation. Note that the values of grand activation come not only from the activation scores of 'Margaret' and 'James' but also from other referents activated during the respective EDUs. One more example of the same kind can be seen in Figure 13.2.[2]

Observation of the evidence, illustrated by Figures 13.1 and 13.2, makes it possible to arrive at several important generalizations.

---

[1] Lines 1401 to 2104 of the text. Most of these lines can be found as examples in Chapter 12. The full text is given as an appendix to Grüning and Kibrik (2005).

[2] Lines 0201 to 0903. The beginning of this excerpt appears below as example (13.2).

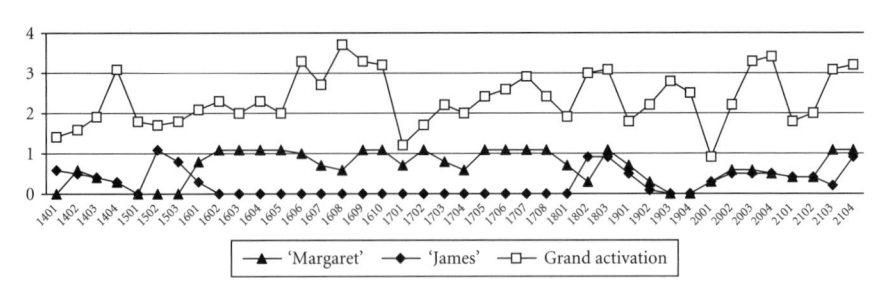

FIGURE 13.1. The dynamics of two protagonist referents' activation and of grand activation in an excerpt from the English story (lines 1401 to 2104)

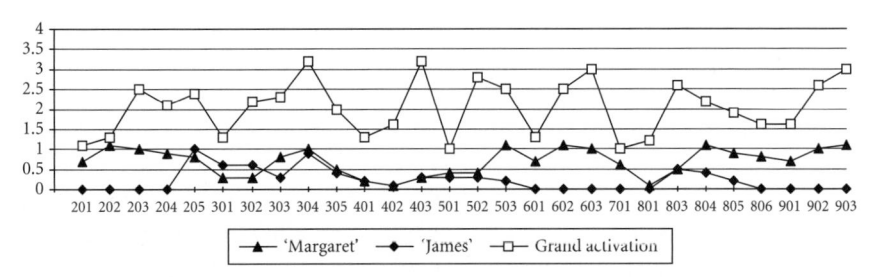

FIGURE 13.2. The dynamics of two protagonist referents' activation and of grand activation in an excerpt from the English story (lines 201 to 903)

First, grand activation varies within the range between 1 and 4, and most of the time is below 3.[3] Thus the variation of grand activation is very moderate, the ratio of its maximal to its minimal value being between 3 and 4. Compare this to the fluctuation between the maximal and zero activation for individual referents (the ratio is mathematically infinite). This observation means that, as discourse unfolds, WM for specific referents is always filled by some information, at least at the level characteristic of the full activation of a single referent. Furthermore, the maximal capacity of WM seems not to exceed four maximal activations of a single referent.

Second, the mean grand activation in all EDUs represented in Figures 13.1 and 13.2 equals 2.2. This suggests that the most typical situation in discourse is having two fully activated referents, or a numerical equivalent of that (several less than fully activated referents).

---

[3] It is important to emphasize that the upper limit on grand activation does not depend on the amount of protagonists in a discourse. Even when there are more than two protagonists, at a given point in discourse not all of them act, and grand activation still remains within the same limits.

13. Cognitive inferences   451

Third, the strongest shifts of grand activation are found at paragraph boundaries. Even a visual examination of the graphs in both figures demonstrates that grand activation values at the beginnings of all paragraphs are local minimums. The mean grand activation at the beginnings of the paragraphs is 1.4. In contrast, in the middle or at the end of paragraphs grand activation gradually builds up to a local maximum. Evidently, one of the cognitive functions of paragraph boundary is activation reset.[4]

These findings appear relevant for the general theory of working memory. Particularly remarkable is the convergence of the result on WM maximal capacity with the results of psychological studies. According to the natural discourse evidence, this maximal capacity does not exceed four maximal activations of a referent. This number cannot be simply coincidental with the figure of four items obtained by psychologists and neuroscientists using a variety of experimental methodologies; see Cowan (2001), Luck and Vogel (1997), Awh et al. (2007) inter alia.

As was discussed in Kibrik (1999: 45–46), there are some differences between the Russian and the English activation patterns. For Russian, the mean grand activation was found to be 1.7 (in contrast to 2.2 found for English). Paragraph boundaries seem to have a less radical significance in Russian compared to English. Both of these tendencies are observed throughout the discourse samples employed in the studies. It is not clear whether those differences can be attributed to a difference between languages, or discourse genres, or are significant at all. These questions remain open for further research.

13.3 Control of working memory

The question of the control of WM is the question of how information comes into WM. As was discussed in Chapter 10 (subsection 10.2.3), many psychologists and neuroscientists currently hold the view that WM is controlled by attention. The controlling role of attention amounts not only to bringing information into WM but also to the maintenance of information in WM. In this section, however, I concentrate on the first of these two controlling functions of attention. Related to the question of control is the

---

[4] Of course, a drop in grand activation at paragraph boundaries is predetermined by the fact that paragraph boundary is a strong activation decreasing factor: each referent is deactivated after a paragraph boundary, and, therefore, the sum of particular ASs necessarily goes down. However, grand activation drop is not a mere artefact of the present approach. The deactivational effect of a paragraph boundary is an inherent fact that needs to be accounted for by any theory of reference in discourse. The observation of grand activation drop is a direct consequence of that inherent fact.

452 IV. Cognitive Multi-Factorial Approach to Referential Choice

question of a source from which information comes into WM. As was again discussed in subsection 10.2.3, attention can be directed to either external stimuli or to long-term memory. Given that attention controls WM, this means that these are two possible sources of information in WM. This issue is not discussed in any detail here. Since this study is based on narrative discourse we can assume that the relevant source of information is the speaker's long-term memory.

As was argued in section 10.3, the linguistic manifestation of attention is referent mention, or reference. Furthermore, the degree of activation in WM is manifested by referential choice; specifically, high activation is manifested as the choice of a reduced referential device. There is thus a quartet of notions linked by the relations of control and manifestation, as represented in Figure 13.3.

Note that the 'control' relation in Figure 13.3 has a temporal dimension. Suggesting that attention controls WM means that what is attended to at moment t_n gets activated in WM at moment t_{n+1}. Likewise, suggesting that referent mention controls or affects referential choice means that referent mention at moment t_n leads to reduced referential choice at moment t_{n+1}.

The dotted single arrow in Figure 13.3 represents the possible control relation between referent mention and subsequent referential choice that can be expected based on what we know from cognitive psychology and neuroscience. If we are able to demonstrate that referent mention actually facilitates the subsequent use of a reduced referential device we would obtain a coherent picture and corroborate, on purely linguistic grounds, that:

- The controlling relation holds between attention and WM, as hypothesized by psychologists and neuroscientists.
- Manifestations of cognitive processes indicated in Figure 13.3 are understood correctly.

Now, according to the model of referential choice developed in Chapters 10 to 12, if a referent is mentioned in EDU n (that is, moment t_n), then (provided

Moments of time	t_n	t_{n+1}
Cognitive processes	ATTENTION	⟶ WORKING MEMORY
	⇓	⇓
Linguistic phenomena	REFERENT MENTION	┄▶ REFERENTIAL CHOICE

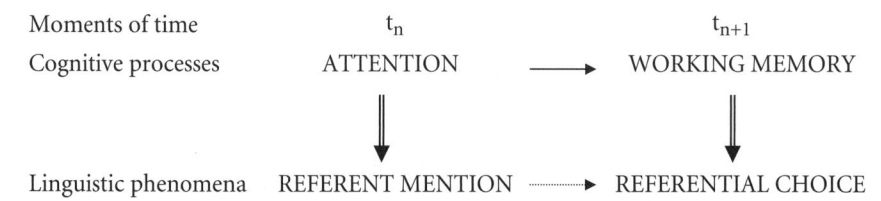

FIGURE 13.3. The quartet of cognitive and linguistic phenomena (single arrows denote the relation of control; double arrows denote the manifestation in linguistic structure)

that the speaker chooses to remention it) its mention in EDU n+1 (that is, moment t_{n+1}) will most likely be a reduced one. The reason is that distance to the previous mention is the strongest factor of reduced reference: if the referent has been mentioned close by (especially along the discourse's rhetorical structure), the chances are very high that a reduced referential device will be selected at the point in question. Therefore, the relation between mention and referential choice is exactly as predicted in Figure 13.3: a recent mention strongly affects referential choice. So we can conclude that the quartet of phenomena depicted in Figure 13.3 actually does operate in a highly coherent and close-knit way.

An even stronger piece of support for this quartet comes from the experimental paradigm established in the work of Tomlin (1995). As has been convincingly demonstrated in that experimental study, focal attention is systematically conveyed by language speakers as the clause subject. If a referent that is focally attended to plays the patient role in its clause, in many languages, including English, speakers consistently use the passive voice or its functional equivalent, thus keeping the 'focal attention = subject' principle intact. In some languages, however, speakers use active voice and normal word order in both agent- and patient-attended clauses, and one such language is Russian. Myachykov and Tomlin (2005) explored this phenomenon in detail and discovered that Russian speakers, when reporting a patient-cued situation, take a 200 msec delay before they verbalize the event. This delay is interpreted as the period of time necessary for restructuring the speaker's attentional distribution. If so, in Russian, as well as in English, focal attention is mapped onto the subject syntactic role. The difference between these two languages is only in the extent to which their grammars are attuned to expressing varying correspondences between focal attention and semantic roles.

As was discussed in Chapters 11 and 12 (see e.g. section 11.5), one of the most powerful activation factors is the antecedent's subjecthood. While a recent mention makes a reduced referential device probable, a recent mention in the subject position makes it almost guaranteed. In both English and Russian, an antecedent's subjecthood can add up to 0.4 to the overall activation of a referent. In both English and Russian discourse samples, 86% of pronouns allowing no referential alternative have subjects as their antecedent. We can thus posit a modification of Figure 13.3, now concentrating on focal attention rather than attention in general, and specifying the memorial status and the corresponding linguistic manifestation, see Figure 13.4.

To recapitulate, attention feeds WM, i.e. what is attended to at moment t_n becomes activated in WM at moment t_{n+1}. (Linguistic moments are elementary

Moments of time	t_n	t_{n+1}
Cognitive processes	FOCAL ATTENTION ⟶	HIGH ACTIVATION IN WM
	⇓	⇓
Linguistic phenomena	MENTION IN SUBJECT POSITION ⟶	USE OF A REDUCED REFERENTIAL DEVICE

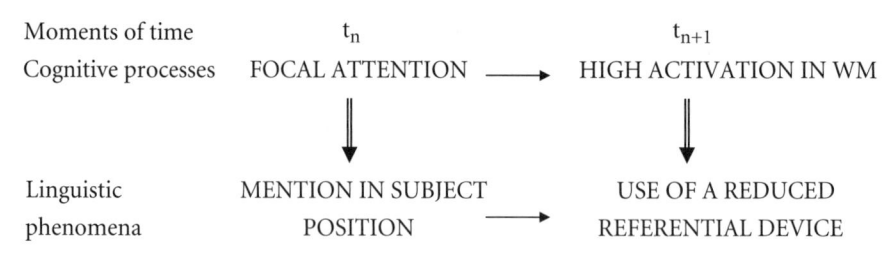

FIGURE 13.4. The interplay of focal attention and high activation in cognition and in discourse (single arrows denote the relation of control; double arrows denote the manifestation in linguistic structure)

discourse units.) Focally attended referents are coded by subjects; at the next moment they become highly activated (even if they were not before) and, if the speaker needs to mention such a referent it is coded by a reduced referential device. As has been argued in Chapter 12, the effect of an antecedent's subjecthood is a short-lived one and expires quite rapidly.

13.4 Forgetting from working memory

How does information get forgotten from WM?[5] There is a long debate in cognitive psychology between two competing hypotheses (for reviews see e.g. Baddeley 1986: 6–71; Cowan and AuBuchon 2008). The first one, sometimes called 'trace decay', suggested that forgetting is a function of time. The second hypothesis, admittedly a more sophisticated one, proposed that information gets forgotten not simply because of the time factor but due to interference of or displacement by other incoming information. This debate was particularly ardent several decades ago, but it is still ongoing in cognitive psychology; see e.g. Baddeley and Logie (1999), Cowan (1999), Oberauer and Kliegl (2006). Sometimes compromise approaches have been proposed; see Baddeley (1990: 46–47) and Altmann and Schunn (2002). The debate on the mechanisms of forgetting in psychology concerns not only working memory but, actually much more centrally, long-term memory. The present discussion, however, is limited to WM only.

In the cognitive model of referential choice put forward here, the factor of time is captured by means of the distance factors. Evidently, distance factors are static, text-based reflections of what is actually time in online language

---

[5] In psychology, it is conventional to use the word 'forgetting' when talking about the decay of information in working memory. The term 'short-term forgetting' is sometimes employed; see e.g. Baddeley (2000: 79).

use. As distance (in its different aspects) becomes greater, activation goes down.[6] That is, the model developed here apparently is compatible with the trace decay hypothesis. What is the linguistic evidence in favour of this view?

First, referents clearly deactivate, even in the absence of other incoming strongly competing referents. Consider an example from the second and third paragraphs of the Margaret story analysed in Chapter 12:

(13.2) 0201 When she woke up,
       0202 she was in the cabin of her own ship.
       0203 It was named The Maggie B. after her,
       0204 and the nice company was her brother, James,
       0205 who was a dear baby.
       0301 A rooster crowed on deck,
       0302 so Margaret knew the day was about to begin.
       0303 She took James out to welcome the sun.
       0304 It warmed them up
       0305 and brightened the sky.

In discourse unit 0304, there are two pronouns referring to three highly activated referents: 'Margaret', 'James', and 'the sun', with activation scores of 1, 0.9, and 1.1, respectively. That is, three highly activated referents cohabit perfectly well within one EDU, and do not preclude each other either from high activation or from pronominal mention.

Now compare this with the situation in discourse unit 0302. Here the referent 'Margaret' is highly unlikely to be mentioned by a pronoun, as its AS (=activation score) is 0.3. Is non-pronominalizability of 'Margaret' in 0302 due to interference of other referents? Candidate referents for such a role would be 'James' (AS = 0.6), mentioned in two immediately preceding EDUs 0204 and 0205, and the referent 'the rooster' (AS = 0.9), newly introduced in the immediately preceding EDU 0205.

Keeping in mind what is permissible in 0304, it looks very implausible that two referents, one of a mid-high AS, the other of a very moderate AS, could possibly displace 'Margaret' from WM and deprive this referent of high activation.[7]

---

[6] As was demonstrated in Chapters 11 and 12, the rate of deactivation can be different for different referents: protagonists and humans deactivate more slowly than other referents. However, deactivation always happens with time, and even for protagonists and humans the distance factors are most powerful.

[7] One could argue that in such cases displacement might still take place, just the displacing information is not referents but, perhaps, other activated information – states or events being spoken of. However, as was discussed in subsection 13.2.1 above, it is likely that working memory for specific referents is a relatively separate section of the cognitive system with its own capacity limitations.

What does really deactivate 'Margaret' since its previous occurrence in 0204 is distance – paragraph, rhetorical, and linear.

The second point potentially supporting the trace decay hypothesis is that a limitation on the number of concurrently activated referents does not necessarily require the concept of displacement or interference. It can be explained by the already stated limitation on the capacity of WM. Since grand activation rarely exceeds 3 and remains below 4, three strongly activated referents, as in 0304, is about as much as there can be in discourse at one time. And this is due not to the displacement effect but to the balanced system of activation factors that activate and deactivate referents in accordance with the limits of the WM store. So, overall, it appears that the 'trace decay' model is compatible with the natural discourse data and can explain deactivation phenomena, as expressed by referential choice. This model, like the simpler one, thus gains some points over the more complicated interference model.

The phenomenon of competition between referents is, however, real. Suppose that there are two highly activated referents at a certain point. Suppose the speaker needs to mention only one of them at that point, and plans to use a reduced form of reference on the basis of the standard pattern: if high activation, then a reduced referential device. But the speaker may preview the addressee's difficulty in telling apart two concurrently activated referents, when trying to understand the reduced referential device. This situation has been extensively discussed in the previous chapters under the name of referential conflict. Languages possess various devices helping to discriminate between concurrently activated referents, for example, gender and number (as in 0304). Referential aids allow a speaker to keep a reduced referential device. When referential aids are not available, referential conflict can prevent the speaker from using a reduced referential form even in a case of a very high activation. As a psychologist would put it, the use of a reduced referential device is inhibited. The important point here is that referential conflict and all processes associated with it are *a separate component* of the referential system; see discussion in Chapter 2, section 2.8. Referential conflict is not an activation (or deactivation) factor, it is a filter coming into play *after* the activation factors computed the ASs of referents (see Figure 10.2 in Chapter 10). So, referential conflict, or interference, can make a speaker act as if the piece of information were forgotten from WM: both under low activation and under irrevocable referential conflict full referential devices will be used. But these two reasons for the similar overt behaviour must be differentiated clearly.

If the discourse data support the trace decay hypothesis of forgetting, there seems to be a clear contradiction between them and the quite advanced cognitive-psychological experimental studies proposing the other alternative:

the interference/displacement hypothesis. A possible explanation of this contradiction is hinted at by the study of Hockey (1973). In that study a difference between the compulsory and the passive strategies of operating WM was emphasized. According to Hockey, under a passive strategy, when the pace of performance is chosen by an experiment participant rather than by an experimenter, the pattern of forgetting approaches the prediction made by the trace decay hypothesis, whereas under a compulsory strategy a pattern more in line with the interference hypothesis is observed.

The problem is that in many psychological experiments the cognitive system of an individual undergoes a degree of pressure that never or rarely occurs in natural conditions. In other words, in experiments, it is not the attentional system of an individual himself but rather the will of an experimenter that exploits WM and brings to it too many referents at a time, and the effect of interference can indeed be observed. It seems quite likely that in natural conditions (under the 'passive' strategy), on the other hand, the attentional system brings as many referents to WM as WM can normally accommodate and process. So the evidence in favour of the interference model of short-term forgetting may be an artefact of particular experimental designs.

13.5 Linguistics and cognitive science

Linguistics is generally viewed as one of the main components of cognitive science. This presumably means that linguistics is both fed by and feeds cognitive science as a broader discipline. True, cognitive linguists have a fair record of taking the data provided by cognitive psychology into serious account; cf., for example, the impact of Rosch and other psychologists on the work of Lakoff (1987), or the psychologically minded linguistic discourse analysis, such as Chafe (1994), Tomlin (1995), or Dickinson and Givón (1997). Chapters 10 through 12 of this part of the book are strongly based on insights from cognitive psychology, as well as cognitive neuroscience. In this chapter I have attempted an exercise of a converse character – an examination of what linguistic analysis can reveal about the general cognitive issues. It must be noted that the contribution of linguistics to cognitive science has been quite modest. Results of cognitive linguistics rarely exert a significant impact upon other branches of cognitive science; see, however, Tomasello (ed.) (1998, 2003).

As was discussed in Chapter 10, the phenomenon of working memory is hotly debated in modern cognitive psychology and cognitive neuroscience. Linguists are largely outside this important discussion. In this chapter I have presented several pieces of evidence that are potentially useful for a general cognitive theory of working memory. Specific aspects of working memory that were assessed here include the WM capacity, attentional control of WM, and short-term forgetting. The second of these aspects also bears on the general theory of attention, in particular its relationship with working memory.

Hopefully, in the future, cognitive discourse analysis will provide a significant contribution to cognitive science. Discourse presents a precious window on cognitive processes and furnishes much more overt, articulate, and detailed information on these hidden processes than most other forms of human behaviour.

Summary

This chapter attempts a linguistic contribution to a general theory of working memory. This contribution is a side effect of the psychologically grounded model of referential choice developed in the previous chapters of this part. Given that we have a cognitively plausible model of reference in discourse, we can look in a novel way at several classic issues in the theory of working memory.

The system of calculating referents' activation scores is set up so that in each elementary discourse unit scores of all referents can be obtained, irrespective of whether a certain referent is mentioned or not. The sum of all referents' activation scores is the measurement called grand activation. Grand activation can be used as an estimate for the capacity of the working memory for specific referents. Working memory has a maximal capacity of four units, where one unit is the maximal activation of an individual referent. Most of the time working memory is half-filled (two units) and does not go empty (below one unit).

The content of working memory is determined by another cognitive process, namely attention. In discourse structure, attended referents are manifested as mentioned referents. Right after a mention, referents become activated in working memory and are prone to reduced reference. If a referent is mentioned in the subject position, which is the linguistic manifestation of focal attention, this leads to a particularly high level of its subsequent activation. We thus have a remarkably coherent picture of relationships between attention and working memory, both at the cognitive and at the linguistic levels.

If a referent is not mentioned for a few discourse moments, it rapidly gets deactivated, or forgotten from working memory. The effect of time is sufficient to explain the phenomenon of deactivation in natural discourse.

14

Further studies based on the cognitive multi-factorial approach

Overview

The CMF approach to referential choice, presented in Chapters 10 to 12, provides an explanatory model accounting for all data points in the explored discourse samples. This approach makes referential choice predictable, and does so in a testable, publicly verifiable way. It also addresses such problematic issues as adequacy of cognitive interpretation, threat of circular argumentation, and the multiplicity of involved factors.

There are, however, several points in that approach that call for further development. First, its mathematical basis is too elementary to be cognitively plausible. In particular, the interaction between factors is mostly additive, which is by far too simplistic. A mathematical approach that would allow a wider range of possible interactions is clearly needed. In section 14.1 an approach based on the method of neural networks is proposed.

Second, the size of the discourse samples explored so far is too small. Limiting the data sets to one hundred items or so is a natural solution at the stage when a novel methodology is created and tested. However, statistical rigour requires much larger data sets. There is obviously a need to apply the CMF approach to a referentially annotated corpus that is several orders of magnitude larger than the samples analysed so far. Section 14.2 outlines the ongoing work on a referentially annotated corpus and presents preliminary results of this work.

Third, only two languages, Russian and English, have been explored with the help of the CMF approach. As was argued in Chapter 7, these two languages have a fairly similar system of referential devices. In order to broaden the cross-linguistic applicability of the proposed framework, it must be tested on a language with a different set of preferred referential options. In section 14.3 an application of the CMF approach to Japanese is described.

Fourth, as with any theory, it is interesting to test this approach in an experimental setting. In section 14.4 I discuss recent studies that aim to test certain aspects of the CMF approach in a series of psycholinguistic experiments.

14.1 The neural network study

The CMF approach, developed in Chapters 10 to 12, has a mathematical component that can be characterized as calculative. This component is important in the CMF approach, as it makes the mapping from activation factors to referential choice fully explicit and verifiable. However, the kind of mathematics, implemented in the calculative approach, is too simplistic to address cognitive processes. In this section a more advanced mathematical apparatus is proposed as a replacement for the calculative method.

This follow-up study was done in collaboration with the German mathematician André Grüning. This section is a concise rendering of our joint work; see Grüning and Kibrik (2002) and Grüning and Kibrik (2005). Some technical details are omitted here; for those I refer the interested reader to Grüning and Kibrik (2005).[1]

14.1.1 *Shortcomings of the calculative method*

There are several points in the calculative method that appear problematic from a mathematical point of view. First, candidate activation factors were included in the list of actual activation factors (see Chapter 11, section 11.4) on the basis of their individual correlation with referential choice. However, it is only all the factors in conjunction that determines the activation score and, ultimately, referential choice. Therefore the strength of correlation of individual factors may be misleading, and the resultant list of relevant activation factors may be less than optimal.

Second, the numerical weights of the individual factors' values were chosen by hand, which not only was a laborious task but also did not allow us to judge the quality or uniqueness of the set of calculated weights.

Third, the interaction between factors was mainly additive, ignoring possible non-linear interdependencies between the factors. Non-linear dependencies are particularly probable, given that some factors interact with others – cf. the discussion of the factor of the syntactic role of the linear antecedent in section 12.5, whose contribution to AS diminishes with the increase of distance to

---

[1] I thank the publishing house John Benjamins for their permission to use the text of that publication in this section. I also thank André Grüning for a very helpful discussion during the preparation of this section.

antecedent.[2] Other factors might be correlated, e.g. animacy and the syntactic role of subject (the distribution of animacy and subjecthood of the antecedent vis-à-vis full NPs vs. pronouns is very similar, indicating a possible intrinsic interrelationship between these).[3] Also, from the cognitive point of view it is unlikely that such a simple procedure as addition can adequately describe the processing of activation in the brain. For an in-depth argument for non-linearity in cognitive modelling see Elman et al. (1996).

Fourth, because of the additive character of factor interaction it was very hard to limit possible activation to a certain range. It would be intuitively natural to posit that activation varies between zero and some maximum, which can, without the loss of generality, be assumed to be 1. However, because of penalizing factors such as paragraph distance that deduct activation it often happens that the activation score turns out to be negative (a consequence of the simple summing in the calculative approach), which makes cognitive interpretation difficult. Also, it was technically difficult to design the numerical system so that the maximal AS value is exactly 1.

In order to solve these problems, the idea of developing a more sophisticated mathematical apparatus emerged, such that:

- Identification of significant factors, numerical weights, and factor interaction would all be interconnected and would be a part of the same task.
- The modelling of factors would be done computationally, by building an optimal model of factors and their interaction.

The study reported in this section is based on the same English data set as the calculative study described in Chapter 12.

14.1.2 *Proposed solution: a neural network method*

There are many well-known machine learning approaches that lend themselves naturally to the problems mentioned above (e.g. variants of decisions tree algorithms, multiple non-linear regression; see section 14.2). Among these, artificial neural network models are special due to their inherent

---

[2] The attribution of different weights to the syntactic role of the linear antecedent, dependent on the linear distance, can already be viewed as an element of non-linear interdependencies in the calculative approach.

[3] As a mathematical consequence, the weights attributed to animacy and antecedent subjecthood are not 'stable': the model would perform almost as well if the numerical weights for these two factors were interchanged or even modified so that their sum remained the same. Thus the concrete single weights of correlated factors have no objective importance on their own, and it is important to single out correlated factors and describe their relationship in order to ascribe an objective meaning to a combination (most simply, the sum) of their weights.

cognitive interpretation (Ellis and Humphreys 1999). The primary aim of this pilot study on a quite small data set is to evaluate whether neural networks are applicable to the problem of referential choice, and if so, to lay the ground for a larger-scale study.[4] In order to keep the present study comparable to the calculative approach, the original data set was used: data from the English sample discourse, see Chapter 12. The goal was to construct an 'optimal' list of factors, i.e. a model that provides maximal descriptional power (all relevant factors identified and included) and at the same time has a minimal descriptional size (just the relevant factors contained and no others).

In the neural network approach, the requirement of complete predictiveness is lifted: it is posited that referential choice can be predicted/explained with a degree of certainty that can be less than 100%.[5] Also, at this time the neural network approach does not make specific claims about cognitive adequacy and activation and there is no such thing as a summary activation score in this approach at its present stage. Activation factors themselves are reinterpreted as mere parameters or variables in the data that are mapped onto referential choice.

The term **artificial neural network** or **net** denotes a variety of different function approximators that are neuro-biologically inspired (Mitchell 1997). Their common property is that they can, in a supervised or unsupervised way, learn to classify data. For this pilot study a simple feed-forward network with the back-propagation learning algorithm was employed.

A feed-forward network consists of nodes that are connected by weights. Every node integrates the activation it gets from its predecessor nodes in a non-linear way and sends it to its successors. The nodes are ordered in layers. Numerical data is presented to the nodes in the input layer, from where the activation is injected into one or more hidden layers, where the actual computation is done. From there activation spreads to the output layer, where the result of the computation is read off. This computed output can be compared to the expected target output, and subsequently the weights (parameters) are adapted so as to minimize the difference between actual output and target (a so-called gradient descent algorithm, of which the back-propagation algorithm is an example; for details see Ellis and Humphreys 1999). Hidden and output nodes also count as the model's weights (parameters) as they have their own 'bias', that is their own level of activation that is present when there is no input at all.

---

[4] With respect to the small data set we would not be better off with any other of the above-mentioned methods as all of them are quite data-intensive.

[5] This might be a desirable feature, e.g. to account for alterable referential devices.

In this supervised learning task the network must learn to predict referential choice from ten factors (Table 14.1). The composition of these ten factors was as follows. Those factors were not included that were judged second-order, or 'exotic' in the original calculative study; see section 12.5. Out of the activation factors found in Table 12.4 only the first six were included, some of them in a simplified fashion (compare the list of values for antecedent role between Tables 14.1 and 12.4). At the same time, several factors were added that appeared irrelevant at an early stage of the calculative study (see section 11.4), in order to check how they perform in the context of the neural network approach – same or differently compared to the calculative approach. Among

TABLE 14.1. Factors used in the original setup of the neural network, their possible values, and the corresponding input nodes. (S, DO, IOag, Obl, Poss mean subject, direct object, agentive indirect object, oblique, and possessor. Pred means predicative use, Pro pronoun, and FNP full noun phrase.)

Factor	Values	Coding	Input Nodes
Animacy	Human, animal, inanimate	Human: 1, animal: 0, inanimate: −1	6
Protagonisthood	Yes/no	Binary	7
Syntactic role of the referential device in its own clause	S, DO, IOag, Obl, Poss	Unary	1–5
Linear distance to the antecedent	Integer	Integer	22
Rhetorical distance to the antecedent	Integer	Integer	23
Paragraph distance to the antecedent	Integer	Integer	24
Syntactic role of the rhetorical antecedent	S, DO, IOag, Obl, Poss, Pred	Unary	8–13
Referential type of the rhetorical antecedent	Pro, FNP	Binary	14
Syntactic role of the linear antecedent	S, DO, IOag, Obl, Poss, Pred	Unary	15–20
Referential type of the linear antecedent	Pro, FNP	Binary	21

these factors were the role of the NP in question in its own clause and the antecedent's referential type. Antecedent's role and antecedent's referential type were considered separately for the linear and the rhetorical antecedents.

In order to input the factors with symbolic values into the net, they have to be converted into numerical values. If the symbolic values denote some gradual property such as animacy, they are converted into one real variable with values between −1 and 1. The same holds true for binary variables. When there was no a priori obvious order in the symbolic values,[6] they were coded unary (e.g. syntactic role), i.e. to every value of that factor corresponds one input node, which is set to one if the factor assumes this value and to zero otherwise.

Thus 24 input nodes and one output node are needed. The output node is trained to predict whether the referent in question is realized as a full noun phrase or as a pronoun.

14.1.3 Simulation 1: full data set

A network with 24 nodes in a single hidden layer was trained on the data set of 102 items[7] from Kibrik (1999) (see Chapter 12) for 1000 epochs.[8] As parts of the training are stochastic, the experiment was repeated several times. In all runs the net learned to predict the data correctly except for a small number (below six) cases. Typically, the misclassifications occurred for the same items in the data set, independently of the run. A closer analysis of a well-trained net with only four misclassifications revealed that three of them were due to referential conflict (which was not among the input factors), that is, in the situation when the full noun phrase is used only because a pronoun (otherwise expected) may turn out ambiguous.

14.1.4 Simulation 2: pruning

The net was intended so that not only did it learn the data but would also make some statements about the importance of the input factors and their interdependency. To achieve this goal the trained net from Simulation 1 was

---

[6] For example, the factor of syntactic role can take the values 'subject', 'direct object', 'indirect object', 'possesive', etc. One might speculate that a hierarchy of these values, similar to the hierarchy of NP accessibility (Keenan and Comrie 1977), might operate in referential choice. But since this is not self-evident, we code such factors unarily so that the network can find its own order of the values as relevant to the task at hand.

[7] As opposed to the study described in Chapter 12, here the syntactic pronouns were included. Note that due to short linear distance all of them are easily predicted correctly.

[8] Technical details for neural network experts: learning parameter is set to 0.2; no momentum; weights were jogged every epoch by maximally 0.1%; input patterns are shuffled. The simulations are run on the SNNS network simulator (http://www-ra.informatik.uni-tuebingen.de/SNNS).

TABLE 14.2 Weights of a typical pruned net. (Nodes 1–24 denote the input nodes, 25 and 26 are the two remaining hidden nodes, and 27 is the output node. The weights connecting a source and a target node are given in parentheses after the source node.)

Target Node	Source nodes (Weights)
25	1 (−2.4) 2 (2.1) 8 (−1.7) 12 (1.9) 14 (−1.6) 16 (−2.4) 22 (−4.7) 24 (−4.9)
26	7 (1.7) 10 (−2.0) 12 (−5.0) 14 (−1.9) 15 (2.8) 16 (−1.8) 21 (−4.2)
27	2 (−3.7) 8 (3.9) 9 (2.0) 15 (2.7) 17 (1.8) 22 (−22.0) 25 (10.9) 26 (−10.0)

subjected to a so-called pruning procedure, which eliminates nodes and weights from the net that contribute to the computation of the result either little or nothing at all. In such a case, a node or weight is selected and eliminated. Then the net is retrained for 100 epochs. If net performance does not drop, the elimination is confirmed; otherwise the deleted node or weight is restored. This procedure is repeated until no further reduction in the size of the net is possible without worsening the performance.

This procedure leads to smaller nets that are easier to analyse and furthermore can reduce the dimensionality of the input data. They have a lower number of weights (parameters): in the case analysed here the number of weights was reduced from 649 for the full net to 26 for the pruned net. The weights of a generic example of a pruned network trained on the data are shown in Table 14.2. As is clear from Table 14.2, there are no weights connecting the input nodes 3, 4, 5, 6, 11, 13, 18, 19, 20, 23 (the meanings of the nodes can be found in Table 14.1). This means that not all input factors or not all their values are relevant for computing the output. Also, all but two hidden nodes have been pruned. So the two remaining suffice to model the interaction between the input factors.

Some input nodes have a direct influence on the output node (27), e.g. the node indicating that the rhetorical antecedent was a possessor (node 9). Others influence the outcome only indirectly by interacting with other nodes, e.g. paragraph distance (node 24), while yet others influence the output both directly and indirectly (node 22). Some nodes enter in multiple ways that seem to cancel each other, e.g. node 14 (referential type of the rhetorical antecedent).

Pruning again is partly a stochastic procedure, as it for example depends ultimately on the random initialization of the network, so the experiment was repeated until it became clear which factors were almost invariably included. It turned out that subject and possessor roles,[9] protagonisthood, subjecthood

---

[9] Interestingly, some hints on the difference in the usage of argumental and possessive pronouns were observed already during the original work on the calculative approach. The fact that the networks

of the antecedent, and referential type of the antecedent are most important, and those nodes related to the rhetorical antecedent are more involved than those for the linear one. As well, the most important distance is rhetorical distance. Evidently, this list of factors and values coincide to a great extent with what was discovered through the trial-and-error procedure in the calculative approach. Thus, at least qualitatively the neural network approach is on the right track, and we can use the results of the pruning case study as a hint as to how to reduce the dimensionality of the input data. This leads us to the next simulation.

14.1.5 Simulation 3: reduced data set

In a third case study a similar net with twelve hidden nodes was trained on a reduced set of only five input factors (corresponding to six input nodes). The following factors' values were included: the values 'subject' and 'possessor' for syntactic role (nodes 1, 2), protagonisthood (node 3), whether the rhetorical antecedent was a subject (node 4), whether it was realized as a pronoun or full NP (node 5), and rhetorical distance (node 6). The new net had twelve hidden nodes, corresponding to 103 weights. On this reduced net, the back-propagation learning algorithm was executed for 500 epochs and then pruning (fifty epochs retraining for each pruning step) with the same weights as before. A small net was formed at the end (23 weights[10]), shown in Figure 14.1, that misclassified only eight out of 102 items. Note that all the retained factors interact strongly, except for protagonisthood (node 3), which has been pruned away.

14.1.6 Simulation 4: cheap data set

Reliable automatic annotators for rhetorical distance and consequently for all factors related to the rhetorical antecedent, as well as for protagonisthood, are not available. Since these factors require comprehension of the contents of the text, they must be annotated by human experts and are therefore costly. So an attempt was made to replace the rhetorical factors included in Simulation 3 by the corresponding linear ones and protagonisthood by animacy. Six input nodes were kept as before, and a seventh node was added to indicate that the linear antecedent was a possessor and an eighth one for paragraph distance to

---

themselves frequently keep the input for the possessive role can be viewed as a corroboration of this observation, and also as a proof that neural networks can be used as an independent tool for discovering regularities in the data. See observations on possessive pronouns in subsection 14.2.3 below.

[10] 23 weights include 18 weights connecting nodes in Figure 14.1, plus five nodes in the hidden and output layers.

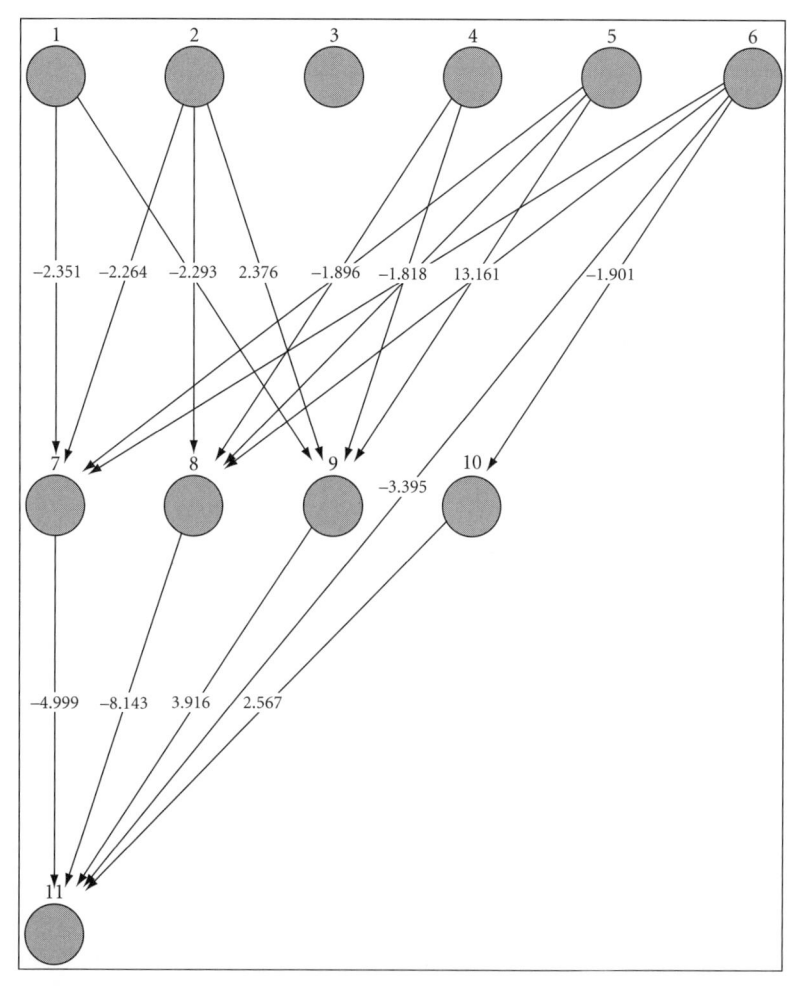

FIGURE 14.1. Net from Simulation 3. (The circles denote the nodes, the arrows the weights connecting the nodes, to which the weight strength is added as a real number. Nodes 1–6 are input nodes, 7–10 the nodes in the hidden layer, and node 11 is the output.)

help the net to overcome the smaller amount of information that is contained in the linear antecedent factors. Training and pruning proceeded as before.

One typical resulting network in this case had 32 weights. Again animacy, which had been substituted for protagonisthood, is disconnected from the rest of the net. On the 102 data items the net produced only six errors (three are due to referential conflict).

Thus, even though the logical structure of the factors and their values was considerably simplified, and none of the factors were included that relate to the rhetorical antecedent, the accuracy (six errors versus four with the full set of factors) did not deteriorate dramatically.

14.1.7 Comparison with the calculative approach

In the calculative model described in Chapter 12, referential choice was modelled by eleven factors using 32 weights, or parameters (counting the number of different numerical weights for all factors' values). The activation score allowed a prediction of the referential choice in five categories. In the study with neural networks, only a binary decision (full NP vs. pronoun) was modelled and the requirement of cognitive adequacy was lifted. The smallest net in the study, in simulation 3, had only 23 weights and five input factors. The best net on the full set of input factors, in Simulations 1 and 2, misclassified only four items, having 26 weights.

Even though the accuracy dropped in the neural network approach (using a reduced set of input factors) as compared to the calculative approach (with the full set of input factors), the model's descriptional length (measured in the number of the model's weights, or free parameters) was reduced by approximately one third and thus yields in this sense a more compact description of the data.

These findings are important in the following respects. Firstly, it is possible to find a smaller set of factors that still allows a relatively good prediction of referential choice, but is much less laborious to extract from a given corpus. Secondly, the descriptional length can be reduced without too severe a drop in accuracy. This means that the networks were able to extract the essential aspects of referential choice as about 100 instances can be described by only 23 weights. Compare this to the worst case in which a learning algorithm needs about 100 free parameters to describe 100 instances. In such a case the algorithm would not have learnt anything essential about referential choice, because it would merely be the list of the 100 instances. The ratio of the number of parameters to the size of data set has a long tradition of being used for judging a model's quality. A high value of this ratio is an indicator for what is known in statistics as overfitting.[11]

---

[11] Overfitting means sticking too closely to the peculiarities of a given training set and not finding the underlying general regularities. Overfitting is roughly the opposite of good generalization of unknown data.

14.1.8 Comparison with Strube and Wolters (2000)

As has been discussed in Chapter 10, the multiplicity of factors affecting referential choice has been a major stumbling block for many students of this phenomenon. Studies reported in various chapters of this Part IV differ sharply from most other research in the area in explicitly addressing the multi-factorial nature of referential choice. However, there is a study that is close in its spirit to this one, namely Strube and Wolters (2000). Strube and Wolters use a similar list of factors to the calculative approach discussed above, except that the costly factors related to the rhetorical antecedent are missing. They analyse a large corpus with several thousand referring expressions for the categorical decision (full NP vs. pronoun) using logistic regression. The logistic regression is a form of linear regression adapted for a binary decision.

Factor interaction and non-linear relations are thus not accounted for in their model, and they present no cognitive interpretation. Still the gist and intention of their study and the present studies – developed independently – largely agree, which provides evidence for the usefulness and appropriateness of quantitative approaches towards referential choice.

14.1.9 Prospects for further neural network research on referential choice

In this section a pilot study is reported, testing whether artificial neural networks are suitable to process the referential choice data. Feed-forward networks were trained on a small set of data. The results show that the nets are able to classify the data almost correctly with respect to the choice of referential device.

Because of the small amount of data for this pilot study, the result must be taken with due care. But these results seem encouraging for developing this approach further and for applying it to a larger data set. This is necessary since neural networks as well as classical statistics need a large amount of data to produce reliable results that are free of artefacts. In the data set used, some situations (i.e. an antecedent that is an indirect object) appear only once, so that no generalization can be made. In a larger study the advantages of the neural network approach can be used fully.[12] In particular, a much better ratio

---

[12] An anonymous reviewer to Grüning and Kibrik (2005) pointed out that there is possibly another interesting application of neural network-based models of referential choice: an application to anaphor resolution. Consider a knowledge-poor anaphor resolution algorithm as a quick-and-dirty first pass that suggests several potential referents for a pronominal mention. Counterchecking the referent mentions in a second pass, a suggested referent could be ruled out if the network does not predict a pronominal mention for it at the point in question. The advantage over anaphor resolution

of descriptional length to the size of data set can be expected to be attained. See section 14.2 below on the ongoing work on a large referential corpus.

Furthermore, it is important to not only model a binary decision (full NP vs. pronoun), but also to have a more fine-grained analysis. The calculative approach has shown the first steps in this direction, allowing for five different categories indicating to what degree a full NP in a particular situation can be replaced by a pronoun and vice versa; see sections 12.2–12.4. A **statistical interpretation** of referential choice can be suggested: if a human expert judges that a particular full NP could be replaced by a pronoun, he/she must have experienced that, in a very similar situation, a writer did indeed realize the other alternative. The expert will be more certain that substitution is suitable if he/she has often experienced the alternative situation. Thus it is promising to replace the five categories of potential referential devices by a continuous result variable that ranges from zero to one and is interpreted as the probability[13] that referential choice realizes a pronoun in the actual situation: 1 means a pronoun with certainty, 0 means a full NP with certainty, and 0.7 means that in 70% of instances a pronoun is realized and a full NP in the remaining 30% of instances. This kind of probabilistic approach may be a more practical replacement for the predictive approach adopted in the calculative method.

14.2 A corpus-based study of referential choice

As was pointed out in Chapter 1 (section 1.8), the observational methodology – one of the major scientific methodologies – has an offspring in modern linguistics, known as corpus methodology. Corpus-based research is now becoming, or perhaps has already become, one of the central kinds of linguistic data analysis. Literature in and about corpus linguistics is exuberant, but see McEnery and Wilson (2001), Biber et al. (2004), Gries and Stefanovich (2006), Plungian (ed.) (2009), inter alia. 'Corpus' is usually understood as a relatively large collection of natural discourse containing an added linguistic annotation of a certain kind and being computer-searchable.

---

algorithms based purely on classical methods would be that computations in a neural network are really fast compared to algorithmic and symbolic computing once the training of the network is finished.

[13] Cf. the probability-oriented discussion of referential choice in Chapter 10, subsection 10.3.2.

In this section I report the recent work in progress on a corpus project involving extensive referential annotation and designed for further research in the cognitive multi-factorial approach.

14.2.1 The RefRhet corpus

In accordance with the conclusions of the previous section, a sufficiently large corpus annotated for coreference was initiated. The leading concern in the selection of discourses for such a corpus was connected to the factor of rhetorical distance. As must be clear from the preceding analysis (see Chapters 11 and 12), this activation factor is simultaneously: (a) the most powerful for predicting referential choice and (b) the most costly in terms of manual annotation. In other words, this parameter cannot be excluded a priori from the list of potentially relevant factors, and therefore it must be annotated. At the same time, annotating it is very labour-intensive as this presupposes producing rhetorical trees for the whole corpus. The best solution to this controversy is using a corpus already annotated for rhetorical structure, and adding all other annotation relevant for referential choice on top of it.

One available corpus of this kind was located: the so-called RST Discourse Treebank distributed by the Linguistic Data Consortium.[14] This corpus was produced by a group of authors led by Daniel Marcu (see Carlson et al. 2003) and contains 385 Wall Street Journal articles (from 1989), annotated for discourse structure in the framework of Rhetorical Structure Theory (RST) of Mann and Thompson (Mann and Thompson 1988, Mann et al. 1992). The articles belong to several genres, including reports, business and legal news, financial analyses, and a number of others. Referents mentioned are, most often, persons, organizations, artefacts, laws, and numbers. The corpus contains 176,383 words and 21,789 elementary discourse units. The corpus is almost two orders of magnitude larger than the discourse sample explored in the Margaret story (Chapter 12, section 12.1). The rhetorical structure annotation of the corpus is consistent and is based on a revised version of RST comprising 78 rhetorical relations that connect elementary discourse units and groups thereof.

We have used the RST Discourse Treebanks as a starting point and processed the texts contained in that corpus, adding extensive **referential annotation**; see below. The resultant product thus consists of two

---

[14] See http://www.ldc.upenn.edu; the page for the RST Discourse Treebank is http://www.ldc.upenn.edu/Catalog/CatalogEntry.jsp?catalogId=LDC2002T07. See also http://www.isi.edu/~marcu/discourse/Corpora.html.

independent components: the original rhetorical annotation from the RST Discourse Treebank and the added referential annotation. The combination of these two components is called below the **RefRhet corpus**. Below I briefly outline the referential annotation in RefRhet; see Kibrik et al. (2010a, 2010b) for further details.

The **scheme** of referential annotation for this corpus was developed by Krasavina and Chiarcos (2007). (This annotation belongs to a family of similar systems; see Poesio and Artstein 2008 for a review.) The scheme is xml-based and relies on the principle of stand-off annotation. In this scheme, the distinction between the primary and the extended schemes has been adopted; so far, only the former has been fully implemented, so in what follows I do not detail the extended scheme. A number of notoriously difficult problems of referential annotation are addressed in the scheme, including discontinuous NPs, complex NPs, affiliation to quoted speech (see section 11.7 on the world boundary filter) and potential ambiguity. A number of principles have been stated explicitly, such as the preference for intra-sentential coreference and the preference for an explicit antecedent.

The scheme includes three kinds of annotation:

- m**a**rkables, that is elements that must be annotated
- coreference relations between markables
- multiple features of markables, relevant for referential choice.

The **markables** to be annotated include definite, demonstrative, and possessive full NPs (headed by a common noun), proper nouns, personal pronouns, and demonstratives. In addition, other NPs are annotated if they serve as antecedents of anaphors (in particular, indefinite full NPs). The **coreference relation** connects every non-first mention of a referent to the immediately preceding antecedent. Chains of coreferential expressions are formed for each referent. The **features** annotated in the RefRhet corpus that are potential activation factors include the following:

Properties of the referent:
- animacy: human vs. inanimate
- protagonisthood

Properties of the projected referential device:
- introductory vs. repeated mention
- discourse world: main discourse world vs. quoted speech
- phrase type: noun phrase vs. prepositional phrase
- grammatical role: subject vs. direct object vs. indirect object

Properties of the antecedent:
- discourse world: main discourse world vs. quoted speech
- phrase type: noun phrase vs. prepositional phrase
- grammatical role: subject vs. direct object vs. indirect object
- referential form: personal pronoun vs. another type of pronoun (e.g. reflexive, relative) vs. proper name vs. *the*-NP vs. possessive NP vs. demonstrative NP

Distance from the projected referential device to the antecedent:
- distance in the number of words
- distance in the number of markables (cf. Hobbs 1976, Wolters 2001, Arnold 2008)
- linear distance, measured in elementary discourse units along the linear discourse structure
- rhetorical distance, measured in elementary discourse units along the hierarchical discourse structure.

NPs and some of their properties were originally identified through an automatic parsing procedure; see Antonova (2004) and Petrova (2004).

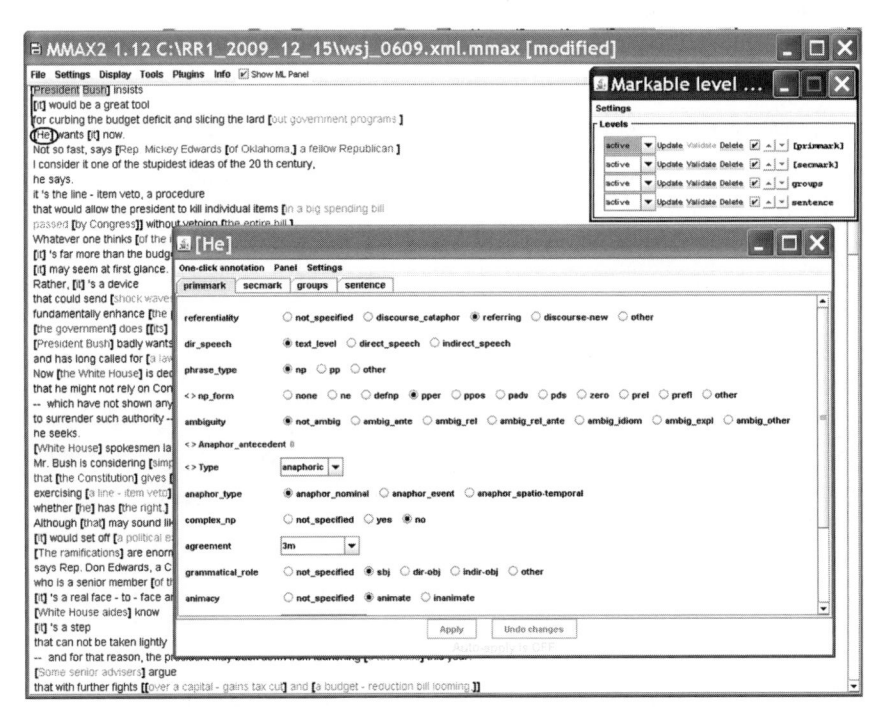

FIGURE 14.2. Windows of the MMAX2 program

Further annotation was performed with the help of the MMAX2 program (Müller and Strube 2006), specifically designed for referential annotation by the company EML Research.[15] An illustration of how the windows of MMAX2 look is provided in Figure 14.2.

In Figure 14.2, in the background window one can see the text with markables annotated with the help of brackets. One referential device, *he*, is marked with an oval (added in this figure by myself for better visibility). A line connects this referential device to its immediate antecedent, shaded in MMAX2 (*President Bush*). In the foreground window one can see the features that are attributed to the given occurrence of *he* in the annotation.

14.2.2 *Measuring rhetorical distance*

As has been shown in the previous chapters, as well as in section 14.1, rhetorical distance (RhD) stands out as a very important activation factor, responsible to a high degree for the resulting referential choice. In this subsection I consider some problems associated with identifying rhetorical distance in RefRhet.

The basic method to compute RhD used in the studies reported in the previous chapters (see sections 11.4 and 12.5) can be formalized as follows:

- move along the graph from the current EDU to the EDU containing the nearest antecedent and count how many horizontal steps you make.

To take a real example from the RST Discourse Treebank, in Figure 14.3 EDU 127 contains two full NPs, *Mr. Schaeffer* and *the couple* that serve as antecedents of further referential expressions. Once we encounter anaphoric pronouns in EDUs 128, 129, and 130, we search along the graph for the nearest antecedent clause that happens to be 127. Rhetorical distances appear to be as shown in Table 14.3; the ways in which they are identified appear quite straightforward.

However, in the course of applying this methodology of RhD calculation to the RefRhet corpus several persistent problems have been encountered. These problems were already acknowledged in Kibrik (1996a, 1999), but were not

---

[15] About 25 specially trained students of the Department of Theoretical and Applied Linguistics, Moscow State University, accomplished the annotation of the corpus, under the supervision of Dmitrij Zalmanov and later Mariya Khudyakova. The MMAX2 web page can be seen at http://mmax2.sourceforge.net.

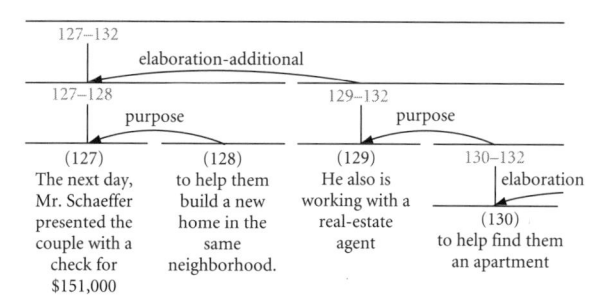

```
              127–132
                  |  elaboration-additional
          127–128                    129–132
              | purpose                  | purpose
      (127)         (128)         (129)        130–132
    The next day,  to help them   He also is      | elaboration
    Mr. Schaeffer  build a new    working with a
    presented the  home in the    real-estate    (130)
    couple with a    same         agent       to help find them
    check for     neighborhood.                an apartment
    $151,000
```

FIGURE 14.3. A fragment of a rhetorical graph from the RST Discourse Treebank

Table 14.3. Rhetorical distances from anaphors back to the antecedents contained in EDU 127 (example in Figure 14.3)

EDU#	Referential device	Rhetorical distance
128	*them*	1
129	*he*	1
130	*them*	2

significant there because of the small size of the data set and the genre properties of the text: it was a narrative which was rhetorically quite monotonous anyway (see Kibrik 2002c), and it was also very homogeneous as a story by one author. In the rest of this subsection I consider two such problems: the problem of multinuclear relations and the problem of multiple antecedents.

Treatment of multinuclear relations. In the graph shown in Figure 14.3 all rhetorical relations are mononuclear (=asymmetric). In the case of mononuclear relations, the contribution of the rhetorical distance is intuitively clear. For example, in terms of the hierarchical discourse structure, EDU 128 is further away from 129 than 127. However, when one deals with multinuclear (=symmetric) structures it is not immediately obvious how to compute and compare RhDs. Consider the configurations in Figure 14.4.

```
          A–C                                      A–C
              mononuclear                              multinuclear
      A–B              C                    A–B                 C
     multinuclear                          multinuclear
    A      B                              A      B
```

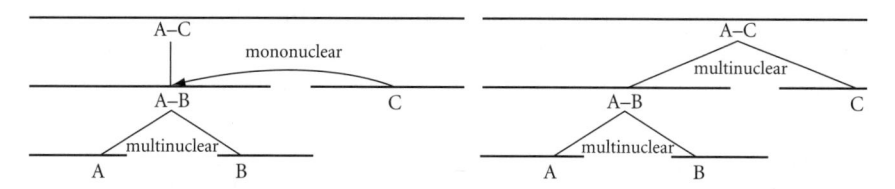

FIGURE 14.4. Mononuclear vs. multinuclear structures

What is the distance from C to A and from C to B? Is it the same or different in the two configurations? And is the distance between C and A–B the same in the two configurations? In Kibrik (1996a) a convention was adopted, according to which the RhD from C to B in Figure 14.4 would be 1 and from C to A it would be 2. That is, a node connected to a symmetrical group was reinterpreted as the satellite of its linearly last member, and both structures in Figure 14.4 were effectively reinterpreted as shown in Figure 14.5.

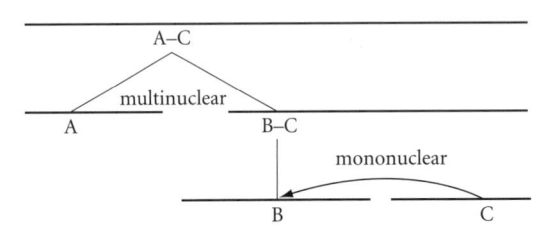

FIGURE 14.5. A reinterpretation of discourse units, connected to multinuclear groups

However, there is evidence that structures in Figures 14.4 and 14.5 are not equivalent in terms of proximity of an anaphor in C to an antecedent in A or B. This is easy to demonstrate with a couple of made-up examples. Example (14.1) corresponds to the configuration in Figure 14.5:

(14.1) John$_J$ was playing and Bill$_B$ was watching a movie because he$_{B,*J}$ was through with his homework

Here the pronoun *he* can only be used with the antecedent *Bill* in clause B. This is primarily due to the different rhetorical distance from C to A and from C to B. Now, example (14.2) corresponds to the configuration in Figure 14.4 (either one of the two represented in this figure[16]):

(14.2) John$_J$ was playing and Bill$_B$ was reading. Then he$_{J\sim B}$ stood up and walked out.

Here the pronoun *he* can in principle corefer to either of the NPs found in clauses A and B, and, therefore, a speaker is unlikely to use a structure as in (14.2), because it creates a referential conflict. Apparently, this situation is due to the multinuclear character of the rhetorical structure. Perhaps the antecedent *Bill* has some privilege over *John*, but this is because of its linear proximity to the anaphor. So, the convention adopted in Kibrik (1996a) actually

---

[16] This made-up, contextless example is ambiguous with respect to the two structures shown in Figure 14.4: without a larger context, it is impossible to decide whether EDU C is a satellite to the group A–B (for example, bearing the 'result' rhetorical relation) or the relation is multinuclear (for example, 'sequence').

smuggles linear proximity into the RhD measurement, and as a result linear distance is taken into account twice.

Thus the prior convention must be replaced.[17] As examples above suggest, the single nucleus of a mononuclear structure (as e.g. 127 within the group 127–128, Figure 14.3) is more accessible as an antecedent clause than the nuclei of multinuclear structures (Figure 14.4). The following convention is proposed:

- when one enters or exits a multinuclear structure on the way through the graph, a penalty of 0.5 is added.

Thus, for example, the rhetorical distance from C to either A or B in Figure 14.4 will be 1.5. Likewise a 0.5 penalty will be charged when an anaphor itself is in a multinuclear structure, for getting out of such a structure. After this suggestion was put forward in Kibrik and Krasavina (2005), it was empirically tested in Chiarcos and Krasavina (2008). They compared the proposed solution to those inferrable from alternative approaches (Grosz and Sidner's 1986 stack model and Cristea et al.'s 1998 Veins Theory) and found that Kibrik and Krasavina's (2005) approach has a 'slight advantage' over the two other approaches.

A number of further issues related to multinuclear groups remain to be resolved. In particular, there may be more than one hierarchical layer of such groups; see Figure 14.6.

The rhetorical distance from C to B is 1.5, that is, 0.5 for getting out of the symmetrical structure C–D plus 1 for one horizontal step (from C–D to B). The question is, what is the RhD from C to A: also 1.5 or 2? In the latter case an

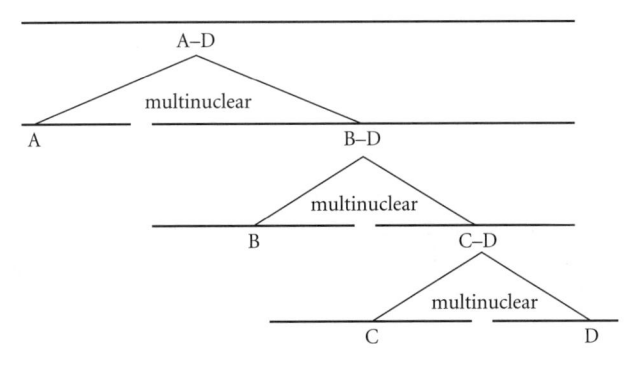

FIGURE 14.6. A multilayer multinuclear structure

---

[17] A different convention was applied to multinuclear groups in Kibrik (1999) (see discussion in section 12.5): in a structure as in Figure 14.4 RhD from C to either A or B was considered 1. This approach also fails to capture the difference between multinuclear and mononuclear groups.

additional 0.5 is charged for getting out of the symmetrical structure B–D. This is an empirical question, and it can only be solved when the stage of fully-fledged testing of the new corpus is reached.

Multiple antecedents. Because of the non-linear character of rhetorical graphs, there may be more than one candidate for an NP's rhetorical antecedent, consider Figure 14.7.

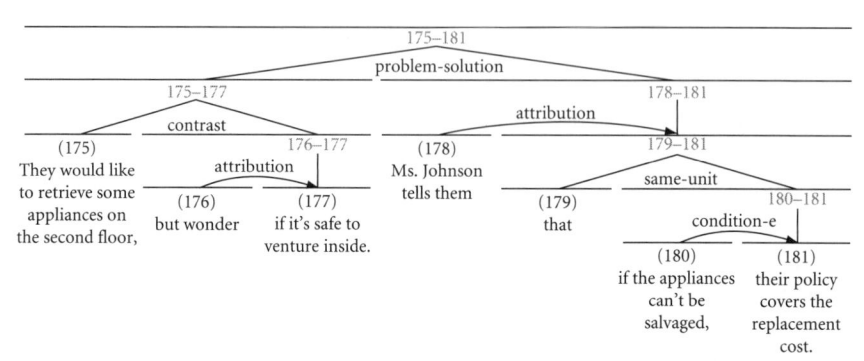

```
                              175–181
                           problem-solution
        175–177                                    178–181
                                                 attribution
                  contrast
   (175)                    176–177         (178)          179–181
They would like           attribution    Ms. Johnson              same-unit
to retrieve some       (176)      (177)   tells them   (179)           180–181
appliances on        but wonder  if it's safe to        that         condition-e
the second floor,                venture inside.
                                                            (180)          (181)
                                                       if the appliances  their policy
                                                          can't be        covers the
                                                          salvaged,       replacement
                                                                             cost.
```

FIGURE 14.7. An example of a rhetorical graph from the RST Discourse Treebank

There is an anaphoric pronoun *them* in 178, and there are two prior coreferential expressions: the pronoun *they* in 175 and the zero anaphor in 176. 176 contains the nearest linear antecedent, but which one is the rhetorical antecedent? Probably the least controversial solution is the following:

- choose the antecedent that is the closest in terms of rhetorical distance.

According to the conventions discussed above, the RhD from 178 to 176 is 3.5 while the RhD from 178 to 175 is 2.5. Therefore, 175 must be chosen as the antecedent clause. This proposal conforms to the principles of the Veins Theory (Cristea et al. 1998).

Of course, one cannot exclude the possibility that occasionally two candidate antecedents would turn out to be at the same rhetorical distance from the anaphor. It is still important to choose one of them as the actual antecedent, because among the factors affecting referential choice are certain antecedent properties, such as its syntactic role in its clause. Among the criteria to be considered are:

- choose the candidate antecedent that is linearly closer to the anaphor
- choose the candidate antecedent that has a more privileged syntactic role
- choose the candidate antecedent that is connected to the anaphor by a tighter rhetorical relation; see subsection 14.2.4.

Once again, choosing between these options remains a task for future empirical research. Beljaev (2009) has compiled a computer program (a plug-in for MMAX2) that automatically computes rhetorical distance in accordance with the above specified conventions.

14.2.3 *First results from the new corpus*

A number of studies have been based on the RefRhet corpus, and a brief account of those is in order here. As is well known, English possessive pronouns have a pattern of use very different from clause participant pronouns (see section 12.1). Specifically, possessive pronouns can be used in reflexive contexts, that is, they can corefer to one of the same clause's participants, especially the subject. Consequently, possessive pronouns very often occur at the distance of 0 to their antecedent. This fact suggests that referential choice in the possessive position cannot be predicted by the same configuration of activation factors as referential choice in clause participant positions. Krasavina (2006) did a pilot comparison of the distribution of possessive and clause participant pronouns in a sample of the RefRhet corpus. Quite expectedly, the rhetorical distance of 0 turned out to be the preferred one for English possessive pronouns (58% of all occurrences), while it is very rare for clause participant pronouns (Krasavina 2006: 175). However, as one can derive from Krasavina's numerical data, under greater rhetorical distances the distribution of clause participant and possessive pronouns is almost equivalent. In particular, if the 'reflexive' uses with the RhD = 0 are excluded, 74% of clause participant pronouns and 73% of possessive pronouns occur at the distance of 1. This suggests that beyond the boundaries of a single clause referential choice in the possessive position can be modelled by the same principles as in clause participant positions.

A more focused study of possessive NPs in RefRhet was conducted by Khudyakova (2010). Khudyakova explored a subcorpus containing 3,128 referential expressions, including 508 in the possessive position and 2,620 in clause participant positions (p. 46). She found out that pronominalization happens in a clause participant position 14% of the time, and in the possessive position 49% of the time. Clearly, this difference is primarily due to the above-mentioned ability of possessive pronouns to occur within the same clause as the antecedent. This is further confirmed by the fact that possessive pronouns have subject antecedents almost twice as frequently as clause participant pronouns (Khudyakova 2010: 60). Khudyakova (2010) also indicated a number of other factors favouring the use of possessive pronouns.

Krasavina (2006: 175ff., 188–191) compared the patterning of singular and plural pronouns. Excluding, for the above-stated reasons, the pronouns appearing at the distance of 0, one can derive from her data that at the rhetorical distance of 1 we find 77% of all singular pronouns and 68% of all plural pronouns. This finding calls for a further exploration: it may be that a referent's number slightly influences referential choice. One possible reason is that some plural referential expressions result from the process of the composition of activated referents; see Kibrik (1992a). There may be some peculiar activation-related effects in this situation. It should be noted, however, that this reasoning must be taken with caution since Krasavina's numerical data did not include evidence for referential options other than the pronominal ones. So what we know at this time is not referential choice per se but the distribution of pronouns only, and these two things are not equivalent.

Krasavina (2006) also explored a number of activation factors and their correlation with referential choice in the RefRhet corpus, including the factors of animacy, protagonisthood, and others. Particularly interesting is her finding related to the interaction between the factors of animacy and rhetorical distance. Consider Table 14.4 below.

This distribution demonstrates that under short distances (no more than 1) animacy does not affect the frequency of pronouns. With due caution, this can be taken to indicate that in such situations animacy does not affect referential choice. Conversely, under greater distances, especially those of three or more, there is a big difference in the frequencies of pronouns. This accords with the system of activation factors and their values, as formulated in

TABLE 14.4. The distribution in a sample of 1,473 clause participant pronouns from the RefRhet corpus, as dependent on animacy and rhetorical distance. The amount of pronouns found under each value of RhD is taken to be 100%: (from Krasavina 2006: 214)

Rhetorical distance:	0	1	2	3 or more
Animate	32 46.38%	432 47.11%	197 59.70%	123 78.34%
Inanimate	37 53.62%	485 52.89%	133 40.30%	34 21.66%
TOTAL	69 100%	917 100%	330 100%	157 100%

Chapters 11 and 12. Animacy, as well as protagonisthood, are factors that affect the rate of referent deactivation. Under short distances, when a referent is fully activated, these factors are not significant. However, at longer distances they make adjustments for referent deactivation. In particular, animate referents deactivate more slowly than inanimate ones.

Finally, among Krasavina's findings based on the RefRhet corpus, I would like to mention those related to demonstratives. Demonstratives are sometimes taken to be among the basic referential devices and to belong to a cline of referential forms; they are then listed as occupying an intermediate position on such a cline, between pronouns and full NPs (Ariel 1990, Gundel et al. 1993). The position taken in this book is very different. As was argued on a number of occasions above (in particular, in Chapter 4, subsection 4.2.1), demonstratives are a much more marked and specialized device than full NPs and pronouns; they are not a part of the basic referential choice. They are used under special conditions as troubleshooters of referential choice, among which the degree of referent activation is only one of the concerns, and probably not the leading one. Krasavina (2004) has shown that Russian demonstratives have a variety of uses that are quite disparate and are only remotely dependent on the level of activation. The same seems to hold true with respect to English demonstratives. Very often they denote not referents but propositional information; see e.g. Webber (1991). Even when they denote referents they pattern quite differently from full NPs and pronouns. According to Krasavina (2006: 194), in a subcorpus of the RefRhet corpus there were only 41 demonstratives per 3,827 full NPs and 3,378 pronouns. That is, demonstratives denoting referents are very unusual and constitute only about 0.057% of all referential expressions and must be characterized as a marginal referential device. Furthermore, among both full NPs and pronouns between 10% and 11% of all instances refer to discourse protagonists, whereas only one out of 41 demonstratives has this feature. It appears that protagonist referents have some special resistance to demonstrative reference.

In another useful paper exploring the RefRhet corpus, Khudyakova (2007) looked at a subcorpus containing 496 referential devices (both full and reduced). She revealed the most typical clusters of the properties found in the antecedents of pronouns such as (pp. 5–6):

- proper name playing the syntactic role of subject and the semantic role of Principal
- animate personal pronoun playing the syntactic role of subject and the semantic role of Principal
- inanimate definite full NP playing the non-Principal semantic role.

Khudyakova also explored the relationship between referential choice and several potential activation factors. She found out that, in the case of subject antecedents, referents are mentioned by reduced NPs twice as frequently as in the case of non-subject antecedents (p. 8). Furthermore, Khudyakova proposed that the antecedent's phrase type (noun phrase vs. prepositional phrase) may be an activation factor itself, independent of the antecedent's syntactic role. She demonstrated (p. 11) that, in the case of a non-subject NP antecedent, one out of four anaphoric mentions is reduced, while in the case of a prepositional antecedent only one out of seven anaphoric mentions is reduced. These and other Khudyakova (2007) quantitative results are summarized in Table 14.5.

Obviously, these quantitative data are only the first step in large-scale modelling of referential choice; compare Table 14.5 with Table 11.6. Note that, contrary to what was found in Chapters 11 and 12, Khudyakova's (2007: 12) results suggest that the antecedent's referential form may actually turn out to be a significant activation factor; see the corresponding line in Table 14.5. Similar claims were previously put forward on a number of occasions; see discussion in subsection 11.4.2. Testing which of the opposite hypotheses is correct remains for further modelling studies.

Khudyakova (2008) explored the question of whether low-level semantic roles, such as agent, experiencer, patient, etc., must be included amongst the activation factors, along with syntactic role and semantic hyperrole (Principal

TABLE 14.5. Quantitative relationships between candidate activation factors and referential choice in the RefRhet corpus, according to Khudyakova (2007)

Antecedent's and referent's properties		Referential choice	
		Full NP	Reduced NP
Antecedent's syntactic role	subject	56%	44%
	non-subject	81%	19%
Antecedent's phrase type	noun phrase	76%	24%
	prepositional phrase	84%	16%
Antecedent's semantic hyperrole	Principal	55%	45%
	non-Principal	77%	23%
Antecedent's referential form	full NP	74%	26%
	reduced NP	54%	46%
Referent's animacy	animate	47%	53%
	inanimate	80%	20%

vs. non-Principal). The conclusion of her paper is that such inclusion is not necessary, as the distinction according to hyperrole provides a sufficiently good result.

Interesting results have been obtained in the study by Linnik (2010). First, she explored the activation factor of protagonisthood. She conducted an experimental study with thirty native speakers of English who identified protagonists in thirty texts from RefRhet. These results were compared with several models of simple automatic protagonisthood annotation. The conclusion was drawn that some of these simple methods, based on the frequency of referent mentions in a text, yield satisfactory identification of protagonisthood. Linnik (2010) also explored the role of zero referent mentions in RefRhet as possible antecedents. (In English written prose zero mentions only occur in certain syntactic positions, such as the subject of non-first coordinate clauses, infinitival clauses, and gerundial clauses.) Linnik arrived at the conclusion that statistically the impact of zero antecedents is negligible and they do not need to be annotated in the corpus.

14.2.4 *Preliminary results of a statistical machine learning study*

At this time (summer 2010) the referential annotation of the RefRhet corpus is about two-thirds complete. Results reported below are based on the part of the corpus containing 237 texts with 110,000 words. These texts contain about 26 thousand markables, among which there are 3,756 reliable pairs 'referential expression – antecedent'. Among the 3,756 referential expressions participating in these pairs, proper names number 1,623 (43%), full NPs based on a common noun number 971 (26%), and third person personal pronouns number 1,162 (31%).

Several machine learning studies have been conducted on the RefRhet corpus; see Kibrik et al. (2010a, 2010b). Statistical modelling has been performed with the use of the Weka system – a collection of machine learning algorithms for data mining tasks (see Hall et al. 2009). Those machine learning algorithms have been chosen that provide more easily interpretable results, including two logical algorithms: the decision tree algorithm C4.5 and the decision rule algorithm JRip. Also, the logistic regression algorithm has been used, as it is more reliable than the logical algorithms and allows one to obtain probabilistic estimates for referential options (see below).

When all candidate activation factors are taken into account, the accuracy of prediction of the twofold referential choice (between full and reduced referential devices), provided by the three above-mentioned algorithms, falls in the range between 85% and 87%. This result appears quite satisfactory.

Compare this to predictions made by individual factors: 74.8% for rhetorical distance to antecedent; 70% for the antecedent's grammatical role; 71.5% for animacy.[18]

An attempt was also made to predict the threefold choice between pronouns, proper names and 'descriptions' (that is, full NPs based on a common noun). In principle, the system of candidate activation factors, developed in the multi-factorial approach (Chapters 11 and 12), is not designed to capture the distinction between proper names and descriptions; they are lumped together in one category 'full NPs'. The difference between these two kinds of full NPs is not sufficiently understood in linguistics; but see Ariel (1990), Downing (1996b), Vieira and Poesio (1999), Stivers et al. (2007). So it is expected that a statistical model of the threefold choice must show results much worse than those for the twofold choice. Indeed the accuracy of prediction turned out much lower, but not too low: between 72% and 74% for different algorithms.[19] Generally, modelling the threefold referential choice is a huge challenge for further studies in reference.

Apparently, a statistical model cannot predict actual referential choice with 100% accuracy. As was discussed in the previous chapters (see especially sections 12.2 and 12.3), there is a difference between categorical and alterable referential devices. For example, sometimes referent activation is so high that a pronoun only is expected, whereas in other contexts either a pronoun or a full NP would work equally well. In discourse, however, the choice is always actually made, even when it is random. If we want our statistical model to always make a specific prediction, it should err at least in some of those instances where referential choice is random. So the further goal of statistical modelling based on the RefRhet corpus is to learn to distinguish between categorical and alterable referential devices. This may be attained by the following probabilistic method.

An algorithm may produce not a predicted referential choice but rather a probabilistic evaluation for each of referential option. When one of the options has a very high probability, a prediction of actual referential choice can be made. In less clear instances random choice may be posited. This is a projected avenue for the improvement of the model's performance. One of the algorithms we employ, namely logistic regression, produces numerical

---

[18] These results for mono-factorial models may appear high, but they are not. The baseline in such counts is determined by the quantitative distribution of referential devices. As was shown above, the share of full and reduced referential devices in the subcorpus is 69% and 31% respectively. That is, if we simply predict that all referential devices are full we would have the accuracy of 69%.

[19] Note that the baseline for this model is 43%, which is the share of proper names in the subcorpus. Apparently, the model shows a big advantage over this baseline.

weights that, most likely, can be used as probabilistic evaluations of referential options. Such evaluations, in turn, can be reinterpreted as activation scores. This may be a path to reintroducing the cognitive interpretation that was largely lost in the statistical studies of reference (see section 14.1), as compared to the calculative model that emphasized activation score as the central component in referential choice.

Among the computational studies in the generation of referential expressions the one that comes the closest to this study in terms of the methodology employed, to the best of my knowledge, is Greenbacker and McCoy (2009). Generally, studies of referential choice (or generation of referential expressions) are not very common in computational linguistics (Dale 1992 seems to be the only monograph on the topic; see Dale 2006 for a more recent review), especially compared to the numerous studies of anaphora resolution; see Mitkov (2002) and Strube (2007) for reviews.

14.2.5 *Additional candidate activation factors*

In the RefRhet corpus almost all variables that had been previously identified as major activation factors (see Chapters 11 and 12) are included in the annotations. A number of other variables, not judged to be activation factors in the studies reported in Chapters 11 and 12, are also included as candidate activation factors, among them the antecedent's referential form. In addition, there are a range of other potential factors proposed by various authors that have so far not been included in the annotations of the RefRhet corpus. Ideally, these must be accounted for in the annotations as well, and then tested for their possible impact upon referential choice. Since machine learning algorithms are computationally very powerful, an unlimited number of candidate factors can be added and tested with the help of this technique. Although these candidate factors have not yet been implemented, it seems useful to show the reader some of the further directions in the studies associated with the RefRhet corpus. Several additional candidate factors are briefly discussed in this subsection.

Implicit causality and type of rhetorical relation. The main reason why the RST Discourse Treebank was chosen as the basis for the RefRhet corpus is this: in the treebank, huge work on the annotation of rhetorical structure has already been implemented. This is very important since rhetorical distance is such a powerful activation factor. However, if one only pays attention to rhetorical distance, the prior work on the construction of the treebank is used only to a very limited degree. That is, the rhetorical graphs are used but specific rhetorical relations are not. In fact, however, specific relations may turn out useful as well.

In Chapter 12, the weak activation factor of predictability was introduced; see also Tily and Piantadosi (2009). This factor operates in contexts in which it is almost inevitable that a referent is mentioned in a certain clause. According to the system outlined in Chapter 12, in such instances a small boost is given to the referent's activation. This phenomenon has been discussed on many occasions in various terms. For example, Li and Thompson (1979: 330) proposed that closeness of a clause's connection to another clause may be among the factors responsible for referential choice. Most approaches paying attention to predictability, however, have looked at it from the perspective of discourse comprehension and anaphora resolution. Predictability is generally important in language use, as in any cognitive task; Schank (2005) lists the ability to predict as the first among the conscious cognitive processes helping an individual to function in the real world.

There is a substantial tradition associated with the notion of 'implicit causality' (e.g. Garvey and Caramazza 1974, Stevenson et al. 1994, 2000, Greene and McKoon 1995, Hudson D'Zmura 1998, Arnold 2001, Miltsakaki 2007, van Berkum et al. 2007). This notion suggests that certain semantic properties of predicates and/or inter-clause connectors provide a bias to what referent is mentioned in a subsequent clause. For example, in the study by Stevenson et al. (1994) experiment participants were asked to continue structures such as *Ken impressed Geoff, so/because he...* and the observed consistent patterns of such continuations were used to make conclusions on how the implicit causality, contained in the predication's semantic roles and in the connector's meaning, 'focuses' one referent among those mentioned in the first clause. In sentences such as the one just cited the connector *so* profiles the first clause's experiencer (Geoff), and the connector *because* the stimulus (Ken). Generally, authors belonging to this tradition recognize a variety of factors involved in the use of pronouns, implicit causality being only one of them; see Stevenson et al. (2000: 254). Also, Stevenson et al. (2000) suggest that the dependency between pronoun resolution and understanding of coherence relations goes both ways: it is sometimes pronoun resolution that helps to establish discourse relations rather than vice versa; see also Vonk et al. (1992).

In the trend of thought initiated by Hobbs (1979), on the other hand, one major factor is emphasized. Hobbs put forward the idea that reference resolution is not an independent process but rather a by-product of establishing inter-clausal coherence in discourse. Kehler (2002) has demonstrated that specific types of coherence (=rhetorical) relations impose specific constraints on discourse referents, thus limiting their interpretation scope. Kehler proposed that preferences in the understanding of pronominal reference 'are not first class resolution heuristics, but instead epiphenomena resulting from the properties of deeper inference processes used to establish different types of coherence relations' (Kehler 2002: 170). For example, one of the major kinds of coherence relations identified in Kehler's approach is cause–effect relations. One relation from this group, namely explanation, is found in sentences such as in (14.3) (Kehler 2002: 162):

(14.3) The city council$_C$ denied the demonstrators$_D$ a permit because
    i. they$_C$ feared violence.
    ii. they$_D$ advocated violence.

As Kehler argues, the semantic interaction between the verbs of the two clauses allows one to establish the explanation relation between the clauses in only one possible way in each of the sentences (14.3i, ii), and reference ascribed to *they* in each case results from such inference. Kehler proposed different inference principles for different types of coherence relations.

In the corpus, it is hard to find natural examples like Kehler's (2002) constructed ones, in which just verb semantics and the relation type alone make the difference. However, slight effects such as the one noted in Chapter 12 are actually observed. Probably, most of the information needed to account for such effects upon referential choice is captured by two kinds of annotation: the type of semantic role (it has been added to the annotation of a portion of the corpus; see Khudyakova 2008), and the type of rhetorical relation (or a set of relations) connecting the current EDU to the antecedent's EDU, which is already available. If the quality of relations between EDUs is taken into account, novel effects may be discovered. It is known that the quality of coherence relations is strongly connected to cognitive representations in language users. For example, it has been demonstrated that various kinds of coherence relations differ in terms of the extent to which they provide a more or less tight, more or less structured relationship between clauses, and, accordingly, they are processed differently (Sanders et al. 1992, Sanders and Noordman 2000).

A theoretical problem associated with the phenomena such as implicit causality or predictability must be noted. As has been argued in Chapter 10, subsection 10.3.4, these factors are more directly related to reference than to referential choice per se. What these factors say is that a certain referent's mention in a given clause is likely. That is, the referent gets more attended to than other referents. This is so from the speaker's perspective, and also from the addressee's perspective (nearly always adopted in implicit causality studies): 'readers use the implicit causality cue in something like "David praised Linda because..." *proactively*, and essentially *predict*, before the pronoun comes along, that the remainder of the sentence will tell us something about Linda' (van Berkum et al. 2007: 167). However, when such prediction is confirmed, and the referent is actually attended to and mentioned, this may be expected to be associated with boosted activation. Whether this happens or not, and when exactly, needs to be thoroughly tested in a corpus study.

Parallelism. It has been noted in a number of studies (e.g. Grober et al. 1978, Stevenson et al. 1995, Chambers and Smyth 1998, Streb et al. 1999, Arnold 2008) that sometimes pronouns are preferentially associated with antecedents appearing in the same or a parallel syntactic role in their clause. This tendency is more salient in those cases when both the anaphor and the antecedent are non-subjects, because, if both of them are subjects, the affinity is easily described through the factor of the antecedent's subjecthood. The factor of parallelism is relatively weak; it is often neutralized by other factors, including the antecedent's subjecthood. Also, it is not only syntactic but also semantic roles that may invoke the parallelism effects, as the two sets of roles do not always accord. For example, Kehler (2002: 161) discussed examples such as the following:

(14.4) Margaret Thatcher is admired by Hillary Clinton, and she worships George W. Bush

According to Kehler, most of his informants understand *she* in (14.4) as referring to 'Hillary Clinton'. This is due to the congruence of the situations described in the two clauses. In terms of Kehler's framework, this congruence, in conjunction with a resemblance relation holding between the clauses, is the basis for associating the pronoun with a certain referent.

The candidate factor of syntactic parallelism can be easily incorporated into the modelling study of referential choice. Various degrees of parallelism can be tested depending on the adopted granularity of roles. For example all non-subjects can be collapsed into one category, or else direct objects can be differentiated from obliques, etc. As for semantic parallelism, it can be implemented if annotation for semantic roles is added.

Other candidate factors. There are a number of factors, generally associated with the notions of topicality or themehood, that need to be taken into account. As is well known, in many languages the earlier linear position of an NP in a clause is associated with higher topicality; see e.g. Tomlin (1995). An antecedent's high topicality can be among the factors affecting referential choice; see e.g. Gernsbacher (1990); Kibrik (2002b); Kaiser and Trueswell

(2011). High topicality is partly accounted for through the factor of antecedent syntactic role, as topicality is strongly associated with subjecthood (Chafe 1994). But it is useful to explore topicality and word order as a separate factor. Topicality can also be conveyed not by word order but by explicit markers such as the preposition *about*. This kind of topicality marking also is among the candidate activation factors. Special syntactic constructions, such as clefts, can also affect subsequent referential choice (Arnold and Griffin 2007: 522).

In Chapter 12, the factor of introductory antecedent was posited. This factor, that can be otherwise called the ordinal number of referent mention, suggests that on the second mention in discourse a referent cannot attain full activation. In some languages, pronominal reference is impossible or unlikely on the second mention; see Kibrik (1991); Diessel (1999: 98); Austin (2001b: 90). Whereas English does not have this property, this factor may be at work in a more covert form.

Ariel (1988: 203–204, 2001: 39ff.) has suggested that (translating Ariel into my terminology) a referent from whose perspective discourse is produced may be more activated. In the study of van Vliet (2002) it was shown that overspecified NPs (those that carry more lexical information than is apparently necessary) may signal a change in perspective, whereas using pronouns may indicate the preservation of the same perspective. Perspective taking is among the most important directions in the further inquiry into discourse reference; cf. the discussion in Chapter 8, subsection 8.6.1 and in Chapter 15, subsection 15.3.3.

In the CMF approach, a whole family of factors modelling the distance to antecedent is used. This idea ultimately goes back to Givón's (1983a) measurement of referential distance. But Givón used another metric in the same study, namely so-called persistence, measured as the number of referent mentions in subsequent discourse. I believe that the intuition behind this measurement is already sufficiently captured by the factor of protagonisthood (see e.g. Chapter 12, section 12.5), but nevertheless persistence can be tested on its own as well.

Among the activation factors implemented in the CMF approach so far, one stands out as being of a completely non-discourse nature but rather dealing with a referent's permanent, ontological features. This is the factor of animacy. In the study of Fraurud (1996) it was proposed that other ontological features of referents, such as individuals vs. functionals, may as well be involved in referential choice. Furthermore, other ontological features may be relevant in the corpus under investigation, for example the class of organizations (such as companies or governments) that constitute a very common referent type in the texts of the RefRhet corpus.[20]

14.3 Another language: Japanese

The CMF approach to referential choice, introduced in the previous chapters, has been applied to one more language, Japanese, in the dissertation of Efimova (2006). Recall from Chapter 3 that Japanese is the best known example of a language that amply uses zero reference. As is demonstrated by Efimova's data (pp. 18ff.), Japanese referential choice primarily amounts to the choice between full NPs and zeroes. Efimova further distinguishes between two kinds of full NPs: those marked and not marked with the topic marker *wa*.

Despite the existence of a rich tradition of reference studies in Japanese (e.g. Hinds (ed.) 1978, Hinds 1984, Clancy 1980, Podlesskaya 1990, Hedberg 1996, Yamamoto 1999, Nariyama 2003: 26, Shimojo 2005 inter alia), Efimova (pp. 48–49) rightly indicates that there are no encompassing studies explaining how various relevant factors interact and collectively predict referential choice. She employs the CMF approach, developed in Kibrik (1996a) for Russian and in Kibrik (1999) for English, because it appears to be universally applicable and typologically adequate (Efimova 2006: 49–51). The goal of her study is to test the applicability of the CMF approach to Japanese data and find out what adjustment will be necessary.

As the point of departure, Efimova uses the same set of candidate activation factors as those employed for Russian in Chapter 11 above. She then performs a statistical test to see which of these factors actually correlate with referential choice in written Japanese narratives (Efimova 2006: 95–98). According to a chi-square test, rhetorical distance displays the strongest correlation with referential choice and is followed by other distance measurements. Other correlations are generally comparable to those found for Russian and English, although there are differences in details. In particular, the factors of the antecedent's syntactic and semantic role appear to be far less powerful in Japanese. The factor of the antecedent's referential form demonstrates the weakest correlation among all factors that exceed the critical chi-square value.

Instead of the referential mappings, shown in Chapters 11 and 12, Efimova uses a different method of relating referential types to activation levels. For each interval on the scale of activation score, she provides a breakdown of referent mentions according to referential type, as in Table 14.6.

---

[20] Some of the factors mentioned in this subsection, along with a number of others, were implemented in a series of machine learning studies in 2011; see Loukachevitch et al. 2011. As a result the accuracy of prediction rose to 89.9% for the twofold task and to 80.9% for the threefold task.

TABLE 14.6. Relationships between activation intervals and frequency of referential expressions in written Japanese discourse (according to Table 8 in Efimova 2006: 114)

Activation score interval	Full NPs without *wa*	Full NPs with *wa*	Zeroes	Total
0 or less	46 (85%)	8 (15%)	0 (0%)	54 (100%)
0.1–0.3	12 (63%)	4 (21%)	3 (16%)	19 (100%)
0.4–0.6	13 (62%)	6 (29%)	2 (9%)	21 (100%)
0.7–0.9	6 (13%)	3 (6%)	38 (81%)	47 (100%)
1 or more	2 (2%)	0 (0%)	113 (98%)	115 (100%)
Total	79	21	156	256

These results suggest that the choice between the two kinds of full NPs cannot be satisfactorily predicted by differences in activation level, especially in the case of high activation. However, the basic referential choice between a full NP and zero works much the same way as in other languages.

A very interesting aspect of Efimova's study is its cross-linguistic component: she explicitly compares referential systems of Russian and Japanese in terms of the CMF approach; see Efimova (2006: 100–103, 125–127). The general conclusion is that the sets of activation factors operating in both languages are very similar. Several differences are noted, though, and the most important one is that in Japanese the syntactic role of a referent mention in its own clause appears to be significant, contrary to Russian: both full NPs with the topic marker *wa* and zero references are strongly biased to the subject position and, conversely, are disfavoured in non-subject positions.[21] Efimova aptly remarks that Russian referential zeroes, when used, display the same tendency. (Remember from Chapter 11 that referential zeroes were rare in my original Russian discourse sample other than in syntactically-controlled environments, and so were not considered in a conclusive way.) This suggests that zeroes may be inherently different from third person pronouns in having a stronger affinity to the subject (or Principal) position.

Another innovative aspect of Efimova (2006) is that it includes a comparison of referential processes in written vs. spoken discourse. She has used both written and spoken retellings of an animation film as her data set. In her spoken corpus, the factor best correlated with referential choice turned out to be linear distance. Rhetorical distance follows it in its degree of correlation (Efimova

---

[21] The fact that zeroes are disfavoured in non-subject positions is a statistical tendency, not a categorical requirement; as was shown in Chapter 3, subsection 3.4.1, Japanese zeroes in principle can occur in all syntactic positions.

2006: 175). More generally, in spoken discourse, compared to written discourse, activation factors display somewhat weaker correlations with referential choice, and referential choice is a bit looser (Efimova 2006: 175–182). Example (14.5) from a spoken retelling is provided as an illustration of deviant referential choice. The zero reference to 'the dog' in the first line is found under quite low activation (linear distance of 6, rhetorical distance of 2 or even 3), while a full NP is used in the following line where activation is supposed to be maximal:

(14.5) Japanese (Efimova 2006: 182)[22]
    a. saishuutekini ee Ø$_d$ neko$_c$ o oidashi-te,
       finally uh cat ACC expel-CONV
    b. sonde inu$_d$ ga ... ee bin ... no futa o ake-te, <...>
       and dog NOM uh jar GEN lid ACC open-CONV
       'Finally he [=the dog] kicked out the cat, and the dog opened the jar's lid, <...>'

Overall, however, the spoken usage of full NPs vs. zeroes appears to be quite similar to what is found in written discourse – compare Table 14.7 with the figures in Table 14.6 above. Under maximal activation, zeroes are used 98% of the time in written discourse, and 97% of the time in spoken discourse. Under minimal activation distributions are also very similar. The greatest difference is found under middle values of activation score.

Finally, Efimova (2006: 183) offers a pilot study of referential choice in spoken Russian discourse. Again, she concludes that referential choice appears to be somewhat looser in spoken Russian compared to the result on written Russian reported in Kibrik (1996a); see Chapter 11.

TABLE 14.7. Relationship between activation intervals and frequency of referential expressions in spoken Japanese discourse (according to Table 15 in Efimova 2006: 180)

Activation score interval	Full NPs without *wa*	Full NPs with *wa*	Zeroes	Total
0 or less	46 (90%)	4 (8%)	1 (2%)	51 (100%)
0.1–0.3	18 (82%)	4 (18%)	0 (0%)	22 (100%)
0.4–0.6	24 (77%)	4 (13%)	3 (10%)	31 (100%)
0.7–0.9	21 (25%)	8 (10%)	55 (65%)	84 (100%)
1 or more	2 (3%)	0	64 (97%)	66 (100%)
Total	111	20	123	254

[22] This is an example from spoken discourse, and it contains some characteristic elements, such as marking of filled and unfilled pauses.

Generally, Efimova's study is a very useful application of the CMF approach. It brings an additional, third, language into the picture, thus rendering the cross-linguistic comparison much more comprehensive. Furthermore, it offers a new dimension for CMF research looking into differences between referential choice in written vs. spoken modes of discourse.

14.4 Activation score, working memory capacity, and reference understanding: psycholinguistic experimental studies

Among the major methods of scientific research, two were primarily employed in the work on the CMF approach: observation (in its variety known as the corpus method) and modelling. Some elements of experimentation were also used; see especially Chapter 12, section 12.3. Of course, it is desirable to test the basic claims of this approach through full-scale experimental studies. Initial psycholinguistic studies of this kind were recently undertaken at the Department of Theoretical and Applied Linguistics, Moscow State University, by Olga V. Fedorova and a group of her students. This is one of the first exercises in the emerging field that can be described as experimental discourse analysis (see also van Berkum in press).

The CMF approach, as described for Russian in Chapter 11, was used for the theoretical point of departure in the studies of Fedorova et al. (2010a, 2010b). These psycholinguistic experimental studies explored how speakers of Russian understand reference in constructed discourses. In these studies, processes of reference understanding (rather than production) were investigated.

The goals of the study of Fedorova et al. (2010a) included the following: to test whether activation scores (as posited in Chapter 11) correlate with the addressees' access to referents of pronouns; to test whether rhetorical distance is a real factor affecting referent activation; to test whether addressees' ability to recover referents correlates with their working memory capacity.

Six experimental discourses were composed, each comprising a bit less than 100 words and two paragraphs. In the first paragraph three human referents were introduced, one being the target referent and two other distractors. In the second paragraph the first two sentences contained no mentions of the human referents, and in the third one a third person pronoun occurred. Each text had three modifications with the rhetorical distance from the pronoun back to the antecedent being 1, 2, and 3 (measured in clauses). Activation factors other than the rhetorical distance were all kept constant in the three versions of the experimental discourse.

In the two preliminary experiments, experimental discourses were screened for the absence of referential conflict and for naturalness. In the main

TABLE 14.8. Percentage of correct answers to the question on the reference of the third person pronoun, based on Appendices 3 and 7 to Fedorova et al. (2010a: 529–530)

Participants, N	Working memory capacity	RhD = 1, AS = 0.7	RhD = 2, AS = 0.5	RhD = 3, AS = 0	Mean
86	Small: 2 to 3	62	38	28	43
17	Medium: 3.5 to 4	85	68	41	65
17	Large: 4.5 to 5	100	94	68	73
120	TOTAL	70	50	35	52

experiment (with 120 participants) an experiment participant read the discourse in the self-paced mode and was thereafter asked to answer a number of questions, including the question addressing the identity of the target referent (mentioned by the third person pronoun). The hypothesis in the main experiment was that errors in referent identification must be primarily due to insufficient referent activation in the participant's working memory. After the participants completed the main experiment, the standard working memory test of Daneman and Carpenter (1980) was run on them. Results of the main experiment are shown in Table 14.8.

As is clear from the unusually neat results in Table 14.8, the percentage of correct answers steadily declines with the increase of rhetorical distance and the corresponding decrease of activation score. At the same time, people with a larger working memory capacity have better access to referents, even those that are insufficiently activated, compared to people with a small working memory capacity.

Several important conclusions can be drawn from this innovative study. First, activation scores are good predictors of addressees' ability to recover referents. Second, rhetorical distance alone can serve as the source of significant changes in activation score. Third, the cognitive component independently identified as working memory in psychology and psycholinguistics is intimately related to referential processes in discourse. All of these conclusions, obtained through a sophisticated experimental procedure, support the cognitive linguistic theory developed in the previous chapters of this part of the book.

Fedorova et al. (2010b) focus on somewhat different results of the same study. In particular, they remark that their study confirms the claim by Otten and van Berkum (2009) that people with lower working memory capacity do not just fail to cope with discourse reference but rather use somewhat different ways to handle it.

Summary

The CMF approach to referential choice, described in the previous chapters of this part of the book, solicits several lines of development. Four such lines, including mathematically sophisticated modelling, amplification of the empirical basis, extension to additional languages, and experimental verification have been discussed in this chapter.

The mathematical component of the original CMF approach can be described as the calculative method. This method has a number of limitations, including the manual selection of activation factors and the simplistic, purely additive, character of the interaction between them. A much more advanced method, based on the machine learning technique known as artificial neural networks, has been applied to the English data set. The networks were trained on the data set, and the results demonstrated that this method is able to classify the data almost correctly with respect to the choice of referential device. A pruning procedure singled out five factors that still allowed for a relatively good prediction of referential choice. Furthermore, it was demonstrated that costly input factors such as rhetorical distance to the antecedent could be replaced by those related to the linear antecedent, which can be more easily derived from a corpus. One can conclude that the machine learning methods have good prospects with respect to referential choice studies, particularly when a sufficiently large data set is available.

The modern approach to large natural discourse data sets is known as the corpus method. A relatively large corpus (over 176,000 words), designed for the development of the CMF approach and named RefRhet, is being developed. This corpus, previously annotated for rhetorical (hierarchical) discourse structure, is being annotated for a number of features, necessary for modelling referential choice. A number of studies have been accomplished on the basis of this corpus, including an improved technique for measuring rhetorical distance, analysis of several individual activation factors, and a statistical machine learning study. A high level of accuracy in the prediction of referential choice has been attained. Also, additional candidate activation factors that can be implemented in the corpus-based study were discussed.

In addition to the CMF studies of Russian and English referential choice, this approach has also been applied to Japanese in the work of Zoya Efimova. Japanese is different from both Russian and English in using zero reference as the dominant reduced referential device. The CMF approach proved to be fully functional with respect to Japanese. The system of activation factors remained essentially the same, although it required several adjustments.

Efimova also extended the CMF approach by comparing referential choice in written and spoken modes of discourse.

The research programme associated with the CMF approach to discourse reference was recently supplemented with a new component: experimental psycholinguistic studies testing the basic premises of this approach. In the work of Olga Fedorova and her associates a number of experiments were run that demonstrated a correlation between a referent's activation score and an addressee's access to the referent. These experiments also showed the significant contribution of rhetorical distance to activation score, as well as the relatedness between working memory and referential processes.

Concluding remarks to Part IV

Chapters 10 to 14, forming Part IV of this book, presented the CMF approach to referential choice in discourse. As is clear from the name of this approach, its two main tenets are: first, a commitment to cognitive explanation and second, the recognition of the multiplicity of factors affecting referential choice. Put simply, numerous factors, grounded in discourse context and in a referent's properties, cumulatively determine a referent's current degree of activation in working memory, called activation score, and activation score is the prime force determining the choice between a full vs. a reduced referential device.

There are two cognitive systems immediately related to reference in discourse. The attentional system is manifested in discourse as reference per se, that is, referent mention. The working memory system, subservient with respect to attention, is responsible for referential choice. Attended referents become activated at the following discourse moment. Whenever a speaker needs to pay attention to a referent, that is mention it, he/she has access to the referent's activation score, as represented in working memory, and chooses a referential device on the basis of this score.

The CMF approach has been applied to the data of two languages: Russian and English. For each of these languages a system of activation factors has been set up, including the factors' values and the corresponding numerical weights. A referent's activation score is calculated as the sum of all relevant weights. Referential mapping describes how activation scores are translated into referential options. Roughly speaking, a low activation results in using a full referential device, and a high activation leads to a reduced referential device. Additional filters, most importantly the referential conflict filter, may interfere in referential choice at a later stage.

The CMF approach is based on the positive knowledge from cognitive psychology and cognitive neuroscience. In turn, it provides some insights into basic questions about working memory, including its capacity, control, and forgetting. In particular, the measurement of grand activation, calculated as the sum of all current activation scores, can be used as an estimate for the specific-referents portion of working memory. The capacity of working memory equals three to four maximal activations of a single referent.

The CMF approach is open to elaboration in several directions, including the application of statistical machine learning methods, development of large corpora annotated for referential features, description of additional languages, and experimental verification.

Even though the main emphasis of this part of the book is on cognitive issues and thus differs from that of the typological Parts II and III, the actual concerns are not as dissimilar as they may seem. As was argued in Chapter 1 (section 1.7), cognitive and typological aspects of any linguistic phenomenon are complementary rather than entirely independent. This claim can be made more concrete in the following way. I view the CMF analyses of specific languages, of the kind that was presented in this part of the book, as an embryonic stage of a future fine-grained linguistic typology in the domain of discourse reference.

To be sure, such typology does not yet exist, but it may become possible one day, if a significant number of languages have detailed accounts of their referential systems in terms of individual activation factors, quantified for their relative contribution. Producing such an account is a laborious task, since one needs to consider all potentially relevant activation factors and sort out their relative contribution and their interaction. But I do not see any way to circumvent such a task if we are interested in a realistic picture of language-specific referential systems. I see the future typology of referential systems as a study involving, among other things, a comparison of the sets of activation factors relevant in particular languages and of their relative significance. In turn, knowledge about linguistic diversity in the realm of referential choice must shed light on the underlying, presumably universal, cognitive processes.

Part V
Broadening the Perspective

Linguistic form is traditionally thought of as consisting of sound. Phonemes make up morphemes, morphemes form words and clauses, etc. Generally, this book follows along the same lines, assuming, most of the time, that reference is performed by means of verbal linguistic devices, having a phonetic shape (unless they are zero). At certain points in the above chapters we briefly considered non-verbal, but vocal elements of linguistic form, that is prosody. Furthermore, there are several aspects that relate reference to another information channel: not just **non-verbal**, but also **non-vocal**. I mean the visual information channel.

The discussion in the previous parts of the book was limited to those instances when referents become attended to and then activated due to their mention in discourse. Of course, it is also possible to attend to and activate referents via visual perception. Human languages are equipped with functional mechanisms to handle such situations, most notably deixis. So it is useful to discuss how deixis relates to the kinds of reference in discourse explored in the previous parts of this book.

We have been concentrating on the verbal referential devices, such as noun phrases. However, there is an important non-verbal and non-vocal way to refer: the **pointing gesture**. There is evidence that pointing is the evolutionary and ontogenetic precursor of verbal reference. So it is important to examine how pointing interacts with the verbal ways of reference in discourse.

There are languages that fundamentally rely on the visual channel of communication: **sign languages** of the deaf. The discussion of reference in human languages would be grossly incomplete if I totally ignored the evidence of sign languages in this book. These issues are considered, even though in an inevitably cursory way, in Chapter 15, forming this part of the book.

15

Reference and visual aspects of discourse

Overview

In this chapter I briefly address several issues related to non-verbal and even non-vocal ways to perform reference. First, there is a mode of reference known as deixis. A referent can be mentioned by a deictic expression if the referent is physically present in the interlocutors' environment and is thus perceptually (most often, visually[1]) available. Deictic expressions involve not just a piece of sound but also a pointing gesture. Therefore, vision is crucially involved in deixis. The functional phenomenon of deixis and the formal phenomenon of pointing, their connectedness and, at the same time, their non-identity, are discussed in section 15.1.

The visual information channel attains the leading role in sign languages, in which linguistic form is not vocal but visual. In section 15.2 the data of Russian Sign Language are introduced, and its referential system is briefly outlined.

Section 15.3 is devoted to one particular kind of pointing that is found in gesticulation accompanying speech. It is virtual pointing, taking place especially in narratives, when a speaker points at referents that are not really but imaginarily stationed in the surrounding space.

15.1 Deixis, exophora, and pointing

Referential choice is fundamentally dependent on the activation of referents in working memory. In the previous chapters, I have mostly addressed referent activation derived from the linguistic structure of discourse, from certain verbal expressions. If a referent was mentioned in prior discourse, that

---

[1] Perception through other senses can also be involved. According to William F. Hanks (the lecture course 'Deixis and indexicality', LSA summer institute, Berkeley, July 2009), in Yucatec (Mayan, eastern Mexico) there is a special deictic element indicating auditory and even olfactory perception.

means, cognitively, that it was attended to. Attention leads to subsequent activation in working memory, and that results in the use of reduced referential devices, such as anaphoric pronouns. Conversely, if a referent was not mentioned in prior discourse, it was not attended to and cannot be expected to be currently activated. As a result, if a speaker needs to mention such a referent, he/she must use a full referential device.

This picture is, however, incomplete. Mentioning things is not the only way to attend to them and to further activate them. In fact, this specifically linguistic kind of attention and activation is quite peculiar. One does not necessarily need to have any discourse at all to have a referent activated. For example, when I notice (that is, attend to) a cat entering this room it gets activated in my working memory just as easily as when someone mentions this cat to me. Undoubtedly, activation on the basis of visual attention is much more fundamental than activation through discourse mention.

The processes of linguistic mention of referents activated through visual attention are known as deixis and exophora. As has been suggested on many occasions (e.g. Lyons 1975), deixis is the ontologic source of anaphoric reference. In this section I briefly discuss deixis and exophora, delineate their boundaries and propose an account of their relationship to anaphora. I also discuss the phenomenon of pointing, closely connected with deixis.

15.1.1 *Deixis*

Reduced referential devices, such as third person pronouns, apart from the anaphoric usage can also be used in a different way, known as **deixis**. It is usually supposed that deixis and anaphora constitute a universal polysemy of pronouns. Both deictic and anaphoric devices are sometimes subsumed under the cover term 'shifters', introduced by Jespersen (1922) and later popularized by Jakobson (1935/1971). To give a simple example of a deictic third person pronoun, imagine the following setting. Two persons are walking down the street, and one of them notices a woman in a funny hat. He points at the woman and tells his friend[2]:

---

[2] In the transcripts of spoken discourse in this chapter I indicate gestures by underlining the portion of speech during which a pointing gesture is observed (or could be observed, in the case of constructed examples). Gestures other than pointing are not shown in transcripts. Discourse transcripts are divided into lines, representing elementary discourse units. Primary accents of elementary discourse units, along with the direction of tone (rising or falling), are marked by means of diacritics ´ and ` on top of accented vowels. Morphological glossing is used to the minimum in this chapter as it is insignificant here. I would like to express my sincere gratitude to Julija Nikolaeva whose assistance and advice were essential in the preparation of this chapter.

(15.1) Look at hèr!

In this constructed example what is attended to is the woman, that is, a referent. It is coded by means of a third person pronoun, accompanied by a non-verbal element, that is a **pointing** gesture. In the following example, the demonstrative pronoun *èti* 'these' is used deictically, in combination with a pointing gesture. (In fact, demonstratives are often particularly firmly associated with pointing gestures; see Levinson 2004 and Diessel 2006.)

(15.2) Russian
Ponjuxaj èti!
smell   these
'Smell these ones!'

Two crucial functional differences of the deictic uses of third person pronouns and demonstratives from the anaphoric ones are the following: first, the referent is perceptually available at the time of reference, and second, deictic reference does not presuppose prior activation of the referent in interlocutors' minds.

It is often claimed that the deictic mechanism depends on the phenomenon of **joint attention** of the speaker and the addressee (see e.g. Diessel 2006 and Louwerse and Bangerter 2005). It is particularly important to emphasize that in deixis the speaker does not simply employ the existing joint attention but intentionally establishes it, that is, instantly attracts the addressee's attention to an element of the perceived environment. To use Lyons's terminology, deixis places a referent into the universe of discourse (Lyons 1977: 673); in Ehlich's words, in deixis the speaker focuses the hearer's attention on a specific item (Ehlich 1982: 325).

The addressee's attention is manipulated by the speaker with the help of a pointing gesture – a crucial formal element of a deictic act of reference. In examples such as (15.1) and (15.2) the fact of pointing is no less meaningful than the use of a verbal referential device. According to the understanding of deixis adopted here, deixis must include some kind of pointing. The converse is not true; as will be discussed below, pointing can occur outside deictic contexts. The phenomenon of pointing is further discussed in subsection 15.1.2.

Since in deixis attention to a referent is established at the time of the referential act, the referent is activated at or immediately after the time of reference. That is, deictic expressions code previously non-activated (new) information (Cornish 2006: 632) – in contrast to anaphora, firmly associated with a referent's prior activation. As has been discussed throughout this book, non-activated information is typically encoded in a fuller, more elaborate way than activated information. In the domain of anaphora, 'more elaborate way' means using full rather than reduced referential devices. However, in the domain of deixis reduced referential devices – pronouns and demonstratives – are common; see examples above. Therefore, in deixis referents' prior non-activation is conveyed primarily not by lexical elaboration but by a different specialized formal element, namely by a pointing gesture. Besides the gestural aspect of form, deictic pronouns are often more elaborate prosodically, being accented – in contrast to anaphoric pronouns that tend to be unaccented clitics. (The relation between pointing and prosody is addressed in subsection 15.1.5).

We thus must recognize that lexically reduced referential devices can in principle be used for non-activated referents. In the previous parts of this book we have seen massive evidence for the claim that a referent's activation in interlocutors' minds is a prerequisite for reduced reference. However, when a pointing gesture establishes a direct link between a referential device and a referent, language users can still be economical and stick to a reduced referential device even in the absence of prior activation. The case of deixis thus points to limits of the correlation between degrees of activation and referential choice. Such correlation, clearly observed in the domain of discourse-induced activation, is not held in the domain of perception-based activation. Due to the support from the pointing gesture, in deixis pronouns strongly intrude in the domain of introductory mention.

Deixis, however, does not require the use of lexically reduced referential devices. Full NPs can perfectly well be used in deictic contexts also. Consider an example from a TV show, in which the speaker pointed at a previously unattended to person in the audience:

(15.3)   Russian (Nikolaeva 2003: 34)
         Ja   xotela by   u   Pavla   sprosit'.
         I   want   PTCL at   Pavel   ask
         'I would like to ask Pavel'

The empirical study by Nikolaeva (2003) demonstrates that full NPs are no less frequently found in deictic contexts than reduced NPs; see also section 15.3.

To recapitulate, deixis is defined here by three foundational properties, the first two functional and the third formal:

- referent's prior non-activation
- referent's perceptual availability at the time of reference
- use of a pointing gesture.

As will be discussed in the subsequent parts of this chapter, these three properties can be realised to a certain degree in various peripheral manifestations of deixis. However, all three of them converge in the prototypical instances.

The outlined definition of deixis is quite restrictive. In the literature a much broader understanding is current that embraces, besides the instances such as in examples (15.1) to (15.3), a whole gamut of other semantic and formal elements, including but not limited to:

- elements of the origo, that is, the egocentric framework defining the parameters of the current speech situation, in particular:
  - first and second person reference
  - spatial and temporal characteristics of the speech situation (so-called *here* and *now*)
- various temporal expressions, including adverbials (such as *then* or *tomorrow*) and tenses; for a concise but ingenious discusson see Levelt (1989: 55–58)
- lexical meanings involving egocentric orientation in space, such as in English *come* (Fillmore 1975)
- relative proximity of items in the perceptual space (Diessel 1999)
- relative social status of discourse participants and/or characters ('social deixis'; Levinson 1983: 61–96).

In my view, such a broad understanding of deixis renders this notion almost vacuous. All of the listed phenomena are outside the notion of deixis as construed here. Note especially that the proposed understanding of deixis does not include locutor pronouns, such as English *I* and *you*. The confusing practice of including both attention-establishing reference (such as *her* coupled with a gesture, see example (15.1)) and the permanently attended to elements of the origo (such as *I*) within one class of deictic expressions goes back to Bühler (1934) and further back to Brugmann (1904). Sometimes locutor pronouns are even cited as deictic elements par excellence, (e.g. Trask 1993: 76, Zubin and Hewitt 1995, Green 2006).

The reason for such confusion is clear: the use of both pointing-accompanied deictic expressions and locutor pronouns is in some way associated with the concept of the origo. However, the role that the origo plays in the functioning of these two groups of expressions is very different. Whereas locutor pronouns are inherently directed at the elements of the origo itself, in deictic reference to the elements of perceived environment the origo participates only as the source from which the pointer comes (see subsection 15.1.2), and with respect to which the target of pointing is located. In accordance with that, locutor pronouns represent referents that are constantly attended to and activated (and do not need to be intentionally brought into the discourse participants' joint attention),[3] while genuine deictic elements, as was discussed above, are directed at those referents that were not previously attended to and activated. So, if *I* is a deictic, it is so in a very different sense from *her* in example (15.1). In fact, it is preferable to think of locutor reference as a distinct type of reference.

The restrictive understanding of deixis is more in line with the etymological meaning of the term (it derives from the Greek root meaning 'point', 'indicate'). The proposed restrictive understanding has precursors in the literature, for example Benveniste (1958).

A vast literature is devoted to the phenomenon of deixis, and it includes both theoretical discussions and cross-linguistic analyses of deictic expressions. To mention just a few important publications of the several last decades, some of which are useful surveys of the work of others, deixis and deictic expressions are discussed in Majtinskaja (1969), Kuryłowicz (1972), Fillmore (1975), Lyons (1975), Jarvella and Klein (eds.) (1982), Weissenborn and Klein (eds.) (1982), Rauh (ed.) (1983), Anderson and Keenan (1987), Levelt (1989: 44–58), Paducheva and Krylov (1992), Diessel (1999), Levinson (2004), Senft (ed.) (2004).

Below I discuss the mechanism of pointing, introduce the phenomenon of exophora and its relation to deixis, and consider how pointing is used in these processes.

15.1.2 *Pointing*

During the last decade or so, the behaviour known as pointing has been in the limelight in linguistic and psychological literature; see e.g. the monograph by Kita (ed.) (2003). The structure of a pointing act is schematically represented in Figure 15.1.

The origo is the centre of coordinates, normally coinciding with the speaker. A number of other terms are used in the literature for the same notion, for example 'the indexical ground' in Hanks (1992). The pointing device, typically represented as a pointing gesture, projects a vector directed

---

[3] The actual situation is somewhat more complex. The unmarked, canonical first and second person reference presupposes the permanent attention to and activation of locutor referents. In accordance with that, locutor reference is normally performed by highly reduced referential devices. However, locutor pronouns may be strong rather than weak, and then they are prosodically prominent and may involve pointing gestures. As was discussed in Chapter 4, subsection 4.5.4, this happens for a number of reasons, including the locutor referents somehow falling out of attention and working memory. In these kinds of atypical occurrences deixis (in my narrow understanding) may in principle be combined with locutor reference.

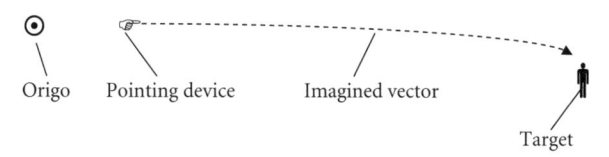

FIGURE 15.1. Elements of a canonical pointing act

from the origo to the target[4] of pointing. The structure represented in Figure 15.1 depicts the most basic, canonical form of pointing. Some deviations from this canon will be accounted for below, some others remain beyond my concern in this chapter.

It is important to emphasize that pointing and deixis are not equal. Pointing is a formal device, while deixis is a functional referential mechanism. As has been suggested above, pointing is among the defining elements of the deictic procedure. However, below we will see that pointing often occurs outside deictic contexts.

Pointing gestures constitute an important phenomenon – in phylogeny, in ontogeny, and in face-to-face communication. As for phylogeny, there is some controversy about whether pointing is found in species other than humans.[5] Butovskaja (2004: 96) suggests that both adolescent and adult chimpanzees use pointing gestures to attract attention to a certain object. Most researchers, however, seem to agree that great apes, the nearest evolutionary relatives of humans, do not use pointing in their natural environment[6] (Krause 1997 and Tomasello et al. 2007: 717–718). In captivity, the situation is more complex. For example, Call and Tomasello (1994) reported instances of referential pointing (and comprehension of human pointing) by two orangutans, an enculturated individual showing a greater proficiency in pointing than simply a captive ape. Liebal et al. (2006) have recorded almost 400 visual gestures of captive orangutans (including approach face, bite or hit intention, offer body part, etc.) but none of these were identified as pointing.

There are more numerous studies of pointing acquisition by captive chimpanzees and its use in apes' communication with humans; see Tomasello et al. (2007: 717–718 for a review). These authors note that pointing only occurs in chimpanzees' directive acts and they 'are not very skillful at comprehending

---

[4] Quine (1971) once observed that pointing is inherently ambiguous, as the vector projected by a pointing gesture potentially intersects a great number of various entities or locations. However, as the subsequent discussion in this chapter demonstrates, in the practice of pointing this problem is not among the most vital ones.

[5] I thank Julia Cissewski for a helpful discussion of certain issues considered in this subsection.

[6] Note that it is pointing gestures that are controversial; the apes' general ability to gesture is not in doubt.

informative pointing gestures' (p. 717) and this is at least partly because apes, when communicating, fail to create 'any kind of joint goal or joint attentional frame of things relevant to a shared activity' (p. 718). In addition, captive chimpanzees do not use pointing in communication between each other, only with humans. Other authors, such as Povinelli et al. (2003), ardently deny the possibility of chimpanzees' pointing under any conditions and claim that the reverse opinion is based on a false interpretation. In general, it appears that only weak precursors of pointing, if any, can be found in great apes, and the ability to point is very close to being exclusively human.

In ontogeny, pointing appears to be one of the earliest communicative behaviours; for recent reviews of literature on the development of pointing see Butterworth (2003), Diessel (2006), Tomasello et al. (2007). The first instances of communicative pointing are usually registered towards the end of the first year of life. At this age babies begin performing a variety of directive, expressive, and informative pointing acts, indicating objects and places of their interest. This ability is clearly related to the already developed ability to understand the other's perception, intentions, attention, and knowledge – the so-called 'theory of mind' (see Tomasello et al. 2007: 716). Thus babies at this age already surpass apes in forming joint attention. It has been demonstrated that the development of pointing is closely connected to linguistic development, as well as to brain lateralization (Butterworth 2003). In particular, the earlier pointing begins, the earlier language is acquired (Bates et al. 1979).

Evidently, pointing communication precedes verbal communication and serves as a basis for the latter's further development. Particularly interesting is the phenomenon of combining verbal and gestural elements – see e.g. Butcher and Goldin-Meadow (2000) and Goldin-Meadow and Butcher (2003). At the period when babies are preparing to proceed from one-word utterances to so-called two-word speech they begin using dyadic constructions comprising a deictic gesture and a lexeme: 'each of the children produced combinations of the following type: gesture conveyed the object of a desired action (e.g. point at a box), and speech conveyed the action itself ('Open'); together, the two modalities conveyed a single proposition (open box)' (Butcher and Goldin-Meadow 2000: 253).[7] So pointing gestures serve as the ontogenetic prototype of referential expressions.

In adult communication, the role of pointing gestures is quite salient. Generally, gesticulation constitutes an important channel of communication

---

[7] Cf. the Louwerse and Bangerter's (2005) substitution hypothesis according to which pointing gestures can substitute for linguistic elements.

and, as is now recognized by many, forms a single unified system closely integrated with vocal language; cf. McNeill (1992), McNeill (ed.) (2000), Goldin-Meadow (2003), Louwerse and Bangerter (2005). Pointing gestures constitute one of the five major types of gesture in the influential classification by McNeill (1992). Krejdlin (2007) states that pointing constitutes the most ancient subsystem of gestures, and for this reason particular languages and cultures converge to a high degree in how they employ pointing. (Studies such as Wilkins 2003, however, illustrate a significant variation across language- and culture-specific ways of pointing.)

Pointing is the most specialized of all gestures in terms of its association with particular verbal expressions, specifically referential expressions; and conversely, reference is closely related to pointing. As was rightly stated by Diessel (2006: 481), 'demonstratives are closely tied to the gestural communicative system. There is no other class of linguistic expressions that is so closely associated with a particular type of gesture than demonstratives'.

Despite being salient in gesture systems, pointing appears not to be among the most frequent gestures. In the quantitative study by Nikolaeva (2003), based on a corpus of recordings of interactive TV shows, 66 gestures on average were found per 100 EDUs. Of all gestures, pointing gestures made up 8%, turning out to be the least frequent gesture type (Nikolaeva's classification comprises five gesture types, partly differing from those of McNeill). Overall, only one out of 18 EDUs on average contains a pointing gesture. In another corpus study currently conducted by Julija Nikolaeva (personal communication) and using film retellings for the data set, pointing gestures constitute a remarkably similar share of all gestures, namely 9.5%. (Note, however, that, according to McNeill 2003, frequency of pointing in different discourse types and even in different parts of the same discourse can be very variable.)

Psychologists and primatologists sometimes insist on a narrow definition of pointing necessarily involving the index finger (Butterworth 2003, Povinelli et al. 2003). From a linguistic or cultural-anthropological point of view, however, other ways of pointing should also be recognized as equivalent to (or being in some kind of distribution with) index-finger pointing (see Wilkins 2003 and Kendon and Versante 2003). Besides index-finger pointing, another finger or thumb, wide hand, head, chin, lips, eyeballs, eyebrows, or actually any other limb can be used in pointing. Occasionally a tool can be employed as well (a teacher's pointer, a wrench used by a car mechanic when talking to a client, etc.).

Moreover, there is a continuum between pointing and handling, roughly of the following kind (cf. Landragin 2007):

(i) out-of-arm-reach, distal pointing;
(ii) within-arm-reach, proximal pointing[8];
(iii) reaching, poking;
(iv) touching, slapping;
(v) holding, handling.

Imagine the following use of a demonstrative.[9] The speaker is a customer at a grocery store choosing a melon and talking to the salesman:

(15.4)   I'll take this one.

This can be uttered in any of the situations (i) to (v), that, is whether the speaker is pointing at the melon, poking, touching, or holding it. Quite obviously, the functional mechanism of deictic reference would be very similar in all of these cases. In all of the cases the speaker is demonstrating the melon to the addressee, thus attracting his/her visual attention to the referent. The scale above is a true continuum, so the borders of pointing are fluid. In terms of Figure 15.1 all these ways of joint attention establishment should qualify as pointing in a broad sense of the term. However important the faculty of pointing (in the narrow sense) is from the developmental perspective, it merges with other ways of attracting the attention of others to objects. In Stokoe's (2000: 395) interesting reasoning about how language might have evolved, originally in the gestural form, the example of deixis provided was an example of holding an object rather than pointing in the literal sense. Butovskaja (2004: 96) informs us that babies both point at and reach towards nearby toys, and only point at remote ones. (Cf., however, Masataka's 2003 argument that the pointing gesture is ontogenetically distinct from the reaching movement.)

15.1.3 Exophora

There is a kind of usage of third person pronouns and demonstratives that shares with deixis the condition of a referent's perceptual availability but is distinct in the timing of cognitive processes of attention and activation. For example, imagine two family members watching the behaviour of their cat, and one of them saying:

(15.5)   She seems restless today, doesn't she?

---

[8] See Maes and de Rooij (2007) on the difference in pointing gestures depending on whether the referent is within or outside arm's reach.

[9] In the example that follows, it is difficult to use a personal pronoun in English. However, some other languages would use a third person pronoun here as easily as in the equivalent of (15.1). So there is no difference in the context of this discussion between third person pronouns and demonstratives.

This usage is outside the technical definition of deixis as it crucially relies on the referent's activation in both interlocutors' minds ***prior*** to the act of reference. In accordance with that, one does not expect to necessarily find a pointing gesture in association with such pronoun usage. This kind of pronoun usage is called situational anaphora, or **exophora**[10] (this phenomenon was discussed by Fillmore 1975, Isard 1975, Lyons 1977, Kibrik 1983, Cornish 1999, Landragin 2007, inter alia). Just as in anaphora, in exophora full NPs can be used under certain circumstances as well – for example, it is easy to imagine *the cat* instead of the first *she* in (15.5).

Exophora thus means mentioning referents that, as in deixis, are perceptually available, but, unlike deixis, are already activated for both the speaker and the addressee, and, as a result, pointing gestures are not necessary – a verbal referential device suffices. (But pointing is not ruled out; see subsection 15.1.5.) In exophora, joint attention is as relevant as it is in deixis. However, it is not established by the speaker at the moment of the act of reference; rather joint attention is reached spontaneously at a previous moment of time through joint eye gaze[11] (or potentially through other modalities, including auditory, tactile, and even olfactory and gustatory), and in the act of reference the speaker takes advantage of the resulting referent activation.

Unlike deixis that is oriented towards previously non-activated referents, exophora thus evokes activated referents. Of course the activation distinction is not binary, it is a continuum with all intermediate stages (see Part IV). Therefore, one cannot expect the distinction between deixis and exophora to be categorical. If a referent is partly deactivated it would be difficult or impossible to identify whether we have an instance of deixis or exophora. However, they are clearly distinct as two prototypes.

In example (15.5) the referent that has provoked the interlocutors' joint attention at the moment prior to reference remains perceptually available. But this is not necessary for exophora. Imagine two people sitting in a moving train and looking through the window. The train passes by a woman walking along the track. One of the passengers says:

(15.6) Did you notice the hat she was wearing?

---

[10] The term was probably first used in Halliday and Hasan (1976). Terminology is quite variable in this domain (see Levinson 2004 for a recent classification of 'phoric' devices); some authors would use 'deixis' including the instances of exophora, while some others prefer the inclusive usage of 'exophora'. I understand these two notions as complementary.

[11] Eye gaze is in fact very important for interactive referential processes. This issue cannot even be cursorily addressed here, but see the recent study by Staudte and Crocker (2009) that contains some reviews and demonstrates that humans strongly rely on gaze in referential processes.

Even though the referent is no longer perceptually available at the time of reference, it became activated through visual attention. This kind of exophora brings us to anaphora. Just like exophora of the kind instantiated in (15.6), anaphora is based on the human ability to keep activated those entities that are not perceptually available. This is the ability once called displacement by Hockett (1958); see also Chafe (1994). The difference between exophora in (15.6) and anaphora is minor: it only concerns the channel of original activation – perceptual in exophora, discourse-based in anaphora.

In principle, one could argue that exophora and anaphora constitute one and the same phenomenon,[12] distinct from deixis: referring to an entity that is already activated in interlocutors' minds; the issue of how it became activated is of rather secondary importance. The prominent status of anaphora in linguistics (and in this book) is mostly due to a linguist's traditional devotion to text. Discourse antecedents do indeed play a role, but no more than any other means of ensuring referents' activation. In exophora, the equivalent of the effect of prior mention on referential choice should be the knowledge that the interlocutors have jointly perceived the referent at the previous moment of time. Probably one of the future directions of the in-depth study of reference must be an integrated theory of exophora and anaphora.

Anaphora is thus ontologically and ontogenetically related to exophora and is in a sense derived from it. This seems particularly likely because vision in many ways underlies cognition, including linguistic cognition (Chafe 1980, Glezer 1993, Kosslyn 1994, Ivanitsky 1996, Zwaan and Kaschak 2006, Holšánová 2008). In the lexicon of various languages, there is a widespread metaphor (in the sense of Lakoff and Johnson 1980) MIND IS VISUAL FIELD, on which expressions such as *I see* (meaning 'I understand'), *it is clear to me*, and the like are based. The relationship of anaphora to exophora is also of a similar fashion: having mentioned/heard something in prior discourse is equivalent to having seen it at the previous moment of time. And being jointly exposed to discourse material is analogous to having had joint eye gaze.

The claim of exophora being the source of anaphora receives further support from a number of developmental studies. It is known that joint visual attention is acquired very early on in ontogeny. According to a number of developmental studies reviewed by Butterworth (2003: 20–21), infants display the beginnings of joint visual attention with an adult as early as the age of four

---

[12] In some terminological systems exophora is a subtype within anaphora (e.g. Cornish 1999).

months or even two months, which is many epochs before the beginning of active language acquisition. This should lead one to believe that exophora is a much more basic process compared to discourse-oriented anaphora.

This point may be potentially contradicted by the findings of Matthews et al. (2006) who have compared the acquisition of referential choice in exophoric and anaphoric contexts. According to their results, at the age of two years children display a better command of referential choice in the presence of a discourse antecedent than in the case of a purely perceptual activation of the referent. I suppose that these results do not necessarily negate the developmental priority of the exophoric pattern in general, for the reason that discourse-based activation is much more explicit than the one based on joint visual attention, and the exophoric experimental setup might have been inherently more complicated for the children.

Under exophora, there are different ways that speakers ensure that a referent is known to the addressee. Besides the immediate perceived environment, a larger shared context may be relevant, as in uses of demonstratives or definite NPs such as *this town, the president, the garden, mum*. Such uses are based on humans' ability to be conscious of the spaces, physical or social, which they are situated in or belong to. This kind of use has been described with the help of the notion of a situational basis by Christophersen (1939: 29–30), and by the term homophora in Halliday and Hasan (1976). Probably there is no discrete boundary between exophora and homophora.

15.1.4 *Relations between deixis, exophora, and anaphora*

It has been suggested on multiple occasions in the literature that it is deixis that serves as the basis for anaphoric usage (see e.g. Bühler 1934, Lyons 1975, Lyons 1977, Ehlich 1982, Kibrik 1983, de Mulder 1992). However, the reasoning in the previous subsection suggests that the foundational source of anaphora is exophora rather than deixis. As the comparison in Table 15.1 indicates, anaphora is different from deixis in all relevant ways while it differs from exophora only in the source of referent activation.

Exophora is the mechanism that lies between deixis and anaphora, and the latter two are related only indirectly. Furthermore, one can suggest that deixis relates to exophora in a similar way to how an introductory[13] mention of a referent relates to a repeated, anaphoric mention. This suggestion is elaborated in Table 15.2.

---

[13] 'Introductory' here refers to any mention of a currently non-activated referent, be it the first mention in the given discourse or not.

TABLE 15.1. A comparison of deixis, exophora, and anaphora

	Source of referent activation	Referent activation prior to the act of reference	Requirement for a pointing gesture or its equivalent
Deixis	Perceived environment	No	Yes
Exophora	Perceived environment	Yes	No
Anaphora	Discourse	Yes	No

TABLE 15.2. A classification of referential processes, based on the timing and source of activation

	Timing of activation	
Source of activation	Referent is not activated before the moment of reference (the speaker intentionally establishes joint attention)	Referent is already activated at the moment of reference (joint attention was established before)
Referent is activated through perceptual attention	(1) Deixis	(3) Exophora
Referent is activated through discourse mention	(2) Introductory discourse mention	(4) Anaphora

Thus deixis is analogous to an introductory discourse mention – the difference is that a referent is presented ostensively rather than verbally. The resemblance between deixis and introductory mention is a functional one. From the point of view of referential devices, similarity is more limited: as has been discussed in subsection 15.1.1, reduced referential devices are common in deixis, while they are not expected in introductory reference. Still in both situations formally elaborate devices are used: pointing is used in deixis, lexical specification in introductory mention.

Note that locutor pronouns do not naturally fit into the scheme shown in Table 15.2. Unlike all other referents, they are exempt from fluctuating levels of activation. By virtue of the very participation in discourse, the speaker and the addressee are constantly activated, and the parameter 'timing of activation' does not naturally apply to them. No specific use of *I* relies in any important way on the previous mentions of the speaker. Also, it would be odd to suggest that the first explicit mention of the speaker in a discourse is somehow introductory.

In light of the scheme given in Table 15.2, it becomes still more evident that there is no firm boundary between deixis and exophora – just as there is none between an introductory and an anaphoric mention. As has been argued throughout this book, referents' activation levels can vary from zero to the maximum, and introductory mentions are simply one pole on this scale. Likewise in deixis.

How are deixis and exophora related to each other? Would it be accurate to propose that deixis in some sense is more basic and underlies exophora? It appears that exophora must be at least as basic. Deixis and exophora have a comparable degree of complexity in terms of the underlying cognitive processes. Both are possible due to the central faculty of human cognition known as 'theory of mind': the ability to realize that another living being is like oneself in perceiving reality, in attending to, remembering, inferring, etc. The difference is that in exophora the speaker knows that the referent is already activated in the addressee, and in deixis the speaker causes the addressee to attend to and, as a consequence, activate the referent. The idea that exophora is at least as basic as deixis finds support in the convincing argument by Butterworth (2003: 20–21) that ontogenetically, joint eye gaze (the basis for exophora) is possible much earlier than the production of pointing (the basis for deixis).

How frequent are deixis and exophora, compared to anaphora? Given that they constitute more basic forms of reference one may expect that they would be more frequently employed in discourse compared to anaphoric expressions. I am not aware of conclusive empirical studies directly assessing frequency of deictic and exophoric referential devices as opposed to anaphoric ones. However, some hints can be gained from the following quantitative data provided by Biber et al. (1999). As is shown in Table 15.3, in a large corpus-based study of English discourses of various registers, Biber et al.

TABLE 15.3. Percentages of situational and anaphoric uses of definite full NPs in several large corpora of English discourses[14]

	Conversation	Fiction	News	Academic prose
situational	55	10	10	10
anaphoric	25	30	30	25

[14] Other types of usages to which the remaining percentages belong include, according to Biber et al. (1999), cataphoric, indirect, generic, idiomatic, and uncertain.

(1999: 266) found that, in conversation, full NPs with a definite article are more frequent in the 'situational' use than in the anaphoric use, while their anaphoric use is significantly more frequent in written registers. Note that Biber et al.'s (1999) situational uses range from the immediate speech situation to a larger shared context and probably embrace deixis and exophora, as well as homophora (see subsection 15.1.3).

15.1.5 *Pointing in deixis and exophora*

Pointing gestures and deixis are intimately connected. Pointing is a formal device that is inherently involved in the functional mechanism of deixis. However, as is always the case with formal devices and functional processes, they cannot be expected to be in a one-to-one correspondence. Pointing or its equivalent, such as holding, appears to be a necessary component of deictic reference. The converse is not true: pointing can be observed with referential processes other than deixis. This situation is parallel to that observed with a verbal referential device that is analogous to pointing: demonstratives. Demonstratives, although being the dedicated device for expressing deixis, can be used in other referential processes too.

Even when a referent is already activated at the time of reference, the speaker may still use a pointing gesture if the entity is perceptually available. This is possible in exophora and even in anaphora. In the following example the first pointing gesture (in line a, illustrated by a screenshot) accompanies a proper name whose referent, the man named Anatolij who was sitting next to the speaker, was exophorically semi-activated at the time of reference. The next gesture (in line e) is associated with a clearly given referent:

(15.7) Russian (Nikolaeva 2003: 82)
    a. <u>My</u>   s   Anatoliem uže   mnogo
       we   with Anatolij already many
       let   očen' rabótaem,
       years very work
       <three intervening clauses>
    e. <u>on</u>   mnogo raz   zavjázyval,
       he   many   times quit
       'Anatolij and I have been working together for many years, <...>
       he was winding it up (drinking) many times'

This example shows that pointing occurs not only with pronouns and demonstratives but also with full NPs (see van der Sluis and Krahmer 2007 and Levy and Fowler 2000); we have seen this before in a deictic context, and encounter it here in an exophoric context. Pointing can also be found with locutor pronouns. So the correspondence between pointing and the verbal referential choice is far from being trivial.

The same concerns the relation between pointing and prosody (cf. McNeill 1992: 84 and Levy and Fowler 2000). In general, there is much in common between gesticulation and prosody; both are 'analogue' systems of communication accompanying the 'digital', segmental component, and they share many foundational properties. Julija Nikolaeva (personal communication) informs me that in her video materials of Russian speech, words to which pointing gestures are connected (both temporally and semantically) invariably have some degree of prosodic prominence, usually a discourse accent, in both deictic and exophoric contexts. Probably there is an association between pointing and accent; cf. the interesting overarching notion of energy expenditure proposed by Levy and Fowler (2000). However, in Russian it is not always the case that a deictic pronoun, accompanied by a pointing gesture, would bear an accent. For instance, in the setting described above for example (15.1), the appropriate Russian phrasing would be:

(15.8) Russian
Posmotrì na neë!
look at her
'Look at her!'

So, despite the non-activated status of the referent, the primary accent would almost obligatorily be found on the verb predicate. Evidently, in this context even a pronoun with a non-activated referent tends to be clitical and resists bearing the primary accent. If a full NP is used, it assumes the primary accent, as is expected for non-activated object referents:

(15.9) Russian
Posmotri na devčònku!
look at gal
'Look at the gal!'

A further example of a Russian clitic pronoun cooccurring with a pointing gesture is discussed in section 15.3, example (15.22d). French is even more telling, as it has a segmental difference between accented and unaccented (clitic) pronouns, and the latter can occasionally cooccur with a pointing gesture; see Cornish (ed.) (2005). Interestingly, English is in sharp contrast to both Russian and French in requiring the accent to be on pronouns conveying non-activated information; see example (15.1). So languages differ in how much prosodic elaboration they require when using a pointing gesture.

Related to this is the question of whether a pointing gesture can be the sole referential device, that is, can cooccur with zero reference in the verbal expression. Generally, it appears that pointing gestures tend to cooccur with explicit referential devices rather than supplant them. However, occasionally a pointing gesture may occur without a corresponding verbal device. This is found in the following example of reference to a locus. In this example, the speaker is representing the direct speech of Don Juan telling Carlos Castañeda to approach an abyss, and is pointing to the front, to the edge of the imagined abyss instead of uttering the demonstrative adverb *tuda* 'there':

(15.10) Russian (Nikolaeva 2003: 45)
         <u>Podojdì</u>!
         approach
         'Go up there!'

Returning to the issue of pointing being not compulsory but allowable in exophora/anaphora, a question arises: how common is pointing in such contexts? Is it rare or comparable in frequency with pointing in deictic contexts? Extant evidence on the relative frequency of deictic and exophoric/anaphoric pointing is scant and partial. O'Neill (1996) has explored differences in the patterns of two-year-old children's pointing (accompanying verbal reference) depending on whether the adult interlocutor already sees the object in question or not (because of being engaged in or disengaged from the child's activity). Thus the design of O'Neill's experiment matches the difference between exophora and deixis. One of her results is that gesturing was significantly more frequent in a deictic setting. This result seems expected, given the role of pointing in the establishment of joint attention. Summarizing observations of several researchers, Levy and Fowler (2000: 219) propose that 'gestures are more likely to occur with presentation of unexpected than of expected lexical information'.[15]

This does not mean, however, that deictic pointing must necessarily be more abundant in discourse compared to exophoric/anaphoric pointing. If there are more instances of exophora/anaphora than deixis, one may eventually find more exophoric/anaphoric pointing in absolute numbers. In Nikolaeva's (2003: 79ff.) study of gestures in Russian conversation, counts were done (conversely to O'Neill 1996) from form to meaning, and 51% of all pointing gestures turned out to be associated with given (that is, activated) and 38% with accessible (semi-activated) referents. New referents accounted

---

[15] Note that this generalization concerns gestures in general, not specifically pointing gestures.

for only 8% of all pointing gestures. (The remaining 3% of pointing gestures were associated with non-specific referents.) Pointing with given information is clearly exophora, pointing with new information is clearly deixis, and pointing with accessible information constitutes an intermediate category. So Nikolaeva's empirical results suggest that pointing under exophora/anaphora is approximately as common as under deixis (51% vs. 46% if we count all instances of pointing with accessible information as deixis) or much more common (89% vs. 8% if we include pointing with accessible information as exophora).

What are the reasons, then, for using pointing in exophoric/anaphoric contexts where a referent is activated anyway? Given the frequency counts just cited, this is an important question. But this is also a very complex question. By way of a first approximation to a reasonable answer, I would mention one factor that readily lends itself as a common reason: pointing occurs in exophora when some kind of contrast between two or more concurrently activated referents is found. In the following example the speaker is telling a story, acting out a policeman talking to a driver who is sitting in his car together with a woman. The policeman has just asked the driver about not being buckled up, and after the driver comes up with an excuse, the policeman refers to the woman, who is anaphorically given due to an explicit reference a few clauses back. When the policeman mentions the woman, he points at a location next to where the imagined interlocutor (the driver) is stationed:

(15.11) Russian (Nikolaeva 2003: 81)
    a. da   ja   ne   pro   vás   govorju,
       PTCL I   not about you   talk

    b. a   pro   sosèdku.
       but   about   neighbour
    'I am talking not about you but about your companion'

In this example there is a contrast between the two referents, and this may be responsible for the use of a pointing gesture concurrently with the verbal reference to the driver's companion.

Among other possible reasons for using pointing, one was offered by McNeill: this is the speaker's need to differentiate between different discourse spaces, such as the subject matter of a narrative, the actual speech situation, the 'metanarrative' level, etc. (McNeill 1992: 188ff.). Evidently, the functions of pointing are in need of further inquiry.

In Nikolaeva's (2003) study, not all pointing gestures were associated with specific reference, either deictic or exophoric. As was mentioned above, 3% of pointing gestures have been characterized as non-specific.[16] Consider an example from a TV show where a participant said, pointing at a psychologist present in the studio:

(15.12) Russian (Nikolaeva 2003: 113)
Vot počemu my i   obraščàemsja poroj   k   psixologam.
this why   we PTCL address   at.times to psychologists
'This is why we address psychologists now and then'

Obviously, in this case pointing participates in a non-specific referent mention, even though it is directed at a specific person. The specific psychologist serves as a substitute for a whole class for psychologists; this is an instance of generic reference. The phenomenon of substitution has been discussed on many occasions in the studies of deixis, with respect to such deictic expressions as pronouns and demonstratives. In an oft-cited example, a medical professor tells his students: *A syringe must be introduced here*, pointing at an area on his own arm but evidently meaning a generic patient's arm.

A whole gamut of terms have been used to describe this phenomenon, including deferred ostension (Quine 1971, Nunberg 1978), analogical deixis (Klein 1982), ostensive metonymy (Paducheva and Krylov 1992: 182ff.), etc.; see also Nunberg (1993). In substitution processes, the intended referent does not have to necessarily be non-specific. In Levelt's (1989: 53) example, a woman is saying about her acquaintance who suffered in an accident *He got a big scar here* while pointing at her own cheek. To take another example, a fisherman may be pointing to the float when saying something like *It is biting!* and referring to a fish. On the other hand, the intended signified of a pointing gesture may be not a referent but a state or event, as in Levelt's (1989: 45) example *Have you seen this?*, in which the speaker points to a vase but refers not to the vase as such but to the fact that it has fresh cracks in it.

This kind of evidence has led some deixis theorists to distinguishing between two entities: a referent and a **demonstratum**. In terms of Figure 15.1 (subsection 15.1.2) the target must be split into these two entities. This distinction is useful for understanding pointing: speakers may point at item X (demonstratum) while meaning item Y (referent). In the most canonical instances, X and Y coincide (see Figure 15.1), but they do not have to. A variety of relations can hold between X and Y, including part-whole or various kinds of association (Clark et al. 1983). Often, the reason for substitution is that Y is

---

[16] In a reanalysis of her 2003 data during a personal communication in 2007, Julija Nikolaeva actually concluded that instances of the non-specific use of pointing were more numerous, probably over 10%.

not at hand – because it is currently absent from the perceived environment (as in the fishing situation), because it is not a specific thing (as is the case with generic referents), etc.

An extension of the substitution pattern is the situation when a speaker points to an empty space, as if a referent were there (see examples (15.10) and (15.11) above). This phenomenon, very common in natural discourse, is discussed in the following two sections (15.2 and 15.3) under the name of virtual pointing.

15.1.6 *Recapitulation*

Concluding this section, it is useful to recapitulate the main points. In both deixis and exophora a referent becomes activated not through a discourse mention but through perception, usually vision. In deixis, attention is brought to a previously unactivated referent, and deixis is thus analogous to introductory discourse mention. In exophora, the speaker exploits the already existing referent's activation, and exophora is thus an analogue of repeated mention in discourse, that is, anaphora.

An important formal phenomenon supplementing verbal referential devices is the pointing gesture, widespread in spoken discourse. Pointing is an important human faculty from a developmental point of view. Pointing is essential in deixis, but can also be found in exophoric and even anaphoric contexts. The notions of pointing and deixis thus should not be confused: deixis is a functional referential process while pointing is a formal device, typically but not exclusively associated with deixis.

The canonical form of pointing involves the origo, the pointer (the index finger), and the target. However, various deviations from this canon occur. The origo may occasionally be associated not with the speaker but with a different character (this phenomenon is discussed below in section 15.3), various limbs or objects can be used as pointing devices, pointing can be replaced by holding, and the target may split into the referent and the demonstratum.

15.2 Reference in a sign language[17]

Linguistic typology, at the incipient stage of its evolution, devoted much attention to the search for 'language types'. As time passed, it became clear that languages differ in myriad ways and do not easily classify into broad

---

[17] This section is a revision of the paper by Kibrik and Prozorova (2007). Pictures in this section were drawn by Evgenija Prozorova. I thank Evgenija for additional assistance in the preparation of this chapter. The collection of the data for the study reported here was possible due to the assistance of the Centre for Deaf Studies and Bilingual Education and its coordinator, Anna Komarova, as well as of

types. Now typologists are busy looking not for language types but for typological parameters, each breaking the set of languages into classes in its own way. However, there is one genuine classification of languages into broad types, and this is the distinction in the leading modality that is used to encode thought; this is the difference between spoken and sign languages.

There are some initial indications of the involvement of sign languages in linguistic typology; cf. several articles on sign language typology in Haspelmath et al. (eds.) (2005). The present book, as is still customary in linguistics, has mostly relied on the assumption that language equals spoken language. But this assumption, strictly speaking, is not correct. Sign languages constitute an important group of languages in their own right, and also a distinct language type. This section pays some tribute to reference in sign languages. The material of a single sign language is discussed, namely Russian Sign Language (RSL). From the existing literature it appears that referential processes in RSL are quite similar to those of other sign languages, but specifying differences and similarities between various sign languages in this domain is an issue for further research.

RSL is used by deaf people in Russia and most other countries of the former Soviet Union. It is a fully-fledged natural language, with its functions, basic features and grammatical processes comparable to those of spoken languages (Kibrik 2008d). RSL still remains only fragmentarily described in linguistic terms. The pioneer of RSL research was Galina L. Zajceva, her work summarized in Zajceva (2000, 2006). There is an overview of RSL grammar by Grenoble (1992). Recent research on RSL includes work on verb morphology (Prozorova 2004), aspect (Shamaro 2006), negation (Kimmelman 2007), reflexivization (Kimmelman 2009b), parts of speech (Kimmelman 2009a), clause structure (Shamaro 2009), word order (Kimmelman 2010), reference in discourse (Prozorova 2006 and Kibrik and Prozorova 2007), local discourse structure (Prozorova 2009) and various other topics.

RSL is a visual-gestural language that employs hands and arms, facial expressions, eye gaze, head and body posture to encode linguistic information. The visual-spatial modality determines the language's specific properties. Signed discourse takes place in a three-dimensional area in front of the signer, further referred to as the **signing arena** (signing space in Bellugi 1972). As will be seen below, this arena and its topology play a significant role in the RSL referential system.

---

school No. 101 for the deaf children in Moscow and Alexander Voskressenski in particular. The contribution of Russian Sign Language consultants, especially Tatiana Davidenko and Roman Parfenov, whose images were used in this section, is gratefully acknowledged.

This study is based on a corpus (657 clauses) of ten RSL retellings of 'The Pear Stories' film (Chafe (ed.) 1980), and builds upon prior studies of other sign languages, primarily American Sign Language (see Klima and Bellugi 1979 and Valli and Lucas 1995).

Main referential devices found in the corpus are:

- full NPs (with a noun sign as the head of the phrase)
- nominal pointing signs (pointing at a referent with an index finger), mostly viewed in the literature in the single function of personal pronouns (for example, Berenz and Ferreira-Brito 1990 and Meier 1990)
- zero expressions.

In this study reference to animate referents alone is considered. There were seven animate referents in the film: six characters that acted individually plus a group of three boys that acted as a single entity. On the whole, to make reference to these characters 487 referential devices were used: 59 full NPs, 27 nominal pointing signs, and 401 zero mentions. Among these three types of referential devices pointing signs require a detailed comment.

15.2.1 *Pointing signs in Russian Sign Language*

In section 15.1 I have delineated a distinction between several referential processes in spoken languages, including deixis, exophora, and anaphora. Among these, deixis is the process most intimately associated with pointing. The use of pointing in RSL is very different from that in spoken languages. Compared to gesticulation accompanying speech, pointing gestures (signs) in RSL are noticeably more distinct and crisp. In RSL, the pointing sign is a conventionalized referential device, it is rather analogous to pronouns or demonstratives of spoken languages: like these, the pointing sign of RSL is used in deixis, exophora, and anaphora, and even for locutor reference (see below). Therefore, the use of pointing by no means contrasts deixis in RSL to other types of reference. Since the data for this study consisted of narrative discourse, instances of pointing in the data were almost exclusively anaphoric. These will be considered in further subsections, whereas here deixis and exophora are briefly discussed.

In RSL, as well as in spoken languages, deictic and exophoric reference takes place when a referent is physically present and perceivable to both the signer and the addressee. To produce a deictic mention of a referent, the signer makes a pointing sign (points with his/her index finger) in the corresponding direction, thus attracting the addressee's attention to the referent. This kind

524   V. *Broadening the Perspective*

FIGURE 15.2. The situation in which (15.13) can be uttered

of situation is schematically depicted in Figure 15.2, and the utterance in (15.13) can be signed in this situation[18]:

(15.13)   Russian Sign Language
          PNT^D ILL
          'He is ill'

In using deictic pointing signs, signers rely on the **perceived space** P[19]; see Figure 15.2. The same is true in the case of exophora, as the following example illustrates.

---

[18] Transcription conventions for RSL used here are as follows. Words in capital letters represent manual signs (e.g. BOY). Multi-word glosses connected by a period are used when more than one English word is required to translate a single sign (GO.AWAY). Dashes between letters indicate a fingerspelled word (P-E-A-R). Words in lower case represent non-conventional signs, i.e. gesticulation (turn around). The superscripts display the spatial information that constitutes a part of the meaning of the sign and is conveyed in the form of the sign as the direction in which the hand moves when producing the sign ($LOOK^D$). To mark the direction, abbreviations are used as follows:

- R – to the right of the signer;
- L – to the left of the signer;
- F – in some distance in front of the signer;
- LF – in some distance to the left of the signer;
- U – above the signer;
- D – at the foot of the signer;
- S – towards the signer;
- C – in two-handed signs: two hands move towards each other.

Arrows in superscripts ($MOVE^{L\to S}$) are used for the predicates that describe the movement path of a referent. The index before the arrow displays the area where the movement begins, while the index after the arrow displays the endpoint of the movement. The pointing signs are glossed as *PNT*.

[19] As was discussed in Chapter 2, an act of reference links a linguistic expression with an entity in the speaker's mind, rather than with an object in the outer world. So in order to be more precise, Figure 17.2 would need to distinguish between the outer, physical space and the inner, mental space that is a perceptual reflection of the outer space. However, as these two spaces are generally isomorphic

(15.14)   Russian Sign Language
          PNT^R TELL   WHAT
          'What was he talking about?'

Example (15.14) is a question about a person situated on the right of the signer who has just told a story that the signer wants the addressee to repeat. The referent, evidently, has been exophorically activated prior to the moment of reference. To refer to that person, the signer pointed with her index finger to the right in the direction of that person. As must be clear by now, the difference is that in (15.13) the referent is first activated at the time of reference (deixis), while in (15.14) it was activated before (exophora).

RSL pointing signs are not only used as nominals as in (15.13) and (15.14), but also have the adnominal (or adjectival) usage (as part of a full NP). In this sense they are analogous to demonstratives in those spoken languages that lack dedicated third person pronouns (see Chapter 4, subsection 4.2.1).

What differentiates RSL (as well as some other sign languages) from spoken languages is that they lack dedicated first and second person singular forms and use the same pointing signs in this function as well. For example, first person singular reference occurs when the signer points to his/her chest. It is only by the direction of the sign that the addressee can judge about the intended person (first, second, or third). (It should be noted that in RSL conversation zero first and second person reference also occurs.) As was mentioned in Chapter 2, subsection 2.3.3, such non-differentiation of all three singular persons is almost unattested in spoken languages.

There is another interesting difference between sign and spoken languages with regard to the system of demonstratives. Spoken languages typically have distal and proximal demonstratives. Some systems include demonstratives that show whether the entity referred to is situated uphill or downhill from the speaker, whether it is visible or not, etc. The majority of spoken languages use a moderate number of categorial distinctions in demonstratives, typically two or three. In Diessel's (2005a) sample of 234 languages, seven languages display no distance contrast, 127 a two-way contrast, 88 a three-way contrast, and twelve a four-way (or more) contrast. In RSL, demonstratives (that is, pointing signs) can be directed at any possible target. This can be interpreted as RSL having just one general demonstrative or, conversely, as an unlimited number of different demonstratives (cf. Liddell 2000).

---

it is allowable to think of a perceived space as an overarching generalization over these two separate spaces.

Like in spoken languages, in order to mention referents that have been activated through a discourse mention rather than via perception the anaphoric procedure is used in RSL. It is based on pointing again, even though the referent is not present in the signer's perceived space. In order to explain how this is possible, the notion of constructed space needs to be introduced.

15.2.2 *The constructed space and virtual pointing*

It has been described in a number of sign language studies, primarily on American and Danish Sign Languages, how reference is being performed when referents are not present in the interlocutors' perceived space (see Klima and Bellugi 1979, Liddell 1990, Winston 1991, Engberg-Pedersen 2003). When first introducing a referent into the discourse, the signer may 'set up' a location for that referent in the signing arena and then make further reference to it by just directing signs towards that location. A referential location can be established in a variety of ways; see Winston (1991) for an exhaustive list.

In the RSL corpus, the most frequent ways to establish the location of a referent are: (1) to use a full NP with an adnominal pointing sign; that is, before or after producing a noun sign for a referent the signer points with the index finger in a particular direction; (2) to use a 'verb of motion and location' (Supalla 1986) or 'classifier predicate' (Supalla 1978); that is, the signer produces a predicate sign in which the movement path/location/orientation of the hand displays the movement path/location/orientation of the referent; see example (15.15) below.

The locations of referents are not chosen at random but demonstrate the way the signer conceptualizes referents, their position, orientation, physical interactions, and even abstract relations between them. Thus, as the discourse goes on, the inner memorial representation of the signer maps onto his/her signing arena. In Figure 15.3, the signer's memorial representation is dubbed **conceived space** C,[20] and its projection onto the signing arena the **constructed space** C'. (The idea of describing referential phenomena of sign languages in terms of 'spaces' was originally developed by Liddell 1995, 2000, 2003 for American Sign Language. The approach proposed here, however, is not identical to that of Liddell.) As must be clear from Figure 15.3, the constructed space is inhabited by (some of) the referents conceived of by the signer.

---

[20] The notion of conceived space is used in this section as a non-technical substitute of working memory, in order to keep a parallelism with the perceived and the constructed spaces.

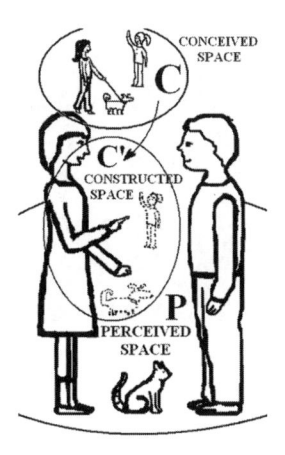

15. Reference and visual aspects of discourse 527

FIGURE 15.3. Spaces employed in referential choice in RSL

According to the evidence from the corpus, the three-dimensional constructed space was used by signers to reproduce the topology of referents in an analogue manner, that is, isomorphically to how the signers remembered them to be located in the Pear Film. For example, at a certain point in the film a specific character (a young man with a goat) was seen as appearing at a distance and moving towards the spectator (see Figure 15.4).

When describing this scene as he remembered it, one signer located a new referent at a distance in front of himself and showed that the person was approaching him:

(15.15) Russian Sign Language

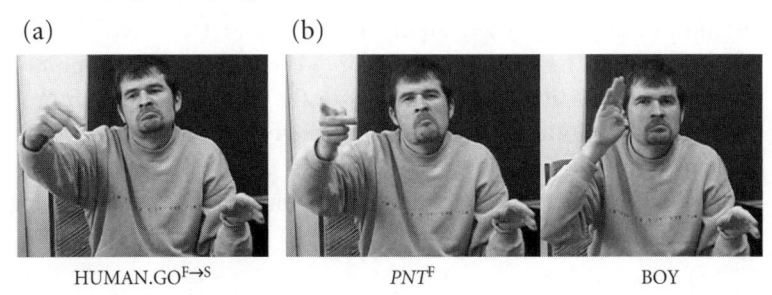

(a)   (b)

HUMAN.GO$^{F \to S}$ PNT^F BOY

a. 'Someone is coming from the front.'
b. 'That is a boy.'

In (15.15a), in order to describe the referent's original location and motion, the signer used a special sign construction in which the movement path of the

FIGURE 15.4. An episode from the Pear Film

hand shows the movement path of the referent and the handshape morpheme displays some salient characteristics of the referent: its form (two-legged), its animacy (by moving the 'legs'). Such handshape morphemes are usually called classifiers. Liddell (1990) argues that classifiers are visible substitutes for the referents in the signer's signing arena (which he compares to a stage on which actors occupy certain positions). The nature of the link between a classifier and a referent this classifier relates to is yet to be clarified.

Clause (15.15b) makes use of the already established location of the referent: a nominal demonstrative is used there. The form of this demonstrative, that is the pointing sign, is exactly the same as that of those pointing signs used in deictic and exophoric reference. However, there is a functional difference: referents are absent from the perceived space. They are found in the constructed space instead; the direction of pointing signs is determined by the location of an imagined referent in the constructed space. This pattern of usage is dubbed here **virtual pointing**.[21] When using virtual pointing signs, the signer points at certain locations in the signing arena that are factually empty but semiotically filled, as they were previously established for the referents in question.

Another retelling of the same Pear Film episode shown in Figure 15.4 appears in the following example:

---

[21] In Kibrik and Prozorova (2007) the term 'quasi-deixis' was used to describe this usage of pointing signs. Here I abandon this term because the technical understanding of deixis, as elaborated in section 15.1, presupposes that the referent in question is not activated prior to the act of reference, and therefore the analogy with deixis appears misleading.

(15.16) Russian Sign Language

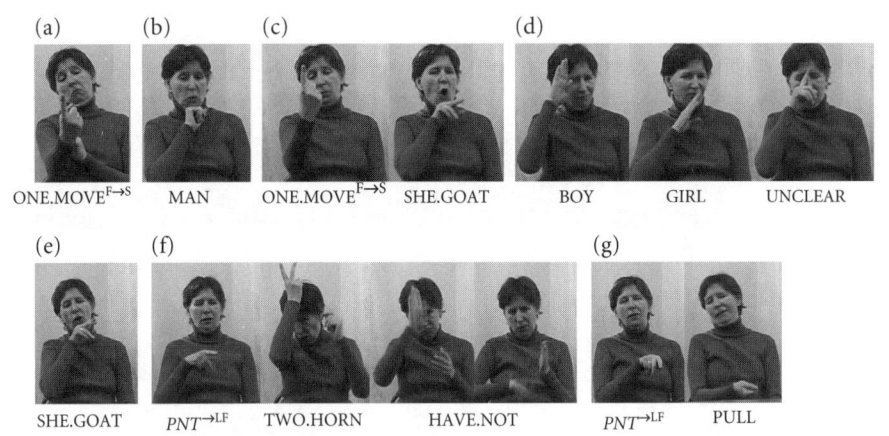

(a)	(b)	(c)	(d)
ONE.MOVE$^{F\to S}$	MAN	ONE.MOVE$^{F\to S}$ SHE.GOAT	BOY GIRL UNCLEAR

(e)	(f)	(g)
SHE.GOAT	PNT$^{\to LF}$ TWO.HORN HAVE.NOT	PNT$^{\to LF}$ PULL

a. 'Someone$_m$ is approaching from the front.

b. Ø$_m$ [=He] is a man.

c. Ø$_m$ is coming with a goat$_g$.

d. Male, female – unclear.

e. Ø$_g$ [=It] is a she-goat:

f. it$_g$ has no horns.

g. He$_m$ is pulling Ø$_g$ [=it].'

In (15.16a) the location of the man in the constructed space was again 'set up' by means of the classifier predicate ONE.MOVE. The signer produces this predicate in a certain location in front of herself. Then she introduces the man's goat, and still later on, in clause (15.16g), produces a pointing sign towards the location established in (15.16a), and by doing so refers to the man. Once again, the virtual pointing sign is formally the same as an exophoric sign that could be used if the man were present at the moment of signing and moving along the same path before the signer's and the addressee's eyes.

Note that the location of a referent in the constructed space can change over time, in accordance with its changes in the signer's memories. This can be seen in the following example. In (15.17a) a new referent, a girl, is introduced into the narrative by means of a full NP with an adnominal pointing sign GIRL *PNT*^{LF}:

(15.17) Russian Sign Language

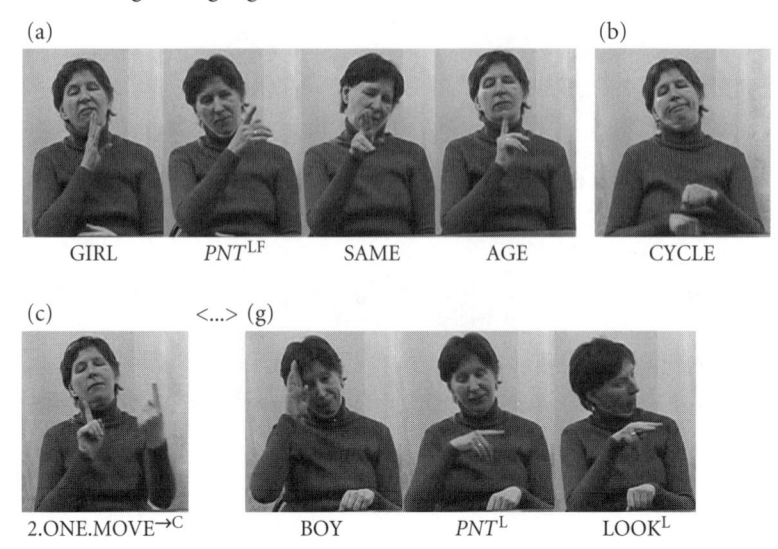

| GIRL | PNT^{LF} | SAME | AGE | CYCLE |

(c)   <...> (g)

| 2.ONE.MOVE$^{\rightarrow C}$ | BOY | PNT^{L} | LOOK^{L} |

a. 'In the front there is a girl$_g$ of the same age.
b. Ø$_g$ [=She] is riding a bicycle.
c. The two of them are moving towards each other.
   <three intervening clauses>
g. The boy looks at her$_g$.'

Indicating the girl's location in (15.17a), the signer directs the pointing sign at a certain point far in front of herself; this is because in the film the girl was approaching the boy from the front, cycling in the opposite direction. Several clauses later on, in (15.17g), the girl is referred to with a nominal pointing sign, now directed to the left of the signer (*PNT^{L}*), because the boy was gazing at the girl especially intently when she came alongside him, that is, was on the left of him. The addressee easily identifies the pointing sign in (15.17g) with the girl, because the signer has visualized the girl's movement path, and the girl's location on the left can be inferred. Note that when using this pointing sign the signer (and the addressee) assume the boy's spatial perspective. This is made clear due to role-shifting (see subsection 15.2.3), that is the signer's facial expression indicating that she is acting for the boy.

15.2.3 Referential choice in Russian Sign Language

In RSL referents are typically introduced into the discourse with full NPs, with or without an adnominal pointing sign. (The only other way of introducing referents is by means of classifiers discussed in subsection 15.2.2.) In the corpus about a half of all full NPs (55) were used in this introductory function.

In order to mention a referent that has some degree of activation, the signer chooses between full NPs (with or without an adnominal pointing sign), zero reference, and nominal pointing signs. In RSL, as in spoken languages, referential choice primarily depends on a referent's activation. Two major factors that influence the total activation score of animate referents have been explored in this study: (1) linear (referential) distance (LinD) to the antecedent; (2) when LinD = 1, the syntactic role of the antecedent (Ant): whether it is the subject (S) or an object (O) of its clause.[22] The results are shown in Table 15.4. Figures in the boxes of the table represent the frequencies of the corresponding referential devices under the given values of the factors.

As can be seen from Table 15.4, zero anaphors are strongly associated with the highest level of activation (LinD = 1; Ant = S). Under this combination of factors, zeroes are used almost exclusively, and, vice versa, the vast majority of all zeroes (342 out of 401, i.e. 85%) are found under this combination of factors' values. In the following two columns (LinD = 1 and Ant = O; LinD = 2) there still exists a preference for zero anaphors, but other referential devices show up strongly. Under LinD $\geq$ 3 the signer is more likely to use the alternative anaphoric device, that is, a full NP. In terms of interaction with activation factors, bare full NPs and full NPs with an adnominal pointing sign pattern more or less similarly, and a fine-grained understanding of this distinction requires further research. Below I lump both of these subtypes together and discuss the patterning of the general category 'full NP'.

Even though full NPs dominate under greater distances to the antecedent, it is sometimes possible to find zero anaphors as well. This suggests that the bottom threshold for the use of zero, the reduced referential option employed in RSL, is lower than the comparable thresholds in the spoken languages explored in Part IV. (This is a hypothetical suggestion; of course, a complete model of referential choice, such as those for Russian and English in Chapters 11 and 12, has not been designed for RSL.)

---

[22] Recall from Chapter 12 that the influence of the antecedent's syntactic role factor rapidly weakens with the increase of distance to the antecedent. Here the assumption was taken that the antecedent's role factor is particularly powerful when the distance is minimal.

Table 15.4. Activation factors and frequencies of referential devices in corpus

factor 1	LinD = 1		LinD=2	LinD ≥3	TOTAL
factor 2	Ant = S	Ant = O			
Full NP, including:	3 (<1%)	8 (33%)	6 (14%)	42 (57%)	59
bare full NP	2 (<1%)	6 (25%)	6 (14%)	28 (38%)	42
full NP with an adnominal demonstrative	1 (<1%)	2 (8%)	0	14 (19%)	17
Nominal demonstrative	1 (<1%)	6 (25%)	8 (19%)	12 (16%)	27
Zero reference	342 (99%)	10 (42%)	29 (67%)	20 (27%)	401
TOTAL	346 (100%)	24 (100%)	43 (100%)	74 (100%)	487

The fact that zero reference is used at significant distances from antecedents has an obvious consequence: chances are high that competing referents may be mentioned between the antecedent and the zero. Therefore, the frequency of possible referential conflicts increases. Which referential aids are employed in RSL to preclude referential conflicts?

According to the evidence from the corpus, ad hoc aids are quite common. The usual semantic (in)compatibility of the clause context with certain referents clearly plays a role. More specifically, certain predicates become associated with particular referents; the most common example in the corpus was the predicate CYCLE as well as HOLD.BICYCLE, associated with the main character of the film – the boy with a bicycle who was stealing pears. Generally, the high load placed on ad hoc aids in the context of zero reference reminds us of comparable phenomena in spoken languages with an extensive use of zeroes (see Van Valin 1987 and the discussion in section 8.2).

However, the most important – and very peculiar – way to distinguish between concurrently activated referents is the so called **role-shifting** (Padden 1986), a resource widespread in sign languages. Role-shifting is a process by which the signer shifts (rotates) the body and/or changes his/her facial expression to demonstrate that he/she is currently 'acting' as a particular referent[23]:

(15.18) Russian Sign Language

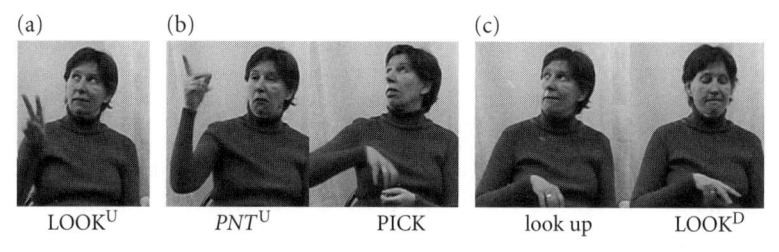

(a)	(b)	(c)
LOOK^U	PNT^U PICK	look up LOOK^D

a. 'Ø$_b$ [=He] looks up.
b. He$_f$ keeps picking pears.
c. Ø$_b$ [=He] looks up and then looks down.'

When signing (15.18a) and (15.18c), the signer is adopting the role of referent b (the boy who wants to steal pears) and makes a wily facial expression. In (15.18b), in contrast, the signer adopts the role of referent f (the farmer) who keeps picking pears from the tree without noticing the boy, and the signer's facial expression thus changes to absent-minded. Now, there is a zero anaphor in (15.18c), used despite the danger of referential conflict. This is possibly due to the facial expression of the signer, turning wily again, and a slight rotation of her body making clear that the referent in question is the boy and not the farmer mentioned in the immediately preceding clause. Role-shifting interestingly contributes to the typology of referential aids proposed in Chapter 8.

Zero anaphors are used prolifically in RSL. In the corpus they make up over 70% of all referential expressions. For an example of a short chain of clauses with coreferential zeroes see example (15.19) below (three clauses). In the corpus, there are instances of much longer chains comprising a dozen clauses or more.

---

[23] This phenomenon somewhat resembles direct speech. Of course, what is 'quoted' in role-shifting is not verbal behaviour but just behaviour.

The second most frequent anaphoric device, that is full NPs, patterns in an almost mirror-image way to zeroes. Full NPs do not occur under the highest level of activation and are the preferred referential device under low activation (LinD $\geq$ 3, 57%). Abstracting away from secondary details, the basic pattern of referential choice in RSL is similar to the one found in many spoken languages and appears as follows:

- high activation $\rightarrow$ use zero NP
- low activation $\rightarrow$ use full NP.

To understand referential choice under intermediate levels of activation, one needs to take more factors into account.

But what about the third referential device, namely nominal pointing signs, or demonstratives? Since they are reduced referential devices, they are often likened to pronouns of spoken languages, and if that were a true analogy one could expect that they should be frequent in the corpus and that their pattern of use should be similar to that of zeroes. However, none of these expectations is confirmed by the facts. The frequency of nominal pointing signs is 4.1 per 100 clauses, and the frequency of all pointing signs (including the adnominal ones) is 6.7 per 100 clauses; compare this to the frequency of zero reference: 61 per 100 clauses.

As for the pattern of use, if pointing signs resemble anything it is full NPs rather than zeroes. Pointing signs do not occur under very high activation (LinD = 1, Ant = S), while their frequency in other columns of Table 15.4 is significant (from 16% to 25%). Under intermediate levels of activation (second and third columns) pointing signs compete with full NPs. Under low activation, however, they are used several times less frequently than full NPs.

This behaviour suggests that pointing signs are not as directly sensitive to the levels of activation as zeroes and full NPs. Relying on both frequency and behaviour, it is safe to conclude that RSL pointing signs should not be likened to third person pronouns of spoken languages; their closer equivalent in spoken languages are demonstratives. Like demonstratives of spoken languages (cf. Krasavina 2004), they are not a part of the basic referential choice and are probably drafted in a variety of particular contexts, yet to be identified. One of these contexts is the referent's object role in its own clause. In the corpus, about 40% of pointing signs appeared in the object position. Evidently, zeroes are somewhat disfavoured in this position and signers resort to pointing signs as an alternative available referential device. It is therefore accurate to call the RSL pointing signs demonstratives.

An interesting question related to nominal demonstratives is the following. If the procedure of virtual pointing is such a powerful device of referent identification, what makes signers use them sparsely under high referential distance and prefer full NPs so much (57% as opposed to 16%)? Consider a typical example of a contrast between a full NP and a demonstrative:

(15.19) Russian Sign Language

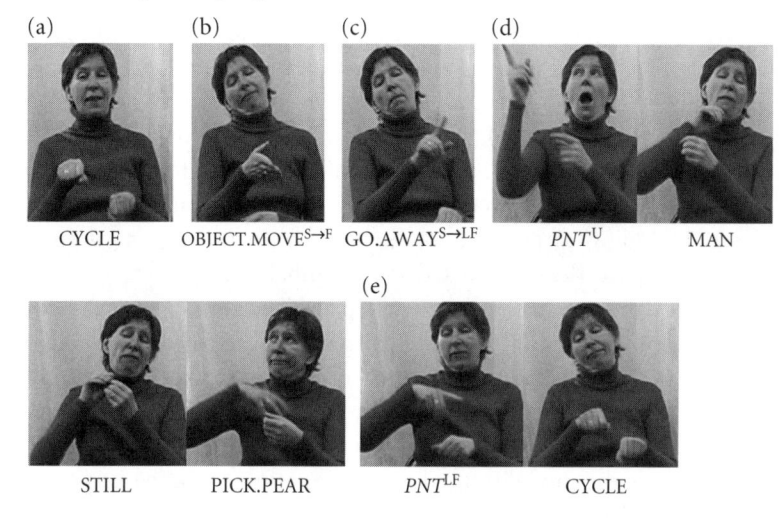

(a)	(b)	(c)	(d)
CYCLE	OBJECT.MOVE$^{S \to F}$	GO.AWAY$^{S \to LF}$	PNT^U MAN

(e)

STILL   PICK.PEAR   PNT^{LF} CYCLE

a. 'Ø$_b$ [=The boy] is cycling.

b. Ø$_b$ [=He] is riding forward.

c. Ø$_b$ [=He] goes away.

d. That man$_f$ is still picking pears.

e. He$_b$ is cycling.'

The referent 'the boy', mentioned in (15.19e), has its nearest antecedent two lines back. In contrast, 'the farmer', mentioned in (15.19d), has its nearest antecedent eleven lines back, and a full NP is used in this situation. This is in spite of the fact that the farmer is still in the same location (up on the tree) engaged in the same activity picking pears. A possible explanation for the preference of full NPs under long distances is that information on the location of a referent in the constructed space can be assumed available only for a limited time and fades afterwards. In example (15.19), the signer had defined the boy's location with the help of the verb GO.AWAY in (15.19c), so in (15.19e) the knowledge of that location is assumed to still be available to the addressee, while the location of the man up on the tree apparently is not taken any longer to be sufficient for referent identification. This observation corroborates the idea that the constructed space is an externalization of working memory. Locations of referents in the constructed space fade away as concepts in working memory do.

15.2.4 Recapitulation

The referential processes known in spoken languages, including deixis, exophora, and anaphora, are found in RSL as well. All of them are served by pointing signs (demonstratives). In anaphoric contexts, pointing is directed towards locations in the signer's arena that have been pre-established as locations of certain referents. In addition to the interlocutors' conceived space (working memory), familiar from what is known about reference in spoken languages, in RSL an additional space, here termed the constructed space, is at work. Constructed space is an external projection of the conceived space, including locations and referents, onto the signing arena. Like the conceived space, the constructed space is inhabited by referents being thought of but not present in the perceived space. The topology of the constructed space is isomorphic to that of the conceived space. When referring to entities in the constructed space by means of demonstratives, signers employ the procedure here termed virtual pointing.

Clearly, a prerequisite for employing the additional constructed space so actively is the modality used for information encoding in sign languages. The referential system of RSL makes primary use of the visual modality, and this allows creating an 'analogue', isomorphic model of the remembered situations.

In anaphoric contexts, the most widely used referential device of RSL is the zero. As in spoken languages, the use of zero anaphors relies exclusively on the conceived space (working memory). Despite the theoretical importance of virtual pointing signs, they are outnumbered by zero anaphors by more than one order of magnitude. The two referential devices immediately sensitive to referent activation are zeroes and full NPs. The use of nominal demonstratives is ruled by a more complex set of factors.

Zero anaphors and full NPs of RSL are quite similar to comparable devices in spoken languages. Pointing signs also have analogues, although not so direct; they are simultaneously demonstratives and pointing gestures of spoken languages. Some referential aids, such as the use of the clause's semantic context, are also parallel between RSL and spoken languages. Furthermore, there are some devices used in RSL for the purposes of reference that usually are not mentioned in the discussions of referential processes in spoken languages. These devices include at least classifier predicates, role-shifting, and the direction of eye gaze. As the following section suggests, some of these devices do play a role in referential processes of spoken languages as well.

15.3 Virtual pointing in speaking

Taking sign languages into consideration encourages one to cast a fresh look at spoken languages. In particular, one notices that in spoken discourse there are traces of using the 'analogue' space as well, that is, spontaneous virtual pointing by the speaker that locates imagined referents in the space in front of him/her in correspondence with their locations in the remembered situation. This phenomenon has been discussed by McNeill (1992: 18, 173) under a somewhat unfortunate name 'abstract pointing'. Probably virtual pointing at least intersects with what Bühler (1934) once called *Deixis am Phantasma* – 'deixis to the imagined'. Virtual pointing often evades the attention of those interested in discourse reference rather than in gesture. This section presents several observations on virtual pointing accompanying Russian speech.

In the study by Nikolaeva (2003), based on a corpus of Russian TV shows' transcripts, 45 pointing gestures per 841 EDUs (roughly equalling clauses) have been identified, and a half of these were instances of virtual pointing. In other words, there were 5.4 pointing gestures per 100 EDUs on average, out of which 2.7 are virtual pointing gestures. Some examples of virtual pointing have already been presented in section 15.1; see examples (15.10) and (15.11).

More relevant in the context of this chapter is the evidence collected by Julija Nikolaeva for her project looking into gesturing in the course of retelling the Pear Film. The identity of the stimulus material with that used for Russian Sign Language (section 15.2) allows us to readily see similarities and differences between virtual pointing in these two different codes. According to Julija Nikolaeva (personal communication), pointing gestures were found in Pear Film retellings (comprising 601 EDUs) with a frequency comparable to what was observed with TV shows: 5.2 per 100 EDUs on average. However, here, unlike TV shows, all of the instances of pointing were virtual pointing, as they were directed at characters not visually present in the environment of discourse. This situation with narrative discourses is fully predictable; cf. McNeill (1992: 93).

15.3.1 *Virtual pointing and activation*

Let us have a look at several examples of virtual pointing in narrative discourse (all of them come from Julija Nikolaeva's Pear Film materials). First of all, virtual pointing is found in contexts of a new referent introduction; these are instances that parallel deixis and could be called virtual deixis.

538   V. Broadening the Perspective

FIGURE 15.5. A screenshot for the pointing gesture in (15.20b)

In the following example, a pointing gesture extends over the whole EDU (15.20b) in which the new referent is introduced[24]:

(15.20)   Russian
    a. әә   Édet,
       uh   rides
    b. i   po   puti   vstrečaet   dèvočku,
       and on   way   meets   girl
    c. tože na   velosipède.
       also on   bicycle
    'He is riding, and on his way he meets a girl, also on a bicycle'

The gesture taking place during (15.20b) is shown in Figure 15.5.

The following example illustrates pointing accompanying accessible (that is, semi-activated) information. In this example the baskets are introduced as a set in (15.21a), and the mentions of subsets in (15.21b, c), with the omitted head noun 'basket', partly rely on this prior activation:

(15.21)   Russian
    a. U   nego   tri   korzíny,
       at   him   three baskets
    b. odna pustája,
       one   empty

---

[24] In this section, in discourse transcription I indicate absolute pauses by three dots, filled pauses by symbols әә and mm (depending on absence or presence of nasalization), and false starts by the '=' symbol.

(b) (c)

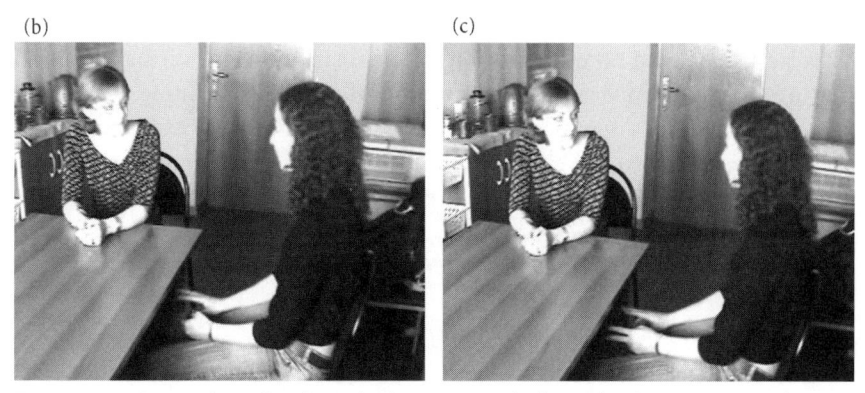

FIGURE 15.6. Screenshots for the pointing gestures in (15.21b, c)

    c. i   dve   pòlnyx.
       and two full
    'He [=the farmer] has three baskets, one empty one and two full ones'

In example (15.21), there are two pointing gestures accompanying the introduction of each subset of baskets. When introducing the empty basket the speaker makes a pointing gesture to the front and a bit to the right with the right open palm, and when introducing the pair of full baskets a quick pointing gesture with the index and the middle fingers of the left hand, directing them to the left of the centre.[25] These two gestures can be seen in Figure 15.6.

It may not be a matter of pure chance that in this example virtual pointing gestures come up in the context of some contrastiveness: the speaker opposes two subsets of baskets. Preliminary observations suggest that contrastiveness is among the factors encouraging pointing gestures; see subsection 15.1.5. Virtual pointing can also accompany mentions of activated information; see the discussion of example (15.22d) below.

In Nikolaeva's corpus of spoken stories the following distribution of virtual pointing gestures with respect to referent activation is found: 29% with new

---

[25] It is interesting to observe that this second gesture may be not an instance of pure pointing; it has an emblematic component suggesting the number of objects (two). ('Emblem' is a traditional term in gesture studies denoting standardized and discrete gestures, such as the OK gesture, that can be described as lexical items; see e.g. Grigor'eva et al. 2001.) However, such aspects of gesture, as well as various kinds of gestures other than pointing (see McNeill 1992 and Nikolaeva 2003) are ignored in this discussion.

referents, 13% with accessible referents, and 48% with given referents[26] (Julija Nikolaeva, personal communication). This distribution of virtual pointing gestures is quite similar to the distribution of (various) pointing gestures in TV shows (see the discussion in subsection 15.1.5 above). These quantitative facts are based on a relatively small number of instances (31 pointing gestures altogether). So they are not conclusive but they do corroborate the findings discussed in subsection 15.1.5: pointing is found in exophoric contexts with a frequency comparable to deictic contexts or even more frequently.

15.3.2 Organization of space in virtual pointing

In order to see that the direction of the two pointing gestures in example (15.21) is not random but immediately reproduces the spatial arrangement of baskets, as the speaker saw them on the screen, consider Figure 15.7; it illustrates how the baskets were seen during the episode of the film that the speaker is retelling at the moment. However, it should be observed that not all virtual pointing gestures display an easily explicable and consistent direction (Nikolaeva 2003: 43–44).

When using virtual pointing gestures in reference to previously non-activated referents, as in example (15.20), the speaker performs two acts at the same moment: he/she mentions a referent and establishes its location in the virtual space. However, these two acts may be separated. This occurs when a virtual pointing gesture is used in reference to an already activated referent, whose location in the virtual space has been pre-established. An example of this is found in the following extract:

two full baskets   the empty basket

FIGURE 15.7. A moment from the Pear Film retold in (15.21)

---

[26] The sum of these percentages is 90%. The remaining 10% were pointing gestures associated not with referents but with times, in contexts such as 'by this moment of time' or 'before that'.

(15.22) Russian
    a. ... əə Kogda on exal po= po doróge,
           uh when he rode FS along road

    b. on əə mm ... <u>poravnjalsja s dévočkoj</u>,
           he uh um aligned with girl

    c. <u>kotoraja tòže exala na velosipede</u>,
        which too rode on bicycle

    d. <u>on</u> zasmotrélsja na neë,
        he gaped at her

    e. ... i əə ego velosiped vre= vrezalsja v kàmen'.
        and uh his bicycle FS smashed in rock

    'As he rode along the road, he passed a girl that also rode a bicycle, he gaped at her, and his bicycle hit a rock'

In line (15.22b) the speaker uses the verb meaning 'passed' or 'aligned' that does not unequivocally help the addressee to visualize the actual spatial arrangement of the event: in the film the girl was approaching the boy from the opposite direction, and this is how the boy and the girl passed (rather than him catching up with her). As can be seen in Figure 15.8, the speaker, in order to supplement and clarify her verbal material, makes an illustrative gesture depicting the opposite movement of the two referents; this gesture is conveyed by double underscore in the transcription. Using both hands, she simultaneously moves her right hand forward and her left hand towards herself. The right and the left hands obviously represent the boy and the girl, respectively, as the boy was riding forward on the right side of the road and the girl was approaching him on his left. The same illustrative gesture is repeated in the next EDU (15.22c), which is a relative clause describing the girl's manner of movement; see Figure 15.9.

This illustrative gesture, occurring twice, strongly resembles what is called 'classifier predicates' in sign language research; see subsection 15.2.2 above.

FIGURE 15.8. Screenshots for the illustrative gesture in (15.22b)

542   V. Broadening the Perspective

FIGURE 15.9. Screenshots for the illustrative gesture in (15.22c)

Evidently, this device is used for establishing the virtual spatial arrangement of referents not only in sign languages but also in gesticulation, though on a less systematic basis.

In the given story, this pre-established arrangement is deployed at the subsequent mention of the referents in line (15.22d). In this line, the speaker produced two pointing gestures, one after another. The first one, performed with the open right palm, is directed forward and approximately coincides in time with uttering the third person pronoun, referring to the boy; see Figure 15.10, (d1). (Actually the period of performing this gesture extends a little into the subsequent predicate.) The second pointing gesture follows the first one and is directed to the left, that is the area where the girl was located with respect to the boy during the event in question. This pointing gesture, performed by two extended fingers of the left hand (the other fingers are half-scrolled), accompanies the mention of the girl; see Figure 15.10, (d2).[27]

(d1)   (d2)

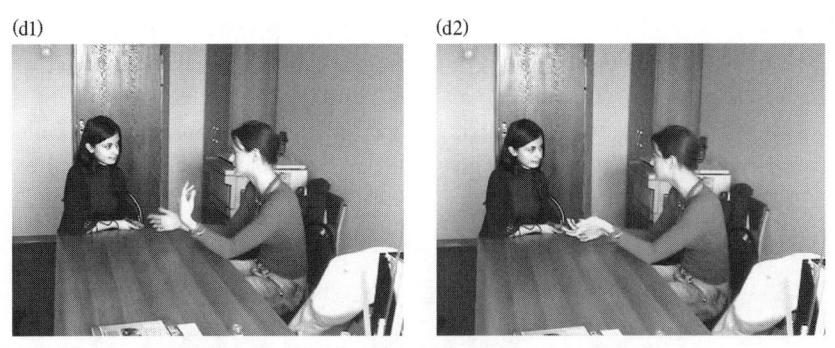

FIGURE 15.10. Screenshots for the two pointing gestures in (15.22d)

---

[27] Julija Nikolaeva (personal communication) suggested that this pointing gesture may be mixed in nature and may contain an illustrative component, denoting not only the girl but also the boy's action of turning and watching the girl.

What we observe here is two pointing gestures corresponding to two clause participants, both of which are highly activated at this time.[28] Therefore these instances of pointing are akin not to deixis but to exophora/anaphora.

An instance of virtual pointing with eye gaze is registered in Julija Nikolaeva's materials. One of the speakers used the nominal demonstrative *tot* that is typically used in Russian for reference to lesser and/or more freshly activated referents (see Chapter 8, subsection 8.6.3). Concurrently with using this demonstrative, the speaker points upward with her eyeballs, as she is referring to the farmer who was sitting on the tree; the spatial arrangement in which the farmer was located high up over the ground was created through the speaker's gestures in previous discourse.

The location of a relevant referent in space does not have to be established necessarily by gestural devices. In the following example (from a TV show) the location of a referent was first indicated by a verbal means. When introducing the two girls sitting across the corridor from her, the speaker used the adverb *naprotiv* 'across, on the opposite side, facing'. On the relevant instance of reference to the girls, the speaker performed a virtual pointing gesture towards a location in front of herself:

(15.23) Russian (Nikolaeva 2003: 115)
 a. i   naprotiv   menja   sideli   dve   devočki-mulátki,
    and   across   me   sat   two   girls-brown
    <20 intervening clauses>

 x. my   tak   s   gotovnost'ju   vtroëm,
    we   so   with   readiness   all.three

 y. vot   èti   dve devočki   naprotiv   i   jà,
    here these   two girls   across   and   I

 z. skazali: "Jà".
    said   I
    'And across from me sat two brown-skinned girls, <...> with such a readiness all the three of us — these two girls and I — said: "Me".'

---

[28] As was discussed in subsection 15.1.5, pointing to referents is generally associated with prosodic prominence of the verbal referential device, such as placement of an accent on a pronoun, but this association is not absolute. The latter point is again corroborated by the two pronouns in (15.22d), accompanied by pointing gestures. As these pronouns convey activated information, and there are no additional semantic effects such as contrastiveness, it is expected that they are produced as unaccented clitics. This is certainly correct with respect to the pronoun *on*, despite the fact that a pointing gesture accompanies this pronoun. As for the second pronoun *neë*, it bears a slight accent, and this may be related to the second pointing gesture whose temporal extent includes this pronoun.

Evidently, for the communicative process there is no difference whether a referent's location was established through a verbal or gestural means. Knowledge of where a referent is stationed in virtual space can be used in either situation with equal ease when the speaker needs to perform a pointing gesture. This parallels the close relatedness between exophora and anaphora discussed in subsection 15.1.3. Verbal and gestural material is jointly used to convey the inner cognitive representation from the speaker to the addressee.

15.3.3 *Perspective taking*

As the analysis of example (15.22) has demonstrated, virtual pointing may be done from the perspective of an external observer: recall the illustrative gesture depicting the relative movement of two referents in (15.22b, c). Subsequent pointing to two participants of the event in (15.22d) again is done from the external perspective: the speaker sees the referents as actors on a stage, and invites the addressee to assume the same perspective.

However, this is not necessarily so in virtual pointing: the speaker may assume the perspective of one of the characters he/she is talking about. In subsection 15.1.5 we have considered two examples that are instances of virtual pointing and involve such perspective taking – (15.10) and (15.11). For example, in (15.11) the speaker talks about a policeman and produces a pointing gesture that replicates a likely gesture made by the policeman himself. However, this gesture is a part of direct quotation from the policeman's speech, so perspective taking here is reflected in a wider context than merely in the pointing gesture itself. (Direct quoting is generally an instance of perspective taking.)

Purer examples of perspective taking instantiated in pointing gestures as such are found in retellings of the Pear Film. For example, in one of the retellings the speaker explains the actions of the boy who was sneakily taking pears while the farmer was on the tree. When referring to the farmer, the speaker uses the nominal demonstrative *tot* 'that', simultaneously pointing upward with her eyeballs. This apparently represents the perspective of the boy, virtually pointing to the man perched up on the ladder. Evidently, the origo, an important element of the structure of pointing (see Figure 15.1), can be stationed variously. Canonically, the origo coincides with the speaker. But occasionally a speaker can detach the origo from him/herself and associate it with another person. Some examples of this kind are discussed by McNeill (1992: 173–175).

The problem of perspective taking has been extensively discussed in the literature on deixis, on discourse, on reported speech, and on gesture; see e.g. Collinson (1937), Langacker (1985), Paducheva and Krylov (1992), Bulygina and Shmelev (1992), Chafe (1994), Duchan et al. (eds.) (1995), McNeill (1992), Helmbrecht (2004: 94–99), Evans (2009); see also the discussion in Chapter 8, subsection 8.6.1. A variety of terms have been used, such as point of view, viewpoint, point of reference, vantage point, centre, shift of origo, etc. As has been recently discussed by Dobrovolsky and Paducheva (2008), any character in discourse can become the 'subject of deixis'. There is a vast literature on the general issue of perspective taking; selected references include Voloshinov (1929: Ch. 3), Paducheva (1995: Part II), Verhagen (2005).

Perspective taking in virtual pointing clearly resembles role-shifting in sign languages; see subsection 15.2.3. The difference is that in RSL role-shifting has acquired the status of a widespread and conventionalized resource, while perspective taking in gesturing has a more spontaneous and fluid character.

15.3.4 *How informative is virtual pointing?*

It is important to know if virtual pointing is functional in helping the speaker to convey reference to the addressee. In other words, does the referential process gain anything from the use of virtual pointing?

There is a rather extensive literature on the functions of gestures in general. Some authors concentrate on the role of gestures in the communication of meaning to the addressee (see e.g. Kendon 1994, Cassell et al. 1998, Cutica and Bucciarelli 2006) while others discuss how they help the speaker him/herself to formulate his/her message (e.g. Alibali et al. 2000, Mol et al. 2008). In application specifically to virtual pointing, this dilemma is discussed in McNeill (2003), but overall it seems to be little studied in the literature.

In example (15.22) one could suppose that, once the referents' relative locations were priorly established, pointing towards those locations somehow assists in the speaker's letting the addressee know the referent. It is curious that exactly during the first illustrative gesture depicting the relative motion of the boy and the girl (see Figure 15.8) the addressee focally watched the speaker's hand movements. In other instances it is quite evident that virtual pointing gestures perform little or no role in communicating meaning to the addressee and, therefore, the speaker uses them only to organize his/her own thought and discourse. For example, the speaker shown in Figures 15.5 and 15.6 generally kept her hands under the desk, entirely or partly beyond the addressee's sight. The following formulation hints at what distinguishes gesticulation from sign languages, both in how pointing is formed and in the organization of spaces: 'Since gestures flash by evanescently, so do their projected spaces. Thus the different kinds of gesture spaces...are swiftly instantiated and sometimes just as swiftly discarded in the interactive flow' (Haviland 2000: 24–25).

15.3.5 Recapitulation

Virtual pointing in gesticulation accompanying Russian speech bears significant similarity to virtual pointing in Russian Sign Language. This resemblance is due to the underlying fact: when formulating a message, the speaker analogically reproduces the inner mental representation existing prior to and independently of any discourse activity. In both systems, a referent's location in the virtual space can be established with one gesture and then assumed to be known at the time of the following one.

We have seen a gestural analogy of 'classifier predicates', sometimes viewed as a hallmark of sign languages. The 'gesture spaces' proposed by Haviland (2000) to account for pointing in gesticulation are partly analogous to the spaces posited in section 15.2 to explain pointing in RSL. The phenomenon of role-shifting, widely attested in sign languages and participating in the preclusion of referential conflicts, also has an analogy with gesticulation: perspective taking that affects the character and direction of virtual pointing.

In terms of frequency, instances of virtual pointing in narrative discourse appear to be similar in gesticulation and in sign languages: in the spoken corpus their frequency is 5.2 instances per 100 EDUs, while in signed discourse it is 4.1 if only nominal pointing signs are considered, and 6.7 if adnominal pointing is included as well.

However, there are substantial differences too. Virtual pointing gestures sometimes remain invisible to the addressee, which does not hinder communication. Signs in sign languages appear as the central and robust coding devices, while gestures accompanying speech are far less systematic and less clear-cut. They are often quick and sloppy, far less acute than virtual pointing signs in RSL. In accordance with that, the spaces employed in gesticulation appear to be less robust that those found in sign languages.

Virtual pointing combines with different degrees of referent activation. This rather free combinability results from the multifunctional character of virtual pointing in speech. At certain times virtual pointing conveys referential information to an addressee, but at other times it is instrumental in simply helping the speaker to organize his/her own cognitive representation.

Summary

Reference in discourse has important facets related to the visual channel of communication. Referents can become attended to and subsequently activated through perception, particularly through vision. Also, the act of reference does not have to be performed by a verbal device; it can be done by a pointing gesture. Several domains where reference interplays with the visual channel of communication have been considered in this chapter, including a theoretical discussion of deixis and exophora, an analysis of referential choice in a sign language, and a discussion of pointing gestures accompanying speech.

Deixis and exophora are two kinds of specific reference, distinct from anaphora. In both deixis and exophora a referent is activated ostensively, through perceptual (normally visual) attention. The difference is that in deixis, attention is attracted to the referent at the time of reference (the referent is previously non-activated), while exophora bears on prior activation of the referent.

An important formal property of deixis is pointing, but pointing is used in exophora and even anaphora as well. The act of pointing involves several components, including the origo, a pointer, and a target. Canonically, the origo coincides with the speaker, a pointer with a speaker's index finger, and a target with the referent of a deictic referential expression. However, all of these canonical correspondences occasionally erode, giving rise to deviant kinds of pointing. The origo may be attached to an alternative person (perspective taking), a pointer can be as different from an index finger as the direction of eye or the act of or holding something, and the target may differ from the referent actually intended by the speaker.

Pointing is an important cognitive phenomenon – in phylogeny, in ontogeny, and in communication. It is one of the distinct abilities of Homo sapiens, related to the faculty known as 'theory of mind'. Pointing as a non-verbal and non-vocal referential device interacts with the verbal component. In the gesticulation accompanying speech, pointing is an extra material element involved in the act of reference alongside verbal devices. It may cooccur with both reduced and full referential devices. Pointing often, but not always, cooccurs with prosodic prominence.

In the sign languages of the deaf the pointing gesture (sign) is an independent referential device, comparable to the demonstratives and personal pronouns of spoken languages. Pointing signs are not very frequent in Russian

Sign Language discourse, as the main referential options are full NP and zero reference.

Russian Sign Language makes use of certain devices that normally do not figure as the most salient elements in discussions of reference in spoken languages, such as 'classifier predicates' and role-shifting. Some traces of similar devices can be noted in gesticulation accompanying speech. Also, in Russian Sign Language the phenomenon of virtual pointing is quite noticeable. Virtual pointing is based on the constructed space that is an external projection of the speaker's working memory. The speaker can position imagined referents in this space and subsequently employ their known loci for reference. An analogous process is also widely used in the gesticulation accompanying speech.

Concluding remarks to Part V

In Parts I–IV of this book, I proceeded on the traditional linguistic assumption that language means the verbal channel of communication. In accordance with that, we looked almost exclusively at verbal devices serving referential processes. At certain points I brought in non-verbal but vocal material, that is prosody. In Part V, however, I focused on non-vocal aspects of discourse reference and considered several referential phenomena that are related to visual communication, including the functional mechanisms of deixis and exophora, the formal mechanism of pointing, and referential processes in gesticulation and in sign languages. A comprehensive and encompassing account of reference in discourse must necessarily acknowledge the existence of both vocal and visual communication channels.

Human communication is inherently multimodal. When we speak or listen, we pay attention not only to words but also to prosody, gestures, and other components of body language. Of course, much is known about each of these informational components, but this knowledge is compartmentalized and isolated. One of the most current challenges of linguistics is creating a multimodal theory of language (Kibrik 2008c), integrating relevant knowledge about all information channels and components.

In the domain of reference studies, some incipient steps have already been made towards integrating verbal and visual information. This has been done primarily in computational linguistics and artificial intelligence; see e.g. Kobsa et al. (1986), Louwerse and Bangerter (2005), Kruijff et al. (2006), van der Sluis and Krahmer (2007), Cassell et al. (2007), Kitazawa et al. (2008), Piwek (2009). Studies reported in Part V of the book can also be seen as a contribution to this end.

16

Conclusion

As I am concluding this book project, I find myself having several emotions. There is a sense of relief in that I have achieved the goals that I originally set out to achieve. There is also a feeling of regret, due to the fact that some aspects of discourse reference have remained outside the scope of the book. And finally there is a feeling of anticipation at what the further explorations of this fascinating research field will bring. I will elaborate on each of these three points in the three sections of this concluding chapter.

16.1 What has been achieved

Perhaps the most important contribution of the book is the combination of cognitive and typological concerns in a study of a linguistic discourse-based phenomenon. In modern linguistics, typology and cognitive studies are separated. Whereas linguistic typology looks into properties of whole languages, cognitive linguistics is interested in the processes within the mind of an individual human being. In my view, these two interests are complementary rather than entirely separate. One cannot fully understand the range and limits of linguistic diversity without knowing the cognitive underpinnings of language use. And, conversely, the knowledge of linguistic diversity sheds light on how humans talk and think. I believe that a combination of cognitive and typological perspectives would be beneficial for the studies of other linguistic phenomena, particularly discourse-oriented ones. There is a general need to overcome the traditional compartmentalization of science: the human mind is single and undivided, and we should think about cross-breeding and integrating various perspectives.

More specifically, the main achievements of this book include the following. First, a comprehensive typologically oriented account of reference in discourse was proposed. The referential function is performed by referential devices, such as noun phrases. Universally, there is a distinction between lexically full and reduced referential devices. The latter devices, including free and bound pronouns and zero reference, constituted the primary focus of the book. Cross-linguistically, bound pronouns are the most frequent reduced device. A distinction is made between languages that consistently prefer a certain reduced device and those that employ various kinds thereof, depending on contextual factors. In pronouns, apart from the bound vs. free distinction, there is another important variable, namely the distinction between tenacious vs. alternating. Tenacious pronouns cooccur within a clause with another mention of the same referent, while alternating pronouns are in a complementary distribution. Both bound and free pronouns can be tenacious and alternating to various degrees.

Second, a consistent distinction is made between two kinds of linguistic devices involved in the referential process: referential devices and referential aids. While the former perform reference per se, the latter help to distinguish between two or more concurrently activated referents. As reduced referential devices have a broad referential potential, they often run the risk of referential conflict, or ambiguity, and there are many means that languages and language users can employ to tell referents apart. All of these means can be conceived of as referent sortings. A typology of referent sortings, functioning as referential aids, is proposed.

Third, I proposed a cognitive theory of discourse reference. In doing so, I use knowledge from neighbouring disciplines exploring the human mind, particularly cognitive psychology and neuroscience. I suggest that reference, or referent mention, is the linguistic equivalent of attending to a referent. Referential choice is a separate process involved when the decision to mention a referent has been made by the speaker. The most basic part of referential choice is choosing between full and reduced devices available in a given language. Referential choice depends on the cognitive component known as working memory: referents that are highly activated in working memory are rendered by reduced referential devices, and referents of low activation by full noun phrases. The current activation of referents can be demonstrated to depend, in turn, on a variety of activation factors – properties of the discourse context or of the referent itself. In accordance with the above, the proposed theory is called the cognitive multi-factorial (CMF) approach to discourse reference. This approach, among other things, contributes to a better understanding of classical issues in working memory, including its capacity, control, and the process of forgetting.

In developing my approach to reference in discourse, I intended to overcome several common stumbling blocks in referential studies. I appeal to positive knowledge from cognitive psychology and neuroscience rather than content myself with general mentalistic concepts – a typical shortcoming of cognitive linguistic analysis. Also, I try to overcome the common circularity in explanations of reference, in which linguistic form is explained by cognitive factors, and the cognitive factors are judged by linguistic form; in the CMF approach referent activation is established independently of actual referential choice. Finally, I acknowledge the multiplicity of factors involved in referential choice rather than attempt to reduce this complex phenomenon to one or two discourse factors.

As is well known, reference and anaphora are often treated as essentially syntactic phenomena, presupposing a kind of syntactic control of the antecedent over the anaphor. In my view, this treatment is generally untenable, as the same referential devices (for example pronouns or zeroes) are used within and across syntactic domains, such as sentences. In principle, one could suggest a difference between two kinds of referential phenomena: the discourse-based majority and the syntactic minority. In a radical formulation, such differentiation is again indefensible: people speak with discourses rather than with sentences, and it would be highly unnatural to posit unrelated rules for the use of referential devices, depending on whether the antecedent is found in the same or in a different sentence. Reference is a fundamentally discourse-based phenomenon, and the general principles of reference, those related to attention and working memory, must be formulated for unrestricted discourse contexts. I concede, however, that certain standard usages in tight and routinized syntactic contexts (such as *Joseph and his brothers* or *Father loved Joseph and Ø always praised him*) may be seen as relatively independent. Syntactic anaphora is a special case of discourse anaphora, the grammaticalization of general discourse-based principles of reference. There also exist certain specialized referential devices for tight syntactic contexts, such as reflexives.

How can this book be used? Apart from its theoretical purport, I believe that some parts of it can be used as a sort of a textbook. The typological parts provide a supposedly comprehensive account of major referential devices. This can be used in advanced courses on linguistic typology and linguistic diversity. Reference, although not traditionally listed among the major typological parameters, is actually omnipresent in discourse and grammar and interacts strongly with many well-established linguistic domains, much researched in typology, including: head-marking vs. dependent-marking; argument type; agreement; alignment; case marking; noun classes, etc. Presumably this study helps to unite all these disparate dimensions of typology into one coherent picture. I also hope that the typological parts of the book should be of use for descriptive linguists working on grammars of individual languages. As for the cognitive part of the book, it is a case study in the kind of cognitive linguistics that is strongly underrepresented nowadays: cognitive discourse analysis. As was mentioned in Chapter 1, contemporary textbooks in cognitive linguistics mostly focus on semantics and largely neglect discourse issues. So this book can also serve as a partial introduction to cognitive discourse analysis.

16.2 What was disregarded

In Chapter 1 of this book I quoted Kozma Prutkov's aphorism 'One cannot embrace the unembraceable'. Inevitably there are certain aspects of discourse reference that could not be addressed even in this rather sizeable book. These aspects can probably be divided into the following categories:

(1) types of reference;
(2) linguistic processes involving reference;
(3) approaches to the study of reference.

The following three subsections are organized in accordance with this list of omissions.

16.2.1 *Types of reference*

In this book I mostly proceeded on the tacit assumption that various mentions of a referent are coreferential. Reality sometimes deviates from this prototype; for example, it may be that the referents of the anaphor and of the antecedent are in a looser relation than precise coincidence. This happens, for example, when one talks about a ship and then uses the expression *the deck*, referring to the deck of the given ship. A variety of terms have been used to delimit these kinds of instances, including **indirect anaphora** (e.g. Cornish 1999), bridging (Clark 1977), inferrables or inferred antecedents (Prince 1992, Ziv 1996), associative anaphora (Hawkins 1978), as well as some others. (See Webber et al. 2003, Schwartz-Friesel 2007, Cornish 2007 for relatively recent useful accounts.) Indirect anaphora can be viewed as the opposite of syntactic anaphora: while in the latter the relationships between the anaphor and the antecedent are fully explicit and structured, in the former they are maximally loose. Indirect anaphora is far from being negligible in terms of frequency. According to the large corpus counts in Biber et al. (1999: 266), the indirect anaphoric uses of definite full NPs account for 5% of all usages in conversation, 10% in fiction, and 15% in news and academic texts. It may seem that the problem of indirect anaphora mostly relates to full NPs, as in the deck example above. However, Stirling (1996) found that out of 1,429 anaphoric expressions in her corpus of spoken Australian English 163 (=11%) were instances of indirect anaphora (p. 72). Out of these, 85 (more than a half of the indirect anaphors, and nearly 6% of all anaphors) were third person personal pronouns. So, at least in certain discourses, both full and reduced referential devices can be used in this fashion, and the omission of indirect anaphora in this book is just a case of inevitable simplification. See also Cornish (ed.) (2005) on indirect exophora.

When discussing referential devices, I focused in the main on the most common, least marked referential devices, especially prosodically weak third person pronouns and zeroes. Occasionally, I looked at **minor referential devices**, such as strong pronouns (Chapter 4, section 4.5). These arise for a number of reasons, including the combination of reduced reference and additional discourse-related concerns, such as contrastiveness or emphasis. In fact, a wide-scale study of how both reduced and full reference, as based on working memory activation, interacts with contrastiveness and emphasis is clearly in order. There is also an interesting class of so-called intensifiers, such as Russian *sam* 'X oneself' (see e.g. A. E. Kibrik 1996, Lyutikova 2002, König and Siemund 2000) that need to be included into the general picture of discourse reference.

As was indicated from the outset (Chapter 2, subsection 2.1.2), I have focused on specific definite reference. More **deviant kinds of reference** were hardly touched upon in the book. The border between specific, definite, and anaphoric referential devices, on the one hand, and other kinds of referential expressions is by no means simple. For example, the indefinite pronoun *one* can be used anaphorically (Mühlhäusler et al. 1990: 193):

(16.1)   One should always look after one's money

On the other hand, third person pronouns can be coreferential to a negative or indefinite pronoun, for example (Mühlhäusler et al. 1990: 230):

(16.2)   If anyone arrives late he can collect his key from the concierge

The literature on the deviant kinds of reference (indefinite, negative, interrogative pronouns, quantified expressions, etc.) is so vast that it would be inappropriate to attempt to review it here. Most of that literature belongs to the logical or formal semantic tradition. I will only mention one important study of indefinite (as well as negative) pronouns combining the functionalist theoretical orientation and the typological approach: the monograph by Haspelmath (1997). The present book deals with specific definite reference because it is the most prototypical kind of reference, and its proper understanding must be useful for subsequent exploration of more deviant kinds.

A little investigated issue in referential studies is the question of **plural reference**. As was pointed out in Chapter 14, subsection 14.2.3, third person plural pronouns pattern slightly differently from singular pronouns. To put it simply, plural referents are less clear-cut and crisp, compared to singular referents, and this has many consequences for establishing identities of plural referents. For example, switch-reference systems often glitch in the cases of plural subjects; see e.g. Bergelson and Kibrik (1995). As is pointed out by Abbott (2010: 203), 'plural pronouns seem to be freer in their referential capabilities than singular pronouns'. Very substantial are the effects associated with plural locutor pronouns. Pronouns such as *we* typically refer to a group, including the speaker and some other people (see e.g. Kibrik 1989; Nunberg 1993). That is, *we* often includes an anaphoric component. As was pointed out by Helmbrecht (2004: 75), plural locutor pronouns are between the singular locutor pronouns and third person person pronouns in terms of how referents are identified, as both the speech act situation and previous discourse are relevant. In other words, plural locutor pronouns are a mixed category. As is becoming clear from recent literature, the procedures of using plural pronouns cannot be fully predicted from what we know about singular pronouns (Koh et al. 2008; Borthen 2010).

In this book, the notion of reference has been reserved for referents, that is living beings and objects. However, this notion may be extended to the bordering types of concepts, that is places and times. **Reference to places** (=spatial/local/locative reference) cannot be discretely and objectively distinguished from reference to objects; cf. a chain of concepts that take different positions on the axis of size: this pen – this table – this room – this building – this town – this country. Each of these entities can be conceptualized as either an object or a location depending on the speaker's goals, even though smaller entities are inherently more inclined to be objects while larger entities are more likely to be viewed as locations. The absence of a strict boundary between object and spatial reference can be seen from the frequent contextual synonymy of expressions such as *there* and *at that place*. **Reference to times** (=temporal reference) can also be viewed as a subtype of reference to objects, since moments and intervals of time can be conceptualized as objects; cf. *then* and *at that moment*. Temporal reference interacts in a complex way with the verb categories of aspect and tense. Spatial and temporal reference has been explored in many studies, such as the various contributions to Jarvella and Klein (eds.) (1982), Duchan et al. (eds.) (1995), Arutjunova and Yanko (eds.) (1997), Hickmann (ed.) (2006), and Aurnage et al. (eds.) (2007); also in Partee (1984), Bulygina (1992), Klein (1994), Givón (1995: 364–372), Hickmann (2003). Much remains to be done to develop a unified account of reference to persons/objects, places, and times.

As was pointed out in subsection 2.1.1, apart from referents, locations, and times, the two other major ontological types of concepts are states and events; these are prototypically expressed by verbal predicates in language. Sometimes the notion of reference is extended to also include events or states, and the term **predicate anaphora** is used. There exist reduced verbal expressions, analogous to pronouns, as in (6.13), and zero verbal expressions, as in (6.14) and (6.15):

(16.3) Not everybody congratulated John. Sam did, but Mary didn't.
(16.4) Who is afraid of the IMF? The Greeks. (title of an article in April 2010)
(16.5) Finished holiday shopping yet? Us neither. (from an ad)

Reduced verbal expressions have been considered in works such as Asher (1993), Lappin and Benmamoun (eds.) (1999), Kehler (2002), Webber et al. (2003); see Huang (2006) for a useful concise account. Even though reduced verbal expressions have sometimes been interpreted as a syntactic phenomenon, they are generally as discourse-based as are referential devices discussed throughout this book. As the examples above demonstrate, reduced verbal expressions may appear in different sentences from their antecedents. Moreover, natural dialogue abounds with contexts in which such reduced expressions appear across turn boundaries. An important open theoretical question associated with reduced verbal expressions is whether they can be explained with the same notion of activation in working memory as was used in the above chapters to explain the reduced mention of referents. Webber et al. (2003) proposed that events in discourse are linked by connections similar to coreference, and this structure is superimposed over the structure of semantic, or rhetorical, relations. A peculiar boundary zone between reference to referents and to events/states is constituted by specialized nouns such as *event*, *fact*, or *situation* (see e.g. Conte 1996). Interestingly, the ontological types of concepts are underdifferentiated in pointing: one can point not only at a referent or a location, but also at an event, and it is not always possible to clearly distinguish to which ontological type the target of pointing belongs.

16.2.2 *Domains of reference*

The perspective upon reference adopted in this book is that pertaining to the speaker. That is, all discussion of reference and referential choice was confined to the domain of production (generation) processes: what the speaker chooses to mention as he/she produces discourse, and what referential options he/she chooses. The complementary perspective is associated with the domain of understanding (comprehension) by the hearer. In fact, most of the existing literature on reference, if explicit at all on which of the two perspectives is pursued, adopts the hearer's perspective. As is well known (see for example Treiman et al. 2003 on psycholinguistic research; Mitkov 2002 on computational linguistic research) traditions in the study of language production and comprehension have long been separated. In real life, however, this separation is far from absolute. In Chapter 2 (section 2.6) and elsewhere I have discussed a number of speaker's referential strategies in accordance with the degree to which he/she takes the addressee's viewpoint into account. Likewise, the hearer models the speaker's mind in the course of discourse comprehension. There is a recent train of thought suggesting that hearers emulate production in order to make comprehension more efficient (see e.g. Pickering and Garrod 2007). So the production and comprehension of referential expressions are not as distinct agendas as they may seem from the literature, including theoretical, experimental, and computational. In this sense I tend to believe that the results of the book may be useful for research in reference comprehension. Incidentally, in reference comprehension the distinction between reference per se (attention) and referential choice (working memory activation) may be less clear-cut than in production.

In order to understand a certain natural skill, it is important to understand how it is acquired. Highly relevant for all discourse-related phenomena, reference being no exception, are the acquisition processes, especially first language acquisition. The literature on the acquisition of reference has grown very large; see the recent papers by Salazar Orvig et al. (2010) and Rozendaal and Baker (2010) and the works cited there. Of course, a comprehensive picture of how a certain phenomenon operates in adult language must involve an account of how it is ontogenetically shaped. Since reference is crucially dependent on the general cognitive abilities of attention and working memory, the study of reference acquisition must be coupled with developmental studies of these basic cognitive functions.

In addition to acquisition, another domain that often helps to understand natural phenomena is the way they operate under complicating conditions. Yet another domain of reference is associated with the discourse of the people suffering neurological or psychiatric disorders. It seems that the literature on reference in patients with such disorders is not abundant. However, there are some studies of reference in aphasics, e.g. Davis and Coelho (2004), and in schizophrenics, e.g. Chaika and Lambe (1989) and Utekhin (2010).

16.2.3 Approaches

During the last several decades, reference in discourse has been subject to a multiplicity of approaches in linguistics and related fields. As must be clear by now, particularly relevant to the approach developed in this book was the work by Chafe (1976, 1994), Fox (1987a), and Tomlin (1987, 1995). Generally consonant to my approach is the influential research tradition founded by Givón (1983a), as well as later kindred traditions of Ariel (1988), Gundel et al. (1993), and Cornish (1999). All these studies were amply cited in the above chapters.

There are, however, a number of other approaches that also focus on reference but were not sufficiently taken into account. The discussion in the book has been problem-oriented rather than approach-oriented, so I would not attempt a detailed review of these various approaches. But I would like to mention at least some of the most salient ones.

There is a long tradition of reference studies in philosophy, logic, and, later, formal semantics. This tradition began in early 20th century with work such as Russell (1905) and was developed in many important studies, such as Quine (1953) and Donnellan (1966). Fundamental notions, such as referent and coreference, were made widely known through this tradition. Useful accounts of the huge philosophical, logical, and/or semantic literature on reference can be found in Bílý (1981), Arutjunova (1982), Evans (1982), Nunberg (1993), Recanati (1993), Shmelev (1995), Geurts (1999), von Heusinger and Egli (eds.) (2000), Kempson et al. (2001), Sainsbury (2005), Sullivan (2006), Merrell (2006), King (2006), Rast (2006), Bach (2008), Abbott (2010). Philosophical and formal approaches to reference do not easily combine with discourse-oriented, cognitive, and typological perspectives, albeit they look, ultimately, at the same or at least related natural phenomena. From my perspective, in the logical-philosophical work too much attention is paid to rather marginal and often paradoxical instances of reference, whereas it is more practical to begin with the most basic kind of reference, which is specific definite reference in discourse.

A very extensive line of research is associated with Centering Theory, going back to computationally oriented studies such as Grosz (1977), Grosz and Sidner (1986), and Gordon et al. (1993) and culminating in Walker et al. (eds.) (1998). More recent work includes Beaver (2004), Poesio et al. (2004), Hardt (2004), inter alia, a useful overview is provided by Joshi et al. (2006), and a critique in Kehler (2002). Centering Theory is, essentially, a heuristic aimed at identifying the currently most attended (or activated) referent in discourse (so-called backward-looking centre, roughly equalling local discourse topic) that is likely to be mentioned at the next moment in discourse. Centering literature is often very readable: many authors in this tradition have a background in computer science and/or mathematics and are used to expressing their thoughts clearly. It is very nice that Centering theorists usually formulate their claims in a testable way. However, there are several limitations that reduce the applicability of Centering Theory as a way to analyse empirical data. Most importantly, it is designed axiomatically and not always in the most natural way. In particular, a singleton backward-looking centre is postulated in every 'utterance' which is hardly tenable; as we have seen in Part IV, it is often the case that two or more referents are highly activated at the same time. Most papers in Walker et al. (eds.) (1998) demonstrate that the rigid axioms and built-in rules of Centering Theory do not survive an encounter with empirical reality. Other problems with Centering Theory are that, first, it is a rather secluded approach and, second, it is too reductionist with respect to the array of factors potentially affecting reference (compare this to the multi-factorial approach developed in Part IV of the book). At the same time, a number of interesting results have been obtained within the Centering framework. For example, Hudson D'Zmura (1998) established that verbs of perception (such as *see, watch*) create an expectation that a description of the perceived scene will follow, and that helps to identify reference.

An original approach to reference, the so-called neo-Gricean pragmatic theory, was proposed by Levinson (1987, 2000) and developed by Huang (2000). The use of reduced referential devices, such as third person pronouns and reflexives, is explained through modified Gricean maxims. In many ways the pragmatic theory is saying things that are compatible with or even equivalent to the cognitive approach, and they can possibly be merged in the future. One particularly useful claim developed within the neo-Gricean theory is the observation that reflexives are a much more marked and exotic referential device, compared to third person pronouns (see Chapter 2, subsection 2.3.1), for the obvious reason that coreference of the participants of one and the same clause is a highly unusual situation. This simple truth is often missed by generative grammarians; cf. the so-called referential economy principle proposed by Burzio (1996).

Within the framework of Langacker's Cognitive Grammar (1987/1991), an approach to referential phenomena was proposed; see Langacker (1996) and van Hoek (1997). This approach relies on the notion of so-called conceptual reference points, that are certain discourse entities defining context for the interpretation of referential expressions. Conceptual reference points can actually be understood as highly activated referents. Syntactic anaphora is viewed as a subcase of discourse anaphora. As van Hoek points out herself, this theory is compatible with the cognitive approaches to reference.

Throughout the book, and in a number of other studies, the following perspective upon discourse reference was adopted. One looks at a certain point or moment in discourse and asks the question as to which referents are activated in the speaker at this time, and to what extent, and how the speaker makes referential choices. However, alternatively one can focus on an individual referent and on how its activation changes over time, or, to use the words of Fretheim et al. (2010), on 'the life span of a given discourse referent, whether ephemeral or sustained'. That is, a referent can be conceived of as passing from one activation state to another, or staying in the same state, or interacting with another referent. This perspective can be called the **dynamics of referent activation**. The dynamics perspective is occasionally adopted in

560   Conclusion

```
        Introduction        Maintenance         Decay          Reintroduction
Non-activated  →  Activated       →  Activated    →  Non-activated   →  Activated
     t₁                t₂                 t₃              t₄                 t₅
────────────────────────────────────────────────────────────────────────→
                                                                          t
```

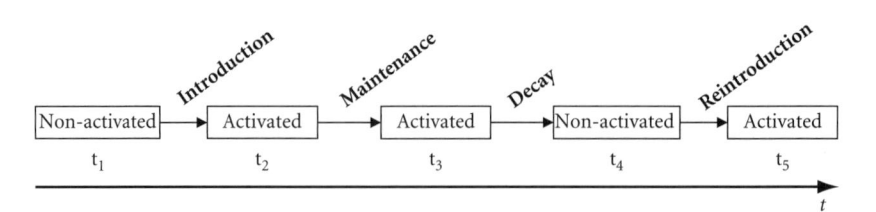

FIGURE 16.1. Dynamics of a single referent's activation

various studies, including Karttunen (1976), Grosz (1977), Noonan (1992: Ch. 10), Hickmann (2003: Ch. 8), Seifart (2005: Ch. 10), partly Givón (1983a), Prince (1981); this perspective is actually characteristic of much work in Centering Theory (Walker et al. (eds.) 1998); see also subsection 13.2.3. Within the dynamics perspective, there is an important difference between an introductory mention of a referent within a discourse and a repeated mention (the terminology once proposed by Gak 1972). Several phases can be distinguished in the 'discourse life' of each referent (Kibrik 1991, 1992a), the most important of which are visualized by a flow chart in Figure 16.1.

The activation dynamics perspective is complementary with respect to the speaker-oriented perspective. A comprehensive picture of reference in discourse should preferably embrace both of these perspectives.

16.3 What is particularly fascinating in future research

When a speaker performs an act of reference, the most basic choice he/she makes is that between a lexically full vs. a reduced referential device. It is this choice that I have been mostly discussing in the above chapters. Unlike reduced devices, lexically full devices that are in principle applicable to a given referent vary immensely. One can use proper names or common nouns, simple or complex noun phrases, etc. The wealth of these choices remained almost entirely outside of the scope of this book. To be sure, the basic choice between full and reduced devices kept us busy enough for many pages. But further inquiry into reference must also involve varieties of full NP mentions. So far, relatively few studies have been devoted to explaining the choice between these varieties; some examples include Arutjunova (1977), Seleznev (1987), Ariel (1990: 34ff.), Vieira and Poesio (1999), Tutin and Viegas (1999), van Deemter (2006), Stivers et al. (2007), Arnold (2008), and Helmbrecht (2009). An important facet of full NP reference is related to what is called perspective taking, or perspectivization, or subjectivity (see Chapter 15, subsection 15.3.3). To give a simple example, the same referent, depending on the speaker's identity and viewpoint, can be called *Susan, his wife, my wife, my mum, that heavenly creature*, etc. Furthermore, the choice between various full NP forms is subject to cognitive analysis, just like the basic referential choice. For example, if I suddenly mention someone called Jim, I assume that in my addressee's cognitive representation there is one Jim out of many by the same name who is somehow more available in long-term memory. The full-scale exploration of all possible referential options, including those by full NPs, is one of the most important frontiers in the future study of discourse reference.

In Chapter 1, subsection 1.4.1, I outlined the general contours of the taxonomy of discourse types. In the main chapters of the book this taxonomy was employed only to a limited extent, but it is in fact highly relevant for discourse reference. There is a clear dependency between referential processes and discourse registers (subsection 1.4.3). All taxonomic variables mentioned in Chapter 1, including mode, genre, passage type, and functional style, affect referential choice. The collection by Fox (ed.) (1996) contains a number of articles on referential processes in specific discourse types in various languages. Other examples of explicit comparisons of referential strategies in various discourse registers and types include Fox (1987a), Biber (1992), Toole (1996), Strube and Wolters (2000), Garrod (2011). To give a concrete illustration, consider the contrastive studies of Japanese pronouns (Clancy 1982, Downing 1996a: 177–179). Although Japanese is strongly committed to zero reference (Chapter 3, section 3.4), occasionally pronouns are used in written discourse. In contrast, 'the relative dearth of pronouns in oral texts is presumably linked to the social constraints on their use ... and it suggests that the status of pronouns as a distinct anaphoric option may be rather tenuous for oral discourse' (Downing 1996a: 179). Sensitivity of referential processes to discourse types does not suggest that people learn new rules of referential choice every time they learn a new discourse type. Each language does have a basic referential system that is further adapted to discourse type. The activation factors of the kind introduced in Chapters 11 and 12 must also be adaptable to mode, genre, and functional style. The nature and plasticity of this adaptation is one of the most interesting directions of further research in discourse reference.

Apart from the variation of referential processes stemming from discourse types, there is of course another kind of variation that is much more central to the concerns of this book. I am referring here to the cross-linguistic variation that was addressed, in one way or another, in most of the above chapters. Appendix 1 contains a questionnaire that might be useful for authors of descriptive accounts of various languages; this questionnaire is aimed at eliciting the crucial parameters of a language's referential system. Hopefully future language grammars may be more easy to search for referential properties than are most of the current descriptive accounts. The kinds of issues addressed in the above-mentioned questionnaire are at a rather coarse level of granularity. A much more refined analysis is required if one attempts to set up, for a random language, an explanatory system of referential choice akin to the analysis of Russian, English, and Japanese reported in Chapters 11, 12, and 14. As was pointed out in section 12.7, one needs to go through a sequence of steps leading to a relatively complete language-specific account of the system of referential choice. Once such accounts are available for a fair number of languages, a comprehensive typology of referential systems may eventually become possible. Any further typology of referential devices must include not only spoken languages but also sign languages briefly introduced in Chapter 15. Generally, sign languages are highly important for any topic in typological research, as they constitute the second major type of human languages, comparable to spoken languages.

In many of the above chapters I used the results of studies obtained within the experimental psycholinguistic paradigm; see Garnham (2001, 2006) for reviews of psycholinguistic research on reference and the most recent collection Gibson and Pearlmutter (eds.) (2011). However, most of the book is based on the observational methodology (see Chapter 1, section 1.8). Also, the modelling method was employed in some chapters of Part IV. My view is that in linguistics, as in other empirical sciences, the best results are achieved when all scientific methodologies are used in conjunction. In the domain of discourse reference the involvement of experimental approaches is now becoming very promising, as psycholinguists are beginning to work with discourses rather than isolated sentences, including in the domain of discourse reference; see e.g. Arnold (2008). Moreover, there is also an emerging neurolinguistic discourse analysis; see e.g. van Berkum (in press). This field is really new, as neurolinguistics, following in the footsteps of psycholinguistics and psychology, has been mostly fond of small-size and decontextualized linguistic phenomena (syllables, words, or constructed sentences at most), rather than natural discourses. Recently the first neurolinguistic studies of referential and related discourse processes have been undertaken; see van Berkum et al. (2007), Nieuwland et al. (2007), Ferstl and Siebörger (2007). One of the important findings is the so-called Nref effect, observed in cases of referential conflict and indicating, among other things, that reference comprehension is performed very rapidly, only a few hundred milliseconds after the acoustic onset of the referential expression. Particularly relevant to the content of this book is the series of psycholinguistic experiments testing the CMF approach, as described in Part IV, by Olga Fedorova and her associates (Fedorova et al. 2010a). Interesting directions of further experimental research include exploring various referential strategies (Chapter 2, section 2.6) and verifying the independence of the referential conflict filter from activation factors (Chapter 2, section 2.8; Part III). This agenda seems very close to the emerging field of social cognitive neuroscience; see Schilbach (2010). I believe that the combination of observational, experimental, and modelling methods will bring the understanding of referential processes to a new qualitative level.

Many advances in the study of discourse reference are associated with the work of computational linguists; see Strube (2006), Byron (2002), Poesio et al. (2004), Mitkov (2002), inter alia. Computational studies are traditionally oriented to large corpora of annotated discourses. There is a recent trend in computational linguistics that expands the empirical basis strongly: the use of open-ended Internet resources, including web-based games for data collection; see e.g. Poesio (2009) (http://anawiki.essex.ac.uk/phrasedetectives/) and Tily and Piantadosi (2009). Such novel methods of empirical research open up new horizons in the study of reference.

Perhaps the most fascinating area in the future exploration of reference has to do with multimodal communication. Conventional language consisting of segmental units can only be artificially treated in separation from prosody and non-vocal communication channels. The tradition of such artificial separation is very strong in linguistics, but it is clear that for a regular language user it makes little difference how his/her messages get through to the addressee: by way of verbal elements, or prosody, or gesture. According to Scollon's (2006) formula, 'any use of language is inescapably multimodal'. Some examples of prosodically informed analysis of reference include Wolters and Byron (2000), Balogh (2003), Cornish (ed.) (2005), Mithun (2007), and Jasinskaja et al. (2007), and some more were mentioned in the above chapters; see Kodzasov (2009) for one of the most innovative general treatments of discourse prosody. In Chapter 15 I considered some connections between verbal and gestural aspects of communication, but that is certainly not enough. The development of multimodal linguistics is one of the most topical issues on the modern agenda (Kibrik 2008c). The emerging new theory of reference must recognize the importance of prosody and visual aspects of communication on a par with the traditional verbal referential devices. This should also combine with the analysis of linguistic diversity since prosodic and gestural devices are as language-specific as verbal material.

These six directions seem to be the most urgent and exciting among the explorations of reference in the foreseeable future. Most of them are connected with the issues addressed in this book. It is highly probable that the study of reference and referential choice will remain among the central concerns of linguistics in the years to come.

Appendix 1

Questionnaire on referential systems for descriptive grammars

An account of referential devices is an essential part of a full description of any language, as necessary as the inventory of tenses or the rules of relative clause formation. In the recent decades, authors of descriptive grammars have begun to acknowledge this fact, and special sections on referential devices, as well as other discourse phenomena, are becoming rightful constituents of language descriptions; see e.g. A. E. Kibrik and Testelets (eds.) (1999) or Olawsky (2006). Much more often, however, information on discourse reference is scattered across various parts of descriptive grammars, such as sections on pronouns, person inflection, or complex sentences. This is true even of some grammars of major languages, such as English; see e.g. Huddleston and Pullum (2005). Relying on the results of this book, I propose below a format of how a language's referential system could be accounted for in a concise and coherent way. An earlier set of suggestions on this issue can be found in Levinsohn (1994); also cf. Staley 2007.

A. Referential devices

    A1. Kinds of full referential devices: proper names, common nouns with and without modifiers

    A2. Locutor reference (first and second person). [Note: because of this book's bias towards third person reference, locutor reference is not further detailed here; but many of the questions in A3 also apply to locutor reference]

    A3. Reduced referential devices (third person)
- Reduced referential devices used in the language: free pronouns vs. bound pronouns vs. zero reference
- Preferred reduced referential device, if any
- In zero reference languages, how are the referents' roles marked?
- The use of the functional analogues of pronouns: demonstratives, classifiers, social nouns, whichever are found in the language

- Double reference pronouns, if they are found in the language
- Compounding of pronouns with clausal categories, such as tense, if that is found in the language
- Strong pronouns:
  - Do they exist as a separate class, or are other devices such as demonstratives used instead?
  - Are they segmentally identical or related to weak free or bound pronouns?
  - What are their prosodic peculiarities?
  - The range of uses
- Sensitivities of reduced referential devices: with respect to:
  - activation level
  - clause participant position
  - various semantic and grammatical contexts (such as coordinate clauses)
- Tenacity vs. alternation of pronouns, including:
  - pronouns in various clause participant positions or hyperroles
  - degrees of tenacity vs. alternation
- In bound pronoun languages, mono- vs. polypersonalism
- Is the phenomenon of agreement found in the language, as distinct from bound pronouns?
- Are there instances in which one can posit bound zero elements?
- If historical information on the language is available, what are the evolutionary precursors of the modern referential system?
- What are the most obvious activation factors leading to the use of reduced referential devices?

B. Referential aids

B1. General
- How much does the language (or language users) care about the preclusion of referential conflicts?
- How many referential aids are found in the language?

B2. Ad hoc referential aids
- Are there examples in which the factors of compatibility and engagement can be demonstrated to participate in the preclusion of referential conflicts?

B3. Conventional referential aids, or referent sortings
- Which of the following are found in the language?:
  - absolute stable sorting (such as noun classes)
  - relative stable sorting (hierarchies)

- broad domain current sorting (such as obviative vs. proximate)
- narrow domain current sorting:
  - perspective-based (such as logophoric pronouns)
  - topicality- or subjecthood-based (such as switch-reference)
  - based on the degree of activation
  - any other?
- For each attested sorting, what is the site of marking, including:
  - on free pronouns
  - on bound pronouns
  - on verbs
  - on special constituents?
- For each attested sorting, what is its basic function in the language, and how is this function related to the preclusion of referential conflicts?
- Are there categories in the language that could potentially be used as referential aids but actually are not?

C. Pointing gestures

- Are they used in deictic contexts?
- Are they used in exophoric contexts?
- What referential devices can they accompany (pronouns, demonstratives, full noun phrases)?
- Do they combine with prosodically weak referential devices?
- What pointing devices can be used (index finger, eye gaze, other limbs, tools)?
- Are instances of virtual pointing attested?

Appendix 2

Map of languages mentioned in the book

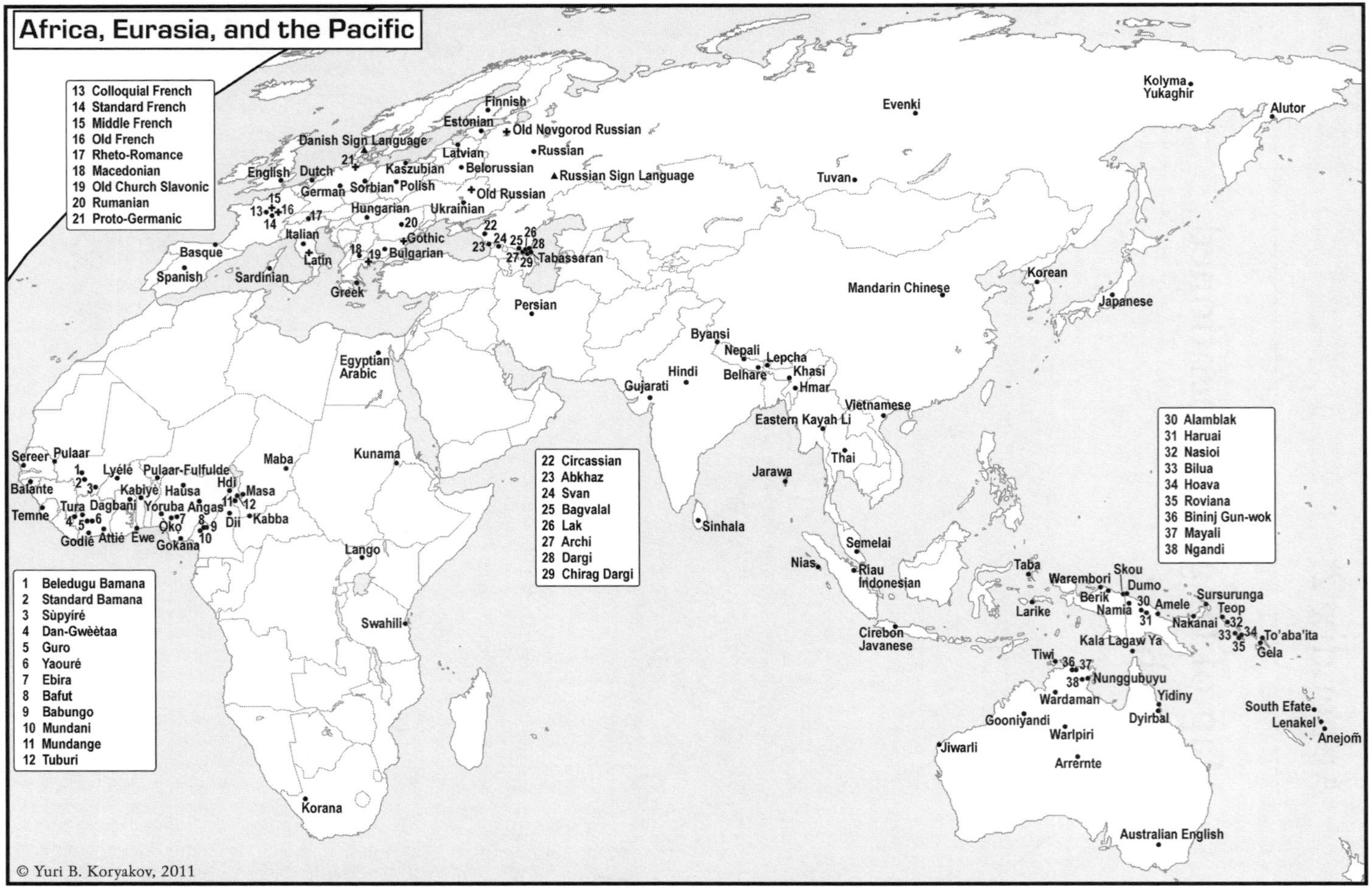
Africa, Eurasia, and the Pacific
13 Colloquial French
14 Standard French
15 Middle French
16 Old French
17 Rheto-Romance
18 Macedonian
19 Old Church Slavonic
20 Rumanian
21 Proto-Germanic
22 Circassian
23 Abkhaz
24 Svan
25 Bagvalal
26 Lak
27 Archi
28 Dargi
29 Chirag Dargi
30 Alamblak
31 Haruai
32 Nasioi
33 Bilua
34 Hoava
35 Roviana
36 Bininj Gun-wok
37 Mayali
38 Ngandi
1 Beledugu Bamana
2 Standard Bamana
3 Sùpyiré
4 Dan-Gwèètaa
5 Guro
6 Yaouré
7 Ebira
8 Bafut
9 Babungo
10 Mundani
11 Mundange
12 Tuburi
Finnish
Estonian
Old Novgorod Russian
Russian
Danish Sign Language
Latvian
Belorussian
Russian Sign Language
English
Dutch
Kaszubian
German
Sorbian
Polish
Old Russian
Hungarian
Ukrainian
Italian
Gothic
Bulgarian
Tabassaran
Basque
Latin
Spanish
Sardinian
Greek
Persian
Evenki
Kolyma Yukaghir
Alutor
Tuvan
Korean
Japanese
Mandarin Chinese
Byansi
Nepali
Lepcha
Hindi
Belhare
Khasi
Gujarati
Hmar
Vietnamese
Eastern Kayah Li
Thai
Jarawa
Sinhala
Egyptian Arabic
Kunama
Maba
Sereer
Pulaar
Lyélé
Pulaar-Fulfulde
Balante
Kabiyé
Hausa
Hdi
Masa
Temne
Tura
Dagbani
Yoruba
Angas
Dii
Kabba
Oko
Godié
Attié
Ewe
Gokana
Lango
Swahili
Korana
Semelai
Nias
Riau Indonesian
Cirebon Javanese
Taba
Warembori
Skou
Dumo
Berik
Namia
Amele
Sursurunga
Teop
Larike
Nakanai
To'aba'ita
Gela
Kala Lagaw Ya
Tiwi
Nunggubuyu
Wardaman
Yidiny
South Efate
Lenakel
Anejom̃
Gooniyandi
Dyirbal
Warlpiri
Jiwarli
Arrernte
Australian English

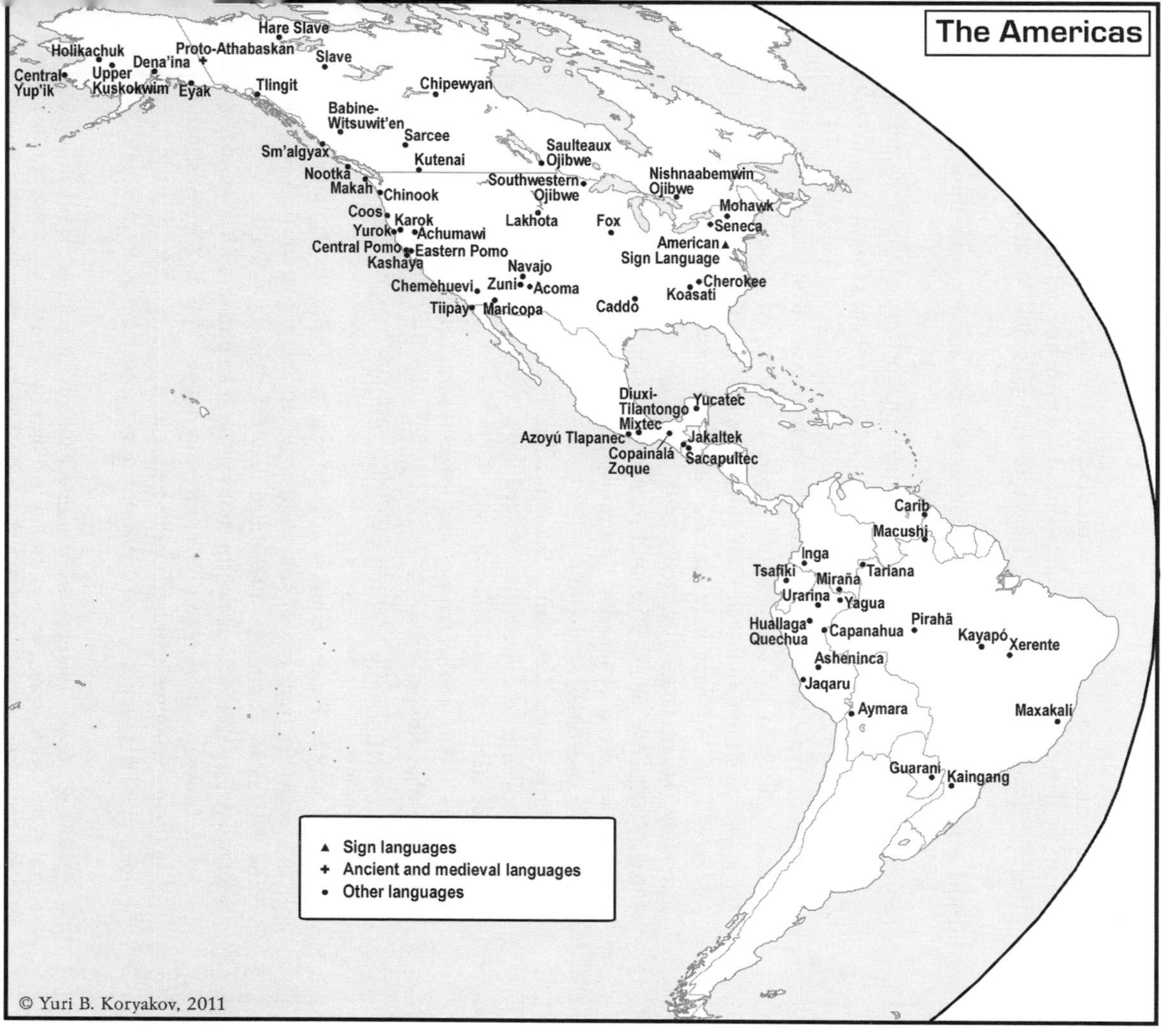
The Americas
Hare Slave
Holikachuk
Proto-Athabaskan
Dena'ina
Slave
Central Yup'ik
Upper Kuskokwim
Eyak
Tlingit
Chipewyan
Babine-Witsuwit'en
Sarcee
Sm'algyax
Kutenai
Saulteaux Ojibwe
Nootka
Makah
Chinook
Southwestern Ojibwe
Nishnaabemwin Ojibwe
Mohawk
Seneca
Coos
Karok
Yurok
Achumawi
Lakhota
Fox
Central Pomo
Eastern Pomo
Kashaya
American Sign Language
Navajo
Chemehuevi
Zuni
Acoma
Cherokee
Koasati
Tiipay
Maricopa
Caddo
Diuxi-Tilantongo Mixtec
Yucatec
Azoyú Tlapanec
Jakaltek
Copainalá Zoque
Sacapultec
Carib
Macushi
Inga
Tsafiki
Tariana
Miraña
Urarina
Yagua
Huallaga Quechua
Capanahua
Pirahã
Kayapó
Xerente
Asheninca
Jaqaru
Aymara
Maxakalí
Guarani
Kaingang
Sign languages
Ancient and medieval languages
Other languages
© Yuri B. Koryakov, 2011

References[1]

Abbott, Barbara (2010). *Reference.* Oxford: Oxford University Press.
Abbott, Miriam (1991). 'Macushi'. In: Desmond C. Derbyshire and Geoffrey K. Pullum (eds.), *Handbook of Amazonian languages.* Vol. 3. Berlin: Mouton de Gruyter, 23–160.
Ädel, Amelie, and Randi Reppen (eds.) (2008). *Corpora and discourse: The challenges of different settings.* Amsterdam: Benjamins.
Adive, John R. (1989). *The verbal piece in Ebira.* Arlington: University of Texas and SIL.
Aikhenvald, Alexandra Y. (2000). *Classifiers: A typology of noun categorization devices.* Oxford: Oxford University Press.
—— (2002). 'Typological parameters for the study of clitics, with special reference to Tariana'. In: R. M. W. Dixon and Alexandra Y. Aikhenvald (eds.), *Word: A cross-linguistic typology.* Cambridge: Cambridge University Press, 42–78.
—— and R. M. W. Dixon (eds.) (2006). *Serial verb constructions: A cross-linguistic typology.* Oxford: Oxford University Press.
Alibali, Martha W., Sotaro Kita, and Amanda J. Young (2000). 'Gesture and the process of speech production: We think, therefore we gesture'. *Language and Cognitive Processes* 15(6), 593–613.
Altmann, Erik M., and Christian D. Schunn (2002). *Integrating decay and interference: A new look at an old interaction.* Proceedings of the 24th Annual Meeting of the Cognitive Science Society. Hillsdale, NJ.
Amidu, Assibi A. (2006). *Pronouns and pronominalizations in Kiswahili grammar.* Köln: Rüdiger Köppe Verlag.
Anderson, John R. (1990). *Cognitive psychology.* 3rd edn. New York: W. H. Freeman and Company.
Anderson, Stephen R., and Edward L. Keenan (1987). 'Deixis'. In: Timothy Shopen (ed.), *Language typology and syntactic description.* Vol. 3. Grammatical categories and the lexicon. Cambridge: Cambridge University Press, 295–309.
Andrews, Avery (1985). 'The major functions of the noun phrase'. In: Timothy Shopen (ed.), *Language typology and syntactic description.* Vol. 1. Clause structure. Cambridge: Cambridge University Press, 62–154.
Antonova, Aleksandra A. (2004). *Algoritm opredelenija antecedentov anaforičeskix*

---

[1] This list of references contains many citations of Russian-language books and papers, originally printed in the Cyrillic script. The titles, publishers, names, etc., are provided in standard Slavicist transliteration. Many authors' and editors' names are given in the same transliteration as well. However, for some authors who have published in English or are otherwise known in a different transliteration that they prefer, such preferred transliteration is given as the main one, while standard transliteration is provided in square brackets. English translations of titles are also given in square brackets.

mestoimenij i avtomatičeskaja referencial'naja razmetka korpusa gazetnyx statej Wall Street Journal [An algorithm for detecting antecedents of anaphoric pronouns and automatic annotation of a corpus of Wall Street Journal articles]. Year paper. Dept. of Theoretical and Applied Linguistics, Moscow State University.

Ariel, Mira (1988). 'Referring and accessibility'. *Journal of Linguistics* 24, 65–87.

—— (1990). *Accessing noun-phrase antecedents*. Croom Helm Linguistics Series. London: Routledge.

—— (2000). 'The development of person agreement markers: From pronouns to higher accessibility markers'. In: Michael Barlow and Suzanne Kemmer (eds.), *Usage-based models of language*. Stanford: SCLI, 197–260.

—— (2001). 'Accessibility theory: An overview'. In: Ted J. M. Sanders, Joost Schilperoord, and Wilbert Spooren (eds.), *Text representation: Linguistic and psycholinguistic aspects*. Amsterdam: Benjamins, 29–88.

—— (2006). *Reference: Maxi-grammar, mini-grammar*. Paper presented at the Conference on Intersentential Pronominal Reference in Child and Adult Language, Berlin, 1–2 December 2006.

Arkhipov, Alexandre V. [Aleksandr V. Arxipov] (2009). *Tipologija komitativnyx konstrukcij* [A typology of comitative constructions]. Moscow: Znak.

Arnold, Jennifer E., Janet G. Eisenband, Sarah Brown-Schmidt, and John C. Trueswell (2000). 'The rapid use of gender information: Evidence of the time course of pronoun resolution from eye tracking'. *Cognition* 76, B13–B26.

—— (2001). 'The effect of thematic roles on pronoun use and frequency of reference continuation'. *Discourse Processes* 31, 137–162.

—— and Zenzi M. Griffin (2007). 'The effect of additional characters on choice of referring expression: Everyone counts'. *Journal of Memory and Language* 56(4), 521–536.

—— (2008). 'Reference production: Production-internal and addressee-oriented processes'. *Language and Cognitive Processes* 23(4), 495–527.

Arnott, David (1970). *The nominal and verbal system of Fula*. Oxford: Oxford University Press.

Arutjunova, Nina D. (1977). 'Nominacija i tekst' [Nomination and text]. In: Boris A. Serebrennikov and Anna A. Ufimceva (eds.), *Jazykovaja nominacija (tipy naimenovanij)*. Moscow: Nauka, 304–357.

—— (1981). 'Faktor adresata' [The addressee factor]. *Izvestija AN SSSR. Serija Literatury i Jazyka* 40(4), 356–367.

—— (1982). 'Lingvističeskie problemy referencii' [Linguistic problems of reference]. In: Nina D. Arutjunova (ed.), *Novoe v zarubežnoj lingvistike, vyp. XIII. Logika i lingvistika*. Moscow: Raduga, 5–40.

—— (ed.) (1988). *Referencija i problemy tekstoobrazovanija* [Reference and the problems of text formation]. Moscow: Nauka.

—— and Tatyana E. Yanko [Tat'jana E. Janko] (eds.) (1997). *Jazyk i vremja* [Language and time]. Moscow: Indrik.

Ashby, William J., and Paola Bentivoglio (2003). 'Preferred argument structure across time and space: A comparative diachronic analysis of French and Spanish'. In: John W. Du Bois, Lorraine E. Kumpf, and William J. Ashby (eds.), *Preferred argument structure: Grammar as architecture for function*. Amsterdam: Benjamins, 61–80.

Asher, Nicholas (1993). *Reference to abstract objects in discourse*. Dordrecht: Kluwer.

Atkinson, Richard C., and Richard M. Shiffrin (1968). 'Human memory: A proposed system and its control processes'. In: Kenneth W. Spence and Janet T. Spence (eds.), *The psychology of learning and motivation: Advances in research and theory*. New York: Academic Press, 89–195.

—— and —— (1971). 'The control of short-term memory'. *Scientific American* 225, 82–90.

Atóyèbí, Joseph Dele (2007). *Examining the pervasiveness of vowel harmony across grammatical structures in Ọ̀kọ*. Leipzig, MPI-EVA. Unpublished.

—— (2009). *A Reference Grammar of Ọ̀kọ*. Ph.D. thesis. Universität Leipzig.

Aurnage, Michel, Maya Hickmann, and Laure Vieu (eds.) (2007). *The categorization of spatial entities in language and cognition*. Amsterdam: Benjamins.

Austin, Peter K. (1981). 'Switch-reference in Australia'. *Language Acquisition* 57, 309–334.

—— (1988). *Complex constructions in Australian languages*. Amsterdam: Benjamins.

—— and Joan Bresnan (1996). 'Non-configurationality in Australian aboriginal languages'. *Natural Language and Linguistic Theory* 14, 215–268.

—— (2001a). 'Word order in a free word order language: The case of Jiwarli'. In: Jane Simpson, David Nash, Mary Laughren, Peter K. Austin, and Barry Alpher (eds.), *Forty years on: Ken Hale and Australian languages*. Canberra: Pacific Linguistics, 305–324.

—— (2001b). 'Zero Arguments in Jiwarli, Western Australia'. *Australian Journal of Linguistics* 21(1), 83–98.

Awh, Edward, Edward E. Smith, and John Jonides (1995). 'Human rehearsal processes and the frontal lobes: PET evidence'. *Annals of the New York Academy of Sciences* 769, 97–118.

—— and John Jonides (2001). 'Overlapping mechanisms of attention and working memory'. *Trends in Cognitive Science* 5(3), 119–126.

—— Edward K. Vogel, and S.-H. Oh (2006). 'Interactions between attention and working memory'. *Neuroscience* 139, 201–208.

—— Brian Barton, and Edward K. Vogel (2007). 'Visual working memory represents a fixed number of items regardless of complexity'. *Psychological Science* 18(7), 622–628.

Baars, Bernard J. (1997). *In the theater of consciousness: The workspace of the mind*. New York: Oxford University Press.

Babaev, Kirill V. (2007). 'K voprosu o proisxoždenii ličnyx okončanij glagola v jazykax mira' [On the issue of the origin of personal verbal endings in the languages of the world]. Paper presented at the Nostratic seminar, Russian State University for the Humanities, Moscow, February 2007.

Babaev, Kirill V. (2008). *Rol' dannyx vnešnego sravnenija dlja rekonstrukcii indoevropejskix pokazatelej lica* [The role of external comparison for the reconstruction of Indo-European person markers]. Ph.D. thesis. Russian State University for the Humanities.

Bach, Kent (2008). On referring and not referring. In: Jeanette K. Gundel and Nancy Hedberg (eds.), *Reference: Interdisciplinary perspectives*. Oxford: Oxford University Press, 13–60.

Baddeley, Alan D., and Graham J. Hitch (1974). 'Working memory'. In: Gordon A. Bower (ed.), *Recent advances in learning and motivation*. New York: Academic Press, 47–90.

—— (1986). *Working memory*. Oxford: Clarendon Press.

—— (1990). *Human memory: Theory and practice*. Needham Heights: Allyn and Bacon.

—— (1993). 'Working memory or working attention?' In: Alan D. Baddeley and Lawrence Weiskrantz (eds.), *Attention: Selection, awareness, and control. A tribute to Donald Broadbent*. New York: Oxford University Press, 152–170.

—— and Robert H. Logie (1999). 'Working memory: The multiple-component model'. In: Akira Miyake and Priti Shah (eds.), *Models of working memory: Mechanisms of active maintenance and executive control*. New York: Cambridge University Press, 28–61.

—— (2000). 'Short-term and working memory'. In: Endel Tulving and Fergus I. M. Craik (eds.), *The Oxford handbook of memory*. Oxford: Oxford University Press, 77–92.

—— (2007). *Working memory, thought, and action*. Oxford: Oxford University Press.

Baker, Mark (1996). *The polysynthesis parameter*. New York: Oxford University Press.

Bakhtin, Mikhail M. [Mixail M. Baxtin] (1953/1986). 'Problema rečevyx žanrov' [The problem of speech genres]. *Mikhail Bakhtin [Mixail Baxtin]. Literaturno-kritičeskie stat'i*. Moscow: Xudožestvennaja literatura, 428–472.

Balogh, Jennifer Elaine (2003). *Pronouns, prosody, and the discourse anaphora weighting approach*. Ph.D. thesis. University of California, San Diego.

Bamberg, Michael G. W. (1987). *The acquisition of narratives: Learning to use language*. Berlin: Mouton de Gruyter.

Baranov, Anatolij N., and Grigorij E. Krejdlin (1992). 'Illokutivnoe vynuždenie v strukture dialoga' [Illocutionary prompting in the structure of a dialogue]. *Voprosy Jazykoznanija* 1992(2), 84–99.

Barlow, Michael (1999). 'Agreement as a discourse phenomenon'. *Folia Linguistica* 33(2), 187–210.

Baron, Naomi (2000). *Alphabet to email: How written English evolved and where it's heading*. London: Routledge.

Barsalou, Lawrence W. (1992). *Cognitive psychology: An overview for cognitive scientists*. Hillsdale, NJ: Erlbaum.

Barss, Andrew (2003). 'Preface'. In: Andrew Barss (ed.), *Anaphora: A reference guide*. Malden, MA: Blackwell, ix–xi.

Bates, Elizabeth A., Laura Benigni, Inge Bretherton, Luigia Camaioni, and Virginia Voltera (1979). 'Cognition and communication from nine to thirteen months: Correlational findings'. In: Elizabeth A. Bates (ed.), *The emergence of symbols: Cognition and communication in infancy*. New York: Academic Press, 69–140.

—— and Brian MacWhinney (eds.) (1989). *The cross-linguistic study of sentence processing*. New York: Cambridge University Press.

—— Antonella Devescovi, and Beverly Wulfeck (2001). 'Psy-cholinguistics: A cross-language perspective'. *Annual Review of Psychology* 51, 369–398.

Bearth, Thomas (2003). 'Syntax'. In: Derek Nurse and Gérard Philippson (eds.), *The Bantu languages*. London: Routledge, 121–142.

Beaver, David I. (2004). 'The optimization of discourse anaphora'. *Linguistics and Philosophy* 27, 3–56.

Beck, David (2002). 'Tsimshianic from a Central Northwest areal perspective'. In: Suzanne Gessner and S.-H. Oh (eds.), *The 37th International Conference on Salish and Neighbouring Languages*. Vancouver: UBC Working Papers in Linguistics, 35–60.

Beeching, Kate (2001). *Un corpus d'entretiens spontanés*. <http://www.uwe.ac.uk/hlss/llas/ces/iclru/corpus.pdf>. Online Database.

Beljaev, Oleg (2009). *Ritoričeskoe rasstojanie v korpuse WSJ Discourse Treebank* [Rhetorical distance in the corpus WSJ Discourse Treebank]. Year paper. Dept. of Theoretical and Applied Linguistics, Moscow State University.

Bellugi, Ursula (1972). 'Studies in sign language'. In: Terrence J. O'Rourke (ed.), *Psycholinguistics and total communication: The State of the Art*. Washington, D.C.: American Annals of the Deaf, 68–83.

Bentivoglio, Paola (1983). 'Topic continuity and discontinuity in discourse: A study of spoken Latin-American Spanish'. In: T. Givón (ed.), *Topic continuity in discourse: A quantitative cross-language study*. Amsterdam: Benjamins, 255–312.

Benveniste, Émile (1958). 'De la subjectivité dans le langage'. *Journal de Psychologie* (Juillet–Septembre).

Berenz, Norine, and Lucinda Ferreira-Brito (1990). 'Pronouns in BCSL and ASL'. In: William H. Edmondson and Fred Karlsson (eds.), *SLR'87: Papers from the 4th International Symposium on Sign Language Research*. International Studies on Sign Language and Communication of the Deaf, Vol. 10. Hamburg: Signum, 26–36.

Bergelson [Bergel'son], Mira B., and Aleksandr E. Kibrik (1981). 'K voprosu ob obščej teorii jazykovoj redukcii' [Towards the general theory of linguistic reduction]. In: Aleksandr S. Narin'jani (ed.), *Formal'noe opisanie struktury estestvennogo jazyka*. Novosibirsk, 147–161.

—— and Andrej A. Kibrik (1987). 'Sistema pereključenija referencii v tuvinskom jazyke' [The system of switch-reference in Tuvan]. *Sovetskaja tjurkologija* 2, 16–32; 4, 30–45.

—— (1988). 'Mestoimennye anaforičeskie sredstva jazyka bamana' [Pronominal anaphoric devices of Bamana]. In: Alexandra Yu. Aikhenvald [Aleksandra Ju.

Ajxenval'd] (ed.), *Tezisy konferencii aspirantov i molodyx sotrudnikov. Jazykoznanie.* Moscow: GRVL Nauka, 13–16.

Bergelson [Bergel'son], Mira B., and Adama Konate (1988). 'Nekotorye sintaksičeskie osobennosti dialekta beledugu v sopostavlenii so standartnym bamana: upotreblenie nulevogo anaforičeskogo elementa' [Some syntactic peculiarities of the Beledugu dialect in comparison to Standard Bamana: The use of the zero anaphoric element]. *Jazyk v Afrike: lingvističeskie problemy sovremennoj afrikanistiki.* Vol. 1. Moscow, 94–103.

—— and Andrej A. Kibrik (1995). 'The system of switch-reference in Tuvan: Converbal and masdar-case forms'. In: Martin Haspelmath and Ekkehard König (eds.), *Converbs in cross-linguistic perspective: Structure and meaning of adverbial verb forms (adverbial participles, gerunds).* Berlin: Mouton de Gruyter, 373–414.

—— (2007). *Pragmatičeskaja i sociokul'turnaja motiviro-vannost' jazykovoj formy* [Pragmatic and sociocultural motivation of linguistic form]. Moscow: Universitetskaja kniga.

Bhat, Darbhe Narayana Shankara (2004). *Pronouns.* Oxford: Oxford University Press.

—— (2005). 'Third-person pronouns and demonstratives'. In: Martin Haspelmath, Matthew Dryer, David Gil, and Bernard Comrie (eds.), *World atlas of language structures.* Oxford: Oxford University Press, 178–181.

Biber, Douglas (1989). 'A typology of English texts'. *Linguistics* 27, 3–43.

—— (1992). 'Using computer-based text corpora to analyze the referential strategies of spoken and written texts'. In: Jan Svartvik (ed.), *Directions in corpus linguistics: Proceedings of Nobel symposium 82.* Berlin: Mouton, 213–252.

—— Stig Johansson, Geoffrey Leech, Susan Conrad, and Edward Finegan (1999). *Longman grammar of spoken and written English.* Harlow: Pearson Education limited.

—— Susan Conrad, and Randi Reppen (2004). *Corpus linguistics: Investigating language structure and use.* Cambridge: Cambridge University Press.

—— (2006). *Dimensions of register variation: A cross-linguistic comparison.* Cambridge: Cambridge University Press.

—— Ulla Connor, and Thomas A. Upton (2007). *Discourse on the move: Using corpus analysis to describe discourse structure.* Amsterdam: Benjamins.

Bickel, Balthasar (2003). 'Referential density in discourse and syntactic typology'. *Language* 79, 708–736.

—— and Johanna Nichols (2005). 'Inflectional synthesis of the verb'. In: Martin Haspelmath, Matthew Dryer, David Gil, and Bernard Comrie (eds.), *World atlas of language structures.* Oxford: Oxford University Press, 94–97.

—— and —— (2007). 'Inflectional morphology'. In: Timothy Shopen (ed.), *Language typology and syntactic description.* Vol. 3. Grammatical categories and the lexicon. Cambridge: Cambridge University Press, 169–240.

Bílý, Milan (1981). *Intrasentential pronominalization and functional sentence perspective.* Lund: Lund University.

Bloomfield, Leonard (1946). 'Algonquian'. In: Harry Hoijer (ed.), *Linguistic structures of native America.* New York: Viking Fund, 85–129.

Boas, Franz (1911). *Handbook of American Indian Languages*. Washington, D.C.: Smithsonian Institution.

Boguslavskaya, Olga Yu. [Ol'ga Ju. Boguslavskaja], and Irina A. Muravyeva [Murav'eva] (1987). 'Mexanizmy anaforičeskoj nominacii' [Mechanisms of anaphoric nomination]. In: Aleksandr E. Kibrik and Aleksandr S. Narin'jani (eds.), *Modelirovanie jazykovoj dejatel'nosti v intellektual'nyx sistemax*. Moscow: Nauka, 78–128.

Bonhoff, Lee E. (1986). 'Yad Dii (Duru) pronouns'. In: Ursula Wiesemann (ed.), *Pronominal systems*. Tübingen: Narr, 103–130.

Bopp, Franz (1833). *Vergleichende Grammatik des Sanskrit, Zend, Griechischen, Lateinischen, Litthauischen, Gothischen und Deutschen*. Berlin: Ferd. Dümmler's Verlagsbuchhandlung (Harrwitz & Gossmann).

Borkovskij, Viktor I., and Petr S. Kuznecov (1979). *Istoričeskaja grammatika russkogo jazyka. Syntaksis. Prostoe predloženie* [A historical grammar of Russian. Syntax. Simple sentence]. Moscow: Nauka.

Boroditsky, Lera (2003). 'Linguistic Relativity'. In: Lynn Nadel (ed.), *Encyclopedia of cognitive science*. London: Macmillan Press, 917–921.

Borthen, Kaja (2010). 'On how we interpret plural pronouns'. *Journal of Pragmatics* 42, 1799–1815.

Bosch, Peter (1983). *Agreement and anaphora: A study of the role of pronouns in syntax and discourse*. London: Academic Press.

—— and Carla Umbach (2006). 'Reference determination for demonstrative pronouns'. Paper presented at the Conference on Intersentential Pronominal Reference in Child and Adult Language. Berlin, 1–2 December 2006.

Bossong, Georg (2003). 'Nominal and/or verbal marking of central actants'. In: Giuliana Fiorentino (ed.), *Romance objects: Transitivity in Romance languages*. Berlin: Mouton de Gruyter, 17–48.

Botley, Simon, and Tony McEnery (eds.) (1999). *Corpus-based and computational approaches to discourse anaphora*. Amsterdam: Benjamins.

Branco, António, Tony McEnery, and Ruslan Mitkov (eds.) (2005). *Anaphora processing: Linguistic, cognitive, and computational modeling*. Amsterdam: Benjamins.

Brennan, Susan E., Marilyn W. Friedman, and Carl J. Pollard (1987). 'A centering approach to pronouns'. In: *Proceedings of the 25th Annual Meeting of the Association for Computational Linguistics (ACL 1987)*. Stanford, 155–162.

Bresnan, Joan, and Sam Mchombo (1987). 'Topic, pronoun, and agreement in Chicheŵa'. *Language* 63(4), 741–782.

—— (2001a). *Lexical-functional syntax*. Oxford: Blackwell.

—— (2001b). 'The emergence of the unmarked pronoun'. In: Géraldine Legendre, Jane Grimshaw, and Sven Vikner (eds.), *Optimality-theoretic syntax*. Cambridge, MA: MIT Press, 113–142.

Broadbent, Donald (1958). *Perception and communication*. New York: Pergamon Press.

Brodskaja, Larisa M. (1988). *Složnopodčinennoe predloženie v evenkijskom jazyke* [The complex subordinate sentence in Evenki]. Novosibirsk: Nauka.

Brown, Gillian, and George Yule (1983). *Discourse analysis*. Cambridge: Cambridge University Press.

Brown, Lea (2003). *Nias: An exception to universals of argument-marking*. Paper presented at the 5th Conference of the Association for Linguistic Typology, Cagliari, Sardinia, September 2003.

Brown, Penelope, and Stephen C. Levinson (1987). *Politeness: Some universals in language usage*. Cambridge: Cambridge University Press.

Brugmann, Karl (1904). 'Die Demonstrativpronomina der indogermanischen Sprachen'. *Abhandlungen der philologisch-historischen Klasse der sächsischen Gesellschaft der Wissenschaften* 22(6).

—— and Berthold Delbrück (1916). *Grundriss der vergleichenden Grammatik der indogermanischen Sprachen*. Vol II. 3–2. Strassburg: Karl J. Trübner.

Bühler, Karl (1934). *Sprachtheorie. Die Darstellungsfunktion der Sprache*. Stuttgart: Gustav Fischer Verlag.

Bulygina, Tat'jana V. (1992). 'Obšċie voprosy dejksisa: vvodnye zamečanija' [General issues in deixis: Introductory remarks]. In: Tat'jana V. Bulygina (ed.), *Čelovečeskij faktor v jazyke. Kommunikacija, modal'nost', dejksis*. Moscow: Nauka, 154–158.

—— and Aleksey D. Shmelev [Aleksej D. Šmelev] (1992). 'Personal'nyj dejksis. Obšċie zamečanija'. [Personal deixis: General remarks]. In: Tat'jana V. Bulygina (ed.), *Čelovečeskij faktor v jazyke. Kommunikacija, modal'nost', dejksis*. Moscow: Nauka, 194–207.

Burquest, Donald (1986). 'The pronoun system of some Chadic languages'. In: Ursula Wiesemann (ed.), *Pronominal systems*. Tübingen: Narr, 71–101.

Burzio, Luigi (1996). 'The role of the antecedent in anaphoric relations'. In: Robert Freidin (ed.), *Current issues in comparative grammar*. Dordrecht: Kluwer, 1–45.

Butcher, Cynthia, and Susan Goldin-Meadow (2000). 'Gesture and the transition from one- to two-word speech: When hand and mouth come together'. In: David McNeill (ed.), *Language and gesture*. Cambridge: Cambridge University Press, 235–257.

Butovskaja, Marina L. (2004). *Neverbal'naja kommunikacija* [Nonverbal communication]. Moscow: Naučnyj mir.

Butt, John, and Carmen Benjamin (2000). *A new reference grammar of modern Spanish*. 3rd edn. London: Arnold.

Butterworth, George (2003). 'Pointing is the royal road to language for babies'. In: Sotaro Kita (ed.), *Pointing: Where language, culture, and cognition meet*. Hillsdale, NJ: Erlbaum, 9–34.

Bybee, Joan, Revere Perkins, and William Pagliuca (1994). *The evolution of grammar: Tense, aspect, and modality in the languages of the world*. Chicago: University of Chicago Press.

Byron, Donna K. (2002). *Resolving pronominal reference to abstract entitis*. Ph.D. thesis. University of Rochester.

Byron, Donna K., Sarah Brown-Schmidt, and Michael K. Tanenhaus (2008). The overlapping distribution of personal and demonstrative pronouns. In: Jeanette K. Gundel and Nancy Hedberg (eds.), *Reference: Interdisciplinary perspectives*. Oxford: Oxford University Press, 143–75.

Caitucoli, Claude (1986). *Douze contes masa*. Berlin: von Dietrich Reimer.

Call, Josep, and Michael Tomasello (1994). 'Production and comprehension of referential pointing by orangutans (Pongo pygmaeus)'. *Journal of Comparative Psychology* 108(4), 307–317.

Campbell, John (2002). *Reference and consciousness*. Oxford: Oxford University Press.

Cardinaletti, Anna, and Michal Starke (1999). 'The typology of structural deficiency: A case study of the three classes of pronouns'. In: Henk van Riemsdijk (ed.), *Clitics in the languages of Europe*. Berlin: Mouton de Gruyter, 145–233.

Carlson, Lynn, Daniel Marcu, and Mary Ellen Okurowski (2003). 'Building a discourse-tagged corpus in the framework of rhetorical structure theory'. In: Jan van Kuppevelt and Ronnie Smith (eds.), *Current directions in discourse and dialogue*. Dordrecht: Kluwer, 85–112.

Carlson, Robert (1987). 'Narrative connectives in Sùpyíré'. In: Russell S. Tomlin (ed.), *Coherence and grounding in discourse*. Amsterdam: Benjamins, 1–19.

—— (1994). *A grammar of Sùpyíré*. Berlin: Mouton de Gruyter.

Carr, Thomas H. (2004). 'A multilevel approach to selective attention: Monitoring environmental space, choosing stimuli for deep processing, and retrieving information from memory'. In: Michael I. Posner (ed.), *Cognitive neuroscience of attention*. New York: The Guilford Press, 56–70.

Cassell, Justine, David McNeill, and Karl-Erik McCullough (1998). 'Speech-gesture mismatches: evidence for one underlying representation of linguistic and non-linguistic information'. *Pragmatics and Cognition* 6(2), 1–34.

—— Stefan Kopp, Paul Tepper, Kim Ferriman, and Kristina Striegnitz (2007). 'Trading spaces: How humans and humanoids use speech and gesture to give directions'. In: Toyoaki Nishida (ed.), *Conversational informatics*. New York: Wiley, 133–160.

Cavanagh, Patrick (2004). 'Attention routines and the architecture of selection'. In: Michael I. Posner (ed.), *Cognitive neuroscience of attention*. New York: The Guilford Press, 13–28.

Čeremisina, Majja I. (1977). 'Deepričastija kak klass form glagola v jazykax raznyx sistem' [Converbs as a class of verb forms in diverse languages]. In: Majja I. Čeremisina (ed.), *Složnoe predloženie v jazykax raznyx sistem*. Novosibirsk: Nauka, 3–28.

—— (1978). 'Monosub"ektnaja konstrukcija: ponjatie i typologija' [Same-subject construction: The concept and a typology]. In: Majja I. Čeremisina (ed.), *Polipredikativnye konstrukcii i ix morfologičeskaja baza*. Novosibirsk: Nauka, 6–33.

Chafe, Wallace (1974). 'Language and consciousness'. *Language* 50, 111–133.

—— (1976). 'Givenness, contrastiveness, definiteness, subjects, topics, and point of view'. In: Charles N. Li (ed.), *Subject and topic*. New York: Academic Press, 25–55.

Chafe, Wallace (1980). 'The deployment of consciousness in the production of a narrative'. In: Wallace Chafe (ed.), *The pear stories: Cognitive, cultural, and linguistic aspects of narrative production*. Norwood: Ablex, 9–50.

—— (ed.) (1980). *The pear stories: Cognitive, cultural, and linguistic aspects of narrative production*. Norwood: Ablex.

—— (1982). 'Integration and involvement in speaking, writing, and oral literature'. In: Deborah Tannen (ed.), *Spoken and written language: Exploring orality and literacy*. Norwood: Ablex, 35–54.

—— (1987). 'Cognitive constraints on information flow'. In: Russell S. Tomlin (ed.), *Linguistic reflections of cognitive events*. Amsterdam: Benjamins, 21–52.

—— (1990a). 'Introduction to a special issue on third-person reference in discourse'. *International Journal of American Linguistics* 56(3), 313–316.

—— (1990b). 'Uses of the defocusing pronominal prefixes in Caddo'. *Anthropological Linguistics* 32(1–2), 57–68.

—— (1994). *Discourse, consciousness, and time: The flow and displacement of conscious experience in speaking and writing*. Chicago: University of Chicago Press.

—— (1996). 'Sketch of Seneca, and Iroquoian language'. In: Ives Goddard (ed.), *Handbook of North American Indians*. Vol. 17. Languages. Washington, D.C.: Smithsonian Institution, 551–579.

—— (2001). 'The analysis of discourse flow'. In: Deborah Schiffrin, Deborah Tannen, and Heidi E. Hamilton (eds.), *Handbook of discourse analysis*. Malden, MA: Blackwell, 673–687.

—— [Uolles Čejf] (2008). 'Rol' introspekcii, nabljudenija i ėksperimentirovanija v ponimanii myšlenija' [The roles of introspection, observation, and experimentation in understanding the mind]. In: Boris M. Velichkovsky [Veličkovskij] and Valery D. Solovyev [Valerij D. Solov'ev] (eds.), *Komp'jutery, mozg, poznanie: uspexi kognitivnyx nauk*. Moscow: Nauka, 163–179.

Chaika, Elaine, and Richard A. Lambe (1989). 'Cohesion in schizophrenic narratives, revisited'. *Journal of Communication Disorders* 22(6), 407–421.

Chambers, Craig G., and Ron Smyth (1998). 'Structural parallelism and discourse coherence: A test of Centering Theory'. *Journal of Memory and Language* 39, 593–608.

Chandrasena Premawardhena, Neelakshi (2002). 'Reference devices in Sinhala'. In: Horst J. Simon and Heike Wiese (eds.), *Pronouns – grammar and representation*. Amsterdam: Benjamins, 63–84.

Chiarcos, Christian, and Olga N. Krasavina (2008). 'Rhetorical distance revisited: A parameterized approach'. In: Anton Benz and Peter Kühnlein (eds.), *Constraints in discourse*. Amsterdam: Benjamins, 97–115.

Christophersen, Paul (1939). *The articles: A study of their theory and use in English*. Copenhagen: Munksgaard.

Chu, Chauncey C. (1998). *A discourse grammar of Mandarin Chinese*. New York: Peter Lang.

Clancy, Patricia M. (1980). 'Referential choice in English and Japanese narrative discourse'. In: Wallace Chafe (ed.), *The pear stories: Cognitive, cultural, and linguistic aspects of narrative production*. Norwood: Ablex, 127–202.

—— (1982). 'Written and spoken style in Japanese narrative discourse'. In: Deborah Tannen (ed.), *Spoken and written language: Exploring orality and literacy*. Norwood: Ablex, 55–76.

—— and Pamela Downing (1987). 'The use of Wa as a cohesion marker in Japanese oral narratives'. In: John Hinds, Senko K. Maynard, and Shoichi Iwasaki (eds.), *Perspectives on topicalization: The case of Japanese 'wa'*. Amsterdam: Benjamins, 3–56.

Clark, Brenda-Joyce (2002). *Noun classifiers*. Ph.D. thesis. UCLA.

Clark, Herbert H. (1977). 'Bridging'. In: Philip N. Johnson-Laird and Peter C. Wason (eds.), *Thinking. Readings in cognitive science*. Cambridge: Cambridge University Press, 411–420.

—— and C. Sengul (1979). 'In search of referents for nouns and pronouns'. *Memory and Cognition* 7, 35–41.

—— Robert Schreuder, and Samuel Buttrick (1983). 'Common ground and the understanding of demonstrative reference'. *Journal of Verbal Learning and Verbal Behavior* 22(2), 245–258.

—— and Deanna Wilkes-Gibbs (1986). 'Referring as a collaborative process'. *Cognition* 22(1), 1–39.

—— and Susan E. Brennan (1991). 'Grounding in communication'. In: Lauren B. Resnick, John M. Levine, and Stephanie D. Teasley (eds.), *Perspectives on socially shared cognition*. Washington, D.C.: APA Books, 127–149.

—— and Adrian Bangerter (2004). 'Changing ideas about reference'. In: Ira A. Noveck and Dan Sperber (eds.), *Experimental Pragmatics*. New York: Palgrave Macmillan, 25–49.

Clements, George N. (1975). 'The logophoric pronoun in Ewe'. *Journal of West African Languages* 10, 142–177.

Cloitre, Marylene, and Thomas G. Bever (1988). 'Linguistic anaphors, levels of representation and discourse'. *Language and Cognitive Processes* 3, 293–322.

Cohen, Jonathan D., Gary Aston-Jones, and Mark S. Gilzenrat (2004). 'A system-level perspective on attention and cognitive control: Guided attention, adaptive gating, conflict monitoring, and exploitation versus exploration'. In: Michael I. Posner (ed.), *Cognitive neuroscience of attention*. New York: The Guilford Press, 71–90.

Cole, Peter (1983). 'Switch-reference in two Quechuan languages'. In: John Haiman and Pamela Munro (eds.), *Switch-reference and universal grammar*. Amsterdam: Benjamins, 1–16.

Collinson, William E. (1937). *Indication. A study of demonstatives, articles, and other 'indicaters'*. Language monographs. Baltimore: Waverly Press.

Comajoan, Llorenç (2006). 'Continuity and episodic structure in Spanish subject reference'. In: J. Clancy Clements and Jiyoung Yoon (eds.), *Functional approaches to Spanish syntax: Lexical semantics, discourse, and transitivity.* Houndmills: Palgrave Macmillan, 53–79.

Company, Concepción Company (2003). 'Transitivity and grammaticalization of object'. In: Giuliana Fiorentino (ed.), *Romance objects: Transitivity in Romance languages.* Berlin: Mouton de Gruyter, 217–260.

Comrie, Bernard (1983). 'Switch-reference in Huichol: A typological study'. In: John Haiman and Pamela Munro (eds.), *Switch-reference and universal grammar.* Amsterdam: Benjamins, 17–38.

—— (1989a). *Language universals and linguistic typology.* 2nd edn. Oxford: Blackwell.

—— (1989b). 'Some general properties of reference-tracking systems'. In: Doug Arnold, Martin Atkinson, Jacques Durand, Claire Grover, and Louisa Sadler (eds.), *Essays on grammatical theory and universal grammar.* Oxford: Clarendon Press, 37–51.

—— (1994). 'Coreference: Between grammar and discourse'. In: *Proceedings of the 18th Annual Meeting of the Kansai Linguistic Society.* Osaka, 1–10.

—— (1998). 'Switch-reference in Haruai: Grammar and discourse'. In: Mark Janse (ed.), *Productivity and creativity: Studies in general and descriptive linguistics in honor of E. M. Uhlenbeck.* Berlin: Mouton de Gruyter, 421–432.

—— (1999). 'Reference-tracking: Description and explanation'. *Sprachtypologie und Universalienforschung* 52(3/4), 335–346.

—— (2005). 'Alignment of case marking'. In: Martin Haspelmath, Matthew Dryer, David Gil, and Bernard Comrie (eds.), *World atlas of language structures.* Oxford: Oxford University Press, 398–405.

Conklin, Harold C. (1962). 'Lexicographical treatment of folk taxonomies'. In: Fred W. Householder and Sol Saporta (eds.), *Problems in lexicography.* Bloomington: Indiana University Press, 119–142.

Conte, Maria-Elisabeth (1996). 'Anaphoric encapsulation'. In: Walter de Mulder and Liliane Tasmowski (eds.), *Coherence and anaphora.* Amsterdam: Benjamins, 1–10.

Cook, Eung-Do (2004). *A grammar of Dëne Sųłiné (Chipewyan).* Winnipeg: University of Manitoba.

Cooke, Joseph R. (1968). *Pronominal reference in Thai, Burmese, and Vietnamese.* Berkeley, CA: University of California Press.

Corbett, Greville G. (1991). *Gender.* Cambridge: Cambridge University Press.

—— (2005a). 'Number of genders'. In: Martin Haspelmath, Matthew Dryer, David Gil, and Bernard Comrie (eds.), *World atlas of language structures.* Oxford: Oxford University Press, 126–129.

—— (2005b). 'Sex-based and non-sex-based gender systems'. In: Martin Haspelmath, Matthew Dryer, David Gil, and Bernard Comrie (eds.), *World atlas of language structures.* Oxford: Oxford University Press, 130–133.

—— (2006). *Agreement.* Cambridge: Cambridge University Press.

Cornish, Francis (1999). *Anaphora, discourse, and understanding: Evidence from English and French.* Oxford: Oxford University Press.

Cornish, Francis (ed.) (2005). *Prosody, discourse deixis and anaphora.* International Symposium on Discourse and Prosody as a Complex Interface, Aix-en-Provence: Université de Provence.
—— (2006). 'Discourse anaphora'. In: Keith Brown (ed.), *Encyclopedia of language and linguistics.* Oxford: Elsevier, 631–638.
—— (2007). 'Indirect pronominal anaphora in English and French: Marginal rarity or unmarked norm? Some psycholinguistic evidence'. In: Monika Schwartz-Friesel, Manfred Consten, and Mareile Knees (eds.), *Anaphors in text: Cognitive, formal and applied approaches to anaphoric reference.* Amsterdam: Benjamins, 21–36.
Corston-Oliver, Simon H. (2003). 'Core arguments and the inversion of the nominal hierarchy in Roviana'. In: John W. Du Bois, Lorraine E. Kumpf, and William J. Ashby (eds.), *Preferred argument structure: Grammar as architecture for function.* Amsterdam: Benjamins, 273–301.
Cowan, Nelson (1988). 'Evolving conceptions of memory storage, selective attention, and their mutual constraints within the human information-processing system'. *Psychological Bulletin* 104(2), 163–191.
—— (1995). *Attention and memory: An integrated framework.* New York: Oxford University Press.
—— (1999). 'An embedded-processes model of working memory'. In: Akira Miyake and Priti Shah (eds.), *Models of working memory: Mechanisms of active maintenance and executive control.* New York: Cambridge University Press, 62–101.
—— (2001). 'The magical number 4 in short-term memory: A reconsideration of mental storage capacity'. *Behavioral and Brain Sciences* 24, 87–185.
—— (2005). *Working memory capacity.* Hove, East Sussex: Psychology Press.
—— (2008). 'What are the differences between long-term, short-term, and working memory?' *Progress in Brain Research* 169, 323–338.
—— and Angela M. AuBuchon (2008). 'Short-term memory loss over time without retroactive stimulus interference'. *Psychonomic Bulletin and Review* 15(1), 230–235.
—— Candice C. Morey, Zhijian Chen, Amanda L. Gilchrist, and Scott Saults (2008). 'Theory and measurement of working memory capacity limits'. *The Psychology of Learning and Motivation* 49, 49–104.
Craig, Colette, and Kenneth Hale (1988). 'Relational preverbs in some languages of the Americas: Typological and historical perspectives'. *Language* 64(2), 312–344.
Creissels, Denis (1991). *Description des langues négro-africaines et théorie syntaxique.* Grenoble: ELLUG.
—— (2000). 'Typology'. In: Bernd Heine and Derek Nurse (eds.), *African languages: An introduction.* Cambridge: Cambridge University Press, 231–258.
—— (2005). 'A typology of subject marker and object marker systems in African languages'. In: Erhard Friedrich Karl Voeltz (ed.), *Studies in African linguistic typology.* Amsterdam: Benjamins, 445–459.
Cresti, Manuela, and Massimo Moneglia (eds.) (2005). *C-ORAL-ROM: Integrated spoken corpora for spoken Romance languages.* Amsterdam: Benjamins.

Crétois, R. P. L. (1973). *Dictionnaire sereer-français*. Vol. 1. Dakar: Centre de linguistique appliquée de Dakar.
Cristea, Dan, Nancy Ide, and Laurent Romary (1998). 'Veins theory: A model of global discourse cohesion and coherence'. In: *Proceedings of the 36th Annual Meeting of the Association for Computational Linguistics and the 17th International Conference on Computational Linguistics (COLING/ACL 1998)*. Montreal, Canada, 281–285.
Croft, William (2001). *Radical construction grammar: Syntactic theory in typological perspective*. Oxford: Oxford University Press.
—— and D. Alan Cruse (2004). *Cognitive linguistics*. Cambridge: Cambridge University Press.
Crowley, Terry (2002). 'Gela'. In: John Lynch, Malcolm Ross, and Terry Crowley (eds.), *The Oceanic languages*. Richmond: Curzon Press, 525–537.
Cruttenden, Alan (1986). *Intonation*. Cambridge: Cambridge University Press.
Cutica, Ilaria, and Monica Bucciarelli (2006). 'Why gestures matter in learning from a discourse'. In: Boris M. Velichkovsky [Veličkovskij], Tatyana V. Chernigovskaya [Tat'jana V. Černigovskaja], Yuri [Jurij] I. Aleksandrov, and Denis N. Akhapkin [Axapkin] (eds.), *The Second Biennial Conference on Cognitive Science*. Vol. 1. Saint-Petersburg: Saint-Petersburg State University, Philological Faculty, 40–41.
Cutler, Anne (ed.) (2005). *Twenty-first century psycholinguistics: Four cornerstones*. London: Routledge.
Cysouw, Michael (2003). *The paradigmatic structure of person marking*. Oxford: Oxford University Press.
Cyxun, Gennadij A. (1968). *Sintaksis mestoimennyx klitik v južnoslavjanskix jazykax* [Syntax of pronominal clitics in South Slavic]. Minsk: Nauka i texnika.
Dahl, Östen (1973). 'On so-called "sloppy identity"'. *Synthese* 26, 81–112.
—— and Kari Fraurud (1996). 'Animacy in grammar and discourse'. In: Thorsten Fretheim and Jeanette K. Gundel (eds.), *Reference and referent accessibility*. Amsterdam: Benjamins, 47–64.
—— (2000). 'Egophoricity in discourse and syntax'. *Functions of Language* 7(1), 37–77.
—— and Maria Koptjevskaja-Tamm (eds.) (2001). *Circum-Baltic languages*. Vols. 1, 2. Amsterdam: Benjamins.
—— (2004). *The growth and maintenance of linguistic complexity*. Amsterdam: Benjamins.
Dale, Robert (1992). *Generating referring expressions*. Cambridge, MA: MIT Press.
—— and Ehud Reiter (1995). 'Computational interpretations of the Gricean maxims in the generation of referring expressions'. *Cognitive Science* 18, 233–263.
—— (2006). 'Generating referring expressions'. In: Keith Brown (ed.), *Encyclopedia of language and linguistics*. Oxford: Elsevier, 761–766.
Daley, Karen Ann (1998). *Vietnamese classifiers in narrative texts*. Arlington: University of Texas.
Daneman, Meredyth, and Patricia A. Carpenter (1980). 'Individual differences in working memory and reading'. *Journal of Verbal Learning and Verbal Behavior* 19, 450–466.

Davis, G. Albyn, and Carl A. Coelho (2004). 'Referential cohesion and logical coherence of narration after closed head injury'. *Brain and Language* 89, 508–523.

de Fockert, Jan W., Geraint Rees, Christopher D. Frith, and Nilli Lavie (2001). 'The role of working memory in visual selective attention'. *Science* 291(March 2), 1803–1806.

de Mulder, Walter (1992). 'Demonstratives and the localist hypothesis'. In: Michel Kefer and Johan van der Auwera (eds.), *Meaning and grammar: Cross-linguistic perspectives*. Berlin: Mouton de Gruyter, 265–278.

—— and Liliane Tasmowski (eds.) (1996). *Coherence and Anaphora*. Amsterdam: Benjamins.

Deco, Gustavo, and Edmund T. Rolls (2003). 'Attention and working memory: A dynamical model of neuronal activity in the prefrontal cortex'. *European Journal of Neuroscience* 18, 2374–2390.

Dell, Gary S., Gail McKoon, and Roger Ratcliff (1983). 'The activation of antecedent information during the processing of anaphoric reference in reading'. *Journal of Verbal Learning and Verbal Behavior* 22(1), 121–132.

Deloria, Ella (1931). *Dakota texts*. Publications of the American Ethnological Society. New York: G. E. Strechert and Co.

Derwing, Bruce L. (1994). 'Experimental linguistics'. In: Ronald E. Asher (ed.), *Encyclopedia of language and linguistics*. Vol. 3. Oxford: Pergamon Press, 1193–1195.

Dickinson, Connie, and T. Givón (1997). 'Memory and conversation: Toward an experimental paradigm'. In: T. Givón (ed.), *Conversation: Cognitive, communicative, and social perspectives*. Amsterdam: Benjamins, 91–132.

—— (2009). 'Reference tracking and evidential/mirative constructions in Tsafiki'. Paper presented at the Conference of the Society for the Study of the Indigenous Languages of the Americas, Berkeley, CA, July 2009.

Diessel, Holger (1999). *Demonstratives: Form, function, and grammaticalization*. Amsterdam: Benjamins.

—— (2005a). 'Distance contrasts in demonstratives'. In: Martin Haspelmath, Matthew Dryer, David Gil, and Bernard Comrie (eds.), *World atlas of language structures*. Oxford: Oxford University Press, 170–173.

—— (2005b). 'Pronominal and adnominal demonstratives'. In: Martin Haspelmath, Matthew Dryer, David Gil, and Bernard Comrie (eds.), *World atlas of language structures*. Oxford: Oxford University Press, 174–177.

—— and Michael Tomasello (2005). 'Particle placement in early child language: A multifactorial analysis'. *Corpus linguistics and Linguistic Theory* 1(1), 89–111.

—— (2006). 'Demonstratives, joint attention, and the evolution of grammar'. *Cognitive Linguistics* 17(4), 443–462.

Dimmendaal, Gerrit J. (2001). 'Logophoric marking and represented speech in African languages as evidential hedging strategies'. *Australian Journal of Linguistics* 21(1), 131–157.

Đình-Hoà, Nguyễn (1997). *Vietnamese*. Amsterdam: Benjamins.

Diop-Fal, Arame (n.d.). *Les nominaux en Sereer-Siin: Parler de Jaxaaw*. Paris: Université de la Sorbonne.

Dixon, R. M. W. (1977). *A grammar of Yidiny*. Cambridge: Cambridge University Press.

—— (1982). 'Noun classes'. In: R. M. V. Dixon (ed.), *Where have all the adjectives gone? And other essays on semantics and syntax*. Berlin: Mouton, 159–184.

Dobrovolsky [Dobrovol'skij], Dmitrij O., and Elena V. Paducheva [Padučeva] (2008). 'Dejksis v otsutstvie govorjaščego: o semantike nemeckix dejktičeskix elementov *hin* i *her*' [Deixis in the absence of a speaker: On the semantics of German deictic elements *hin* and *her*]. In: Aleksandr E. Kibrik (ed.), *Computational Linguistics and Intellectual Technologies. Papers from the Annual International Conference 'Dialogue' (2008). Bekasovo, Moscow region*. Moscow: Izdatel'stvo RGGU, 140–146.

Dolinin, Konstantin A. (2004). 'Socialističeskij realizm v lingvistike (k istorii funkcional'noj stilistiki v SSSR)' [Socialist realism in linguistics: Towards a history of functional stylistics in the USSR]. In: Ljudmila A. Verbickaja (ed.), *Teoretičeskie problemy jazykoznanija*. Saint-Petersburg: Filfak SPbGU, 607–620.

Donnellan, Keith S. (1966). 'Reference and definite descriptions'. *Philosophical Review* 75, 281–304.

Donohue, Mark (1999a). *Warembori*. München: LINCOM Europa.

—— (1999b). 'A most agreeable language'. Paper presented at the Meeting of the Australian Linguistics Society, Perth, 30 September 1999.

—— (2004). *Skou grammar*. Unpublished.

Dooley, Robert A., and Stephen H. Levinsohn (2001). *Analyzing discourse: A manual of basic concepts*. Dallas, TX: SIL International.

Downing, Pamela (1986). 'The anaphoric use of classifiers in Japanese'. In: Colette Grinevald Craig (ed.), *Noun classes and categorization*. Amsterdam: Benjamins, 345–375.

—— (1996a). *Numeral classifier systems: The case of Japanese*. Amsterdam: Benjamins.

—— (1996b). 'Proper names as a referential option in English conversation'. In: Barbara A. Fox (ed.), *Studies in anaphora*. Amsterdam: Benjamins, 95–143.

Dryer, Matthew S. (1992a). 'A comparison of the obviation systems of Kutenai and Algonquian'. In: William Cowan (ed.), *Papers of the 23rd Algonquian Conference*. Ottawa: Carleton University, 119–163.

—— (1992b). 'The Greenbergian word order correlations'. *Language* 68, 81–138.

—— (2005a). 'Expression of pronominal subjects'. In: Martin Haspelmath, Matthew Dryer, David Gil, and Bernard Comrie (eds.), *World atlas of language structures*. Oxford: Oxford University Press, 410–413.

—— (2005b). 'Position of pronominal possessive affixes'. In: Martin Haspelmath, Matthew Dryer, David Gil, and Bernard Comrie (eds.), *World atlas of language structures*. Oxford: Oxford University Press, 234–237.

—— (2005c). 'Position of tense-aspect affixes'. In: Martin Haspelmath, Matthew Dryer, David Gil, and Bernard Comrie (eds.), *World atlas of language structures*. Oxford: Oxford University Press, 282–285.

Du Bois, John W. (1987). 'The discourse basis of ergativity'. *Language* 63, 805–855.
—— Susanna Cumming, Stephan Schuetze-Coburn, and Danae Paolino (1992). *Discourse transcription*. Santa Barbara Papers in Linguistics, Vol. 4. Santa Barbara: UCSB.
—— Wallace L. Chafe, Charles Meyer, and Sandra A. Thompson (2000). *Santa Barbara corpus of spoken American English*. Part 1. Philadelphia: Linguistic Data Consortium.
—— (2003). 'Argument structure: Grammar in use'. In: John W. Du Bois, Lorraine E. Kumpf, and William J. Ashby (eds.), *Preferred argument structure: Grammar as architecture for function*. Amsterdam: Benjamins, 11–60.
—— Lorraine E. Kumpf, and William J. Ashby (eds.) (2003). *Preferred argument structure: Grammar as architecture for function*. Amsterdam: Benjamins.
Duchan, Judith Felson, Gail A. Bruder, and Lynne E. Hewitt (eds.) (1995). *Deixis in narrative: A cognitive science perspective*. Hillsdale, NJ: Erlbaum.
Dulichenko [Duličenko], Aleksandr D. (2005). 'Kašubskij jazyk' [Kashubian]. In: Aleksandr M. Moldovan, Sergej S. Skorvid, Andrej A. Kibrik, Natal'ja V. Rogova, Ekaterina I. Jakuškina, Aleksej F. Žuravlev, and Svetlana M. Tolstaja (eds.), *Jazyki mira: slavjanskie jazyki*. Moscow: Academia, 383–403.
Duponceau, Peter Steven (1819). Report of the corresponding secretary to the Committee, of his progress in the investigation committed to him of the general character and forms of the languages of the American Indians. Read 12 January, 1819. *Transactions of the Historical and Literary Committee* 1.
Duranti, Alessandro, and Elinor Ochs (1979). 'Left-dislocation in Italian conversation'. In: T. Givón (ed.), *Discourse and syntax*. New York: Academic Press, 377–418.
Durie, Mark (1997). 'Grammatical structures in verb serialization'. In: Alex Alsina, Joan Bresnan, and Peter Sells (eds.), *Complex predicates*. Stanford: CSLI, 289–354.
Dutta Baruah, P. N., and V. L. T. Bapui (1996). *Hmar grammar*. Manasagangotri: Central Institute of Indian Languages.
Efimova, Valerija S. (2004). 'Mestoimenie pervogo lica v staroslavjanskom jazyke – svidetel'stva evangel'skix tekstov' [First person pronouns in Old Church Slavonic – evidence from the texts of Gospels]. In: Tatyana [Tat'jana] M. Nikolaeva (ed.), *Verbal'naja i neverbal'naja opory prostranstva mežfrazovyx svjazej*. Moscow: Jazyki slavjanskoj kul'tury, 179–188.
Efimova, Zoya [Zoja] V. (2006). *Referencial'naja struktura narrativa v japonskom jazyke (v sopostavlenii s russkim)* [Referential structure of narrative in Japanese, as compared to Russian]. Ph.D. thesis. Institute of Linguistics, Russian State University for the Humanities.
Efremov, Nikolaj N. (1980). 'O parnosti monosub"ektnyx i raznosub"ektnyx jakutskix temporal'nyx polipredikativnyx konstrukcij' [On the pairedness of same-subject and different-subject temporal multi-clausal constructions in Yakut]. In: Majja I. Čeremisina (ed.), *Infinitnye formy glagola*. Novosibirsk: Institut istorii, filosofii i filologii, SO AN SSSR, 59–74.

Ehlich, Konrad (1982). 'Anaphora and deixis: Same, similar, or different?' In: Robert J. Jarvella and Wolfgang Klein (eds.), *Speech, place and action: Studies in deixis and related topics*. Chichester: Wiley, 315–338.

Ehrlich, Kate (1983). 'Eye movements in pronoun assignment'. In: Keith Rayner (ed.), *Eye movements in reading: Perceptual and language processes*. New York: Academic Press, 253–268.

Ellis, Rob, and Glyn W. Humphreys (1999). *Connectionist Psychology*. East Sussex: Psychology Press.

Elman, Jeffrey L., Elizabeth A. Bates, Mark H. Johnson, Annette Karmiloff-Smith, Domenico Parisi, and Kim Plunkett (1996). *Rethinking innateness: A connectionist perspective on development (Neural Networks and Connectionist Modeling)*. Cambridge, MA: MIT Press.

Engberg-Pedersen, Elisabeth (2003). 'From pointing to reference and predication: Pointing signs, eyegaze, and head and body orientation in Danish Sign Language'. In: Sotaro Kita (ed.), *Pointing: Where language, culture, and cognition meet*. Mahwah, NJ: Erlbaum, 269–292.

Engle, Randall W., and Michael J. Kane (2004). 'Executive attention, working memory capacity, and a two-factor theory of cognitive control'. In: Brian H. Ross (ed.), *The Psychology of Learning and Motivation*. Vol. 44. New York: Academic Press, 145–199.

Evans, Gareth (1982). *The varieties of reference*. Oxford: Oxford University Press.

Evans, Nicholas (2002). 'The true status of grammatical object affixes: Evidence from Bininj Gun-wok'. In: Nicholas Evans and Hans-Jürgen Sasse (eds.), *Problems of polysynthesis*. Studia typologica. Vol. 4. Berlin: Akademie Verlag, 15–50.

—— and Hans-Jürgen Sasse (2002). 'Introduction: Problems of polysynthesis'. In: Nicholas Evans and Hans-Jürgen Sasse (eds.), *Problems of polysynthesis*. Studia typologica. Vol. 4. Berlin: Akademie Verlag, 1–14.

—— (2009). *Some problems in the typology of quotation: A canonical approach*. Paper presented at the 8th Conference of the Association for Linguistic Typology, Berkeley, CA, July 2009.

Evans, Vyvyan, and Melanie Green (2006). *Cognitive linguistics: An introduction*. Mahwah, NJ: Erlbaum.

Everett, Caleb (2009). 'A reconsideration of the motivations for preferred argument structure'. *Studies in Language* 33(1), 1–24.

Everett, Daniel T. (1986). 'Pirahã'. In: Desmond C. Derbyshire and Geoffrey K. Pullum (eds.), *Handbook of Amazonian languages*. Vol. 1. Berlin: Mouton de Gruyter, 200–325.

Ewing, Michael C. (2001). 'Reference and recovery in Cirebon Javanese'. *Australian Journal of Linguistics* 21(1), 25–47.

Fagyal, Zsuzsanna, Douglas Kibbee, and Fred Jenkins (2006). *French: A linguistic introduction*. Cambridge: Cambridge University Press.

Falikman, Marija V. (2006). *Vnimanie* [Attention]. Obščaja psixologija (General editor Boris S. Bratus), Vol. 4. Moscow: Academia.

Fauconnier, Gilles (1994). *Mental spaces: Aspects of meaning construction in natural language.* Cambridge, MA: MIT Press.

Faw, Bill (2003). 'Pre-frontal executive committee for perception, working memory, attention, long-term memory, motor control, and thinking: A tutorial review'. *Consciousness and Cognition* 12, 83–139.

Faye, Souleymane (1982). *Morphologie du verbe sérère.* Les langues nationales au Sénégal, n° 84. Dakar: Centre de Linguistique Appliquée de Dakar.

—— (1985). *Morphologie du nom sérère: Système nominal et alternance consonantique.* Les langues nationales au Sénégal, n° 10. Dakar: Centre de Linguistique Appliquée de Dakar.

Fedorova, Olga V., and Ekaterina V. Pechenkova (2007). 'When "Colorless green ideas ..." meet working memory span'. In: Valery D. Solovyev, Ekaterina V. Pechenkova, and Vladimir N. Polyakov (eds.), *Proceedings of the 9th International Conference 'Cognitive Modeling in Linguistics'.* Kazan': Izdatel'stvo Kazanskogo universiteta, 22–31.

—— —— A. Delikishkina [Delikiškina], Svetlana A. Malyutina [Maljutina], Anna M. Uspenskaya [Uspenskaja], and Anastasija A. Fejn (2010a). 'Èksperimental'nyj podxod k issledovaniju referencii v diskurse: interpretacija anaforičeskogo mestoimenija v zavisimosti ot ritoričeskogo rasstojanija do ego antecedenta' [Experimental approach to reference in discourse: Effects of rhetorical structure on pronoun interpretation]. In: Aleksandr E. Kibrik (ed.), *Computational Linguistics and Intellectual Technologies. Papers from the Annual International Conference 'Dialogue' (2010).* Bekasovo, Moscow region. Moscow: Izdatel'stvo RGGU, 525–530.

—— —— —— —— and —— (2010b). 'Sovmestnoe ili razdel'noe ispol'zovanie verbal'nyx resursov rabočej pamjati v processe ponimanija predloženij' [Shared or separate use of verbal working memory resources in sentence understanding]. In: Tatyana V. Chernigovskaya [Tat'jana V. Černigovskaja] (ed.), *The 4th International Conference on Cognitive Science.* Tomsk, 554–555.

Fernández-Ordóñez, Inés (2000). 'Leísmo, laísmo y loísmo'. In: Ignacio Bosque and Violeta Demonte (eds.), *Gramática descriptiva de la lengua española.* Vol. 1. Sintaxis básica de las clases de palabras. Madrid: Espasa, 1317–1398.

Fernández Soriano, Olga (2000). 'El pronombre personal. Formas I distribuciones. Pronombres átonos y tónicos'. In: Ignacio Bosque and Violeta Demonte (eds.), *Gramática descriptiva de la lengua española.* Vol. 1. Sintaxis básica de las clases de palabras, Madrid: Espasa, 1209–1274.

Ferstl, Evelyn C., and Florian Th. Siebörger (2007). 'Neuroimaging studies of coherence processes'. In: Monika Schwartz-Friesel, Manfred Consten, and Mareile Knees (eds.), *Anaphors in text: Cognitive, formal and applied approaches to anaphoric reference.* Amsterdam: Benjamins, 225–240.

Figurovskij, Ivan A. (1948). 'Ot sintaksisa predloženija k sintaksisu celogo teksta' [From the syntax of sentence towards the syntax of whole text]. *Russkij Jazyk v Škole* 1948(3).

Fillmore, Charles (1975). *Santa Cruz lectures on deixis*. Bloomington: Indiana University Linguistics Club.

Fischer, Olga, Muriel Norde, and Harry Perridon (eds.) (2004). *Up and down the cline: The nature of grammaticalization*. Amsterdam: Benjamins.

Foley, William, and Robert D. Van Valin Jr. (1984). *Functional syntax and universal grammar*. Cambridge: Cambridge University Press.

Fontaine, Carmen (1985). *Application de méthodes quantitatives en diachronie: l'inversion du sujet en français*. M.A. thesis. UQAM.

Foraker, Stephani, and Brian McElree (2007). 'The role of prominence in pronoun resolution: Active versus passive representations'. *Journal of Memory and Language* 56(3), 357–383.

Fortescue, Michael (2006). 'The origins of the Wakashan classificatory verbs of location and handling'. *Anthropological Linguistics* 48(3), 266–287.

Fougeron [Fužero], Irina, and Jean Breillard [Žan Brejar] (2004). 'Mestoimenie "ja" i postroenie diskursivnyx svjazej v sovremennom russkom jazyke' [The pronoun "ja" and the construction of discourse links in modern Russian]. In: Tatyana [Tat'jana] M. Nikolaeva (ed.), *Verbal'naja i neverbal'naja opory prostranstva mežfrazovyx svjazej*. Moscow: Jazyki slavjanskoj kul'tury, 147–166.

Fox, Barbara A. (1987a). *Discourse structure and anaphora in written and conversational English*. Cambridge: Cambridge University Press.

—— (1987b). 'Anaphora in popular written English narratives'. In: Russell S. Tomlin (ed.), *Coherence and grounding in discourse*. Amsterdam: Benjamins, 157–174.

—— Makoto Hayashi, and Robert Jasperson (1996). 'Resources and repair: A cross-linguistic study of syntax and repair'. In: Elinor Ochs, Emanuel A. Schegloff, and Sandra A. Thompson (eds.), *Interaction and grammar*. Cambridge: Cambridge University Press, 185–237.

—— (ed.) (1996). *Studies in anaphora*. Amsterdam: Benjamins.

Frajzyngier, Zygmunt, and Erin Shay (2000). *A grammar of Hdi*. Berlin: Mouton de Gruyter.

Francik, E. P. (1985). *Referential choice and focus of attention in narratives (discourse anaphora, topic continuity, language production)*. Ph.D. thesis. Stanford University.

Franklin, Karl J. (1983). 'Some features of interclausal reference in Kewa'. In: John Haiman and Pamela Munro (eds.), *Switch-reference and universal grammar*. Amsterdam: Benjamins, 39–50.

Franks, Steven, and Tracy Holloway King (2000). *A handbook of Slavic clitics*. Oxford: Oxford University Press.

Fraurud, Kari (1996). 'Cognitive ontology and NP form'. In: Thorsten Fretheim and Jeanette K. Gundel (eds.), *Reference and referent accessibility*. Amsterdam: Benjamins, 65–88.

Fretheim, Thorstein, and Jeanette K. Gundel (eds.) (1996). *Reference and referent accessibility*. Amsterdam: Benjamins.

—— Kaja Borthen, and Heidi Brøseth (2010). 'Introduction: Linguistic and cognitive aspects of reference'. *Journal of Pragmatics* 42, 1765–1769.

Fukumura, Kumiko, and Roger P. G. van Gompel (2009). 'Speakers use their own, privileged discourse model to determine referents' accessibility during the production of referring expressions'. Paper presented at the Production of Referring Expressions Conference: Bridging the Gap between Computational and Empirical Approaches to Reference (PRE-CogSci), Amsterdam, 29 July 2009.

Funahashi, Shintaro (2006). 'Prefrontal cortex and working memory processes'. *Neuroscience* 139(1), 251–261.

Gaden, Henri (1913). *Le Pulaar. Dialecte peul du Fouta Sénégalais*. Vol. 1. Étude morphologique. Textes. Paris: Leroux.

Gair, James W., Barbara Lust, K. V. Subbarao, and Kashi Wali (2000). 'Introduction'. In: Barbara Lust, Kashi Wali, James W. Gair, and K. V. Subbarao (eds.), *Lexical anaphors and pronouns in selected South Asian languages: A principled typology*. Berlin: Mouton de Gruyter, 1–48.

Gak, Vladimir G. (1972). 'Povtornaja nominacija i ee stilističeskoe ispol'zovanie' [Repeated mention and its stylistic use]. *Voprosy francuzskoj filologii. Trudy MGPU im. V. I. Lenina*. Moscow: MGPI, 129–136.

—— (1979). *Teoretičeskaja grammatika francuzskogo jazyka. Morfologija* [A theoretical grammar of French. Morphology]. Moscow: Vysšaja škola.

Galambos, Sylvia Joseph (1980). 'A clarification of the notion of topic: Evidence from popular spoken French'. In: Jody Kreiman and Almerindo E. Ojeda (eds.), *Papers from the parasession on pronouns and anaphora*. Chicago Linguistic Society. Chicago: University of Chicago Press, 125–138.

Galperin, Ilya R. [Il'ja R. Gal'perin] (1981). *Tekst kak ob"ekt lingvističeskogo issledovanija* [Text as an object of linguistic exploration]. Moscow: Nauka.

Garnham, Alan (2001). *Mental models and the interpretation of anaphora. Essays in cognitive psychology*. Philadelphia, PA: Psychology Press.

—— (2006). 'Reference: Psycholinguistic approach'. In: Keith Brown (ed.), *Encyclopedia of language and linguistics*. Oxford: Elsevier, 427–433.

Garrod, Simon C., David Freudenthal, and Elizabeth Boyle (1994). 'The role of different types of anaphor in the on-line resolution of sentences in a discourse'. *Journal of Memory and Language* 33, 39–68.

—— (2011). 'Referential processing in monologue and dialogue with and without access to real world referents'. In: Edward Gibson and Neal J. Pearlmutter (eds.), *The processing and acquisition of reference*. Cambridge, MA: MIT Press, 273–294.

Garvey, Catherine, and Alfonso Caramazza (1974). 'Implicit causality in verbs'. *Linguistic Inquiry* 5, 459–464.

Gasparov, Boris (2001). *Old Church Slavonic*. München: LINCOM Europa.

Gathercole, Susan E. (ed.) (1996). *Models of short-term memory*. Hove, East Sussex: Psychology Press.

Gavins, Johanna (2006). 'Text world theory'. In: Keith Brown (ed.), *Encyclopedia of language and linguistics*. Oxford: Elsevier, 628–630.

Geeraerts, Dirk (2006). *Lectal factors and the multivariate nature of linguistic phenomena*. In: Boris M. Velichkovsky [Veličkovskij], Tatyana V. Chernigovskaya [Tat'jana V. Černigovskaja], Jury [Jurij] I. Aleksandrov, and Denis N. Akhapkin [Axapkin] (eds.), *The Second Biennial Conference on Cognitive Science*. Vol. 1. Saint-Petersburg: Saint-Petersburg State University, Philological Faculty, 62–63.

—— (ed.) (2006). *Cognitive linguistics: Basic readings*. Berlin: Mouton de Gruyter.

—— and Hubert Cuyckens (eds.) (2007). *The Oxford handbook of cognitive linguistics*. Oxford: Oxford University Press.

Geluykens, Ronald (1994). *The pragmatics of discourse anaphora in English: Evidence from conversational repair*. Berlin: Mouton de Gruyter.

Genetti, Carol (1994). *A descriptive and historical account of the Dolakha Newari dialect*. Tokyo: Institute for the Study of Languages and Cultures of Asia and Africa.

—— and Laura D. Crain (2003). 'Beyond preferred argument structure: Sentences, pronouns, and given referents in Nepali'. In: John W. Du Bois (ed.), *Preferred argument structure: Grammar as architecture for function*. Amsterdam: Benjamins, 197–224.

Gernsbacher, Morton Ann (1990). *Language comprehension as structure building*. Hillsdale, NJ: Erlbaum.

—— and David Hargreaves (1992). 'The privilege of primacy: Experimental data and cognitive explanation'. In: Doris L. Payne (ed.), *Pragmatics of word order flexibility*. Amsterdam: Benjamins, 83–116.

Geurts, Bart (1999). *Presuppositions and pronouns*. Amsterdam: Elsevier.

Gibson, Edward, and Neal J. Pearlmutter (eds.) (2011). *The processing and acquisition of reference*. Cambridge, MA: MIT Press.

Gil, David (1993). 'Nominal and verbal quantification'. *Sprachtypologie und Universalienforschung* 46, 275–317.

—— (1999). 'Riau Indonesian as a pivotless language'. In: Ekaterina V. Rakhilina [Raxilina] and Yakov G. Testelets [Jakov G. Testelec] (eds.), *Tipologija i teorija jazyka: ot opisanija k ob"jasneniju*. Moscow: Jazyki russkoj kul'tury, 187–211.

—— (2005). 'Towards a typology of isolating languages: A cross-linguistic experiment'. Paper presented at the 4th International School in Linguistic Typology and Anthropology, Tsaxkadzor, Armenia, September 2005.

Giora, Rachel, and Cher-Leng Lee (1996). 'Unstressed pronouns in Mandarin Chinese'. In: Thorsten Fretheim and Jeanette K. Gundel (eds.), *Reference and referent accessibility*. Amsterdam: Benjamins, 113–140.

Givón, T. (1976). 'Topic, pronoun, and grammatical agreement'. In: Charles N. Li (ed.), *Subject and topic*. New York: Academic Press, 149–188.

—— (ed.) (1979). *Discourse and syntax*. New York: Academic Press.

—— (ed.) (1983). *Topic continuity in discourse: A quantitative cross-language study*. Amsterdam: Benjamins.

Givón, T. (1983a). 'Topic continuity in discourse: An introduction'. In: T. Givón (ed.), *Topic continuity in discourse: A quantitative cross-language study.* Amsterdam: Benjamins, 1–42.

—— (1983b). 'Topic continuity in spoken English'. In: T. Givón (ed.), *Topic continuity in discourse: A quantitative cross-language study.* Amsterdam: Benjamins, 345–363.

—— (1990). *Syntax: A functional-typological introduction.* Vol. 2. Amsterdam: Benjamins.

—— (1993). 'Coherence in text, coherence in mind'. *Pragmatics and Cognition* 1(2), 171–227.

—— (ed.) (1994). *Voice and inversion.* Amsterdam: Benjamins.

—— (1995). *Functionalism and grammar.* Amsterdam: Benjamins.

—— (2001). *Syntax: A functional-typological introduction.* Vols. 1, 2. Amsterdam: Benjamins.

—— (2005). *Context as other minds: The pragmatics of sociality, cognition and communication.* Amsterdam: Benjamins.

Glenberg, Arthur (1997). 'What memory is for'. *Behavioral and Brain Sciences* 20(1), 1–55.

Glezer, Vadim D. (1993). *Zrenie i myšlenie* [Vision and cognition]. Saint-Petersburg: Nauka.

Goddard, Ives (1990). 'Aspects of the topic structure of Fox narratives: Proximate shifts and the use of overt and inflectional NPs'. *International Journal of American Linguistics* 56(3), 317–340.

Goldberg, Adele E. (ed.) (1996). *Conceptual structure, discourse and language.* Stanford: CSLI.

Goldin-Meadow, Susan (2003). *Hearing gesture: How our hands help us think.* Cambridge: Cambridge University Press.

—— and Cynthia Butcher (2003). 'Pointing toward two-word speech in young children'. In: Sotaro Kita (ed.), *Pointing: Where language, culture, and cognition meet.* Mahwah, NJ: Erlbaum, 85–108.

Goldman-Rakic, Patricia S. (1987). 'Circuitry of the prefrontal cortex and the regulation of behavior by representational memory'. In: Vernon B. Mountcastle, Fred Plum, and Stephen R. Geiger (eds.), *Handbook of neurobiology.* Bethesda: American Physiological Society, 373–417.

Gordon, Peter C., Barbara J. Grosz, and Laura A. Gilliom (1993). 'Pronouns, names, and the centering of attention in discourse'. *Cognitive Science* 17(3), 311–347.

Gorelova, Lilija M. (1980). 'Modeli polipredikativnyx konstrukcij v ėvenkijskom jazyke' [Models of polypredicative constructions in Evenki]. In: Majja I. Čeremisina (ed.), *Polipredikativnye konstrukcii i ix morfologičeskaja baza.* Novosibirsk: Nauka, 83–96.

Graesser, Arthur C., and Sharon M. Goodman (1985). 'Implicit knowledge, question answering, and the representation of expository text'. In: Bruce K. Britton and John B. Black (eds.), *Understanding expository text: A theoretical and practical handbook for analyzing explanatory text.* Hillsdale, NJ: Erlbaum, 109–172.

Graesser, Arthur C., Morton Ann Gernsbacher, and Susan R. Goldman (eds.) (2003). *Handbook of discourse processes*. Mahwah, NJ: Erlbaum.

Green, John N. (1997). 'Spanish'. In: Martin Harris and Nigel Vincent (eds.), *The Romance languages*. London: Routledge, 79–130.

Green, Keith (2006). 'Deixis and anaphora: Pragmatic approaches'. In: Keith Brown (ed.), *Encyclopedia of language and linguistics*. Oxford: Elsevier, 415–417.

Greenbacker, Charles F., and Kathleen F. McCoy (2009). 'Feature selection for reference generation as informed by psycholinguistic research'. Paper presented at the Production of Referring Expressions Conference: Bridging the Gap between Computational and Empirical Approaches to Reference (PRE-CogSci), Amsterdam, 29 July 2009.

Greenberg, Joseph H. (1963). 'Some universals of grammar with particular reference to the order of meaningful elements'. In: Joseph H. Greenberg (ed.), *Universals of language*. Cambridge, MA: MIT Press, 73–113.

—— (1986). 'Introduction: Some reflections or pronominal systems'. In: Ursula Wiesemann (ed.), *Pronominal systems*. Tübingen: Narr, xvii–xxi.

Greene, Steven B., and Gail McKoon (1995). 'Telling something we can't know: Experimental approaches to verbs exhibiting implicit causality'. *Psychological Science* 6, 262–270.

Grenoble, Lenore (1992). 'An overview of Russian Sign Language'. *Sign Language Studies* 77, 321–338.

—— (1998). *Deixis and information packaging in Russian discourse*. Amsterdam: Benjamins.

—— (2001). 'Conceptual reference points, pronouns and conversational structure in Russian'. *Glossos* 1.

Gries, Stefan Th. (2001). 'Particle placement in English: A multifactorial investigation'. In: Ruth M. Brend, Alan K. Melby, and Arle R. Lommel (eds.), *LACUS Forum XXVII: Speaking and comprehending*. Fullerton: LACUS, 19–32.

—— and Anatol Stefanovich (2006). *Corpora in cognitive linguistics: Corpus-based approaches to syntax and lexis*. Berlin: Mouton de Gruyter.

Grigor'eva, Svetlana A., Nikolaj V. Grigor'ev, and Grigorij E. Krejdlin (2001). *Slovar' jazyka russkix žestov* [A dictionary of Russian gestures]. Moscow: Jazyki russkoj kul'tury.

Grimes, Joseph (1975). *The thread of discourse*. The Hague: Mouton.

—— (ed.) (1978). *Papers in discourse*. Arlington: SIL.

Grinevald, Colette (2000). 'A morphosyntactic typology of classifiers'. In: Gunter Senft (ed.), *Systems of nominal classification*. Cambridge: Cambridge University Press, 50–92.

Grinevald Craig, Colette (1977). *The Structure of Jacaltec*. Austin: University of Texas.

—— (1986). 'Jacaltec noun classifiers: A study in language and culture'. In: Colette Grinevald Craig (ed.), *Noun classes and categorization*. Amsterdam: Benjamins, 263–294.

Grinevald Craig, Colette (1992). 'Classifiers in a functional perspective'. In: Michael Fortescue, Peter Harder, and Lars Kristoffersen (eds.), *Layered structure and reference in a functional perspective*. Amsterdam: Benjamins, 277–301.

Grober, Ellen H., William Beardsley, and Alfonso Caramazza (1978). 'Parallel function strategy in pronoun assignment'. *Cognition* 6, 117–133.

Grosz, Barbara (1977). 'The representation and use of focus in a system for understanding dialogues'. In: *Proceedings of the 5th International Joint Conference on Artificial Intelligence*. Cambridge, 67–76.

—— and Candace Sidner (1986). 'Attention, intentions, and the structure of discourse'. *Computational Linguistics* 12, 175–204.

Grüning, André, and Andrej A. Kibrik (2002). 'Referential choice and activation factors: A neural network approach'. In: Antonio Branco, Tony McEnery, and Ruslan Mitkov (eds.), *Proceedings of the 4th Discourse Anaphora and Anaphor Resolution Colloquium (DAARC 2002)*. Lisbon: Edições Colibri, 81–86.

—— and —— (2005). 'Modelling referential choice in discourse: A cognitive calculative approach and a neural network approach'. In: António Branco, Tony McEnery, and Ruslan Mitkov (eds.), *Anaphora processing: Linguistic, cognitive and computational modelling*. Amsterdam: Benjamins, 163–198.

Guentchéva, Zlatka (1993). *Thématisation de l'objet en bulgare*. Berne: Peter Lang.

Gundel, Jeanette K. (1980). 'Zero NP-anaphora in Russian: A case of topic-prominence'. In: Jody Kreiman and Almerindo E. Ojeda (eds.), *Papers from the parasession on pronouns and anaphora*. Chicago: Chicago Linguistic Society, 139–146.

—— Nancy Hedberg, and Ron Zacharski (1993). 'Cognitive status and the form of referring expressions in discourse'. *Language* 69(2), 274–307.

—— Dimitrios Ntelitheos, and Melinda Kowalsky (2006). 'Theory of mind and the acquisition of referring expressions by children'. Paper presented at the Conference on Intersentential Pronominal Reference in Child and Adult Language. Berlin, 1–2 December 2006.

—— and Nancy Hedberg (eds.) (2008). *Reference: Interdisciplinary perspectives*. Oxford: Oxford University Press.

Gunlogson, Christine (2001). 'Third-person object prefixes in Babine-Witsuwit'en'. *International Journal of American Linguistics* 67(4), 365–395.

Hagège, Claude (1974). 'Les pronoms logophoriques'. *Bulletin de la Société de Linguistique de Paris* 69, 287–310.

Haile, Berard (1941). *Learning Navaho*. St. Michaels: St. Michaels Press.

Haiman, John, and Pamela Munro (1983). 'Introduction'. In: John Haiman and Pamela Munro (eds.), *Switch-reference and universal grammar*. Amsterdam: Benjamins, ix–xv.

—— and —— (eds.) (1983). *Switch-reference and universal grammar*. Amsterdam: Benjamins.

—— (1985). *Natural syntax: Iconicity and erosion*. Cambridge: Cambridge University Press.

Hale, Kenneth (1973). 'A note on subject-object inversion in Navajo'. In: Braj B. Kachru, Robert Lees, Yakov Malkiel, Angelina Pietrangeli, and Sol Saporta (eds.), *Papers in linguistics in honor of Henry and Renee Kahane*. Urbana: University of Illinois Press, 300–309.

—— (1983). 'Warlpiri and the grammar of non-configurational languages'. *Natural Language and Linguistic Theory* 1(1), 5–47.

Hall, Mark, Eibe Frank, Geoffrey Holmes, Bernhard Pfahringer, Peter Reutemann, and Ian H. Witten (2009). *The WEKA data mining software: An update*. SIGKDD Explorations, Vol. 11(1). New York: ACM.

Halliday, Michael A. K., and Ruqaiya Hasan (1976). *Cohesion in English*. London: Longman.

Halpern, Aaron L. (1998). 'Clitics'. In: Andrew Spencer and Arnold M. Zwicky (eds.), *Handbook of morphology*. Oxford: Blackwell, 101–122.

Hanks, William F. (1992). 'The indexical ground of deictic reference'. In: Alessandro Duranti and Charles Goodwin (eds.), *Rethinking context, language as an interactive phenomenon*. Cambridge: Cambridge University Press, 43–77.

Hanna, Joy E., Michael K. Tanenhaus, and John C. Trueswell (2003). 'The effects of common ground and perspective on domains of referential interpretation'. *Journal of Memory and Language* 49, 43–61.

Hardt, Daniel (2004). *Dynamic centering*. Paper presented at the Workshop on Reference Resolution and its Applications (ACL 2004), Barcelona, 21–26 August 2004.

Harris, Martin (1997). 'French'. In: Martin Harris and Nigel Vincent (eds.), *The Romance languages*. London: Routledge, 209–245.

—— and Nigel Vincent (eds.) (1997). *The Romance languages*. London: Routledge.

Harris, Zellig (1952). 'Discourse analysis'. *Language* 28, 1–30.

Hartmann, Peter (1964). 'Text, Texte, Klassen von Texten'. *Bogawus* 12, 15–25.

Hartsuiker, Robert J., and Pashiera N. Barkhuysen (2006). 'Language production and working memory: The case of subject–verb agreement'. *Language and Cognitive Processes* 21(1/2/3), 181–204.

Haspelmath, Martin (1997). *Indefinite pronouns*. Oxford: Oxford University Press.

—— Ekkehard König, Wulf Oesterreicher, and Wolfgang Raible (eds.) (2001). *Language typology and language universals: An international handbook*. Berlin: de Gruyter.

—— (2002). *Understanding morphology*. London: Arnold.

—— Matthew Dryer, David Gil, and Bernard Comrie (eds.) (2005). *World atlas of language structures*. Oxford: Oxford University Press.

—— —— —— and —— (eds.) (2008). *World atlas of language structures*. München: Max Planck Digital Library. http://wals.info/

Haviland, John (2000). 'Pointing, gesture spaces, and mental maps'. In: David McNeill (ed.), *Language and gesture*. Cambridge: Cambridge University Press, 13–46.

Hawkins, John (1978). *Definiteness and indefiniteness: A study in reference and grammaticality prediction*. London: Croom Helm.

Hazy, Thomas E., Michael J. Frank, and Randall C. O'Reilly (2006). 'Banishing the homunculus: Making working memory work'. *Neuroscience* 139(1), 105–118.
Head, Brian (1979). 'Respect degrees in pronominal reference'. In: Joseph H. Greenberg, Charles A. Ferguson, and Edith A. Moravcsik (eds.), *Universals of human language*. Vol. 3. Word structure. Stanford: Stanford University Press, 151–211.
Heap, David (2000). *La variation grammaticale en géolinguistique: Les pronoms sujet en roman central*. München: LINCOM Europa.
Heath, Jeffrey (1975). 'Some functional relationships in grammar'. *Language* 51, 89–104.
—— (1983). 'Referential tracking in Nunggubuyu'. In: John Haiman and Pamela Munro (eds.), *Switch-reference and universal grammar*. Amsterdam: Benjamins, 129–150.
—— (1984). *Functional grammar of Nunggubuyu*. Canberra: Australian Institute of Aboriginal studies.
Hedberg, Nancy (1996). 'Word order and cognitive status in Mandarin'. In: Thorsten Fretheim and Jeanette K. Gundel (eds.), *Reference and referent accessibility*. Amsterdam: Benjamins, 179–192.
Heine, Bernd, and Ulrike Claudi (1986). *On the rise of grammatical categories*. Berlin: Reimer.
Helasvuo, Marja-Liisa (2003). 'Argument splits in Finnish grammar and discourse'. In: John W. Du Bois, Lorraine E. Kumpf, and William J. Ashby (eds.), *Preferred argument structure: Grammar as architecture for function*. Amsterdam: Benjamins, 247–272.
Helmbrecht, Johannes (2004). *Personal pronouns – form, function, and grammaticalization*. Habilitation thesis. University of Erfurt.
—— (2005). 'Politeness distinctions in pronouns'. In: Martin Haspelmath, Matthew Dryer, David Gil, and Bernard Comrie (eds.), *World atlas of language structures*. Oxford: Oxford University Press, 186–190.
—— (2009). 'On the typology of proper names'. Paper presented at the 8th Conference of the Association for Linguistic Typology, Berkeley, CA, July 2009.
Herring, Susan C. (ed.) (1996). *Computer-mediated communication: Linguistic, social and cross-cultural perspectives*. Amsterdam: Benjamins.
Hewitt, Brian George (1979). *Abkhaz*. Amsterdam: North-Holland.
—— (2005). *Abkhazian folk tales (with grammatical introduction, translation, notes, and vocabulary)*. München: LINCOM Europa.
Hickmann, Maya (2003). *Children's discourse: Person, space and time across languages*. Cambridge Studies in Linguistics. Cambridge: Cambridge University Press.
—— (ed.) (2006). *Space in languages: Linguistic systems and cognitive categories*. Amsterdam: Benjamins.
Himmelmann, Nikolaus P. (1996). 'Demonstratives in narrative discourse: A taxonomy of universal uses'. In: Barbara A. Fox (ed.), *Studies in anaphora*. Amsterdam: Benjamins, 205–254.

Hinds, John (ed.) (1978). *Anaphora in discourse*. Edmonton: Linguistic Research Inc.
—— (1984). 'Topic maintenance in Japanese narratives and Japanese conversational interaction'. *Discourse Processes* 7, 465–482.
Hirst, Graeme (1981). *Anaphora in natural language understanding: A survey*. Berlin: Springer.
Hobbs, Jerry R. (1976). *Pronoun resolution*. New York: City College.
—— (1979). 'Coherence and coreference'. *Cognitive Science* 3, 67–90.
Hockett, Charles (1958). *A course in modern linguistics*. New York: Macmillan Press.
Hockey, Robert (1973). 'Rate of presentation in running memory and direct manipulation of input processing strategies'. *Quarterly Journal of Experimental Psychology* 25, 104–111.
Holler, Anke, and Lisa Irmen (2007). 'Empirically assessing effects of the Right Frontier Constraint'. In: António Branco (ed.), *Anaphora: Analysis, algorithms, and applications*. Berlin: Springer, 15–27.
Holšánová, Jana (2008). *Discourse, vision, and cognition*. Amsterdam: Benjamins.
Hopkins, Elizabeth B. (1986). 'Pronouns and pronoun fusions in Yaouré'. In: Ursula Wiesemann (ed.), *Pronominal systems*. Tübingen: Narr, 191–203.
Horton, William S. (2009). 'Memory and other limits on audience design in reference production'. Paper presented at the Production of Referring Expressions Conference: Bridging the Gap between Computational and Empirical Approaches to Reference (PRE-CogSci), Amsterdam, 29 July 2009.
Hualde, José Ignacio, and Jon Ortiz de Urbina (eds.) (2003). *A grammar of Basque*. Berlin: Mouton de Gruyter.
Huang, Yan (2000). *Anaphora: A cross-linguistic study*. Oxford: Oxford University Press.
—— (2006). 'Anaphora, cataphora, exophora, logophoricity'. In: Keith Brown (ed.), *Encyclopedia of language and linguistics*. Oxford: Elsevier, 231–237.
Huddleston, Rodney, and Geoffrey K. Pullum (2005). *A student's introduction to English grammar*. Cambridge: Cambridge University Press.
Hudson D'Zmura, Susan (1998). 'Control and event structure: The view from the center'. In: Marilyn A. Walker, Aravind K. Joshi, and Ellen F. Prince (eds.), *Centering theory in discourse*. Oxford: Clarendon Press, 71–88.
Hutchisson, Don (1986). 'Sursurunga pronouns and the special use of quadral numbers'. In: Ursula Wiesemann (ed.), *Pronominal systems*. Tübingen: Narr, 1–20.
Ide, Nancy, and Dan Cristea (2000). 'A hierarchical account of referential accessibility'. Proceedings of the 38th Annual Meeting of the Association for Computational Linguistics (ACL 2000). Hong Kong, China.
Ingram, David (1978). 'Typology and universals of pronouns'. In: Joseph H. Greenberg, Charles A. Ferguson, and Edith A. Moravcsik (eds.), *Universals of human language*. Vol. 3. Word structure. Stanford: Stanford University Press, 213–247.

Isard, Stephen (1975). 'Changing the context'. In: Edward L. Keenan (ed.), *Formal semantics of natural language*. London: Cambridge University Press, 287–296.
Ishikawa, Kiyoshi (1998). *A network theory of reference*. Bloomington: Indiana University Linguistics Club.
Ivanitsky, Aleksey M. [Aleksej M. Ivanickij] (1996). 'Mozgovaja osnova sub"ektivnyx pereživanij: gipoteza informacionnogo sinteza' [The brain basis of subjective experiences: The hypothesis of information synthesis]. *Žurnal Vysšej Nervnoj Dejatel'nosti* 46(2), 241–252.
—— O. V. Sysoeva, I. R. Ilyuchenok, and A. I. Streltsova (2008). 'Brain semantic systems, attention and memory'. Paper presented at the 3rd International Conference on Cognitive Science, Moscow, June 2008.
Ivanov, Valerij V. (1982). 'Istorija vremennyx form glagola' [History of verbal tense forms]. In: Ruben I. Avanesov and Valerij V. Ivanov (eds.), *Istoričeskaja grammatika russkogo jazyka. Morfologija. Glagol*. Moscow: Nauka, 25–131.
Iwasaki, Shoichi (1992). *Subjectivity in grammar and discourse: Theoretical considerations and a case study of Japanese spoken discourse*. Amsterdam: Benjamins.
Jacobsen, William, Jr., (1967). 'Switch-reference in Hokan-Coahuiltecan'. In: Dell H. Hymes and William E. Bittle (eds.), *Studies in southwestern ethnolinguistics: Meaning and history in the languages of the American Southwest*. The Hague: Mouton, 238–263.
—— (1980). 'Inclusive/exclusive: A diffused pronominal category in native Western North America'. In: Jody Kreiman and Almerindo E. Ojeda (eds.), *Papers from the parasession on pronouns and anaphora*. Chicago: Chicago Linguistic Society, 204–227.
—— (1983). 'Typological and genetic notes on switch-reference systems in North American languages'. In: John Haiman and Pamela Munro (eds.), *Switch-reference and universal grammar*. Amsterdam: Benjamins, 151–184.
Jaggar, Philip J. (2001). *Hausa*. Amsterdam: Benjamins.
Jakobson, Roman (1935/1971). 'Shifters, verbal categories, and the Russian verb'. In: *Selected writings of Roman Jakobson*. Vol. 2. Word and language. The Hague: Mouton, 130–147.
—— (1935/1971). 'Les enclitiques slaves'. In: *Selected writings of Roman Jakobson*. Vol. 2. Word and language. The Hague: Mouton, 16–22.
James, William (1890). *The principles of psychology*. New York: Holt.
Jarvella, Robert J., and Wolfgang Klein (eds.) (1982). *Speech, place, and action: Studies in deixis and related topics*. New York: Wiley.
Jasinskaja, Ekaterina, Ulrike Kölsch, and Jörg Mayer (2007). 'Nuclear accent placement and other prosodic parameters as cues to pronoun resolution'. In: António Branco (ed.), *Anaphora: Analysis, algorithms, and applications*. Berlin: Springer, 1–14.
Jelinek, Eloise (1984). 'Empty categories, case, and configurationality'. *Natural Language and Linguistic Theory* 2(1), 39–76.

Jelinek, Eloise (1985). *The projection principle and the argument type parameter.* Unpublished.
Jensen, Ole (2006). 'Maintenance of multiple working memory items by temporal segmentation'. *Neuroscience* 139(1), 237–249.
Jespersen, Otto (1922). *Language, its nature, development and origin.* London: Allen and Unwin.
Johnstone, Barbara (2002). *Discourse analysis.* Malden, MA: Blackwell.
Joseph, Brian (2002). 'The word in Modern Greek'. In: R. M. W. Dixon and Alexandra Y. Aikhenvald (eds.), *Word: A cross-linguistic typology.* Cambridge: Cambridge University Press, 243–265.
Joshi, Aravind K., Rashmi Prasad, and Eleni Miltsakaki (2006). 'Anaphora resolution: Centering theory approach'. In: Keith Brown (ed.), *Encyclopedia of language and linguistics.* Oxford: Elsevier, 223–230.
Judge, Anne, and F. G. Healey (1990). *A reference grammar of modern French.* London: Arnold.
Kacnel'son, Solomon D. (1972). *Tipologija jazyka i rečevoe myšlenie* [The typology of language and verbal thinking]. Leningrad: Nauka.
Kahneman, Daniel, and Anne Treisman (1984). 'Changing views of attention and automaticity'. In: Raja Parasuraman (ed.), *Varieties of attention.* New York: Academic Press, 29–61.
Kaiser, Elsi, and Katrin Hiietam (2003). 'A Comparison of the referential properties of third person pronouns in Finnish and Estonian'. *University of Tromsø Working Papers on Language and Linguistics* 31(4), 654–667.
—— (2008). 'Multiple dimensions in anaphor resolution'. Paper presented at the 3rd International Conference on Cognitive Science, Moscow, June 2008.
—— and John Trueswell (2011). 'Investigating the interpretation of pronouns and demonstratives in Finnish: Going beyond salience'. In: Edward Gibson and Neal J. Pearlmutter (eds.), *The processing and acquisition of reference.* Cambridge, MA: MIT Press, 323–354.
Kameyama, Megumi (1998). 'Intrasentential centering: A case study'. In: Marilyn A. Walker, Aravind K. Joshi, and Ellen F. Prince (eds.), *Centering theory in discourse.* Oxford: Clarendon Press, 89–114.
—— (1999). 'Stressed and unstressed pronouns: Complimentary preferences'. In: Peter Bosch and Rob van der Sandt (eds.), *Focus: Linguistic, cognitive and computational perspectives.* Cambridge: Cambridge University Press, 306–321.
Kärkkäinen, Elisa (1996). 'Preferred argument structure and subject role in American English conversational discourse'. *Journal of Pragmatics* 25, 675–701.
Karttunen, Lauri (1976). 'Discourse referents'. In: James McCawley (ed.), *Syntax and Semantics.* Vol. 7. New York: Academic Press, 363–385.
Kastner, Sabine, and Leslie G. Ungerleider (2000). 'Mechanisms of visual attention in the human cortex'. *Annual Review of Neuroscience* 23, 315–341.
Keenan, Edward (1976). 'Towards a universal definition of "Subject"'. In: Charles N. Li (ed.), *Subject and topic.* New York: Academic Press, 303–334.

Keenan, Edward, and Bernard Comrie (1977). 'Noun phrase accessibility and Universal Grammar'. *Linguistic Inquiry* 8(1), 63–98.

Kehler, Andrew (2002). *Coherence, reference, and the theory of grammar*. Stanford: CSLI.

—— (2008). Rethinking the SMASH approach to pronoun interpretation. In: Jeanette K. Gundel and Nancy Hedberg (eds.), *Reference: Interdisciplinary perspectives*. Oxford: Oxford University Press, 95–122.

Kemmer, Suzanne (1993). *The middle voice*. Amsterdam: Benjamins.

Kempson, Ruth M., Wilfried Meyer-Viol, and Dov M. Gabbay (2001). *Dynamic syntax: The flow of language understanding*. Malden, MA: Blackwell.

Kendon, Adam (1994). 'Do gestures communicate? A review'. *Research on Language and Social Interaction in Grammar* 27, 175–200.

—— and Laura Versante (2003). 'Pointing by hand in "Neapolitan"'. In: Sotaro Kita (ed.), *Pointing: Where language, culture, and cognition meet*. Mahwah, NJ: Erlbaum, 109–137.

Keysar, Boaz, Dale J. Barr, Jennifer A. Balin, and Jason S. Brauner (2000). 'Taking perspective in conversation: The role of mutual knowledge in comprehension'. *Psychological Science* 11, 32–37.

—— Shuhong Lin, and Dale J. Barr (2003). 'Limits on theory of mind use in adults'. *Cognition* 89(1), 25–41.

Khudyakova, Mariya V. [Marija V. Xudjakova] (2007). *Referencial'nyj vybor v zavisimosti ot svojstv antecedenta v anglijskom jazyke* [Referential choice and its dependence of the antecedent's properties in English]. Year paper. Dept. of Theoretical and Applied Linguistics, Moscow State University.

—— (2008). *Referencial'nyj vybor v zavisimosti ot semantičeskoj roli antecedenta v anglijskom jazyke* [English referential choice and its dependence on the antecedent's semantic role]. Year paper. Dept. of Theoretical and Applied Linguistics, Moscow State University.

—— (2010). *Posessornye IG i referencial'nyj vybor v anglijskoj delovoj proze (na materiale korpusa, annotirovannogo po referencii)* [Possessor NPs and referential choice in English business prose (on the material of a referentially annotated corpus)]. Diploma thesis. Dept. of Theoretical and Applied Linguistics, Moscow State University.

Kibrik, Aleksandr E. (1977a). *Opyt strukturnogo opisanija arčinskogo jazyka. T. 2. Taksonomičeskaja grammatika* [A structural description of Archi. Vol. 2. A taxonomic grammar]. Moscow: Izdatel'stvo Moskovskogo universiteta.

—— (1977b). *Opyt strukturnogo opisanija arčinskogo jazyka. T. 3. Dinamičeskaja grammatika* [A structural description of Archi. Vol. 3. A dynamic grammar]. Moscow: Izdatel'stvo Moskovskogo universiteta.

—— (1977c). 'O sootnošenii ponjatija sintaksičeskogo podčinenija s ponjatijami soglasovanija, upravlenija i primykanija' [The notion of syntactic subordination, as compared to the notions of agreement, government, and adjunction]. *Problemy*

teoretičeskoj i ėksperimental'noj lingvistiki. Moscow: Izdatel'stvo Moskovskogo universiteta.
—— (1983). 'Lingvističeskie postulaty' [Linguistic postulates]. *Mexanizmy vyvoda i pererabotki znanij v sistemax ponimanija jazyka. Trudy po iskusstvennomu intellektu. Učenye zapiski Tartusskogo universiteta, vyp.* 621. 24–39.
—— (1996). 'Svjazannye upotreblenija leksemy SAM (sistemno-kognitivnyj analiz)' [Bound uses of the lexeme SAM (a systemic cognitive analysis)]. In: Tatyana [Tat'jana] M. Nikolaeva (ed.), *Rusistika. Slavistika. Indoevropeistika. Sbornik k 60-letiju Andreja Anatol'eviča Zaliznjaka*. Moscow: Indrik, 494–509.
—— (1997). 'Beyond subject and object: Toward a comprehensive relational typology'. *Linguistic Typology* 1(3), 279–346.
—— (1998). 'Kognitivno orientirovannaja tipologija' [Cognitively oriented typology]. *Vestnik RGNF* 3, 156–160.
—— and Yakov G. Testelets [Jakov G. Testelec] (eds.) (1999). *Elementy caxurskogo jazyka v tipologičeskom osveščenii* [Elements of Tsakhur with a typological interpretation]. Moscow: Nasledie.
—— Sandro V. Kodzasov, and Irina A. Muravyeva [Murav'eva] (2000). *Jazyk i fol'klor aljutorcev* [Alutor language and folklore]. Moscow: Nasledie.
—— (2003). *Konstanty i peremennye jazyka* [Constants and variables of language]. Saint-Petersburg: Aletejja.
Kibrik, Andrej A. (1983). 'Ob anafore, dejksise i ix sootnošenii' [On anaphora, deixis, and the relation between them]. In: Aleksandr S. Narin'jani (ed.), *Razrabotka i primenenie lingvističeskix processorov*. Novosibirsk: VC SO AN SSSR, 88–106.
—— (1984). *Povtornaja nominacija: tipy i mexanizmy* [Repeated mention: Types and mechanisms]. Diploma thesis. Dept. of Structural and Applied Linguistics, Moscow State University.
—— (1987a). 'Mexanizmy ustranenija referencial'nogo konflikta' [Mechanisms of referential conflict removal]. In: Aleksandr E. Kibrik and Aleksandr S. Narin'jani (eds.), *Modelirovanie jazykovoj dejatel'nosti v intellektual'nyx sistemax*. Moscow: Nauka, 128–145.
—— (1987b). 'Fokusirovanie vnimanija i mestoimenno-anaforičeskaja nominacija' [Focusing of attention and pronominal anaphora]. *Voprosy Jazykoznanija* 1987(3), 79–90.
—— (1988). *Tipologija sredstv oformlenija anaforičeskix svjazej* [A typology of anaphoric links representation]. Ph.D. thesis. Institut Jazykoznanija AN SSSR.
—— (1990a). 'Mestoimenija: morfologičeskie, sintaksičeskie i diskursivnye aspekty' [Pronouns: Morphological, syntactic, and discourse aspects]. In: Fedor M. Berezin and Elena S. Kubrjakova (eds.), *Teorija grammatiki: leksiko-grammatičeskie klassy i razrjady slov*. Moscow: INION AN SSSR, 139–201.
—— (1990b). '"Poslelogi" v navaxo: poterja statusa časti reči' [Navajo "postpostions": The loss of the part-of-speech status]. In: Vladimir M. Alpatov (ed.), *Časti reči: teorija i tipologija*. Moscow: Nauka, 234–253.

Kibrik, Andrej A. (1991). 'Maintenance of reference in sentence and discourse'. In: Winfred P. Lehmann and Helen-Jo J. Hewitt (eds.), *Language typology 1988: Typological models in reconstruction*. Amsterdam: Benjamins, 57–84.

—— (1992a). 'Dynamics of attention focus in narrative discourse: The Pulaar case'. *Languages of the World* 4, 4–12.

—— (1992b). 'Relativization in polysynthetic languages'. *International Journal of American Linguistics* 58(2), 135–157.

—— (1994). 'Anaphora in Russian narrative discourse: A cognitive calculative account'. Paper presented at the Symposium on Anaphora, Estes Park, Colorado, May 1994.

—— (1995). 'Podderžanie referencii v serer' [Reference-maintenance in Sereer]. In: Viktor A. Vinogradov and Antonina I. Koval [Koval'] (eds.), *Problemy izučenija jazykov Afriki*. Moscow: Institut Jazykoznanija RAN, 62–69.

—— (1996a). 'Anaphora in Russian narrative discourse: A cognitive calculative account'. In: Barbara A. Fox (ed.), *Studies in anaphora*. Amsterdam: Benjamins, 255–304.

—— (1996b). 'Jazyk ne tak nelep, kak kažetsja (lično-čislovoe glagol'noe soglasovanie v svanskom jazyke)' [Language is not as absurd as it seems (person–number agreement in Svan)]. In: Tatyana [Tat'jana] M. Nikolaeva (ed.), *Rusistika. Slavistika. Indoevropeistika. Sbornik k 60-letiju Andreja Anatol'eviča Zaliznjaka*. Moscow: Indrik, 478–493.

—— (1996c). 'Transitivity decrease in Athabaskan languages: Actor-affecting propositional derivations'. In: Eloise Jelinek, Sally Midgette, Keren Rice, and Leslie Saxon (eds.), *Studies in Athabaskan linguistics*. Albuquerque: UNM Press, 259–304.

—— and Vladimir A. Plungian [Plungjan] (1997). 'Funkcionalizm' [Functionalism]. In: Andrej A. Kibrik, Irina M. Kobozeva, and Irina A. Sekerina (eds.), *Fundamental'nye napravlenija sovremennoj amerikanskoj lingvistiki*. Moscow: Izdatel'stvo Moskovskogo universiteta, 276–339.

—— (1999). 'Cognitive inferences from discourse observations: Reference and working memory'. In: Karen van Hoek, Andrej A. Kibrik, and Leo Noordman (eds.), *Discourse studies in cognitive linguistics. Proceedings of the 5th International Cognitive Linguistics Conference*. Amsterdam: Benjamins, 29–52.

—— (2000). 'A cognitive calculative approach towards discourse anaphora'. In: Paul Baker, Andrew Hardie, Tony McEnery, and Anna Siewierska (eds.), *The 3rd Discourse Anaphora and Reference Resolution Colloquium (DAARC 2000)*. Lancaster: Lancaster University Centre for Computer Corpus Research on Language, 72–82.

—— (2001a). 'Reference-maintenance in discourse'. In: Martin Haspelmath, Ekkehard König, Wulf Oesterreicher, and Wolfgang Raible (eds.), *Language typology and language universals: An international handbook*. Berlin: de Gruyter, 1123–1141.

Kibrik, Andrej A. (2001b). 'Cognitive discourse analysis: Some results'. In: T. Enikő Németh (ed.), *Cognition in language use: Selected papers from the 7th International*

Pragmatics Conference. Vol. 1. Antwerp: International Pragmatics Association, 164–180.

—— (2001c). 'Polisintetičeskie jazyki' [Polysynthetic languages], *Ènciklopedija Krugosvet*, <http://www.krugosvet.ru/articles/77/1007729/1007729a1.htm>.

—— (2001d). 'Navajo dative: Two bi- or not two bi-?' Paper presented at the SSILA Meeting, Santa Barbara, July 2001.

—— (2002a). 'A typologically oriented portrait of the Athabaskan language family'. In: Vera I. Podlesskaya [Podlesskaja] (ed.), *Tret'ja zimnjaja tipologičeskaja škola: meždunarodnaja škola po lingvističeskoj tipologii i antropologii*. Moscow: Izdatel'stvo RGGU, 38–48.

—— (2002b). 'Plus or minus switch-reference: Referential strategies in Tuvan'. In: Rais G. Buxaraev, Valery D. Solovyev [Valerij D. Solov'ev], and Džavdet S. Sulejmanov (eds.), *Trudy kazanskoj školy po komp'juternoj i kognitivnoj lingvistike (TEL 2002)*. Kazan': Otečestvo, 269–296.

—— (2002c). 'Discourse types, genre schemata, and rhetorical relations'. Paper presented at the 6th Conference on Conceptual Structure, Discourse, and Language, Rice University, Houston, Texas, 11–14 October 2002.

—— (2003). *Analiz diskursa v kognitivnoj perspektive* [Discourse analysis in a cognitive perspective]. Habilitation thesis. Institut Jazykoznanija RAN.

—— (2004). 'Zero anaphora vs. zero person marking in Slavic: A chicken/egg dilemma?' In: António Branco, Ruslan Mitkov, and Tony McEnery (eds.), *Proceedings of the 5th Discourse Anaphora and Anaphor Resolution Colloquium (DAARC 2004)*. Lisbon: Edições Colibri, 87–90.

—— Abdoulaye [Abdulaj] Y. Ba, and Antonina I. Koval [Koval'] (2005). 'Skazanie "Ljubov'", ili "Dingiral", na jazyke pular' [The Pulaar saga 'Love', or 'Dingiral']. In: Antonina I. Koval [Koval'] (ed.), *Afrikanskaja skazka-III. K issledovaniju jazyka fol'klora*. Moscow: Vostočnaja literatura RAN, 399–479.

—— and Olga N. Krasavina (2005). 'A corpus study of referential choice: The role of rhetorical structure'. In: Irina M. Kobozeva, Aleksandr S. Narin'jani, and Vladimir P. Selegej (eds.), *Computational Linguistics and Intellectual Technologies. Papers from the Annual International Conference 'Dialogue' (2005)*. Zvenigorod, Moscow region. Moscow: Nauka, 561–569.

—— (2006). 'Multi-factorial choices in speaking'. In: Boris M. Velichkovsky [Veličkovskij], Tatyana V. Chernigovskaya [Tat'jana V. Černigovskaja], Yuri [Jurij] I. Aleksandrov, and Denis N. Akhapkin [Axapkin] (eds.), *The Second Biennial Conference on Cognitive Science*. Vol. 1. Saint-Petersburg: Saint-Petersburg State University, Philological Faculty, 86–87.

—— and Vera I. Podlesskaya [Podlesskaja] (2006). 'Problema segmentacii ustnogo diskursa i kognitivnaja sistema govorjaščego' [The problem of spoken discourse segmentation and the speaker's cognitive system]. In: Valery D. Solovyev [Valerij D. Solov'ev] (ed.), *Kognitivnye issledovanija*. Vol. 1. Moscow: Institut psixologii RAN, 138–158.

Kibrik, Andrej A., and Evgenija V. Prozorova (2007). 'Referential choice in signed and spoken languages'. In: António Branco, Tony McEnery, Ruslan Mitkov, and Fátima Silva (eds.), *The 6th Discourse Anaphora and Anaphor Resolution Colloquium (DAARC 2007)*. Porto: Centro de Linguistica da Universidade do Porto, 41–46.

—— (2008a). 'Est' li predloženie v ustnoj reči?' [Is sentence valid in spoken language?]. In: Alexandre V. Arkhipov [Aleksandr V. Arxipov], Leonid M. Zakharov [Zaxarov], Andrej A. Kibrik, Aleksandr E. Kibrik, Irina M. Kobozeva, Olga [Ol'ga] F. Krivnova, Ekaterina A. Lyutikova [Ljutikova], and Olga [Ol'ga] V. Fedorova (eds.), *Fonetika i nefonetika. K 70-letiju Sandro V. Kodzasova*. Moscow: Jazyki slavjanskix kul'tur, 104–115.

—— (2008b). 'Finitnost' i diskursivnaja funkcija klauzy (na primere karačaevo-balkarskogo jazyka)' [Finiteness and the discourse function of a clause: Karachay-Balkar evidence]. In: Vladimir A. Plungian [Plungjan] (ed.), *Grammatičeskie kategorii v diskurse*. Moscow: Gnozis, 131–166.

—— (2008c). 'Multimodal'naja lingvistika: napravlenija issledovanij' [Multimodal linguistics: Directions of research]. In: Vladimir N. Polyakov [Poljakov] (ed.), *Cognitive Modelling in Linguistics. Proceedings of the Xth International Conference*. Becici, Montenegro: Kazan' State University Press, 132–145.

—— (2008d). 'On the importance of Russian Sign Language linguistic research'. In: Anna A. Komarova and Nadežda A. Čauš'jan (eds.), *Linguistic rights of the deaf: Materials of the International Conference*. Moscow: OOOI VOG, 393–399.

—— and Vera I. Podlesskaya [Podlesskaja] (eds.) (2009). *Rasskazy o snovidenijax: korpusnoe issledovanie ustnogo russkogo diskursa* [Night Dream Stories: A corpus study of spoken Russian discourse]. Moscow: Jazyki slavjanskix kul'tur.

—— (2009a). 'Modus, žanr i drugie parametry klassifikacii diskursov' [Mode, genre, and other parameters of discourse classification]. *Voprosy Jazykoznanija* 2009(2), 3–21.

—— (2009b). *Basics of referential systems: Sorting things out*. Paper presented at the 7th Discourse Anaphora and Anaphor Resolution Colloquium (DAARC 2009), Goa, India, 5–6 November 2009.

—— Grigorij B. Dobrov, Dmitrij A. Zalmanov, Anastasija S. Linnik, and Natalia V. Loukachevitch [Natal'ja V. Lukaševič] (2010a). 'Referencial'nyj vybor kak mnogofaktornyj verojatnostnyj process' [Referential choice as a multi-factorial probabilistic process]. In: Aleksandr E. Kibrik (ed.), *Computational Linguistics and Intellectual Technologies. Papers from the Annual International Conference 'Dialogue' (2010). Bekasovo, Moscow region*. Moscow: Izdatel'stvo RGGU, 173–181.

—— —— —— and Natalia V. Loukachevitch (2010b). 'Referential choice as a probabilistic multi-factorial process'. In: Tatyana V. Chernigovskaya [Tat'jana V. Černigovskaja] (ed.), *The 4th International Conference on Cognitive Science*. Vol. 1. Tomsk, June 2010 56–67.

—— (2011). 'Cognitive discourse analysis: local discourse structure'. In: Marcin Grygiel and Laura A. Janda (eds.), *Slavic linguistics in a cognitive framework*. Frankfurt am Main: Peter Lang, 273–304.

Kibrik, Andrej A. (in press a). 'What's in the head of head-marking languages?' In: Pirkko Suihkonen, Bernard Comrie, and Valery Solovyev (eds.) *Proceedings of the international Symposium on the typology of argument structure and grammatical relations in languages spoken in Europe and North and Central Asia. Kazan' State University, Russia, May 2004.* Amsterdam: Benjamins.

—— (in press b). 'Discourse semantics and the form of the verb predicate in Karachay-Balkar: A corpus-based and experimental study'. In: Balthasar Bickel, Lenore Grenoble, David A. Peterson, and Alan Timberlake (eds.), *What's where why? Language typology and historical contingency: A festschrift to honor Johanna Nichols.* Amsterdam: Benjamins.

—— (in preparation). *Referential Choice in Tuvan.*

Kim, Myung-Hee, Leslie Stirling, and Nicholas Evans (2001). 'Narrative structure and referring expressions in Australian languages'. Paper presented at the 4th Conference of the Association for Linguistic Typology, Santa Barbara, 22 July 2001.

Kimmelman [Kimmel'man], Vadim (2007). *Otricanie v RŽJa. Osnovnye osobennosti* [Negation in RSL. Main peculiarities]. Year paper. Institute of Linguistics, Russian State University for the Humanities.

—— (2009a). 'Parts of speech in Russian Sign Language: The role of iconicity and economy'. *Sign Language and Linguistics* 12(2), 161–186.

—— (2009b). *Reflexive pronouns in Russian Sign Language and Sign Language of the Netherlands.* M.A. thesis. University of Amsterdam.

—— (2010). *Bazovyj porjadok slov v russkom žestovom jazyke* [Basic word order in Russian Sign Language]. Diploma thesis. Institute of Linguistics, Russian State University for the Humanities.

King, Jeffrey (2006). 'Anaphora: Philosophical aspects'. In: Keith Brown (ed.), *Encyclopedia of language and linguistics.* Oxford: Elsevier, 238–240.

Kita, Sotaro (ed.) (2003). *Pointing: Where language, culture, and cognition meet.* Mahwah, NJ: Erlbaum.

Kitazawa, Shigeyoshi, Shinya Kiriyama, Tomohiko Kasami, Shogo Ishikawa, Naofumi Otani, Hiroaki Horiuchi, and Yoichi Takebayashi (2008). *A multimodal infant behavior annotation for developmental analysis of demonstrative expressions.* Proceedings of the 6th International Language Resources and Evaluation (LREC 2008). Marrakech, Morocco, 28–30 May 2008.

Klein, Wolfgang (1982). 'Local deixis in route direction'. In: Robert J. Jarvella and Wolfgang Klein (eds.), *Speech, place and action: Studies in deixis and related topics.* New York: Wiley, 161–182.

—— (1994). *Time in language.* London: Routledge.

Klein-Andreu, Flora (1996). 'Anaphora, deixis, and the evolution of Latin *ille*'. In: Barbara A. Fox (ed.), *Studies in anaphora.* Amsterdam: Benjamins, 305–332.

Klima, Edward S., and Ursula Bellugi (1979). *The Signs of language.* Cambridge, MA: Harvard University Press.

Kobsa, Alfred, Jürgen Allgayer, Carola Reddig, Norbert Reithinger, Dagmar Schmauks, Karin Harbusch, and Wolfgang Wahlster (1986). 'Combining deictic gestures and natural language for referent identification'. In: *Proceedings of the 11th International Conference on Computational Linguistics.* Bonn, Germany, 356–361.

Kodzasov, Sandro V. (2009). *Issledovanija v oblasti russkoj prosodii* [Studies in the field of Russian prosody]. Moscow: Jazyki slavjanskix kul'tur.

Koh, Sungryong, Anthony J. Sanford, Charles Clifton Jr., and Eugene J. Dawydiak (2008). Good-enough representation in plural and singular pronominal reference. In: Jeanette K. Gundel and Nancy Hedberg (eds.), *Reference: Interdisciplinary perspectives.* Oxford: Oxford University Press, 123–42.

Konate, Adama (1989). *Sopostavitel'nyj analiz dialektov beledugu i bamako jazyka bamana (fonetika, grammatika)* [A comparative analysis of the Beledugu and Bamako dialects of Bamana (Phonetics and grammar)]. Ph.D. thesis. Institute of Linguistics, Academy of Sciences of the USSR.

Kong, Kenneth (1998). 'Are simple business request letters really simple? A comparison of Chinese and English business request letters'. *Text* 18(1), 103–141.

König, Ekkehard, and Peter Siemund (2000). 'Intensifiers and reflexives: A typological perspective'. In: Zygmunt Frajzyngier and Tracy S. Curl (eds.), *Reflexives: Forms and functions.* Amsterdam: Benjamins, 41–74.

Koolen, Ruud, Albert Gatt, Martijn Goudbeek, and Emiel Krahmer (2009). 'Need I say more? On factors causing referential overspecification'. Paper presented at the Production of Referring Expressions Conference: Bridging the Gap between Computational and Empirical Approaches to Reference (PRE-CogSci), Amsterdam, 29 July 2009.

Kosslyn, Stephen M. (1994). *Image and brain: The resolution of the imagery debate.* Cambridge, MA: MIT Press.

Koval [Koval'], Antonina I., and Galina V. Zubko (1986). *Jazyk fula* [The Fula language]. Moscow: Nauka.

—— (1997). 'Imennye kategorii v pular-ful'ful'de' [Nominal categories in Pulaar-Fulfulde]. In: Viktor A. Vinogradov (ed.), *Osnovy afrikanskogo jazykoznanija. Imennye kategorii.* Moscow: Aspekt Press, 92–220.

—— (1999). 'Jazyk ustnogo èposa ful'be i zatekstovaja kul'turnaja informacija' [The language of Fulbe oral epic and implied cultural information]. In: Viktor Ja. Porxomovskij and Natal'ja N. Semenjuk (eds.), *Ustnye formy literaturnogo jazyka: istorija i sovremennost'.* Moscow: Editorial URSS, 219–237.

Krasavina, Olga [Ol'ga] N. (2004). 'Upotreblenie ukazatel'noj gruppy v russkom povestvovatel'nom diskurse' [The use of demonstrative NPs in Russian narrative discourse]. *Voprosy Jazykoznanija* 2004(3), 51–68.

—— (2006). *Korpusno-orientirovannoe issledovanie referencii (principy annotacii i analiz dannyx)* [A corpus-oriented study of reference (principles of annotation and data analysis)]. Ph.D. thesis. Dept. of Theoretical and Applied Linguistics, Moscow State University.

—— and Christian Chiarcos (2007). 'PoCoS – Potsdam Coreference Scheme'. In: Proceedings of the Conference of the Asssociation for Computational Linguistics (LAW). Prague, Czech Republic, 156–163.

Krause, Mark A. (1997). 'Comparative perspectives on pointing and joint attention in children and apes'. *International Journal of Comparative Psychology* 3, 137–157.

Kreiman, Jody, and Almerindo E. Ojeda (eds.) (1980). *Papers from the parasession on pronouns and anaphora*. Chicago: Chicago Linguistic Society.

Krejdlin, E., and Aleksandr S. Chekhov [Čexov] (1988). *Sootnošenie semantiki, aktual'nogo členenija i pragmatiki v leksikografičeskom opisanii anaforičeskix mestoimenij (na materiale mestoimenij gruppy TOT)* [Semantics, theme-rheme articulation, and pragmatics in the lexicographic description of anaphoric pronouns (on the basis of the pronouns of the TOT-group)]. Problemnaja gruppa po èksperimental'noj i prikladnoj lingvistike. Predvaritel'nye publikacii, Vol. 178. Moscow: Institut Russkogo Jazyka AN SSSR.

—— (2007). 'Mexanizmy vzaimodejstvija verbal'nyx i neverbal'nyx edinic v dialoge. Dejktičeskie žesty i ix tipy'. [Mechanisms of interaction between verbal and nonverbal units in dialogue. Deictic gestures and their types]. In: Leonid L. Iomdin, Natal'ja I. Laufer, Aleksandr S. Narin'jani, and Vladimir P. Selegej (eds.), *Computational Linguistics and Intellectual Technologies. International Conference 'Dialogue 2007' Proceedings. Bekasovo, Moscow region*. Moscow: Izdatel'stvo RGGU, 320–327.

Kresin, Susan C. (1998). 'Deixis and thematic hierarchies in Russian narrative discourse'. *Journal of Pragmatics* 30, 421–435.

Kruijff, Geert-Jan M., John D. Kelleher, and Nick Hawes (2006). 'Information fusion for visual reference resolution in dynamic situated dialogue'. In: Elisabeth Andre, Laila Dybkjaer, Wolfgang Minker, Heiko Neumann, and Michael Weber (eds.), *Perception and Interactive Technologies*. Berlin: Springer, 117–128.

Krupa, Viktor (1976). 'A semantic typology of personal pronouns'. *Asian and African Studies* 12, 149–155.

Kruspe, Nicole (2004). *A grammar of Semelai*. Cambridge: Cambridge University Press.

Kuiper, Albertha, and Joy Oram (1991). 'A syntactic sketch of Diuxi-Tilantongo Mixtec'. In: Henty C. Bradley and Barbara E. Hollenbach (eds.), *Studies in the syntax of Mixtecan languages*. Vol. 3. Arlington: University of Texas at Arlington, 179–409.

Kumar, Pramod (2006). 'Jarawa morphology'. Paper presented at the Max Planck Institute for Evolutionary Anthropology, 7 November 2006.

Kumaxov, Muxaddin A. (1974). 'O strukture predloženija v jazykax polisintetičeskogo tipa' [On clause structure in polysynthetic languages]. *Universalii i tipologičeskie issledovanija: meščaninovskie čtenija*. Moscow: Nauka, 125–134.

Kuryłowicz, Jerzy (1972). 'The role of deictic elements in linguistic evolution'. *Semiotica* 5(2), 174–183.

Laidig, Wyn D., and Carol J. Laidig (1990). 'Larike pronouns: Duals and trials in a Central Moluccan language'. *Oceanic Linguistics* 29(2), 87–109.

Lakoff, George (1976). 'Pronouns and reference'. In: James McCawley (ed.), *Syntax and Semantics*. Vol. 7. New York: Academic Press, 275–335.

—— and Mark Johnson (1980). *Metaphors we live by*. Chicago: University of Chicago Press.

Lakoff, George (1987). *Women, fire, and dangerous things.* Chicago: University of Chicago Press.
—— (1990). 'The invariance hypothesis: Is abstract reason based on image-schemas?' *Cognitive Linguistics* 1(1), 39–74.
—— and Rafael E. Núñez (2000). *Where mathematics comes from.* New York: Basic Books.
Lambrecht, Knud (1981). *Topic, antitopic and verb agreement in non-standard French.* Amsterdam: Benjamins.
—— (1994). *Information structure and sentence form. Topic, focus, and the mental representation of discourse referents.* Cambridge: Cambridge University Press.
Landragin, Frédéric (2007). 'Taking situational factors into account when resolving anaphora: An approach based on salience and events'. In: António Branco, Tony McEnery, Ruslan Mitkov, and Fátima Silva (eds.), *Proceedings of the 6th Discourse Anaphora and Anaphor Resolution Colloquium (DAARC 2007).* Porto: Centro de Linguística da Universidade do Porto, 71–76.
Langacker, Ronald (1985). 'Observations and speculations on subjectivity'. In: John Haiman (ed.), *Iconicity in syntax.* Amsterdam: Benjamins, 109–150.
—— (1987/1991). *Foundations of cognitive grammar.* Vols. 1, 2. Stanford: Stanford University Press.
—— (1996). 'Conceptual grouping and pronominal anaphora'. In: Barbara A. Fox (ed.), *Studies in anaphora.* Amsterdam: Benjamins, 333–378.
—— (2001). 'Discourse in cognitive grammar'. *Cognitive Linguistics* 12(2), 143–188.
Lappin, Shalom, and Elabbas Benmamoun (eds.) (1999). *Fragments: Studies in ellipsis and gapping.* New York: Oxford University Press.
Leafgren, John (2002). *Degrees of explicitness.* Amsterdam: Benjamins.
Lebedev, Mikhail, Adam Messinger, Jerlad D. Kralik, and Steven P. Wise (2004). 'Representation of attended versus remembered locations in prefrontal cortex'. *PLoS Biology* 2(11), 1919–1935.
Lébikaza, Kézié Koyenzi (1999). *Grammaire kabiyè: Une analyse systematique.* Köln: Rüdiger Köppe Verlag.
Leer, Jeffry A. (1991). *The schetic categories of the Tlingit verb.* Ph.D. thesis. University of Chicago.
Legendre, Géraldine (2000). 'Morphological/prosodic alignment of Bulgarian clitics'. In: Joost Dekkers, Frank van der Leeuw, and Jeroen van de Weijer (eds.), *Optimality Theory: Phonology, syntax, acquisition.* Amsterdam: Benjamins, 423–464.
Leger, Rudolf (2005). 'Logophoric pronouns in the Southern Bole-Tangale languages'. Paper presented at the 4th International School in Linguistic Typology and Anthropology, Tsaxkadzor, Armenia, September 2005.
Lehmann, Christian (1995). *Thoughts on grammaticalization.* München: LINCOM Europa.
Levelt, Willem J. M. (1989). *Speaking: From intention to articulation.* Cambridge, MA: MIT Press.
Levinsohn, Stephen H. (1994). 'Field procedures for the analysis of participant reference in a monologue discourse'. In: Stephen H. Levinsohn (ed.), *Discourse features of ten languages of West-Central Africa.* Dallas: SIL, 109–121.

Levinson, Stephen C. (1983). *Pragmatics*. Cambridge: Cambridge University Press.
—— (1987). 'Pragmatics and the grammar of anaphora'. *Journal of Linguistics* 23, 379–434.
—— (2000). *Presumptive meanings: The theory of generalized conversational implicature*. Cambridge, MA: MIT Press.
—— (2004). 'Deixis and pragmatics'. In: Laurence R. Horn and Gregory Ward (eds.), *Handbook of pragmatics*. Malden, MA: Blackwell, 97–121.
Levy, Elena, and Carol A. Fowler (2000). 'The role of gestures and other graded language forms in the grounding of reference in perception'. In: David McNeill (ed.), *Language and gesture*. Cambridge: Cambridge University Press, 215–234.
Li, Charles N., and Sandra A. Thompson (1976). 'Subject and topic: A new typology of languages'. In: Charles N. Li (ed.), *Subject and topic*. New York: Academic Press, 457–489.
—— and —— (1979). 'Third-person pronouns and zero-anaphora in Chinese discourse'. In: T. Givón (ed.), *Discourse and syntax*. New York: Academic Press, 311–335.
Lichtenberk, Frantisek (1996). 'Patterns of anaphora in To'aba'ita narrative discourse'. In: Barbara A. Fox (ed.), *Studies in anaphora*. Amsterdam: Benjamins, 379–412.
—— (1997). 'Head-marking and objecthood'. In: Joan Bybee, John Haiman, and Sandra A. Thompson (eds.), *Essays on language function and language type. Dedicated to T. Givón*. Amsterdam: Benjamins, 301–322.
Liddell, Scott K. (1990). 'Four functions of a locus: Reexamining the structure of space in ASL'. In: Ceil Lucas (ed.), *Sign language research: Theoretical Issues*. Washington, D.C.: Gallaudet University Press, 176–198.
—— (1995). 'Real, surrogate, and token space: Grammatical consequences in ASL'. In: Karen Emmorey and Judy S. Reilly (eds.), *Language, gesture, and space*. Hillsdale, NJ: Erlbaum, 19–41.
—— (2000). 'Blended spaces and deixis in sign languages'. In: David McNeill (ed.), *Language and gesture*. Cambridge: Cambridge University Press, 331–357.
—— (2003). *Grammar, gesture, and meaning in American Sign Language*. Cambridge: Cambridge University Press.
Liebal, Katja, Simone Pika, and Michael Tomasello (2006). 'Gestural communication of orangutans (Pongo pygmaeus)'. *Gesture* 6(1), 1–38.
Linde, Charlotte (1979). 'Focus of attention and the choice of pronouns in discourse'. In: T. Givón (ed.), *Discourse and syntax*. New York: Academic Press, 337–354.
Linnik, Anastasija S. (2010). *Lingvističeskoe obespečenie statističeskogo analiza korpusa, razmečennogo po referencii* [Linguistic support for the statistical analysis of a referentially annotated corpus]. Diploma thesis. Dept. of Theoretical and Applied Linguistics, Moscow State University.
Logan, Gordon D. (1995). 'Linguistic and conceptual control of visual spatial attention'. *Cognitive Psychology* 28, 103–174.
Logan, Harold Jeffrrey (2001). *A collection of Saulteaux texts with translations and linguistic analyses*. M.A. thesis. University of Regina.

Longacre, Robert E. (1983a). *The grammar of discourse*. New York: Plenum Press.

—— (1983b). 'Switch-reference in two distinct linguistic areas: Wojokeso (Papua New Guinea) and Guanano (Northern South America)'. In: John Haiman and Pamela Munro (eds.), *Switch-reference and universal grammar*. Amsterdam: Benjamins, 185–208.

Lord, Carol, and Kathleen Dahlgren (1997). 'Participant and event anaphora in newspaper articles'. In: Joan Bybee, John Haiman, and Sandra A. Thompson (eds.), *Essays on language function and language type. Dedicated to T. Givón*. Amsterdam: Benjamins, 323–356.

Loukachevitch, Natalia V. [Natal'ja V. Lukaševič], Grigorij B. Dobrov, Andrej A. Kibrik, Mariya V. Khudyakova [Marija V. Xudjakova], and Anastasija S. Linnik (2011). 'Factors of referential choice: Computational modelling'. In: *Computational Linguistics and Intellectual Technologies. Papers from the Annual International Conference 'Dialogue' (2011). Bekasovo, Moscow region*. Moscow: Izdatel'stvo RGGU, 458–467.

Louwerse, Max M., and Adrian Bangerter (2005).'Focusing attention with deictic gestures and linguistic expressions'. In: Bruno G. Bara, Lawrence Barsalou, and Monica Bucciarelli (eds.), *The Annual Conference of the Cognitive Science Society*. Stresa, Italy, 21–23 July 2005: Erlbaum, 1331–1336.

Luck, Steven J., and Edward K. Vogel (1997). 'The capacity of visual working memory for features and conjunctions'. *Nature* 390 (20 November 1997), 279–281.

Lungstrum, Richard W. (1995). *Switch-reference and the structure of Lakhota narrative discourse*. Ph.D. thesis. University of Pennsylvania.

Lupyan, Gary, and Rick Dale (2010). 'Language structure is partly determined by social structure'. *PLoS ONE* 5(1).

Lust, Barbara, Kashi Wali, James W. Gair, and K. V. Subbarao (eds.) (2002). *Lexical anaphors and pronouns in selected South Asian languages: A principled typology*. Berlin: Mouton de Gruyter.

Lynch, John (1982). 'Anejom̃ grammar sketch'. In: John Lynch (ed.), *Papers in linguistics of Melanesia*. Vol. 4. Canberra: Australian National University, 93–154.

—— (1983). 'Switch-reference in Lenakel'. In: John Haiman and Pamela Munro (eds.), *Switch-reference and universal grammar*. Amsterdam: Benjamins, 209–222.

—— (2002). 'Anejom̃'. In: John Lynch, Malcolm Ross, and Terry Crowley (eds.), *The Oceanic languages*. Richmond: Curzon Press, 723–752.

Lyons, John (1975). 'Deixis as the source of reference'. In: Edward L. Keenan (ed.), *Formal semantics of natural language*. Cambridge: Cambridge University Press, 61–83.

—— (1977). *Semantics*. Vol. 2. Cambridge: Cambridge University Press.

Lyutikova [Ljutikova], Ekaterina A. (2001). 'Anaforičeskie sredstva' [Anaphoric devices]. In: Aleksandr E. Kibrik (ed.), *Bagvalinskij jazyk. Grammatika. Teksty. Slovari*. Moscow: Nasledie, 615–682.

—— (2002). *Kognitivnaja tipologija: refleksivy i intensifikatory* [Cognitive typology: Reflexives and intensifiers]. Moscow: IMLI RAN.

Maes, Alfons (1996). 'The markedness of abstract-object anaphors in discourse'. In: Walter de Mulder and Liliane Tasmowski (eds.), *Coherence and anaphora*. Amsterdam: Benjamins, 161–183.

—— and Christ de Rooij (2007). '(How) do demonstratives code distance?' In: António Branco, Tony McEnery, Ruslan Mitkov, and Fátima Silva (eds.), *Proceedings of the 6th Discourse Anaphora and Anaphor Resolution Colloquium (DAARC 2007)*. Porto: Centro de Linguística da Universidade do Porto, 83–89.

Mahootian, Shahrzad, and Lewis Gebhardt (1997). *Persian*. London: Routledge.

Majtinskaja, Klara E. (1969). *Mestoimenija v jazykax raznyx sistem* [Pronouns in the languages of various systems]. Moscow: Nauka.

Makarov, Mixail L. (2003). *Osnovy teorii diskursa* [Foundations of the theory of discourse]. Moscow: Gnozis.

Malchukov [Mal'čukov], Andrej L. (2009). 'Taksis v evenskom jazyke' [Taxis in Even]. In: Viktor S. Khrakovsky [Xrakovskij] (ed.), *Tipologija taksisnyx konstrukcij*. Moscow: Znak, 828–864.

Mann, William C., and Sandra A. Thompson (1988). 'Rhetorical structure theory: Toward a functional theory of text organization'. *Text* 8(3), 243–281.

—— Christian Matthiessen, and Sandra A. Thompson (1992). 'Rhetorical structure theory and text analysis'. In: William C. Mann and Sandra A. Thompson (eds.), *Discourse description: Diverse analyses of a fund-raising text*. Amsterdam: Benjamins, 39–78.

—— and Sandra A. Thompson (eds.) (1992). *Discourse description: Diverse analyses of a fund-raising text*. Amsterdam: Benjamins.

Marchese, Lynell (1986). 'Godié'. In: Ursula Wiesemann (ed.), *Pronominal systems*. Tübingen: Narr, 217–256.

Markus, Olga (2007). 'Independent personal pronouns in Athabaskan: Their forms and functions'. In: Andrea Berez, Suzanne Gessner, Leslie Saxon, and Siri Tuttle (eds.), *Working papers in Athabaskan languages*. Vol. 6. Fairbanks: Alaska Native Language Center, 67–82.

Marslen-Wilson, William, Elena Levy, and Lorraine K. Tyler (1982). 'Producing interpretable discourse: The establishment and maintenance of reference'. In: Robert J. Jarvella and Wolfgang Klein (eds.), *Speech, place and action: Studies in deixis and related topics*. Chichester: Wiley, 339–378.

Martin, Jim R., and David Rose (2008). *Genre relations: Mapping culture*. London: Equinox.

Masataka, Nobuo (2003). 'From index-finger extension to index-finger pointing: Ontogenesis of pointing in preverbal infants'. In: Sotaro Kita (ed.), *Pointing: Where language, culture, and cognition meet*. Mahwah, NJ: Erlbaum, 69–84.

Maslova, Elena (2003). *A grammar of Kolyma Yukaghir*. Berlin: Mouton de Gruyter.

—— and Tatjana Nikitina (2007). *Stochastic universals and dynamics of cross-linguistic distributions: The case of alignment types*. Unpublished.

Mathesius, Vilém (1939). 'O tak zvaném aktuálním členění věty'. *Slovo a slovesnost* 5, 171–174.

Matsumoto, Kazuko (2003). *Intonation units in Japanese conversation: Syntactic, informational, and functional structures*. Amsterdam: Benjamins.

Matthews, Danielle E., Elena V. M. Lieven, Anna Theakston, and Michael Tomasello (2006). 'The effect of perceptual availability and prior discourse on young children's use of referring expressions'. *Applied Psycholinguistics* 27, 403–422.

—— —— and Michael Tomasello (2009). 'The development of reference from two to four years'. Paper presented at the Production of Referring Expressions Conference: Bridging the Gap between Computational and Empirical Approaches to Reference (PRE-CogSci), Amsterdam, 29 July 2009.

Mattissen, Johanna (2002). 'Dependent-head synthesis in Nivkh – with an outlook on polysynthesis in the Far Northeast'. In: Nicholas Evans and Hans-Jürgen Sasse (eds.), *Problems of polysynthesis*. Studia typologica. Vol. 4. Berlin: Akademie Verlag, 135–166.

McCarthy, John (2002). *A thematic guide to optimality theory*. Cambridge: Cambridge University Press.

McElree, Brian (2001). 'Working memory and focal attention'. *Journal of Experimental Psychology: Learning, Memory, and Cognition* 27(3), 817–835.

—— Stephani Foraker, and Lisbeth Dyer (2003). 'Memory structures that subserve sentence comprehension'. *Journal of Memory and Language* 48, 67–91.

McEnery, Tony, and Andrew Wilson (2001). *Corpus linguistics: An introduction*. Edinburgh: Edinburgh University Press.

McKay, Graham R. (1978). 'Pronominal person and number categories in Rembarrnga and Djeebbana'. *Oceanic Linguistics* 17, 27–37.

McLendon, Sally (1996). 'Sketch of Eastern Pomo, a Pomoan language'. In: Ives Goddard (ed.), *Handbook of North American Indians. Vol. 17. Languages*. Washington, D.C.: Smithsonian Institution, 507–550.

McNeill, David (1992). *Hand and mind: What gestures reveal about thought*. Chicago: University of Chicago Press.

—— (ed.) (2000). *Language and gesture*. Cambridge: Cambridge University Press.

—— (2003). 'Pointing and morality in Chicago'. In: Sotaro Kita (ed.), *Pointing: Where language, culture, and cognition meet*. Mahwah, NJ: Erlbaum, 293–306.

Meier, Richard P. (1990). 'Person deixis in ASL'. In: Susan D. Fischer and Patricia Siple (eds.), *Theoretical issues in sign language research*. Vol. 1. Chicago: University of Chicago Press, 175–190.

Mel'nik, Andrej D., and Elena V. Mnacakanjan (2010). 'ĖĖG-korreljaty različij meždu kategorijami "živoe" i "neživoe" v zadače kategorizacii zritel'nyx stimulov u čeloveka' [EEG-correlates of the differences between the categories 'animate' and 'inanimate' in the categorization task for visual stimuli in humans]. In: Tatyana V. Chernigovskaya [Tat'jana V. Černigovskaja] (ed.), *The 4th International Conference on Cognitive Science*. Vol. 1., June 2010 Tomsk, 410–411.

Merrell, Floyd (2006). 'Reference: Semiotic theory'. In: Keith Brown (ed.), *Encyclopedia of language and linguistics*. Oxford: Elsevier, 433–440.

Miestamo, Matti (2005). *Standard negation: The negation of declarative verbal main clauses in a typological perspective.* Berlin: Mouton de Gruyter.

Miller, George A. (1956). 'The magical number seven, plus or minus two: Some limits on our capacity for processing information'. *Psychological Review* 63, 81–97.

—— Eugene Galanter, and Karl H. Pribram (1960). *Plans and the structure of behavior.* New York: Holt, Rinehart & Winston.

Miller, Jim, and Regina Weinart (1998). *Spontaneous spoken language: Syntax and discourse.* Oxford: Clarendon Press.

Miller, Philip H., and Ivan A. Sag (1997). 'French clitic movement without clitics or movement'. *Natural Language and Linguistic Theory* 15(3), 573–639.

Miltsakaki, Eleni (2007). 'A rethink of the relationship between salience and anaphora resolution'. In: António Branco, Tony McEnery, Ruslan Mitkov, and Fátima Silva (eds.), *Proceedings of the 6th Discourse Anaphora and Anaphor Resolution Colloquium (DAARC 2007).* Porto: Centro de Linguística da Universidade do Porto, 91–96.

Mitchell, Tom M. (1997). *Machine learning.* Boston: McGraw-Hill.

Mithun, Marianne (1986a). 'Disagreement: The case of pronominal affixes and nouns'. In: Deborah Tannen (ed.), *Proceedings of the Georgetown University Round Table Conference on Language and Linguistics.* Washington, D.C.: Georgetown University Press, 50–66.

—— (1986b). 'The convergence of noun classification systems'. In: Colette Craig (ed.), *Noun classes and categorization.* Amsterdam: Benjamins, 379–398.

—— (1986c). 'When zero isn't there'. In: Vassiliki Nikoforidou, Mary VanClay, Mary Niepokuj, and Deborah Feder (eds.), *Berkeley Linguistics Society* 12. 195–211.

—— (1987). 'Is basic word order universal?' In: Russell S. Tomlin (ed.), *Coherence and grounding in discourse.* Amsterdam: Benjamins, 281–328.

—— (1990). 'Third-person reference and the function of pronouns in Central Pomo natural speech'. *International Journal of American Linguistics* 56(3), 361–376.

—— (1991). 'The development of bound pronominal paradigms'. In: Winfred P. Lehmann and Helen-Jo Jakusz Hewitt (eds.), *Language typology 1988: Typological models in reconstruction.* Amsterdam: Benjamins, 85–104.

—— (1993). '"Switch-reference": Clause combining in Central Pomo'. *International Journal of American Linguistics* 59, 119–136.

—— (1999). *The languages of native North America.* Cambridge: Cambridge University Press.

—— (2003). 'Pronouns and agreement: The information status of pronominal affixes'. *Transactions of the Philological Society* 101(2), 235–278.

—— (2007). 'Freedom and prosody: Mohawk independent pronouns in spontaneous speech'. Paper presented at the LSA/SSILA Meeting. Anaheim, January 2007.

Mitkov, Ruslan (2002). *Anaphora resolution.* London: Longman.

Miyake, Akira, and Priti Shah (eds.) (1999). *Models of working memory: Mechanisms of active maintenance and executive control.* Cambridge: Cambridge University Press.

Mol, Lisette, Emiel Krahmer, Alfons Maes, and Marc Swerts (2008). *Audience design and gesticulation*. Proceedings of the 3rd International Conference on Cognitive Science. Moscow, 110–111.

Moldovan, Aleksandr M., Sergej S. Skorvid, Andrej A. Kibrik, Natal'ja V. Rogova, Ekaterina I. Jakuškina, Aleksej F. Žuravlev, and Svetlana M. Tolstaja (eds.) (2005). *Jazyki mira: slavjanskie jazyki* [Languages of the world: Slavic languages]. Moscow: Academia.

Monachesi, Paola (2005). *The verbal complex in Romance*. Oxford: Oxford University Press.

Moneglia, Massimo (2005). 'The C-ORAL-ROM resource'. In: Manuela Cresti and Massimo Moneglia (eds.), *C-ORAL-ROM: Integrated corpora for spoken Romance languages*. Amsterdam: Benjamins, 1–70.

Mosel, Ulrike (2010). 'The fourth person in Teop'. In: John Bowden, Nikolaus Himmelmann, and Makolm Ross (eds.), *A journey through Austronesian and Papuan linguistic and cultural space: Papers in honour of Andrew K. Pawley*. Canberra: Pacific Linguistics, 391–404.

Moser, Rosmarie (2004). *Kabba: A Nilo-Saharan language of the Central African Republic*. München: LINCOM Europa.

Mous, Maarten (2007). *Grammatical sketch of Seereer*. Unpublished.

Mühlhäusler, Peter, Rom Harré, Anthony Holiday, and Michael Freyne (1990). *Pronouns and people: The linguistic construction of social and personal identity*. Oxford: Blackwell.

—— (2001). 'Personal pronouns'. In: Martin Haspelmath, Ekkehard König, Wulf Oesterreicher, and Wolfgang Raible (eds.), *Language typology and language universals: An international handbook*. Vol. 1. Berlin: de Gruyter, 741–747.

Mulder, Jean (1994). *Ergativity in Coast Tsimshian (Sm'algyax)*. Berkeley, CA: University of California Press.

Müller, Christoph, and Michael Strube (2006). 'Multi-Level Annotation of Linguistic Data with MMAX2'. In: Sabine Braun, Kurt Kohn, and Joybrato Mukherjee (eds.), *Corpus technology and language pedagogy: New resources, new tools, new methods*. Frankfurt: Peter Lang, 197–214.

Müller, Olga (2004). 'Why there is no y-/b- alternation in Dena'ina'. *Working papers in Athabaskan languages* 4, 99–114.

Munro, Pamela (1980). 'Studies on switch-reference'. *UCLA Papers in Syntax 8*. Los Angeles: Dept. of Linguistics, UCLA, 89–118.

Myachykov, Andriy, and Michael I. Posner (2005). 'Attention in language'. In: Laurent Itti, Geraint Rees, and John K. Tsotsos (eds.), *Neurobiology of Attention*. Burlington, MA: Elsevier Academic Press, 324–329.

—— and Russell S. Tomlin (2005). *Talking about fish in Russian: The interface between attention and syntax in the production of discourse*. Glasgow. Unpublished.

—— —— and Michael I. Posner (2005). 'Attention and empirical studies of grammar'. *The Linguistic Review* 22, 347–364.

Myachykov, Andriy, Michael I. Posner, and Russell S. Tomlin (2007). 'A parallel interface for language and cognition in sentence production: Theory, method, and experimental evidence'. *The Linguistic Review* 24, 455–472.

Myhill, John, and Junko Hibiya (1988). 'The discourse function of clause chaining'. In: John Haiman and Sandra A. Thompson (eds.), *Clause combining in grammar and discourse*. Amsterdam: Benjamins, 361–398.

—— and —— (2001). 'Typology and discourse analysis'. In: Deborah Schiffrin, Deborah Tannen, and Heidi E. Hamilton (eds.), *Handbook of discourse analysis*. Malden, MA: Blackwell, 161–174.

Naden, Anthony J. (1986). 'Western Oti/Volta pronoun systems'. In: Ursula Wiesemann (ed.), *Pronominal systems*. Tübingen: Narr, 257–284.

Nariyama, Shigeko (2001). 'Argument structure as another reference-tracking system with reference to ellipsis'. *Australian Journal of Linguistics* 21(1), 99–129.

—— (2003). *Ellipsis and reference tracking in Japanese*. Amsterdam: Benjamins.

—— (2007). 'Ellipsis and markedness: Examining the meaning of ellipsis'. In: António Branco, Tony McEnery, Ruslan Mitkov, and Fátima Silva (eds.), *The 6th Discourse Anaphora and Anaphor Resolution Colloquium (DAARC 2007)*. Porto: Centro de Linguística da Universidade do Porto, 97–102.

Németh, T. Enikő (ed.) (2001). *Cognition in language use*. Antwerp: International Pragmatics Association.

Nesset, Tore (2008). *Abstract phonology in a concrete model: Cognitive linguistics and the morphology-phonology interface*. Berlin: Mouton de Gruyter.

Nevis, Joel A., Brian D. Joseph, Dieter Wanner, and Arnold M. Zwicky (1994). *Clitics: A comprehensive bibliography 1892–1991*. Amsterdam: Benjamins.

Nevskaja, Irina A. (1993). *Formy deepričastnogo tipa v šorskom jazyke* [Converb-like forms in Shor]. Novosibirsk: Izdatel'stvo Novisibirskogo Universiteta.

Newman, Stanley (1996). 'Sketch of the Zuni language'. In: Ives Goddard (ed.), *Handbook of North American Indians. Vol. 17. Languages*. Washington, D.C.: Smithsonian Institution, 483–506.

Newmeyer, Frederic J. (1991). 'Functional explanation in linguistics'. *Language and Communication* 11, 3–28.

Nichols, Johanna (1983). 'Switch-reference in the Northeast Caucasus'. In: John Haiman and Pamela Munro (eds.), *Switch-reference and universal grammar*. Amsterdam: Benjamins, 245–266.

—— (1984). 'Functional theories of language'. *Annual Review of Anthropology* 13, 97–117.

—— (1985). 'Grammatical marking of theme'. In: Michael Flier and Richard Brecht (eds.), *Issues in Russian morphosyntax*. UCLA Slavic Studies. Vol. 10. Columbus: Slavica, 170–186.

—— (1986). 'Head-marking and depending-marking grammar'. *Language* 62, 56–119.

—— (1992). *Linguistic diversity in space and time*. Chicago: University of Chicago Press.

Nichols, Johanna and Balthasar Bickel (2005a). 'Locus of marking in possessive noun phrases'. In: Martin Haspelmath, Matthew Dryer, David Gil, and Bernard Comrie (eds.), *World atlas of language structures*. Oxford: Oxford University Press, 102–105.
—— and Balthasar Bickel (2005b). 'Locus of marking in the clause'. In: Martin Haspelmath, Matthew Dryer, David Gil, and Bernard Comrie (eds.), *World atlas of language structures*. Oxford: Oxford University Press, 98–101.
Nieuwland, Mante S., Marte Otten, and Jos J. A. van Berkum (2007). 'Who are you talking about? Tracking discourse-level referential processing with ERPs'. *Journal of Cognitive Neuroscience* 19, 228–236.
—— and Jos J. A. van Berkum (2008). 'The neurocognition of referential ambiguity in language comprehension'. *Language and Linguistics Compass* 2/4, 603–630.
Nikolaeva, Julija V. (2003). *Illjustrativnye žesty: semantika i osobennosti verbal'nogo konteksta* [Illustrative gestures: Semantics and the properties of the verbal context]. Diploma thesis. Dept. of Theoretical and Applied Linguistics, Moscow State University.
Nikolaeva, Tatyana [Tat'jana] M. (1978). 'Lingvistika teksta: sovremennoe sostojanie i perspektivy' [Text linguistics: Current state and perspectives]. In: Tatyana [Tat'jana] M. Nikolaeva (ed.), *Novoe v zarubežnoj lingvistike, vyp. VIII. Lingvistika teksta*. Moscow: Progress, 5–42.
—— (2000). *Ot zvuka k tekstu* [From sound to text]. Moscow: Jazyki russkoj kul'tury.
—— (2004). 'Funkcii russkogo "ja" v indoevropejskoj perspektive' [Functions of Russian 'I' in an Indo-European perspective]. In: Tatyana [Tat'jana] M. Nikolaeva (ed.), *Verbal'naja i neverbal'naja opory prostranstva mežfrazovyx svjazej*. Moscow: Jazyki slavjanskoj kul'tury, 167–178.
—— (2008). *Neparadigmatičeskaja lingvistika (Istorija 'bluždajuščix častic')* [Non-paradigmatic linguistics (The history of 'vagile particles')]. Moscow: Jazyki slavjanskoj kul'tury.
Noonan, Michael (1992). *A grammar of Lango*. Berlin: Mouton de Gruyter.
Nordlinger, Rachel, and Louisa Sadler (2000). 'Tense as a nominal category'. In: Miriam Butt and Tracy Holloway King (eds.), *LFG'00 Conference*. Berkeley, CA: CSLI.
Norman, Donald A. (1968). 'Toward a theory of memory and attention'. *Psychological Review* 75, 522–536.
Nunberg, Geoffrey D. (1978). *The pragmatics of reference*. Bloomington: Indiana University Linguistics Club.
—— (1993). 'Indexicality and deixis'. *Linguistics and Philosophy* 16(1), 1–43.
Nuyts, Jan (2007). 'Cognitive linguistics and functional linguistics'. In: Dirk Geeraerts and Hubert Cuyckens (eds.), *The Oxford handbook of cognitive linguistics*. Oxford: Oxford University Press, 543–565.
O'Donnell, Michael (1994). *Sentence analysis and generation – a systemic perspective*. Ph.D. thesis. Dept. of Linguistics, University of Sydney.

O'Neill, Daniela (1996). 'Two-year-old children's sensitivity to a parent's knowledge state when making requests'. *Child Development* 67(2), 659–677.

Obata, Kazuko (2003). *A grammar of Bilua: A Papuan language of the Solomon Islands.* Canberra: Pacific Linguistics.

Oberauer, Klaus, and Reinhold Kliegl (2006). 'A formal model of capacity limits in working memory'. *Journal of Memory and Language* 55(4), 601–626.

Olawsky, Knut J. (1999). *Aspects of Dagbani grammar.* München: LINCOM Europa.

—— (2006). *A grammar of Urarina.* Berlin: Mouton de Gruyter.

Oswalt, Robert L. (1983). 'Interclausal reference in Kashaya'. In: John Haiman and Pamela Munro (eds.), *Switch-reference and universal grammar.* Amsterdam: Benjamins, 267–290.

Otten, Marte, and Jos J. A. van Berkum (2009). 'Does working memory capacity affect the ability to predict upcoming words in discourse?'. *Brain Research* 1291, 92–101.

Padden, Carol A. (1986). 'Verbs and role-shifting in American Sign Language'. In: Carol A. Padden (ed.), *Fourth National Symposium on Sign Language Research and Teaching.* Silver Spring: National Association of the Deaf, 44–57.

Paducheva [Padučeva], Elena V. (1965). 'O strukture abzaca' [On the structure of paragraph]. *Trudy po znakovym sistemam* II, 284–292.

—— (1985). *Vyskazyvanie i ego sootnesennost' s dejstvitel'nost'ju* [Utterance and its relation to reality]. Moscow: Nauka.

—— and Sergej A. Krylov (1992). 'Obščie voprosy dejksisa' [General issues in deixis]. In: Tat'jana V. Bulygina (ed.), *Čelovečeskij faktor v jazyke. Kommunikacija, modal'nost', dejksis.* Moscow: Nauka, 158–194.

—— (1995). *Semantičeskie issledovanija* [Semantic studies]. Moscow: Škola Jazyki russkoj kul'tury.

Palmer, Bill (2009). *VSO clause order and the VP: The case of Oceanic.* Paper presented at the 8th Conference of the Association for Linguistic Typology, Berkeley, CA, July 2009.

Palmer, Frank, Rodney Huddleston, and Geoffrey K. Pullum (2002). 'Inflectional morphology and related matters'. In: Rodney Huddleston and Geoffrey K. Pullum (eds.), *The Cambridge grammar of the English language.* Cambridge: Cambridge University Press, 1565–1619.

Paltridge, Brian (2006). *Discourse analysis: An introduction.* London: Continuum.

Paraboni, Ivandré, Kees van Deemter, and Judith Masthoff (2007). 'Generating referring expressions: Making referents easy to identify'. *Computational Linguistics* 33(2), 229–254.

Parasuraman, Raja (ed.) (1984). *Varieties of attention.* New York: Academic Press.

Parker, Elisabeth (1986). 'Mundani pronouns'. In: Ursula Wiesemann (ed.), *Pronominal systems.* Tübingen: Narr, 131–165.

Partee, Barbara H. (1984). 'Nominal and temporal anaphora'. *Linguistics and Philosophy* 7(3), 287–324.

Pashler, Harold (1998). *Psychology of attention.* Cambridge, MA: MIT Press.

Pavlova, Elizaveta (2010). *Vzaimosvjaz' meždu markirovaniem lica v glagole i v podležaščnom mestoimenii v russkom jazyke* [Relationship between person marking on the verb and on subject pronoun in Russian]. Year paper. Dept. of Theoretical and Applied Linguistics, Moscow State University.

Payne, Doris L., and Thomas E. Payne (1990). 'Yagua'. In: Desmond C. Derbyshire and Geoffrey K. Pullum (eds.), *Handbook of Amazonian languages*. Vol. 2. Berlin: Mouton de Gruyter, 249–474.

Payne, Thomas E. (1993). *The twins stories: Participant coding in Yagua narrative*. Berkeley, CA: University of California Press.

Pensalfini, Robert J. (2006). 'Configurationality'. In: Keith Brown (ed.), *Encyclopedia of language and linguistics*. Oxford: Elsevier, 23–27.

Petrova, Anna (2004). *Avtomatičeskoe ustanovlenie referencii imennyx grupp i pritjažatel'nyx mestoimenij v anglijskom tekste* [Automatic identification of the reference of noun phrases and possessive pronouns in English text]. Year paper. Dept. of Theoretical and Applied Linguistics, Moscow State University.

Piaget, Jean (1923). *Le langage et la pensée chez l'enfant*. Neuchâtel: Delachaux et Niestlé.

Pichl, W. J. (1963). 'Les classes nominales et leur fonctions en sérère'. In: *Actes du 2e. Colloque International de Linguistique Négro-Africaine*. Dakar, 271–273.

Pickering, Martin J., and Simon Garrod (2004). 'Toward a mechanistic psychology of dialogue'. *Behavioral and Brain Sciences* 27, 169–225.

—— and —— (2007). 'Do people use language production to make predictions during comprehension?' *Trends in Cognitive Science* 11(3), 105–110.

Piwek, Paul (2009). 'Salience and pointing in multimodal reference'. Paper presented at the Production of Referring Expressions Conference: Bridging the Gap between Computational and Empirical Approaches to Reference (PRE-CogSci), Amsterdam, 29 July 2009.

Plungian [Plungjan], Vladimir A. (2003). *Obščaja morfologija. Vvedenie v problematiku* [General morphology. Introduction to topical issues]. 2nd edn. Moscow: Editorial URSS.

—— (ed.) (2009). *Nacional'nyj korpus russkogo jazyka: 2006–2008. Novye rezul'taty i perspektivy* [Russian National Corpus: 2006–2008. New results and perspectives]. St. Petersburg: Nestor-Istorija.

Podlesskaya [Podlesskaja], Vera I. (1990). *Voprosy leksičeskoj i sintaksičeskoj semantiki: anafora v sovremennom japonskom jazyke* [Issues in lexical and syntactic semantics: Anaphora in modern Japanese]. Moscow: Nauka.

—— (2010). 'Parameters for typological variation of placeholders'. In: Nino Amiridze, Boyd H. Davis, and Margaret Maclagan (eds.), *Fillers, pauses, and placeholders*. Amsterdam: Benjamins, 11–32.

Poesio, Massimo, Rosemary Stevenson, Barbara di Eugenio, and Janet Hitzeman (2004). 'Centering: A parametric theory and its instantiations'. *Computational Linguistics* 30, 309–363.

Poesio, Massimo, and Ron Artstein (2008). 'Anaphoric annotation in the ARRAU Corpus'. In: *Proceedings of the 6th International Language Resources and Evaluation Conference (LREC 2008)*. Marrakech, Morocco, 28–30 May 2008.

—— (2009). 'Play your way to an annotated corpus: Games with a purpose and anaphoric annotation'. Paper presented at the 7th Discourse Anaphora and Anaphor Resolution Colloquium (DAARC 2009), Goa, India, 5–6 November 2009.

Polyakov [Poljakov], Vladimir N., and Valery D. Solovyev [Valerij D. Solov'ev] (2006). *Komp'juternye modeli i metody v typologii i komparativistike* [Computational models and methods in typological and comparative linguistics]. Kazan': Kazan' State University Press.

Popovich, Harold (1986). 'The nominal reference system of Maxakalí.' In: Ursula Wiesemann (ed.), *Pronominal systems*. Tübingen: Narr, 351–358.

Posner, Michael I. (1989). 'May I have your attention please?', *Proceedings of the Science and Public Policy Seminars*. Washington, D.C., 17 March 1989.

—— and Steven E. Petersen (1990). 'The attention system of the human brain.' *Annual Review of Neuroscience* 13, 25–42.

—— (1994). 'Attention: The mechanisms of consciousness.' *Proceedings of the National Academy of Sciences* 91(August), 7398–7403.

—— (ed.) (2004). *Cognitive neuroscience of attention*. New York: The Guilford Press.

Postle, Bradley R. (2006). 'Working memory as an emergent property of the mind and brain.' *Neuroscience* 139(1), 23–38.

Povinelli, Daniel J., Jesse M. Bering, and Steve Giambrone (2003). 'Chimpanzees' "pointing": Another error of the argument by analogy'. In: Sotaro Kita (ed.), *Pointing: Where language, culture, and cognition meet*. Hillsdale, NJ: Erlbaum, 35–68.

Prasad, Rashmi (2003). *Constraints on the generation of referring expressions, with special reference to Hindi*. Ph.D. thesis. Department of Linguistics, University of Pennsylvania.

Premack, David G., and Guy Woodruff (1978). 'Does the chimpanzee have a theory of mind?' *Behavioral and Brain Sciences* 1, 515–526.

Press, Margaret L. (1980). *Chemehuevi: A grammar and lexicon*. Berkeley, CA: University of California Press.

Prince, Ellen F. (1981). 'Toward a taxonomy of given-new information'. In: Peter Cole (ed.), *Radical pragmatics*. New York: Academic Press, 223–256.

—— (1992). 'The ZPG letter: Subjects, definiteness and information-status'. In: William Mann and Sandra A. Thompson (eds.), *Discourse description: Diverse analyses of a fund-raising text*. Amsterdam: Benjamins, 295–325.

Prince, Gerald (1982). *Narratology: The form and function of narrative*. Berlin: Mouton.

Propp, Vladimir Ja. (1928). *Morfologija skazki* [Morphology of folk tale]. Leningrad: Academia.

Prozorova, Evgenija V. (2004). *Morfologičeskaja složnost' glagola v russkom žestovom jazyke* [Morphological complexity of verbs in Russian Sign Language]. Diploma thesis. Dept. of Theoretical and Applied Linguistics, Moscow State University.

—— (2006). *Referencial'nye xarakteristiki imennyx grupp v russkom žestovom jazyke* [Referential properties of NPs in Russian Sign Language]. Diploma thesis. Dept. of Theoretical and Applied Linguistics, Moscow State University.

—— (2009). *Markery lokal'noj struktury diskursa v russkom žestovom jazyke* [Markers of local discourse structure in Russian Sign Language]. Ph.D. thesis. Dept. of Theoretical and Applied Linguistics, Moscow State University.

Pu, Ming-Ming (2001). 'Cognitive and pragmatic aspects of zero anaphora: A cross-linguistic study'. In: T. Enikő Németh (ed.), *Cognition in language use: Selected papers from the 7th International Pragmatics Conference.* Vol. 1. Antwerp: International Pragmatics Association, 333–349.

Quine, Willard Van Orman (1953). 'Reference and modality'. In: *Quine, Willard Van Orman. From a logical point of view.* Cambridge, MA: Harvard University Press, Chapter VIII.

—— (1971). 'The inscrutability of reference'. In: Danny D. Steinberg and Leon A. Jakobovits (eds.), *Semantics: An interdisciplinary reader in philosophy, linguistics and psychology.* Cambridge: Cambridge University Press, 142–154.

Rast, Erich Hermann (2006). *Reference and indexicality.* Ph.D. thesis. Roskilde University.

Rauh, Gisa (ed.) (1983). *Essays on deixis.* Tübingen: Narr.

Recanati, François (1993). *Direct reference: From language to thought.* Oxford: Blackwell.

Reed, Judy, and David L. Payne (1986). 'Asheninca (Campa) pronominals'. In: Ursula Wiesemann (ed.), *Pronominal systems.* Tübingen: Narr, 323–332.

Reichard, Gladys A. (1951). *Navaho grammar.* New York: Augustin.

Renkema, Jan (2004). *Introduction to discourse studies.* Amsterdam: Benjamins.

—— (ed.) (2009). *Discourse, of course: An overview of research in discourse studies.* Amsterdam: Benjamins.

Repovš, Grega, and Maja Bresjanac (2006). 'Cognitive neuroscience of working memory: A prologue'. *Neuroscience* 139(1), 1–3.

Rhodes, Richard (1997). 'On pronominal systems'. In: Irén Hegedus, Peter A. Michalove, and Alexis Manaster Ramer (eds.), *Indo-European, Nostratic, and beyond: Festschrift for Vitalij V. Shevoroshkin.* Washington, D.C.: Journal of Indo-European Studies, Monograph Number 22, 293–319.

Rice, Keren (1989). *A grammar of Slave.* Berlin: Mouton de Gruyter.

—— (2000). *Morpheme order and semantic scope: Word formation in the Athapaskan verb.* Cambridge: Cambridge University Press.

—— (2003). 'Doubling of agreement in Slave (Northern Athapaskan)'. In: Andrew Carnie and Heidi Harley (eds.), *Form and function: Essays in honor of Eloise Jelinek.* Amsterdam: Benjamins, 51–78.

Rising, David P. (1992). *Switch-reference in Koasati discourse*. Arlington: University of Texas.

Rizzi, Luigi (1982). *Issues in Italian Syntax*. Dordrecht: Foris.

Roberts, John R. (1997). 'Switch-reference in Papua New Guinea: A preliminary survey'. In: Andrew Pawley (ed.), *Papers in Papuan linguistics*. Vol. 3. Canberra: Australian National University, 101–241.

Robertson, Cathy, and Kim Kirsner (2000). 'Indirect memory measures in spontaneous discourse in normal and amnesic subjects'. *Language and Cognitive Processes* 15(2), 203–222.

Rozendaal, Margot, and Anne Baker (2010). 'The acquisition of reference: Pragmatic aspects and the influence of language input'. *Journal of Pragmatics* 42, 1866–1879.

Rubadeau, Patrice Marie (1996). *A descriptive study of clitics in four Slavic languages: Serbo-Croatian, Bulgarian, Polish, and Czech*. Ph.D. thesis. University of Michigan.

Russell, Bertrand (1905). 'On denoting'. *Mind* 14: 479–493.

Russell, Kevin (1996). 'Does obviation mark point of view?' In: John D. Nichols and Argen C. Ogg (eds.), *Nikotwasik iskwahtem, paskihtepayih! Studies in honor of H. C. Wolfart. Algonquian and Iroquoian Linguistics, Memoir 13*. Winnipeg, 367–382.

Sacks, Harvey, Emanuel Schegloff, and Gail Jefferson (1974). 'A simplest systematics for the organization of turn-taking in conversation'. *Language* 50(1), 696–735.

Sainsbury, R. M. (2005). *Reference without referents*. Oxford: Oxford University Press.

Salazar Orvig, Anne, Haydé Marcos, Aliyah Morgenstern, Rouba Hassan, Jocelyne Leber-Marin, and Jacques Parès (2010). 'Dialogical beginnings of anaphora: The use of third person pronouns before the age of 3'. *Journal of Pragmatics* 42, 1842–1865.

Sampson, Geoffrey, David Gil, and Peter Trudgill (eds.) (2009). *Language Complexity as an Evolving Variable*. Oxford: Oxford University Press.

Sanders, Ted J. M., Wilbert P. M. Spooren, and Leo G. M. Noordman (1992). 'Toward a taxonomy of coherence relations'. *Discourse Processes* 15, 1–35.

—— and Leo G. M. Noordman (2000). 'The role of coherence relations and their linguistic markers in text processing'. *Discourse Processes* 29, 37–60.

—— and Wilbert P. M. Spooren (2007). 'Discourse and text structure'. In: Dirk Geeraerts and Hubert Cuyckens (eds.), *The Oxford handbook of cognitive linguistics*. Oxford: Oxford University Press, 916–942.

Sapir, Edward, and Harry Hoijer (1942). *Navaho texts*. Iowa City: Linguistic Society of America.

—— and —— (1967). *The phonology and morphology of the Navaho language*. Berkeley, CA: University of California Press.

Savel'eva-Trofimova, Ol'ga A. (2008). *Neklauzal'nye diskursivnye edinicy (na materiale korpusa 'Rasskazy o snovidenijax')* [Non-clausal discourse units: Evidence from the corpus 'Night Dream Stories']. Diploma thesis. Dept. of Theoretical and Applied Linguistics, Moscow State University.

Schacter, Daniel, Anthony D. Wagner, and Randy L. Buckner (2000). 'Memory systems of 1999'. In: Endel Tulving and Fergus I. M. Craik (eds.), *The Oxford handbook of memory*. Oxford: Oxford University Press, 627–644.

Schank, Roger (2005). *Cognition! Teaching kids to think*. http://www.rogerschank.com/books/How-education-needs-to-be-fixed.html

Schaub, Willi (1985). *Babungo*. London: Croom Helm.

Schegloff, Emanuel, and Harvey Sacks (1973). 'Opening up closings'. *Semiotica* 7(4), 289–327.

Schiffrin, Deborah, Deborah Tannen, and Heidi E. Hamilton (eds.) (2001). *The handbook of discourse analysis*. Malden, MA: Blackwell.

—— (2006). *In other words: Variation in reference and narrative*. Cambridge: Cambridge University Press.

Schilbach, Leonhard (2010). 'A second-person approach to other minds'. *Nature Reviews Neuroscience* 11, 264–274.

Schlösser, Ralf G. M., Gerd Wagner, and Heinrich Sauer (2006). 'Assessing the working memory network: Studies with functional magnetic resonance imaging and structural equation modeling'. *Neuroscience* 139(1), 91–103.

Schober, Michael F., and Herbert H. Clark (1989). 'Understanding by addressees and overhearers'. *Cognitive Psychology* 21, 211–232.

Schröger, Erich, Axel Mecklinger, and Angela D. Friederici (eds.) (2000). *Working on working memory*. Leipzig: Leipziger Universitaetsverlag.

Schütze, Carson (2006). 'Data and evidence'. In: Keith Brown (ed.), *Encyclopedia of language and linguistics*. Oxford: Elsevier, 356–363.

Schwartz, Linda (1986). 'The function of free pronouns'. In: Ursula Wiesemann (ed.), *Pronominal systems*. Tübingen: Narr, 405–436.

—— and Timothy Dunnigan (1986). 'Pronouns and pronominal categories in Southwestern Ojibwe'. In: Ursula Wiesemann (ed.), *Pronominal systems*. Tübingen: Narr, 285–322.

Schwartz-Friesel, Monika (2007). 'Indirect anaphora in text: A cognitive account'. In: Monika Schwartz-Friesel, Manfred Consten, and Mareile Knees (eds.), *Anaphors in text: Cognitive, formal and applied approaches to anaphoric reference*. Amsterdam: Benjamins, 3–20.

—— Manfred Consten, and Mareile Knees (eds.) (2007). *Anaphors in text: Cognitive, formal and applied approaches to anaphoric reference*. Amsterdam: Benjamins.

Schwegler, Armin (1990). *Analyticity and syntheticity: A diachronic perspective with a special reference to Romance languages*. Berlin: Mouton de Gruyter.

Scollon, Ron, and Suzanne Wong Scollon (2001). *Intercultural communication: A discourse approach*. Malden, MA: Blackwell.

—— (2006). 'Multimodality and the language of politics'. In: Keith Brown (ed.), *Encyclopedia of language and linguistics*. Oxford: Elsevier, 386–387.

Seifart, Frank (2005). *The structure and use of shape-based noun classes in Miraña (north-west Amazon)*. Ph.D. thesis. Radboud University.

Seleznev, Mikhail [Mixail] G. (1987). 'Referencija i nominacija' [Reference and nomination]. In: Aleksandr E. Kibrik and Aleksandr S. Narin'jani (eds.), *Modelirovanie jazykovoj dejatel'nosti v intellektual'nyx sistemax*. Moscow: Nauka, 64–78.

Seliverstova, Ol'ga N. (1988). *Mestoimenija v jazyke i reči* [Pronouns in language and speech]. Moscow: Nauka.

Senft, Gunter (ed.) (2004). *Deixis and demonstratives in Oceanic languages*. Canberra: Pacific Linguistics.

Seo, Seunghyun (2001). *The frequency of null subjects in Russian, Polish, Bulgarian and Serbo-Croatian: An analysis according to morphosyntactic environments*. Ph.D. thesis. Dept. of Slavic languages and literatures, Indiana University.

Shah, Priti, and Akira Miyake (1999). 'Models of working memory: An introduction'. In: Akira Miyake and Priti Shah (eds.), *Models of working memory: Mechanisms of active maintenance and executive control*. Cambridge: Cambridge University Press, 1–27.

Shamaro, Elena Yu. [Elena Ju. Šamaro] (2006). 'Nekotorye fakty vido-vremennoj sistemy RŽJa' [Certain facts of the aspectual-temporal system of RSL]. In: Anna A. Komarova (ed.), *Sovremennye aspekty žestovogo jazyka*. Moscow, 180–191.

—— (2009). *Povtorenie predikata v narrativax na russkom žestovom jazyke* [Predicate repetition in RSL narratives]. Diploma thesis. Dept. of Theoretical and Applied Linguistics, Moscow State University.

Shcherba [Ščerba], Lev V. (1955). *Fonetika francuzskogo jazyka* [French phonetics]. Moscow: Izdatel'stvo literatury na inostrannyx jazykax.

Shields, Kenneth C. (1992). *A history of Indo-European verb morphology*. Amsterdam: Benjamins.

Shimojo, Mitsuaki (2005). *Argument encoding in Japanese conversation*. Houndmills: Palgrave Macmillan.

Shmelev, Aleksey D. [Aleksej D. Šmelev] (1995). *Referencial'nye mexanizmy russkogo jazyka* [Referential mechanisms in Russian]. Habilitation thesis. MPGU.

Shopen, Timothy (ed.) (2007). *Language typology and syntactic description*. 2nd edn., Cambridge: Cambridge University Press.

Showalter, Catherine (1986). 'Pronouns in Lyélé'. In: Ursula Wiesemann (ed.), *Pronominal systems*. Tübingen: Narr, 205–216.

Siewierska, Anna (1999). 'From anaphoric pronoun to grammatical agreement marker: Why objects don't make it'. *Folia Linguistica* 33(2), 225–251.

—— (2004). *Person*. Cambridge: Cambridge University Press.

—— (2005a). 'Alignment of verbal person marking'. In: Martin Haspelmath, Matthew Dryer, David Gil, and Bernard Comrie (eds.), *World atlas of language structures*. Oxford: Oxford University Press, 406–409.

—— (2005b). 'Gender distinctions in independent personal pronouns'. In: Martin Haspelmath, Matthew Dryer, David Gil, and Bernard Comrie (eds.), *World atlas of language structures*. Oxford: Oxford University Press, 182–185.

—— (2005c). 'Order of person markers on the verb'. In: Martin Haspelmath, Matthew Dryer, David Gil, and Bernard Comrie (eds.), *World atlas of language structures*. Oxford: Oxford University Press, 422–425.

Siewierska, Anna (2005d). 'Third-person zero of verbal person marking'. In: Martin Haspelmath, Matthew Dryer, David Gil, and Bernard Comrie (eds.), *World atlas of language structures*. Oxford: Oxford University Press, 418–421.

—— (2005e). 'Verbal person marking'. In: Martin Haspelmath, Matthew Dryer, David Gil, and Bernard Comrie (eds.), *World atlas of language structures*. Oxford: Oxford University Press, 414–417.

—— and Dik Bakker (2005). 'The Agreement cross-reference continuum: Person marking in FG'. In: Casper de Groot and Kees Hengeveld (eds.), *Morphosyntactic expression in Functional Grammar*. Berlin: Mouton de Gruyter, 203–248.

Silverstein, Michael (1976). 'Hierarchy of features and ergativity'. In: R. M. W. Dixon (ed.), *Grammatical categories in Australian languages*. Canberra: Australian institute of Aboriginal studies, 112–171.

Simon, Horst J., and Heike Wiese (2002). 'Grammatical properties of pronouns and their representations: An exposition'. In: Horst J. Simon and Heike Wiese (eds.), *Pronouns – grammar and representation*. Amsterdam: Benjamins, 1–22.

—— and —— (eds.) (2002). *Pronouns – grammar and representation*. Amsterdam: Benjamins.

Skribnik, Elena K. (1980). 'O sisteme deepričastij v sovremennom burjatskom jazyke' [On the system of converbs in modern Buryat]. *Narody i jazyki Sibiri*. Novosibirsk: Nauka, 94–110.

—— (1988). *Polipredikativnye sintetičeskie predloženija v burjatskom jazyke* [Polypredicative synthetic sentences in Buryat]. Novosibirsk: Nauka.

Slobin, Dan I. (2003). 'Language and thought online: Cognitive consequences of linguistic relativity'. In: Deirdre Gentner and Susan Goldin-Meadow (eds.), *Language in mind: Advances in the study of language and thought*. Cambridge, MA: MIT Press, 157–192.

Smith, Carlota (2003). *Modes of discourse: The local structure of texts*. Cambridge: Cambridge University Press.

Smith, Edward E., and John Jonides (1997). 'Working memory: A view from neuroimaging'. *Cognitive Psychology* 33, 5–42.

Sokolovskaja, Natal'ja K. (1980). 'Nekotorye semantičeskie universalii v sisteme ličnyx mestoimenij' [Some semantic universals in the system of personal pronouns]. *Teorija i tipologija mestoimenij*. Moscow: Nauka, 84–103.

Solganik, Grigorij Ja. (2003). *Stilistika teksta* [Text stylistics]. Moscow: Nauka.

Solnit, David B. (1997). *Eastern Kayah Li. Grammar, texts, glossary*. Honolulu: University of Hawai'i Press.

Soto, David, John Hodson, Pia Rotshtein, and Glyn W. Humphreys (2008). 'Automatic guidance of attention from working memory'. *Trends in Cognitive Science* 12(9), 342–348.

Spencer, Andrew (1998). *Morphological theory*. Oxford: Blackwell.

—— and Ana Luís (2009). 'On clitics and canons'. Paper presented at the 8th Conference of the Association for Linguistic Typology, Berkeley, CA, July 2009.

Spruit, Arie (1986). *Abkhaz studies*. Ph.D. thesis. Leiden University.
Staley, William E. (2007). Referent management in Olo: A cognitive perspective. SIL International
Staudte, Maria, and Matthew W. Crocker (2009). 'Producing and resolving multi-modal referring expressions in human-robot interaction in grammar'. Paper presented at the Production of Referring Expressions Conference: Bridging the Gap between Computational and Empirical Approaches to Reference (PRE-CogSci), Amsterdam, 29 July 2009.
Steele, Susan (1978). 'Word order variation: A typological study'. In: Joseph H. Greenberg, Charles A. Ferguson, and Edith A. Moravcsik (eds.), *Universals of human language*. Vol. 4. Syntax. Stanford: Stanford University Press, 585–623.
Stevenson, Rosemary J., Rosalind A. Crawley, and David Kleinman (1994). 'Thematic roles, focus and the representation of events'. *Language and Cognitive Processes* 9, 519–548.
—— A. W. R. Nelson, and K. Stenning (1995). 'The role of parallelism in strategies of pronoun comprehension'. *Language and Speech* 38, 393–418.
—— Alistair Knott, Jon Oberlander, and Sharon McDonald (2000). 'Interpreting pronouns and connectives: Interactions among focusing, thematic roles and coherence relations'. *Language and Cognitive Processes* 15(3), 225–262.
Stirling, Leslie (1993). *Switch-reference and discourse representation*. Cambridge: Cambridge University Press.
—— (1996). 'Metonymy and anaphora'. In: Walter de Mulder and Liliane Tasmowski (eds.), *Coherence and anaphora*. Amsterdam: Benjamins, 69–88.
—— (2001). 'The multifunctionality of anaphoric expressions: Typological perspective'. *Australian Journal of Linguistics* 21(1), 7–23.
—— (2002). 'Deixis and anaphora'. In: Rodney Huddleston and Geoffrey K. Pullum (eds.), *The Cambridge grammar of the English language*. Cambridge: Cambridge University Press, 1449–1564.
Stivers, Tanya, Nick J. Enfield, and Stephen C. Levinson (2007). 'Person reference in interaction'. In: Nick J. Enfield and Tanya Stivers (eds.), *Person reference in interaction: Linguistic, cultural, and social perspectives*. Cambridge: Cambridge University Press, 1–20.
Stokoe, William C. (2000). 'Gesture to sign'. In: David McNeill (ed.), *Language and gesture*. Cambridge: Cambridge University Press, 388–399.
Stoll, Sabine, and Balthasar Bickel (2009). 'How deep are differences in referential density?' In: Elena Lieven, Jiansheng Guo, Nancy Budwig, Susan Ervin-Tripp, Keiko Nakamura, and Şeyda Özçalişkan (eds.), *Cross-linguistic approaches to the psychology of language: Research in the traditions of Dan Slobin*. London: Psychology Press, 543–555.
Stone, Gerald (1993a). 'Cassubian'. In: Bernard Comrie and Greville G. Corbett (eds.), *The Slavonic languages*. London: Routledge, 759–794.
—— (1993b). 'Sorbian'. In: Bernard Comrie and Greville G. Corbett (eds.), *The Slavonic languages*. London: Routledge, 593–685.

Streb, Judith, Frank Rösler, and Erwin Henninghausen (1999). 'Event-related responses to pronoun and proper name anaphor in parallel and nonparallel discourse structures'. *Brain and Language* 70, 273–286.

—— Erwin Henninghausen, and Frank Rösler (2004). 'Different anaphoric expressions are investigated by event-related brain potentials'. *Journal of Psycholinguistic Research* 33(3), 175–201.

Strube, Michael, and Maria Wolters (2000). 'A Probabilistic genre-independent model of pronominalization'. *Proceedings of the 1st Meeting of the North American Chapter of the Association for Computational Linguistics.* Seattle, 29 April – 4 May 2000, 18–25.

—— (2006). 'Statistical anaphora and coreference resolution'. In: Keith Brown (ed.), *Encyclopedia of language and linguistics.* Oxford: Elsevier, 216–221.

—— (2007). 'Corpus-based and machine learning approaches to anaphora resolution'. In: Monika Schwartz-Friesel, Manfred Consten, and Mareile Knees (eds.), *Anaphors in text: Cognitive, formal and applied approaches to anaphoric reference.* Amsterdam: Benjamins, 207–224.

Sugamoto, Nobuko (1989). 'Pronominality: A noun–pronoun continuum'. In: Roberta Corrigan, Fred Eckman, and Michael Noonan (eds.), *Linguistic categorization.* Amsterdam: Benjamins, 267–291.

Sullivan, Arthur (2006). 'Reference: Philosophical theories'. In: Keith Brown (ed.), *Encyclopedia of language and linguistics.* Oxford: Elsevier, 420–427.

Supalla, Ted (1978). 'The morphology of verbs of motion and location in American Sign Language'. In: Frank Caccamise and Doin Hicks (eds.), *ASL in a bilingual, bicultural context. Proceedings of The Second National Symposium on Sign Language Research and Teaching.* Coronado: National Association of the Deaf, 27–45.

—— (1986). 'The classifier system in American Sign Language'. In: Colette Craig (ed.), *Noun classes and categorization.* Amsterdam: Benjamins, 181–214.

Sussex, Roland, and Paul Cubberley (2006). *The Slavic languages.* Cambridge: Cambridge University Press.

Švedova, Natal'ja Ju. (1998). *Mestoimenie i smysl* [Pronoun and meaning]. Moscow: Azbukovnik.

Swales, John (1990). *Genre analysis: English in academic and research settings.* Cambridge: Cambridge University Press.

Sylla, Yèro (1982). *Grammaire moderne du pulaar.* Dakar: Les Nouvelles Éditions Africaines.

Taboada, Maite, and William C. Mann (2006). 'Rhetorical structure theory: Looking back and moving ahead'. *Discourse Studies* 8, 423–459.

Takubo, Yukinori, and Satoshi Kinsui (1997). 'Discourse management in terms of mental spaces'. *Journal of Pragmatics* 28(6), 741–758.

Talmy, Leonard (2003). *Toward a cognitive semantics.* Vol. 2. Typology and process in concept structuring. Cambridge, MA: MIT Press.

Tao, L. (1996). 'Topic discontinuity and zero anaphora in Chinese discourse: Cognitive strategies in discourse processing'. In: Barbara A. Fox (ed.), *Studies in anaphora*. Amsterdam: Benjamins, 487–514.

Tatevosov, Sergei [Sergej] G. (2002). *Semantika sostavljajuščix imennoj gruppy: kvantornye slova* [The semantics of noun phrase constituents: Quantifiers]. Moscow: IMLI RAN.

Testelets, Yakov G. [Jakov G. Testelec], and Svetlana Yu. [Ju.] Toldova (1998). 'Refleksivnye mestoimenija v dagestanskix jazykax i tipologija refleksiva' [Reflexive pronouns in Daghestanian languages and the typology of reflexives]. *Voprosy Jazykoznanija* 1998(4).

Theeuwes, Jan, and Stefan van der Stigchel (2006). 'Faces capture attention: Evidence from inhibition of return'. *Visual Cognition* 13(6), 657–665.

Thieberger, Nicholas (2006). *A grammar of South Efate, an Oceanic language of Vanuatu*. Honolulu: University of Hawai'i Press.

Thompson, Chad (1989). *Voice and obviation in Athabaskan and other languages*. Ph.D. thesis. Dept. of Linguistics, University of Oregon.

—— (1996). 'The history and function of the yi-/bi- alternation in Athabaskan'. In: Eloise Jelinek, Sally Midgette, Keren Rice, and Leslie Saxon (eds.), *Athabaskan language studies: Essays in honor of Robert W. Young*. Albuquerque: University of New Mexico Press, 365–395.

Thompson, Laurence C. (1965). *Vietnamese reference grammar*. Honolulu: University of Hawai'i Press.

Thompson, Sandra A., and Elizabeth Couper-Kuhlen (2005). 'The clause as a locus of grammar and interaction'. *Discourse Studies* 7, 481–506.

Tily, Harry, and Steven Piantadosi (2009). 'Refer efficiently: Use less informative expressions for more predictable meanings'. Paper presented at the Production of Referring Expressions Conference: Bridging the Gap between Computational and Empirical Approaches to Reference (PRE-CogSci), Amsterdam, 29 July 2009.

Timberlake, Alan (2004). *A reference grammar of Russian*. Cambridge: Cambridge University Press.

Tomasello, Michael (ed.) (1998). *The new psychology of language: Cognitive and functional approaches to language structure*. Vol. 1. Mahwah, NJ: Erlbaum.

—— (ed.) (2003). *The new psychology of language: Cognitive and functional Approaches to language structure*. Vol. 2. Mahwah, NJ: Erlbaum.

—— Malinda Carpenter, and Ulf Liszkowski (2007). 'A New look at infant pointing'. *Child Development* 78(3), 705–722.

—— (2008). *Origins of human communication*. Cambridge, MA: MIT Press.

Tomlin, Russell S. (1986). *Basic word order: Functional principles*. London: Croom Helm.

—— (1987). 'Linguistic reflections of cognitive events'. In: Russell S. Tomlin (ed.), *Coherence and grounding in discourse*. Amsterdam: Benjamins, 455–479.

—— and Ming-Ming Pu (1991). 'The management of reference in Mandarin discourse'. *Cognitive Linguistics* 2(1), 65–95.

Tomlin, Russell S. (1995). 'Focal attention, voice and word order: An experimental cross-linguistic study'. In: Pamela Downing and Michael Noonan (eds.), *Word order in discourse*. Amsterdam: Benjamins, 517–554.

—— (1997). 'Mapping conceptual representations into linguistic representations: The role of attention in grammar'. In: Jan Nuyts and Eric Pederson (eds.), *Language and conceptualization*. Cambridge: Cambridge University Press, 162–189.

Toole, Janine (1996). 'The effect of genre on referential choice'. In: Thorsten Fretheim and Jeanette K. Gundel (eds.), *Reference and referent accessibility*. Amsterdam: Benjamins, 263–290.

Townsend, Charles E., and Laura A. Janda (1996). *Common and comparative Slavic: Phonology and inflection (with special attention to Russian, Polish, Czech, Serbo-Croatian, Bulgarian)*. Columbus: Slavica.

Trask, Robert L. (1993). *A dictionary of grammatical terms in linguistics*. London: Routledge.

Treiman, Rebecca, Charles E. Clifton Jr., Antje S. Meyer, and Lee H. Wurm (2003). 'Language comprehension and production'. In: Alice F. Healy and Robert W. Proctor (eds.), *Comprehensive handbook of psychology*. Vol. 4. Experimental psychology. New York: Wiley, 527–548.

Treisman, Anne (2008). 'Broad or narrow focus of attention: How does it determine what we see?' Paper presented at the 3rd International Conference on Cognitive Science, Moscow, June 2008.

Turk, Monica J. (2007). 'Self-referential gestures in conversation'. *Discourse Studies* 9(4), 558–566.

Tutin, Agnès, and Evelyne Viegas (1999). 'Generating coreferential anaphoric definite NPs'. In: Simon Botley and Tony McEnery (eds.), *Corpus-based and computational approaches to discourse anaphora*. Amsterdam: Benjamins, 227–247.

Usikova, Rina P. (2005). 'Makedonskij jazyk' [Macedonian]. In: Aleksandr M. Moldovan, Sergej S. Skorvid, Andrej A. Kibrik, Natal'ja V. Rogova, Ekaterina I. Jakuškina, Aleksej F. Žuravlev, and Svetlana M. Tolstaja (eds.), *Jazyki mira: slavjanskie jazyki*. Moscow: Academia, 102–139.

Utekhin, Ilya V. [Il'ja V. Utexin] (2010). 'Javlenija meta-urovnja v sovmestnoj dejatel'nosti i social'noe raspredelenie kognitivnogo processa' [Meta-level of joint activity and the social distribution of cognition]. Paper presented at the 4th International Conference on Cognitive Science, Tomsk, June 2010.

Valentine, J. Randolph (2001). *Nishnaabemwin reference grammar*. Toronto: University of Toronto Press.

Valli, Clayton, and Ceil Lucas (1995). *Linguistics of American Sign Language: An introduction*. Washington, D.C.: Gallaudet University Press.

van Berkum, Jos J. A., Arnout W. Koornneef, Marte Otten, and Mante S. Nieuwland (2007). 'Establishing reference in language comprehension: An electrophysiological perspective'. *Brain Research* 1146, 158–171.

van Berkum, Jos J. A. (in press). 'The electrophysiology of discourse and conversation'. In: Michael Spivey, Marc F. Joanisse, and Ken McRae (eds.), *The Cambridge Handbook of Psycholinguistics*. Cambridge: Cambridge University Press.

van Deemter, Kees (2006). 'Generating referring expressions that involve gradable properties'. *Computational Linguistics* 32(2), 195–222.

van den Berg, Helma (2004). 'Coordinating constructions in Daghestanian languages'. In: Martin Haspelmath (ed.), *Coordinating constructions*. Amsterdam: Benjamins, 197–226.

van de Auwera, Johan, and Ludo Lejeune (2005). 'The morphological imperative'. In: Martin Haspelmath, Matthew Dryer, David Gil, and Bernard Comrie (eds.), *World atlas of language structures*. Oxford: Oxford University Press, 286–289.

—— and Jan Nuyts (2007). 'Cognitive linguistics and language typology'. In: Dirk Geeraerts and Hubert Cuyckens (eds.), *The Oxford handbook of cognitive linguistics*. Oxford: Oxford University Press, 1074–1091.

van der Sluis, Ielka, and Emiel Krahmer (2007).'Generating multimodal referring expressions'. *Discourse Processes* 44(3), 145–174.

van Dijk, Teun A. (1972). *Some aspects of text grammars: a study in theoretical linguistics and poetics*. The Hague: Mouton.

—— and Walter Kintsch (1983). *Strategies of discourse comprehension*. New York: Academic Press.

—— (ed.) (1985). *Handbook of discourse analysis*. New York: Academic Press.

—— (ed.) (1997). *Discourse studies: A multidisciplinary introduction*. Vols. 1, 2. London: Sage Publications.

van Hoek, Karen (1997). *Anaphora and conceptual structure*. Chicago: University of Chicago Press.

—— Andrej A. Kibrik, and Leo Noordman (eds.) (1999). *Discourse studies in cognitive linguistics*. Amsterdam: Benjamins.

Van Linden, An, Jean-Christophe Verstraete, and Kristin Davidse (eds.) (2010). *Formal evidence in grammaticalization research*. Amsterdam: Benjamins.

Van Valin, Robert D., Jr. (1977). *Aspects of Lakhota syntax*. Ph.D. thesis. University of California Press.

—— (1985). 'Case marking and the structure of the Lakhota clause'. In: Johanna Nichols and Anthony Woodbury (eds.), *Grammar inside and outside the clause*. Cambridge: Cambridge University Press, 363–413.

—— (1987). 'Aspects of the interaction of syntax and pragmatics: Discourse coreference mechanisms and the typology of grammatical systems'. In: Jef Verschueren and Marcella Bertucceli-Papi (eds.), *The pragmatic perspective: Selected papers from the 1985 International Pragmatics Conference*. Amsterdam: Benjamins, 513–531.

—— (1990). 'Functionalism, anaphora, and syntax'. *Studies in Language* 14, 169–219.

—— (1993). 'A synopsis of Role and Reference Grammar'. In: Robert D. Van Valin Jr. (ed.), *Advances in Role and Reference Grammar*. Amsterdam: Benjamins, 1–164.

Van Valin, Robert D., Jr. and Randy J. LaPolla (1997). *Syntax: Structure, meaning and function.* Cambridge: Cambridge University Press.

van Vliet, Sarah (2002). 'Overspecified NPs marking conceptual shifts in narrative discourse'. In: Hans Broekhuis and Paula Fikkert (eds.), *Linguistics in the Netherlands 2002.* Amsterdam: Benjamins, 187–198.

Vance, Barbara S. (1997). *Syntactic change in medieval French: Verb-second and null subjects.* Dordrecht: Kluwer.

Velichkovsky, Boris M., Markus Joos, Jens R. Helmert, and Sebastian Pannasch (2005). 'Two visual systems and their eye movements: Evidence from static and dynamic scene perception'. In: Bruno G. Bara, Lawrence Barsalou, and Monica Bucciarelli (eds.), *The Annual Conference of the Cognitive Science Society.* Stresa, Italy, 21–23 July 2005: Erlbaum, 2283–2288.

Venditty, Jennifer J., Matthew Stone, Preetham Nanda, and Paul Tepper (2001). *Toward an account of accented pronoun interpretation in discourse context: Evidence from eye-tracking.* Rutgers Center for Cognitive Science and Dept. of Computer Science. Report.

Verhagen, Arie (2005). *Constructions of intersubjectivity: Discourse, syntax, and cognition.* Oxford: Oxford University Press.

Vieira, Renata, and Massimo Poesio (1999). 'Processing definite descriptions in corpora'. In: Simon Botley and Tony McEnery (eds.), *Corpus-based and computational approaches to discourse anaphora.* Amsterdam: Benjamins, 189–212.

Vol'f, Elena M. (1974). *Grammaitika i semantika mestoimenij* [Grammar and semantics of pronouns]. Moscow: Nauka.

Voloshinov [Vološinov], Valentin N. (1929). *Marksizm i filosofija jazyka* [Marxism and the philosophy of language]. Leningrad: Priboj.

von Heusinger, Klaus, and Urs Egli (eds.) (2000). *Reference and anaphoric relations.* Dordrecht: Kluwer.

von Humboldt, Wilhelm (1836/1988). *On language: The diversity of human language-structure and its influence on the mental development of mankind.* Translated by Peter Heath. Cambridge: Cambridge University Press.

von Stutterheim, Christian, and Ralf Nüse (2003). 'Processes of conceptualization in language production: Language-specific perspectives and event construal'. *Linguistics* 41(5), 851–881.

Vonk, Wietske, Lettica G. M. M. Hustinx, and Wim H. G. Simons (1992). 'The use of referential expressions in structuring discourse'. *Language and Cognitive Processes* 73, 301–333.

Vydrine, Valentin F. (2005). 'Pronoms personnels gouro'. *Journal of West African Languages* 21(1–2), 83–107.

Vydrine [Vydrin], Valentin F. (2006). 'Ličnye mestoimenija v južnyx mande' [Personal pronouns in Southern Mande]. In: Nikolaj N. Kazanskij (ed.), *Acta Linguistica Petropolitana.* Saint-Petersburg: Nauka, 327–413.

Vydrine [Vydrin], Valentin F. (in preparation). 'Vostočnyj jakuba (dan-gueta)' [Eastern Yakuba (Dan-Gwèètaa)]. In: Valentin F. Vydrine [Vydrin] (ed.), *Jazyki mira: jazyki mande*. Moscow: Academia.

—— (2010). 'Ešče raz o sub"ektnyx mestoimenijax v južnyx mande: mestoimenija ili predikativnye pokazateli' [Once more on 'subject pronouns' in Southern Mande: Pronouns or predicative markers?]. In: Viktor A. Vinogradov (ed.), *Osnovy afrikanskogo jazykoznanija. Sintaksis immenyx i glagol'nyx grupp*. Moscow: Academia, 385–400.

Vygotsky, Lev S. (1934/1994). *Thought and language*. Cambridge, MA: MIT Press.

Walker, Marilyn A., Aravind K. Joshi, and Ellen F. Prince (eds.) (1998). *Centering theory in discourse*. Oxford: Clarendon Press.

Wanner, Dieter (1987). *The development of Romance clitic pronouns: From Latin to Old Romance*. Berlin: Mouton de Gruyter.

Watkins, Laurel (1993). 'The discourse function of Kiowa switch-reference'. *International Journal of American Linguistics* 59(2), 137–164.

Webber, Bonnie Lynn (1991). 'Structure and ostension in the interpretation of discourse deixis'. *Natural Language and Cognitive Processes* 2(6), 107–135.

—— Matthew Stone, Aravind K. Joshi, and Alistair Knott (2003). 'Anaphora and discourse structure'. *Computational Linguistics* 29(4), 545–587.

Weber, David J. (1986). 'Huallaga Quechua pronouns'. In: Ursula Wiesemann (ed.), *Pronominal systems*. Tübingen: Narr, 333–350.

Weerman, Fred (1989). *The V2 conspiracy: A synchronic and a diachronic analysis of verbal positions in German languages*. Dordrecht: Foris.

Weissenborn, Jürgen, and Wolfgang Klein (eds.) (1982). *Here and there: Crosslinguistic studies in deixis and demonstration*. Amsterdam: Benjamins.

Westrum, Peter N., and Ursula Wiesemann (1986). 'Berik pronouns'. In: Ursula Wiesemann (ed.), *Pronominal systems*. Tübingen: Narr, 37–46.

Wheelock, Frederic M. (1995). *Wheelock's Latin, revised by Richard A. LaFleur*. 5th edn. New York: Harper Perennial.

Whistler, Kenneth (1985). 'Focus, perspective, and inverse person marking in Nootkan'. In: Johanna Nichols and Anthony Woodbury (eds.), *Grammar inside and outside the clause*. Cambridge: Cambridge University Press, 227–267.

Wichmann, Søren (2007). 'The reference-tracking system of Tlapanec: Between obviation and switch reference'. *Studies in Language* 31(4), 801–827.

—— (2008). 'Case relations in a head-marking language: Verb-marked cases in Tlapanec'. In: Andrej Malchukov and Andrew Spencer (eds.), *Handbook of Case*. Oxford: Oxford University Press, 797–807.

—— and Eric W. Holman (2009). *Assessing temporal stability for linguistic typological features*. München: LINCOM Europa.

Wiemer, Björn (1997). *Diskursreferenz im Polnischen und Deutschen (aufgezeigt an der narrativen Rede ein- und zweisprachiger Schüler)*. München: Otto Sagner Verlag.

Wiesemann, Ursula (1982). 'Switch-reference in Bantu languages'. *Journal of West African languages* 12(2), 42–57.

Wiesemann, Ursula (ed.) (1986). *Pronominal systems*. Tübingen: Narr.
—— (1986a). 'Grammaticalized coreference'. In: Ursula Wiesemann (ed.), *Pronominal systems*. Tübingen: Narr, 437–463.
—— (1986b). 'Preface'. In: Ursula Wiesemann (ed.), *Pronominal systems*. Tübingen: Narr, vii–ix.
—— (1986c). 'The pronoun systems of some Jê and Macro-Jê languages'. In: Ursula Wiesemann (ed.), *Pronominal systems*. Tübingen: Narr, 359–380.
Wilkins, David P. (1988). 'Switch-reference in Mparntwe Arrernte (Aranda): Form, function, and problems of identity'. In: Peter K. Austin (ed.), *Complex sentence constructions in Australian languages*. Amsterdam: Benjamins, 141–176.
—— (2000). 'Ants, ancestors and medicine: A semantic and pragmatic account of classifier constructions in Arrernte (Central Australia)'. In: Gunter Senft (ed.), *Systems of nominal classification*. Cambridge: Cambridge University Press, 147–216.
—— (2003). 'Why pointing with the index finger is not a universal (in sociocultural and semiotic terms)'. In: Sotaro Kita (ed.), *Pointing: Where language, culture, and cognition meet*. Mahwah, NJ: Erlbaum, 171–216.
Willie, MaryAnn (1991). *Navajo pronouns and obviation*. Ph.D. thesis. Dept. of Linguistics, University of Arizona.
Winston, Elizabeth A. (1991). 'Spatial referencing and cohesion in an American Sign Language Text'. *Sign Language Studies* 73, 379–409.
Wischer, Ilse, and Gabriele Diewald (eds.) (2002). *New reflections on grammaticalization*. Amsterdam: Benjamins.
Wolfart, H. Christoph (1996). 'Sketch of Cree, an Algonquian language'. In: Ives Goddard (ed.), *Handbook of North American Indians. Vol. 17. Languages*. Washington, D.C.: Smithsonian Institution, 390–439.
Wolters, Maria, and Donna K. Byron (2000). 'Prosody and the resolution of pronominal anaphora'. In: *Proceedings of the 18th International Conference on Computational Linguistics* (COLING 2000), 919–925.
—— (2001). *Towards entity status*. Ph.D. thesis. Institut für Kommunikationsforschung und Phonetik, Universität Bonn.
Woodbury, Anthony (1983). 'Switch-reference, syntactic organization, and rhetorical structure in Central Yup'ik Eskimo'. In: John Haiman and Pamela Munro (eds.), *Switch-reference and universal grammar*. Amsterdam: Benjamins, 291–316.
Woodward, Todd S., Tara A. Cairo, Christian C. Ruff, Yoshio Takane, Michael A. Hunter, and Elton T. C. Ngan (2006). 'Functional connectivity reveals load dependent neural systems underlying encoding and maintenance in verbal working memory'. *Neuroscience* 139(1), 317–325.
Wouk, Fay (2008). 'The syntax of intonation units in Sasak'. *Studies in Language* 32(1), 137–162.
Wundt, Wilhelm Max (1911). *Einführung in die Psychologie*. Leipzig: Dürr.
Yamamoto, Mutsumi (1999). *Animacy and reference: A cognitive approach to corpus linguistics*. Amsterdam: Benjamins.
Yokoyama, Olga (1986). *Discourse and word order*. Amsterdam: Benjamins.

Young, Robert W., and William Morgan, Sr. (1987). *The Navajo language: A grammar and colloquial dictionary*. Revised edn. Albuquerque: University of New Mexico Press.

—— William Morgan, Sr., and Sally Midgette (1992). *Analytical lexicon of Navajo*. Albuquerque: University of New Mexico Press.

Zajceva, Galina L. (2000). *Žestovaja reč'. Daktilologija* [Sign Language. Fingerspelling]. Moscow: Vlados.

—— (2006). *Žest i slovo* [Gesture and word]. Moscow.

Zaliznjak, Andrej A. (1995). *Drevnenovgorodskij dialekt* [Old Novgorod dialect]. Moscow: Jazyki russkoj kul'tury.

—— (2008). *Drevnerusskie ėnklitiki* [Old Russian enclitics]. Moscow: Jazyki slavjanskoj kul'tury.

Zelinsky-Wibbelt, Cornelia (2000). *Discourse and the continuity of reference: Representing mental categorization*. Berlin: Mouton de Gruyter.

Zemskaja, Elena A., Margarita V. Kitajgorodskaja, and Evgenij N. Širjaev (1981). *Russkaja razgovornaja reč'. Obščie voprosy. Slovoobrazovanie. Sintaksis* [Russian colloquial speech. General issues. Word formation. Syntax]. Moscow: Nauka.

Ziv, Yael (1996). 'Pronominal reference to inferred antecedents'. In: Walter de Mulder and Liliane Tasmowski (eds.), *Coherence and anaphora*. Amsterdam: Benjamins, 55–67.

Zribi-Hertz, Anna (ed.) (1997). *Les pronoms: Morphologie, syntaxe et typologie*. Saint-Denis: Presses Universitaires de Vincennes.

Zubin, David A., and Lynne E. Hewitt (1995). 'The deictic center: A theory of deixis in narrative'. In: Judith Felson Duchan, Gail A. Bruder, and Lynne E. Hewitt (eds.), *Deixis in narrative: A cognitive science perspective*. Hillsdale, NJ: Erlbaum, 129–158.

Zúñiga, Fernando (2006). *Deixis and alignment: Inverse systems in indigenous language of the Americas*. Amsterdam: Benjamins.

Zvegincev, Vladimir A. (1996). *Mysli o lingvistike* [Thoughts about linguistics]. Moscow: Izdatel'stvo Moskovskogo universiteta.

Zwaan, Rolf A., and Michael P. Kaschak (2006). 'Language, visual cognition and motor action'. In: Keith Brown (ed.), *Encyclopedia of language and linguistics*. Oxford: Elsevier, 648–651.

Zwicky, Arnold M. (1985). 'Clitics and particles'. *Language* 61(2), 283–305.

Index of languages

Purely areal, non-genealogical, language groupings appear in quote marks.

Abkhaz (Abkhaz-Adyghean) 92–98, 99 n. 25, 100, 101, 102, 119, 143, 144, 145, 152, 155, 157, 175, 176, 188, 196, 197, 198, 199, 203, 204, 205, 207, 208, 210, 211, 212, 213, 214, 236, 254, 255, 278, 298–299, 303
Abkhaz-Adyghean 101, 205
Achumawi (Palaihnihan) 140 n.
Acoma (Keresan) 140 n.
Alamblak (Sepik, "Papuan") 322
Algonquian (Algic) 89 n., 101, 205, 311, 313, 345
Altaic 326
Alutor (Chukchi-Koryakan) 138, 140
Amele (Madang, "Papuan") 322
American Sign Language 523, 526, 527
AnejoM̃ (Southern Oceanic, Austronesian) 218, 220, 225, 270
Angas (Chadic, Afro-Asiatic) 316–317
Apachean (Na-Dene) 239, 245–246, 279
Arabic (Semitic, Afro-Asiatic):
  Egyptian Arabic 153
Arawakan 101
Archi (Nakh-Daghestanian) 319, 336
Arrernte (Pama-Nyungan) 90, 132, 145, 346
Asheninca (Arawakan) 205
Athabaskan (Na-Dene) 154, 232, 234, 239–248, 259, 279, 281, 282, 283, 300, 302
Atlantic 334, 347, 355
Attié (Kwa) 320
Austro-Asiatic 112
Austronesian 326
Aymara (Aymaran) 140 n.
Azoyú Tlapanec (Oto-Manguean) 331–332

Babine-Witsuwit'en (Na-Dene) 246–247, 255, 279, 282
Babungo (Bantoid, Benue-Congo) 176–177, 277, 278
Bafut (Bantoid, Benue-Congo) 321, 322, 325
Bagvalal (Nakh-Daghestanian) 319
Balante (Atlantic) 122

Bamana (Mande):
  Beledugu Bamana 111–112
  standard Bamana 111, 313
Bambara, *see* Bamana
Bantu (Benue-Congo) 101
Basque (isolate of Europe) 98
Belhare (Kiranti, Sino-Tibetan) 337
Belorussian (East Slavic, Indo-European) 275
Benue-Congo 90
Berik (Tor-Kwerba, "Papuan") 219
Bilua (Central Solomon, "Papuan") 195–196, 203, 278
Bininj Gun-wok (Gunwinyguan, "Non-Pama-Nyungan") 205
Bulgarian (South Slavic, Indo-European) 152, 262–263, 268, 277, 279, 283
Byansi (Western Himalayish, Sino-Tibetan) 217

Caddo (Caddoan) 325
Capanahua (Panoan) 323
Carib (Cariban) 140 n.
Cariban 101
Cassubian, *see* Kaszubian
Central Pomo (Pomoan) 319
Central Yup'ik (Eskimo-Aleut) 140 n., 205, 208, 325
Chadic (Afro-Asiatic) 142, 319
Chemehuevi (Uto-Aztecan) 87–88
Cherokee (Iroquoian) 133
Chinese (Sinitic, Sino-Tibetan):
  Mandarin Chinese 134, 144, 145, 162–164, 166, 180, 267, 277, 278, 285, 292, 327, 335, 336
Chinook (Chinookan) 205
Chipewyan (Na-Dene) 242
Circassian (Abkhaz-Adyghean) 205
Coast Thimshian, *see* Sm'algyax
Coos (Coosan) 140 n.
Copainalá Zoque (Mixe-Zoque) 140 n.

Index of languages

Dagbani (Gur) 79, 82
Daghestanian (Nakh-Daghestanian) 207, 229–230
Dan-Gwèètaa (Mande) 136–138, 141, 142, 143, 144, 145, 147, 196–197, 203, 232, 316
Danish Sign Language 526
Dargi (Nakh-Daghestanian) 229
   Chirag Dargi 229–230
Dena'ina (Na-Dene) 247
Dëne Sųłiné, *see* Chipewyan
Dii (Adamawa-Ubangi) 142
Diuxi-Tilantongo Mixtec (Oto-Manguean) 320
Dumo (Sko, "Papuan") 217
Dutch (Germanic, Indo-European) 217, 331
Dyirbal (Pama-Nyungan) 327

Eastern Kayah Li (Karen, Sino-Tibetan) 164–165, 314–315
Eastern Pomo (Pomoan) 145
East Slavic (Indo-European) 90, 217, 260, 273, 275, 280, 283
Ebira (Nupoid, Benue-Congo) 191–192, 203, 278
English (Germanic, Indo-European) 8, 15, 20, 26, 27, 28, 32, 33, 34, 38, 39, 40, 41, 43–45, 49, 51, 52, 55, 62, 64, 72, 74–77, 78, 82, 84–86, 89, 90, 91, 92, 94, 112, 119, 123, 125, 126, 127, 129 n., 134, 148, 149, 150, 152, 155, 160, 170–172, 176–180, 182, 183, 187, 203, 205, 208, 210, 214–217, 221–226, 228, 230, 231, 232, 234, 237, 241, 252, 260, 265, 267, 274, 277, 278, 281, 282, 285, 291, 292, 296, 303, 315, 326, 336, 337, 338, 346, 383, 384, 387, 391, 393, 405, 428–444, 451, 453, 460–490, 505, 510, 515, 517
   Australian English 553
Eskimo-Aleut 101
Estonian (Uralic) 331
Evenki (Tungusic) 217
Ewe (Kwa) 317–318

Finnish (Uralic) 145, 171, 331
Fox (Algic) 313
French (Romance, Indo-European) 122, 156, 157, 183, 217, 230, 255, 256, 273, 276, 280, 282, 285, 300, 517
   colloquial French 122, 206, 248, 252–260, 278, 279, 281, 283, 300
   Middle French 249, 250, 259, 280, 283

Old French 217, 250–251, 259, 276, 280, 282
   standard French 206, 223, 250–254, 259, 279, 283
Fula, *see* Pulaar-Fulfulde
Fuuta-Tooro, *see* Pulaar

Gela (Southeast Solomonic Oceanic, Austronesian) 142, 173, 175, 193, 203
German (Germanic, Indo-European) 78, 85, 129, 145, 208, 214–217, 223–227, 230, 236, 237, 264, 267, 274, 280, 285, 331
Germanic (Indo-European) 77, 90, 91 n. 15, 186, 214–228, 230, 237, 239, 250, 251, 259, 260, 264, 266, 267, 270, 274–275, 280, 281, 282, 283, 331
Godié (Kru) 154, 201, 203
Gokana (Cross River, Benue-Congo) 318
Gooniyandi (Bunaban, "Non-Pama-Nyungan") 140 n.
Gothic (Germanic, Indo-European) 224
Greek (Hellenic, Indo-European) 261, 386–387
Guaraní (Tupian) 140 n.
Gujarati (Indo-Aryan, Indo-European) 319
Gur 79, 82, 85, 90, 119
Guro (Mande) 142 n.

Hanis, *see* Coos
Haruai (Upper Yuat, "Papuan") 322, 323
Hausa (Chadic, Afro-Asiatic) 80–81, 142, 187, 190
Hdi (Chadic, Afro-Asiatic) 183 n.
Himalayish (Sino-Tibetan) 327
Hindi (Indo-Aryan, Indo-European) 165, 285
Hmar (Kuki-Chin, Sino-Tibetan) 193
Hoava (Meso-Melanesian Oceanic, Austronesian) 203 n.
Holikachuk (Na-Dene) 241
Huallaga Quechua (Quechuan) 152, 213
Hungarian (Uralic) 140 n.

Indo-European 147, 152, 158, 194, 212, 215, 217, 239, 260, 261, 273, 275, 280, 281
Indonesian (Sundic, Austronesian):
   Riau Indonesian 42, 121
Inga (Quechuan) 153
Iroquoian 101
Italian (Romance, Indo-European) 222, 249

Index of languages 637

Jakaltek (Mayan) 128–130, 132, 296, 346
Jamul, *see* Tiipay
Japanese (isolate of East Asia) 20, 43, 74, 76, 77, 104, 107–111, 112, 113, 114, 119, 121, 122, 126–127, 131–132, 134, 135, 153, 160, 162, 163, 166, 175, 186, 227, 233, 234, 235, 270, 278, 285, 292, 293, 308, 327, 335, 364, 490–492, 495, 561, 562
Jaqaru (Aymaran) 140 n.
Jarawa (South Andamanese) 123, 169
Javanese (Sundic, Austronesian): Cirebon Javanese 122, 127 n., 293
Jiwarli (Pama-Nyungan) 104 n., 127

Kabba (Central Sudanic) 199, 203, 278
Kabiyè (Gur) 79 n. 8
Kaingang (Macro-Ge) 90, 324–325
Kala Lagaw Ya (Pama-Nyungan) 95
Karok (Karok-Shasta) 140 n.
Kartvelian 101
Kashaya (Pomoan) 323
Kaszubian (West Slavic, Indo-European) 275
Kayapó (Macro-Ge) 324
Khasi (Austro-Asiatic) 217
Koasati (Muskogean) 340, 341 n. 5
Kolyma Yukaghir (Yukaghir) 321–322, 323
Korana (Central Khoisan) 296–297, 303
Korean (isolate of East Asia) 112
Kunama (isolate of East Africa) 140 n.
Kutenai (isolate of North America) 305, 313

Lak (Nakh-Daghestanian) 229, 230
Lakhota (Siouan) 205, 234–235, 324
Lango (Western Nilotic, Eastern Sudanic) 318
Larike (Central Moluccan, Austronesian) 93, 199–200, 203
Latin (Italic, Indo-European) 146, 152, 185, 186, 210–214, 224–227, 236, 239, 248, 249, 251, 253, 256, 260, 261, 264, 274, 278, 279, 281, 283, 319
Latvian (Baltic, Indo-European) 217
Lenakel (Southern Oceanic, Austronesian) 325
Lepcha (Sino-Tibetan) 90
Lyélé (Gur) 78–79, 80, 82, 119, 144, 145, 148, 150, 152, 154, 158, 175, 181, 182, 202, 203, 225–227, 278

Maba (Maban) 140 n.
Macedonian (South Slavic, Indo-European) 263, 264, 277, 283

Macushi (Cariban) 199
Makah (Wakashan) 140 n.
Mande 142, 143
Maricopa (Yuman) 140 n.
Masa (Chadic, Afro-Asiatic) 173, 175, 278
Maxakalí (Macro-Ge) 319
Mayali (Gunwinyguan, "Non-Pama-Nyungan") 95
Mayan 101
Mesquakie, *see* Fox
Miraña (Bora-Witotoan) 296, 345
Mohawk (Iroquoian) 154, 155
Mongolic 326
Mundange (Adamawa-Ubangi) 317
Mundani (Bantoid, Benue-Congo) 336
Muskogean 101

Na-Dene 101, 239
Nakanai (Western Oceanic, Austronesian) 174
Nakh-Daghestanian 319, 326
Namia (Sepik, "Papuan") 90
Nasioi (East Bougainville, "Papuan") 296
Navajo (Na-Dene) 74–77, 93, 119, 125–126, 138–140, 144, 145, 151, 152, 154, 176, 196, 202, 203, 205, 208, 209–210, 213, 235, 236, 239–248, 255, 273, 278, 279, 281, 282, 283, 285, 301, 304–306, 309, 311, 336
Nepali (Indo-Aryan, Indo-European) 171
Ngandi (Gunwinyguan, "Non-Pama-Nyungan") 303
Nias (Sundic, Austronesian) 141, 169
"*Non-Pama-Nyungan*" 101, 295
Nootka (Wakashan) 313
Nunggubuyu (Gunwinyguan, "Non-Pama-Nyungan") 140 n., 205, 290, 299

Oceanic (Austronesian) 142
Ojibwe (Algic):
 Nishnaabemwin Ojibwe 311–312
 Saulteaux Ojibwe 312
 Southwestern Ojibwe 151, 153
Ókó (Okoid, Benue-Congo) 87, 192
Old Church Slavonic (South Slavic, Indo-European) 260–261, 262, 267–268, 283
Omotic (Afro-) 319

Pama-Nyungan 90, 102, 112
"*Papuan*" 142, 217, 322, 326
Persian (Iranian, Indo-European) 96
Pirahã (Mura) 314

Index of languages

Polish (West Slavic, Indo-European) 85, 135, 264–267, 269, 271, 275, 279, 281, 283, 331
Pomoan 90
Proto-Athabaskan (Na-Dene) 242, 279, 281
Proto-Germanic (Germanic, Indo-European) 280
Pulaar-Fulfulde (Atlantic) 180, 296, 297, 303, 347, 353
  Pulaar 285, 334, 346, 347–355, 356, 358, 359

Rheto-Romance (Romance, Indo-European) 217, 251
Romance (Indo-European) 148, 187, 193, 217, 248–251, 253, 259, 260, 261, 263, 273, 274, 279, 281, 282, 283
Roviana (Meso-Melanesian Oceanic, Austronesian) 171, 172
Rumanian (Romance, Indo-European) 249
Russian (East Slavic, Indo-European) 28, 38, 45, 60, 72, 78, 84, 85, 125, 145, 150, 152, 154, 157, 165, 178, 180–181, 182, 217, 226, 264–275, 277, 278, 280, 283, 285, 307, 327–331, 337, 342–345, 364, 388, 391, 396–427, 443, 444, 451, 453, 481, 491–492, 503, 504, 516–520, 522, 537–546, 554
  Old Novgorod Russian 268–270
  Old Russian 154, 260–261, 265 n., 267–273, 280, 283
Russian Sign Language 122 n., 521–536, 545, 546, 548

Sacapultec (Mayan) 208
Salishan 101
Sarcee (Na-Dene) 246
Sardinian (Romance, Indo-European) 249
Seereer, *see* Sereer
Semelai (Austro-Asiatic) 193, 203
Seneca (Iroquoian) 138, 205, 299
Senegalese (Atlantic) 347, 355
Senegambian, *see* Senegalese
Sereer (Atlantic) 325, 334, 336, 346, 355–359
Serer-Sine, *see* Sereer
Sinhala (Indo-Aryan, Indo-European) 126, 306–307
Sino-Tibetan 112
Siouan 101, 205
Skou (Sko, "Papuan") 219–220, 227, 237
Slave (Na-Dene) 247
  Hare Slave 154

Slavic (Indo-European) 148, 260, 261, 263, 264, 267, 268, 273, 274, 279, 281, 283, 331
Sm'algyax (Tsimshianic) 145–146
Sorbian (West Slavic, Indo-European) 275
South Efate (Southern Oceanic, Austronesian) 200, 203
South Slavic (Indo-European) 194, 260, 261–263, 283
Spanish (Romance, Indo-European) 72, 85, 86, 142, 143, 144, 146, 147, 148, 153, 155–157, 168, 172, 174, 175, 184, 187–190, 191, 193, 203, 205, 207, 213, 222–223, 236, 248, 249, 250, 251, 253, 254, 259, 262, 278, 281, 283, 285
Sùpyíré (Senufo, possibly Gur) 79, 82, 324
Sursurunga (Meso-Melanesian Oceanic, Austronesian) 142
Svan (Kartvelian) 98–101, 213
Swahili (Bantu, Benue-Congo) 164

Taba (South Halmahera, Austronesian) 217
Tabassaran (Nakh-Daghestanian) 230
Tai-Kadai 112
Tariana (Arawakan) 297, 303
Temne (Atlantic) 153
Teop (Meso-Melanesian Oceanic, Austronesian) 315
Thai (Tai-Kadai) 292
Tiipay (Yuman) 140 n.
Tiwi (isolate of Australia) 197
Tlingit (Na-Dene) 239, 242
To'aba'ita (Southeast Solomonic Oceanic, Austronesian) 166–167, 181, 193, 203, 278
Toqabaqita, *see* To'aba'ita
Tsafiki (Barbacoan) 320
Tsúùt'íná, *see* Sarcee
Tuburi (Adamawa-Ubangi) 317
Tura (Mande) 142 n.
Turkic 126, 275, 280, 326
Tuvan (Turkic) 165, 232, 285, 305, 326 n.

Ukrainian (East Slavic, Indo-European) 275
Upper Kuskokwim (Na-Dene) 198, 199, 203, 232, 234, 235, 240–242, 245–246, 278, 279, 282, 301–303
Uralic 275, 280, 331
Urarina (isolate of South America) 174–175, 278, 293, 299
Uto-Aztecan 101

Index of languages

Vietnamese (Austro-Asiatic) 130–131, 133–134, 303, 306

Wardaman (Gunwinyguan, "Non-Pama-Nyungan") 140 n.
Warembori (Lower Mamberamo, "Papuan") 198, 203
Warlpiri (Pama-Nyungan) 143–144, 145, 147
Western Nilotic (Eastern Sudanic) 319
West Slavic (Indo-European) 273, 275

Xerente (Macro-Ge) 142

Yagua (Peba-Yaguan) 194–195, 202, 203, 204
Yaouré (Mande) 138
Yidiny (Pama-Nyungan) 106, 112, 113, 119, 153, 160, 161, 278
Yoruba (Yoruboid, Benue-Congo) 87
Yucatec (Mayan) 501 n.
Yurok (Algic) 140 n.

Zuni (isolate of North America) 175

Index of terms

Boldfaced are those page numbers in which a term is defined, explained, or introduced. Those terms that are central to the conceptual system of this book are **boldfaced**. *Italicized* are more general terms, not specific to this book's conceptual system, but appearing very often. For all italicized terms and for particularly frequent boldfaced terms, only a selection of pages is indicated, in order to avoid extremely long lists of page numbers. In cross-references inside a term family, the tilde ($\sim$) replaces the headword of a term family.

accent 14, 46, 82, 85, 274, 517, *see also* prosodic prominence
accessibility 41, 52, 53, 127, 163, 366, 386, 422
accusativity 169, 170, *see also* alignment, accusative
activation (in working memory) **53–56**, 327–332, 342–345, 378–384, 448
aggregate 61, 64, 391, 426, 439
attentional 52
degree of 55, 61, 108, 163, 165, 277, 312, 315, 331, 332, 342, 381, 383, 429, 447, 452, 531, 566, *see also* referent sorting, current, narrow domain
grand 448–**449**, 450–451, 456, 497
lesser and/or fresh 328, 330, 345, *see also* referent sorting, current, narrow domain
level of 161–168, *see also* degree of $\sim$
maintenance of 54, 370–374, 381, 451, 560
activation cost 57
activation factor **61**, 363, **390–394**, 402–416, 435–441
actual 402, 406, 407, 460
animacy 392, 406–408, 411, **413**, 436, **439**–440, 463, 472, 480–482, *see also* rate-of-deactivation correction
antecedent's phrase type 473, 482
antecedent's referential form/type 405, 407–408, 463, 473
antecedent's role 405, 409, 411, **412**, 436, **439**, 473, *see also* subjecthood
candidate 402, 406, 408, 460, 472, 482–485, 489, 490
discourse world 472–473, *see also* quoting; world boundary filter
distance 403–405, 435, 454, 473
hierarchical, *see* rhetorical $\sim$
in the number of markables 473, *see also* markable
in the number of words 473
linear (LinD) 403–404, 408, 411, 413–414, **435**, **436**, 463, 473, 531–532
paragraph 405, 409, 411, **414**, 435, **439**, 463, 473, *see also* discourse structure, global
referential 132, 390, 403, 489, 531, *see also* linear $\sim$
rhetorical (RhD) 404, 408, **410**–412, **435**–**438**, 463, 473–480, 490, 493, *see also* discourse structure, hierarchical
sentence 405, 407–408
implicit causality 387, 440, 485, 486–488, *see also* predictability $\sim$
introductory antecedent 436, 441, 489
potential, *see* candidate $\sim$
parallelism 488
persistence 489
predictability 436, 440–441, 486–487
protagonisthood 332, 406–408, 411, **413**, 436, **440**, 463, 472, 480, 483, *see also* rate-of-deactivation correction
referential device's phrase type 472
referential device's role 405, 407–408, 463, 472
related to discourse context 61, 64, 366, 390, 392, 394, 403–406, 551
related to the referent's properties 61, 64, 366, 392, 394, 406, 439, 472, 551
sloppy identity 410–411, 415, 420
supercontiguity 436, 440–441
temporal/spatial shift 436, 440–441
topicality 488–489

Index of terms

type of rhetorical relation 486–487
weak referent 436, 440–441
activation scale 378, 379, 428, 432, 434, 435
activation score (AS) **392**, 416–420, 423, 434, 435, 439, 441–442, 460–462, 485, 491, 493–494
activation threshold 54, **378**–380, 435, 531
addressee 17, **48**–50, 56–60, 62–67, 556–557
addressee factor 56, *see also* theory of mind
adverbial participle 326, 425, *see also* converb
affix 83, 89, 254
personal 92, 97, 100, 204, 208, 210–213, *see also* verb, person marking in
afterthought 98, 154, *see also* referential device, position of, retrospective
agreement 204, **207**, 214–231
anaphoric 295
gender 129 n., 229
Germanic pattern of 186, 216–221, 224, 225, 230, 264, 266, 274, 275
monopersonal 205, 207, 229, 230
number 207
person 207, 224–231, *see also* verb, person marking in
polypersonal 205, 229
alternation 96, 187 n., 202, *see also* pronoun, alternating
alignment (in communication) 58–59
alignment (of core arguments) **27**, 28, 58, 161, 168, 169, 552
accusative 27, 28, 172, 174, 204, 302 n. 3
active 27, 100, 104, 169, 194, 199, 204, 324
ergative 27, 92, 169, 171, 204, 230, 302 n. 3
neutral 169
tripartite 204
ambiguity, *see* referential conflict
anaphor 35, 49
anaphora 35–37, **49**, 512–516, *see also* reference; mention, repeated
associative, *see* indirect ∼
discourse 36, 552, 559
indirect 54, **553**–554
predicate **555**–556
situational, *see* exophora
syntactic 36, 168, 206 n., 208, **552**, 553, 559
antecedent 35, 49, **55**, 405, 553
explicit 49, 472
immediate 35, 353 n., 382, 472, 474

linear, *see* activation factor, distance, linear
rhetorical, *see* activation factor, distance, rhetorical
anterior cingulate cortex 368
anthropology 11
anti-reflexive 315, *see also* referent sorting, current, narrow domain
antitopic 60, *see also* referential device, position of, retrospective
aphasics 557
areal grouping 282
areal pattern 112, 114, 275, 319, 331
argumenthood 98, 202, *see also* clause participant, argument
argument type 202, 552, *see also* pronoun, tenacious
article:
definite 32–34, 39, 49, 128, 129, 197, 348, 516
indefinite 34
artificial intelligence 9, 549
artificial neural network 461, **462**–470
attention 53, **368**–369, 372–377, 381–387, 452–454
capacity of, *see* attention span
focal 55, 56, **369**, 370, 383–385, 405, 439, 453–454
focused 368, *see also* focal ∼
focus of 52, 53, 325, 369, 372, 383, 447, *see also* focal ∼
involuntary 368
joint 503, 506, 508, 510, 511, 514, 518
neural grounds of 374–375
object-based 368
spaced-based 368
to meaning 383
visual 3, 383, 502, 510, 512, 513
voluntary 368
attention focus, *see* focal attention
attention span 377
attentional system 368, 383, 457
anterior 368
attenuation, *see* reduction
attribute 53, *see also* modifier

back-propagation learning algorithm 462, 466
backward-looking center 385, 558
body language 46, 549, *see also* gesture

boundness 96, 101, 145, 187, 190–191, 201–204, 253–255, 276, 279–281, *see also* pronoun, bound
bridging, *see* anaphora, indirect

calculative approach 392–393, **407**, 416–421, 436, 441–442, 460–463, 466, 468–470
case:
  accusative 26, 94, 138–140, 149, 157, 188, 198, 209, 240–243, 246, 247, 263, 348, 356, 399
  dative 28, 100, 109–111, 148, 188, 255, 259, 261, 263, 399, 400, 412, 423
  ergative 94, 146
  genitive 111, 399
  narrative 100
  nominative 28, 55, 84, 89, 99, 139, 142, 146, 157, 198, 234, 240, 242, 259, 348, 353, 356, 399
  oblique 94, 139, 140, 165, 241, 243, 245–247, 261, 279, 300, 348, 356
  verb-marked 94–95
categorization 17, 127, **295**, 303, 333, 346–347, 359, *see also* referent sorting, stable, absolute; taxonomy
Centering Theory 385, 405, 558–560
channel 46, 500, 549, *see also* multimodality
  visual 501–548
  vocal 46
  non-vocal **46**–47, **499**, 563, *see also* visual ~
choice 14–**15**, 119, *see also* referential choice
  grammatical 15, 20, 119
  lexical 20, 46, 397
  multi-factorial 61, 390–393
classificatory verb stem 300–303
classifier **127**–133, 296–298, 302–303
  general categorical 130
  in sign language 526, **528**, 529, 531, 536, 541, 546
  kin 130
  modifying 130
  noun 128, 129, 132
  numeral 128, 131, 132
  verbal 128, 132, 300
clausal category, *see* pronoun, marked for clausal categories
clause:
  complement 182, 316, 317
  converbal 400
  coordinate 79, 160, 177–182, 215, 227, 265, 272, 277, 400, 422, 423, 430, 565
  dependent 174 n., 182, 318–319
  elliptical 154
  gerundial 44, 483
  imperative 176
  main 44, 316, 321, 436
  independent 400, 422
  participial **300**
  subordinate 188, 400
clause chain 299, 326, 340, 377, 533
clause coordination 79, 160, **176**–180, 196, 265, 430
clause participant **27**, 44–46, 80, 88, 168–176, 203, 204, 479, 480, 543, 565
  actant, *see* argument ~
  adjunct 26, 27, 44, 97, 98, 101, 241, 377, 389, *see also* non-argument ~
  argument **27**, 94–95
    core 27, 94, 95, 98, 129, 138, 143, 168, 199, 316
    non-core 27, 94, 109, 110, 204 241, 341, 405, 478
  circumstant, *see* non-argument ~
  complement, *see* argument ~
  non-argument **27**, 138
  oblique **27**, 122, 139, 140, 245
  privileged **27**, 206, 212, 229
clause subordination 181
clefting 154, 369
clitic **82**–86, *see also* pronoun, clitic
  fixed 84
  local 84
  mobile 84
  phrasal 84
  pronominal, *see* pronoun, clitic
  simple 85–86
  special 85–86
clitic climbing 188, 254
clitic doubling 188, *see also* pronoun, tenacious
cognitive commitment 15–16, 22, 366
Cognitive Grammar 16, 559
cognitive linguistics 15–18, 22, 385, 445, 457, 551, 552
cognitive multi-factorial (CMF) approach **60–61**, 363–395, 396–427, 428–444, 445–458, 459–497
cognitive neuroscience 16, 18, 53, 338, 366–375, 386, 445–458, 563

cognitive psychology 16, 18, 53, 366–375, 386, 445–458, 562
cognitive science 53, 363, 445, 457–458
common noun 33, 34, 37, 38, 52, 472, 483, 484, 560, 564, *see also* referential device, full
communication 9, 12, 17, 42, 56, 507–509, 544–546, 549, 563
compatibility with the context of the clause 292–293
complement construction 319, 326
computational linguistics 59, 485, 549, 563
concept 7, 31, 32, 54, 122, 370, 375, 535, 555, 556
conceptual reference point 559
conceptualization 7, 17, 31, 40, 526, 555
consciousness 17, 52, 155, 366, 368, 384, 385–386
consistency (in referential choice), *see* language, consistent
contrastiveness 46, 84, 150, 151, 154, 155, 211, 261, 270, 539, 554
converb 326, 425
conversation 8, 40, 41, 43, 55, 89, 156, 170, 375, 515, 553
coordinate construction 80, 153, 177–179, 251
coordinate noun phrase, *see* coordinate phrase
coordinate phrase 112, 150
coreference 35, 39, 41, 97, 319, 339, 471–472, 558
coreference relation 472
corpus 34, 38, 39, 114, 156, 178, 523, 537, 553
corpus linguistics 24, 470, 493

deactivation 54, 157, 374, 382, 425, 447, 455, **456**, 481, *see also* working memory, forgetting from
decay 371, 454–457, 560
deconflicter, *see* referential aid
deference 134, 306
deferred ostension, *see* pointing, substitution in
defocusing 325
definiteness 129, 247, *see also* article, definite; noun phrase, full, definite
degree of formality **13**, 252
demonstrative 41, 100, 123–**127**, 129, 130, 135, 153, 157, 234, 319, 327, 331, 348, 355, 356, 399, 420, 425, 481, 503, 509, 516, 518, 525, 532, 534–536

demonstratum **520**–521
dependent-marking **102**–104, 552, *see also* language, dependent-marking
description 33, 37, *see also* common noun; referential device, full
deixis 37, 47, 55, 501–502, **503**–507, 510–520, 523, 545
analogical, *see* pointing, substitution in
social 307, 505
Deixis am Phantasma, *see* pointing, virtual
different-subject (DS) **320**–326, 336, 339–341, 358, *see also* switch-reference
direct vs. inverse marking 305
discourse 11–21, **24**–26, 36
expository 109
narrative 13, 47, 109, 311, 313, 452, 490, 523, 537, 546
discourse analysis 11–15, 28
cognitive 15–18, 21–23, 457–458, 552
experimental 17, 24–25, 58, 162, 343, 383, 387, 432–434, 453, 483, 493–494, 557, 563
functional 17–18, 20, 23
neurolinguistic 210, 338, 562
typological 19, 23
discourse marker 15, 45, 251
discourse structure 13–15, 163, 323, 404, 458
global 13–**14**, 309, 390, 391, 392, 403, 405, 414
hierarchical 14–15, 323, 392, **403**–405, 473, *see also* Rhetorical Structure Theory
linear 15, 323, 358, 392, 403–405, 473
local 13–14, 309, 390, 392, 403, 405
discourse type 13, 15, 43, 156, 376, 509, 561, *see also* register; taxonomy, of discourses
discourse unit 61, 403
elementary (EDU) **14**, 376–377, 397, 452–453
displacement 37, 512
distribution:
areal, *see* geographical ~
genealogical 89–90, 101–102, 112–113, 221 n.
geographical 89–90, 101–102, 112–114, 221 n.
double expression 186, *see also* representation, double
dummy subject 258
dynamics of referent's activation 449–450, 559–560

elicitation 24
ellipsis 109, 178, 216, 222, *see also* zero reference

ellipsis (*cont.*)
   initial 180
emphasis 9, 88, 154, 155, 157, 270–272, 554
engagement 294
entity, *see* referent
episodic boundary 390, 440, *see also* discourse structure, global
ergativity 169, 172, *see also* alignment, ergative
event 4, **6**, 7, 13, 31, 37, 228, 320, 377, 520, 555, 556
eye gaze 511, 512, 515, 522, 536, 543
exophora 37, 49, 55, 510, **511**–513, 513–516, 516–521
experimentation **24**–26, 432–434, 493–494

feed-forward network 462, 469
fiction 8, 40, 41, 43, 55, 89, 170, 515, 553
freeness 96, 101, 190–191, *see also* pronoun, free
functional style **13**, 561

gender 62–63, 65, 128, 295–303, 337, *see also* noun class
genealogical pattern 112
genre **12**, 13, 15, 51, 109, 426, 451, 471, 475, 561
genre schema 12
gerund 6, 188, 190, *see also* converb
gesticulation 508, 517, 523, 542, 546, *see also* gesture
gesture 41, 46–47, 507, 509, 518, 539, 545, 546
   illustrative 15, 541, 542, 544, 545
   pointing 47, 68, **499**, 503, 504, 506–511, 514, 518–519, 566
givenness **34**, 41–42, 53, 108, 127, 172, 247, 386
grammar 15, 16, 56, 61, 76, 78, 91, 118, 202, 230 n. 39, 322, 552
grammaticalization **36**, 133, 224, 225, 405, 430, 552
great apes 507, 508
   chimpanzee 507, 508
   orangutan 507

head-marking **102**–104, 552, *see also* language, head-marking
hierarchy **14**, 189, 294, 323, 338–339, 375, 464 n., *see also* referent sorting, stable, relative; discourse structure, hierarchical
   animacy 68, **304**–306, 311 n., 312, 332
   givenness 41–42
   honorific 134, **306**–308, 332

historical shift 239, 281
hyperrole 27, 28, 95, 168–172, 184, 229, 405, 482, 483, 565
   A 26, 28, 103, 104, 146
   Absolutive 27, 28, 171–172
   Actor 27, 194, 204, 229, 322
   Agentive 27, 28, 171–172
   P 26, 28, 103, 104, 146
   Patientive 27, 28, 168–171, 193–195, 195–197, 198–199, 199–200
   Principal 27, 28, 168–171, 191–193, 195–197, 199–200
   S 26, 28
   Sole 27, 28, 130, 161, 171, 172, 233, 302
   Undergoer 27, 194, 199, 204, 229

identifiability 32, 42, *see also* definiteness
imagining 5, 31, 37, 507, 519, 528, 537
inconsistency (in referential choice) 68, 77, 101, **160**, 161, 175, *see also* language, inconsistent
indefiniteness 196–197, *see also* article, indefinite; noun phrase, full, indefinite
inference 292, 487; *see also* compatibility with the context of the clause
information:
   accessible 57, 477, 518, 519, 538, 530, 538, *see also* activation cost
   active **54**, 57–58, 378
   given **34**–35, 42, 54, 57, 84, 331, 518, 540, *see also* givenness; activation cost
   inactive **54**, 57–58, 378
   new **34**–35, 49, 50, 54, 57, 331, 519, *see also* activation cost
   semiactive **54**, 57–58, **378**
instantiation (of a referent) 96, **186**, 218, 219, 220, 225, 240, 277
intensifier 554
intention 56, 155, 368, 508
interaction of activation factors 61, 367, 391, 393, 416, **460**–461, 465, 469, 480, 498
interference 371, 454–457
interview 109
intonation unit 14, 57–58, 376
inverse 304–305, 312, *see also* direct vs. inverse marking

language:
   analytic 113, 144–145
   configurational 91

consistent 77, 115–117, **160**, 175
dependent-marking 102, 245
double-marking 103 n. 31
head-marking 102, 103, 104, 197, 259
inconsistent 77, **160**, 175
insensitive, *see* consistent ~
isolating 113
mode of existence:
  offline **16**–17
  online **16**–17
moderately synthetic 144–146
no-marking 113
nominal argument 94, 101
non-configurational 91
null-marking, *see* no-marking ~
polysynthetic **102**–103, 114, 144, 145, 151, 154, 196, 204, 205, 208–210, 239, 241, 254, 256
pronominal argument 94, 101
pure, *see* consistent ~
sensitive, *see* inconsistent ~
subject-prominent 90–91
topic-prominent 90
type of 115–116, 144, 146, 202–203, 239, 521–522, 562
light subject constraint 55, 170
linguistic disourse analysis, *see* discourse analysis
linguistic diversity 19, 20, 22, 23, 67, 73, 498, 550, 552, 561–563
linguistic typology 19–21, 21–23, 550, 552
  large-scale 19, 20, 92
  small-scale 19, 20
linking 5, **6**, 75, 76, 97, 100, 137, 225, 226
location 7, 31, 535, 536, 545, 546, 555, 556
logic 30, 31, 33, 52, 558
logophoricity 315–320, 326, 332
long-term memory (LTM) 5, 42, 369, 370, 374, 375, 452, 454, 561

machine learning 461, 483–485
maintenance of reference, *see* reference-maintenance
management of reference 50, *see also* referential choice
markable **472**–474, 483
membership **123**, 333
mental source 316, 319, 326, 333
mention 5, 9, 35, 50, **53**, **376**, *see also* reference
  first 9, 35, 38, 47, 54, 60, 353, 379, 411, 418

introductory 378, 472, 504, 513– 515, 521, 560
prior 35, 37, 43, 382, 390, 405, 512, *see also* antecedent
repeated 10, 35, 181, 376, 382, 472, 513, 521, 560
subsequent 9, 10, 34, 35, 47, 542
metaphor 7, 26, 96, 386, 512
  computer 16
mind 31, 56–58, 66, 155, 366, 512, 557
MMAX2 program 473–474, 479
modelling **25**, 48, 392–394, 416, 441 460–469, 470–490
mode of discourse **11**, 12, 14, 15, 51, 252, 491–493, 561
  electronic 12
  internal 12
  spoken 11–12, 38, 50, 55, 60, 64, 84, 108, 132, 160, 172, 178–180, 249, 262, 330, 355, 376, 377, 491–493, 537–546, 553
  written 11–12, 107, 160, 178, 249, 262, 377, 387, 397, 429, 483, 490–493, 516, 561
morphological complexity 73, 114, 117–118
modifier 31, 37–38, 41, 121, 295, 400
motor control 375
multimodality 549, 563
multiplicity of activation factors 61, 363, 390–393
multirepresentation 96, 98 n.23, 202, 206, *see also* representation; pronoun, tenacious

neo-Gricean pragmatic theory 559
neural network, *see* artificial neural network
news 8, 43, 170, 171, 553
Night Dream Stories corpus 38, 84, 157, 181–182
node:
  in neural network 462, 464, 465, 466, 467
  hidden 465, 466
  input 463–467
  output 462, 464, 465
  in rhetorical tree 14, 41, 404, 438, 476
non-topic 322, 329, 360
non-verbal devices 47, **499**, 503, *see also* prosody
non-vocal devices 15, 47, **499** *see also* body language
noun class 128, 129, **295**–303, 335, 336, 338, 339, 345–347, 347–355, 355–359,

see also referent sorting, stable, absolute
  basis for classification 295, 300–303, 347–348
noun phrase (NP):
  full, *see* referential device, full
    definite 34, 41, 42, 189, 513, 515, 553
    indefinite 42, 167, 189, 196, 197, 234, 243, 263
    possessive 32, 197, 232, 472, 473
    reduced, *see* referential device, reduced
    suppressed 436, 439
Nref effect 562
nucleus 82, 318, 324, 403, 477, *see also* rhetorical relation
number 299–300

observation **23–26**, 470, 562
obviative 311, **312**, 313, 345, 566, *see also* referent sorting, current, broad domain
one new idea constraint 50
ontogeny 507–510, 512, 515, 557
Optimality Theory 392 n.
origo 42, **505**–507, 521, 544, 545
ostensive metonymy, *see* pointing, substitution in

paragraph boundary 163, 317, 405, 414, 415, 431, 433, 440, 451, *see also* discourse structure, global
passage **12–13**, 353–355, 561
  argumentative 12
  descriptive 12
  expository 12
  instructive 12
  narrative 12, 13, 412
pausing 14, 15, 57, 58, 107 n., 150, 173 n., 255, 257 n., 351 n., 492 n., 538 n.
Pear Film 48, 189, 523, 527, 528, 537, 540, 544
perception 5, 370, 375, 497, 504, 508, 521, 526
person 40, 43, 122, 299–300, *see also* verb, person marking in
personal desinence 152, 155, 190, 210–213, 230, 239, 249, 250, 252, 260, 267, 273, 274, *see also* verb, person marking in
personal ending 146, 168, 215, 276, *see also* verb, person marking in
perspective taking 489, 544–547, 560, *see also* logophoricity
  in pointing gesture 544–545, 546
perspectivization, *see* perspective taking
philosophy 9, 30, 31, 558
phylogeny 507
plane of thought/talk 6, 75, 76, 97, 105, 137, 226
pointer 505–507, 521
pointing 37, 506–510, 516–521, *see also* gesture, pointing
  abstract, *see* virtual ~
  development of 508, 521
  substitution in 508 n., 520
  target of 505, 507, 520, 521, 556
  virtual 521, 526–**528**, 529–530, 534, 536, **537–546**, 566
point of view 311, 545
polypersonalism 247, 248, 281, 565
posterior parietal area 374
pragmatic system 292, *see also* compatibility with the context of the clause
Preferred Argument Structure 171–172
prefrontal cortex 374
prepositional phrase 472, 473, 482
pro-drop 76–77, 221
pronominal affix 95, 98, 187, 197–199, 206, 207, 239, 313, *see also* verb, person marking in
pronominal salience 276–283
pronoun 37, 39–40, 43, 75, 120, **121**, *see also* referential device, reduced
  accented 46, 82, 86, 149, 150, 155, *see also* strong ~
  affixal, *see* bound ~
  alternating 96, 187, 191, 197–201
  anaphoric 49, 82, 96, 121, 132, 161, 206, 215, 366, 385, 423, 474, 502, 504, *see also* anaphor
  anti-logophoric 320, *see also* referent sorting, current, narrow domain
  bound 74, 75–77, 92–104, 186–187, 204–207
  clitic **82**, 85, 89, 146, 196, 219, 220, 517, *see also* weak ~
    contextually 85, 86, 272
    inherently 85, 86, 263, 268
  compound, *see* double reference ~; ~ marked for clausal categories
  demonstrative, *see* demonstrative
  double reference 136–140, 157, 565
  double-referring, *see* double reference ~
  emphatic, *see* strong ~

Index of terms

first person 121, 122, 152, 155–157, 252, 261, 267, 275, 315, 429, 525, see also locutor ~
fourth person 75, 136, 209, **309**–311, 320, see also referent sorting, current, broad domain
free 74, **75**–77, 78–92, 215–220
fused, see double reference ~
indefinite 33, 228, 234, 554
insensitive, see referential device, reduced, insensitive
interrogative 167, 243, 554
locutor 40, **42**–43, 121, 122, 125, 138, 139, 160, 161, 208, 229, 233, 234, 240, 268–272, 339, 397, 399, 505, 506, 514, 517, 523, 525, 555, 564
plural 43, 555
logophoric **315**–320, 336, 339, 566, see also logophoricity; referent sorting, current, narrow domain
marked for clausal categories 140–147
negative 33, 554
non-locutor 42–43, 122, 160, 161, 176, 233, 234, 240, 272
object 82, 168, 249, 262, 264
personal 33–34, 40, 43, 120–123, see also third person ~
portmanteau, see double reference ~
possessive 45, 93, 97, 101, 186, 204, 280, 308, 388, 399, 430, 479
prosodically prominent 85, 150, 263, see also accented ~; strong ~
reciprocal 210, 314, 399
reflexive 41, 45, 210, 314, 399, 430, 473, 559
long-distance 41, 136, 319, 335, 336
second person 154, 156, 176, 213, 231, 252, see also locutor ~
sensitive, see referential device, reduced, sensitive
separate, see free ~
strong 82, 84–86, 88, **147**–157, 162, 220, 227, 239, 258, 263, 269, 554
dedicated 150, 153
subject 89, 155, 180, 215, 248, 259
tenacious 80–81, **96**–98, 186–197, 200–204
third person 40–**43**, 121, 125, 399, 429, see also non-locutor ~
analogue of 123–124
dedicated 44, 123–127, 319
unaccented 46, 82, 86, 150, see also weak ~
weak 39, 40, 75, **82**–88, 151
proper name 32, 34, 35, 37, 38, 52, 306, 309, 473, 481, 483, 484, 516, 560, 564, see also referential device, full
prose 267, 483
academic 8, 170, 515, 553
narrative 396–427, 428–444
prosodic independence 82
prosodic prominence 148, 149, 150, 151, 517, 543
prosody 46–47, 151, 178, 517, 563
protagonist 4, 75 n., 108–111, 130, 177, 179, 264, 309–314, 322, 325, 331–332, 392, **406**, 429, 449, 450, 481, see also activation factor, protagonisthood
proximate **311**–313, 345, 566, see also referent sorting, current, broad domain
pruning 464–466, 467
psycholinguistics 18, 338, 493–494, 562
quoting 315–316, 320, 352, 358, 399, 412, 414, 424, 429, 438, 472–473, 533, 544

rate-of-deactivation correction 440
recoverability 386, **387**–388, 389
reduction 46–47, 66, 86, 150
redundancy 59, 188, 228, 271, 307
reference 3–5, 8–10, 30–**31**
act of 5, 47, 62, 65, 72, 105, 108, 290, 381, 503, 511, 514, 524 n., 528 n., 560
deviant kinds of 34, 544
introductory 49, 54, see also mention, introductory
local, see ~ to places
locative, see ~ to places
locutor 42–43, 121, 122, 160, 506, 525
plural 377 n., 480, **554**–555
repeated 9, 49, see also mention, repeated
spatial, see ~ to places
steadiness of 383–385
temporal, see ~ to times
third person 65, 108, 157, 160, 161, 175, 222, 233, 308, see also pronoun, third person
to places 31, 555
to times 31, 555
reference-maintenance 50, see also referential choice
reference-tracking 50, 309, 327, 339, see also referential choice; referential conflict

648 Index of terms

referent 4–7, 31–34, 339, 447
  activated 43, 46, 53–57, 65, 373
  non-activated 46, 49, 55, 153, 171, 226,
    227, 373, 503, 504, 511, 517, 540, 560
  semi-activated 516, 518, 538
referent introduction 9, 75, 247, 330, 331,
    526, 529, 531, 537–539, 543, 560
referent reactivation 413, see also referent
    reintroduction
referent reintroduction 413, 560
referent sorting 64, 108, 136, 294, 328, 333,
    338–347, 359, 551, see also referential
    aid, conventional
  current 294, 308, 336, 347, 356, 358
    broad domain 308–314
    narrow domain 314–332
    supernarrow domain 314, 315
  stable 294, 308, 347, 356
    absolute 294–304, 335, 565
    relative 304–308, 565
referent-tracking, see reference-tracking
referential aid 65, 287, 290–291, 332
  ad hoc 291–295, 292, 332–333, 335–338,
    343, 352, 425, 532
  conventional 291, 292–295, 332–333,
    335–339, 343, 344, 353–355, 359
  dedicated 322, 339, 359
  site of expression 294–299, 309, 326, 337–338
referential annotation 471, 472, 474, 483
  scheme of 472
referential choice 15, 48–55, 377–381
  basic 39, 41, 42, 48, 54, 151, 291, 380, 406,
    407, 422, 481, 491, 534, 561
  main law of 53–54, 378–380
  model of 61, 64, 393–394
  troubleshooters of 127, 481
referential conflict 58, 62–63, 287, 290–291
  preclusion of 63–68, 290–291, 333,
    335–339, 342–350, 424, 532, 546
referential conflict filter 63–64, 394,
    424–425, 443, 456, 562
referential continuity 161, 341
  degree of 161, 339, 340 n.
referential device 5–6, 37–48
  acquisition of 513, 557
  actual 416, 432, 434, 442
  alterable 401–402, 407, 431–432, 443, 484
  attested 431, 435, see also actual ~
  basic 37, 41, 51, 398, 400, 416, 431, 441,
    481, 491, 534

categorical 379–380, 402, 407, 431–432,
    443, 484
comprehension of 44, 51, 57, 64, 204,
    372, 486, 556, 557, 562
full 38–42, 295, 378
generation of 485, 556, see also
    production of ~
global 309
lexically full, see full ~
local 309
position of 44–45
  clause participant 26, 44, 77, 168–176,
    191–204, 212
  possessive 45
  prospective 45
  retrospective 45
potential 416–417, 431, 435, 441–442, 470
production of 23, 25, 48, 51, 56, 58,
    63–65, 204, 338, 372, 385, 387, 447,
    556, 557
reduced 39–42, 71, 73–76, 378, 504
  alternating, see pronoun, alternating
  ancillary 225–227, 399 n.
  bound, see pronoun, bound
  dominant 43, 117–118, 225, 163, 232,
    235, 239, 274, 276, 495, see also
    preferred ~
  default 78, 107, 266, see also preferred ~
  free, see pronoun, free
  fully-fledged 226, 249, 274 n., 277,
  insensitive 166, 181, 196, 202, 206, 208,
    243, 263, 277
  major 68, 73–77, 90, 115, 147, 154, 175,
    231, 276, 443
  marginal 124, 133, 135, 481
  minor 40, 90, 420, 443, 554
  non-zero, see overt ~
  overt 43–44, 121, see also pronoun
  preferred 73, 121, 148, 160, 171, 179 n.
    18, 182, 227, 230, 239, 278, 280
  sensitive 112, 160–161, 189, 202, 204–206
  tenacious, see pronoun, tenacious
  zero, see zero
understanding of 7, 17, 493, 556, see also
    comprehension of ~
referential economy principle 559
referential element, see referential device
referential expression, see referential device
referential mapping 416–420, 432, 434–435,
    441, 497

Index of terms

referential option 41–42, **48**, 161, 169, 379, 408, 431, 441, 561, *see also* referential choice; referential device
referential status 31–34
　autonomous 32
　non-specific 32, 34, 247, 400, 590
　　attributive 32, 33
　　existential 32
　　generic 32, 33, 193, 520
　　universal 32
　predicative 32, 463
　specific:
　　definite 6, **32**–34, 34–37, 40, 247, 263, 447, 554
　　indefinite 32, 33, 193, 255, 261, 309
referential strategy 59–60
　egocentric **59**, 62, 64, 65, 66, 67, 380, 417
　optimal **59**, 64, 65, 67, 417
　overprotective **59**, 64, 67, 380, 417
referential systems 15, 21, 238–239, 283, 536, 561
　diachrony of 238–240
　typology of 248, 363, 444, 490, 498, 562
referential tracking, *see* reference-tracking
referral 6
referring, *see* reference
referring expression, *see* referential device
RefRhet corpus 471–474, 479–485, 490
register 8, **13**, 34, 40, 51, 170, 178, 189, 249, 426, 515–516
repeated name penalty 51
representation (of a referent) 21, 71–72, 98, 220, 424, 225
　double 75, 96, 98, 186, *see also* pronoun, tenacious
resolution:
　anaphora 393, 469 n., 485, 486, *see also* referential device, comprehension
　pronoun 46, 486, *see also* referential device, comprehension
　reference 59, 393, *see also* referential device, comprehension
rhetorical graph 410, 437, 438, 475, 478, 485
rhetorical relation 14, 403, 410, 412, 422, 438, 471, 475, 476, 478, 485–487, 566, *see also* Rhetorical Structure Theory
　asymmetric, *see* mononuclear
　mononuclear 403, 404, 475, 477
　multinuclear 403, 438, 475–477
　symmetric, *see* multinuclear

Rhetorical Structure Theory (RST) 14, 318 n, 323, 403, 437, 471
rhetorical tree 404, 471, *see also* rhetorical graph
Role and Reference Grammar 78
role-shifting 530, **533**, 536, 545, 546 *see also* perspective taking
RST Discourse Treebank 471, 472, 474, 475, 478, 485
Russian National Corpus 327–329, 342–343

salience 52, 125, 183, 366, **386**–387
same-subject (SS) **320**–326, 336, 339–341, 425, *see also* switch-reference
sample:
　discourse 108, 134, 156, 266, 329, 393, 397–398, 429–431, 443
　language 19, 21, 77, 89, 90, 103, 114, 146, 175, 339, 525
satellite 318, 403, 476, *see also* rhetorical relation
schizophrenics 557
semantic role 27, 80, 94, 123, 322, 405, 408, 411, 412, 421, 453, 481, 482, 486–488, 490
　agent 27, 92, 186, 229, 312, 482
　agent-like 27, 169
　benefactive 45, 92, 245
　comitative 27, 92, 94, 245
　experiencer 27, 482, 486
　goal 186
　location 27
　patient 27, 92, 292, 312, 482
　patient-like 27, 169
　possessor 186, 197, 219, 232, 389, 465
　recipient 27, 92, 95, 99, 109, 110, 188, 193
semiclitic, *see* pronoun, clitic, contextually
sensitivity (in referential choice) **160**, 168, 175, 277, *see also* referential device, reduced, sensitive
sentence 10, 36, 173 n. 13, 177–179, 317, 338, 353–355, 552, 556, 562
short-term memory, *see* working memory
sign 523, 526
　pointing 523–526, 528–531, 534, 536, 546
sign languages of the deaf 12, 499, 522–526, 533, 536, 537, 542, 545, 546, 562
signing arena 522, 526, 528, 536
signing space, *see* signing arena
social status noun 124, 131, **133**–135, 306 *see also* deference; honorific hierarchy
sociology 11

space (in sign languages):
  conceived 526, 536
  constructed 526–531, 535, 536
  gesture spaces 546
  perceived 524–526, 528, 536
speaker 5, 9, 15, 17, 31, 42, **48**–50, 56–60, 62–67, 506, 556
spoken languages 12, 522, 523, 525, 526, 531, 532, 534, 536–538, 562
starting point 170
state 4, **6**, 7, 13, 31, 520, 555, 556
statistical analysis 468–470, 484–485
story 12, 51, 397, 429, 475
stress 84, 254, *see also* prosodic prominence
subjecthood 229, 320–327, 332, 405, 443, 453, 454, 461, 465, 488, 489, 566, *see also* syntactic role, subject
subjectivity, *see* perspective taking
subject/tense/mood particle 217–218, *see also* pronoun, marked for clausal categories
switch-reference **320**–327, 335–337, **339**–342, 357, 359, 566, *see also* referent sorting, current, narrow domain
syntactic role:
  object 28, 79, 80, 109, 137, 138, 168, 170, 188–190, 261–263, 386, 430, 531
    direct 28, 174, 181, 189, 266, 317, 389, 436, 439, 463, 464, 472, 473
    indirect 189, 262, 317, 463, 464, 472, 473
  subject 28, 55, 79, 80, 109, 137, 138, 141, 142, 169, 170, 173–175, 215, 221, 222, 383, 405, 412, 439, 453–454

taxonomy:
  ethnocultural 347, 352, 359
  of concepts 31
  of discourses 11–13, 561
  referential, *see* referent sorting, stable, absolute
tenacity 68, 81, **96**, 187–197, 201–206, 235, 252–255, 263, 276, 279–282, *see also* pronoun, tenacious
themehood, *see* topicality
theme, *see* clause topic
theory of mind **56**–57, 59, 508, 515
thinking 52, 53, 56, 75, 375, 522, 545
time 7, 31, 403, 454, 458, 555
topic:
  anticipatory 45, 98

clause 51, 55, 170, 313, 322, 328, 329, 333, 383, 385, 405, 490, 491 *see also* referential device, position of, prospective
contrastive 41
discourse 311, 558
topicality 305, 315, 320–327, 332, 405, 566, *see also* referent sorting, current, narrow domain; activation factor, topicality
topicalization 149, 154
topic chain 55, *see also* referential continuity
topic continuity 422, *see also* referential continuity
Two-Character Effect 56
typological calculus 19 n., 184
typological feature 90, 102, 113, *see also* typological parameter
typological parameter 76, 89, 102–104, 201, 275, 278, 294, 309, 333, 522, 552
typology, *see* linguistic typology

unirepresentation 202, *see also* representation; pronoun, alternating

verb:
  bipersonal 213–214
  intransitive 27, 161, 210, 233
  monopersonal 210–213
  person marking in 92–104, 233, 266, 267, 275
  polypersonal 208–210
  transitive 27, 115, 166, 181, 210, 214
verbal devices 499, 549, 563
verbal person marker 115, 204, 213–216, 221, 224, 225, 230, 267, *see also* verb, person marking in; pronoun, bound; agreement, person
verb-second principle 217, 223, 239–240, 259
verb serialization 180–181
visual-spatial modality 522, 536, *see also* channel, visual

Wackernagel position 268
word 83–89, 253, 268
word order 14, 23, 104, 217, 335, 489, 522
working memory (WM) 52, **53**, 54–56, **369**–384, 445–446, 493–494, *see also* activation
  capacity of 446–451
  control of 451–454
  encoding into 371, 372, 387

for specific referents 446–447
forgetting from 454–457
fractioning of 370, 375, 446–447
measurement of 447–448
model of 369–372
neural grounds of 374–375
relatedness to attention 372–374, 381–384, 452–454
relatedness to language 52–54, 377–380, 446–457
World Atlas of Language Structures (WALS) 19, 91, 103, 113, 115, 118, 146, 252, 275, 346

world boundary filter 394, 423–**424**, 425, 472

zero 74, 75–77, 104–115, *see also* zero reference
bound 186, 231–236, 565
free 186, 227, 231–236, 283
morphological, *see* bound ∼
syntactic, *see* free ∼
zero anaphor, *see* zero
zero anaphora, *see* zero reference
zero reference 43–44, 74, 75, 104–115, 153, 281–282, 422–423